2018/19
FACTS & FIGURES

TABLES FOR THE CALCULATION OF DAMAGES

2018/19
FACTS & FIGURES

TABLES FOR THE CALCULATION OF DAMAGES

Compiled and Edited by:

Members of the Professional Negligence Bar Association

General Editor: Simon Levene

Editors:

Chris Daykin CB FIA
Vitek Frenkel FCA MAE
Peter Jennings
William Latimer-Sayer QC
Tejina Mangat
Harry Trusted

SWEET & MAXWELL

THOMSON REUTERS

Published in 2018 by Thomson Reuters, trading as Sweet & Maxwell.
Registered in England and Wales. Company number 1679046.
Registered Office and address for service: 5 Canada Square, Canary Wharf, London E14 5AQ.

For further information on our products and services, visit *http://www.sweetandmaxwell.co.uk*.

Designed and typeset by Wright & Round Ltd, Gloucestershire
Printed and bound in Great Britain by Ashford Colour Press, Gosport, Hants

No natural forests were destroyed to make this product; only farmed timber was used and re-planted.

ISBN 978-0-414-06712-7

A CIP catalogue record for this book is available from the British Library.

All rights reserved. Crown Copyright material is reproduced with the permission of the Controller of HMSO and the Queen's Printer for Scotland.

No part of this publication may be reproduced or transmitted in any form or by any means, or stored in any retrieval system of any nature without prior written permission, except for permitted fair dealing under the Copyright, Designs and Patents Act 1988, or in accordance with the terms of a licence issued by the Copyright Licensing Agency in respect of photocopying and/or reprographic reproduction. Application for permission for other use of copyright material including permissions to reproduce extracts in other published works shall be made to the publishers. Full acknowledgement of author, publisher and source must be given.

Material is contained in this publication for which publishing permission has been sought, and for which copyright is acknowledged. Permission to reproduce such material cannot be granted by the publishers and application must be made to the copyright holder.

Thomson Reuters, the Thomson Reuters Logo and Sweet & Maxwell ® are trademarks of Thomson Reuters.

© Professional Negligence Bar Association 2018

ACKNOWLEDGMENTS

We are very grateful to the following contributors:

- Dr Victoria Wass of Cardiff Business School for updating *B6: Step-by-step guide to finding the annual estimates for hourly pay in **ASHE SOC 2000 6115*** and for providing the guide to the ASHE earnings tables at *F7: Average earning statistics*.

- Rodney Nelson Jones of Field Fisher Waterhouse and Lexis Nexis for allowing us to use and to develop his table for the calculation of special damages interest in *C4: Special and general damages interest*.

- Keith Carter & Associates for the research undertaken for the preparation of the tables F5 on Regional Unemployment Statistics.

- Melissa Chapman and the Family Law Bar Association for their permission to use table I1 & I2 and Gary Vaux, Head of Money Advice, Hertfordshire County Council for updating *I1: Social security benefits (non means-tested)* and *I2: Social security benefits and tax credits (means-tested)*.

- Lynne Bradey, Partner at Wrigleys, for updating *I3: Personal injury trusts*.

- Christine Bunting, Director of Hyphen Law, for her contribution to J1, J2 and J3 on Court of Protection and Deputyship Costs.

- Alison Somek of Somek & Associates Ltd and James Rowley QC of Byrom Street Chambers, for their work on *K1: Care and attendance*.

- Nicholas Leviseur for preparing the notes for *L3: The Motability Scheme*.

- Margaret McDonald, specialist costs counsel of Kenworthy's Chambers, for updating *M1: Senior Court Costs Office Guideline Rates for Summary Assessment*.

- Craig Ford of Enable Law for his help with the PULHHEEMS rating table for *M5: Medical reference intervals and scales*.

We are very grateful to the following organisations for kindly granting us permission to use their material:

- The HMSO for their permission to use *Table C2: Real and nominal interest rates and price inflation*. Crown Copyright is reproduced with the permission of HMSO.

- The Office for National Statistics for the data reported in *A3: Life Tables and Projected Life Tables, E1: Retail Prices Index, E2: Inflation table, F6: Average earnings index; F7: Average weekly earnings* and *F8: Average earnings statistics*.

- HM Revenue & Customs and HMSO for their permission to use the material in *L2: Taxation of car and fuel benefits*.

Acknowledgments

- Sweet & Maxwell for their permission to use the tables from *Kemp & Kemp: The Quantum of Damages* at *C3: Special investment account rates* and *C8: Judgment debt interest rates (England and Wales)*.

- W. Green for their permission to use *C9: Judicial rates of interest (Scotland)*.

- FTSE Russell for their permission to use the FTSE 100 Index at *D1: Share price index*.

- Halifax; IHS Markit for providing the up-to-date material for *E3: House price indices* and *E4: Average semi-detached house prices by region*.

- *Intuition Communication Ltd for their permission to reproduce figures from their website www.privatehealth.co.uk at K4: Hospital self-pay (uninsured) charges.*

- *National Health Services for data reported in K5: NHS charges.*

- APIL for their permission to reproduce the APIL/FOIL Serious Injury Guide at *K7*.

- The RAC Motoring Services in conjunction with Emmerson Hill Associates, who compiled the illustrative running costs at *L1: Motoring costs*.

- Bauer Media, publishers of Parker's Car Price Guide, upon whose figures the calculations in *L4: The costs of buying and replacing cars* are based.

- Collins Debden Australia for their permission to reproduce the perpetual calendar, as featured in the International Management Diary, at *M3: Perpetual calendar*.

INTRODUCTION TO THE TWENTY-THIRD EDITION

"I've got £100 here, and it will take me two minutes to count it out."

Jim Bowen (1937–2018)

The editorial team

This year's editorial team is (in reverse alphabetical order) Harry Trusted, Tejina Mangat, Simon Levene, William Latimer-Sayer QC, Peter Jennings, Vitek Frenkel and Chris Daykin. We are grateful to Sohini Banerjee and Skye O'Neill of Sweet & Maxwell for keeping us in order, and making sure that we do not oversleep.

The year's news

With all respect to those whose leading cases have taken them to the Privy Council or the Supreme Court, there have been no startling developments on issues of quantum in the last 12 months.

Just as we were going to press last year, the government announced that consultation on the discount rate was now closed, and an announcement would follow on 3 August 2017. It did not, and we went to press wondering whether a major part of the book was about to become obsolete—say, on the day after publication[1]. Complicated plans were drawn up. In the end, of course, we need not have worried; at the time of writing (15 May 2018) the rate remains at -0.75 per cent. Or at least, that is the view of the Government; defendants think differently, and regularly draft counter-schedules using a discount rate of one per cent, which is what it is believed the rate *will* be, one of these days.

And then the 2018 Civil Liability Bill was published. It is now grinding its way through parliament, in a bathchair apparently propelled by Rip van Winkle. If the Bill is passed in its present form, the effect on the discount rate will be that:

- The Lord Chancellor will be obliged to review the discount rate every three years.

- An expert panel will be established to conduct the review, and the Treasury will also be consulted. No reason is given for the latter's inclusion. The Treasury pays out more in personal injury damages each year than any insurer, and can presumably be trusted to represent the interests of all defendants.

- The discount rate should be that which "a recipient of relevant damages could reasonably be expected to achieve if the recipient invested the relevant damages for the purpose of securing that (a) the relevant damages would meet those losses and costs for which they are awarded; (b) the relevant damages would meet those losses and costs at the time or times when they fall to be met by the relevant damages; and (c) the relevant damages would be exhausted at the end of the period for which they are awarded."

- The claimant (who never asked to become an investor, and presumably never wanted to take risks with all he has) will no longer be assumed to invest risk-free for the purpose of calculating

---

[1] We tried to find out, but in the end we were forced to conclude that nothing had changed since Charles Dickens wrote Chapter 10 of *Little Dorrit*, entitled "Containing the whole Science of Government".

Introduction to the Twenty-Third Edition

the quantum of damages. The Lord Chancellor is to assume that damages will be invested with "more risk than a very low level of risk, but less risk than would ordinarily be accepted by a prudent and properly advised individual investor who has different financial aims." The bill helpfully goes on to say that this "does not limit the assumptions which the Lord Chancellor may make"[2]—which makes careful wording of the bill superfluous.

The expert panel will be chaired by the Government Actuary, and four other members appointed by the Lord Chancellor. These four must include an actuary, an economist, an expert in "consumer matters as relating to investments" and someone with experience of managing investments.

Other news

The same Bill, incidentally, attempts to regulate claims for whiplash injuries. It is not at all clear why a separate tariff of general damages is needed for whiplash claims; the perceived (or at any rate, alleged) problem was *fraudulent* claims, not a lack of judicial consistency. The symptoms of whiplash are allegedly often faked. One would have thought that many other injuries depend on subjective reporting of symptoms—psychiatric conditions and tinnitus, for example. Others, such as Raynaud's phenomenon, are seldom witnessed by the reporting expert. Amputations might be harder to fake, but one should remember the Victorian murderer Charles Peace, who was missing a finger from his right hand; to conceal this deformity from the police, he wore a prosthetic arm with no hand at all.[3]

After an opaque definition of "whiplash injury"—which is to be defined further in Regulations—the Bill provides that where the whiplash injury lasts for two years or less[4]:

- General damages will be an amount specified in regulations made by the Lord Chancellor. This includes damages for minor psychological injury[5] associated with the whiplash. (In theory, this means that a claimant may be better off claiming for the psychological injury alone.)

- There can be an uplift (defined in Regulations) in (undefined) "exceptional circumstances".

- A solicitor may not settle a whiplash claim without "seeing appropriate evidence of the whiplash injury".

None of this, of course, could possibly increase the cost of litigation—any more than the reforms of civil procedure over the last two decades have done.

Our readers

As always, we welcome feedback and suggestions from our readers. If there is anything in the way of data or worked examples that you would find helpful, please let us know. Even if you only want to tell us about missing commas, we would like to hear from you.

Envoi

To remind our readers that there may be more than one answer to even the starkest mathematical question, if we ask "What is 2 + 2?":

---

[2] Perish the thought.
[3] Peace was hanged in 1879, having (appropriately enough) been fingered by an accomplice.
[4] Subject to the claimant's failure to mitigate the effect of the injury. Unfortunately, the Bill does not tell us what steps could be taken to mitigate a whiplash injury. Aspirin, perhaps.
[5] It is assumed that the parliamentary draftsman sees no difference between the concepts of "psychological" and "psychiatric".

Introduction to the Twenty-Third Edition

- a mathematician will answer "4";
- a physicist will answer "between 3.5 and 4.5";
- an engineer will answer "4—but say 40 to be on the safe side"; and
- an accountant will answer "What would you like it to be?"

Finally, and to emphasise that there is nothing new under the sun, the uncertainty of future projections is highlighted in the poem by George Outram[6]:

The Annuity

gaed to spend a week in Fife –
An unco week it proved to be –
For there I met a waesome wife
Lamentin' her viduity.
Her grief brak out sae fierce and fell,
I thought her heart wad burst the shell;
And – I was sae left to mysel' –
I sell't her an annuity.

The bargain lookit fair eneugh –
She just was turned o' saxty-three –
I couldna guessed she'd prove sae teugh,
By human ingenuity.
But years have come, and years have gane,
And there she's yet as stieve as stane –
The limmer's growin' young again,
Since she got her annuity.

She's crined' awa' to bane and skin,
But that, it seems, is nought to me;
She's like to live – although she's in
The last stage o' tenuity.

She munches wi' her wizen'd gums,
An' stumps about on legs o' thrums;
But comes, as sure as Christmas comes,
To ca' for her annuity.

I read the tables drawn wi' care
For an insurance company;
Her chance o' life was stated there,
Wi' perfect perspicuity.
But tables here or tables there,
She's lived ten years beyond her share,
An' 's like to live a dozen mair,
To ca' for her annuity…

The water-drop wears out the rock,
As this eternal jaud wears me;
I could withstand the single shock,
But not the continuity.
It's pay me here, an' pay me there,
An' pay me, pay me, evermair –
I'll gang demented wi' despair –
I'm charged for her annuity.

This would be echoed by André-François Raffray, a 47-year-old French lawyer, who sold an annuity to a 90-year-old woman called Jeanne Calment; what could go wrong? Thirty years later, when he died, she was still going strong, and his widow inherited the obligation to pay Mme Calment the 30,000 francs a year. When she eventually died at the age of 122, she was the oldest woman in the world—a condition that she ascribed in part to a diet rich in olive oil and foie gras. She ate up to a kilo of chocolate a week.

We wish our readers *bon appétit*.

Simon Levene

12 King's Bench Walk
Temple, London
EC4Y 7EL

1 June 2018
chambers@12kbw.co.uk
T: 020 7583 0811

---

[6] 1805–56.

CONTENTS

Group A—Ogden Tables and Related Materials
A1	-0.75 per cent discount tables "at a glance"	3
A2	Nil discount tables "at a glance"	10
A3	Life tables and projected life tables	16
A4	Loss of earnings multipliers adjusted for education, disability and employment status	22
A5	Multipliers for fixed periods and at intervals	36
A6	Tables of deferred loss	42
A7	Table of adjustments to multiplier for Fatal Accidents Acts dependency	46
A8	The Ogden Tables	47
A9	The Lord Chancellor's statement, 27 February 2017	125

Group B—Damages
B1	General damages table following *Heil v Rankin* and *Simmons v Castle*	131
B2	Bereavement damages	134
B3	*Auty v National Coal Board* (pension claims)	135
B4	*Roberts v Johnstone* (accommodation claims)	137
B5	Periodical payments	138
B6	Step-by-step guide to finding the annual estimates for hourly pay in ASHE SOC 2000 6115	140

Group C—Interest Rates
C1	Interest base rates	145
C2	Real and nominal interest rates and price inflation	146
C3	Special investment account rates	148
C4	Special and general damages interest	149
C5	Base rate + 10 per cent	151
C6	Number of days between two dates	152
C7	Decimal years	153
C8	Judgment debt interest rates (England and Wales)	154
C9	Judicial rates of interest (Scotland)	154

Group D—Investment
D1	Share price index (FTSE 100)	157
D2	Graph of share price index	158
D3	Index-linked stock	159

Group E—Prices
E1	Retail Prices Index	165
E2	Inflation table	167
E3	House price indices	168
E4	Average semi-detached house prices by region	170
E5	How prices have changed over 12 years	170

Group F—Earnings
F1	Earnings losses in personal injury and fatal accident cases	173
F2	Lost years	177

Contents

F3	Payroll documents	179
F4	National minimum wage	181
F5	Regional unemployment statistics	183
F6	Average weekly earnings index	189
F7	Average weekly earnings	190
F8	Average earnings statistics	191
F9	Public sector comparable earnings	213

Group G—Tax and National Insurance

G1	Net equivalents to a range of gross annual income figures	217
G2	Illustrative net earnings calculations	228
G3	Income tax reliefs and rates	229
G4	National Insurance contributions	232
G5	VAT registration thresholds and rates	236

Group H—Pension

H1	Net equivalents to a range of gross annual pension figures	239
H2	Illustrative net pension calculations	241
H3	Note on pension losses	243
H4	State pension age timetables	248

Group I—Benefits, Allowances, Charges

I1	Social security benefits (non-means-tested)	253
I2	Social security benefits and tax credits (means-tested)	256
I3	Personal injury trusts	261
I4	Claims for loss of earnings and maintenance at public expense	272
I5	Foster care allowances	272

Group J—Court of Protection

J1	Note on the Court of Protection	277
J2	The incidence of deputyship costs over a claimant's life	287
J3	Deputyship costs	289

Group K—Carer Rates and Rehabilitation

K1	Care and attendance	295
K2	Nannies, cleaners and school fees	312
K3	DIY, gardening and housekeeping	313
K4	Hospital self-pay (uninsured) charges	315
K5	NHS charges	316
K6	The 2015 Rehabilitation Code	317
K7	APIL/FOIL Serious Injury Guide	329

Group L—Motoring and Allied Material

L1	Motoring costs	339
L2	Taxation of car and fuel benefits	343
L3	The Motability Scheme	345
L4	The costs of buying and replacing cars	346
L5	Time, speed and distance	352

Group M—Other Information

M1	Senior Court Costs Office Guideline Rates for Summary Assessment	357

M2	Conversion formulae	360
M3	Perpetual calendar	362
M4	Religious festivals	365
M5	Medical reference intervals and scales	366

Group A
Ogden Tables and Related Materials

A1: **-0.75 per cent discount tables "at a glance"**

A2: **Nil discount tables "at a glance"**

A3: **Life tables and projected life tables**

A4: **Loss of earnings multipliers adjusted for education, disability and employment status**

A5: **Multipliers for fixed periods and at intervals**

A6: **Combination tables**

A7: **Table of adjustments to multiplier for Fatal Accidents Acts dependency**

A8: **The Ogden Tables**

A9: **The Lord Chancellor's statement, 27 February 2017**

A1: -0.75 per cent discount tables "at a glance"

The following tables comprise the -0.75 per cent columns from Ogden Tables 1–26 (Supplementary Tables). However, we now include columns for loss of earnings to, and loss of pension from, ages 66, 67, 68 and 69, which have been obtained by interpolation.

The method of interpolation for the multiplier for loss of earnings to pension age is as recommended in paragraph 13 of the Explanatory Notes to the 7th Edition of the Ogden Tables (see Table A8).

The Ogden Tables for loss of earnings are not extended below age 16. The appropriate starting figure for loss of earnings where an equivalent age below age 16 is required has been calculated as the difference between the multiplier for life and the multiplier from the equivalent retirement age.

Readers are reminded that the figures for loss of earnings must be adjusted in accordance with Section B of the Explanatory Notes to the Ogden Tables (Contingencies other than mortality) reproduced in Table A8. Multipliers already adjusted for these contingencies are set out in Table A4.

The multiplier for loss of pension commencing at ages 66 to 69 is calculated as the difference between the multiplier for life, as set out in tables 1 and 2 of the Ogden Tables, and the calculated multiplier to pension age.

> Multipliers for loss of earnings/loss of pension to and from ages 66 to 69 are shown at the back of Table A1 for a -0.75 per cent discount rate and at the back of Table A2 for a Nil discount rate.

A1: -0.75 per cent discount tables "at a glance"

-0.75 per cent discount tables "at a glance"—MALE

Age at date of trial	Table 1 Pecuniary loss for life	Table 3 Loss of earnings to age 50	Table 5 Loss of earnings to age 55	Table 7 Loss of earnings to age 60	Table 9 Loss of earnings to age 65	Table 11 Loss of earnings to age 70	Table 13 Loss of earnings to age 75	Table 15 Loss of pension from age 50	Table 17 Loss of pension from age 55	Table 19 Loss of pension from age 60	Table 21 Loss of pension from age 65	Table 23 Loss of pension from age 70	Table 25 Loss of pension from age 75
0	128.73							68.85	61.71	54.40	46.96	39.47	32.00
1	127.21							68.47	61.34	54.05	46.64	39.17	31.73
2	125.07							67.74	60.68	53.44	46.08	38.67	31.30
3	122.92							67.02	60.01	52.83	45.53	38.18	30.87
4	120.79							66.30	59.34	52.22	44.98	37.69	30.45
5	118.67							65.59	58.68	51.62	44.43	37.21	30.03
6	116.57							64.88	58.03	51.02	43.89	36.73	29.61
7	114.49							64.18	57.38	50.42	43.36	36.25	29.20
8	112.42							63.48	56.74	49.84	42.83	35.79	28.80
9	110.36							62.79	56.10	49.25	42.30	35.32	28.39
10	108.32							62.10	55.46	48.67	41.78	34.86	27.99
11	106.29							61.42	54.84	48.10	41.26	34.40	27.60
12	104.29							60.75	54.22	47.54	40.76	33.95	27.21
13	102.30							60.09	53.61	46.98	40.25	33.51	26.83
14	100.33							59.44	53.00	46.43	39.76	33.07	26.45
15	98.38							58.79	52.41	45.88	39.27	32.64	26.08
16	96.45	38.30	44.63	51.10	57.67	64.24	70.74	58.15	51.82	45.35	38.79	32.21	25.71
17	94.55	37.02	43.31	49.73	56.23	62.75	69.20	57.53	51.24	44.82	38.31	31.79	25.35
18	92.66	35.75	41.99	48.36	54.82	61.28	67.67	56.91	50.67	44.30	37.85	31.38	24.99
19	90.80	34.50	40.69	47.01	53.41	59.83	66.16	56.30	50.11	43.79	37.39	30.98	24.65
20	88.96	33.25	39.40	45.67	52.02	58.38	64.66	55.71	49.57	43.29	36.94	30.58	24.31
21	87.14	32.02	38.12	44.34	50.64	56.95	63.17	55.12	49.02	42.80	36.50	30.19	23.97
22	85.33	30.79	36.84	43.02	49.27	55.53	61.69	54.54	48.48	42.31	36.05	29.80	23.63
23	83.53	29.57	35.58	41.71	47.92	54.12	60.23	53.96	47.95	41.82	35.61	29.41	23.30
24	81.75	28.37	34.33	40.41	46.57	52.72	58.77	53.38	47.42	41.34	35.18	29.03	22.97
25	79.99	27.17	33.09	39.12	45.23	51.33	57.33	52.82	46.90	40.86	34.76	28.65	22.65
26	78.25	25.98	31.85	37.85	43.91	49.96	55.91	52.27	46.39	40.40	34.34	28.29	22.34
27	76.52	24.80	30.63	36.58	42.59	48.60	54.49	51.73	45.89	39.95	33.93	27.93	22.03
28	74.81	23.63	29.42	35.32	41.29	47.24	53.09	51.18	45.39	39.49	33.52	27.57	21.72
29	73.11	22.47	28.21	34.07	39.99	45.90	51.69	50.64	44.89	39.03	33.11	27.21	21.41
30	71.43	21.31	27.02	32.84	38.71	44.57	50.31	50.11	44.41	38.59	32.72	26.86	21.11
31	69.77	20.17	25.84	31.61	37.44	43.25	48.95	49.60	43.93	38.16	32.33	26.52	20.82
32	68.14	19.04	24.67	30.40	36.19	41.95	47.60	49.10	43.48	37.74	31.96	26.19	20.54
33	66.54	17.92	23.51	29.20	34.95	40.67	46.27	48.62	43.03	37.34	31.59	25.87	20.27
34	64.94	16.80	22.36	28.01	33.71	39.39	44.95	48.14	42.59	36.93	31.23	25.55	20.00
35	63.36	15.70	21.21	26.83	32.49	38.12	43.63	47.66	42.15	36.53	30.87	25.24	19.73
36	61.80	14.60	20.08	25.65	31.28	36.87	42.33	47.19	41.72	36.14	30.52	24.93	19.46
37	60.25	13.51	18.95	24.49	30.07	35.62	41.05	46.73	41.29	35.75	30.17	24.62	19.20
38	58.71	12.43	17.84	23.34	28.88	34.39	39.76	46.28	40.87	35.37	29.83	24.32	18.94
39	57.18	11.36	16.73	22.19	27.69	33.16	38.49	45.82	40.45	34.99	29.48	24.02	18.68
40	55.66	10.29	15.63	21.05	26.52	31.94	37.23	45.37	40.04	34.61	29.15	23.72	18.43
41	54.16	9.23	14.53	19.92	25.35	30.73	35.98	44.93	39.63	34.24	28.82	23.43	18.18
42	52.68	8.18	13.45	18.80	24.19	29.54	34.74	44.51	39.24	33.88	28.49	23.15	17.94
43	51.22	7.13	12.37	17.69	23.04	28.35	33.52	44.09	38.85	33.53	28.18	22.87	17.70
44	49.77	6.10	11.30	16.59	21.91	27.18	32.30	43.68	38.47	33.18	27.87	22.60	17.47
45	48.34	5.06	10.24	15.49	20.78	26.01	31.10	43.28	38.10	32.85	27.56	22.33	17.24
46	46.92	4.04	9.19	14.41	19.66	24.86	29.91	42.88	37.74	32.51	27.26	22.06	17.01
47	45.52	3.02	8.14	13.33	18.55	23.72	28.73	42.50	37.38	32.19	26.97	21.81	16.79
48	44.14	2.01	7.10	12.27	17.45	22.58	27.56	42.13	37.04	31.87	26.68	21.56	16.58
49	42.78	1.00	6.07	11.21	16.37	21.46	26.41	41.78	36.71	31.57	26.41	21.31	16.37
50	41.44		5.05	10.16	15.29	20.36	25.27	41.44	36.39	31.28	26.15	21.08	16.17
51	40.12		4.03	9.12	14.22	19.26	24.14		36.09	31.00	25.90	20.86	15.98
52	38.82		3.01	8.08	13.17	18.18	23.03		35.81	30.74	25.66	20.64	15.80
53	37.55		2.01	7.06	12.12	17.11	21.93		35.55	30.49	25.43	20.44	15.62
54	36.30		1.00	6.04	11.08	16.05	20.85		35.30	30.26	25.22	20.25	15.45

-0.75 per cent discount tables "at a glance"—MALE *continued*

Age at date of trial	Table 1 Pecuniary loss for life	Table 3 Loss of earnings to age 50	Table 5 Loss of earnings to age 55	Table 7 Loss of earnings to age 60	Table 9 Loss of earnings to age 65	Table 11 Loss of earnings to age 70	Table 13 Loss of earnings to age 75	Table 15 Loss of pension from age 50	Table 17 Loss of pension from age 55	Table 19 Loss of pension from age 60	Table 21 Loss of pension from age 65	Table 23 Loss of pension from age 70	Table 25 Loss of pension from age 75
55	35.07			5.02	10.05	15.00	19.78		35.07	30.05	25.02	20.07	15.30
56	33.87			4.01	9.03	13.96	18.72			29.86	24.84	19.91	15.15
57	32.69			3.01	8.01	12.93	17.67			29.68	24.68	19.76	15.02
58	31.52			2.00	7.00	11.91	16.63			29.51	24.52	19.61	14.88
59	30.35			1.00	5.99	10.89	15.60			29.35	24.36	19.47	14.75
60	29.19				4.98	9.87	14.57			29.19	24.21	19.32	14.62
61	28.05				3.98	8.87	13.55				24.06	19.18	14.49
62	26.92				2.99	7.87	12.55				23.94	19.05	14.38
63	25.82				1.99	6.88	11.55				23.83	18.94	14.27
64	24.74				1.00	5.90	10.57				23.74	18.84	14.17
65	23.70					4.92	9.60				23.70	18.78	14.10
66	22.68					3.94	8.64					18.74	14.04
67	21.69					2.96	7.68					18.73	14.01
68	20.73					1.98	6.73					18.75	14.00
69	19.78					0.99	5.78					18.79	14.00
70	18.85						4.84					18.85	14.02
71	17.92						3.88						14.04
72	17.00						2.93						14.07
73	16.07						1.96						14.11
74	15.15						0.99						14.16
75	14.22												14.22
76	13.32												
77	12.44												
78	11.58												
79	10.77												
80	9.99												
81	9.27												
82	8.61												
83	7.99												
84	7.42												
85	6.89												
86	6.38												
87	5.90												
88	5.44												
89	5.00												
90	4.59												
91	4.21												
92	3.85												
93	3.52												
94	3.22												
95	2.96												
96	2.74												
97	2.55												
98	2.37												
99	2.21												
100	2.06												

A1: -0.75 per cent discount tables "at a glance"

-0.75 per cent discount tables "at a glance"—FEMALE

Age at date of trial	Table 2 Pecuniary loss for life	Table 4 Loss of earnings to age 50	Table 6 Loss of earnings to age 55	Table 8 Loss of earnings to age 60	Table 10 Loss of earnings to age 65	Table 12 Loss of earnings to age 70	Table 14 Loss of earnings to age 75	Table 16 Loss of pension from age 50	Table 18 Loss of pension from age 55	Table 20 Loss of pension from age 60	Table 22 Loss of pension from age 65	Table 24 Loss of pension from age 70	Table 26 Loss of pension from age 75
0	135.52							75.34	68.08	60.62	52.96	45.17	37.29
1	133.87							74.89	67.66	60.22	52.59	44.82	36.97
2	131.69							74.13	66.95	59.57	52.00	44.29	36.51
3	129.52							73.38	66.25	58.93	51.42	43.77	36.05
4	127.36							72.63	65.56	58.29	50.84	43.25	35.60
5	125.21							71.88	64.87	57.65	50.26	42.74	35.15
6	123.07							71.14	64.18	57.02	49.69	42.22	34.70
7	120.96							70.41	63.50	56.40	49.12	41.72	34.25
8	118.85							69.68	62.83	55.78	48.56	41.22	33.81
9	116.77							68.96	62.16	55.16	48.00	40.72	33.38
10	114.70							68.25	61.50	54.56	47.45	40.23	32.95
11	112.65							67.54	60.85	53.96	46.91	39.74	32.53
12	110.62							66.84	60.20	53.36	46.37	39.26	32.11
13	108.60							66.15	59.55	52.77	45.83	38.78	31.69
14	106.60							65.47	58.92	52.19	45.31	38.32	31.28
15	104.62							64.79	58.29	51.62	44.79	37.85	30.88
16	102.65	38.53	44.98	51.60	58.38	65.26	72.17	64.12	57.67	51.05	44.27	37.39	30.48
17	100.71	37.25	43.65	50.22	56.94	63.77	70.62	63.46	57.06	50.49	43.76	36.94	30.08
18	98.78	35.98	42.33	48.85	55.52	62.29	69.09	62.80	56.45	49.93	43.26	36.49	29.69
19	96.88	34.72	41.02	47.49	54.11	60.82	67.56	62.16	55.86	49.39	42.77	36.05	29.31
20	94.99	33.46	39.72	46.14	52.71	59.37	66.05	61.53	55.27	48.85	42.28	35.62	28.94
21	93.12	32.22	38.43	44.80	51.32	57.92	64.55	60.90	54.69	48.32	41.80	35.20	28.57
22	91.26	30.99	37.15	43.47	49.93	56.49	63.06	60.27	54.11	47.79	41.33	34.77	28.20
23	89.41	29.76	35.87	42.15	48.56	55.06	61.58	59.65	53.54	47.26	40.85	34.35	27.83
24	87.58	28.54	34.61	40.84	47.20	53.65	60.12	59.03	52.97	46.74	40.37	33.93	27.46
25	85.76	27.34	33.36	39.54	45.85	52.25	58.66	58.43	52.40	46.22	39.91	33.51	27.10
26	83.97	26.14	32.12	38.25	44.52	50.86	57.22	57.83	51.85	45.72	39.45	33.11	26.75
27	82.19	24.95	30.89	36.97	43.19	49.48	55.78	57.24	51.30	45.22	39.00	32.71	26.40
28	80.42	23.78	29.66	35.70	41.87	48.11	54.36	56.65	50.76	44.72	38.55	32.31	26.06
29	78.68	22.61	28.45	34.45	40.56	46.76	52.96	56.07	50.23	44.23	38.11	31.92	25.72
30	76.95	21.45	27.25	33.20	39.27	45.41	51.56	55.50	49.70	43.75	37.68	31.53	25.39
31	75.24	20.30	26.05	31.96	37.98	44.08	50.17	54.94	49.18	43.28	37.25	31.16	25.06
32	73.54	19.15	24.87	30.73	36.71	42.76	48.80	54.39	48.67	42.81	36.83	30.78	24.74
33	71.86	18.02	23.69	29.51	35.45	41.44	47.44	53.84	48.17	42.35	36.42	30.42	24.42
34	70.20	16.90	22.53	28.30	34.19	40.14	46.09	53.30	47.67	41.89	36.00	30.05	24.11
35	68.54	15.78	21.37	27.10	32.95	38.85	44.75	52.76	47.17	41.44	35.60	29.69	23.79
36	66.91	14.67	20.22	25.91	31.71	37.57	43.42	52.24	46.68	40.99	35.19	29.34	23.49
37	65.29	13.57	19.09	24.73	30.49	36.30	42.10	51.72	46.20	40.56	34.80	28.99	23.19
38	63.69	12.48	17.96	23.56	29.28	35.05	40.80	51.20	45.73	40.12	34.41	28.64	22.89
39	62.10	11.40	16.84	22.40	28.07	33.80	39.50	50.70	45.26	39.70	34.02	28.30	22.59
40	60.52	10.33	15.72	21.25	26.88	32.56	38.22	50.19	44.80	39.27	33.64	27.96	22.30
41	58.96	9.26	14.62	20.11	25.70	31.33	36.95	49.70	44.34	38.86	33.27	27.63	22.02
42	57.42	8.20	13.53	18.98	24.52	30.12	35.69	49.22	43.90	38.45	32.90	27.31	21.74
43	55.90	7.15	12.44	17.85	23.36	28.91	34.44	48.74	43.46	38.05	32.54	26.99	21.46
44	54.39	6.11	11.36	16.74	22.20	27.72	33.20	48.28	43.03	37.65	32.18	26.67	21.19
45	52.90	5.08	10.29	15.63	21.06	26.53	31.97	47.82	42.61	37.27	31.84	26.37	20.93
46	51.42	4.05	9.23	14.53	19.93	25.36	30.76	47.38	42.19	36.89	31.50	26.06	20.66
47	49.96	3.03	8.18	13.45	18.80	24.20	29.56	46.94	41.79	36.52	31.16	25.77	20.41
48	48.53	2.01	7.13	12.37	17.69	23.05	28.37	46.52	41.40	36.16	30.84	25.48	20.16
49	47.11	1.00	6.09	11.30	16.59	21.91	27.19	46.11	41.02	35.81	30.52	25.20	19.92
50	45.71		5.06	10.24	15.50	20.78	26.03	45.71	40.65	35.47	30.22	24.93	19.69
51	44.33		4.04	9.19	14.41	19.67	24.88		40.29	35.14	29.92	24.66	19.45
52	42.97		3.02	8.14	13.34	18.56	23.73		39.94	34.82	29.63	24.40	19.23
53	41.62		2.01	7.10	12.27	17.46	22.61		39.61	34.52	29.35	24.15	19.01
54	40.29		1.00	6.07	11.22	16.38	21.49		39.29	34.22	29.08	23.91	18.80

-0.75 per cent discount tables "at a glance"—FEMALE *continued*

Age at date of trial	Table 2 Pecuniary loss for life	Table 4 Loss of earnings to age 50	Table 6 Loss of earnings to age 55	Table 8 Loss of earnings to age 60	Table 10 Loss of earnings to age 65	Table 12 Loss of earnings to age 70	Table 14 Loss of earnings to age 75	Table 16 Loss of pension from age 50	Table 18 Loss of pension from age 55	Table 20 Loss of pension from age 60	Table 22 Loss of pension from age 65	Table 24 Loss of pension from age 70	Table 26 Loss of pension from age 75
55	38.99			5.05	10.17	15.30	20.38		38.99	33.94	28.82	23.68	18.60
56	37.70			4.03	9.12	14.24	19.29			33.67	28.57	23.46	18.41
57	36.43			3.02	8.09	13.18	18.20			33.41	28.34	23.25	18.22
58	35.17			2.01	7.06	12.13	17.13			33.16	28.11	23.04	18.04
59	33.92			1.00	6.04	11.08	16.06			32.92	27.88	22.84	17.86
60	32.68				5.02	10.05	15.00			32.68	27.66	22.63	17.68
61	31.45				4.01	9.02	13.95				27.44	22.43	17.50
62	30.24				3.00	8.00	12.91				27.24	22.24	17.33
63	29.04				2.00	6.98	11.88				27.04	22.06	17.16
64	27.88				1.00	5.98	10.86				26.88	21.90	17.01
65	26.74					4.98	9.86				26.74	21.76	16.88
66	25.63					3.98	8.86					21.65	16.77
67	24.55					2.99	7.87					21.56	16.68
68	23.49					1.99	6.88					21.50	16.61
69	22.45					1.00	5.90					21.45	16.55
70	21.41						4.92					21.41	16.49
71	20.39						3.94						16.44
72	19.35						2.96						16.39
73	18.31						1.98						16.33
74	17.27						0.99						16.28
75	16.23												16.23
76	15.20												
77	14.19												
78	13.21												
79	12.27												
80	11.39												
81	10.56												
82	9.78												
83	9.06												
84	8.39												
85	7.76												
86	7.16												
87	6.59												
88	6.05												
89	5.53												
90	5.05												
91	4.60												
92	4.18												
93	3.81												
94	3.48												
95	3.20												
96	2.96												
97	2.75												
98	2.56												
99	2.38												
100	2.21												

A1: -0.75 per cent discount tables "at a glance"

A1: -0.75 per cent discount tables for retirement ages 66 to 69—MALE

Age at date of trial	Loss of earnings to age 66	Loss of earnings to age 67	Loss of earnings to age 68	Loss of earnings to age 69	Age at date of trial	Loss of pension from age 66	Loss of pension from age 67	Loss of pension from age 68	Loss of pension from age 69
16	58.97	60.27	61.59	62.91	16	37.53	36.24	34.93	33.58
17	57.52	58.82	60.13	61.44	17	37.07	35.79	34.49	33.15
18	56.09	57.38	58.68	59.98	18	36.61	35.35	34.06	32.73
19	54.68	55.95	57.24	58.53	19	36.16	34.91	33.63	32.32
20	53.27	54.54	55.81	57.10	20	35.72	34.47	33.20	31.91
21	51.89	53.14	54.40	55.67	21	35.28	34.04	32.78	31.50
22	50.51	51.75	53.00	54.26	22	34.85	33.63	32.37	31.10
23	49.14	50.37	51.61	52.86	23	34.43	33.21	31.97	30.70
24	47.78	49.00	50.23	51.47	24	34.00	32.80	31.57	30.31
25	46.43	47.65	48.87	50.10	25	33.59	32.40	31.18	29.93
26	45.10	46.30	47.51	48.73	26	33.18	31.99	30.79	29.55
27	43.78	44.97	46.17	47.38	27	32.78	31.60	30.40	29.18
28	42.46	43.64	44.83	46.03	28	32.38	31.21	30.02	28.80
29	41.16	42.34	43.51	44.70	29	31.99	30.84	29.65	28.44
30	39.87	41.04	42.21	43.38	30	31.60	30.46	29.29	28.08
31	38.59	39.75	40.91	42.08	31	31.22	30.09	28.93	27.74
32	37.33	38.48	39.63	40.79	32	30.85	29.72	28.58	27.40
33	36.07	37.21	38.36	39.51	33	30.49	29.37	28.23	27.07
34	34.83	35.96	37.10	38.24	34	30.14	29.02	27.89	26.73
35	33.60	34.72	35.85	36.98	35	29.79	28.68	27.56	26.41
36	32.38	33.49	34.61	35.74	36	29.44	28.35	27.23	26.09
37	31.17	32.27	33.38	34.50	37	29.10	28.01	26.90	25.77
38	29.97	31.06	32.16	33.27	38	28.77	27.68	26.58	25.46
39	28.77	29.86	30.95	32.05	39	28.43	27.36	26.27	25.15
40	27.59	28.67	29.75	30.84	40	28.11	27.04	25.96	24.85
41	26.42	27.49	28.56	29.64	41	27.78	26.73	25.65	24.55
42	25.25	26.31	27.38	28.46	42	27.47	26.42	25.35	24.26
43	24.10	25.15	26.21	27.28	43	27.15	26.11	25.06	23.97
44	22.95	24.00	25.05	26.11	44	26.85	25.82	24.76	23.69
45	21.82	22.86	23.91	24.96	45	26.56	25.53	24.48	23.41
46	20.69	21.73	22.77	23.81	46	26.26	25.24	24.20	23.14
47	19.58	20.61	21.64	22.68	47	25.98	24.97	23.93	22.88
48	18.48	19.50	20.53	21.55	48	25.70	24.70	23.67	22.62
49	17.39	18.40	19.42	20.44	49	25.44	24.44	23.42	22.38
50	16.30	17.32	18.33	19.34	50	25.18	24.19	23.17	22.14
51	15.23	16.24	17.25	18.25	51	24.93	23.95	22.94	21.91
52	14.17	15.17	16.18	17.18	52	24.70	23.72	22.71	21.69
53	13.12	14.12	15.12	16.11	53	24.48	23.50	22.50	21.48
54	12.08	13.07	14.07	15.06	54	24.27	23.30	22.30	21.29
55	11.04	12.03	13.02	14.01	55	24.07	23.10	22.12	21.11
56	10.01	11.00	11.99	12.98	56	23.88	22.92	21.94	20.94
57	8.99	9.98	10.96	11.95	57	23.71	22.74	21.77	20.77
58	7.98	8.96	9.94	10.93	58	23.55	22.58	21.60	20.62
59	6.97	7.95	8.93	9.91	59	23.40	22.43	21.45	20.46
60	5.97	6.95	7.93	8.90	60	23.26	22.29	21.30	20.31
61	4.97	5.95	6.93	7.90	61	23.12	22.16	21.17	20.18
62	3.97	4.96	5.93	6.90	62	23.00	22.04	21.05	20.06
63	2.98	3.97	4.94	5.91	63	22.90	21.94	20.95	19.95
64	1.99	2.98	3.96	4.93	64	22.81	21.85	20.87	19.87
65	1.00	1.99	2.97	3.95	65	22.75	21.80	20.81	19.81
66		1.00	1.99	2.97	66	22.73	21.76	20.78	19.77
67			1.00	1.98	67		21.76	20.77	19.76
68				0.99	68			20.79	19.78
69					69				19.82

See notes at the start of section A1 for details of methodology

A1: -0.75 per cent discount tables for retirement ages 66 to 69—FEMALE

Age at date of trial	Loss of earnings to age 66	Loss of earnings to age 67	Loss of earnings to age 68	Loss of earnings to age 69	Age at date of trial	Loss of pension from age 66	Loss of pension from age 67	Loss of pension from age 68	Loss of pension from age 69
16	59.74	61.10	62.48	63.86	16	42.95	41.61	40.23	38.83
17	58.29	59.64	61.01	62.38	17	42.46	41.12	39.76	38.36
18	56.85	58.20	59.55	60.91	18	41.97	40.64	39.29	37.91
19	55.43	56.76	58.10	59.46	19	41.48	40.17	38.83	37.46
20	54.02	55.34	56.67	58.01	20	41.00	39.70	38.37	37.01
21	52.61	53.92	55.25	56.58	21	40.53	39.23	37.91	36.57
22	51.22	52.52	53.83	55.16	22	40.07	38.78	37.46	36.13
23	49.84	51.13	52.43	53.74	23	39.60	38.33	37.02	35.70
24	48.47	49.75	51.04	52.34	24	39.14	37.88	36.59	35.27
25	47.11	48.38	49.66	50.95	25	38.68	37.43	36.15	34.85
26	45.77	47.03	48.29	49.57	26	38.23	36.99	35.72	34.43
27	44.43	45.68	46.94	48.20	27	37.79	36.56	35.30	34.02
28	43.10	44.34	45.59	46.85	28	37.36	36.13	34.88	33.61
29	41.79	43.02	44.25	45.50	29	36.93	35.71	34.47	33.21
30	40.48	41.70	42.93	44.17	30	36.50	35.30	34.07	32.82
31	39.19	40.40	41.62	42.84	31	36.08	34.89	33.67	32.43
32	37.90	39.10	40.31	41.53	32	35.67	34.48	33.28	32.04
33	36.63	37.82	39.02	40.23	33	35.26	34.08	32.89	31.66
34	35.37	36.55	37.74	38.94	34	34.86	33.69	32.50	31.29
35	34.11	35.29	36.47	37.66	35	34.46	33.31	32.12	30.92
36	32.87	34.03	35.21	36.39	36	34.07	32.92	31.75	30.56
37	31.64	32.79	33.96	35.13	37	33.68	32.54	31.38	30.20
38	30.42	31.56	32.72	33.88	38	33.30	32.17	31.02	29.84
39	29.20	30.34	31.49	32.64	39	32.92	31.80	30.66	29.49
40	28.00	29.13	30.27	31.41	40	32.55	31.44	30.30	29.14
41	26.81	27.93	29.06	30.19	41	32.19	31.08	29.95	28.80
42	25.63	26.74	27.86	28.98	42	31.83	30.73	29.61	28.47
43	24.46	25.56	26.67	27.79	43	31.47	30.39	29.28	28.14
44	23.30	24.39	25.49	26.60	44	31.13	30.05	28.95	27.82
45	22.15	23.23	24.33	25.43	45	30.79	29.71	28.62	27.50
46	21.01	22.09	23.17	24.26	46	30.46	29.39	28.30	27.19
47	19.88	20.95	22.03	23.11	47	30.13	29.07	28.00	26.89
48	18.76	19.82	20.89	21.97	48	29.81	28.76	27.69	26.60
49	17.65	18.71	19.77	20.84	49	29.50	28.46	27.40	26.31
50	16.55	17.60	18.66	19.72	50	29.20	28.16	27.11	26.03
51	15.46	16.50	17.56	18.61	51	28.91	27.88	26.83	25.76
52	14.38	15.42	16.46	17.51	52	28.63	27.60	26.56	25.49
53	13.31	14.34	15.38	16.42	53	28.35	27.34	26.30	25.24
54	12.24	13.27	14.31	15.34	54	28.09	27.08	26.05	24.99
55	11.19	12.21	13.24	14.27	55	27.83	26.83	25.80	24.75
56	10.14	11.16	12.19	13.21	56	27.58	26.58	25.56	24.53
57	9.10	10.12	11.14	12.16	57	27.35	26.35	25.33	24.30
58	8.07	9.08	10.10	11.11	58	27.12	26.12	25.11	24.09
59	7.05	8.05	9.06	10.07	59	26.90	25.90	24.89	23.87
60	6.03	7.03	8.03	9.04	60	26.69	25.69	24.68	23.66
61	5.01	6.01	7.02	8.02	61	26.48	25.49	24.48	23.46
62	4.00	5.00	6.00	7.00	62	26.28	25.30	24.29	23.27
63	3.00	4.00	5.00	5.99	63	26.10	25.13	24.12	23.10
64	2.00	3.00	3.99	4.99	64	25.94	24.97	23.97	22.94
65	1.00	2.00	2.99	3.99	65	25.79	24.83	23.83	22.81
66		1.00	2.00	2.99	66	25.67	24.71	23.72	22.70
67			1.00	1.99	67		24.61	23.62	22.61
68				1.00	68			23.54	22.54
69					69				22.48

See notes at the start of section A1 for details of methodology

A2: Nil discount tables "at a glance"

Tables at 0.0%

MALE

Age at date of trial	Table 1 Pecuniary loss for life	Table 3 Loss of earnings to age 50	Table 5 Loss of earnings to age 55	Table 7 Loss of earnings to age 60	Table 9 Loss of earnings to age 65	Table 11 Loss of earnings to age 70	Table 13 Loss of earnings to age 75	Table 15 Loss of pension from age 50	Table 17 Loss of pension from age 55	Table 19 Loss of pension from age 60	Table 21 Loss of pension from age 65	Table 23 Loss of pension from age 70	Table 25 Loss of pension from age 75
0	88.96							39.61	34.80	30.06	25.41	20.90	16.58
1	88.31							39.70	34.87	30.10	25.44	20.91	16.56
2	87.22							39.59	34.76	30.00	25.33	20.81	16.47
3	86.12							39.49	34.65	29.89	25.23	20.70	16.37
4	85.01							39.37	34.54	29.78	25.12	20.60	16.28
5	83.89							39.26	34.43	29.67	25.01	20.50	16.18
6	82.78							39.14	34.32	29.56	24.90	20.39	16.08
7	81.66							39.03	34.20	29.45	24.80	20.29	15.98
8	80.55							38.91	34.09	29.34	24.69	20.19	15.88
9	79.43							38.80	33.97	29.22	24.58	20.08	15.79
10	78.31							38.68	33.86	29.11	24.47	19.97	15.69
11	77.19							38.56	33.74	29.00	24.36	19.87	15.59
12	76.07							38.44	33.63	28.88	24.25	19.76	15.49
13	74.96							38.33	33.51	28.77	24.14	19.66	15.39
14	73.84							38.21	33.40	28.66	24.03	19.56	15.29
15	72.73							38.10	33.29	28.55	23.92	19.45	15.20
16	71.61	33.63	38.44	43.18	47.80	52.26	56.51	37.99	33.17	28.44	23.82	19.35	15.10
17	70.51	32.63	37.44	42.18	46.80	51.26	55.50	37.88	33.06	28.33	23.71	19.25	15.01
18	69.41	31.64	36.45	41.18	45.80	50.25	54.49	37.77	32.96	28.23	23.61	19.15	14.92
19	68.31	30.65	35.46	40.19	44.80	49.26	53.49	37.67	32.85	28.12	23.51	19.06	14.82
20	67.22	29.66	34.47	39.20	43.81	48.26	52.48	37.57	32.75	28.02	23.41	18.96	14.74
21	66.13	28.66	33.48	38.21	42.82	47.26	51.48	37.46	32.65	27.92	23.31	18.87	14.65
22	65.04	27.67	32.49	37.21	41.82	46.27	50.48	37.36	32.55	27.82	23.21	18.77	14.55
23	63.94	26.68	31.49	36.22	40.83	45.27	49.48	37.26	32.45	27.72	23.11	18.67	14.46
24	62.85	25.69	30.50	35.23	39.84	44.27	48.48	37.16	32.34	27.62	23.01	18.58	14.37
25	61.76	24.70	29.52	34.24	38.85	43.28	47.48	37.06	32.24	27.52	22.91	18.48	14.28
26	60.68	23.71	28.53	33.25	37.86	42.29	46.48	36.96	32.15	27.42	22.82	18.39	14.20
27	59.59	22.72	27.54	32.27	36.87	41.29	45.48	36.87	32.06	27.33	22.73	18.30	14.11
28	58.51	21.73	26.55	31.28	35.88	40.30	44.48	36.77	31.96	27.23	22.63	18.21	14.02
29	57.42	20.74	25.56	30.29	34.89	39.31	43.49	36.68	31.86	27.13	22.53	18.11	13.93
30	56.34	19.76	24.57	29.30	33.90	38.32	42.49	36.58	31.76	27.04	22.44	18.02	13.85
31	55.27	18.77	23.59	28.32	32.92	37.33	41.50	36.50	31.68	26.95	22.35	17.93	13.76
32	54.20	17.78	22.61	27.34	31.94	36.35	40.52	36.42	31.60	26.86	22.26	17.85	13.69
33	53.15	16.80	21.63	26.36	30.96	35.37	39.54	36.35	31.52	26.79	22.18	17.77	13.61
34	52.09	15.82	20.65	25.38	29.99	34.40	38.56	36.27	31.44	26.71	22.10	17.69	13.53
35	51.03	14.83	19.67	24.40	29.01	33.42	37.58	36.20	31.36	26.63	22.02	17.61	13.45
36	49.98	13.85	18.69	23.43	28.03	32.45	36.60	36.13	31.29	26.55	21.94	17.53	13.38
37	48.93	12.86	17.71	22.45	27.06	31.47	35.62	36.06	31.22	26.47	21.87	17.45	13.30
38	47.87	11.88	16.73	21.48	26.08	30.50	34.64	35.99	31.14	26.40	21.79	17.37	13.23
39	46.82	10.89	15.75	20.50	25.11	29.52	33.67	35.92	31.07	26.32	21.71	17.30	13.15
40	45.76	9.91	14.76	19.52	24.13	28.55	32.69	35.85	31.00	26.24	21.63	17.22	13.07
41	44.71	8.92	13.78	18.54	23.16	27.57	31.71	35.79	30.93	26.17	21.55	17.14	13.00
42	43.67	7.93	12.80	17.57	22.19	26.60	30.74	35.73	30.86	26.10	21.48	17.07	12.93
43	42.62	6.95	11.82	16.59	21.22	25.63	29.77	35.68	30.80	26.03	21.41	16.99	12.86
44	41.59	5.96	10.84	15.62	20.25	24.66	28.80	35.63	30.74	25.97	21.34	16.92	12.79
45	40.55	4.97	9.86	14.64	19.28	23.70	27.83	35.58	30.69	25.91	21.27	16.85	12.72
46	39.52	3.98	8.88	13.67	18.31	22.73	26.87	35.54	30.64	25.85	21.21	16.79	12.65
47	38.49	2.99	7.90	12.70	17.34	21.77	25.90	35.50	30.59	25.79	21.15	16.72	12.59
48	37.47	1.99	6.92	11.73	16.38	20.81	24.95	35.47	30.55	25.74	21.09	16.66	12.52
49	36.45	1.00	5.93	10.75	15.41	19.85	23.99	35.46	30.52	25.70	21.04	16.60	12.46

Nil discount tables "at a glance"—MALE *continued*

Age at date of trial	Table 1 Pecuniary loss for life	Table 3 Loss of earnings to age 50	Table 5 Loss of earnings to age 55	Table 7 Loss of earnings to age 60	Table 9 Loss of earnings to age 65	Table 11 Loss of earnings to age 70	Table 13 Loss of earnings to age 75	Table 15 Loss of pension from age 50	Table 17 Loss of pension from age 55	Table 19 Loss of pension from age 60	Table 21 Loss of pension from age 65	Table 23 Loss of pension from age 70	Table 25 Loss of pension from age 75
50	35.45		4.95	9.78	14.46	18.90	23.04	35.45	30.50	25.66	20.99	16.55	12.41
51	34.45		3.97	8.81	13.50	17.95	22.10		30.49	25.64	20.96	16.51	12.36
52	33.47		2.98	7.84	12.54	17.00	21.16		30.49	25.62	20.93	16.47	12.31
53	32.49		1.99	6.87	11.59	16.06	20.23		30.50	25.62	20.91	16.43	12.27
54	31.53		1.00	5.90	10.63	15.12	19.30		30.53	25.63	20.90	16.41	12.23
55	30.58			4.93	9.68	14.19	18.37		30.58	25.65	20.90	16.39	12.20
56	29.64			3.95	8.73	13.25	17.46			25.69	20.91	16.39	12.18
57	28.71			2.97	7.77	12.32	16.54			25.74	20.94	16.39	12.17
58	27.78			1.99	6.82	11.39	15.63			25.80	20.97	16.40	12.16
59	26.85			1.00	5.85	10.45	14.71			25.86	21.00	16.40	12.15
60	25.92				4.89	9.51	13.79			25.92	21.03	16.41	12.13
61	25.00				3.92	8.58	12.87				21.07	16.42	12.12
62	24.08				2.95	7.64	11.96				21.12	16.44	12.12
63	23.17				1.98	6.70	11.05				21.20	16.47	12.12
64	22.28				0.99	5.77	10.15				21.29	16.52	12.13
65	21.42					4.83	9.25				21.42	16.59	12.16
66	20.57					3.88	8.36					16.69	12.21
67	19.74					2.93	7.46					16.81	12.28
68	18.93					1.97	6.56					16.96	12.37
69	18.12					0.99	5.66					17.13	12.47
70	17.32						4.75					17.32	12.58
71	16.53						3.83						12.70
72	15.72						2.89						12.83
73	14.92						1.95						12.97
74	14.10						0.99						13.12
75	13.29												13.29
76	12.48												
77	11.70												
78	10.93												
79	10.19												
80	9.49												
81	8.83												
82	8.22												
83	7.65												
84	7.13												
85	6.63												
86	6.16												
87	5.71												
88	5.27												
89	4.86												
90	4.47												
91	4.10												
92	3.76												
93	3.44												
94	3.16												
95	2.91												
96	2.69												
97	2.50												
98	2.34												
99	2.18												
100	2.04												

A2: Nil discount tables "at a glance"

Nil discount tables "at a glance"—FEMALE

Age at date of trial	Table 2 Pecuniary loss for life	Table 4 Loss of earnings to age 50	Table 6 Loss of earnings to age 55	Table 8 Loss of earnings to age 60	Table 10 Loss of earnings to age 65	Table 12 Loss of earnings to age 70	Table 14 Loss of earnings to age 75	Table 16 Loss of pension from age 50	Table 18 Loss of pension from age 55	Table 20 Loss of pension from age 60	Table 22 Loss of pension from age 65	Table 24 Loss of pension from age 70	Table 26 Loss of pension from age 75
0	92.57							42.98	38.10	33.26	28.47	23.78	19.22
1	91.86							43.07	38.16	33.30	28.50	23.79	19.21
2	90.77							42.97	38.06	33.20	28.40	23.69	19.12
3	89.68							42.87	37.96	33.10	28.30	23.60	19.02
4	88.58							42.77	37.86	33.00	28.21	23.50	18.93
5	87.49							42.67	37.76	32.90	28.11	23.41	18.84
6	86.38							42.56	37.66	32.80	28.01	23.31	18.75
7	85.28							42.46	37.56	32.70	27.91	23.21	18.65
8	84.18							42.36	37.45	32.60	27.81	23.11	18.56
9	83.07							42.25	37.35	32.49	27.70	23.01	18.46
10	81.97							42.15	37.24	32.39	27.60	22.92	18.37
11	80.86							42.04	37.14	32.29	27.50	22.82	18.28
12	79.76							41.94	37.04	32.18	27.40	22.72	18.18
13	78.65							41.83	36.93	32.08	27.30	22.62	18.09
14	77.55							41.73	36.83	31.98	27.20	22.53	18.00
15	76.44							41.62	36.72	31.88	27.10	22.43	17.91
16	75.34	33.82	38.72	43.57	48.34	53.01	57.53	41.52	36.62	31.78	27.00	22.33	17.81
17	74.24	32.82	37.72	42.57	47.34	52.01	56.52	41.42	36.52	31.67	26.90	22.24	17.72
18	73.14	31.83	36.72	41.57	46.34	51.00	55.51	41.32	36.42	31.58	26.80	22.14	17.63
19	72.05	30.83	35.73	40.57	45.34	50.00	54.51	41.22	36.32	31.48	26.71	22.05	17.54
20	70.96	29.83	34.73	39.57	44.34	49.00	53.50	41.12	36.23	31.38	26.61	21.96	17.45
21	69.86	28.84	33.73	38.58	43.34	48.00	52.50	41.03	36.13	31.29	26.52	21.86	17.36
22	68.77	27.84	32.74	37.58	42.34	47.00	51.49	40.93	36.03	31.19	26.42	21.77	17.27
23	67.67	26.85	31.74	36.58	41.35	46.00	50.49	40.82	35.93	31.09	26.32	21.67	17.18
24	66.57	25.85	30.74	35.58	40.35	44.99	49.48	40.72	35.83	30.99	26.23	21.58	17.09
25	65.48	24.85	29.75	34.59	39.35	43.99	48.48	40.62	35.73	30.89	26.13	21.48	17.00
26	64.38	23.86	28.75	33.59	38.35	42.99	47.47	40.53	35.63	30.79	26.03	21.39	16.91
27	63.29	22.86	27.76	32.59	37.35	41.99	46.47	40.43	35.54	30.70	25.94	21.30	16.82
28	62.20	21.87	26.76	31.60	36.36	40.99	45.46	40.33	35.44	30.60	25.84	21.21	16.74
29	61.11	20.87	25.77	30.60	35.36	39.99	44.46	40.24	35.34	30.51	25.75	21.11	16.65
30	60.02	19.88	24.77	29.61	34.36	39.00	43.46	40.15	35.25	30.41	25.66	21.03	16.56
31	58.94	18.88	23.78	28.62	33.37	38.00	42.46	40.06	35.16	30.32	25.57	20.94	16.48
32	57.86	17.89	22.79	27.62	32.38	37.01	41.46	39.97	35.07	30.23	25.48	20.85	16.39
33	56.77	16.89	21.79	26.63	31.38	36.01	40.46	39.88	34.98	30.14	25.39	20.76	16.31
34	55.69	15.90	20.80	25.64	30.39	35.02	39.47	39.79	34.89	30.05	25.30	20.68	16.23
35	54.61	14.91	19.81	24.65	29.40	34.02	38.47	39.70	34.80	29.96	25.21	20.59	16.14
36	53.53	13.92	18.82	23.66	28.41	33.03	37.47	39.62	34.72	29.88	25.13	20.50	16.06
37	52.46	12.92	17.83	22.67	27.42	32.04	36.48	39.54	34.63	29.79	25.04	20.42	15.98
38	51.38	11.93	16.84	21.68	26.43	31.05	35.49	39.45	34.55	29.71	24.95	20.33	15.90
39	50.31	10.94	15.85	20.69	25.44	30.06	34.49	39.37	34.46	29.62	24.87	20.25	15.82
40	49.24	9.95	14.86	19.70	24.45	29.07	33.50	39.29	34.38	29.54	24.79	20.17	15.73
41	48.17	8.95	13.87	18.71	23.47	28.08	32.51	39.22	34.30	29.46	24.70	20.08	15.66
42	47.10	7.96	12.88	17.73	22.48	27.10	31.53	39.14	34.23	29.38	24.62	20.00	15.58
43	46.04	6.97	11.89	16.74	21.50	26.11	30.54	39.07	34.15	29.30	24.54	19.93	15.50
44	44.98	5.97	10.90	15.75	20.51	25.13	29.55	39.01	34.08	29.23	24.47	19.85	15.43
45	43.93	4.98	9.91	14.77	19.53	24.15	28.57	38.94	34.02	29.16	24.40	19.78	15.35
46	42.87	3.99	8.92	13.79	18.55	23.17	27.59	38.89	33.95	29.09	24.32	19.70	15.28
47	41.83	2.99	7.93	12.80	17.57	22.19	26.62	38.83	33.89	29.02	24.26	19.63	15.21
48	40.79	2.00	6.95	11.82	16.59	21.22	25.64	38.79	33.84	28.97	24.19	19.57	15.14
49	39.76	1.00	5.96	10.84	15.62	20.25	24.67	38.76	33.80	28.92	24.14	19.51	15.08
50	38.73		4.97	9.86	14.65	19.28	23.71	38.73	33.76	28.87	24.08	19.45	15.02
51	37.71		3.98	8.88	13.67	18.31	22.75		33.73	28.83	24.03	19.39	14.96
52	36.69		2.99	7.90	12.70	17.35	21.78		33.70	28.79	23.99	19.34	14.90
53	35.68		1.99	6.92	11.73	16.39	20.83		33.68	28.76	23.95	19.29	14.85
54	34.68		1.00	5.94	10.76	15.43	19.87		33.68	28.74	23.91	19.25	14.80

A2: Nil discount tables "at a glance"

Nil discount tables "at a glance"—FEMALE *continued*

Age at date of trial	Table 2 Pecuniary loss for life	Table 4 Loss of earnings to age 50	Table 6 Loss of earnings to age 55	Table 8 Loss of earnings to age 60	Table 10 Loss of earnings to age 65	Table 12 Loss of earnings to age 70	Table 14 Loss of earnings to age 75	Table 16 Loss of pension from age 50	Table 18 Loss of pension from age 55	Table 20 Loss of pension from age 60	Table 22 Loss of pension from age 65	Table 24 Loss of pension from age 70	Table 26 Loss of pension from age 75
55	33.68			4.95	9.79	14.47	18.92		33.68	28.73	23.89	19.21	14.76
56	32.69			3.97	8.82	13.51	17.97			28.73	23.87	19.19	14.72
57	31.71			2.98	7.85	12.55	17.02			28.73	23.86	19.16	14.69
58	30.74			1.99	6.88	11.59	16.08			28.74	23.86	19.14	14.66
59	29.76			1.00	5.91	10.64	15.13			28.76	23.85	19.12	14.62
60	28.78				4.93	9.68	14.19			28.78	23.85	19.10	14.59
61	27.80				3.95	8.72	13.24				23.85	19.08	14.55
62	26.83				2.97	7.76	12.30				23.86	19.06	14.52
63	25.86				1.99	6.80	11.36				23.88	19.06	14.50
64	24.91				1.00	5.85	10.43				23.92	19.07	14.48
65	23.98					4.89	9.50				23.98	19.10	14.49
66	23.07					3.92	8.57					19.15	14.51
67	22.18					2.95	7.64					19.22	14.54
68	21.29					1.98	6.70					19.32	14.59
69	20.42					0.99	5.77					19.43	14.65
70	19.55						4.83					19.55	14.72
71	18.67						3.88						14.79
72	17.79						2.93						14.86
73	16.89						1.97						14.93
74	15.99						0.99						15.00
75	15.08												15.08
76	14.17												
77	13.28												
78	12.40												
79	11.56												
80	10.77												
81	10.02												
82	9.31												
83	8.65												
84	8.03												
85	7.45												
86	6.89												
87	6.36												
88	5.85												
89	5.36												
90	4.90												
91	4.47												
92	4.08												
93	3.72												
94	3.41												
95	3.14												
96	2.91												
97	2.70												
98	2.52												
99	2.35												
100	2.18												

A2: Nil discount tables "at a glance"

A2: Nil discount tables for retirement ages 66 to 69 – MALE

Age at date of trial	Loss of earnings to age 66	Loss of earnings to age 67	Loss of earnings to age 68	Loss of earnings to age 69	Age at date of trial	Loss of pension from age 66	Loss of pension from age 67	Loss of pension from age 68	Loss of pension from age 69
16	48.70	49.59	50.48	51.37	16	22.91	22.02	21.13	20.24
17	47.69	48.59	49.48	50.36	17	22.82	21.92	21.03	20.15
18	46.69	47.58	48.48	49.37	18	22.72	21.83	20.93	20.04
19	45.69	46.59	47.48	48.37	19	22.62	21.72	20.83	19.94
20	44.69	45.59	46.48	47.37	20	22.53	21.63	20.74	19.85
21	43.70	44.59	45.48	46.38	21	22.43	21.54	20.65	19.75
22	42.71	43.60	44.48	45.38	22	22.33	21.44	20.56	19.66
23	41.71	42.61	43.49	44.38	23	22.23	21.33	20.45	19.56
24	40.72	41.61	42.50	43.39	24	22.13	21.24	20.35	19.46
25	39.73	40.62	41.50	42.40	25	22.03	21.14	20.26	19.36
26	38.74	39.63	40.51	41.40	26	21.94	21.05	20.17	19.28
27	37.75	38.64	39.52	40.41	27	21.84	20.95	20.07	19.18
28	36.77	37.65	38.53	39.42	28	21.74	20.86	19.98	19.09
29	35.78	36.66	37.54	38.43	29	21.64	20.76	19.88	18.99
30	34.79	35.68	36.56	37.44	30	21.55	20.66	19.78	18.90
31	33.80	34.69	35.57	36.45	31	21.47	20.58	19.70	18.82
32	32.83	33.71	34.60	35.47	32	21.37	20.49	19.60	18.73
33	31.85	32.73	33.61	34.50	33	21.30	20.42	19.54	18.65
34	30.87	31.75	32.64	33.52	34	21.22	20.34	19.45	18.57
35	29.90	30.78	31.66	32.54	35	21.13	20.25	19.37	18.49
36	28.92	29.80	30.68	31.56	36	21.06	20.18	19.30	18.42
37	27.94	28.83	29.71	30.59	37	20.99	20.10	19.22	18.34
38	26.97	27.85	28.73	29.61	38	20.90	20.02	19.14	18.26
39	25.99	26.88	27.75	28.64	39	20.83	19.94	19.07	18.18
40	25.02	25.90	26.78	27.66	40	20.74	19.86	18.98	18.10
41	24.04	24.93	25.81	26.69	41	20.67	19.78	18.90	18.02
42	23.07	23.96	24.84	25.72	42	20.60	19.71	18.83	17.95
43	22.11	22.99	23.87	24.75	43	20.51	19.63	18.75	17.87
44	21.14	22.02	22.90	23.79	44	20.45	19.57	18.69	17.80
45	20.17	21.06	21.94	22.82	45	20.38	19.49	18.61	17.73
46	19.20	20.09	20.97	21.85	46	20.32	19.43	18.55	17.67
47	18.24	19.13	20.01	20.89	47	20.25	19.36	18.48	17.60
48	17.27	18.17	19.05	19.93	48	20.20	19.30	18.42	17.54
49	16.32	17.20	18.09	18.98	49	20.13	19.25	18.36	17.47
50	15.35	16.25	17.14	18.02	50	20.10	19.20	18.31	17.43
51	14.41	15.29	16.19	17.07	51	20.04	19.16	18.26	17.38
52	13.45	14.35	15.24	16.12	52	20.02	19.12	18.23	17.35
53	12.50	13.40	14.30	15.18	53	19.99	19.09	18.19	17.31
54	11.55	12.45	13.35	14.24	54	19.98	19.08	18.18	17.29
55	10.59	11.51	12.41	13.30	55	19.99	19.07	18.17	17.28
56	9.65	10.56	11.47	12.36	56	19.99	19.08	18.17	17.28
57	8.70	9.61	10.52	11.43	57	20.01	19.10	18.19	17.28
58	7.74	8.67	9.58	10.49	58	20.04	19.11	18.20	17.29
59	6.80	7.72	8.64	9.54	59	20.05	19.13	18.21	17.31
60	5.83	6.77	7.69	8.61	60	20.09	19.15	18.23	17.31
61	4.88	5.82	6.75	7.67	61	20.12	19.18	18.25	17.33
62	3.91	4.87	5.80	6.72	62	20.17	19.21	18.28	17.36
63	2.95	3.90	4.85	5.79	63	20.22	19.27	18.32	17.38
64	1.98	2.94	3.90	4.84	64	20.30	19.34	18.38	17.44
65	0.99	1.98	2.94	3.89	65	20.43	19.44	18.48	17.53
66		0.99	1.97	2.93	66	20.57	19.58	18.60	17.64
67			0.99	1.97	67		19.74	18.75	17.77
68				0.99	68			18.93	17.94
69					69				18.12

See notes at the start of section A1 for details of methodology

A2: Nil discount tables for retirement ages 66 to 69 – FEMALE

Age at date of trial	Loss of earnings to age 66	Loss of earnings to age 67	Loss of earnings to age 68	Loss of earnings to age 69	Age at date of trial	Loss of pension from age 66	Loss of pension from age 67	Loss of pension from age 68	Loss of pension from age 69
16	49.27	50.21	51.14	52.08	16	26.07	25.13	24.20	23.26
17	48.27	49.20	50.14	51.07	17	25.97	25.04	24.10	23.17
18	47.27	48.20	49.14	50.07	18	25.87	24.94	24.00	23.07
19	46.27	47.20	48.14	49.07	19	25.78	24.85	23.91	22.98
20	45.27	46.20	47.14	48.07	20	25.69	24.76	23.82	22.89
21	44.27	45.20	46.14	47.07	21	25.59	24.66	23.72	22.79
22	43.27	44.20	45.13	46.07	22	25.50	24.57	23.64	22.70
23	42.27	43.20	44.13	45.06	23	25.40	24.47	23.54	22.61
24	41.28	42.20	43.13	44.06	24	25.29	24.37	23.44	22.51
25	40.28	41.21	42.13	43.06	25	25.20	24.27	23.35	22.42
26	39.28	40.21	41.13	42.06	26	25.10	24.17	23.25	22.32
27	38.28	39.21	40.13	41.06	27	25.01	24.08	23.16	22.23
28	37.28	38.21	39.14	40.06	28	24.92	23.99	23.06	22.14
29	36.29	37.21	38.14	39.07	29	24.82	23.90	22.97	22.04
30	35.29	36.22	37.15	38.07	30	24.73	23.80	22.87	21.95
31	34.29	35.22	36.15	37.08	31	24.65	23.72	22.79	21.86
32	33.30	34.22	35.16	36.08	32	24.56	23.64	22.70	21.78
33	32.31	33.23	34.16	35.09	33	24.46	23.54	22.61	21.68
34	31.31	32.24	33.17	34.09	34	24.38	23.45	22.52	21.60
35	30.32	31.25	32.18	33.10	35	24.29	23.36	22.43	21.51
36	29.33	30.26	31.18	32.11	36	24.20	23.27	22.35	21.42
37	28.34	29.27	30.19	31.12	37	24.12	23.19	22.27	21.34
38	27.36	28.28	29.20	30.13	38	24.02	23.10	22.18	21.25
39	26.37	27.29	28.21	29.14	39	23.94	23.02	22.10	21.17
40	25.38	26.30	27.23	28.15	40	23.86	22.94	22.01	21.09
41	24.39	25.32	26.24	27.16	41	23.78	22.85	21.93	21.01
42	23.41	24.33	25.25	26.17	42	23.69	22.77	21.85	20.93
43	22.42	23.35	24.27	25.19	43	23.62	22.69	21.77	20.85
44	21.44	22.36	23.29	24.21	44	23.54	22.62	21.69	20.77
45	20.46	21.39	22.31	23.23	45	23.47	22.54	21.62	20.70
46	19.48	20.41	21.33	22.25	46	23.39	22.46	21.54	20.62
47	18.50	19.43	20.35	21.28	47	23.33	22.40	21.48	20.55
48	17.53	18.45	19.38	20.30	48	23.26	22.34	21.41	20.49
49	16.55	17.48	18.41	19.33	49	23.21	22.28	21.35	20.43
50	15.58	16.51	17.44	18.36	50	23.15	22.22	21.29	20.37
51	14.61	15.54	16.47	17.39	51	23.10	22.17	21.24	20.32
52	13.64	14.58	15.51	16.43	52	23.05	22.11	21.18	20.26
53	12.67	13.61	14.54	15.47	53	23.01	22.07	21.14	20.21
54	11.70	12.64	13.57	14.51	54	22.98	22.04	21.11	20.17
55	10.74	11.67	12.61	13.54	55	22.94	22.01	21.07	20.14
56	9.77	10.71	11.65	12.58	56	22.92	21.98	21.04	20.11
57	8.80	9.75	10.69	11.62	57	22.91	21.96	21.02	20.09
58	7.83	8.78	9.72	10.66	58	22.91	21.96	21.02	20.08
59	6.86	7.81	8.76	9.70	59	22.90	21.95	21.00	20.06
60	5.90	6.85	7.80	8.74	60	22.88	21.93	20.98	20.04
61	4.92	5.89	6.83	7.78	61	22.88	21.91	20.97	20.02
62	3.94	4.91	5.87	6.82	62	22.89	21.92	20.96	20.01
63	2.97	3.94	4.91	5.86	63	22.89	21.92	20.95	20.00
64	1.99	2.96	3.93	4.90	64	22.92	21.95	20.98	20.01
65	1.00	1.99	2.96	3.93	65	22.98	21.99	21.02	20.05
66		1.00	1.98	2.95	66	23.07	22.07	21.09	20.12
67			0.99	1.98	67		22.18	21.19	20.20
68				0.99	68			21.29	20.30
69					69				20.42

See notes at the start of section A1 for details of methodology

A3: Life tables and projected life tables

National Life Tables, United Kingdom

Period expectation of life
Based on data for the years 2014–2016

Office for National Statistics

Age	\multicolumn{5}{c}{Males}	\multicolumn{5}{c}{Females}
x	m_x	q_x	l_x	d_x	e_x	m_x	q_x	l_x	d_x	e_x
0	0.004234	0.004225	100000.0	422.5	79.17	0.003521	0.003515	100000.0	351.5	82.86
1	0.000306	0.000306	99577.5	30.5	78.51	0.000246	0.000246	99648.5	24.5	82.15
2	0.000163	0.000163	99547.1	16.2	77.53	0.000137	0.000137	99624.0	13.6	81.17
3	0.000127	0.000127	99530.8	12.6	76.54	0.000105	0.000105	99610.4	10.4	80.18
4	0.000090	0.000090	99518.2	8.9	75.55	0.000081	0.000081	99599.9	8.1	79.19
5	0.000092	0.000092	99509.3	9.2	74.56	0.000067	0.000067	99591.8	6.7	78.20
6	0.000091	0.000091	99500.1	9.0	73.57	0.000074	0.000074	99585.1	7.3	77.20
7	0.000085	0.000085	99491.1	8.5	72.57	0.000074	0.000074	99577.8	7.4	76.21
8	0.000066	0.000066	99482.6	6.5	71.58	0.000060	0.000060	99570.4	6.0	75.21
9	0.000085	0.000085	99476.1	8.5	70.58	0.000069	0.000069	99564.4	6.8	74.22
10	0.000094	0.000094	99467.6	9.4	69.59	0.000059	0.000059	99557.6	5.9	73.22
11	0.000100	0.000100	99458.2	9.9	68.60	0.000061	0.000061	99551.7	6.1	72.23
12	0.000095	0.000095	99448.3	9.5	67.60	0.000060	0.000060	99545.6	6.0	71.23
13	0.000101	0.000101	99438.8	10.0	66.61	0.000106	0.000106	99539.6	10.6	70.24
14	0.000125	0.000125	99428.8	12.4	65.62	0.000112	0.000112	99529.0	11.1	69.24
15	0.000158	0.000158	99416.4	15.7	64.62	0.000138	0.000138	99517.9	13.7	68.25
16	0.000213	0.000213	99400.7	21.2	63.63	0.000161	0.000161	99504.2	16.0	67.26
17	0.000296	0.000296	99379.5	29.4	62.65	0.000154	0.000154	99488.2	15.3	66.27
18	0.000414	0.000414	99350.1	41.1	61.67	0.000209	0.000209	99472.9	20.7	65.28
19	0.000453	0.000453	99308.9	44.9	60.69	0.000209	0.000209	99452.1	20.8	64.30
20	0.000472	0.000472	99264.0	46.9	59.72	0.000205	0.000205	99431.3	20.4	63.31
21	0.000508	0.000508	99217.1	50.4	58.75	0.000220	0.000220	99410.9	21.9	62.32
22	0.000499	0.000499	99166.7	49.5	57.78	0.000219	0.000219	99389.1	21.7	61.34
23	0.000556	0.000556	99117.2	55.1	56.80	0.000232	0.000232	99367.3	23.1	60.35
24	0.000549	0.000548	99062.1	54.3	55.84	0.000231	0.000231	99344.3	22.9	59.36
25	0.000586	0.000586	99007.8	58.0	54.87	0.000249	0.000249	99321.3	24.7	58.38
26	0.000627	0.000627	98949.8	62.0	53.90	0.000273	0.000273	99296.6	27.2	57.39
27	0.000631	0.000630	98887.8	62.3	52.93	0.000271	0.000271	99269.4	26.9	56.41
28	0.000667	0.000667	98825.4	65.9	51.96	0.000327	0.000327	99242.5	32.5	55.42
29	0.000698	0.000698	98759.5	68.9	51.00	0.000351	0.000351	99210.0	34.8	54.44
30	0.000743	0.000742	98690.6	73.3	50.03	0.000385	0.000385	99175.2	38.1	53.46
31	0.000764	0.000763	98617.3	75.3	49.07	0.000412	0.000412	99137.1	40.9	52.48
32	0.000900	0.000900	98542.0	88.7	48.11	0.000468	0.000467	99096.2	46.3	51.50
33	0.000886	0.000885	98453.4	87.2	47.15	0.000492	0.000492	99049.9	48.7	50.52
34	0.000969	0.000969	98366.2	95.3	46.19	0.000531	0.000531	99001.2	52.6	49.55
35	0.001027	0.001026	98270.9	100.8	45.24	0.000589	0.000589	98948.6	58.2	48.57
36	0.001096	0.001096	98170.1	107.6	44.28	0.000655	0.000655	98890.4	64.8	47.60
37	0.001145	0.001144	98062.5	112.2	43.33	0.000680	0.000679	98825.6	67.1	46.63
38	0.001325	0.001324	97950.3	129.7	42.38	0.000758	0.000758	98758.5	74.8	45.67
39	0.001371	0.001370	97820.6	134.1	41.44	0.000812	0.000812	98683.6	80.1	44.70
40	0.001564	0.001562	97686.5	152.6	40.49	0.000943	0.000943	98603.6	93.0	43.74
41	0.001690	0.001689	97533.9	164.7	39.55	0.000969	0.000969	98510.6	95.5	42.78
42	0.001747	0.001746	97369.2	170.0	38.62	0.001090	0.001089	98415.1	107.2	41.82
43	0.001919	0.001917	97199.3	186.3	37.69	0.001162	0.001162	98308.0	114.2	40.86
44	0.002137	0.002134	97012.9	207.1	36.76	0.001287	0.001286	98193.8	126.3	39.91
45	0.002219	0.002217	96805.9	214.6	35.84	0.001465	0.001464	98067.5	143.5	38.96
46	0.002390	0.002387	96591.3	230.5	34.91	0.001535	0.001534	97923.9	150.2	38.02
47	0.002659	0.002656	96360.7	255.9	34.00	0.001634	0.001633	97773.7	159.7	37.07
48	0.002740	0.002736	96104.8	262.9	33.09	0.001771	0.001769	97614.0	172.7	36.13
49	0.003024	0.003020	95841.9	289.4	32.18	0.001876	0.001874	97441.4	182.6	35.20
50	0.003352	0.003346	95552.5	319.7	31.27	0.002143	0.002141	97258.8	208.2	34.26

A3: Life tables and projected life tables

Period expectation of life
Based on data for the years 2014–2016

Age	\multicolumn{5}{c}{Males}	\multicolumn{5}{c}{Females}
x	m_x	q_x	l_x	d_x	e_x	m_x	q_x	l_x	d_x	e_x
51	0.003484	0.003478	95232.8	331.2	30.37	0.002349	0.002347	97050.6	227.7	33.33
52	0.003735	0.003728	94901.6	353.8	29.48	0.002540	0.002537	96822.8	245.6	32.41
53	0.004005	0.003997	94547.8	377.9	28.59	0.002788	0.002784	96577.2	268.9	31.49
54	0.004414	0.004404	94169.8	414.8	27.70	0.003002	0.002998	96308.3	288.7	30.58
55	0.004995	0.004983	93755.1	467.2	26.82	0.003355	0.003349	96019.6	321.6	29.67
56	0.005383	0.005369	93287.9	500.8	25.95	0.003632	0.003625	95698.0	346.9	28.77
57	0.005858	0.005841	92787.1	541.9	25.09	0.003990	0.003982	95351.0	379.7	27.87
58	0.006488	0.006467	92245.2	596.5	24.23	0.004252	0.004243	94971.3	403.0	26.98
59	0.007163	0.007138	91648.7	654.2	23.39	0.004810	0.004798	94568.3	453.7	26.09
60	0.008005	0.007973	90994.5	725.5	22.55	0.005272	0.005258	94114.5	494.9	25.22
61	0.008743	0.008705	90269.0	785.8	21.73	0.005669	0.005653	93619.7	529.2	24.35
62	0.009480	0.009435	89483.2	844.3	20.92	0.006315	0.006295	93090.4	586.0	23.48
63	0.010563	0.010508	88638.9	931.4	20.11	0.006821	0.006798	92504.4	628.9	22.63
64	0.011523	0.011457	87707.5	1004.9	19.32	0.007383	0.007356	91875.5	675.8	21.78
65	0.012418	0.012341	86702.6	1070.0	18.54	0.007932	0.007901	91199.7	720.5	20.94
66	0.013365	0.013277	85632.6	1136.9	17.76	0.008772	0.008734	90479.2	790.2	20.10
67	0.014402	0.014299	84495.7	1208.2	16.99	0.009407	0.009363	89689.0	839.7	19.27
68	0.015849	0.015724	83287.5	1309.7	16.23	0.010574	0.010519	88849.2	934.6	18.45
69	0.017636	0.017481	81977.9	1433.1	15.49	0.011580	0.011513	87914.6	1012.2	17.64
70	0.019534	0.019345	80544.8	1558.2	14.75	0.013094	0.013008	86902.5	1130.5	16.84
71	0.021786	0.021551	78986.6	1702.2	14.03	0.014518	0.014413	85772.0	1236.3	16.06
72	0.024146	0.023858	77284.4	1843.8	13.33	0.016174	0.016044	84535.8	1356.3	15.28
73	0.026669	0.026318	75440.5	1985.5	12.65	0.018226	0.018061	83179.5	1502.3	14.52
74	0.030434	0.029978	73455.1	2202.1	11.97	0.020130	0.019930	81677.1	1627.8	13.78
75	0.033535	0.032982	71253.0	2350.1	11.33	0.022491	0.022241	80049.3	1780.4	13.05
76	0.036620	0.035962	68903.0	2477.9	10.70	0.025465	0.025145	78268.9	1968.0	12.34
77	0.040718	0.039906	66425.1	2650.8	10.08	0.027964	0.027579	76300.9	2104.3	11.64
78	0.045248	0.044247	63774.3	2821.8	9.48	0.031363	0.030879	74196.6	2291.1	10.96
79	0.050351	0.049114	60952.6	2993.6	8.89	0.035326	0.034713	71905.5	2496.1	10.29
80	0.057138	0.055551	57958.9	3219.7	8.32	0.040802	0.039987	69409.4	2775.4	9.65
81	0.063428	0.061479	54739.2	3365.3	7.78	0.045875	0.044846	66634.0	2988.3	9.03
82	0.072131	0.069620	51373.9	3576.7	7.26	0.052508	0.051165	63645.7	3256.4	8.43
83	0.081866	0.078647	47797.3	3759.1	6.77	0.060210	0.058450	60389.2	3529.8	7.85
84	0.091641	0.087626	44038.2	3858.9	6.30	0.068667	0.066387	56859.5	3774.8	7.31
85	0.103836	0.098711	40179.3	3966.2	5.86	0.077555	0.074660	53084.7	3963.3	6.79
86	0.115705	0.109377	36213.1	3960.9	5.45	0.088787	0.085013	49121.4	4175.9	6.30
87	0.130200	0.122242	32252.2	3942.6	5.06	0.101213	0.096337	44945.5	4329.9	5.84
88	0.147528	0.137393	28309.6	3889.5	4.69	0.114430	0.108237	40615.6	4396.1	5.41
89	0.163145	0.150840	24420.1	3683.5	4.36	0.130420	0.122436	36219.4	4434.6	5.01
90	0.183289	0.167902	20736.6	3481.7	4.04	0.148635	0.138353	31784.9	4397.5	4.64
91	0.200370	0.182124	17254.8	3142.5	3.76	0.163695	0.151311	27387.4	4144.0	4.30
92	0.222813	0.200479	14112.3	2829.2	3.48	0.183918	0.168430	23243.4	3914.9	3.98
93	0.249339	0.221700	11283.1	2501.5	3.23	0.204108	0.185206	19328.5	3579.8	3.68
94	0.278319	0.244320	8781.6	2145.5	3.01	0.233708	0.209256	15748.7	3295.5	3.41
95	0.302173	0.262511	6636.1	1742.1	2.82	0.255562	0.226606	12453.2	2822.0	3.17
96	0.329315	0.282757	4894.1	1383.8	2.64	0.279396	0.245149	9631.2	2361.1	2.96
97	0.344012	0.293524	3510.2	1030.3	2.49	0.300215	0.261032	7270.2	1897.7	2.76
98	0.388481	0.325296	2479.9	806.7	2.31	0.334203	0.286353	5372.4	1538.4	2.55
99	0.414017	0.343011	1673.2	573.9	2.19	0.370395	0.312518	3834.0	1198.2	2.38
100	0.457723	0.372477	1099.3	409.5	2.07	0.396048	0.330584	2635.8	871.4	2.23

Source: Office for National Statistics licensed under the Open Government licence V.I.O.

A3: Life tables and projected life tables

Expectations of life table

Expectations of life for age attained in 2018 allowing for projected changes in mortality assumed in the 2016-based population projections produced by the Office for National Statistics.

United Kingdom

Age	Males	Females	Age	Males	Females
0	89.6	92.2	51	34.2	36.7
1	88.8	91.4	52	33.2	35.7
2	87.7	90.3	53	32.1	34.7
3	86.6	89.2	54	31.1	33.7
4	85.5	88.1	55	30.1	32.6
5	84.4	87.0	56	29.1	31.6
6	83.2	85.9	57	28.2	30.6
7	82.1	84.7	58	27.2	29.6
8	81.0	83.6	59	26.2	28.6
9	79.8	82.5	60	25.3	27.7
10	78.7	81.4	61	24.3	26.7
11	77.6	80.3	62	23.4	25.7
12	76.5	79.2	63	22.5	24.8
13	75.3	78.1	64	21.6	23.8
14	74.2	76.9	65	20.7	22.9
15	73.1	75.8	66	19.9	22.0
16	71.9	74.7	67	19.0	21.0
17	70.8	73.6	68	18.1	20.1
18	69.7	72.5	69	17.3	19.2
19	68.6	71.4	70	16.5	18.3
20	67.5	70.3	71	15.6	17.5
21	66.4	69.2	72	14.8	16.6
22	65.2	68.1	73	14.0	15.7
23	64.1	67.0	74	13.3	14.9
24	63.0	65.9	75	12.5	14.1
25	61.9	64.7	76	11.8	13.3
26	60.8	63.6	77	11.1	12.5
27	59.7	62.5	78	10.4	11.8
28	58.6	61.4	79	9.7	11.0
29	57.5	60.4	80	9.1	10.3
30	56.4	59.3	81	8.5	9.6
31	55.3	58.2	82	7.9	8.9
32	54.3	57.1	83	7.3	8.3
33	53.2	56.0	84	6.8	7.7
34	52.1	54.9	85	6.3	7.1
35	51.0	53.8	86	5.8	6.5
36	49.9	52.7	87	5.3	6.0
37	48.9	51.6	88	4.9	5.5
38	47.8	50.6	89	4.5	5.1
39	46.7	49.5	90	4.1	4.6
40	45.7	48.4	91	3.8	4.3
41	44.6	47.3	92	3.5	3.9
42	43.6	46.3	93	3.2	3.6
43	42.5	45.2	94	3.0	3.3
44	41.4	44.1	95	2.7	3.1
45	40.4	43.1	96	2.5	2.8
46	39.4	42.0	97	2.3	2.6
47	38.3	40.9	98	2.2	2.4
48	37.3	39.9	99	2.0	2.2
49	36.2	38.8	100	1.9	2.0
50	35.2	37.8			

Source: Office for National Statistics

A3: Life tables and projected life tables

Notes:

1. National life tables of various kinds and population projections have been produced for a considerable period, formerly by the Government Actuary's Department and, since February 2006, by the Office for National Statistics. The Decennial Life Tables for England and Wales combined and for Scotland are based on data for the three-year period around a Census. Between Censuses, life tables known as National Life Tables (formerly named Interim Life Tables) are produced which are based on data for the numbers in the population and the deaths by age and sex for the latest three-year period available. These National Life Tables are produced for the United Kingdom as a whole, Great Britain, England and Wales and also for each individual country of the United Kingdom. It is intended to update the life tables in *Facts and Figures* every year, using the latest data then available.

The historical life tables

2. The latest published Decennial Life Tables are the English Life Tables No.17 (ELT No.17). These are based on data on the numbers in the population and the numbers of deaths by age and sex for 2010–2012 (the three years around the 2011 Census). The latest published decennial life tables for Scotland are the Scottish Life Tables 2000–2002, based on data for the three years 2000 to 2002.

3. Data from the Decennial Life Table, ELT No.15, based on data for 1990–1992, formed the mortality assumptions underlying the calculations of the multipliers in Tables 1–18 of the 4th edition of the Ogden Tables. Tables of multipliers using mortality from the Decennial Life Tables are no longer reproduced in the Ogden Tables.

4. The tables reproduced on pages 16 and 17 are the latest available National Life Tables for the United Kingdom (based on data for 2014–2016). These life tables are based on historical data (and expectations of life which are calculated using these data), and effectively assume that the mortality rate for a given age and sex will remain constant in future years. They provide a measure of mortality for that particular period but are not a good indication of how long someone of a given age now is expected to live.

5. There have been large improvements in mortality rates over the last 100 years or so. For estimating how long someone of a given age is expected to live it is reasonable to assume that mortality rates will continue to improve in future

Projected mortality

6. The table reproduced on page 18 is the latest available official projection of expectations of life for the United Kingdom making allowance for expected future changes in mortality for individuals of specified ages in 2018. This table allows for the projected changes in mortality assumed in the 2016-based population projections produced by the Office for National Statistics and published in October 2017. It should be noted that this is a more recent projection of mortality than that used to prepare the 7th edition of the Ogden Tables. However, because of reductions made to the future mortality improvement factors in the latest ONS projections, the expectations of life are in fact lower at most ages (apart from males under 20) than the expectations of life shown in the 0.0% a year column of Tables 1 and 2 of the Ogden Tables (see Note 10).

7. As a rough approximation to the mortality assumptions of the 2016-based projections, the Ogden Tables may be used with the following adjustments to the age of the claimant:

A3: Life tables and projected life tables

Age of Males	Increase (Reduction) in age	Age of Females	Increase (Reduction) in age
Up to 20	($\frac{1}{2}$ year)	Up to 35	$\frac{1}{2}$ year
20 to 49	None	35 and over	1 year
50 to 64	$\frac{1}{2}$ year		
65 and over	1 year		

8. At Appendix A to the Introduction to the 4th edition of the Ogden Tables there is an extract from ELT No.15, which shows graphs indicating rates of mortality expressed in percentages of the 1911 rates of mortality on a logarithmic scale. They demonstrate in stark fashion the improvement in longevity which has taken place since 1911.

9. The sole exception in some recent years has been small increases in the mortality of young males in their 30s due to increases in deaths caused by HIV infection and AIDS; suicide rates and alcohol-related mortality have also increased for men at young ages in some years. However, even if this slight worsening of mortality were to continue, the effects on the tables of multipliers (in the Ogden Tables) would not be significant.

10. The Office for National Statistics carries out official population projections for the United Kingdom and constituent countries, usually every two years. In particular, these projections include assumptions of improving mortality rates at most ages in the years following the base year of the projections. The latest projections were based on 2016 and were published in October 2017.

11. Tables 1–26 of the 7th edition of the Ogden Tables give multipliers based on the projected mortality rates underlying the 2008-based principal population projections for the United Kingdom. These take as their base the estimated numbers in the population by sex and age in the constituent countries of the United Kingdom in mid-2008. The projections and the underlying assumptions are available on the website of the Office for National Statistics at: *http://www.ons.gov.uk/peoplepopulationandcommunity/populationandmigration/populationprojections/bulletins/nationalpopulationprojections/2015-10-29*.

12. Multipliers in earlier editions of the Ogden Tables were based on historical or projected mortality rates for the population of England and Wales combined. However, the Ogden Tables are used extensively in Scotland and Northern Ireland. Although it would be possible to produce separate Tables based on projected mortality rates for Scotland and for Northern Ireland, it was agreed for the 6th edition that rather than have three separate sets of tables there should be one set calculated using mortality rates from the population projections of the United Kingdom as a whole and this was continued in the 7th edition.

13. The Ogden Tables take account of the possibilities that a claimant may live for different periods, e.g. die soon or live to be very old. As mentioned above, the mortality assumptions for the 7th edition relate to the general population of the United Kingdom. Although comparable expectations of life are available for the constituent countries of the United Kingdom (and statistics are available which give a measure of variations in mortality between regions and areas), the Ogden Tables are recommended for use unadjusted regardless of location within the United Kingdom or for other potentially relevant factors such as earnings level, educational background, lifestyle or health status. Unless there is clear evidence in an individual case to support the view that the claimant concerned is "atypical" and can be expected to experience a significantly shorter or longer than average lifespan, to an extent greater than would be encompassed by variations in place of residence, lifestyle and general health status, no further increase or reduction should be

A3: Life tables and projected life tables

made for mortality alone. Examples of an atypical claimant might be a lifelong heavy smoker, someone suffering from a head injury or epilepsy, an immobile patient or more likely a combination of adverse factors.

14. Where a claimant is thought to be atypical, medical or other relevant expert evidence should be sought on the possible impact of any condition on life expectancy. For large cases where it is thought appropriate to argue, on medical evidence or for other reasons, that the situation of the claimant is atypical, an actuary should be consulted on how an appropriate adjustment may be made to the Ogden Tables.

15. The mortality tables in this section and those underlying the Ogden Tables do not make any allowance for contingencies other than mortality. Appropriate adjustments for such contingencies are considered in section A4.

A4: Loss of earnings multipliers adjusted for education, disability and employment status

The Ogden Tables dealing with loss of earnings (Ogden tables 3–14) are subject to adjustment for contingencies other than mortality (Ogden paras 26–44). The tables which follow incorporate those factors without the need for further calculation.

The contingencies are whether the claimant was in employment or not, whether he was disabled or not, and his educational or skill level. Earlier editions (1st–5th) of the Ogden Tables and of *Facts & Figures*, based on earlier research, made adjustments for the general state of the economy; the nature of the claimant's employment, whether clerical or manual; and for different geographical areas of the country. These are not used in the latest edition as more recent research has shown that when adjustments are made for education, disability and educational attainment the difference made by these other factors is small.

Employment

Employed
Those who at the time of the accident are employed, self-employed or on a government training scheme.

Not employed
All others (including those temporarily out of work, full-time students and unpaid family workers).

Disability

Disabled
A person is classified as being disabled if all three of the following conditions in relation to the ill-health or disability are met:

(i) he or she has either a progressive illness or an illness which has or is expected to last for over a year,

and

(ii) he or she satisfies the Equality Act definition that the impact of the disability substantially limits the person's ability to carry out normal day-to-day activities,

and

(iii) his or her condition affects either the kind **or** the amount of paid work they can do.

Not disabled.
All others.

Paragraph 35 of the Ogden notes (section A8 in this book) gives examples of the ways in which a disability may limit one's day-to-day activities.

Educational attainment means the highest level of education attained by the claimant. It is a shorthand for the level of skill and includes equivalent non-academic qualifications.

Degree or equivalent.

A4: Loss of earnings multipliers adjusted for education, etc.

This includes professional qualifications, for example as a nurse.

GCSE grades A–C, O levels, or CSE grade 1, up to A-levels or equivalent.
In the tables which follow this is called "Good GCSE level education or equivalent".

Qualifications below GCSE grade C or CSE grade 1 or equivalent, or no qualifications.
In the tables which follow this is called "Education below good GCSE level".

There are 12 tables each for men and women arranged in the following order.

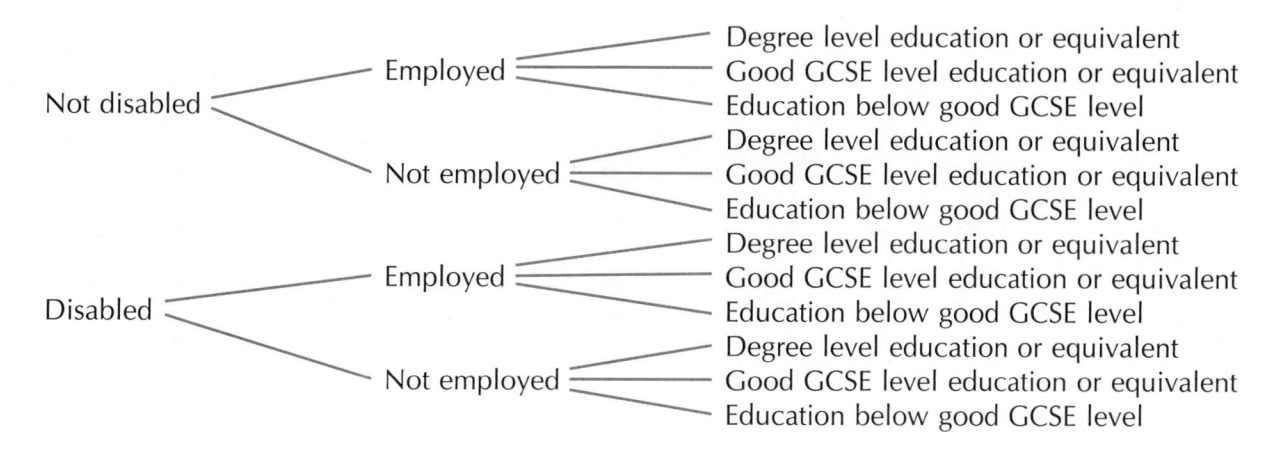

```
                          ┌── Degree level education or equivalent
              ┌─ Employed ─── Good GCSE level education or equivalent
Not disabled ─┤            └── Education below good GCSE level
              │                ┌── Degree level education or equivalent
              └─ Not employed ─── Good GCSE level education or equivalent
                               └── Education below good GCSE level
                          ┌── Degree level education or equivalent
              ┌─ Employed ─── Good GCSE level education or equivalent
Disabled ─────┤            └── Education below good GCSE level
              │                ┌── Degree level education or equivalent
              └─ Not employed ─── Good GCSE level education or equivalent
                               └── Education below good GCSE level
```

Thus if the claimant is a 32-year-old male solicitor, employed before the accident at a salary of £40,000, not disabled and proposing to retire at 60, the first table on the next page gives the multiplier for loss of earnings to age 60 as 27.97.

By using the tables for disabled claimants it is possible to obtain an estimate of the claimant's residual earning capacity, with an "inbuilt" allowance for employment risks which would otherwise require a separate *Smith v Manchester* award. Thus if the accident has seriously affected the solicitor's ability to work as a solicitor, and he is now employed at a salary of £25,000, the seventh table gives a multiplier of 17.94 for his new earning capacity to age 60. This approach will not always be suitable and there will be cases where a *Smith v Manchester* or *Blamire* award is still needed.

The 6th edition of the Ogden Tables had an adjustment factor for persons aged 16–19 with a degree level education. This caused difficulties. The 7th edition (para.41) recommends that in the case of someone who has not yet reached the age at which it is likely that he would start work, there should be an assessment of the level of education he would have attained, the age he would have started work, and whether he would have been employed or not. The multiplier appropriate to that age and those conditions should then be discounted for early receipt (for the period between the date of trial and the putative date of starting work).

The notes to the Ogden Tables do not provide specific adjustment factors for ages above 54 on the basis that, above that age, the likely course of someone's employment will depend on individual circumstances and the use of statistical averages may be inappropriate.

The adjustment factors as stated in the Ogden Tables are usually constant over a five year age range. This sometimes gives the appearance of anomalies or discontinuities in the figures—for example, in some tables a claimant of 18 or 19 has a smaller multiplier than one in his or her early 20s. The editors have been advised that this is the correct approach.

The tables use the -0.75 per cent discount rate.

A4: Loss of earnings multipliers adjusted for education, etc.

ND E Deg

Loss of earnings: not disabled; employed; degree level education or equivalent

Age	\multicolumn{6}{c}{Male to retiring age}	Age	\multicolumn{6}{c}{Female to retiring age}
	50	55	60	65	70	75		50	55	60	65	70	75
16							16						
17			See introductory notes				17			See introductory notes			
18							18						
19							19						
20	30.59	36.25	42.02	47.86	53.71	59.49	20	29.78	35.35	41.06	46.91	52.84	58.78
21	29.46	35.07	40.79	46.59	52.39	58.12	21	28.68	34.20	39.87	45.67	51.55	57.45
22	28.33	33.89	39.58	45.33	51.09	56.75	22	27.58	33.06	38.69	44.44	50.28	56.12
23	27.20	32.73	38.37	44.09	49.79	55.41	23	26.49	31.92	37.51	43.22	49.00	54.81
24	26.10	31.58	37.18	42.84	48.50	54.07	24	25.40	30.80	36.35	42.01	47.75	53.51
25	25.27	30.77	36.38	42.06	47.74	53.32	25	24.33	29.69	35.19	40.81	46.50	52.21
26	24.16	29.62	35.20	40.84	46.46	52.00	26	23.26	28.59	34.04	39.62	45.27	50.93
27	23.06	28.49	34.02	39.61	45.20	50.68	27	22.21	27.49	32.90	38.44	44.04	49.64
28	21.98	27.36	32.85	38.40	43.93	49.37	28	21.16	26.40	31.77	37.26	42.82	48.38
29	20.90	26.24	31.69	37.19	42.69	48.07	29	20.12	25.32	30.66	36.10	41.62	47.13
30	19.61	24.86	30.21	35.61	41.00	46.29	30	19.09	24.25	29.55	34.95	40.41	45.89
31	18.56	23.77	29.08	34.44	39.79	45.03	31	18.07	23.18	28.44	33.80	39.23	44.65
32	17.52	22.70	27.97	33.29	38.59	43.79	32	17.04	22.13	27.35	32.67	38.06	43.43
33	16.49	21.63	26.86	32.15	37.42	42.57	33	16.04	21.08	26.26	31.55	36.88	42.22
34	15.46	20.57	25.77	31.01	36.24	41.35	34	15.04	20.05	25.19	30.43	35.72	41.02
35	14.13	19.09	24.15	29.24	34.31	39.27	35	14.04	19.02	24.12	29.33	34.58	39.83
36	13.14	18.07	23.09	28.15	33.18	38.10	36	13.06	18.00	23.06	28.22	33.44	38.64
37	12.16	17.06	22.04	27.06	32.06	36.95	37	12.08	16.99	22.01	27.14	32.31	37.47
38	11.19	16.06	21.01	25.99	30.95	35.78	38	11.11	15.98	20.97	26.06	31.19	36.31
39	10.22	15.06	19.97	24.92	29.84	34.64	39	10.15	14.99	19.94	24.98	30.08	35.16
40	9.06	13.75	18.52	23.34	28.11	32.76	40	9.19	13.99	18.91	23.92	28.98	34.02
41	8.12	12.79	17.53	22.31	27.04	31.66	41	8.24	13.01	17.90	22.87	27.88	32.89
42	7.20	11.84	16.54	21.29	26.00	30.57	42	7.30	12.04	16.89	21.82	26.81	31.76
43	6.27	10.89	15.57	20.28	24.95	29.50	43	6.36	11.07	15.89	20.79	25.73	30.65
44	5.37	9.94	14.60	19.28	23.92	28.42	44	5.44	10.11	14.90	19.76	24.67	29.55
45	4.35	8.81	13.32	17.87	22.37	26.75	45	4.42	8.95	13.60	18.32	23.08	27.81
46	3.47	7.90	12.39	16.91	21.38	25.72	46	3.52	8.03	12.64	17.34	22.06	26.76
47	2.60	7.00	11.46	15.95	20.40	24.71	47	2.64	7.12	11.70	16.36	21.05	25.72
48	1.73	6.11	10.55	15.01	19.42	23.70	48	1.75	6.20	10.76	15.39	20.05	24.68
49	0.86	5.22	9.64	14.08	18.46	22.71	49	0.87	5.30	9.83	14.43	19.06	23.66
50		4.19	8.43	12.69	16.90	20.97	50		4.35	8.81	13.33	17.87	22.39
51		3.30	7.48	11.66	15.79	19.79	51		3.43	7.81	12.25	16.72	21.15
52		2.44	6.54	10.67	14.73	18.65	52		2.54	6.84	11.21	15.59	19.93
53		1.61	5.65	9.70	13.69	17.54	53		1.67	5.89	10.18	14.49	18.77
54		0.79	4.77	8.75	12.68	16.47	54		0.83	5.04	9.31	13.60	17.84

See introductory notes as regards claimants over 54 at date of trial

See introductory notes as regards claimants over 54 at date of trial

A4: Loss of earnings multipliers adjusted for education, etc.

ND E GCSE

Loss of earnings: not disabled; employed; good GCSE level education or equivalent

Age	\multicolumn{6}{c	}{Male to retiring age}	Age	\multicolumn{6}{c}{Female to retiring age}
	50	55	60	65	70	75		50	55	60	65	70	75
16	34.47	40.17	45.99	51.90	57.82	63.67	16	31.21	36.43	41.80	47.29	52.86	58.46
17	33.32	38.98	44.76	50.61	56.48	62.28	17	30.17	35.36	40.68	46.12	51.65	57.20
18	32.18	37.79	43.52	49.34	55.15	60.90	18	29.14	34.29	39.57	44.97	50.45	55.96
19	31.05	36.62	42.31	48.07	53.85	59.54	19	28.12	33.23	38.47	43.83	49.26	54.72
20	30.59	36.25	42.02	47.86	53.71	59.49	20	27.44	32.57	37.83	43.22	48.68	54.16
21	29.46	35.07	40.79	46.59	52.39	58.12	21	26.42	31.51	36.74	42.08	47.49	52.93
22	28.33	33.89	39.58	45.33	51.09	56.75	22	25.41	30.46	35.65	40.94	46.32	51.71
23	27.20	32.73	38.37	44.09	49.79	55.41	23	24.40	29.41	34.56	39.82	45.15	50.50
24	26.10	31.58	37.18	42.84	48.50	54.07	24	23.40	28.38	33.49	38.70	43.99	49.30
25	25.00	30.44	35.99	41.61	47.22	52.74	25	22.97	28.02	33.21	38.51	43.89	49.27
26	23.90	29.30	34.82	40.40	45.96	51.44	26	21.96	26.98	32.13	37.40	42.72	48.06
27	22.82	28.18	33.65	39.18	44.71	50.13	27	20.96	25.95	31.05	36.28	41.56	46.86
28	21.74	27.07	32.49	37.99	43.46	48.84	28	19.98	24.91	29.99	35.17	40.41	45.66
29	20.67	25.95	31.34	36.79	42.23	47.55	29	18.99	23.90	28.94	34.07	39.28	44.49
30	19.39	24.59	29.88	35.23	40.56	45.78	30	18.23	23.16	28.22	33.38	38.60	43.83
31	18.35	23.51	28.77	34.07	39.36	44.54	31	17.26	22.14	27.17	32.28	37.47	42.64
32	17.33	22.45	27.66	32.93	38.17	43.32	32	16.28	21.14	26.12	31.20	36.35	41.48
33	16.31	21.39	26.57	31.80	37.01	42.11	33	15.32	20.14	25.08	30.13	35.22	40.32
34	15.29	20.35	25.49	30.68	35.84	40.90	34	14.37	19.15	24.06	29.06	34.12	39.18
35	14.13	19.09	24.15	29.24	34.31	39.27	35	13.57	18.38	23.31	28.34	33.41	38.49
36	13.14	18.07	23.09	28.15	33.18	38.10	36	12.62	17.39	22.28	27.27	32.31	37.34
37	12.16	17.06	22.04	27.06	32.06	36.95	37	11.67	16.42	21.27	26.22	31.22	36.21
38	11.19	16.06	21.01	25.99	30.95	35.78	38	10.73	15.45	20.26	25.18	30.14	35.09
39	10.22	15.06	19.97	24.92	29.84	34.64	39	9.80	14.48	19.26	24.14	29.07	33.97
40	9.06	13.75	18.52	23.34	28.11	32.76	40	8.88	13.52	18.28	23.12	28.00	32.87
41	8.12	12.79	17.53	22.31	27.04	31.66	41	7.96	12.57	17.29	22.10	26.94	31.78
42	7.20	11.84	16.54	21.29	26.00	30.57	42	7.05	11.64	16.32	21.09	25.90	30.69
43	6.27	10.89	15.57	20.28	24.95	29.50	43	6.15	10.70	15.35	20.09	24.86	29.62
44	5.37	9.94	14.60	19.28	23.92	28.42	44	5.25	9.77	14.40	19.09	23.84	28.55
45	4.35	8.81	13.32	17.87	22.37	26.75	45	4.32	8.75	13.29	17.90	22.55	27.17
46	3.47	7.90	12.39	16.91	21.38	25.72	46	3.44	7.85	12.35	16.94	21.56	26.15
47	2.60	7.00	11.46	15.95	20.40	24.71	47	2.58	6.95	11.43	15.98	20.57	25.13
48	1.73	6.11	10.55	15.01	19.42	23.70	48	1.71	6.06	10.51	15.04	19.59	24.11
49	0.86	5.22	9.64	14.08	18.46	22.71	49	0.85	5.18	9.61	14.10	18.62	23.11
50		4.19	8.43	12.69	16.90	20.97	50		4.25	8.60	13.02	17.46	21.87
51		3.30	7.48	11.66	15.79	19.79	51		3.39	7.72	12.10	16.52	20.90
52		2.44	6.54	10.67	14.73	18.65	52		2.54	6.84	11.21	15.59	19.93
53		1.61	5.65	9.70	13.69	17.54	53		1.67	5.89	10.18	14.49	18.77
54		0.79	4.77	8.75	12.68	16.47	54		0.83	5.04	9.31	13.60	17.84

See introductory notes as regards claimants over 54 at date of trial

See introductory notes as regards claimants over 54 at date of trial

A4: Loss of earnings multipliers adjusted for education, etc.

ND E <GCSE

Loss of earnings: not disabled; employed; education below good GCSE level

Age	\multicolumn{6}{c}{Male to retiring age}	Age	\multicolumn{6}{c}{Female to retiring age}
	50	55	60	65	70	75		50	55	60	65	70	75
16	32.56	37.94	43.44	49.02	54.60	60.13	16	24.66	28.79	33.02	37.36	41.77	46.19
17	31.47	36.81	42.27	47.80	53.34	58.82	17	23.84	27.94	32.14	36.44	40.81	45.20
18	30.39	35.69	41.11	46.60	52.09	57.52	18	23.03	27.09	31.26	35.53	39.87	44.22
19	29.33	34.59	39.96	45.40	50.86	56.24	19	22.22	26.25	30.39	34.63	38.92	43.24
20	28.93	34.28	39.73	45.26	50.79	56.25	20	22.75	27.01	31.38	35.84	40.37	44.91
21	27.86	33.16	38.58	44.06	49.55	54.96	21	21.91	26.13	30.46	34.90	39.39	43.89
22	26.79	32.05	37.43	42.86	48.31	53.67	22	21.07	25.26	29.56	33.95	38.41	42.88
23	25.73	30.95	36.29	41.69	47.08	52.40	23	20.24	24.39	28.66	33.02	37.44	41.87
24	24.68	29.87	35.16	40.52	45.87	51.13	24	19.41	23.53	27.77	32.10	36.48	40.88
25	24.18	29.45	34.82	40.25	45.68	51.02	25	19.68	24.02	28.47	33.01	37.62	42.24
26	23.12	28.35	33.69	39.08	44.46	49.76	26	18.82	23.13	27.54	32.05	36.62	41.20
27	22.07	27.26	32.56	37.91	43.25	48.50	27	17.96	22.24	26.62	31.10	35.63	40.16
28	21.03	26.18	31.43	36.75	42.04	47.25	28	17.12	21.36	25.70	30.15	34.64	39.14
29	20.00	25.11	30.32	35.59	40.85	46.00	29	16.28	20.48	24.80	29.20	33.67	38.13
30	18.97	24.05	29.23	34.45	39.67	44.78	30	16.09	20.44	24.90	29.45	34.06	38.67
31	17.95	23.00	28.13	33.32	38.49	43.57	31	15.23	19.54	23.97	28.49	33.06	37.63
32	16.95	21.96	27.06	32.21	37.34	42.36	32	14.36	18.65	23.05	27.53	32.07	36.60
33	15.95	20.92	25.99	31.11	36.20	41.18	33	13.52	17.77	22.13	26.59	31.08	35.58
34	14.95	19.90	24.93	30.00	35.06	40.01	34	12.68	16.90	21.23	25.64	30.11	34.57
35	13.97	18.88	23.88	28.92	33.93	38.83	35	12.31	16.67	21.14	25.70	30.30	34.91
36	12.99	17.87	22.83	27.84	32.81	37.67	36	11.44	15.77	20.21	24.73	29.30	33.87
37	12.02	16.87	21.80	26.76	31.70	36.53	37	10.58	14.89	19.29	23.78	28.31	32.84
38	11.06	15.88	20.77	25.70	30.61	35.39	38	9.73	14.01	18.38	22.84	27.34	31.82
39	10.11	14.89	19.75	24.64	29.51	34.26	39	8.89	13.14	17.47	21.89	26.36	30.81
40	9.06	13.75	18.52	23.34	28.11	32.76	40	8.26	12.58	17.00	21.50	26.05	30.58
41	8.12	12.79	17.53	22.31	27.04	31.66	41	7.41	11.70	16.09	20.56	25.06	29.56
42	7.20	11.84	16.54	21.29	26.00	30.57	42	6.56	10.82	15.18	19.62	24.10	28.55
43	6.27	10.89	15.57	20.28	24.95	29.50	43	5.72	9.95	14.28	18.69	23.13	27.55
44	5.37	9.94	14.60	19.28	23.92	28.42	44	4.89	9.09	13.39	17.76	22.18	26.56
45	4.35	8.81	13.32	17.87	22.37	26.75	45	4.11	8.33	12.66	17.06	21.49	25.90
46	3.47	7.90	12.39	16.91	21.38	25.72	46	3.28	7.48	11.77	16.14	20.54	24.92
47	2.60	7.00	11.46	15.95	20.40	24.71	47	2.45	6.63	10.89	15.23	19.60	23.94
48	1.73	6.11	10.55	15.01	19.42	23.70	48	1.63	5.78	10.02	14.33	18.67	22.98
49	0.86	5.22	9.64	14.08	18.46	22.71	49	0.81	4.93	9.15	13.44	17.75	22.02
50		4.19	8.43	12.69	16.90	20.97	50		4.10	8.29	12.56	16.83	21.08
51		3.30	7.48	11.66	15.79	19.79	51		3.27	7.44	11.67	15.93	20.15
52		2.44	6.54	10.67	14.73	18.65	52		2.45	6.59	10.81	15.03	19.22
53		1.61	5.65	9.70	13.69	17.54	53		1.63	5.75	9.94	14.14	18.31
54		0.79	4.77	8.75	12.68	16.47	54		0.82	4.98	9.20	13.43	17.62

See introductory notes as regards claimants over 54 at date of trial

See introductory notes as regards claimants over 54 at date of trial

A4: Loss of earnings multipliers adjusted for education, etc.

ND NE Deg

Loss of earnings: not disabled; not employed; degree level education or equivalent

Age	Male to retiring age						Age	Female to retiring age					
	50	55	60	65	70	75		50	55	60	65	70	75
16							16						
17							17						
18			See introductory notes				18			See introductory notes			
19							19						
20	29.59	35.07	40.65	46.30	51.96	57.22	20	28.11	33.36	38.76	44.28	49.87	55.48
21	28.50	33.93	39.46	45.07	50.69	56.22	21	27.06	32.28	37.63	43.11	48.65	54.22
22	27.40	32.79	38.29	43.85	49.42	54.90	22	26.03	31.21	36.51	41.94	47.45	52.97
23	26.32	31.67	37.12	42.65	48.17	53.60	23	25.00	30.13	35.41	40.79	46.25	51.73
24	25.25	30.55	35.96	41.45	46.92	52.31	24	23.97	29.07	34.31	39.65	45.07	50.50
25	24.18	29.45	34.82	40.25	45.68	51.02	25	22.69	27.69	32.82	38.06	43.37	48.69
26	23.12	28.35	33.69	39.08	44.46	49.76	26	21.70	26.66	31.75	36.95	42.21	47.49
27	22.07	27.26	32.56	37.91	43.25	48.50	27	20.71	25.64	30.69	35.85	41.07	46.30
28	21.03	26.18	31.43	36.75	42.04	47.25	28	19.74	24.62	29.63	34.75	39.93	45.12
29	20.00	25.11	30.32	35.59	40.85	46.00	29	18.77	23.61	28.59	33.66	38.81	43.96
30	18.54	23.51	28.57	33.68	38.78	43.77	30	17.37	22.07	26.89	31.81	36.78	41.76
31	17.55	22.48	27.50	32.57	37.63	42.59	31	16.44	21.10	25.89	30.76	35.70	40.64
32	16.56	21.46	26.45	31.49	36.50	41.41	32	15.51	20.14	24.89	29.74	34.64	39.53
33	15.59	20.45	25.40	30.41	35.38	40.25	33	14.60	19.19	23.90	28.71	33.57	38.43
34	14.62	19.45	24.37	29.33	34.27	39.11	34	13.69	18.25	22.92	27.69	32.51	37.33
35	13.35	18.03	22.81	27.62	32.40	37.09	35	12.62	17.10	21.68	26.36	31.08	35.80
36	12.41	17.07	21.80	26.59	31.34	35.98	36	11.74	16.18	20.73	25.37	30.06	34.74
37	11.48	16.11	20.82	25.56	30.28	34.89	37	10.86	15.27	19.78	24.39	29.04	33.68
38	10.57	15.16	19.84	24.55	29.23	33.80	38	9.98	14.37	18.85	23.42	28.04	32.64
39	9.66	14.22	18.86	23.54	28.19	32.72	39	9.12	13.47	17.92	22.46	27.04	31.60
40	8.44	12.82	17.26	21.75	26.19	30.53	40	8.06	12.26	16.58	20.97	25.40	29.81
41	7.57	11.91	16.33	20.79	25.20	29.50	41	7.22	11.40	15.69	20.05	24.44	28.82
42	6.71	11.03	15.42	19.84	24.22	28.49	42	6.40	10.55	14.80	19.13	23.49	27.84
43	5.85	10.14	14.51	18.89	23.25	27.49	43	5.58	9.70	13.92	18.22	22.55	26.86
44	5.00	9.27	13.60	17.97	22.29	26.49	44	4.77	8.86	13.06	17.32	21.62	25.90
45	3.90	7.88	11.93	16.00	20.03	23.95	45	3.66	7.41	11.25	15.16	19.10	23.02
46	3.11	7.08	11.10	15.14	19.14	23.03	46	2.92	6.65	10.46	14.35	18.26	22.15
47	2.33	6.27	10.26	14.28	18.26	22.12	47	2.18	5.89	9.68	13.54	17.42	21.28
48	1.55	5.47	9.45	13.44	17.39	21.22	48	1.45	5.13	8.91	12.74	16.60	20.43
49	0.77	4.67	8.63	12.60	16.52	20.34	49	0.72	4.38	8.14	11.94	15.78	19.58
50		3.64	7.32	11.01	14.66	18.19	50		3.24	6.55	9.92	13.30	16.66
51		2.82	6.38	9.95	13.48	16.90	51		2.42	5.51	8.65	11.80	14.93
52		2.02	5.41	8.82	12.18	15.43	52		1.69	4.56	7.47	10.39	13.29
53		1.27	4.45	7.64	10.78	13.82	53		1.01	3.55	6.14	8.73	11.31
54		0.59	3.56	6.54	9.47	12.30	54		0.44	2.67	4.94	7.21	9.46

See introductory notes as regards claimants over 54 at date of trial

See introductory notes as regards claimants over 54 at date of trial

A4: Loss of earnings multipliers adjusted for education, etc.

ND NE GCSE

Loss of earnings: not disabled; not employed; good GCSE level education or equivalent

Age	\multicolumn{6}{c}{Male to retiring age}	Age	\multicolumn{6}{c}{Female to retiring age}
	50	55	60	65	70	75		50	55	60	65	70	75
16	32.56	37.94	43.44	49.02	54.60	60.13	16	29.67	34.63	39.73	44.95	50.25	55.57
17	31.47	36.81	42.27	47.80	53.34	58.82	17	28.68	33.61	38.67	43.84	49.10	54.38
18	30.39	35.69	41.11	46.60	52.09	57.52	18	27.70	32.59	37.61	42.75	47.96	53.20
19	29.33	34.59	39.96	45.40	50.86	56.24	19	26.73	31.59	36.57	41.66	46.83	52.02
20	29.26	34.67	40.19	45.78	51.37	56.90	20	25.43	30.19	35.07	40.06	45.12	50.20
21	28.18	33.55	39.02	44.56	50.12	55.59	21	24.49	29.21	34.05	39.00	44.02	49.06
22	27.10	32.42	37.86	43.36	48.87	54.29	22	23.55	28.23	33.04	37.95	42.93	47.93
23	26.02	31.31	36.70	42.17	47.63	53.00	23	22.62	27.26	32.03	36.91	41.85	46.80
24	24.97	30.21	35.56	40.98	46.39	51.72	24	21.69	26.30	31.04	35.87	40.77	45.69
25	23.91	29.12	34.43	39.80	45.17	50.45	25	20.51	25.02	29.66	34.39	39.19	44.00
26	22.86	28.03	33.31	38.64	43.96	49.20	26	19.61	24.09	28.69	33.39	38.15	42.92
27	21.82	26.95	32.19	37.48	42.77	47.95	27	18.71	23.17	27.73	32.39	37.11	41.84
28	20.79	25.89	31.08	36.34	41.57	46.72	28	17.84	22.25	26.78	31.40	36.08	40.77
29	19.77	24.82	29.98	35.19	40.39	45.49	29	16.96	21.34	25.84	30.42	35.07	39.72
30	18.33	23.24	28.24	33.29	38.33	43.27	30	16.09	20.44	24.90	29.45	34.06	38.67
31	17.35	22.22	27.18	32.20	37.20	42.10	31	15.23	19.54	23.97	28.49	33.06	37.63
32	16.37	21.22	26.14	31.12	36.08	40.94	32	14.36	18.65	23.05	27.53	32.07	36.60
33	15.41	20.22	25.11	30.06	34.98	39.79	33	13.52	17.77	22.13	26.59	31.08	35.58
34	14.45	19.23	24.09	28.99	33.88	38.66	34	12.68	16.90	21.23	25.64	30.11	34.57
35	13.19	17.82	22.54	27.29	32.02	36.65	35	11.68	15.81	20.05	24.38	28.75	33.12
36	12.26	16.87	21.55	26.28	30.97	35.56	36	10.86	14.96	19.17	23.47	27.80	32.13
37	11.35	15.92	20.57	25.26	29.92	34.48	37	10.04	14.13	18.30	22.56	26.86	31.15
38	10.44	14.99	19.61	24.26	28.89	33.40	38	9.24	13.29	17.43	21.67	25.94	30.19
39	9.54	14.05	18.64	23.26	27.85	32.33	39	8.44	12.46	16.58	20.77	25.01	29.23
40	8.33	12.66	17.05	21.48	25.87	30.16	40	7.44	11.32	15.30	19.35	23.44	27.52
41	7.48	11.77	16.14	20.53	24.89	29.14	41	6.67	10.53	14.48	18.50	22.56	26.60
42	6.63	10.89	15.23	19.59	23.93	28.14	42	5.90	9.74	13.67	17.65	21.69	25.70
43	5.78	10.02	14.33	18.66	22.96	27.15	43	5.15	8.96	12.85	16.82	20.82	24.80
44	4.94	9.15	13.44	17.75	22.02	26.16	44	4.40	8.18	12.05	15.98	19.96	23.90
45	3.90	7.88	11.93	16.00	20.03	23.95	45	3.25	6.59	10.00	13.48	16.98	20.46
46	3.11	7.08	11.10	15.14	19.14	23.03	46	2.59	5.91	9.30	12.76	16.23	19.69
47	2.33	6.27	10.26	14.28	18.26	22.12	47	1.94	5.24	8.61	12.03	15.49	18.92
48	1.55	5.47	9.45	13.44	17.39	21.22	48	1.29	4.56	7.92	11.32	14.75	18.16
49	0.77	4.67	8.63	12.60	16.52	20.34	49	0.64	3.90	7.23	10.62	14.02	17.40
50		3.64	7.32	11.01	14.66	18.19	50		2.78	5.63	8.53	11.43	14.32
51		2.82	6.38	9.95	13.48	16.90	51		2.06	4.69	7.35	10.03	12.69
52		2.02	5.41	8.82	12.18	15.43	52		1.39	3.74	6.14	8.54	10.92
53		1.27	4.45	7.64	10.78	13.82	53		0.82	2.91	5.03	7.16	9.27
54		0.59	3.56	6.54	9.47	12.30	54		0.35	2.12	3.93	5.73	7.52

See introductory notes as regards claimants over 54 at date of trial

See introductory notes as regards claimants over 54 at date of trial

A4: Loss of earnings multipliers adjusted for education, etc.

ND NE <GCSE

Loss of earnings: not disabled; not employed; education below good GCSE level

Age	\multicolumn{6}{c}{Male to retiring age}	Age	\multicolumn{6}{c}{Female to retiring age}
	50	55	60	65	70	75		50	55	60	65	70	75
16	31.41	36.60	41.90	47.29	52.68	58.01	16	22.73	26.54	30.44	34.44	38.50	42.58
17	30.36	35.51	40.78	46.11	51.46	56.74	17	21.98	25.75	29.63	33.59	37.62	41.67
18	29.32	34.43	39.66	44.95	50.25	55.49	18	21.23	24.97	28.82	32.76	36.75	40.76
19	28.29	33.37	38.55	43.80	49.06	54.25	19	20.48	24.20	28.02	31.92	35.88	39.86
20	27.60	32.70	37.91	43.18	48.46	53.67	20	20.08	23.83	27.68	31.63	35.62	39.63
21	26.58	31.64	36.80	42.03	47.27	52.43	21	19.33	23.06	26.88	30.79	34.75	38.73
22	25.56	30.58	35.71	40.89	46.09	51.20	22	18.59	22.29	26.08	29.96	33.89	37.84
23	24.54	29.53	34.62	39.77	44.92	49.99	23	17.86	21.52	25.29	29.14	33.04	36.95
24	23.55	28.49	33.54	38.65	43.76	48.78	24	17.12	20.77	24.50	28.32	32.19	36.07
25	22.28	27.13	32.08	37.09	42.09	47.01	25	16.68	20.35	24.12	27.97	31.87	35.78
26	21.30	26.12	31.04	36.01	40.97	45.85	26	15.95	19.59	23.33	27.16	31.02	34.90
27	20.34	25.12	30.00	34.92	39.85	44.68	27	15.22	18.84	22.55	26.35	30.18	34.03
28	19.38	24.12	28.96	33.86	38.74	43.53	28	14.51	18.09	21.78	25.54	29.35	33.16
29	18.43	23.13	27.94	32.79	37.64	42.39	29	13.79	17.35	21.01	24.74	28.52	32.31
30	17.26	21.89	26.60	31.36	36.10	40.75	30	13.51	17.17	20.92	24.74	28.61	32.48
31	16.34	20.93	25.60	30.33	35.03	39.65	31	12.79	16.41	20.13	23.93	27.77	31.61
32	15.42	19.98	24.62	29.31	33.98	38.56	32	12.06	15.67	19.36	23.13	26.94	30.74
33	14.52	19.04	23.65	28.31	32.94	37.48	33	11.35	14.92	18.59	22.33	26.11	29.89
34	13.61	18.11	22.69	27.31	31.91	36.41	34	10.65	14.19	17.83	21.54	25.29	29.04
35	12.56	16.97	21.46	25.99	30.50	34.90	35	9.94	13.46	17.07	20.76	24.48	28.19
36	11.68	16.06	20.52	25.02	29.50	33.86	36	9.24	12.74	16.32	19.98	23.67	27.35
37	10.81	15.16	19.59	24.06	28.50	32.84	37	8.55	12.03	15.58	19.21	22.87	26.52
38	9.94	14.27	18.67	23.10	27.51	31.81	38	7.86	11.31	14.84	18.45	22.08	25.70
39	9.09	13.38	17.75	22.15	26.53	30.79	39	7.18	10.61	14.11	17.68	21.29	24.89
40	8.03	12.19	16.42	20.69	24.91	29.04	40	6.20	9.43	12.75	16.13	19.54	22.93
41	7.20	11.33	15.54	19.77	23.97	28.06	41	5.56	8.77	12.07	15.42	18.80	22.17
42	6.38	10.49	14.66	18.87	23.04	27.10	42	4.92	8.12	11.39	14.71	18.07	21.41
43	5.56	9.65	13.80	17.97	22.11	26.15	43	4.29	7.46	10.71	14.02	17.35	20.66
44	4.76	8.81	12.94	17.09	21.20	25.19	44	3.67	6.82	10.04	13.32	16.63	19.92
45	3.74	7.58	11.46	15.38	19.25	23.01	45	2.64	5.35	8.13	10.95	13.80	16.62
46	2.99	6.80	10.66	14.55	18.40	22.13	46	2.11	4.80	7.56	10.36	13.19	16.00
47	2.23	6.02	9.86	13.73	17.55	21.26	47	1.58	4.25	6.99	9.78	12.58	15.37
48	1.49	5.25	9.08	12.91	16.71	20.39	48	1.05	3.71	6.43	9.20	11.99	14.75
49	0.74	4.49	8.30	12.11	15.88	19.54	49	0.52	3.17	5.88	8.63	11.39	14.14
50		3.54	7.11	10.70	14.25	17.69	50		2.18	4.40	6.67	8.94	11.19
51		2.74	6.20	9.67	13.10	16.42	51		1.62	3.68	5.76	7.87	9.95
52		1.99	5.33	8.69	12.00	15.20	52		1.09	2.93	4.80	6.68	8.54
53		1.27	4.45	7.64	10.78	13.82	53		0.64	2.27	3.93	5.59	7.24
54		0.59	3.56	6.54	9.47	12.30	54		0.27	1.64	3.03	4.42	5.80

See introductory notes as regards claimants over 54 at date of trial

See introductory notes as regards claimants over 54 at date of trial

Sweet & Maxwell

A4: Loss of earnings multipliers adjusted for education, etc.

D E Deg

Loss of earnings: disabled; employed; degree level education or equivalent

Age	\multicolumn{6}{c}{Male to retiring age}	Age	\multicolumn{6}{c}{Female to retiring age}
	50	55	60	65	70	75		50	55	60	65	70	75
16							16						
17			See introductory notes				17			See introductory notes			
18							18						
19							19						
20	20.28	24.03	27.86	31.73	35.61	39.44	20	21.41	25.42	29.53	33.73	38.00	42.27
21	19.53	23.25	27.05	30.89	34.74	38.53	21	20.62	24.60	28.67	32.84	37.07	41.31
22	18.78	22.47	26.24	30.05	33.87	37.63	22	19.83	23.78	27.82	31.96	36.15	40.36
23	18.04	21.70	25.44	29.23	33.01	36.74	23	19.05	22.96	26.98	31.08	35.24	39.41
24	17.31	20.94	24.65	28.41	32.16	35.85	24	18.27	22.15	26.14	30.21	34.34	38.48
25	16.30	19.85	23.47	27.14	30.80	34.40	25	17.22	21.02	24.91	28.89	32.92	36.96
26	15.59	19.11	22.71	26.35	29.98	33.55	26	16.47	20.24	24.10	28.05	32.04	36.05
27	14.88	18.38	21.95	25.55	29.16	32.69	27	15.72	19.46	23.29	27.21	31.17	35.14
28	14.18	17.65	21.19	24.77	28.34	31.85	28	14.98	18.69	22.49	26.38	30.31	34.25
29	13.48	16.93	20.44	23.99	27.54	31.01	29	14.24	17.92	21.70	25.55	29.46	33.36
30	12.57	15.94	19.38	22.84	26.30	29.68	30	13.30	16.90	20.58	24.35	28.15	31.97
31	11.90	15.25	18.65	22.09	25.52	28.88	31	12.59	16.15	19.82	23.55	27.33	31.11
32	11.23	14.56	17.94	21.35	24.75	28.08	32	11.87	15.42	19.05	22.76	26.51	30.26
33	10.57	13.87	17.23	20.62	24.00	27.30	33	11.17	14.69	18.30	21.98	25.69	29.41
34	9.91	13.19	16.53	19.89	23.24	26.52	34	10.48	13.97	17.55	21.20	24.89	28.58
35	9.11	12.30	15.56	18.84	22.11	25.31	35	9.63	13.04	16.53	20.10	23.70	27.30
36	8.47	11.65	14.88	18.14	21.38	24.55	36	8.95	12.33	15.81	19.34	22.92	26.49
37	7.84	10.99	14.20	17.44	20.66	23.81	37	8.28	11.64	15.09	18.60	22.14	25.68
38	7.21	10.35	13.54	16.75	19.95	23.06	38	7.61	10.96	14.37	17.86	21.38	24.89
39	6.59	9.70	12.87	16.06	19.23	22.32	39	6.95	10.27	13.66	17.12	20.62	24.10
40	5.87	8.91	12.00	15.12	18.21	21.22	40	6.20	9.43	12.75	16.13	19.54	22.93
41	5.26	8.28	11.35	14.45	17.52	20.51	41	5.56	8.77	12.07	15.42	18.80	22.17
42	4.66	7.67	10.72	13.79	16.84	19.80	42	4.92	8.12	11.39	14.71	18.07	21.41
43	4.06	7.05	10.08	13.13	16.16	19.11	43	4.29	7.46	10.71	14.02	17.35	20.66
44	3.48	6.44	9.46	12.49	15.49	18.41	44	3.67	6.82	10.04	13.32	16.63	19.92
45	2.78	5.63	8.52	11.43	14.31	17.11	45	3.05	6.17	9.38	12.64	15.92	19.18
46	2.22	5.05	7.93	10.81	13.67	16.45	46	2.43	5.54	8.72	11.96	15.22	18.46
47	1.66	4.48	7.33	10.20	13.05	15.80	47	1.82	4.91	8.07	11.28	14.52	17.74
48	1.11	3.91	6.75	9.60	12.42	15.16	48	1.21	4.28	7.42	10.61	13.83	17.02
49	0.55	3.34	6.17	9.00	11.80	14.53	49	0.60	3.65	6.78	9.95	13.15	16.31
50		2.68	5.38	8.10	10.79	13.39	50		3.04	6.14	9.30	12.47	15.62
51		2.14	4.83	7.54	10.21	12.79	51		2.46	5.61	8.79	12.00	15.18
52		1.63	4.36	7.11	9.82	12.44	52		1.84	4.97	8.14	11.32	14.48
53		1.09	3.81	6.54	9.24	11.84	53		1.25	4.40	7.61	10.83	14.02
54		0.54	3.26	5.98	8.67	11.26	54		0.63	3.82	7.07	10.32	13.54

See introductory notes as regards claimants over 54 at date of trial

See introductory notes as regards claimants over 54 at date of trial

A4: Loss of earnings multipliers adjusted for education, etc.

D E GCSE

Loss of earnings: disabled; employed; good GCSE level education or equivalent

Age	\multicolumn{5}{c}{Male to retiring age}	Age	\multicolumn{5}{c}{Female to retiring age}
	50	55	60	65	70	75		50	55	60	65	70	75
16	21.07	24.55	28.11	31.72	35.33	38.91	16	16.57	19.34	22.19	25.10	28.06	31.03
17	20.36	23.82	27.35	30.93	34.51	38.06	17	16.02	18.77	21.59	24.48	27.42	30.37
18	19.66	23.09	26.60	30.15	33.70	37.22	18	15.47	18.20	21.01	23.87	26.78	29.71
19	18.98	22.38	25.86	29.38	32.91	36.39	19	14.93	17.64	20.42	23.27	26.15	29.05
20	18.29	21.67	25.12	28.61	32.11	35.56	20	14.72	17.48	20.30	23.19	26.12	29.06
21	17.61	20.97	24.39	27.85	31.32	34.74	21	14.18	16.91	19.71	22.58	25.48	28.40
22	16.93	20.26	23.66	27.10	30.54	33.93	22	13.64	16.35	19.13	21.97	24.86	27.75
23	16.26	19.57	22.94	26.36	29.77	33.13	23	13.09	15.78	18.55	21.37	24.23	27.10
24	15.60	18.88	22.23	25.61	29.00	32.32	24	12.56	15.23	17.97	20.77	23.61	26.45
25	14.67	17.87	21.12	24.42	27.72	30.96	25	12.30	15.01	17.79	20.63	23.51	26.40
26	14.03	17.20	20.44	23.71	26.98	30.19	26	11.76	14.45	17.21	20.03	22.89	25.75
27	13.39	16.54	19.75	23.00	26.24	29.42	27	11.23	13.90	16.64	19.44	22.27	25.10
28	12.76	15.89	19.07	22.30	25.51	28.67	28	10.70	13.35	16.07	18.84	21.65	24.46
29	12.13	15.23	18.40	21.59	24.79	27.91	29	10.17	12.80	15.50	18.25	21.04	23.83
30	11.08	14.05	17.08	20.13	23.18	26.16	30	9.87	12.54	15.27	18.06	20.89	23.72
31	10.49	13.44	16.44	19.47	22.49	25.45	31	9.34	11.98	14.70	17.47	20.28	23.08
32	9.90	12.83	15.81	18.82	21.81	24.75	32	8.81	11.44	14.14	16.89	19.67	22.45
33	9.32	12.23	15.18	18.17	21.15	24.06	33	8.29	10.90	13.57	16.31	19.06	21.82
34	8.74	11.63	14.57	17.53	20.48	23.37	34	7.77	10.36	13.02	15.73	18.46	21.20
35	7.54	10.18	12.88	15.60	18.30	20.94	35	7.57	10.26	13.01	15.82	18.65	21.48
36	7.01	9.64	12.31	15.01	17.70	20.32	36	7.04	9.71	12.44	15.22	18.03	20.84
37	6.48	9.10	11.76	14.43	17.10	19.70	37	6.51	9.16	11.87	14.64	17.42	20.21
38	5.97	8.56	11.20	13.86	16.51	19.08	38	5.99	8.62	11.31	14.05	16.82	19.58
39	5.45	8.03	10.65	13.29	15.92	18.48	39	5.47	8.08	10.75	13.47	16.22	18.96
40	4.94	7.50	10.10	12.73	15.33	17.87	40	5.27	8.02	10.84	13.71	16.61	19.49
41	4.43	6.97	9.56	12.17	14.75	17.27	41	4.72	7.46	10.26	13.11	15.98	18.84
42	3.93	6.46	9.02	11.61	14.18	16.68	42	4.18	6.90	9.68	12.51	15.36	18.20
43	3.42	5.94	8.49	11.06	13.61	16.09	43	3.65	6.34	9.10	11.91	14.74	17.56
44	2.93	5.42	7.96	10.52	13.05	15.50	44	3.12	5.79	8.54	11.32	14.14	16.93
45	2.43	4.92	7.44	9.97	12.48	14.93	45	2.74	5.56	8.44	11.37	14.33	17.26
46	1.94	4.41	6.92	9.44	11.93	14.36	46	2.19	4.98	7.85	10.76	13.69	16.61
47	1.45	3.91	6.40	8.90	11.39	13.79	47	1.64	4.42	7.26	10.15	13.07	15.96
48	0.96	3.41	5.89	8.38	10.84	13.23	48	1.09	3.85	6.68	9.55	12.45	15.32
49	0.48	2.91	5.38	7.86	10.30	12.68	49	0.54	3.29	6.10	8.96	11.83	14.68
50		2.47	4.98	7.49	9.98	12.38	50		2.83	5.73	8.68	11.64	14.58
51		1.97	4.47	6.97	9.44	11.83	51		2.34	5.33	8.36	11.41	14.43
52		1.47	3.96	6.45	8.91	11.28	52		1.81	4.88	8.00	11.14	14.24
53		0.98	3.46	5.94	8.38	10.75	53		1.25	4.40	7.61	10.83	14.02
54		0.50	3.02	5.54	8.03	10.43	54		0.66	4.01	7.41	10.81	14.18

See introductory notes as regards claimants over 54 at date of trial

See introductory notes as regards claimants over 54 at date of trial

A4: Loss of earnings multipliers adjusted for education, etc.

D E <GCSE

Loss of earnings: disabled; employed; education below good GCSE level

Age	\multicolumn{6}{c}{Male to retiring age}	Age	\multicolumn{6}{c}{Female to retiring age}
	50	55	60	65	70	75		50	55	60	65	70	75
16	12.26	14.28	16.35	18.45	20.56	22.64	16	9.63	11.25	12.90	14.60	16.32	18.04
17	11.85	13.86	15.91	17.99	20.08	22.14	17	9.31	10.91	12.56	14.24	15.94	17.66
18	11.44	13.44	15.48	17.54	19.61	21.65	18	9.00	10.58	12.21	13.88	15.57	17.27
19	11.04	13.02	15.04	17.09	19.15	21.17	19	8.68	10.26	11.87	13.53	15.21	16.89
20	12.64	14.97	17.35	19.77	22.18	24.57	20	8.37	9.93	11.54	13.18	14.84	16.51
21	12.17	14.49	16.85	19.24	21.64	24.00	21	8.06	9.61	11.20	12.83	14.48	16.14
22	11.70	14.00	16.35	18.72	21.10	23.44	22	7.75	9.29	10.87	12.48	14.12	15.77
23	11.24	13.52	15.85	18.21	20.57	22.89	23	7.44	8.97	10.54	12.14	13.77	15.40
24	10.78	13.05	15.36	17.70	20.03	22.33	24	7.14	8.65	10.21	11.80	13.41	15.03
25	11.41	13.90	16.43	19.00	21.56	24.08	25	6.84	8.34	9.89	11.46	13.06	14.67
26	10.91	13.38	15.90	18.44	20.98	23.48	26	6.54	8.03	9.56	11.13	12.72	14.31
27	10.42	12.86	15.36	17.89	20.41	22.89	27	6.24	7.72	9.24	10.80	12.37	13.95
28	9.92	12.36	14.83	17.34	19.84	22.30	28	5.95	7.42	8.93	10.47	12.03	13.59
29	9.44	11.85	14.31	16.80	19.28	21.71	29	5.65	7.11	8.61	10.14	11.69	13.24
30	8.52	10.81	13.14	15.48	17.83	20.12	30	6.44	8.18	9.96	11.78	13.62	15.47
31	8.07	10.34	12.64	14.98	17.30	19.58	31	6.09	7.82	9.59	11.39	13.22	15.05
32	7.62	9.87	12.16	14.48	16.78	19.04	32	5.75	7.46	9.22	11.01	12.83	14.64
33	7.17	9.40	11.68	13.98	16.27	18.51	33	5.41	7.11	8.85	10.64	12.43	14.23
34	6.72	8.94	11.20	13.48	15.76	17.98	34	5.07	6.76	8.49	10.26	12.04	13.83
35	6.12	8.27	10.46	12.67	14.87	17.02	35	5.37	7.27	9.21	11.20	13.21	15.22
36	5.69	7.83	10.00	12.20	14.38	16.51	36	4.99	6.87	8.81	10.78	12.77	14.76
37	5.27	7.39	9.55	11.73	13.89	16.01	37	4.61	6.49	8.41	10.37	12.34	14.31
38	4.85	6.96	9.10	11.26	13.41	15.51	38	4.24	6.11	8.01	9.96	11.92	13.87
39	4.43	6.52	8.65	10.80	12.93	15.01	39	3.88	5.73	7.62	9.54	11.49	13.43
40	4.01	6.10	8.21	10.34	12.46	14.52	40	3.93	5.97	8.08	10.21	12.37	14.52
41	3.60	5.67	7.77	9.89	11.98	14.03	41	3.52	5.56	7.64	9.77	11.91	14.04
42	3.19	5.25	7.33	9.43	11.52	13.55	42	3.12	5.14	7.21	9.32	11.45	13.56
43	2.78	4.82	6.90	8.99	11.06	13.07	43	2.72	4.73	6.78	8.88	10.99	13.09
44	2.38	4.41	6.47	8.54	10.60	12.60	44	2.32	4.32	6.36	8.44	10.53	12.62
45	1.97	3.99	6.04	8.10	10.14	12.13	45	2.13	4.32	6.56	8.85	11.14	13.43
46	1.58	3.58	5.62	7.67	9.70	11.66	46	1.70	3.88	6.10	8.37	10.65	12.92
47	1.18	3.17	5.20	7.23	9.25	11.20	47	1.27	3.44	5.65	7.90	10.16	12.42
48	0.78	2.77	4.79	6.81	8.81	10.75	48	0.84	2.99	5.20	7.43	9.68	11.92
49	0.39	2.37	4.37	6.38	8.37	10.30	49	0.42	2.56	4.75	6.97	9.20	11.42
50		2.02	4.06	6.12	8.14	10.11	50		2.38	4.81	7.29	9.77	12.23
51		1.65	3.74	5.83	7.90	9.90	51		1.98	4.50	7.06	9.64	12.19
52		1.23	3.31	5.40	7.45	9.44	52		1.54	4.15	6.80	9.47	12.10
53		0.84	2.97	5.09	7.19	9.21	53		1.09	3.83	6.63	9.43	12.21
54		0.43	2.60	4.76	6.90	8.97	54		0.57	3.46	6.40	9.34	12.25

See introductory notes as regards claimants over 54 at date of trial

See introductory notes as regards claimants over 54 at date of trial

A4: Loss of earnings multipliers adjusted for education, etc.

D NE Deg

Loss of earnings: disabled; not employed; degree level education or equivalent

Age	\multicolumn{6}{c	}{Male to retiring age}	Age	\multicolumn{6}{c}{Female to retiring age}
	50	55	60	65	70	75		50	55	60	65	70	75
16							16						
17			See introductory notes				17			See introductory notes			
18							18						
19							19						
20	17.62	20.88	24.21	27.57	30.94	34.27	20	19.41	23.04	26.76	30.57	34.43	38.31
21	16.97	20.20	23.50	26.84	30.18	33.48	21	18.69	22.29	25.98	29.77	33.59	37.44
22	16.32	19.53	22.80	26.11	29.43	32.70	22	17.97	21.55	25.21	28.96	32.76	36.57
23	15.67	18.86	22.11	25.40	28.68	31.92	23	17.26	20.80	24.45	28.16	31.93	35.72
24	15.04	18.19	21.42	24.68	27.94	31.15	24	16.55	20.07	23.69	27.38	31.12	34.87
25	13.04	15.88	18.78	21.71	24.64	27.52	25	13.67	16.68	19.77	22.93	26.13	29.33
26	12.47	15.29	18.17	21.08	23.98	26.84	26	13.07	16.06	19.13	22.26	25.43	28.61
27	11.90	14.70	17.56	20.44	23.33	26.16	27	12.48	15.45	18.49	21.60	24.74	27.89
28	11.34	14.12	16.95	19.82	22.68	25.48	28	11.89	14.83	17.85	20.94	24.06	27.18
29	10.79	13.54	16.35	19.20	22.03	24.81	29	11.31	14.23	17.23	20.28	23.38	26.48
30	9.16	11.62	14.12	16.65	19.17	21.63	30	9.44	11.99	14.61	17.28	19.98	22.69
31	8.67	11.11	13.59	16.10	18.60	21.05	31	8.93	11.46	14.06	16.71	19.40	22.07
32	8.19	10.61	13.07	15.56	18.04	20.47	32	8.43	10.94	13.52	16.15	18.81	21.47
33	7.71	10.11	12.56	15.03	17.49	19.90	33	7.93	10.42	12.98	15.60	18.23	20.87
34	7.22	9.61	12.04	14.50	16.94	19.33	34	7.44	9.91	12.45	15.04	17.66	20.28
35	5.97	8.06	10.20	12.35	14.49	16.58	35	6.63	8.98	11.38	13.84	16.32	18.80
36	5.55	7.63	9.75	11.89	14.01	16.09	36	6.16	8.49	10.88	13.32	15.78	18.24
37	5.13	7.20	9.31	11.43	13.54	15.60	37	5.70	8.02	10.39	12.81	15.25	17.68
38	4.72	6.78	8.87	10.97	13.07	15.11	38	5.24	7.54	9.90	12.30	14.72	17.14
39	4.32	6.36	8.43	10.52	12.60	14.63	39	4.79	7.07	9.41	11.79	14.20	16.59
40	3.40	5.16	6.95	8.75	10.54	12.29	40	3.93	5.97	8.08	10.21	12.37	14.52
41	3.05	4.79	6.57	8.37	10.14	11.87	41	3.52	5.56	7.64	9.77	11.91	14.04
42	2.70	4.44	6.20	7.98	9.75	11.46	42	3.12	5.14	7.21	9.32	11.45	13.56
43	2.35	4.08	5.84	7.60	9.36	11.06	43	2.72	4.73	6.78	8.88	10.99	13.09
44	2.01	3.73	5.47	7.23	8.97	10.66	44	2.32	4.32	6.36	8.44	10.53	12.62
45	1.32	2.66	4.03	5.40	6.76	8.09	45	1.42	2.88	4.38	5.90	7.43	8.95
46	1.05	2.39	3.75	5.11	6.46	7.78	46	1.13	2.58	4.07	5.58	7.10	8.61
47	0.79	2.12	3.47	4.82	6.17	7.47	47	0.85	2.29	3.77	5.26	6.78	8.28
48	0.52	1.85	3.19	4.54	5.87	7.17	48	0.56	2.00	3.46	4.95	6.45	7.94
49	0.26	1.58	2.91	4.26	5.58	6.87	49	0.28	1.71	3.16	4.65	6.13	7.61
50		1.21	2.44	3.67	4.89	6.06	50		1.16	2.36	3.57	4.78	5.99
51		0.93	2.10	3.27	4.43	5.55	51		0.85	1.93	3.03	4.13	5.22
52		0.66	1.78	2.90	4.00	5.07	52		0.60	1.63	2.67	3.71	4.75
53		0.42	1.48	2.55	3.59	4.61	53		0.36	1.28	2.21	3.14	4.07
54		0.20	1.21	2.22	3.21	4.17	54		0.16	0.97	1.80	2.62	3.44

See introductory notes as regards claimants over 54 at date of trial

See introductory notes as regards claimants over 54 at date of trial

A4: Loss of earnings multipliers adjusted for education, etc.

D NE GCSE

Loss of earnings: disabled; not employed; good GCSE level education or equivalent

Age	\multicolumn{6}{c}{Male to retiring age}	Age	\multicolumn{6}{c}{Female to retiring age}
	50	55	60	65	70	75		50	55	60	65	70	75
16	18.77	21.87	25.04	28.26	31.48	34.66	16	13.49	15.74	18.06	20.43	22.84	25.26
17	18.14	21.22	24.37	27.55	30.75	33.91	17	13.04	15.28	17.58	19.93	22.32	24.72
18	17.52	20.58	23.70	26.86	30.03	33.16	18	12.59	14.82	17.10	19.43	21.80	24.18
19	16.91	19.94	23.03	26.17	29.32	32.42	19	12.15	14.36	16.62	18.94	21.29	23.65
20	15.30	18.12	21.01	23.93	26.85	29.74	20	11.04	13.11	15.23	17.39	19.59	21.80
21	14.73	17.54	20.40	23.29	26.20	29.06	21	10.63	12.68	14.78	16.94	19.11	21.30
22	14.16	16.95	19.79	22.66	25.54	28.38	22	10.23	12.26	14.35	16.48	18.64	20.81
23	13.60	16.37	19.19	22.04	24.90	27.71	23	9.82	11.84	13.91	16.02	18.17	20.32
24	13.05	15.79	18.59	21.42	24.25	27.03	24	9.42	11.42	13.48	15.58	17.70	19.84
25	11.14	13.57	16.04	18.54	21.05	23.51	25	8.75	10.68	12.65	14.67	16.72	18.77
26	10.65	13.06	15.52	18.00	20.48	22.92	26	8.36	10.28	12.24	14.25	16.28	18.31
27	10.17	12.56	15.00	17.46	19.93	22.34	27	7.98	9.88	11.83	13.82	15.83	17.85
28	9.69	12.06	14.48	16.93	19.37	21.77	28	7.61	9.49	11.42	13.40	15.40	17.40
29	9.21	11.57	13.97	16.40	18.82	21.19	29	7.24	9.10	11.02	12.98	14.96	16.95
30	7.25	9.19	11.17	13.16	15.15	17.11	30	6.65	8.45	10.29	12.17	14.08	15.98
31	6.86	8.79	10.75	12.73	14.71	16.64	31	6.29	8.08	9.91	11.77	13.66	15.55
32	6.47	8.39	10.34	12.30	14.26	16.18	32	5.94	7.71	9.53	11.38	13.26	15.13
33	6.09	7.99	9.93	11.88	13.83	15.73	33	5.59	7.34	9.15	10.99	12.85	14.71
34	5.71	7.60	9.52	11.46	13.39	15.28	34	5.24	6.98	8.77	10.60	12.44	14.29
35	4.40	5.94	7.51	9.10	10.67	12.22	35	4.42	5.98	7.59	9.23	10.88	12.53
36	4.09	5.62	7.18	8.76	10.32	11.85	36	4.11	5.66	7.25	8.88	10.52	12.16
37	3.78	5.31	6.86	8.42	9.97	11.49	37	3.80	5.35	6.92	8.54	10.16	11.79
38	3.48	5.00	6.54	8.09	9.63	11.13	38	3.49	5.03	6.60	8.20	9.81	11.42
39	3.18	4.68	6.21	7.75	9.28	10.78	39	3.19	4.72	6.27	7.86	9.46	11.06
40	2.37	3.59	4.84	6.10	7.35	8.56	40	2.38	3.62	4.89	6.18	7.49	8.79
41	2.12	3.34	4.58	5.83	7.07	8.28	41	2.13	3.36	4.63	5.91	7.21	8.50
42	1.88	3.09	4.32	5.56	6.79	7.99	42	1.89	3.11	4.37	5.64	6.93	8.21
43	1.64	2.85	4.07	5.30	6.52	7.71	43	1.64	2.86	4.11	5.37	6.65	7.92
44	1.40	2.60	3.82	5.04	6.25	7.43	44	1.41	2.61	3.85	5.11	6.38	7.64
45	1.01	2.05	3.10	4.16	5.20	6.22	45	0.91	1.85	2.81	3.79	4.78	5.75
46	0.81	1.84	2.88	3.93	4.97	5.98	46	0.73	1.66	2.62	3.59	4.56	5.54
47	0.60	1.63	2.67	3.71	4.74	5.75	47	0.55	1.47	2.42	3.38	4.36	5.32
48	0.40	1.42	2.45	3.49	4.52	5.51	48	0.36	1.28	2.23	3.18	4.15	5.11
49	0.20	1.21	2.24	3.27	4.29	5.28	49	0.18	1.10	2.03	2.99	3.94	4.89
50		0.91	1.83	2.75	3.66	4.55	50		0.76	1.54	2.33	3.12	3.90
51		0.69	1.55	2.42	3.27	4.10	51		0.57	1.29	2.02	2.75	3.48
52		0.48	1.29	2.11	2.91	3.68	52		0.39	1.06	1.73	2.41	3.08
53		0.30	1.06	1.82	2.57	3.29	53		0.22	0.78	1.35	1.92	2.49
54		0.14	0.85	1.55	2.25	2.92	54		0.09	0.55	1.01	1.47	1.93

See introductory notes as regards claimants over 54 at date of trial

See introductory notes as regards claimants over 54 at date of trial

A4: Loss of earnings multipliers adjusted for education, etc.

D NE <GCSE

Loss of earnings: disabled; not employed; education below good GCSE level

Age	\multicolumn{6}{c	}{Male to retiring age}	Age	\multicolumn{6}{c}{Female to retiring age}
	50	55	60	65	70	75		50	55	60	65	70	75
16	9.58	11.16	12.78	14.42	16.06	17.69	16	7.32	8.55	9.80	11.09	12.40	13.71
17	9.26	10.83	12.43	14.06	15.69	17.30	17	7.08	8.29	9.54	10.82	12.12	13.42
18	8.94	10.50	12.09	13.71	15.32	16.92	18	6.84	8.04	9.28	10.55	11.84	13.13
19	8.63	10.17	11.75	13.35	14.96	16.54	19	6.60	7.79	9.02	10.28	11.56	12.84
20	7.98	9.46	10.96	12.48	14.01	15.52	20	5.69	6.75	7.84	8.96	10.09	11.23
21	7.68	9.15	10.64	12.15	13.67	15.16	21	5.48	6.53	7.62	8.72	9.85	10.97
22	7.39	8.84	10.32	11.82	13.33	14.81	22	5.27	6.32	7.39	8.49	9.60	10.72
23	7.10	8.54	10.01	11.50	12.99	14.46	23	5.06	6.10	7.17	8.26	9.36	10.47
24	6.81	8.24	9.70	11.18	12.65	14.10	24	4.85	5.88	6.94	8.02	9.12	10.22
25	6.52	7.94	9.39	10.86	12.32	13.76	25	4.37	5.34	6.33	7.34	8.36	9.39
26	6.24	7.64	9.08	10.54	11.99	13.42	26	4.18	5.14	6.12	7.12	8.14	9.16
27	5.95	7.35	8.78	10.22	11.66	13.08	27	3.99	4.94	5.92	6.91	7.92	8.92
28	5.67	7.06	8.48	9.91	11.34	12.74	28	3.80	4.75	5.71	6.70	7.70	8.70
29	5.39	6.77	8.18	9.60	11.02	12.41	29	3.62	4.55	5.51	6.49	7.48	8.47
30	4.90	6.21	7.55	8.90	10.25	11.57	30	3.22	4.09	4.98	5.89	6.81	7.73
31	4.64	5.94	7.27	8.61	9.95	11.26	31	3.05	3.91	4.79	5.70	6.61	7.53
32	4.38	5.67	6.99	8.32	9.65	10.95	32	2.87	3.73	4.61	5.51	6.41	7.32
33	4.12	5.41	6.72	8.05	9.35	10.64	33	2.70	3.55	4.43	5.32	6.22	7.12
34	3.86	5.14	6.44	7.75	9.06	10.34	34	2.54	3.38	4.25	5.13	6.02	6.91
35	3.14	4.24	5.37	6.50	7.62	8.73	35	2.21	2.99	3.79	4.61	5.44	6.27
36	2.92	4.02	5.13	6.26	7.37	8.47	36	2.05	2.83	3.63	4.44	5.26	6.08
37	2.70	3.79	4.90	6.01	7.12	8.21	37	1.90	2.67	3.46	4.27	5.08	5.89
38	2.49	3.57	4.67	5.78	6.88	7.95	38	1.75	2.51	3.30	4.10	4.91	5.71
39	2.27	3.35	4.44	5.54	6.63	7.70	39	1.60	2.36	3.14	3.93	4.73	5.53
40	1.54	2.34	3.16	3.98	4.79	5.58	40	1.34	2.04	2.76	3.49	4.23	4.97
41	1.38	2.18	2.99	3.80	4.61	5.40	41	1.20	1.90	2.61	3.34	4.07	4.80
42	1.23	2.02	2.82	3.63	4.43	5.21	42	1.07	1.76	2.47	3.19	3.92	4.64
43	1.07	1.86	2.65	3.46	4.25	5.03	43	0.93	1.62	2.32	3.04	3.76	4.48
44	0.92	1.70	2.49	3.29	4.08	4.85	44	0.79	1.48	2.18	2.89	3.60	4.32
45	0.56	1.13	1.70	2.29	2.86	3.42	45	0.56	1.13	1.72	2.32	2.92	3.52
46	0.44	1.01	1.59	2.16	2.73	3.29	46	0.45	1.02	1.60	2.19	2.79	3.38
47	0.33	0.90	1.47	2.04	2.61	3.16	47	0.33	0.90	1.48	2.07	2.66	3.25
48	0.22	0.78	1.35	1.92	2.48	3.03	48	0.22	0.78	1.36	1.95	2.54	3.12
49	0.11	0.67	1.23	1.80	2.36	2.91	49	0.11	0.67	1.24	1.82	2.41	2.99
50		0.51	1.02	1.53	2.04	2.53	50		0.51	1.02	1.55	2.08	2.60
51		0.36	0.82	1.28	1.73	2.17	51		0.36	0.83	1.30	1.77	2.24
52		0.24	0.65	1.05	1.45	1.84	52		0.24	0.65	1.07	1.48	1.90
53		0.14	0.49	0.85	1.20	1.54	53		0.14	0.50	0.86	1.22	1.58
54		0.06	0.36	0.66	0.96	1.25	54		0.06	0.36	0.67	0.98	1.29

See introductory notes as regards claimants over 54 at date of trial

See introductory notes as regards claimants over 54 at date of trial

A5: Multipliers for fixed periods and at intervals

Introductory notes

1. The purpose of the table is to provide a means of calculating an appropriate multiplier which will produce the present day equivalent of a cost recurring, either continuously or at fixed intervals, over a given number of years. It does not allow for mortality or contingencies.

2. The table is based on a discount rate of -0.75 per cent per annum. The Lord Chancellor fixed the discount rate under the Damages Act 1996 (from 20 March 2017) at -0.75 per cent, leaving open the possibility of a different rate in exceptional cases such as the effect of tax on large sums. In recent editions of this book, the range of discount rates was extended as a result of the decision in *Helmot v Simon*.[1] Readers requiring tables at -1.5 per cent or 1 per cent per annum should refer to the 2013/14 edition and for tables at 2.5 per cent per annum to the 2016/17 edition.

3. It is assumed that yearly loss is incurred at the *end* of each year in which the loss arises. (Continuous loss obviously accrues from day to day throughout the period. Weekly and monthly losses can in practice be treated as continuous.) For example:

    For expenditure assumed to recur every seven years the expenditure is shown as arising at the end of years seven, 14, and so on.

4. The table contains a number of columns: the number of years; the multiplier for a single payment in *n* years' time; that for a continuous loss over a period of *n* years; that for annual payments in the sense of a series of payments at intervals of one year; and those for payments at intervals of two, three, four and so on years.

5. The figures in the continuous column reproduce those in Table 28 of the Ogden Tables at a discount rate of -0.75 per cent, and hence make no allowance for mortality. For continuous loss for rest of life or up to a particular age, where due allowance should be made for mortality, the multiplier should be derived from Tables 1 to 14 of the Ogden Tables. In large and complex cases, where allowance for mortality could be material to the value of payments at fixed intervals, the advice of an actuary should be sought. Multipliers allowing for mortality are provided in A6 for situations where there is a payment for life but deferred for a number of years.

6. The multiplier for a single payment in *n* years' time (second column) is the same as the discount factor for deferment for the next *n* years.

7. The table shows a multiplier appropriate to each year in which expenditure is to be incurred, and also cumulative multipliers for expenditure up to the end of that year. For example, at -0.75 per cent discount:

    The multiplier for expenditure at the end of year 10 is 1.078. Thus the current lump sum required to provide £100 in 10 years' time is £107.80.

    And similarly:

    - £100 a year continuously over the next 10 years has a present value of £1,039;

---

[1] [2010] GCA 31.

- £100 payable at the end of each of the next 10 years has a present value of £1,043;

- £100 payable at the end of two, four, six, eight and 10 years a present value of £523 (row 10, two-yearly column); and

- £100 payable at the end of three, six and nine years a present value of £314 (row 9, three-yearly column).

The cumulative multipliers do not include an immediate payment; where one is needed in addition to the recurring payments add 1.00 to the multiplier.

8. The multipliers have been rounded to two places of decimals. To use the table to value payments *for life* for a given periodicity, find the expectation of life from Table 1 or 2 of the Ogden Tables at 0.0 per cent. Then take the value in the relevant frequency column at this duration or at the nearest duration shorter than this duration which has a non-zero entry. If a different expectation of life is advised by an actuary or medical expert for an atypical case then that expectation of life should be used. As an example, for a 40 year old female, the Ogden Table 2 expectation of life is 49.24 (also available from the table on page 12). The value of payments every 4 years would be 14.67, for every 7 years would be 8.69 and for every 10 years would be 4.85.

Multipliers where there is evidence of life expectancy

9. In some cases there is medical evidence of the particular claimant's life expectancy. As more distant losses have higher present value, the possibility of dying earlier than expected has less effect on the multiplier than that of dying later than expected. The multiplier for life of someone whose life expectancy is *n* years will therefore be higher than the multiplier for a fixed period of *n* years. The difference varies with sex and age and can be quite significant at a discount rate of -0.75[2] per cent. It is recommended to find the equivalent age for the specified life expectancy, as recommended in paragraph 20 of the Ogden notes (Section A8 of this book), and use the appropriate Ogden Tables at -0.75 per cent for that age.

10. If the conditions set out in the cases of *Sarwar v Ali*[3] and *Burton v Kingsbury*[4] for the estimation of life expectancy are met, then it is appropriate to adopt a multiplier from term certain tables (such as the tables in this section and in Tables 27 and 28 of the Ogden Tables) with no further adjustment for mortality. In all other cases an adjustment to the fixed term multipliers should be adopted for mortality.

Adjustment of fixed term multipliers for mortality

11. For the reasons discussed above in relation to cases where there is evidence of life expectancy, in all cases where the period of loss is dependent on someone's life the multiplier for a fixed period will be lower than the true multiplier. In appropriate cases the fixed term multipliers can be increased by the method discussed in paragraph 20 of the Ogden notes (Table A8 of this book), which calculates an equivalent age based on reduced life expectation.

---

[2] This relation holds only for life multipliers. Multipliers for fixed periods or up to a specified age will be lower if allowance is made for survival than if Tables 27 and 28 are used. It is still recommended to proceed by finding the equivalent age for the specified life expectancy but ensuring that the period for which the calculation is made is maintained.
[3] [2007] EWHC 2091 (QB).
[4] [2007] EWHC 2091 (QB).

A5: Multipliers for fixed periods and at intervals

12. For example:

The claimant is aged 53 and seven months. On the basis of evidence his life expectancy has been determined to be 30 years. For the first 12 years he will need care at £10,000 a year and will incur expenditure on equipment of £5,000 at the end of every four years (i.e. after four, eight and 12 years). For the remaining 18 years he will need care at £20,000 a year and will incur expenditure on equipment of £6,000 at the end of every three years (i.e. after 15, 18, 21, 24, 27 and 30 years).

For a continuous loss of 30 years (e.g. required to value the future care expenditure) the multipliers—from the continuous loss column of Table A5 at -0.75 per cent—are:

	First 12 years	Remaining 18 years[5]	30 years
Care:	12.56	21.10	33.66

The equivalent age to be adopted is calculated from interpolation of the 0% column in the life multipliers shown at Table 1 of the Ogden Tables, as follows:

55 year old multiplier for life at 0%	30.58
56 year old multiplier for life at 0%	29.64

$$\left(\frac{30.58 - 30.00}{30.58 - 29.64}\right) \times 56 + \left(\frac{30.00 - 29.64}{30.58 - 29.64}\right) \times 55 = 55.62$$

The life multiplier at a discount rate of -0.75 per cent for a male aged 55.62 is shown at Table 1 of the Ogden Tables to be 34.33. It is not 33.66 (the multiplier for a continuous loss for 30 years allowing only for compound interest), because the possibility of dying later than expected affects the multiplier more than the possibility of dying earlier. The fixed term multipliers for care are therefore too low and need to be increased by a factor of 34.33/33.66 = 101.99 per cent.

Multipliers for care (as set out above) adjusted for mortality (that is multiplied by 101.99 per cent):

	First 12 years	Remaining 18 years	30 years
Care:	12.81	21.52	34.33

For expenditure at fixed intervals (i.e. non-continuous) over a period of 30 years (i.e. required to value the future equipment expenditure) the multipliers—from the appropriate frequency of loss columns of Table A5 at -0.75 per cent—are:

	First 12 years[6]	Remaining 18 years[7]	30 years[8]
Equipment:	3.19	7.12	33.78

To allow for mortality these multipliers must be increased by 101.99 per cent as above.

---

[5] Calculated by subtraction, taking 12.56 for the first 12 years from 33.66 for 30 years.
[6] 12-year multiplier for 4-yearly replacements.
[7] Calculated by subtraction: 30-year multiplier for 3-yearly replacements 11.35 (Table A5) less 12-year multiplier for 3-yearly replacements 4.23 (Table A5)—see point 13.
[8] 30-year multiplier for a one-yearly frequency of loss.

A5: Multipliers for fixed periods and at intervals

Multipliers for equipment adjusted for mortality (that is multiplied by 101.99 per cent):

	First 12 years	Remaining 18 years	30 years
Equipment:	3.25	7.26	34.33

Modifications

13. Multipliers for continuous loss for periods other than entire years can be obtained by interpolation:

    For continuous payments for 10 and 11 years the multipliers are 10.39 and 11.47. So, for weekly or monthly payments for 10 years 3 months (i.e. 10.25 years) the multiplier is:

    10.39 + (10.25 − 10.00) × (11.47 − 10.39) = 10.39 + (0.25 × 1.08) = 10.66

14. Multipliers for payments beginning after a deferred period can be derived by subtraction or by multiplying by a factor from the single payment column;

    Multipliers for five-yearly payments for 15 and for 50 years are 3.24 and 12.37;

    So the multiplier for five-yearly payments from years 20 to 50 inclusive is 12.37 − 3.24 = 9.13;

    Multiplier for one payment after 18 years is 1.145;

    So the multiplier for five-yearly payments from years 38–68 inclusive is 9.13 × 1.145 = 10.45.

    Multipliers allowing for mortality are provided in A6 for situations where there is a payment for life but deferred for a number of years.

15. Multipliers for irregular payments can be found by adding individual figures from the single payment column.

A5: Multipliers for fixed periods and at intervals

Multipliers at -0.75 per cent discount

n	Single payment	Continuous loss	\multicolumn{13}{c}{Frequency of payments in years}
			\multicolumn{13}{c}{The figures below do not include a payment at the start (i.e. at time zero)}
			1	2	3	4	5	6	7	8	10	12	15	20
1	1.008	1.00	1.01											
2	1.015	2.02	2.02	1.02										
3	1.023	3.03	3.05		1.02									
4	1.031	4.06	4.08	2.05		1.03								
5	1.038	5.10	5.11				1.04							
6	1.046	6.14	6.16	3.09	2.07			1.05						
7	1.054	7.19	7.21						1.05					
8	1.062	8.25	8.28	4.15		2.09				1.06				
9	1.070	9.31	9.35		3.14									
10	1.078	10.39	10.43	5.23			2.12				1.08			
11	1.086	11.47	11.51											
12	1.095	12.56	12.61	6.33	4.23	3.19		2.14				1.09		
13	1.103	13.66	13.71											
14	1.111	14.76	14.82	7.44						2.17				
15	1.120	15.88	15.94		5.35		3.24						1.12	
16	1.128	17.00	17.07	8.57		4.32					2.19			
17	1.137	18.14	18.20											
18	1.145	19.28	19.35	9.71	6.50				3.29					
19	1.154	20.43	20.50											
20	1.162	21.58	21.67	10.87		5.48	4.40				2.24			1.16
21	1.171	22.75	22.84		7.67				3.34					
22	1.180	23.93	24.02	12.05										
23	1.189	25.11	25.21											
24	1.198	26.30	26.40	13.25	8.87	6.68		4.48		3.39		2.29		
25	1.207	27.51	27.61				5.61							
26	1.216	28.72	28.83	14.47										
27	1.225	29.94	30.05		10.09									
28	1.235	31.17	31.29	15.70		7.91				4.57				
29	1.244	32.41	32.53											
30	1.253	33.66	33.78	16.96	11.35		6.86	5.74			3.49		2.37	
31	1.263	34.92	35.05											
32	1.272	36.18	36.32	18.23		9.18				4.66				
33	1.282	37.46	37.60		12.63									
34	1.292	38.75	38.89	19.52										
35	1.301	40.04	40.20				8.16			5.87				
36	1.311	41.35	41.51	20.83	13.94	10.49			7.05			3.60		
37	1.321	42.67	42.83											
38	1.331	43.99	44.16	22.16										
39	1.341	45.33	45.50		15.28									
40	1.351	46.68	46.85	23.51		11.85	9.51			6.01	4.85			2.51
41	1.362	48.03	48.21											
42	1.372	49.40	49.58	24.89	16.65			8.42	7.24					
43	1.382	50.78	50.97											
44	1.393	52.16	52.36	26.28		13.24								
45	1.403	53.56	53.76		18.06		10.92						3.78	
46	1.414	54.97	55.18	27.69										
47	1.425	56.39	56.60											
48	1.435	57.82	58.04	29.13	19.49	14.67		9.86		7.45	5.04			
49	1.446	59.26	59.48						8.69					
50	1.457	60.71	60.94	30.58			12.37				6.30			
51	1.468	62.17	62.41		20.96									
52	1.479	63.65	63.89	32.06		16.15								
53	1.490	65.13	65.38											
54	1.502	66.63	66.88	33.57	22.46			11.36						
55	1.513	68.14	68.39				13.89							
56	1.524	69.65	69.92	35.09		17.68			10.22	8.97				
57	1.536	71.18	71.45		24.00									
58	1.547	72.73	73.00	36.64										
59	1.559	74.28	74.56											
60	1.571	75.84	76.13	38.21	25.57	19.25	15.46	12.93			7.87	6.61	5.35	4.08

Multipliers at -0.75 per cent discount

n	Single payment	Continuous loss	1	2	3	4	5	6	7	8	10	12	15	20
			\multicolumn{13}{c}{Frequency of payments in years}
			\multicolumn{13}{c}{The figures below do <u>not</u> include a payment at the start (i.e. at time zero)}
61	1.583	77.42	77.71											
62	1.595	79.01	79.31	39.80										
63	1.607	80.61	80.91		27.17					11.82				
64	1.619	82.22	82.53	41.42		20.87					10.59			
65	1.631	83.85	84.16				17.09							
66	1.644	85.49	85.81	43.07	28.82				14.57					
67	1.656	87.14	87.46											
68	1.668	88.80	89.13	44.73		22.54								
69	1.681	90.47	90.81		30.50							9.57		
70	1.694	92.16	92.51	46.43			18.78			13.52				
71	1.707	93.86	94.21											
72	1.720	95.57	95.93	48.15	32.22	24.25		16.29		12.31		8.33		
73	1.732	97.30	97.67											
74	1.746	99.04	99.41	49.89										
75	1.759	100.79	101.17		33.98		20.54						7.11	
76	1.772	102.56	102.94	51.67		26.03								
77	1.785	104.33	104.73						15.30					
78	1.799	106.13	106.53	53.46	35.78				18.09					
79	1.813	107.93	108.34											
80	1.826	109.75	110.17	55.29		27.85	22.37			14.14	11.39			5.91
81	1.840	111.59	112.01		37.62									
82	1.854	113.43	113.86	57.14										
83	1.868	115.29	115.73											
84	1.882	117.17	117.61	59.03	39.50	29.74		19.97	17.18		10.21			
85	1.896	119.06	119.51				24.26							
86	1.911	120.96	121.42	60.94										
87	1.925	122.88	123.34		41.42									
88	1.940	124.81	125.28	62.88		31.67				16.08				
89	1.954	126.76	127.24											
90	1.969	128.72	129.20	64.85	43.39		26.23	21.94			13.36		9.07	
91	1.984	130.70	131.19							19.17				
92	1.999	132.69	133.19	66.84		33.67								
93	2.014	134.69	135.20		45.41									
94	2.029	136.72	137.23	68.87										
95	2.045	138.75	139.28				28.28							
96	2.060	140.80	141.34	70.93	47.47	35.73		24.00		18.14		12.27		
97	2.076	142.87	143.41											
98	2.091	144.96	145.50	73.02					21.26					
99	2.107	147.06	147.61		49.57									
100	2.123	149.17	149.73	75.15		37.86	30.40				15.49			8.03

1. The single payment column is the appropriate multiplier for one payment in *n* years' time.
2. The continuous loss column is for loss accruing from day to day: in practice it is appropriate for weekly and monthly losses as well.
3. The column headed "1" is for a series of payments at yearly intervals *at the end of each year* for *n* years. If you want an immediate payment as well, add 1.
4. The remaining columns similarly show the multiplier for a series of payments at intervals of two, three, and so on years. If an immediate payment is to be included, add 1.
5. Thus at -0.75 per cent discount
   – £100 paid after 10 years has a present value of £107.80;
   – £100 a year continuously over the next 10 years has a present value of £1,039;
   – £100 at the end of each of the next 10 years has a present value of £1,043;
   – £100 at the end of two, four, six, eight and 10 years has a present value of £523 (row 10, two-yearly column);
   – £100 at the end of three, six and nine years has a present value of £314 (row 9, three-yearly column); and
   – £100 now and after two, four, six and eight years (but not the 10th year) has a present value of £515 (row 8, two-yearly column, plus one).

A6: Tables of deferred loss

Introductory notes

Part 1

1. The first table that follows is intended for use when a claimant will suffer a loss over a specified number of years, but that loss will not start to run immediately. The figures in the table have been derived from first principles, but they are the same as combining Ogden Tables 27 and 28 at -0.75 per cent per annum.

2. For example:

    a. The claimant is now 30 years old. The Court has decided that he has a reduced expectation of life of 30 years, to the age of 60. For the last 20 years of his life he is expected to need nursing care at a cost of £7,500 a year. His nursing needs will therefore start in 10 years' time.

    b. At -0.75 per cent per annum discount, the multiplier for a period of 20 years is 21.58 [Ogden Table 28].

    c. At -0.75 per cent per annum discount, a loss that will not occur for another 10 years should be adjusted by multiplying it by 1.0782 [Ogden Table 27].

    d. The appropriate multiplier is therefore (21.58 × 1.0782) = 23.27 (to two decimal places).

    e. Compare the figure in the table that follows for 20 years of loss and 10 years before the loss starts to run.[1]

    But see paras 20–33 of the Ogden notes.

3. The following points should also be remembered:

    a. Ogden Table 27 (Discounting Factors for Term Certain) gives the discount factor for a period of complete years. So, in the example above, where the date of trial is 23 August 2018, the need for nursing care is assumed to start on 23 August 2028.

    b. Ogden Table 28 (Multipliers for Pecuniary Loss for Term Certain) assumes that the loss will occur continuously throughout the year, e.g. weekly or monthly bills for nursing care.

---

[1] Note that sometimes the result of making the calculation using Table 28 and Table 27 and multiplying together the rounded figures from each will differ in the second decimal place from the figures in the table which follows, which is calculated exactly without rounding at the intermediate stages.

A6: Tables of deferred loss

Combination grid for different terms certain and different deferment periods (Discount rate -0.75% per annum)

Years of loss	\multicolumn{16}{c}{Years before loss starts to run}	Years of loss
	1	2	3	4	5	6	7	8	9	10	12.5	15	20	25	30	35	40	
1	1.01	1.02	1.03	1.03	1.04	1.05	1.06	1.07	1.07	1.08	1.10	1.12	1.17	1.21	1.26	1.31	1.36	1
2	2.03	2.05	2.06	2.08	2.09	2.11	2.12	2.14	2.16	2.17	2.21	2.26	2.34	2.43	2.53	2.62	2.72	2
3	3.06	3.08	3.10	3.13	3.15	3.17	3.20	3.22	3.25	3.27	3.33	3.40	3.53	3.66	3.80	3.95	4.10	3
4	4.09	4.12	4.15	4.18	4.22	4.25	4.28	4.31	4.35	4.38	4.46	4.55	4.72	4.90	5.09	5.29	5.49	4
5	5.13	5.17	5.21	5.25	5.29	5.33	5.37	5.41	5.45	5.49	5.60	5.70	5.92	6.15	6.39	6.63	6.89	5
6	6.18	6.23	6.28	6.33	6.37	6.42	6.47	6.52	6.57	6.62	6.74	6.87	7.13	7.41	7.69	7.99	8.29	6
7	7.24	7.30	7.35	7.41	7.46	7.52	7.58	7.63	7.69	7.75	7.90	8.05	8.36	8.68	9.01	9.35	9.71	7
8	8.31	8.37	8.43	8.50	8.56	8.63	8.69	8.76	8.82	8.89	9.06	9.23	9.59	9.95	10.34	10.73	11.14	8
9	9.38	9.45	9.52	9.60	9.67	9.74	9.82	9.89	9.96	10.04	10.23	10.43	10.83	11.24	11.67	12.12	12.58	9
10	10.46	10.54	10.62	10.70	10.78	10.87	10.95	11.03	11.11	11.20	11.41	11.63	12.07	12.54	13.02	13.52	14.04	10
11	11.55	11.64	11.73	11.82	11.91	12.00	12.09	12.18	12.27	12.36	12.60	12.84	13.33	13.84	14.37	14.93	15.50	11
12	12.65	12.75	12.85	12.94	13.04	13.14	13.24	13.34	13.44	13.54	13.80	14.06	14.60	15.16	15.74	16.34	16.97	12
13	13.76	13.86	13.97	14.07	14.18	14.29	14.40	14.51	14.61	14.73	15.01	15.29	15.88	16.49	17.12	17.77	18.46	13
14	14.88	14.99	15.10	15.22	15.33	15.45	15.56	15.68	15.80	15.92	16.22	16.53	17.16	17.82	18.51	19.22	19.95	14
15	16.00	16.12	16.24	16.37	16.49	16.61	16.74	16.87	16.99	17.12	17.45	17.78	18.46	19.17	19.90	20.67	21.46	15
16	17.13	17.26	17.39	17.52	17.66	17.79	17.92	18.06	18.20	18.33	18.68	19.04	19.77	20.52	21.31	22.13	22.98	16
17	18.27	18.41	18.55	18.69	18.83	18.97	19.12	19.26	19.14	19.55	19.93	20.30	21.08	21.89	22.73	23.60	24.51	17
18	19.42	19.57	19.72	19.87	20.02	20.17	20.32	20.47	20.63	20.78	21.18	21.58	22.41	23.27	24.16	25.09	26.05	18
19	20.58	20.74	20.89	21.05	21.21	21.37	21.53	21.69	21.86	22.02	22.44	22.87	23.75	24.66	25.60	26.58	27.60	19
20	21.75	21.91	22.08	22.24	22.41	22.58	22.75	22.92	23.10	23.27	23.71	24.16	25.09	26.05	27.05	28.09	29.17	20
21	22.92	23.10	23.27	23.45	23.62	23.80	23.98	24.16	24.35	24.53	25.00	25.47	26.45	27.46	28.52	29.61	30.75	21
22	24.11	24.29	24.47	24.66	24.84	25.03	25.22	25.41	25.60	25.80	26.29	26.79	27.81	28.88	29.99	31.14	32.33	22
23	25.30	25.49	25.68	25.88	26.07	26.27	26.47	26.67	26.87	27.07	27.59	28.11	29.19	30.31	31.47	32.68	33.94	23
24	26.50	26.70	26.91	27.11	27.31	27.52	27.73	27.94	28.15	28.36	28.90	29.45	30.58	31.75	32.97	34.23	35.55	24
25	27.72	27.92	28.14	28.35	28.56	28.78	29.00	29.21	29.44	29.66	30.22	30.80	31.98	33.20	34.48	35.80	37.17	25
26	28.94	29.15	29.38	29.60	29.82	30.05	30.27	30.50	30.73	30.96	31.55	32.15	33.39	34.67	36.00	37.38	38.81	26
27	30.17	30.39	30.62	30.86	31.09	31.32	31.56	31.80	32.04	32.28	32.89	33.52	34.80	36.14	37.53	38.97	40.46	27
28	31.41	31.64	31.88	32.12	32.37	32.61	32.86	33.10	33.35	33.61	34.25	34.90	36.23	37.62	39.07	40.57	42.12	28
29	32.65	32.90	33.15	33.40	33.65	33.91	34.16	34.42	34.68	34.94	35.61	36.28	37.68	39.12	40.62	42.18	43.80	29
30	33.91	34.17	34.43	34.69	34.95	35.21	35.48	35.75	36.02	36.29	36.98	37.68	39.13	40.63	42.19	43.80	45.48	30
31	35.18	35.45	35.71	35.98	36.26	36.53	36.81	37.08	37.36	37.65	38.36	39.09	40.59	42.15	43.76	45.44	47.18	31
32	36.46	36.73	37.01	37.29	37.57	37.86	38.14	38.43	38.72	39.01	39.75	40.51	42.06	43.68	45.35	47.09	48.90	32
33	37.74	38.03	38.32	38.61	38.90	39.19	39.49	39.79	40.09	40.39	41.16	41.94	43.55	45.22	46.95	48.75	50.62	33
34	39.04	39.34	39.63	39.93	40.23	40.54	40.84	41.15	41.46	41.78	42.57	43.38	45.04	46.77	48.57	50.43	52.36	34
35	40.35	40.65	40.96	41.27	41.58	41.89	42.21	42.53	42.85	43.18	44.00	44.83	46.55	48.34	50.19	52.12	54.12	35
36	41.66	41.98	42.30	42.61	42.94	43.26	43.59	43.92	44.25	44.58	45.43	46.29	48.07	49.91	51.83	53.82	55.88	36
37	42.99	43.31	43.64	43.97	44.30	44.64	44.98	45.32	45.66	46.00	46.88	47.77	49.60	51.50	53.48	55.53	57.66	37
38	44.33	44.66	45.00	45.34	45.68	46.03	46.37	46.72	47.07	47.43	48.33	49.25	51.14	53.10	55.14	57.26	59.45	38
39	45.67	46.02	46.36	46.71	47.07	47.42	47.78	48.14	48.51	48.87	49.80	50.75	52.69	54.72	56.81	58.99	61.26	39
40	47.03	47.38	47.74	48.10	48.47	48.83	49.20	49.57	49.95	50.33	51.28	52.26	54.26	56.34	58.50	60.75	63.08	40
41	48.39	48.76	49.13	49.50	49.87	50.25	50.63	51.01	51.40	51.79	52.77	53.77	55.84	57.98	60.20	62.51	64.91	41
42	49.77	50.15	50.53	50.91	51.29	51.68	52.07	52.47	52.86	53.26	54.27	55.30	57.43	59.63	61.92	64.29	66.76	42
43	51.16	51.55	51.94	52.33	52.72	53.12	53.52	53.93	54.34	54.75	55.79	56.85	59.03	61.29	63.64	66.08	68.62	43
44	52.56	52.95	53.35	53.76	54.16	54.57	54.99	55.40	55.82	56.24	57.31	58.40	60.64	62.97	65.38	67.89	70.49	44
45	53.97	54.37	54.78	55.20	55.62	56.04	56.46	56.89	57.32	57.75	58.85	59.96	62.26	64.65	67.13	69.71	72.38	45
Years of loss	1	2	3	4	5	6	7	8	9	10	12.5	15	20	25	30	35	40	Years of loss
	\multicolumn{16}{c}{Years before loss starts to run}	

A6: Tables of deferred loss

Part 2

4. The following tables are intended for use when a claimant will suffer a loss for the rest of life, but that loss will not start to run immediately. These tables allow for mortality and are therefore consistent with Ogden Tables 1 to 26. The period of deferment is represented by m. When m is zero the factors correspond to Tables 1 and 2 of the Ogden Tables at the relevant ages. Some other combinations correspond to other tables in the Ogden Tables. For example, the multiplier for a male age 40 with a 20 year period of deferment is 34.61. This is the same as Table 19 of the Ogden Tables at age 40.

5. If a multiplier is required for a specific number of payments after a period of deferment, the combination table on the previous page can be used with mortality ignored.

6. If there is medical evidence of the particular claimant's life expectancy, it will usually be appropriate to follow the approach set out in paragraph 20 of the Explanatory Notes to the 7th edition of the Ogden Tables to find the effective age for which the expectation of life in accordance with the mortality tables underlying the Ogden Tables (from the 0.0% per annum column of Table 1 or 2 of the Ogden Tables as appropriate) would be equal to the deemed life expectancy. This effective age can then be used as the starting age in order to apply the following table to find a multiplier for a series of payments for life which is deferred for a given period.

7. For example, the claimant is a female aged 30 and a payment of £5,000 a year is expected to start after 15 years. The multiplier from the female tables at -0.75 per cent per annum for age 30 at the start and a period of deferment of 15 years is 61.13. The value of this loss is thus £5,000 × 61.13 = £305,650.

8. In another example the claimant is a male aged 45, who would have a normal expectation of life of 40.55 (from Table 1 of the Ogden Tables at 0.0% per annum). On the basis of medical evidence he is deemed to have an expectation of life of only 25 years. His deemed age is thus 61 (from Table 1 of Ogden at 0.0%). A multiplier is required for a continuous payment for the rest of life starting 10 years from now. The multipliers from the table below are 19.32 for a male aged 60 at the date of calculation and 9.62 for a male aged 70 at the date of calculation. For a male aged 61 at the date of calculation the multiplier required is 19.32 × 9/10 + 9.62 × 1/10 = 18.35.

9. The following points should also be remembered:

   a. When applying the multipliers to claims for loss of earnings, this table (along with the Ogden Tables themselves) only take into account the discount rate and mortality. They do not take into accounts other factors such as employment status or disability and the impact that such factors may be expected to have on the likelihood of continuing to be employed up to normal retirement age. Where appropriate a discount should be applied for these contingencies other than mortality in accordance with Section B of the Explanatory Notes of the 7th edition of the Ogden Tables.

   b. The multipliers in the tables below assume that payments are made continually (or on a weekly or monthly basis) once they come into payment.

10. If a multiplier at -0.75 per cent per annum is required for future continuous payment for just m years, this can be obtained by subtracting the relevant multiplier in the following tables for payments deferred for m years from the corresponding whole life multiplier from Table 1 or 2 of the Ogden Tables.

A6: Tables of deferred loss

Multipliers at -0.75 per cent for future continuous annual payments for life deferred *m* years (Males)

Starting age

m	0	10	20	30	40	50	60	70	80
0	128.73	108.32	88.96	71.43	55.66	41.44	29.19	18.85	9.99
1	127.73	107.31	87.96	70.42	54.66	40.44	28.19	17.86	9.02
2	126.72	106.30	86.95	69.41	53.65	39.43	27.20	16.88	8.10
3	125.71	105.28	85.93	68.40	52.63	38.42	26.20	15.91	7.23
4	124.69	104.26	84.91	67.37	51.61	37.41	25.20	14.95	6.41
5	123.66	103.22	83.87	66.34	50.59	36.39	24.21	14.02	5.64
6	122.63	102.18	82.84	65.31	49.56	35.37	23.22	13.10	4.93
7	121.58	101.13	81.79	64.26	48.52	34.35	22.24	12.20	4.28
8	120.53	100.07	80.73	63.21	47.47	33.33	21.26	11.31	3.67
9	119.47	99.01	79.67	62.16	46.43	32.30	20.29	10.46	3.12
10	118.40	97.94	78.60	61.09	45.37	31.28	19.32	9.62	2.63
11	117.33	96.86	77.53	60.02	44.31	30.25	18.36	8.82	2.19
12	116.25	95.77	76.44	58.95	43.25	29.22	17.41	8.04	1.80
13	115.15	94.68	75.35	57.87	42.18	28.20	16.47	7.29	1.45
14	114.05	93.57	74.25	56.78	41.11	27.17	15.54	6.57	1.16
15	112.95	92.46	73.15	55.68	40.04	26.15	14.62	5.89	0.91
20	107.29	86.79	67.51	50.11	34.61	21.08	10.27	3.04	0.20
25	101.42	80.91	61.70	44.41	29.15	16.17	6.48	1.20	0.02
30	95.34	74.84	55.71	38.59	23.72	11.57	3.49	0.33	0.00
35	89.04	68.57	49.57	32.72	18.43	7.50	1.48	0.05	0.00
40	82.52	62.10	43.29	26.86	13.42	4.20	0.45	0.00	0.00

Multipliers at -0.75 per cent for future continuous annual payments for life deferred *m* years (Females)

Starting age

m	0	10	20	30	40	50	60	70	80
0	135.52	114.70	94.99	76.95	60.52	45.71	32.68	21.41	11.39
1	134.52	113.70	93.99	75.94	59.52	44.71	31.68	20.42	10.41
2	133.51	112.68	92.97	74.93	58.51	43.70	30.68	19.43	9.46
3	132.50	111.67	91.96	73.91	57.49	42.69	29.67	18.44	8.55
4	131.47	110.64	90.93	72.89	56.47	41.67	28.67	17.46	7.68
5	130.44	109.61	89.90	71.86	55.44	40.65	27.66	16.49	6.85
6	129.41	108.56	88.85	70.82	54.40	39.62	26.65	15.54	6.07
7	128.36	107.51	87.81	69.77	53.36	38.59	25.65	14.59	5.34
8	127.31	106.46	86.75	68.72	52.31	37.56	24.64	13.66	4.65
9	126.25	105.39	85.69	67.65	51.26	36.52	23.64	12.74	4.01
10	125.18	104.32	84.61	66.58	50.19	35.47	22.63	11.84	3.42
11	124.10	103.24	83.53	65.51	49.13	34.43	21.63	10.95	2.89
12	123.02	102.15	82.45	64.43	48.05	33.38	20.64	10.09	2.41
13	121.93	101.05	81.35	63.34	46.97	32.33	19.65	9.25	1.98
14	120.83	99.95	80.25	62.24	45.89	31.27	18.66	8.44	1.61
15	119.72	98.83	79.14	61.13	44.80	30.22	17.68	7.66	1.28
20	114.05	93.14	73.46	55.50	39.27	24.93	12.93	4.22	0.32
25	108.16	87.24	67.59	49.70	33.64	19.69	8.57	1.81	0.04
30	102.06	81.12	61.53	43.75	27.96	14.61	4.90	0.55	0.00
35	95.73	74.79	55.27	37.68	22.30	9.90	2.23	0.10	0.00
40	89.16	68.25	48.85	31.53	16.79	5.86	0.74	0.01	0.00

A7: Table of adjustments to multiplier for Fatal Accidents Acts dependency

These tables deal with the risk in dependency cases that the deceased would not have survived until trial. They are derived from the Explanatory Notes of the Ogden Tables, para.64 onwards (approved as correct by the Supreme Court in *Knauer v Ministry of Justice*[1]).

PRE-TRIAL damages (factor to be applied to damages from date of accident to trial)

Age of deceased at date of accident	Male	3	6	9	Female	3	6	9
10		1.00	1.00	1.00		1.00	1.00	1.00
20		1.00	1.00	1.00		1.00	1.00	1.00
30		1.00	1.00	0.99		1.00	1.00	1.00
40		1.00	0.99	0.99		1.00	1.00	0.99
50		0.99	0.99	0.98		1.00	0.99	0.99
60		0.99	0.97	0.94		0.99	0.98	0.97
65		0.98	0.95	0.91		0.99	0.97	0.95
70		0.97	0.92	0.86		0.98	0.95	0.91
75		0.94	0.87	0.78		0.96	0.91	0.84
80		0.90	0.79	0.67		0.93	0.84	0.75

Period from accident to trial (or cessation of dependency if earlier)

POST-TRIAL damages (factor to be applied to damages from date of trial to retirement age)

Age of deceased at date of accident	Male	3	6	9	Female	3	6	9
10		1.00	1.00	1.00		1.00	1.00	1.00
20		1.00	1.00	0.99		1.00	1.00	1.00
30		1.00	0.99	0.99		1.00	1.00	0.99
40		0.99	0.99	0.98		1.00	0.99	0.99
50		0.99	0.97	0.95		0.99	0.98	0.97
60		0.97	0.93	0.88		0.98	0.96	0.92
65		0.96	0.90	0.82		0.97	0.93	0.88
70		0.93	0.84	0.71		0.96	0.89	0.80
75		0.88	0.73	0.55		0.92	0.81	0.66
80		0.83	0.59	0.37		0.86	0.68	0.48

Period from accident to trial

POST-RETIREMENT damages (for the period of dependency after retirement age)

1. First obtain the multiplier for the whole of life dependency by the following steps:

    (a) determine, from 0% tables, the expectation of life which the deceased would have had at date of trial (or shorter period for which s/he would have provided the dependency);

    (b) determine the expected period for which the dependant would have been able to receive the dependency (for a widow, normally her life expectancy from 0% tables; for a child, normally the period until it reaches adulthood);

    (c) take the lesser of the two periods; and

    (d) treat the resulting period as a term certain and look up the multiplier for that period (Table A5, continuous loss column).

2. Obtain the multiplier for dependency from date of trial to retirement age. Do not adjust it for contingencies other than mortality. Do not apply the factors in the Post-Trial table above.

3. Subtract the multiplier for dependency to retirement age (2) from the whole life multiplier (1). Multiply by the factor in the Post-Trial table above.

    Post-retirement multiplier = [Stage 1 figure *minus* Stage 2 figure] × Post-Trial factor.

[1] [2016] UKSC 9.

A8: The Ogden Tables

Actuarial tables with explanatory notes for use in personal injury and fatal accident cases.

Prepared by an Inter-Professional Working Party of Actuaries, Lawyers, Accountants and other interested parties.

7th edition prepared by the Government Actuary's Department.

Table of Contents	Page
Introduction to 7th edition	49
Explanatory Notes	53
Section A: General	53
Section B: Contingencies other than mortality	60
Section C: Summary of personal injury applications	67
Section D: Application of tables to fatal accident cases	72
Section E: Concluding remarks	83

Tables 1–26

Table 1: Multipliers for pecuniary loss for life (males)	85
Table 2: Multipliers for pecuniary loss for life (females)	87
Table 3: Multipliers for loss of earnings to pension age 50 (males)	89
Table 4: Multipliers for loss of earnings to pension age 50 (females)	90
Table 5: Multipliers for loss of earnings to pension age 55 (males)	91
Table 6: Multipliers for loss of earnings to pension age 55 (females)	92
Table 7: Multipliers for loss of earnings to pension age 60 (males)	93
Table 8: Multipliers for loss of earnings to pension age 60 (females)	94
Table 9: Multipliers for loss of earnings to pension age 65 (males)	95
Table 10: Multipliers for loss of earnings to pension age 65 (females)	96
Table 11: Multipliers for loss of earnings to pension age 70 (males)	97
Table 12: Multipliers for loss of earnings to pension age 70 (females)	98
Table 13: Multipliers for loss of earnings to pension age 75 (males)	99
Table 14: Multipliers for loss of earnings to pension age 75 (females)	100
Table 15: Multipliers for loss of pension commencing age 50 (males)	101
Table 16: Multipliers for loss of pension commencing age 50 (females)	102
Table 17: Multipliers for loss of pension commencing age 55 (males)	103
Table 18: Multipliers for loss of pension commencing age 55 (females)	104
Table 19: Multipliers for loss of pension commencing age 60 (males)	105

A8: The Ogden Tables

Table 20: Multipliers for loss of pension commencing age 60 (females)   107
Table 21: Multipliers for loss of pension commencing age 65 (males)   109
Table 22: Multipliers for loss of pension commencing age 65 (females)   111
Table 23: Multipliers for loss of pension commencing age 70 (males)   113
Table 24: Multipliers for loss of pension commencing age 70 (females)   115
Table 25: Multipliers for loss of pension commencing age 75 (males)   117
Table 26: Multipliers for loss of pension commencing age 75 (females)   119

Tables 27 and 28 (Tables for term certain)

Table 27: Discounting factors for term certain   121
Table 28: Multipliers for pecuniary loss for term certain   123
Actuarial formulae and basis   124

Introduction to the 7th edition

"When it comes to the explanatory notes we must make sure that they are readily comprehensible. We must assume the most stupid circuit judge in the country and before him are the two most stupid advocates. All three of them must be able to understand what we are saying"

Sir Michael Ogden QC, on his explanatory notes to the 1st edition of the Ogden Tables.[1]

1. The Working Party has been eager to see a new set of these tables published, as there have been changes in the official projections of future mortality rates for the UK since the previous, 6th edition was published which produce significant changes in the values of some of the multipliers. The Working Party is grateful that the Ministry of Justice has agreed to fund the production of this edition of the Ogden Tables.

Purpose of the tables

2. These tables are designed to assist those concerned with calculating lump sum damages for future losses in personal injury and fatal accident cases in the UK.

3. The methodology is long-established whereby multipliers are applied to the present day value of a future annual loss (net of tax in the case of a loss of earnings and pension) with the aim of producing a lump sum equivalent to the capitalised value of the future losses. In essence, the multiplier is the figure by which an annual loss is multiplied in order to calculate a capitalised sum, taking into account accelerated receipt, mortality risks and, in relation to claims for loss of earnings and pension, discounts for contingencies other than mortality.

4. This methodology was endorsed by the House of Lords in the famous case of **Wells v Wells**.[2] In that case the court determined that the discount rate should be based on the yields on Index Linked Government Stock. The discount rate is now fixed by the Lord Chancellor of the day pursuant to his powers under the Damages Act 1996. The above method was further endorsed by Lord Chancellor Irvine in his decision of July 2001, when he fixed the Discount Rate as being 2.5 per cent. He also gave his reasons for his decision, which reasons appear now to be less than happy in the light of the financial turmoil which has since occurred. I will deal with this below. In my view, this present rate is long out of date and does not reflect the substantial reduction in yields on Index Linked Government Stocks since 2001. The present Lord Chancellor Clarke has agreed to review it although his decision may not be available for several months.

First decision of the Working Party

5. It was decided that, with funding now obtained, a new set of tables, based on the most recent mortality rates produced by the Office for National Statistics (ONS), with as few other revisions as possible, should be issued as quickly as was realistically achievable.

Second decision of the Working Party

6. It was decided that, due to the passage of time and the changed circumstances since the tables were first produced, the text of the Explanatory Notes will require a substantial re-write in order to bolster

---

[1] Memoirs of Sir Michael Ogden QC, *Variety is the Spice of Legal Life*, p.182 (Lewes: The Book Guild, 2002).
[2] [1999] 1 A.C. 345.

A8: The Ogden Tables

its usefulness to practitioners. Not only is there a need to change the language, but the effect of other decided cases has made this a task of importance. The intention of the Working party is to accomplish this re-writing in the next (eighth) edition, which will rely on the further updated mortality projections due to be produced by the ONS later in 2011. It is hoped that the 8th edition will be available in autumn 2012.

Third decision of the Working Party

7. Developments in Guernsey and the review of the discount rate currently being carried out by the Lord Chancellor (see further, below, in respect of both matters) caused the Working Party to decide to include in this edition tables with discount rate columns which range between minus 2 per cent and plus 3 per cent.

8. It is not, we believe, the purpose of these tables or the role of the Working Party to advocate a discount rate, but merely to provide the tools so that, whatever the rate should be, personal injury and fatal accident claims may be quantified.

9. The revised spread of discount rates will assist comparison between lump sums and periodical payments, a process required by the Damages Act 1996, to be more accurately appreciated. The present value of periodical payments is substantially higher than lump sums calculated using the current discount rate of 2.5 per cent. Brooke L.J. remarked in para.34 of the ***Flora v Wakom***[3] judgment: "The fact that these two quite different mechanisms now sit side by side in the same Act of Parliament does not in my judgment mean that the problems that infected the operation of the one should be allowed to infect the operation of the other." This imbalance is a factor which any Lord Chancellor ought to take into account.

Fourth decision of the Working Party

10. The Working Party decided not to increase further the number of tables to reflect different possible retirement ages. The multipliers for retirement ages which do not conform strictly with the five-yearly intervals between 50 and 75 can be calculated with reasonable accuracy by interpolation. We would be interested to learn of other views on this decision which might cause us to think again.

Helmot v Simon

11. The judgment in ***Helmot v Simon***[4] in the Court of Appeal of the Island of Guernsey (September 14, 2010), presided over by Sumption J.A., could be truly described as a decision which has had after-effects. The results have rippled the waters within the English legal establishment, even though the decision creates no precedent in England.

12. The first point to make about the case is that the Damages Act 1996 (as amended) does not apply in Guernsey. Consequentially, neither the 2.5 per cent discount rate prescribed under the power provided by s.1 applies nor is there any power to make an award by way of a periodical payment.

12. The original lump sum award made at first instance on January 14, 2010 was for damages in the sum of £9.3 million plus interest. The court used a single discount rate of 1 per cent for all future losses. The claimant had argued for differential rates of 0.5 per cent for non-earnings-related losses and of

---

[3] [2006] EWCA Civ 1103; [2007] 1 W.L.R. 282.
[4] [2009–10] G.L.R. 465.

minus 1.5 per cent for earnings-related losses. Some eight months later these arguments succeeded on appeal and the final amount of the award was increased to more than £14 million. Permission has been granted to appeal the decision to the Privy Council.

14. The consequences in England and Wales have been profound. The Lord Chancellor has indicated his intention to reconsider the discount rate and at the time of writing is in the process of doing so. It has also emphasised the disparity between lump sum awards and the provision of periodical payments, to the detriment of lump sum awards, when the discount rate is inappropriate, it not having been revised for a period of 10 years.

Mortality data

15. Projections of future mortality rates are usually produced on a two-yearly basis by the ONS as part of the production of national population projections for the United Kingdom and its constituent countries. Multipliers published in the 6th edition of the Ogden Tables were calculated using mortality rates from the 2004-based projections; this new edition provides multipliers based on mortality rates from the most recent, 2008-based, projections. The 2006-based projections showed rather higher projected life expectancies at many ages than those in the 2004-based projections. The 2008-based projections suggest slightly higher projected life expectancies than those in the 2006-based projections, but which are of relatively little significance in terms of the values of the multipliers at most ages.

16. There is much debate among demographers about whether the factors that have led to the significant improvements in mortality in recent years can continue unabated, thus adding some uncertainty to any projections of future mortality. While the Working Party has continued to use the official projections made by the ONS of future mortality rates in the UK, we propose to monitor developments as new evidence becomes available.

Contingencies other than mortality

17. We have persuaded Dr Victoria Wass to join the Working Party. She has suggested changes to the definition of "disabled" and also clarified some of the language in the Explanatory Notes. We anticipate some further suggestions for amendment in the 8th edition.

18. The Working Party notes that there have been a number of cases in which judges have made significant adjustments to the suggested discount factors. In particular the approach of the trial judges to the calculation of future loss of earnings in **Conner v Bradman**[5] and **Clarke v Maltby**[6] has generated some debate. These issues will be discussed in detail when drafting the 8th edition and consideration will be given to whether or not the Explanatory Notes need amendment, especially as regards the circumstances in which it might be appropriate to depart from the suggested non-mortality reduction factors and the size of any adjustments that are made. In the meantime, practitioners performing such calculations are referred to the helpful article by Dr Wass, *"Discretion in the Application of the New Ogden Six Multipliers: The Case of Conner v Bradman and Company"*,[7] which highlights some of the relevant issues.

---

[5] [2007] EWHC 2789 (QB).
[6] [2010] EWHC 1201 (QB).
[7] [2008] J.P.I.L. 2, 154–163.

Fatal Accidents Act calculations and the "Actuarially Recommended Approach"

19. This is dealt with in detail in Section D of the Explanatory Notes. To those comments I would add one qualification which is that the Court of Appeal in **Fletcher v A Train & Sons Ltd**[8] was sufficiently concerned with the consequence of following the reasoning of the House of Lords in **Cookson v Knowles**[9] that it unanimously gave the unsuccessful appellant permission to appeal to the House of Lords on the point; the appeal was subsequently compromised.

20. The Scottish Parliament has since enacted the Damages (Scotland) Act 2011 dealing with the same point and in so doing has demonstrated that it agrees with the point that our predecessors had made on this topic.

21. Section 7(1)(d) of the Damages (Scotland) Act 2011 provides for the multiplier to be calculated at the date of the proof (trial) and the losses over the period between the fatal accident and the proof to be calculated separately, subject to a factor for possible early death, with interest added. Multipliers are determined from the tables based on the age of the deceased had he/she survived to the date of proof. This is the same as our actuarially recommended approach.

Concluding remarks

22. The changes to the Explanatory Notes in this edition are minor; it is the figures that have been updated.

23. As I have previously stated, the figures for the tables themselves are produced by the Government Actuary's Department according to long-established principles.

24. The other matters discussed are the subject of careful and detailed analysis by the members of the Working Party. Its discussions are never less than uninhibited and I am grateful to those members of the Working Party (listed inside the front cover) who give their time and energy to attend the meetings and ensure that all is done which ought to be done.

25. I begin to believe that the journey made by Jason and the Argonauts in search of the Golden Fleece is as nothing in comparison with the desire of those involved in these tables to make the assessment of future losses as simple and accurate as they possibly can be, whilst remaining as clear as we can be in explaining the actual process of calculating the figures. I am conscious that we may not always succeed in that ambition.

Robin de Wilde QC   1 August 2012

---

[8] [2008] EWCA Civ 413; [2008] 4 All E.R. 699.
[9] [1979] A.C. 566.

A8: The Ogden Tables

Explanatory Notes

Section A: General

Purpose of tables

1. The tables have been prepared by the Government Actuary's Department. They provide an aid for those assessing the lump sum appropriate as compensation for a continuing future pecuniary loss or consequential expense or cost of care in personal injury and fatal accident cases.

Application of tables

2. The tables set out multipliers. These multipliers enable the user to assess the present capital value of future annual loss (net of tax) or annual expense calculated on the basis of various assumptions which are explained below. Accordingly, to find the present capital value of a given annual loss or expense, it is necessary to select the appropriate table, find the appropriate multiplier and then multiply the amount of the annual loss or expense by that figure.

3. Tables 1–26 deal with annual loss or annual expense extending over three different periods of time. In each case there are separate tables for men and women.

— In Tables 1 and 2 the loss or expense is assumed to begin immediately and to continue for the whole of the rest of the claimant's life.

— In Tables 3–14 the loss or expense is assumed to begin immediately but to continue only until the claimant's retirement or earlier death.

— In Tables 15–26 it is assumed that the annual loss or annual expense will not begin until the claimant reaches retirement but will then continue for the whole of the rest of his or her life. These tables all make due allowance for the chance that the claimant may not live to reach the age of retirement.

Mortality assumptions

4. The tables are based on a reasonable estimate of the future mortality likely to be experienced by average members of the population alive today and are based on projected mortality rates for the United Kingdom as a whole. The Office for National Statistics publishes population projections on a regular basis which include estimates of the extent of future improvements in mortality. Tables 1–26 in this edition show the multipliers which result from the application of these projected mortality rates which were derived from the principal 2008-based population projections for the United Kingdom, which were published in October 2009. (Further details of these projections can be found on the ONS website at: *http://www.ons.gov.uk/ons/rel/npp/national-population-projections/2008-based-projections/index/html.)*

5. The tables do not assume that the claimant dies after a period equating to the expectation of life, but take account of the possibilities that the claimant will live for different periods, e.g. die soon or live to be very old. The mortality assumptions relate to the general population of the United Kingdom. However, unless there is clear evidence in an individual case to support the view that the individual is atypical and will enjoy longer or shorter expectation of life, no further increase or reduction is required for mortality alone.

Use of tables

6. To find the appropriate figure for the present value of a particular loss or expense, the user must first choose that table which relates to the period of loss or expense for which the individual claimant is to be compensated and to the gender of the claimant, or, where appropriate, the claimant's dependants.

7. If, for some reason, the facts in a particular case do not correspond with the assumptions on which one of the tables is based (e.g. it is known that the claimant will have a different retiring age from that assumed in the tables), then the tables can only be used if an appropriate allowance is made for this difference; for this purpose the assistance of an actuary should be sought, except for situations where specific guidance is given in these explanatory notes.

Rate of return

8. The basis of the multipliers set out in the tables is that the lump sum will be invested and yield income (but that over the period in question the claimant will gradually reduce the capital sum, so that at the end of the period it is exhausted). Accordingly, an essential factor in arriving at the right figure is the choice of the appropriate rate of return.

9. The annual rate of return currently to be applied is 2.5 per cent (net of tax), as fixed by the Lord Chancellor on June 25, 2001, and reassessed on July 27, 2001, under the provisions of the Damages Act 1996 s.1. An annual rate of return of 2.5 per cent was also set for Scotland by the Scottish Ministers on February 8, 2002. The Lord Chancellor may make a fresh determination of this rate, after receiving advice from the Government Actuary and the Treasury (and, in Scotland, the Scottish Ministers after consultation with the Government Actuary). In order to allow the tables to continue to be used should a new discount rate be specified, the tables are accordingly shown for a range of possible annual rates of return ranging from −2 per cent to 3 per cent, in steps of 0.5 per cent, rather than the range 0.0 per cent to 5.0 per cent as in the 6th edition. This change has been made because multipliers at negative rates are useful for the financial evaluation of periodical payments in the exercise which is required by the Damages Act in all cases for comparison with lump sums. In addition, it is recognised that multipliers based on discount rates of more than 3 per cent are currently not generally required, and a recent case heard in the Channel Islands (**Helmot v Simon**[10]) has made an award based on negative discount rates.

10. The figures in the 0% column show the multiplier without any discount for interest and provide the expectations of life (Tables 1 and 2) or the expected period over which a person would have provided a dependency (up to retirement age Tables 3–14 or from pension age Tables 15–26). These are supplied to assist in the calculation of multipliers in Fatal Accidents Act cases (see Section D).

11. Section 1(2) of the Damages Act 1996 makes provision for the courts to make variations to the discount rate if any party to the proceedings shows that it is more appropriate in the case in question. Variations to the discount rate under this provision have, however, been rejected by the Court of Appeal in the cases of **Warriner v Warriner**[11] and **Cooke & Others v United Bristol Health Care & Others**.[12]

12. Previous editions of these tables explained how the current yields on index-linked government bonds could be used as an indicator of the appropriate real rate of return for valuing future income

---

[10] [2009–10] G.L.R. 465.
[11] [2002] EWCA Civ 81; [2002] 1 W.L.R. 1703.
[12] [2003] EWCA Civ 1370; [2004] 1 W.L.R. 251.

streams. Such considerations were endorsed by the House of Lords in **Wells v Wells** and the same argumentation was adopted by the Lord Chancellor when he set the rate on commencement of s.1 of the Damages Act 1996. In cases outwith the scope of these tables, the advice of an actuary should be sought.

Different retirement ages

13. In para.7 above, reference was made to the problem that will arise when the claimant's retiring age is different from that assumed in the tables. Such a problem may arise in valuing a loss or expense beginning immediately but ending at retirement; or in valuing a loss or expense which will not begin until the claimant reaches retirement but will then continue until death. Tables are provided for retirement ages of 50, 55, 60, 65, 70 and 75. Where the claimant's actual retiring age would have been between two of the retirement ages for which tables are provided, the correct multiplier can be obtained by consideration of the tables for retirement age immediately above and below the actual retirement age, keeping the period to retirement age the same. Thus a woman of 42 who would have retired at 58 can be considered as being in between the cases of a woman of 39 with a retirement age of 55 and a woman of 44 with a retirement age of 60. The steps to take are as follows:

(1) Determine between which retirement ages, for which tables are provided, the claimant's actual retirement age R lies. Let the lower of these ages be A and the higher be B.

(2) Determine how many years must be subtracted from the claimant's actual retirement age to get to A and subtract that period from the claimant's age. If the claimant's age is x, the result of this calculation is $(x + A - R)$.

(3) Look up this new reduced age in the table corresponding to retirement age A at the appropriate rate of return. Let the resulting multiplier be M.

(4) Determine how many years must be added to the claimant's actual retirement age to get to B and add that period to the claimant's age. The result of this calculation is $(x + B - R)$.

(5) Look up this new increased age in the table corresponding to retirement age B at the appropriate rate of return. Let the resulting multiplier be N.

(6) Interpolate between M and N. In other words, calculate:

$(B - R) \times M + (R - A) \times N$

and divide the result by $[(B - R) + (R - A)]$, (or equivalently $[B - A]$).

14. In the example given in para.13, the steps would be as follows:

(1) R is 58, A is 55 and B is 60.

(2) Subtracting three years from the claimant's age gives 39.

(3) Looking up age 39 in Table 6 (for retirement age 55) gives 13.10 at a rate of return of 2.5 per cent.

(4) Adding two years to the claimant's age gives 44.

(5) Looking up age 44 in Table 8 (for retirement age 60) gives 13.03 at a rate of return of 2.5 per cent.

(6) Calculating $2 \times 13.10 + 3 \times 13.03$ and dividing by $(60 - 58) + (58 - 55)$ [equals 5] gives 13.06 as the multiplier.

15. When the loss or expense to be valued is that from the date of retirement to death, and the claimant's date of retirement differs from that assumed in the tables, a different approach is necessary, involving the following three steps.

(1) Assume that there is a present loss which will continue for the rest of the claimant's life and from Table 1 or 2 establish the value of that loss or expense over the whole period from the date of assessment until the claimant's death.

(2) Establish the value of such loss or expense over the period from the date of assessment until the claimant's expected date of retirement following the procedure explained in paras 13 and 14, above.

(3) Subtract the second figure from the first. The balance remaining represents the present value of the claimant's loss or expense between retirement and death.

16. If the claimant's actual retirement age would have been earlier than 50, or later than 75, the advice of an actuary should be sought.

Younger ages

17. Tables 1 and 2, which concern pecuniary loss for life, and Tables 15–26, which concern loss of pension from retirement age, have been extended down to age 0. In some circumstances the multiplier at age 0 is slightly lower than that at age 1; this arises because of the relatively high incidence of deaths immediately after birth.

18. Tables for multipliers for loss of earnings (Tables 3–14) have not been extended below age 16. In order to determine the multiplier for loss of earnings for someone who has not yet started work, it is first necessary to determine an assumed age at which the claimant would have commenced work and to find the appropriate multiplier for that age from Tables 3–14, according to the assumed retirement age. This multiplier should then be multiplied by the deferment factor from Table 27 which corresponds to the appropriate rate of return and the period from the date of the trial to the date on which it is assumed that the claimant would have started work. A similar approach can be used for determining a multiplier for pecuniary loss for life where the loss is assumed to commence a fixed period of years from the date of the trial. For simplicity the factors in Table 27 relate purely to the impact of compound interest and ignore mortality. At ages below 30 this is a reasonable approximation but at higher ages it would normally be appropriate to allow explicitly for mortality and the advice of an actuary should be sought.

Contingencies

19. Tables 1–26 make reasonable provision for the levels of mortality which members of the population of the United Kingdom alive today may expect to experience in future. The tables do not take account of the other risks and vicissitudes of life, such as the possibility that the claimant would for periods have ceased to earn due to ill-health or loss of employment. Nor do they take account of the fact that many people cease work for substantial periods to care for children or other dependants. Section B suggests ways in which allowance may be made to the multipliers for loss of earnings, to allow for certain risks other than mortality.

Impaired lives

20. In some cases, medical evidence may be available which asserts that a claimant's health impairments are equivalent to adding a certain number of years to their current age, or to treating the

individual as having a specific age different from their actual age. In such cases, Tables 1 and 2 can be used with respect to the deemed higher age. For the other tables the adjustment is not so straightforward, as adjusting the age will also affect the assumed retirement age, but the procedures described in paras 13–15 may be followed, or the advice of an actuary should be sought. In other cases, the medical evidence may state that the claimant is likely to live for a stated number of years. This is often then treated as requiring payment to be made for a fixed period equal to the stated life expectancy and using Table 28 to ascertain the value of the multiplier. In general, this is likely to give a multiplier which is too high since this approach does not allow for the distribution of deaths around the expected length of life. For a group of similarly impaired lives of the same age, some will die before the average life expectancy and some after; allowing for this spread of deaths results in a lower multiplier than assuming payment for a term certain equal to the life expectancy. In such cases, it is preferable to look up the age in the 0 per cent column in Tables 1 or 2 for which the value of the multiplier at 0 per cent is equal to the stated life expectancy. The relevant multipliers are then obtained from the relevant tables using this age. Take, for example, an impaired male life which is stated to have a life expectancy of 20 years. By interpolation, the age for which the multiplier in the 0 per cent column in Table 1 is 20 is:

$$(20 - 19.74)/(20.57 - 19.74) \times 66 + (20.57 - 20)/(20.57 - 19.74) \times 67$$

which equals 66.7 years.

The value of the whole of life multiplier is then obtained from the 2.5 per cent column of Table 1 for age 66.7 years:

$$(67 - 66.7) \times 15.38 + (66.7 - 66) \times 14.90$$

which equals 15.04 (compared to 15.78 for the value for a term certain of 20 years using the 2.5 per cent column of Table 28).

Fixed period

21. In cases where pecuniary loss is to be valued for a fixed period, the multipliers in Table 28 may be used. These make no allowance for mortality or any other contingency but assume that regular frequent payments (e.g. weekly or monthly) will continue throughout the period. These figures should in principle be adjusted if the periodicity of payment is less frequent, especially if the payments in question are annually in advance or in arrears.

Variable future losses or expenses

22. The tables do not provide an immediate answer when the annual future loss or expense is likely to change at given points in time in the future. The most common examples will be where:

(a) the claimant's lost earnings would have increased on a sliding scale or changed due to promotion; or

(b) the claimant's care needs are likely to change in the future, perhaps because it is anticipated that a family carer will not be able to continue to provide help.

In such situations it is usually necessary to split the overall multiplier, whether for working life or whole of life, into segments, and then to apply those smaller segmented multipliers to the multiplicand appropriate for each period.

A8: The Ogden Tables

There are a variety of methods which could be used for splitting a multiplier, especially where the age at which a payment is increased or decreased, or stops or begins, is one which is tabulated in Tables 1–26. The following examples serve to illustrate how multipliers might be split using the "apportionment method". This method can be extended for use in cases where none of the ages at which payments change are tabulated.

Example 1—Variable future earnings

23. The claimant is female, a graduate with a degree, aged 25 at date of settlement/trial. Her probable career progression, in the absence of injury, would have provided her with salary increases at ages 30, 35 and 40; thereafter she would have continued at the same level to age 60, when she would have stepped down from full-time work to work part-time until 70. Post-accident she is now incapable of working.

The multiplicands for lost future earnings are:

    Age 25–30:   £16,000 a year

    Age 30–35:   £25,000 a year

    Age 35–40:   £35,000 a year

    Age 40–60:   £40,000 a year

    Age 60–70:   £20,000 a year

The multipliers for each stage of her career are calculated as follows:

(1) The working-life will be 45 years and the Multiplier from Table 12 for that period taking into account mortality risks but without any discounts for any other contingencies will be 26.73.

(2) The multiplier for a term certain of 45 years (ignoring mortality risks) from Table 28 is 27.17.

(3) The multiplier from Table 28 should be split so that each individual segment of the whole working life period (45 years) is represented by a figure. So, the first five years is represented by a multiplier for a term certain of five years, namely 4.70; the next five years is represented by a multiplier of 4.16 (being the difference between the figure for a term certain of 10 years, namely 8.86 and the figure for a term certain of five years, namely 4.70); the next five years by 3.68 (i.e. the 15-year figure of 12.54 less the 10 year figure of 8.86); the next 20 years by 10.89 (i.e. the difference between the 35-year figure which is 23.43 and the 15-year figure of 12.54); then, the final 10 years by the balance of 3.74 (the residual figure being 27.17 less 23.43).

(4) Each of those smaller segmented multipliers can be shown as a percentage or fraction of the whole: so, for the first five years the segmented multiplier of 4.70 is 17.30 per cent of the whole figure of 27.17, and so on for each segment of the 45-year period.

(5) The working life multiplier from Table 12 can now be split up in identical proportions to the way in which the Table 28 multiplier has been treated above: thus the first five-year period is now represented by a multiplier of 4.62, which is calculated by taking 17.30 per cent of 26.73. Each segmented multiplier is calculated in the same way.

(6) Having now obtained multipliers for each segment of working life, taking into account mortality risks, it is then necessary to discount those figures for "contingencies other than mortality". The

discount factor from Table C (using the column for a female, not disabled, with degree level education) is 0.89. So, the figure of 4.62 for the first five-year period now becomes 4.11 (i.e. 4.62 × 0.89). Again, treat each segmented multiplier in the same way.

(7) The multiplicand for each segment of working life is now multiplied by the appropriate segmented multiplier to calculate the loss for that period. The sum total of those losses represents the full sum for loss of future earnings (ignoring any mitigation).

(8) The figures are set out in tabular form below and give a total lump sum award of £716,260:

Ages	Period (years)	Table 28	% Split	Table 12	Discounted Multipliers (Table C) (× 0.89)	Net Annual Earnings £	£ Loss
25–30	5	4.70	17.30	4.62	4.11	16,000	65,760
30–35	5	4.16	15.31	4.09	3.64	25,000	91,000
35–40	5	3.68	13.54	3.62	3.22	35,000	112,700
40–60	20	10.89	40.08	10.71	9.53	40,000	381,200
60–70	10	3.74	13.77	3.68	3.28	20,000	65,600
Totals:	45 years	27.17	100.00	26.73	23.79		**716,260**

N.B. the figures in the above table have been rounded at each step of the calculation so the totals shown are not necessarily the sum of the individual multipliers in the columns

Example 2—Variable future care costs

24. A male aged 20 years at the date of settlement/trial requires personal care support for life. He has a normal life expectation for his age. Significant changes in his care regime are anticipated at age 30 and again at age 50.

The multiplicands for care costs are:

Age 20–30:   £30,000 a year

Age 30–50:   £60,000 a year

Age 50 for rest of life: £80,000 a year

The multipliers for each stage of the care regime are calculated as follows:

(1) The life expectation will be 67.22 years (from the 0 per cent column of Table 1) and the multiplier for that period taking into account mortality risks (from Table 1) will be 32.10.

(2) The multiplier for a term certain of 67.22 years (ignoring mortality risks) from Table 28 lies between 32.75 (for 67 years) and 32.94 (for 68 years) and is calculated thus:

(68 − 67.22) × 32.75 + (67.22 − 67) × 32.94 = 32.79.

(3) The multiplier from Table 28 should be split so that each individual segment of the whole period of life expectation is represented by a figure. So, the first 10 years (20–30) are represented by a multiplier of 8.86; the next 20 years (30–50) are represented by a multiplier of 12.33 (being the difference between the 30-year figure of 21.19 and the 10-year figure of 8.86); then, the final

years (50 to death) are represented by the balance of 11.60 (being the difference between the term certain multiplier of 32.79 and the 30-year figure of 21.19).

(4) Each of those smaller segmented multipliers can be shown as a percentage or fraction of the whole: so, for the first 10 years the segmented multiplier of 8.86 is 27.02 per cent of the whole figure of 32.79, and so on for each segment of the life period.

(5) The life multiplier from Table 1 can now be split up in the way in which the Table 28 multiplier was treated above and in identical proportions: thus the first 10-year period is now represented by a multiplier of 8.67 which is calculated by taking 27.02 per cent of 32.10.

(6) The figures are set out in tabular form below and give a total lump sum award of £1,893,100:

Age (years)	Table 28 (67.22 years) Split multipliers	% Split (of Table 28) figure	Table 1 (multiplier allowing for mortality)	Care costs £ a year	Total £
20–30	8.86	27.02%	8.67	30,000	260,100
30–50	12.33	37.60%	12.07	60,000	724,200
50 till death	11.60	35.38%	11.36	80,000	908,800
Totals	32.79 (no mortality discount)	100.00%	32.10 life multiplier		**1,893,100**

N.B. the figures in the above table have been rounded at each step of the calculation.

Spouse's pensions

25. If doubt exists whether the tables are appropriate to a particular case which appears to present significant difficulties of substance, it would be prudent to take actuarial advice. This might be appropriate in relation to the level of spouse's benefits, if these are to be assessed, since these are not readily valued using Tables 1–26. As a rough rule of thumb, if spouse's benefits are to be included when valuing pension loss from normal pension age, the multipliers in Tables 15–26 should be increased by 5 per cent for a female claimant (i.e. benefits to the male spouse) and by 14 per cent for a male claimant if the spouse's pension would be half of the pension that the member was receiving at death. If the spouse's pension would be payable at a rate of two-thirds the member's pension at death the multipliers should be increased by 7 per cent for a female claimant and by 18 per cent for a male claimant.

Section B: Contingencies other than mortality

26. As stated in para.19, the tables for loss of earnings (Tables 3–14) take no account of risks other than mortality. This section shows how the multipliers in these tables may be reduced to take account of these risks.

27. Tables of factors to be applied to the existing multipliers were first introduced in the 2nd edition of the Ogden Tables. These factors were based on work commissioned by the Institute of Actuaries and carried out by Professor S. Haberman and Mrs D. S. F. Bloomfield.[13] Although there was some debate within the actuarial profession about the details of the work, and in particular about the scope for developing it further, the findings were broadly accepted and were adopted by the Government

---

[13] "Work time lost to sickness, unemployment and stoppages: measurement and application" (1990) 117 *Journal of the Institute of Actuaries*, 533–595.

Actuary and the other actuaries who were members of the Working Party when the 2nd edition of the Tables was published and remained unchanged until the 6th edition.

28. Some related work was published in 2002 by Lewis, McNabb and Wass.[14] For the publication of the 6th edition of the Ogden Tables, the Ogden Working Party was involved in further research into the impact of contingencies other than mortality carried out by Professor Richard Verrall, Professor Steven Haberman and Mr Zoltan Butt of City University, London and, in a separate exercise, by Dr Victoria Wass of Cardiff University. Their findings were combined to produce the tables of factors given in section B of the 6th edition and repeated here.

29. The Haberman and Bloomfield paper relied on data from the Labour Force Surveys for 1973, 1977, 1981 and 1985 and English Life Tables No. 14 (1980–82). The Labour Force Survey (LFS) was originally designed to produce a periodic cross-sectional snapshot of the working age population and collects information on an extensive range of socio-economic and labour force characteristics. Since the winter of 1992/3, the LFS has been carried out on a quarterly basis, with respondents being included in the survey over five successive quarters. The research of Professor Verrall *et al.* and Dr Wass used data from the Labour Force Surveys conducted from 1998–2003 to estimate the probabilities of movement of males and females between different states of economic activity, dependent on age, sex, employment activity and level of disability. These probabilities permit the calculation of the expected periods in employment until retirement age, dependent on the initial starting state of economic activity, disability and educational attainment. These can then be discounted at the same discount rate that is used for obtaining the relevant multiplier from Tables 3–14, in order to give a multiplier which takes into account only those periods the claimant would be expected, on average, to be in work. These discounted working life expectancy multipliers can be compared to those obtained assuming the person remained in work throughout, to obtain reduction factors which give the expected proportion of time to retirement age which will be spent in employment.

30. The factors described in subsequent paragraphs are for use in calculating loss of earnings up to retirement age. The research work did not investigate the impact of contingencies other than mortality on the value of future pension rights. Some reduction to the multiplier for loss of pension would often be appropriate when a reduction is being applied for loss of earnings. This may be a smaller reduction than in the case of loss of earnings because the ill-health contingency (as opposed to the unemployment contingency) may give rise to significant ill-health retirement pension rights. A bigger reduction may be necessary in cases where there is significant doubt whether pension rights would have continued to accrue (to the extent not already allowed for in the post-retirement multiplier) or in cases where there may be doubt over the ability of the pension fund to pay promised benefits. In the case of a defined contribution pension scheme, loss of pension rights may be allowed for, simply by increasing the future earnings loss (adjusted for contingencies other than mortality) by the percentage of earnings which the employer contributes to the scheme represent.

31. The methodology proposed in paras 33–42 describes one method for dealing with contingencies other than mortality. If this methodology is followed, in many cases it will be appropriate to increase or reduce the discount in the tables to take account of the nature of a particular claimant's disabilities. It should be noted that the methodology does not take into account the pre-accident employment history. The methodology also provides for the possibility of valuing more appropriately the possible mitigation of loss of earnings in cases where the claimant is employed after the accident or is considered capable of being employed. This will in many cases enable a more accurate assessment to be made of the mitigation of loss. However, there may be some cases when the *Smith v Manchester Corporation* or *Blamire* approach remains applicable or otherwise where a precise mathematical approach is inapplicable.

---

[14] "Methods of calculating damages for loss of future earnings" (2002) 2 *Journal of Personal Injury Law*, 151–165.

32. The suggestions which follow are intended as a "ready reckoner" which provides an initial adjustment to the multipliers according to the employment status, disability status and educational attainment of the claimant when calculating awards for loss of earnings and for any mitigation of this loss in respect of potential future post-injury earnings. Such a ready reckoner cannot take into account all circumstances and it may be appropriate to argue for higher or lower adjustments in particular cases. In particular, it can be difficult to place a value on the possible mitigating income when considering the potential range of disabilities and their effect on post-work capability, even within the interpretation of disability set out in para.35. However, the methodology does offer a framework for consideration of a range of possible figures with the maximum being effectively provided by the post-injury multiplier assuming the claimant was not disabled and the minimum being the case where there is no realistic prospect of post-injury employment.

The deduction for contingencies other than mortality

33. Under this method, multipliers for loss of earnings obtained from Tables 3–14 are multiplied by factors to allow for the risk of periods of non-employment and absence from the workforce because of sickness.

34. The research by Professor Verrall et al. and Dr Wass referred to in paras 28 and 29 demonstrated that the key issues affecting a person's future working life are employment status, disability status and educational attainment.

35. The definitions of employed/not employed, disabled/not disabled and educational attainment used in this analysis and which should be used for determining which factors to apply to the multipliers to allow for contingencies other than mortality are as follows:

Employed	Those who at the time of the accident are employed, self-employed or on a government training scheme.
Not employed	All others (including those temporarily out of work, full-time students and unpaid family workers).
Disabled	A person is classified as being disabled if all three of the following conditions in relation to the ill-health or disability are met:

    (i) the person has an illness or a disability which has lasted or is expected to last for over a year or is a progressive illness,

    (ii) the person satisfies the Equality Act 2010 definition that the impact of the disability substantially limits the person's ability to carry out normal day to day activities, and

    (iii) their condition affects either the kind **or** the amount of paid work they can do.

Not disabled	All others.

Normal day to day activities are those which are carried out by most people on a daily basis, and we are interested in disabilities/health problems which have a substantial adverse effect on respondent's ability to carry out these activities.

There are several ways in which a disability or health problem may affect the respondent's day to day activities:

Mobility—for example, unable to travel short journeys as a passenger in a car, unable to walk other than at a slow pace or with jerky movements, difficulty in negotiating stairs, unable to use one or more forms of public transport, unable to go out of doors unaccompanied.

Manual dexterity—for example, loss of functioning in one or both hands, inability to use a knife and fork at the same time, or difficulty in pressing buttons on a keyboard.

Physical co-ordination—for example, the inability to feed or dress oneself; or to pour liquid from one vessel to another except with unusual slowness or concentration.

Problems with bowel/bladder control—for example, frequent or regular loss of control of the bladder or bowel. Occasional bedwetting is not considered a disability.

Ability to lift, carry or otherwise move everyday objects (for example, books, kettles, light furniture)—for example, inability to pick up a weight with one hand but not the other, or to carry a tray steadily.

Speech—for example, unable to communicate (clearly) orally with others, taking significantly longer to say things. A minor stutter, difficulty in speaking in front of an audience, or inability to speak a foreign language would not be considered impairments.

Hearing—for example, not being able to hear without the use of a hearing aid, the inability to understand speech under normal conditions or over the telephone.

Eyesight—for example, while wearing spectacles or contact lenses—being unable to pass the standard driving eyesight test, total inability to distinguish colours (excluding ordinary red/green colour blindness), or inability to read newsprint.

Memory or ability to concentrate, learn or understand—for example, intermittent loss of consciousness or confused behaviour, inability to remember names of family or friends, unable to write a cheque without assistance, or an inability to follow a recipe.

Perception of risk of physical danger—for example, reckless behaviour putting oneself or others at risk, mobility to cross the road safely. This excludes (significant) fear of heights or under-estimating risk of dangerous hobbies.

Three levels of educational attainment are defined for the purposes of the tables as follows:

D   Degree or equivalent or higher.

GE–A   GCSE grades A–C up to A levels or equivalents.

O   Below GCSE C or CSE 1 or equivalent or no qualifications.

The following table gives a more detailed breakdown of the allocation of various types of educational qualification to each of the three categories above and is based on the allocations used in the research by Professor Verrall, et al. and Dr Wass.

A8: The Ogden Tables

Categories of highest educational attainment

D Degree or equivalent or higher	GE–A GCSE grades A–C up to A levels or equivalent	O Below GCSE grade C or CSE grade 1 or equivalent or no qualifications
Any degree (first or higher) Other higher education qualification below degree level Diploma in higher education	A or AS level or equivalent O level, GCSE grade A–C or equivalent	CSE below grade 1 GCSE below grade C
NVQ level 4 or 5	NVQ level 2 or 3	NVQ level 1 or equivalent
HNC/HND, BTEC higher, etc	BTEC/SCOTVEC first or general diploma OND/ONC, BTEC/SCOTVEC national	BTEC first or general certificate SCOTVEC modules or equivalent
RSA higher diploma	RSA diploma, advanced diploma or certificate	RSA other
Teaching, Nursing, etc	GNVQ intermediate or advanced	GNVQ/GVSQ foundation level
	City and Guilds craft or advanced craft	City and Guilds other
	SCE higher or equivalent Trade apprenticeship Scottish 6th year certificate (CSYS)	YT/ YTP certificate Other qualifications No qualification Don't know

Note: "educational attainment" is used here as a proxy for skill level, so that those in professional occupations such as law, accountancy, nursing, etc. who do not have a degree ought to be treated as if they do have one.

36. The research also considered the extent to which a person's future working life expectancy is affected by individual circumstances such as occupation and industrial sector, geographical region and education. The researchers concluded that the most significant consideration was the highest level of education achieved by the claimant and that, if this was allowed for, the effect of the other factors was relatively small. As a result, the Working Party decided to propose adjustment factors which allow for employment status, disability status and educational attainment only. This is a change from earlier editions of the Ogden Tables where adjustments were made for types of occupation and for geographical region.

37. A separate assessment is made for: (a) the value of earnings the claimant would have received if the injury had not been suffered, and (b) the value of the claimant's earnings (if any) taking account of the injuries sustained. The risk of non-employment is significantly higher post-injury due to the impairment. The loss is arrived at by deducting (b) from (a).

38. In order to calculate the value of the earnings the claimant would have received, if the injury had not been suffered, the claimant's employment status and the disability status need to be determined as at the date of the accident (or the onset of the medical condition) giving rise to the claim, so that the correct table can be applied. For the calculation of future loss of earnings (based on actual pre-accident earnings and also future employment prospects), Tables A and C should be used for claimants who were not disabled at the time of the accident, and Tables B and D should be used for those with a pre-existing disability. In all of these tables the three left hand columns are for those who were employed at the time of the accident and the three right hand columns are for those who were not.

A8: The Ogden Tables

39. In order to calculate the value of the actual earnings that a claimant is likely to receive in the future (i.e. after settlement or trial), the employment status and the disability status need to be determined as at the date of settlement or trial. For claimants with a work-affecting disability at that point in time, Tables B and D should be used. The three left hand columns will apply in respect of claimants actually in employment at date of settlement or trial and the three right hand columns will apply in respect of those who remain non-employed at that point in time.

40. The factors in Tables A–D allow for the interruption of employment for bringing up children and caring for other dependants.

41. In the case of those who at the date of the accident have not yet reached the age at which it is likely they would have started work, the relevant factor will be chosen based on a number of assessments of the claimant's likely employment had the injury not occurred. The relevant factor from the tables would be chosen on the basis of the level of education the claimant would have been expected to have attained, the age at which it is likely the claimant would have started work, together with an assessment as to whether the claimant would have become employed or not. The work multiplier will also have to be discounted for early receipt using the appropriate factor from Table 27 for the number of years between the claimant's age at the date of trial and the age at which it is likely that he/she would have started work.

42. Tables A–D include factors up to age 54 only. For older ages the reduction factors increase towards 1 at retirement age for those who are employed and fall towards 0 for those who are not employed. However, where the claimant is older than 54, it is anticipated that the likely future course of employment status will be particularly dependent on individual circumstances, so that the use of factors based on averages would not be appropriate. Hence reduction factors are not provided for these older ages.

Table A
Loss of earnings to pension age 65 (males—not disabled)

Age at date of trial	Employed D	Employed GE–A	Employed O	Not employed D	Not employed GE–A	Not employed O
16–19		0.90	0.85		0.85	0.82
20–24	0.92	0.92	0.87	0.89	0.88	0.83
25–29	0.93	0.92	0.89	0.89	0.88	0.82
30–34	0.92	0.91	0.89	0.87	0.86	0.81
35–39	0.90	0.90	0.89	0.85	0.84	0.80
40–44	0.88	0.88	0.88	0.82	0.81	0.78
45–49	0.86	0.86	0.86	0.77	0.77	0.74
50	0.83	0.83	0.83	0.72	0.72	0.70
51	0.82	0.82	0.82	0.70	0.70	0.68
52	0.81	0.81	0.81	0.67	0.67	0.66
53	0.80	0.80	0.80	0.63	0.63	0.63
54	0.79	0.79	0.79	0.59	0.59	0.59

Table B
Loss of earnings to pension age 65 (males—disabled)

Age at date of trial	Employed D	Employed GE–A	Employed O	Not employed D	Not employed GE–A	Not employed O
16–19		0.55	0.32		0.49	0.25
20–24	0.61	0.55	0.38	0.53	0.46	0.24
25–29	0.60	0.54	0.42	0.48	0.41	0.24
30–34	0.59	0.52	0.40	0.43	0.34	0.23
35–39	0.58	0.48	0.39	0.38	0.28	0.20
40–44	0.57	0.48	0.39	0.33	0.23	0.15
45–49	0.55	0.48	0.39	0.26	0.20	0.11
50	0.53	0.49	0.40	0.24	0.18	0.10
51	0.53	0.49	0.41	0.23	0.17	0.09
52	0.54	0.49	0.41	0.22	0.16	0.08
53	0.54	0.49	0.42	0.21	0.15	0.07
54	0.54	0.50	0.43	0.20	0.14	0.06

Table C
Loss of earnings to pension age 60 (females—not disabled)

Age at date of trial	Employed D	Employed GE–A	Employed O	Not employed D	Not employed GE–A	Not employed O
16–19		0.81	0.64		0.77	0.59
20–24	0.89	0.82	0.68	0.84	0.76	0.60
25–29	0.89	0.84	0.72	0.83	0.75	0.61
30–34	0.89	0.85	0.75	0.81	0.75	0.63
35–39	0.89	0.86	0.78	0.80	0.74	0.63
40–44	0.89	0.86	0.80	0.78	0.72	0.60
45–49	0.87	0.85	0.81	0.72	0.64	0.52
50	0.86	0.84	0.81	0.64	0.55	0.43
51	0.85	0.84	0.81	0.60	0.51	0.40
52	0.84	0.84	0.81	0.56	0.46	0.36
53	0.83	0.83	0.81	0.50	0.41	0.32
54	0.83	0.83	0.82	0.44	0.35	0.27

Table D
Loss of earnings to pension age 60 (females—disabled)

Age at date of trial	Employed D	Employed GE–A	Employed O	Not employed D	Not employed GE–A	Not employed O
16–19		0.43	0.25		0.35	0.19
20–24	0.64	0.44	0.25	0.58	0.33	0.17
25–29	0.63	0.45	0.25	0.50	0.32	0.16
30–34	0.62	0.46	0.30	0.44	0.31	0.15
35–39	0.61	0.48	0.34	0.42	0.28	0.14
40–44	0.60	0.51	0.38	0.38	0.23	0.13
45–49	0.60	0.54	0.42	0.28	0.18	0.11
50	0.60	0.56	0.47	0.23	0.15	0.10
51	0.61	0.58	0.49	0.21	0.14	0.09
52	0.61	0.60	0.51	0.20	0.13	0.08
53	0.62	0.62	0.54	0.18	0.11	0.07
54	0.63	0.66	0.57	0.16	0.09	0.06

The factors in Tables A–D will need to be reviewed if the discount rate changes.

Different pension ages

43. The factors in the preceding tables assume retirement at age 65 for males and age 60 for females. It is not possible to calculate expected working life times assuming alternative retirement ages from the LFS data, since the employment data in the LFS are collected only for the working population, assumed to be aged between 16 and 64 for males and between 16 and 59 for females. Where the retirement age is different from age 65 for males or age 60 for females, it is suggested that this should be ignored and the reduction factor and the adjustments thereto be taken from the above tables for the age of the claimant as at the date of trial with no adjustment, i.e. assume that the retirement age is age 65 for males and age 60 for females. However, if the retirement age is close to the age at the date of trial, then it may be more appropriate to take into account the circumstances of the individual case.

44. It should be noted that the reduction factors in Tables A, B, C and D are based on data for the period 1998–2003. Whilst the reduction factors and adjustments allow for the age-specific probabilities of moving into, or out of, employment over future working life time, based on data for the period 1998–2003, the methodology assumes that these probabilities remain constant over time; there is no allowance for changes in these age-specific probabilities beyond this period. It is also assumed that there will be no change in disability status or educational achievement after the date of the accident. Future changes in the probabilities of moving into, and out of, employment are especially difficult to predict with any certainty. It is the intention that the factors should be reassessed from time to time as new data becomes available.

Section C: Summary of personal injury applications

45. To use the tables the guidance below should be followed:

(1) Choose the table relating to the appropriate sex of the claimant and period of loss or expense (e.g. loss for life, or loss of earnings to a set retirement age). Where loss of earnings is concerned, and none of the tables is relevant because the claimant's expected age of retirement differs from that assumed in the tables, the procedure in paras 13–16 of the explanatory notes should be followed.

(2) Choose the appropriate discount column (currently 2.5 per cent).

A8: The Ogden Tables

(3) In that column find the appropriate figure for the claimant's age at trial ("the basic multiplier").

Loss of earnings

(4) When calculating **loss of earnings**, the tables should be used when a multiplier/multiplicand approach is appropriate. If it is, the basic multiplier should be adjusted to take account of contingencies other than mortality. These contingencies include the claimant's employment and disability status and educational qualifications. The basic multiplier should be multiplied by the appropriate figure taken from Tables A–D. It may be necessary at this stage to modify the resulting figure further to allow for circumstances specific to the claimant.

This process gives "the adjusted table multiplier".

(5) Multiply the net annual loss (the multiplicand) by the adjusted table multiplier to arrive at a figure which represents the capitalised value of the future loss of earnings.

(6) If the claimant has a residual earning capacity, allowance should be made for any post-accident vulnerability on the labour market: the following paragraphs show one way of doing this, although there may still be cases where a conventional **Smith v City of Manchester** award is appropriate.

Where it is appropriate to do so, repeat steps 1–5 above, replacing the pre-accident employment and disability status with the post-accident employment and disability status in step 4 and replacing the net annual loss by the assumed new level of net earnings at step 5. It will only be necessary to reconsider the claimant's educational attainments if these have changed between the accident and the date of trial or settlement.

The result will represent the capitalised value of the claimant's likely post-accident earnings. It is important to note that, when carrying out this exercise, the *degree* of residual disability may have a different effect on residual earnings depending on its relevance to the claimant's likely field of work. For example, the loss of a leg may have less effect on a sedentary worker's earnings than on a manual worker's.

(7) Deduct the sum yielded by step 6 from that yielded by step 5 to obtain the net amount of loss of earnings allowing for residual earning capacity. Where the above methodology is used there will usually be no need for a separate **Smith v City of Manchester** award.

Lifetime losses

(8) Where a **loss** will continue **for life**, follow steps 1–3, above, to find the appropriate multiplier in the table.

Where the normal life expectancy given by the table is inapplicable the approach set out in para.20, using the lifetime tables rather than Table 28, is the correct approach.

(9) This figure may need adjustment to allow for the particular circumstances of the claimant.

(10) Multiply the annual loss or expense by the multiplier as adjusted.

Variable annual losses

(11) In cases where there will be different losses at different periods it may be necessary to split the multiplier. The approach set out at paras 22–24 should be followed.

A8: The Ogden Tables

Fixed period and deferred losses

(12) Where a loss will continue over a fixed period, the appropriate multiplier can be found in Table 28.

(13) Where a loss will not commence until some future date, multiply the appropriate multiplier by a discount figure taken from Table 27 (the use of which is explained in para.18). This paragraph does not apply to loss of pensions, which have their own tables.

Examples

46. The following are examples of the use of the tables in illustrative personal injury cases with simplified assumptions.

Example 3

47. The claimant is female, aged 35 at the date of the trial. She has three A levels, but not a degree, and was in employment at the date of the accident at a salary of £25,000 a year net of tax. She was not disabled before the accident. As a result of her injuries, she is now disabled and has lost her job but has found part-time employment at a salary of £5,000 a year net of tax. Her loss of earnings to retirement age of 60 is assessed as follows:

(1) Look up Table 8 for loss of earnings to pension age 60 for females.

(2) The appropriate rate of return is determined to be 2.5 per cent (the rate currently set under s.1 of the Damages Act 1996).

(3) Table 8 shows that, on the basis of a 2.5 per cent rate of return, the multiplier for a female aged 35 is 18.43.

(4) Now take account of risks other than mortality. Allowing for the claimant being employed, not disabled and having achieved A levels at the date of trial, Table C would require 18.43 to be multiplied by 0.86, resulting in a revised multiplier of 15.85.

(5) The damages for loss of earnings are assessed as £396,250 (15.85 × £25,000).

(6) Allow for mitigation of loss of earnings in respect of post-injury earnings. As before, Table 8 shows that, on the basis of a 2.5 per cent rate of return, the multiplier for a female aged 35 is 18.43.

(7) Now take account of risks other than mortality. Allowing for the claimant being employed, disabled and having achieved A levels at the date of trial, Table D would require 18.43 to be multiplied by 0.48, resulting in a revised multiplier of 8.85.

(8) The amount of mitigation for post-injury earnings is assessed as £44,150 (8.85 × £5,000).

(9) Hence award for loss of earnings after allowing for mitigation is £396,250 − £44,250 = £352,00.

Example 4

48. The claimant is male, aged 48 at the date of the trial. He has no educational qualifications. His retirement age was 65, he was employed at the time of the accident and his pre-retirement multiplicand has been determined as £20,000 a year net of tax. He was not disabled before the accident.

As a result of his injuries, he is now disabled and has lost his job. The multiplicand for costs of care is deemed to be £50,000 a year. He is unemployed at the date of trial but has been assessed as capable of finding work with possible future earnings of £5,000 a year net of tax. His loss of earnings to retirement age of 65 is assessed as follows:

(1) Look up Table 9 for loss of earnings to pension age 65 for males.

(2) The appropriate rate of return is determined to be 2.5 per cent (the rate currently set under s.1 of the Damages Act 1996).

(3) Table 9 shows that, on the basis of a 2.5 per cent rate of return, the multiplier for a male aged 48 is 13.42.

(4) Now take account of risks other than mortality. Allowing for the claimant being employed, not disabled and having no educational qualifications at the date of trial, Table A would require 13.42 to be multiplied by 0.86, resulting in a revised multiplier of 11.54.

(5) The damages for loss of earnings are assessed as £230,800 (11.54 × £20,000).

(6) Allow for mitigation of loss of earnings in respect of post-injury earnings. As before, Table 9 shows that, on the basis of a 2.5 per cent rate of return, the multiplier for a male aged 48 is 13.42.

(7) Now take account of risks other than mortality. Allowing for the claimant being unemployed and disabled with no educational qualifications at the date of trial, Table B would require 13.42 to be multiplied by 0.11, resulting in a revised multiplier of 1.48.

(8) The amount of mitigation for post-injury earnings is assessed as £7,400 (1.48 × £5,000).

(9) Hence award for loss of earnings after allowing for mitigation is £230,800 − £7,400 = £223,400.

49. The damages for cost of care are assessed as follows:

(1) Look up Table 1 for the multiplier at age 48.

(2) The appropriate rate of return is 2.5 per cent.

(3) Table 1 shows that, on the basis of a 2.5 per cent rate of return, the multiplier at age 48 is 23.51.

(4) No adjustment is made for risks other than mortality.

(5) The damages for cost of care are assessed at £1,175,500 (23.51 × £50,000).

Example 5

50. The claimant is female, aged 14 at the date of the trial. She is expected to achieve a degree and to be in employment thereafter on a salary, in current terms, of £30,000 a year net of tax. She was not disabled before the accident. As a result of her injuries, she is now disabled—she is still expected to achieve a degree and to be in employment, but with an average salary in current terms of £20,000 net of tax. She will be aged 21 when she completes her degree. Her loss of earnings to retirement age of 60 is assessed as follows:

(1) Look up Table 8 for loss of earnings to pension age 60 for females.

(2) The appropriate rate of return is determined to be 2.5 per cent (the rate currently set under s.1 of the Damages Act 1996).

(3) Table 8 shows that, on the basis of a 2.5 per cent rate of return, the multiplier for a female graduate aged 21 is 24.83. This needs to be discounted back to age 14. The factor at 2.5 per cent for a period for deferment for seven years is 0.8413 from Table 27, giving a total multiplier of 24.83 × 0.8413 = 20.89.

(4) Now take account of risks other than mortality. Allowing for the claimant at age 21 assessed as achieving a degree, being employed and not disabled, Table C would require 20.89 to be multiplied by 0.89, resulting in a revised multiplier of 18.59.

(5) The damages for loss of earnings are assessed as £557,700 (18.59 × £30,000).

(6) Allow for mitigation of loss of earnings in respect of post-injury earnings. As before, Table 8 shows that, on the basis of a 2.5 per cent rate of return, the multiplier for a female graduate aged 21 is 24.83. As before, after discounting for seven years to age 14 the multiplier is reduced to 24.83 × 0.8413 = 20.89.

(7) Now take account of risks other than mortality. Allowing for the claimant at age 21 assessed as achieving a degree, being employed and disabled, Table D would require 20.89 to be multiplied by 0.64, resulting in a revised multiplier of 13.37.

(8) The amount of mitigation for post-injury earnings is assessed as £267,400 (13.37 × £20,000).

(9) Hence award for loss of earnings after allowing for mitigation is £557,700 − £267,400 = £290,300.

Example 6

51. The claimant is male, aged 40 at the date of the trial. He has achieved O levels. He was unemployed at the time of the accident. His potential pre-retirement multiplicand has been determined as £15,000 a year net of tax. He was disabled before the accident. As a result of his injuries, he has been assessed as having no future prospect of employment. His loss of earnings to retirement age of 65 is assessed as follows:

(1) Look up Table 9 for loss of earnings to pension age 65 for males.

(2) The appropriate rate of return is determined to be 2.5 per cent (the rate currently set under s.1 of the Damages Act 1996).

(3) Table 9 shows that, on the basis of a 2.5 per cent rate of return, the multiplier for a male aged 40 is 18.09.

(4) Now take account of risks other than mortality. Allowing for the claimant being unemployed, disabled and having achieved O levels at the date of trial, Table A would require 18.09 to be multiplied by 0.23, resulting in a revised multiplier of 4.16.

(5) The damages for loss of earnings are assessed as £62,400 (4.16 × £15,000).

A8: The Ogden Tables

(6) As the claimant has been assessed as having no future prospect of employment following the accident, there is no mitigation of loss of earnings in respect of post-injury earnings.

(7) Hence award for loss of earnings after allowing for mitigation is £62,400.

Section D: Application of tables to fatal accident cases

52. The current approach of the courts, except in Scotland, is to assess the multiplier as at the date of death (***Cookson v Knowles***[15]).

53. That approach was criticised by the Law Commission in their Report 263 (*Claims for Wrongful Death*). The Law Commission recommended that multipliers should be assessed as at the date of trial and that the multipliers derived from the Ogden Tables should only take effect from the date of trial. The Law Commission stressed that the current approach incorporates an actuarial flaw in that it incorporates a discount for early receipt in the period prior to trial or assessment.

54. The Working Party, then under the Chairmanship of the late Sir Michael Ogden QC, considered that the Law Commission's criticism was valid. In the Fourth Edition of the Tables published in August 2000, the Working Party set out guidance in Section D of the Explanatory Notes on how damages should be calculated in such cases. We refer to that guidance below as the actuarially recommended approach. We note that the actuarially recommended approach has been adopted in the Damages (Scotland) Act 2011. For further details see paras 20–21 in the Introduction.

55. However, the courts have considered themselves bound by ***Cookson v Knowles*** and hence have not followed the actuarially recommended approach (***White v Esab***,[16] ***H v S***[17] and ***Fletcher v A Train & Sons Ltd***[18]).

The basic law in England and Wales

56. Under the Fatal Accidents Act the loss is that of the dependants, i.e. those who relied upon the deceased for support. They may claim that part of the deceased's income (whether earnings, pension, unearned income or state benefits) that the deceased would have spent on them. They may also claim the loss of the services such as DIY, domestic/household or childcare which the deceased would have undertaken and from which they would have benefited. The position of each dependant must be considered separately.

57. Each head of dependency must be considered separately. For each head of claim for each dependant the court calculates a multiplicand. This is calculated on the basis of what is known at the date of trial. For pre-trial losses, the actual loss to date of trial is calculated. Interest is added. For post-trial losses the multiplicand is calculated as at the date of trial.

58. A multiplier for the period of dependency is applied to the multiplicand to arrive at an overall lump sum for each head of dependency.

59. The remainder of section D deals with how to approach the calculations in fatal accident claims. Three approaches are put forward. Paragraphs 60–63 set out the current approach. The actuarially

---

[15] [1979] A.C. 556.
[16] [2002] P.I.Q.R. Q6.
[17] [2002] EWCA Civ. 792, [2003] Q.B. 965.
[18] [2008] EWCA Civ. 413, [2008] 4 All E.R. 699.

recommended approach is then set out at paras 64–81. Example 7 illustrates the application of both these approaches whilst Examples 8 and 9 show the actuarially recommended approach applied to more complex situations—these examples make up paras 82–87. The final paragraphs of section D, 88–90, offer an alternative approach using multipliers selected from the date of death.

The current approach

60. Under the approach currently followed by the courts, the multiplier is calculated as at the date of death. However, when making that calculation the court is entitled to take into account matters that have arisen between death and trial. For example, ***Williamson v Thorneycroft***[19] in which the deceased's widow died after her husband but before trial, her dependency terminated at her death. See also, ***Corbett v Barking, Havering & Brentwood HA***.[20]

61. There are two periods to be determined:

(i) the expected period from date of death in which the deceased would have been capable of providing the dependency; and

(ii) the expected period from the date of the death in which the dependant would have been able to receive the dependency.

The shorter of those two periods provides the basis for the multiplier.

62. In respect of each of those periods consideration must be given as to what discount should be made for contingencies other than mortality. The most obvious contingencies other than mortality fall into the following three categories:

(i) Factors relating to the deceased. For example, the deceased's health may have been such as to seriously affect his ability to provide services or work until retirement age. In relation to earnings the starting point for the adjustment factor should be the figures contained in Tables A–D.

(ii) Factors relating to the dependant. For example, at trial it may be proved that a dependant has a significantly reduced life expectancy.

(iii) Factors relating to the relationship of the deceased and the dependant. For example, an unmarried couple who were on the point of separation before the deceased died. See also s.3 (4) of the Act and ***Drew v Abassi***.[21]

63. The assessment of the multiplier involves the following steps:

(1) Determine the expected period from the date of death for which the deceased would have been capable of providing the dependency.

(2) Discount that period for early receipt using the appropriate table as at the date of death and a discount rate of 2.5 per cent.

(3) Apply any adjustment to the above figure to reflect contingencies other than mortality.

[19] [1940] 2 K.B. 658.
[20] [1991] 2 Q.B. 408.
[21] Court of Appeal, May 24, 1995.

A8: The Ogden Tables

(4) Determine the expected period from date of death for which the dependant would have been able to receive the dependency.

(5) Discount that period for early receipt using the appropriate table as at the date of death at a discount rate of 2.5 per cent.

(6) Apply any adjustment to the figure in (5) to reflect contingencies other than mortality.

(7) Take the lower of the figures in (3) and (6) above. That is the overall multiplier from date of death.

(8) Subtract the period elapsed from date of death to date of trial. Losses in this period will be treated as in effect special damages and will attract an award of interest.

(9) The balance of the multiplier will be the multiplier for the post-trial multiplicand.

The actuarially recommended approach

64. Whereas in personal injury cases the problem to be solved is that of setting a value on an income stream during the potential life of one person (the claimant), the situation is generally more complicated in fatal accident cases. Here the compensation is intended to reflect the value of an income stream during the lifetime of one or more dependants of the deceased (or the expected period for which the dependants would have expected to receive the dependency, if shorter) but limited according to the expectation of how long the deceased would have been able to provide the financial support, had he or she not been involved in the fatal accident.

65. In principle, therefore, the compensation for post-trial dependency should be based on the present value at the date of the trial of the dependency during the expected future joint lifetime of the deceased and the dependant or claimant (had the deceased survived naturally to the date of the trial), subject to any limitations on the period of dependency and any expected future changes in the level of dependency, for example, on attaining retirement age. In addition there should be compensation for the period between the date of accident and the date of trial.

66. A set of actuarial tables to make such calculations accurately would require tables similar to Tables 1–26 but for each combination of ages as at the date of the trial of the deceased and the dependant to whom compensation is to be paid. The Working Party concluded that this would not meet the criterion of simplicity of application which was a central objective of these tables and recommends that, in complex cases, or cases where the accuracy of the multiplier is thought by the parties to be of critical importance and material to the resulting amount of compensation (for example, in cases potentially involving very large claims where the level of the multiplicand is unambiguously established), the advice of a professionally qualified actuary should be sought. However, for the majority of cases, a certain amount of approximation will be appropriate, bearing in mind the need for a simple and streamlined process, and taking into consideration the other uncertainties in the determination of an appropriate level of compensation. The following paragraphs describe a methodology using Tables 1–26 which can be expected to yield satisfactory answers.

(i) Damages for the period from the fatal accident to the date of trial

67. The period of pre-trial dependency will normally be equal to the period between the date of the fatal accident and the date of the trial, substituting where appropriate the lower figure of the expected period for which the deceased would have provided the dependency, had he or she not been killed in

the accident, or if the period of dependency would have been limited in some way, for example, if the dependant is a child.

68. A deduction may be made for the risk that the deceased might have died anyway, in the period between the date of the fatal accident and the date at which the trial takes place. In many cases this deduction will be small and could usually be regarded as de minimis. The need for a deduction becomes more necessary the longer the period from the date of accident to the date of trial and the older the deceased at the date of death. As an illustration of the order of magnitude of the deduction, Table E shows some examples of factors by which the multiplier should be multiplied for different ages of the deceased and for different periods from the date of accident to the date of the trial.

Table E
Factor by which pre-trial damages should be multiplied to allow for the likelihood that the deceased would not in any case have survived to provide the dependency for the full period to the date of trial

Age of deceased at date of accident	Period from date of accident to date of trial or date of cessation of dependency, if earlier (years)					
	Male deceased			Female deceased		
	3	6	9	3	6	9
10	1.00	1.00	1.00	1.00	1.00	1.00
20	1.00	1.00	1.00	1.00	1.00	1.00
30	1.00	1.00	0.99	1.00	1.00	1.00
40	1.00	0.99	0.99	1.00	1.00	0.99
50	0.99	0.99	0.98	1.00	0.99	0.99
60	0.99	0.97	0.94	0.99	0.98	0.97
65	0.98	0.95	0.91	0.99	0.97	0.95
70	0.97	0.92	0.86	0.98	0.95	0.91
75	0.94	0.87	0.78	0.96	0.91	0.84
80	0.90	0.79	0.67	0.93	0.84	0.75

N.B. The factor for a period of zero years is clearly 1.00. Factors for other ages and periods not shown in the table may be obtained approximately by interpolation.

69. The resultant multiplier, after application of any discount for the possibility of early death of the deceased before the date of trial, even had the accident not taken place, is to be applied to the multiplicand, which is determined in the usual way. Interest will then be added up to the date of trial on the basis of special damages.

(ii) Damages from the date of trial to retirement age

70. The assessment of the multiplier involves the following steps:

(1) Determine the expected period from the date of the trial for which the deceased would have been able to provide the dependency (see para.71).

(2) Determine the expected period for which the dependant would have been able to receive the dependency (see paras 71 and 72).

(3) Take the lesser of the two periods.

(4) Treat the resulting period as a term certain for which the multiplier is to be determined and look up the figure in Table 28 for this period at the appropriate rate of interest.

(5) Apply any adjustment for contingencies other than mortality in accordance with section B.

A8: The Ogden Tables

(6) If necessary, make an allowance for the risk that the deceased might have died anyway before the date of the trial (see para.73).

71. The expected periods at (1) and (2) of para.70 may be obtained from the 0% column of the appropriate table at the back of this booklet. For (1), Tables 3–14 will be relevant, according to the sex of the deceased and the expected age of retirement. The age at which the table should be entered is the age which the deceased would have been at the date of the trial. For (2), Tables 1 and 2 can be used, according to the sex of the dependant and looking up the table at the age of the dependant at the date of the trial.

72. If the period for which the dependency would have continued is a short fixed period, as in the case of a child, the figure at (2) would be the outstanding period at the date of the trial.

73. A deduction may be made for the risk that the deceased might have died anyway before the date of trial. The need for such a deduction becomes more necessary the longer the period from the date of accident to the date of trial and the older the deceased at the date of death. As an illustration of the order of magnitude of the deduction, Table F shows some examples of the factor by which the multiplier, determined as above, should be multiplied for different ages of the deceased and for different periods from the date of accident to the date of the trial.

Table F
Factor by which post-trial damages should be multiplied to allow for the likelihood that the deceased would not in any case have survived to the date of trial in order to provide any post-trial dependency

Age of deceased at date of accident	Period from date of accident to date of trial (years)					
	Male deceased			Female deceased		
	3	6	9	3	6	9
10	1.00	1.00	1.00	1.00	1.00	1.00
20	1.00	1.00	0.99	1.00	1.00	1.00
30	1.00	0.99	0.99	1.00	1.00	0.99
40	0.99	0.99	0.98	1.00	0.99	0.99
50	0.99	0.97	0.95	0.99	0.98	0.97
60	0.97	0.93	0.88	0.98	0.96	0.92
65	0.96	0.90	0.82	0.97	0.93	0.88
70	0.93	0.84	0.71	0.96	0.89	0.80
75	0.88	0.73	0.55	0.92	0.81	0.66
80	0.83	0.59	0.37	0.86	0.68	0.48

N.B. The factor for a period of zero years is clearly 1.00. Factors for other ages and periods not shown in the table may be obtained approximately by interpolation.

74. The resulting multiplier, after application of any discount for the possibility of early death of the deceased before the date of trial, even had the accident not taken place, is to be applied to the appropriate multiplicand, determined in relation to dependency as assessed for the period up to retirement age.

75. If there are several dependants, to whom damages are to be paid in respect of their own particular lifetime (or for a fixed period of dependency), separate multipliers should be determined for each and multiplied by the appropriate multiplicand using the procedure in paras 70–74. The total amount of damages is then obtained by adding the separate components. If a single multiplicand is determined, but the damages are to be shared among two or more dependants so long as they are each alive, or during a period of common dependency, then the multiplier will be calculated using the procedure in paras 70–74. However, at step (2) of para.70 the expected period will be the longest of the expected periods for which the dependency might last.

(iii) Damages for the period of dependency after retirement age

76. The method described in paras 70–75 for pre-retirement age dependency cannot satisfactorily be applied directly to post-retirement age dependency with a sufficient degree of accuracy. We therefore propose a method which involves determining the multiplier by looking at dependency for the rest of life from the date of trial and then subtracting the multiplier for dependency up to retirement age.

77. The assessment of the multiplier for whole of life dependency involves the following steps:

(1) Determine the expectation of life which the deceased would have had as at the date of trial, or such lesser period for which the deceased would have been able to provide the dependency (see para.78).

(2) Determine the expected period for which the dependant would have been able to receive the dependency (see para.78).

(3) Take the lesser of the two periods.

(4) Treat the resulting period as a term certain for which the multiplier is to be determined and look up the figure in Table 28 for this period at the appropriate rate of interest.

78. The expected periods at (1) and (2) of para.77 may be obtained from the 0% column of the appropriate table at the back of this booklet. For (1), Tables 1 or 2 will be relevant, according to the sex of the deceased. The age at which the table should be entered is the age which the deceased would have attained at the date of the trial. For (2), Tables 1 and 2 can be used, according to the sex of the dependant and looking up the table at the age of the dependant at the date of the trial.

79. Deduct the corresponding multiplier for post-trial pre-retirement dependency, as determined in paras 70–75, but without any adjustment for contingencies other than mortality, or that the deceased may have died anyway before the date of trial. The result is the multiplier for post-retirement dependency, which must then be applied to the appropriate multiplicand, assessed in relation to dependency after retirement age. The adjustment for contingencies other than mortality in respect of the damages for the period of dependency after retirement age will often be less than that required for pre-retirement age damages (see para.30).

80. A deduction may finally be made for the risk that the deceased might have died anyway before the date of trial. The need for such a deduction becomes more necessary the longer the period from the date of accident to the date of trial and the older the deceased at the date of death. As an illustration of the order of magnitude of the deduction, Table F shows some examples of the factor by which the multiplier, determined as above, should be multiplied for different ages of the deceased and for different periods from the date of accident to the date of the trial. The factors for this purpose are exactly the same deductions as used in the calculation at paras 70–75.

81. The layout of paras 70–80 is based on the assumption that the dependency provided by the deceased would have changed at retirement age. This may not be appropriate in some cases, particularly in the important case of the deceased wife and mother whose contribution has been solely in the home or in the case of an adult child caring for an elderly parent or parents. In cases like this, where the deceased might have provided the dependency throughout their lifetime, paras 76–80 should be ignored and paras 70–75 used, with the difference that the expected period required at step (1) of para.70 should be a whole of life expectancy, taken from Tables 1 and 2. This is also the approach to use when the deceased was already a pensioner.

A8: The Ogden Tables

Examples

82. Paragraphs 83 and 84 give calculations of damages awards for Example 7, calculated using first the current approach and then the actuarially recommended approach.

Example 7

83. The dependant is female, aged 38 at the date of the trial, which is taking place three years after the date of the fatal accident which killed her husband, at that time aged 37, on whom she was financially dependent. The deceased had A levels, was in employment and in good health with no disability at the time of the fatal accident. The dependant was, at the date of death, and is at the date of trial, in good health. Their relationship was stable. The court has determined a multiplicand of £30,000 up to the deceased's normal retirement age of 65 with no financial dependency post-age 65, nor any services dependency. The damages are to be calculated as follows:

The current approach

(1) The deceased would have been capable of providing the financial dependency to the dependant for the period of 28 years from the date of his death aged 37 to his 65th birthday.

(2) The appropriate Table is 9. Using the 2.5 per cent column the multiplier = 19.64.

(3) Adjustment factor for contingencies other than mortality (in accordance with section B) for an employed male aged 37 with A levels and who is not disabled = 0.9 to give a multiplier of 19.64 × 0.9 = 17.68.

(4) The expected period for which the dependant would have been able to receive the dependency was between the ages of 35 and 63.

(5) The appropriate Tables are 8 and 10, and using the 2.5 per cent column the multiplier = 19.91.

(6) The parties were married so section 3(4) does not apply. The relationship was stable. The dependant was and is in good health. The court is unlikely to make much of an adjustment to the figure in (5) above to reflect contingencies other than mortality.

(7) The lower of the two figures is that in (3) above, namely 17.68.

(8) The period that has elapsed between date of death and date of trial is three years. The pre-trial loss is therefore £30,000 × 3 = £90,000.

(9) Interest at half rate from date of death to date of trial: three years at 3 per cent a year = 9 per cent.
£90,000 × 9% = £8,100.

(10) The post-trial multiplier is 14.68 (17.68 − 3).

(11) The post trial loss is therefore 14.68 × £30,000 = £440,400.

(12) Total financial dependency is therefore £90,000 + £8,100 + £440,400 = £538,500.

A8: The Ogden Tables

The actuarially recommended approach

84. Applying this approach to Example 7 set out above:

Pre-trial damages:

(1)   Period between fatal accident and trial: three years.

(2)   Factor for possible early death (Table E for male aged 37 and three years) = 1.00.

(3)   Pre-trial damages = 3 × 1.00 × £30,000 = £90,000 (plus interest as special damages).

(4)   Interest at half rate from date of death to date of trial: three years at 3 per cent a year = 9 per cent.
£90,000 × 9% = £8,100.

Post-trial damages:

(1)   Expected period for which the deceased would have provided the dependency (Table 9 at 0 per cent for male aged 40, the age as at the date of trial): 24.13.

(2)   Expected period for which the dependant would have been able to receive the dependency (Table 2 at 0 per cent for female aged 38): 51.38.

(3)   Lesser of two periods at (1) and (2) = 24.13.

(4)   Multiplier for term certain of 24.13 years at 2.5 per cent rate of return = 18.18.

(5)   Adjustment factor for contingencies other than mortality (in accordance with section B) for an employed male aged 40 with A levels and who was not disabled = 0.88 to give a multiplier of 18.18 × 0.88 = 16.00.

(6)   Adjustment factor for the risk that the deceased might have died anyway before the date of trial (Table F for male aged 37 and three years): 0.99 to give a multiplier of 16.00 × 0.99 = 15.84.

(7)   Post-trial damages = 15.84 × £30,000 = £475,200.

(8)   Total financial dependency is therefore £90,000 + £8,100 + £475,200 = £573,300.

85. Examples 8 and 9 in the following paragraphs set out two further examples to show the application of the actuarially recommended approach to more complex examples.

Example 8

86. The dependant is female, aged 50 at the date of the trial, which is taking place four years after the date of the fatal accident which killed the man, at that time aged 47, on whom she was financially dependent. The deceased was in employment at the time of the fatal accident, was not disabled and had achieved A levels. The court has determined a multiplicand, up to the deceased's normal retirement age of 60, of £50,000 and has decided that post-retirement damages should be payable based on a multiplicand of £30,000. The damages are to be calculated as follows:

Sweet & Maxwell

A8: The Ogden Tables

Pre-trial damages:

(1) Period between fatal accident and trial: four years.

(2) Factor for possible early death (Table E for male aged 47 and four years): 0.99.

(3) Pre-trial damages = 4 × 0.99 × £50,000 = £198,000 (plus interest as special damages).

Post-trial pre-retirement damages:

(1) Expected period for which the deceased would have provided the dependency (Table 7 at 0% for male aged 51, the age as at the date of trial): 8.81.

(2) Expected period for which the dependant would have been able to receive the dependency (Table 2 at 0 per cent for female aged 50): 38.73.

(3) Lesser of two periods at (1) and (2) = 8.81.

(4) Multiplier for term certain of 8.81 years at 2.5 per cent rate of return (interpolating between the values for 8 and 9 in Table 28) = (9 − 8.81) × 7.26 + (8.81 − 8) × 8.07 = 7.92.

(5) Adjustment factor for contingencies other than mortality (in accordance with section B) for an employed male aged 51 with A levels and who was not disabled = 0.82 to give a multiplier of 7.92 × 0.82 = 6.49.

(6) Adjustment factor for the risk that the deceased might have died anyway before the date of trial (Table F for male aged 47 and four years): 0.99 to give a multiplier of 6.49 × 0.99 = 6.43.

(7) Post-trial pre-retirement damages = 6.43 × £50,000 = £321,500.

Post-retirement damages:

(1) Expectation of life of deceased at date of trial (Table 1 at 0 per cent for male aged 51): 34.45.

(2) Expected period for which the dependant would have been able to receive the dependency (Table 2 at 0 per cent for female aged 50): 38.73.

(3) Lesser of two periods at (1) and (2) = 34.45.

(4) Multiplier for term certain of 34.45 years at 2.5 per cent rate of return (interpolating between the values for 34 and 35 in Table 28) = (35 − 34.45) × 23.01 + (34.45 − 34) × 23.43 = 23.20.

(5) Deduct multiplier for post-trial pre-retirement damages before application of adjustment factors for contingencies other than mortality and for the risk that the deceased might have died anyway before the date of trial: 23.20 − 7.92 = 15.28.

(6) Adjustment factor for the risk that the deceased might have died anyway before the date of trial (Table F for male aged 47 and four years): 0.99 to give a multiplier of 15.28 × 0.99 = 15.13.

(7) Post-retirement damages = 15.13 × £30,000 = £453,900.

Example 9

87. There are two dependants, respectively a child aged 10 and a male aged 41 at the date of the trial, which is taking place three years after the date of the fatal accident which killed the woman, at that

time aged 35, on whom both were financially dependent. She had a degree and worked in London for a computer company. The court has determined a multiplicand, up to the deceased's normal retirement age of 62, of £50,000 for the male dependant and £10,000 for the child, up to the age of 21, and has decided that post-retirement damages should be payable based on a multiplicand of £20,000. The damages are to be calculated as follows:

Pre-trial damages:

(1) Period between fatal accident and trial: three years.

(2) Factor for possible early death (Table E for female aged 35 and three years): 1.00.

(3) Pre-trial damages = 3 × 1.00 × (£50,000 + £10,000) = £180,000 (plus interest as special damages).

Post-trial pre-retirement damages:

(1) Expected period for which the deceased would have provided the dependency should be based on female aged 38 at the date of trial with retirement age of 62. First calculate as though deceased were aged 36 and had retirement age of 60 (Table 8 at 0% for female aged 36): 23.66.

Then calculate as though deceased were aged 41 and had retirement age of 65 (Table 10 at 0 per cent for female aged 41): 23.47.

Interpolate for age 38 with retirement age of 62 = (3 × 23.66 + 2 × 23.47)/5 = 23.58.

(2) Expected period for which the male dependant would have been able to receive the dependency (Table 1 at 0 per cent for male aged 41): 44.71.

Expected period for which child would have been able to receive the dependency = 11.00.

(3) Lesser of two periods at (1) and (2) = 11.00 (in case of child)

= 23.58 (in case of man).

(4) Multiplier for term certain of 11 years at 2.5 per cent (Table 28): 9.63.

Multiplier for term certain of 23.58 years at 2.5 per cent rate of return (interpolating between the values for 23 and 24 in Table 28)

= (24 − 23.58) × 17.55 + (23.58 − 23) × 18.11 = 17.87.

(5) Adjustment factor for contingencies other than mortality (in accordance with section B) for an employed female aged 38 with a degree and who was not disabled = 0.89 (does not apply to child) to give a multiplier of 17.87 × 0.89 = 15.90.

(6) Adjustment factor for the risk that the deceased might have died anyway before the date of trial (Table F for female aged 35 and three years): 1.00, so multipliers are 9.63 and 15.90 respectively.

(7) Pre-retirement damages = 9.63 × £10,000 + 15.90 × £50,000

= £96,300 + £795,000 = £891,300.

A8: The Ogden Tables

Post-retirement damages:

(1) Expectation of life of deceased at date of trial (Table 2 at 0 per cent for female aged 38): 51.38.

(2) Expected period for which the dependant would have been able to receive the dependency (Table 1 at 0 per cent for male aged 41): 44.71 (no post retirement dependency for child).

(3) Lesser of two periods at (1) and (2) = 44.71.

(4) Multiplier for term certain of 44.71 years at 2.5 per cent rate of return (interpolating between the values for 42 and 43 in Table 28)

= (45 − 44.71) × 26.83 + (44.71 − 44) × 27.17 = 27.07.

(5) Deduct multiplier for post-trial pre-retirement damages before application of adjustment factors for contingencies other than mortality and for the risk that the deceased might have died anyway before the date of trial: 27.07 − 17.87 = 9.20.

(6) Adjustment factor for the risk that the deceased might have died anyway before the date of trial (Table F for female aged 35 and three years) = 1.00, so multiplier is 9.20 × 1.00 = 9.20.

(7) Post-retirement damages = 9.20 × £20,000 = £184,000.

An Alternative approach

88. If the court wishes to select multipliers from the date of death, it is essential to ensure that the period before the trial does not include a discount for early receipt. This could be achieved by selecting multipliers from the 0% columns of the appropriate tables and then applying the discount for early receipt to the period after the trial (using the discount rate set under s.1 of the Damages Act 1996). The calculation of the multiplier involves the following steps:

(1) Determine the expected period for which the deceased would have provided the dependency at the date of death.

(2) Deduct the period between accidental death and date of trial to give post-trial period.

(3) Determine the expected post-trial period for which the dependant would have been able to receive the dependency.

(4) Take the lesser of two periods at (2) and (3).

(5) Take the multiplier for term certain for the period calculated at (4) at 2.5 per cent rate of return (from Table 28).

(6) Apply any adjustment factor to the figure in (5) to reflect contingencies other than mortality (in accordance with section B). This will give the multiplier for the post-trial multiplicand.

89. Applying this approach to Example 7 set out above:

(1) Expected period for which the deceased would have provided the dependency (Table 9 at 0 per cent for male aged 37, the age as at the date of death): 27.06.

(2) Deduct period between accidental death and date of trial of three years to give post-trial period: 24.06.

(3) Expected post-trial period for which the dependant would have been able to receive the dependency (Table 2 at 0 per cent for female aged 38): 51.38.

(4) Lesser of two periods at (2) and (3) = 24.06.

(5) Multiplier for term certain of 24.06 years at 2.5 per cent rate of return (Table 28) = 18.14.

(6) Adjustment factor for contingencies other than mortality (in accordance with section B) for an employed male aged 37 with A levels and who was not disabled = 0.90 to give a multiplier of 18.14 × 0.90 = 16.33.

(7) Pre-trial damages = 3 × £30,000 = £90,000 (plus interest as special damages of £8,100).

(8) Post-trial damages = 16.33 × £30,000 = £489,900.

(9) Total financial dependency therefore £90,000 + £8,100 + £489,900 = £588,000.

90. As can be seen, the three methodologies (the current approach, the actuarially recommended approach and this alternative approach) give three different amounts of damages in relation to Example 7, namely £538,500 for the current approach used by the courts, £573,300 using the actuarially recommended approach, and £588,000 using this alternative approach. The size of the disparities between the three methods depends on the length of the period between the date of death and the date of trial; if the example had assumed a period of six years then the differences would have been greater.

Section E: Concluding remarks

91. These tables are designed to assist the courts to arrive at suitable multipliers in a range of possible situations. However, they do not cover all possibilities and in more complex situations, such as where there are significant pension rights, advice should be sought from a Fellow of the Institute and Faculty of Actuaries.

GEORGE RUSSELL FIA
Deputy Government Actuary
London
August 2012

A8: The Ogden Tables

Notes

On 27 February 2017 the Lord Chancellor announced that under the provisions of Section 1 of the Damages Act 1996 the prescribed discount rate to be taken into account by the courts when assessing lump sum damages awards for personal injury would be lowered from 2.5 per cent to -0.75 per cent with effect from 20 March 2017. Tables of multipliers in the current 7th edition of the Ogden Tables are not tabulated at a discount rate of -0.75 per cent. Hence supplementary tables have been issued which provide multipliers at the current tabulated discount rates together with multipliers calculated at a discount rate of -0.75 per cent.

These supplementary tables to the 7th edition of the Ogden Tables provide all the tables of multipliers in the 7th edition of the Ogden Tables with the addition of a column of multipliers in each table calculated at a rate return of -0.75 per cent. These multipliers have been calculated using the same mortality rates and other assumptions underlying the tables in the 7th edition. The multipliers at other rates of discount are the same as those published in the 7th edition. The other tables of factors in the explanatory notes to the 7th edition have not been revised at this time.

These supplementary tables are not available in hard copy format from The Stationery Office.

Government Actuary's Department
March 2017

Table 1: Multipliers for pecuniary loss for life (males)

Age at date of trial	\-2.0%	\-1.5%	\-1.0%	\-0.75%	\-0.5%	0.0%	0.5%	1.0%	1.5%	2.0%	2.5%	3.0%	Age at date of trial
0	264.76	195.32	147.14	128.73	113.22	88.96	71.35	58.34	48.60	41.17	35.41	30.89	0
1	259.11	191.95	145.15	127.21	112.06	88.31	71.00	58.18	48.54	41.18	35.46	30.96	1
2	252.28	187.68	142.46	125.07	110.35	87.22	70.30	57.73	48.24	40.98	35.33	30.87	2
3	245.58	183.46	139.78	122.92	108.64	86.12	69.58	57.26	47.94	40.78	35.19	30.78	3
4	239.02	179.29	137.12	120.79	106.93	85.01	68.86	56.78	47.62	40.56	35.05	30.68	4
5	232.59	175.19	134.48	118.67	105.22	83.89	68.12	56.30	47.29	40.34	34.90	30.58	5
6	226.29	171.15	131.87	116.57	103.52	82.78	67.39	55.80	46.96	40.12	34.75	30.47	6
7	220.14	167.18	129.29	114.49	101.83	81.66	66.65	55.31	46.63	39.89	34.59	30.36	7
8	214.13	163.28	126.74	112.42	100.15	80.55	65.90	54.80	46.28	39.65	34.42	30.24	8
9	208.23	159.43	124.21	110.36	98.48	79.43	65.15	54.29	45.93	39.41	34.25	30.13	9
10	202.47	155.64	121.71	108.32	96.81	78.31	64.39	53.78	45.58	39.16	34.08	30.00	10
11	196.83	151.92	119.23	106.29	95.15	77.19	63.63	53.25	45.22	38.91	33.90	29.87	11
12	191.33	148.26	116.79	104.29	93.50	76.07	62.86	52.72	44.85	38.65	33.72	29.74	12
13	185.95	144.67	114.37	102.30	91.87	74.96	62.09	52.19	44.47	38.39	33.53	29.61	13
14	180.69	141.14	111.98	100.33	90.24	73.84	61.32	51.65	44.10	38.12	33.34	29.47	14
15	175.56	137.67	109.62	98.38	88.63	72.73	60.55	51.11	43.71	37.84	33.14	29.32	15
16	170.55	134.27	107.30	96.45	87.02	71.61	59.77	50.56	43.32	37.57	32.94	29.17	16
17	165.66	130.93	105.00	94.55	85.44	70.51	58.99	50.01	42.93	37.28	32.73	29.02	17
18	160.89	127.66	102.74	92.66	83.86	69.41	58.22	49.46	42.53	37.00	32.52	28.87	18
19	156.25	124.45	100.52	90.80	82.31	68.31	57.44	48.91	42.14	36.71	32.31	28.71	19
20	151.72	121.31	98.32	88.96	80.76	67.22	56.66	48.35	41.73	36.41	32.10	28.55	20
21	147.28	118.22	96.15	87.14	79.23	66.13	55.88	47.78	41.32	36.11	31.87	28.39	21
22	142.94	115.17	94.00	85.33	77.70	65.04	55.09	47.21	40.90	35.81	31.64	28.22	22
23	138.69	112.17	91.87	83.53	76.18	63.94	54.30	46.63	40.48	35.49	31.41	28.04	23
24	134.54	109.22	89.77	81.75	74.67	62.85	53.51	46.05	40.05	35.17	31.17	27.86	24
25	130.49	106.33	87.69	79.99	73.17	61.76	52.71	45.46	39.61	34.85	30.92	27.67	25
26	126.54	103.50	85.65	78.25	71.69	60.68	51.91	44.87	39.17	34.51	30.67	27.48	26
27	122.69	100.72	83.63	76.52	70.22	59.59	51.11	44.28	38.73	34.18	30.42	27.28	27
28	118.90	97.98	81.63	74.81	68.74	58.51	50.30	43.67	38.27	33.83	30.15	27.08	28
29	115.20	95.28	79.64	73.11	67.28	57.42	49.49	43.06	37.81	33.48	29.88	26.87	29
30	111.59	92.63	77.69	71.43	65.83	56.34	48.68	42.45	37.34	33.12	29.60	26.65	30
31	108.09	90.04	75.78	69.77	64.40	55.27	47.87	41.83	36.87	32.76	29.32	26.44	31
32	104.68	87.52	73.89	68.14	62.99	54.20	47.06	41.22	36.40	32.39	29.04	26.21	32
33	101.36	85.04	72.04	66.54	61.60	53.15	46.26	40.60	35.92	32.02	28.75	25.99	33
34	98.10	82.61	70.21	64.94	60.21	52.09	45.45	39.98	35.44	31.65	28.46	25.75	34
35	94.92	80.21	68.39	63.36	58.83	51.03	44.63	39.35	34.95	31.26	28.15	25.51	35
36	91.82	77.86	66.60	61.80	57.46	49.98	43.82	38.71	34.45	30.87	27.84	25.27	36
37	88.78	75.55	64.83	60.25	56.10	48.93	43.00	38.07	33.95	30.47	27.53	25.01	37
38	85.81	73.27	63.08	58.71	54.74	47.87	42.18	37.42	33.44	30.06	27.20	24.75	38
39	82.89	71.03	61.35	57.18	53.39	46.82	41.35	36.77	32.91	29.65	26.86	24.48	39
40	80.05	68.83	59.63	55.66	52.05	45.76	40.51	36.11	32.39	29.22	26.52	24.20	40
41	77.27	66.67	57.94	54.16	50.72	44.71	39.68	35.44	31.85	28.79	26.17	23.91	41
42	74.56	64.55	56.28	52.68	49.41	43.67	38.84	34.77	31.31	28.35	25.81	23.62	42
43	71.92	62.47	54.63	51.22	48.10	42.62	38.01	34.10	30.76	27.91	25.45	23.32	43
44	69.34	60.43	53.01	49.77	46.81	41.59	37.17	33.42	30.21	27.45	25.08	23.01	44
45	66.82	58.43	51.41	48.34	45.52	40.55	36.33	32.73	29.65	26.99	24.70	22.69	45
46	64.36	56.46	49.83	46.92	44.25	39.52	35.49	32.05	29.08	26.53	24.31	22.37	46
47	61.96	54.53	48.28	45.52	42.99	38.49	34.65	31.35	28.51	26.05	23.91	22.04	47
48	59.63	52.64	46.74	44.14	41.74	37.47	33.81	30.66	27.94	25.57	23.51	21.70	48
49	57.35	50.79	45.24	42.78	40.50	36.45	32.97	29.97	27.36	25.09	23.10	21.36	49
50	55.14	48.99	43.76	41.44	39.29	35.45	32.14	29.27	26.78	24.60	22.69	21.01	50
51	52.99	47.23	42.31	40.12	38.09	34.45	31.31	28.58	26.19	24.11	22.27	20.65	51
52	50.90	45.51	40.89	38.82	36.91	33.47	30.48	27.88	25.61	23.61	21.85	20.29	52
53	48.87	43.83	39.49	37.55	35.74	32.49	29.67	27.19	25.02	23.11	21.42	19.92	53
54	46.90	42.19	38.12	36.30	34.60	31.53	28.85	26.50	24.43	22.61	20.99	19.55	54

Table 1: Multipliers for pecuniary loss for life (males) *continued*

Age at date of trial	-2.0%	-1.5%	-1.0%	-0.75%	-0.5%	0.0%	0.5%	1.0%	1.5%	2.0%	2.5%	3.0%	Age at date of trial
55	44.99	40.60	36.79	35.07	33.47	30.58	28.04	25.81	23.85	22.11	20.56	19.18	55
56	43.15	39.04	35.48	33.87	32.37	29.64	27.25	25.13	23.26	21.60	20.12	18.80	56
57	41.35	37.53	34.19	32.69	31.28	28.71	26.45	24.45	22.67	21.09	19.68	18.42	57
58	39.59	36.04	32.93	31.52	30.19	27.78	25.65	23.76	22.08	20.58	19.23	18.02	58
59	37.87	34.57	31.67	30.35	29.11	26.85	24.85	23.07	21.47	20.05	18.77	17.62	59
60	36.17	33.12	30.42	29.19	28.04	25.92	24.04	22.36	20.86	19.51	18.30	17.20	60
61	34.52	31.69	29.19	28.05	26.97	25.00	23.23	21.65	20.24	18.96	17.81	16.77	61
62	32.91	30.30	27.98	26.92	25.92	24.08	22.43	20.95	19.62	18.41	17.33	16.34	62
63	31.36	28.95	26.80	25.82	24.89	23.17	21.63	20.25	19.00	17.86	16.84	15.90	63
64	29.85	27.63	25.65	24.74	23.88	22.28	20.85	19.55	18.38	17.31	16.35	15.47	64
65	28.40	26.37	24.54	23.70	22.90	21.42	20.08	18.87	17.77	16.77	15.86	15.03	65
66	27.02	25.14	23.46	22.68	21.94	20.57	19.33	18.20	17.17	16.24	15.38	14.60	66
67	25.68	23.96	22.41	21.69	21.01	19.74	18.59	17.54	16.58	15.70	14.90	14.16	67
68	24.38	22.81	21.39	20.73	20.10	18.93	17.86	16.88	15.99	15.17	14.42	13.73	68
69	23.13	21.69	20.39	19.78	19.21	18.12	17.14	16.23	15.40	14.64	13.93	13.29	69
70	21.91	20.60	19.41	18.85	18.32	17.32	16.41	15.58	14.81	14.10	13.44	12.84	70
71	20.70	19.52	18.43	17.92	17.44	16.53	15.69	14.92	14.21	13.55	12.94	12.38	71
72	19.52	18.44	17.46	17.00	16.56	15.72	14.96	14.25	13.60	12.99	12.43	11.91	72
73	18.34	17.38	16.49	16.07	15.67	14.92	14.22	13.57	12.97	12.42	11.90	11.42	73
74	17.18	16.32	15.52	15.15	14.79	14.10	13.47	12.89	12.34	11.83	11.36	10.92	74
75	16.04	15.27	14.56	14.22	13.90	13.29	12.72	12.19	11.70	11.24	10.81	10.40	75
76	14.93	14.25	13.62	13.32	13.03	12.48	11.97	11.50	11.05	10.64	10.25	9.88	76
77	13.86	13.26	12.70	12.44	12.18	11.70	11.24	10.82	10.42	10.05	9.69	9.36	77
78	12.83	12.31	11.82	11.58	11.36	10.93	10.53	10.15	9.79	9.46	9.15	8.85	78
79	11.86	11.40	10.97	10.77	10.57	10.19	9.84	9.50	9.19	8.89	8.61	8.34	79
80	10.94	10.55	10.17	9.99	9.82	9.49	9.18	8.88	8.60	8.34	8.09	7.85	80
81	10.10	9.75	9.43	9.27	9.12	8.83	8.56	8.30	8.05	7.82	7.60	7.38	81
82	9.33	9.03	8.74	8.61	8.47	8.22	7.98	7.75	7.53	7.33	7.13	6.94	82
83	8.62	8.36	8.11	7.99	7.88	7.65	7.44	7.24	7.05	6.87	6.69	6.53	83
84	7.97	7.74	7.53	7.42	7.32	7.13	6.94	6.76	6.59	6.43	6.28	6.13	84
85	7.36	7.16	6.98	6.89	6.80	6.63	6.47	6.31	6.16	6.02	5.88	5.75	85
86	6.79	6.62	6.46	6.38	6.31	6.16	6.02	5.88	5.75	5.62	5.50	5.39	86
87	6.25	6.11	5.97	5.90	5.83	5.71	5.58	5.46	5.35	5.24	5.14	5.04	87
88	5.74	5.62	5.50	5.44	5.38	5.27	5.16	5.06	4.96	4.87	4.78	4.69	88
89	5.26	5.15	5.05	5.00	4.95	4.86	4.76	4.68	4.59	4.51	4.43	4.35	89
90	4.81	4.72	4.64	4.59	4.55	4.47	4.39	4.31	4.24	4.17	4.10	4.03	90
91	4.40	4.32	4.25	4.21	4.17	4.10	4.04	3.97	3.91	3.85	3.79	3.73	91
92	4.01	3.94	3.88	3.85	3.82	3.76	3.70	3.65	3.59	3.54	3.49	3.44	92
93	3.65	3.59	3.54	3.52	3.49	3.44	3.39	3.34	3.30	3.25	3.21	3.17	93
94	3.33	3.29	3.24	3.22	3.20	3.16	3.11	3.07	3.03	2.99	2.96	2.92	94
95	3.06	3.02	2.98	2.96	2.94	2.91	2.87	2.84	2.80	2.77	2.74	2.71	95
96	2.83	2.79	2.76	2.74	2.72	2.69	2.66	2.63	2.60	2.57	2.54	2.52	96
97	2.62	2.59	2.56	2.55	2.53	2.50	2.48	2.45	2.42	2.40	2.37	2.35	97
98	2.44	2.41	2.38	2.37	2.36	2.34	2.31	2.29	2.27	2.24	2.22	2.20	98
99	2.27	2.25	2.22	2.21	2.20	2.18	2.16	2.14	2.12	2.10	2.08	2.06	99
100	2.11	2.09	2.07	2.06	2.06	2.04	2.02	2.00	1.98	1.97	1.95	1.93	100

Table 2: Multipliers for pecuniary loss for life (females)

Age at date of trial	\-2.0%	\-1.5%	\-1.0%	\-0.75%	\-0.5%	0.0%	0.5%	1.0%	1.5%	2.0%	2.5%	3.0%	Age at date of trial
0	285.20	208.39	155.57	135.52	118.70	92.57	73.74	59.95	49.69	41.92	35.94	31.26	0
1	279.01	204.72	153.41	133.87	117.45	91.86	73.36	59.76	49.62	41.91	35.97	31.32	1
2	271.81	200.28	150.65	131.69	115.73	90.77	72.67	59.33	49.34	41.73	35.86	31.24	2
3	264.75	195.89	147.91	129.52	114.00	89.68	71.97	58.88	49.05	41.55	35.73	31.16	3
4	257.83	191.56	145.19	127.36	112.28	88.58	71.27	58.43	48.75	41.35	35.60	31.08	4
5	251.06	187.30	142.49	125.21	110.56	87.49	70.56	57.97	48.45	41.15	35.47	30.99	5
6	244.43	183.11	139.83	123.07	108.85	86.38	69.85	57.50	48.14	40.95	35.34	30.89	6
7	237.94	178.98	137.18	120.96	107.15	85.28	69.13	57.03	47.83	40.74	35.19	30.80	7
8	231.59	174.92	134.57	118.85	105.46	84.18	68.40	56.55	47.51	40.52	35.05	30.70	8
9	225.38	170.93	131.98	116.77	103.77	83.07	67.67	56.06	47.18	40.30	34.90	30.60	9
10	219.31	167.00	129.43	114.70	102.10	81.97	66.94	55.57	46.85	40.08	34.75	30.49	10
11	213.37	163.14	126.90	112.65	100.43	80.86	66.20	55.07	46.52	39.85	34.59	30.38	11
12	207.57	159.34	124.40	110.62	98.78	79.76	65.46	54.57	46.18	39.62	34.42	30.27	12
13	201.89	155.60	121.92	108.60	97.13	78.65	64.71	54.07	45.83	39.38	34.26	30.15	13
14	196.33	151.93	119.48	106.60	95.49	77.55	63.96	53.55	45.47	39.13	34.09	30.03	14
15	190.91	148.32	117.06	104.62	93.86	76.44	63.21	53.03	45.12	38.88	33.91	29.90	15
16	185.61	144.77	114.67	102.65	92.25	75.34	62.45	52.51	44.75	38.62	33.73	29.77	16
17	180.42	141.28	112.31	100.71	90.64	74.24	61.70	51.99	44.38	38.37	33.55	29.64	17
18	175.36	137.86	109.98	98.78	89.05	73.14	60.94	51.46	44.01	38.10	33.36	29.51	18
19	170.42	134.50	107.68	96.88	87.46	72.05	60.17	50.92	43.63	37.83	33.16	29.37	19
20	165.60	131.20	105.42	94.99	85.89	70.96	59.41	50.38	43.25	37.56	32.97	29.22	20
21	160.88	127.95	103.17	93.12	84.33	69.86	58.64	49.84	42.86	37.28	32.76	29.08	21
22	156.26	124.76	100.95	91.26	82.78	68.77	57.86	49.28	42.47	36.99	32.56	28.92	22
23	151.72	121.60	98.74	89.41	81.22	67.67	57.08	48.72	42.06	36.70	32.34	28.76	23
24	147.29	118.50	96.56	87.58	79.68	66.57	56.29	48.16	41.65	36.40	32.12	28.60	24
25	142.97	115.46	94.41	85.76	78.15	65.48	55.50	47.58	41.23	36.09	31.89	28.43	25
26	138.74	112.47	92.28	83.97	76.63	64.38	54.71	47.01	40.81	35.78	31.66	28.26	26
27	134.61	109.53	90.18	82.19	75.12	63.29	53.92	46.43	40.38	35.46	31.42	28.08	27
28	130.57	106.65	88.11	80.42	73.62	62.20	53.12	45.84	39.95	35.14	31.18	27.90	28
29	126.63	103.81	86.05	78.68	72.13	61.11	52.32	45.25	39.51	34.81	30.93	27.71	29
30	122.78	101.02	84.03	76.95	70.65	60.02	51.52	44.65	39.06	34.47	30.68	27.51	30
31	119.02	98.29	82.03	75.24	69.18	58.94	50.71	44.05	38.61	34.13	30.41	27.31	31
32	115.34	95.60	80.06	73.54	67.72	57.86	49.90	43.44	38.15	33.78	30.15	27.11	32
33	111.75	92.97	78.11	71.86	66.27	56.77	49.09	42.83	37.68	33.42	29.87	26.89	33
34	108.24	90.37	76.18	70.20	64.83	55.69	48.27	42.21	37.21	33.06	29.59	26.67	34
35	104.80	87.81	74.27	68.54	63.40	54.61	47.45	41.58	36.73	32.69	29.31	26.45	35
36	101.45	85.31	72.39	66.91	61.98	53.53	46.63	40.95	36.24	32.31	29.01	26.22	36
37	98.17	82.84	70.53	65.29	60.57	52.46	45.81	40.31	35.75	31.93	28.71	25.98	37
38	94.97	80.42	68.69	63.69	59.17	51.38	44.98	39.67	35.25	31.54	28.40	25.74	38
39	91.83	78.04	66.88	62.10	57.78	50.31	44.15	39.03	34.74	31.14	28.09	25.48	39
40	88.77	75.71	65.08	60.52	56.39	49.24	43.31	38.37	34.23	30.73	27.76	25.23	40
41	85.78	73.41	63.31	58.96	55.02	48.17	42.48	37.71	33.71	30.32	27.43	24.96	41
42	82.86	71.16	61.56	57.42	53.66	47.10	41.64	37.05	33.18	29.90	27.09	24.69	42
43	80.01	68.94	59.84	55.90	52.31	46.04	40.80	36.38	32.65	29.47	26.75	24.41	43
44	77.23	66.77	58.14	54.39	50.97	44.98	39.95	35.71	32.11	29.03	26.39	24.12	44
45	74.52	64.65	56.46	52.90	49.64	43.93	39.11	35.03	31.56	28.59	26.03	23.82	45
46	71.87	62.56	54.81	51.42	48.32	42.87	38.27	34.35	31.01	28.14	25.67	23.52	46
47	69.28	60.51	53.17	49.96	47.02	41.83	37.42	33.67	30.45	27.69	25.29	23.21	47
48	66.77	58.50	51.57	48.53	45.73	40.79	36.58	32.98	29.89	27.23	24.91	22.90	48
49	64.32	56.54	50.00	47.11	44.46	39.76	35.74	32.30	29.33	26.76	24.53	22.58	49
50	61.93	54.62	48.44	45.71	43.20	38.73	34.90	31.61	28.76	26.29	24.14	22.25	50
51	59.60	52.73	46.91	44.33	41.95	37.71	34.06	30.91	28.19	25.81	23.74	21.92	51
52	57.33	50.88	45.40	42.97	40.71	36.69	33.22	30.22	27.61	25.33	23.33	21.57	52
53	55.11	49.07	43.92	41.62	39.49	35.68	32.38	29.52	27.02	24.84	22.92	21.22	53
54	52.96	47.30	42.46	40.29	38.28	34.68	31.55	28.82	26.44	24.34	22.50	20.87	54

Table 2: Multipliers for pecuniary loss for life (females) *continued*

Age at date of trial	Multiplier calculated with allowance for projected mortality from the 2008–based population projections and rate of return of												Age at date of trial
	-2.0%	-1.5%	-1.0%	-0.75%	-0.5%	0.0%	0.5%	1.0%	1.5%	2.0%	2.5%	3.0%	
55	50.86	45.57	41.02	38.99	37.09	33.68	30.71	28.12	25.84	23.84	22.07	20.51	55
56	48.83	43.88	39.61	37.70	35.91	32.69	29.88	27.42	25.25	23.34	21.64	20.14	56
57	46.84	42.22	38.23	36.43	34.75	31.71	29.05	26.72	24.65	22.83	21.21	19.76	57
58	44.89	40.60	36.86	35.17	33.59	30.74	28.22	26.01	24.05	22.31	20.76	19.37	58
59	42.99	38.99	35.50	33.92	32.44	29.76	27.39	25.29	23.43	21.78	20.30	18.98	59
60	41.12	37.41	34.16	32.68	31.30	28.78	26.55	24.57	22.81	21.24	19.83	18.57	60
61	39.30	35.86	32.83	31.45	30.16	27.80	25.70	23.84	22.18	20.69	19.35	18.15	61
62	37.52	34.33	31.52	30.24	29.03	26.83	24.86	23.11	21.54	20.13	18.86	17.72	62
63	35.79	32.84	30.24	29.04	27.92	25.86	24.02	22.38	20.90	19.57	18.37	17.28	63
64	34.11	31.39	28.98	27.88	26.83	24.91	23.19	21.65	20.26	19.01	17.87	16.84	64
65	32.50	29.99	27.76	26.74	25.77	23.98	22.38	20.93	19.63	18.45	17.38	16.40	65
66	30.94	28.64	26.58	25.63	24.73	23.07	21.58	20.23	19.00	17.89	16.88	15.96	66
67	29.44	27.32	25.43	24.55	23.72	22.18	20.78	19.52	18.38	17.34	16.39	15.52	67
68	27.99	26.05	24.30	23.49	22.72	21.29	20.00	18.83	17.76	16.78	15.89	15.07	68
69	26.57	24.80	23.19	22.45	21.74	20.42	19.22	18.13	17.13	16.22	15.39	14.62	69
70	25.19	23.57	22.10	21.41	20.76	19.55	18.44	17.43	16.50	15.65	14.87	14.15	70
71	23.83	22.35	21.01	20.39	19.79	18.67	17.65	16.72	15.86	15.07	14.35	13.68	71
72	22.47	21.14	19.92	19.35	18.81	17.79	16.85	16.00	15.20	14.48	13.80	13.18	72
73	21.13	19.93	18.83	18.31	17.82	16.89	16.04	15.25	14.53	13.86	13.24	12.66	73
74	19.80	18.72	17.73	17.27	16.82	15.99	15.21	14.50	13.84	13.23	12.66	12.13	74
75	18.48	17.53	16.64	16.23	15.83	15.08	14.38	13.74	13.14	12.58	12.06	11.58	75
76	17.20	16.35	15.57	15.20	14.84	14.17	13.55	12.97	12.43	11.92	11.45	11.01	76
77	15.95	15.21	14.51	14.19	13.87	13.28	12.72	12.20	11.72	11.27	10.84	10.45	77
78	14.75	14.10	13.50	13.21	12.93	12.40	11.91	11.45	11.02	10.62	10.24	9.88	78
79	13.62	13.05	12.52	12.27	12.03	11.56	11.13	10.72	10.34	9.98	9.64	9.32	79
80	12.56	12.07	11.61	11.39	11.17	10.77	10.38	10.02	9.69	9.37	9.07	8.78	80
81	11.58	11.15	10.75	10.56	10.37	10.02	9.68	9.36	9.06	8.78	8.51	8.26	81
82	10.67	10.30	9.95	9.78	9.62	9.31	9.02	8.74	8.48	8.23	7.99	7.76	82
83	9.83	9.51	9.21	9.06	8.92	8.65	8.39	8.15	7.92	7.70	7.49	7.29	83
84	9.06	8.78	8.52	8.39	8.27	8.03	7.81	7.59	7.39	7.19	7.01	6.83	84
85	8.34	8.10	7.87	7.76	7.65	7.45	7.25	7.06	6.88	6.71	6.55	6.40	85
86	7.66	7.45	7.25	7.16	7.07	6.89	6.72	6.56	6.40	6.25	6.11	5.97	86
87	7.01	6.84	6.67	6.59	6.51	6.36	6.21	6.07	5.93	5.80	5.68	5.56	87
88	6.41	6.26	6.11	6.05	5.98	5.85	5.72	5.60	5.48	5.37	5.26	5.16	88
89	5.84	5.71	5.59	5.53	5.47	5.36	5.25	5.15	5.05	4.95	4.86	4.77	89
90	5.31	5.20	5.10	5.05	5.00	4.90	4.81	4.72	4.64	4.55	4.47	4.40	90
91	4.82	4.73	4.64	4.60	4.55	4.47	4.40	4.32	4.25	4.18	4.11	4.04	91
92	4.37	4.29	4.22	4.18	4.15	4.08	4.01	3.95	3.89	3.83	3.77	3.71	92
93	3.97	3.90	3.84	3.81	3.78	3.72	3.67	3.61	3.56	3.51	3.46	3.41	93
94	3.62	3.56	3.51	3.48	3.46	3.41	3.36	3.31	3.27	3.22	3.18	3.14	94
95	3.32	3.27	3.23	3.20	3.18	3.14	3.10	3.06	3.02	2.98	2.94	2.91	95
96	3.06	3.02	2.98	2.96	2.94	2.91	2.87	2.84	2.80	2.77	2.74	2.71	96
97	2.84	2.80	2.77	2.75	2.74	2.70	2.67	2.64	2.61	2.58	2.56	2.53	97
98	2.64	2.61	2.58	2.56	2.55	2.52	2.49	2.47	2.44	2.42	2.39	2.37	98
99	2.45	2.42	2.40	2.38	2.37	2.35	2.32	2.30	2.28	2.26	2.23	2.21	99
100	2.27	2.25	2.22	2.21	2.20	2.18	2.16	2.14	2.12	2.10	2.08	2.06	100

A8: The Ogden Tables

Table 3: Multipliers for loss of earnings to pension age 50 (males)

Age at date of trial	\-2.0%	\-1.5%	\-1.0%	\-0.75%	\-0.5%	0.0%	0.5%	1.0%	1.5%	2.0%	2.5%	3.0%	Age at date of trial
	Multiplier calculated with allowance for projected mortality from the 2008–based population projections and rate of return of												
16	48.26	43.90	40.05	38.30	36.65	33.63	30.94	28.55	26.42	24.51	22.80	21.26	16
17	46.31	42.26	38.66	37.02	35.47	32.63	30.10	27.84	25.81	24.00	22.36	20.89	17
18	44.40	40.64	37.29	35.75	34.30	31.64	29.25	27.12	25.20	23.47	21.91	20.51	18
19	42.54	39.04	35.93	34.50	33.14	30.65	28.41	26.39	24.57	22.94	21.45	20.11	19
20	40.71	37.48	34.58	33.25	31.99	29.66	27.55	25.66	23.94	22.39	20.99	19.71	20
21	38.91	35.93	33.25	32.02	30.84	28.66	26.70	24.92	23.30	21.84	20.50	19.29	21
22	37.16	34.41	31.94	30.79	29.70	27.67	25.84	24.17	22.65	21.27	20.01	18.86	22
23	35.44	32.92	30.63	29.57	28.56	26.68	24.97	23.41	21.99	20.69	19.51	18.42	23
24	33.75	31.44	29.34	28.37	27.43	25.69	24.10	22.65	21.32	20.11	18.99	17.96	24
25	32.10	29.99	28.06	27.17	26.31	24.70	23.23	21.88	20.65	19.51	18.46	17.49	25
26	30.48	28.56	26.80	25.98	25.19	23.71	22.36	21.11	19.96	18.90	17.92	17.01	26
27	28.89	27.15	25.55	24.80	24.08	22.72	21.47	20.32	19.26	18.27	17.36	16.52	27
28	27.34	25.76	24.31	23.63	22.97	21.73	20.59	19.53	18.55	17.64	16.79	16.00	28
29	25.81	24.40	23.08	22.47	21.87	20.74	19.70	18.73	17.83	16.99	16.21	15.48	29
30	24.32	23.05	21.87	21.31	20.78	19.76	18.81	17.92	17.10	16.33	15.61	14.94	30
31	22.86	21.73	20.67	20.17	19.69	18.77	17.91	17.11	16.36	15.66	15.00	14.38	31
32	21.43	20.43	19.49	19.04	18.61	17.78	17.01	16.29	15.61	14.97	14.37	13.81	32
33	20.03	19.15	18.31	17.92	17.53	16.80	16.11	15.46	14.85	14.28	13.73	13.22	33
34	18.66	17.88	17.15	16.80	16.47	15.82	15.20	14.63	14.08	13.57	13.08	12.62	34
35	17.31	16.64	16.00	15.70	15.40	14.83	14.29	13.78	13.30	12.84	12.41	11.99	35
36	16.00	15.42	14.87	14.60	14.34	13.85	13.38	12.93	12.51	12.10	11.72	11.35	36
37	14.70	14.21	13.74	13.51	13.29	12.86	12.46	12.07	11.70	11.35	11.01	10.69	37
38	13.44	13.02	12.62	12.43	12.24	11.88	11.53	11.20	10.88	10.58	10.29	10.01	38
39	12.19	11.85	11.52	11.36	11.20	10.89	10.60	10.32	10.05	9.79	9.54	9.31	39
40	10.98	10.69	10.42	10.29	10.16	9.91	9.67	9.43	9.21	8.99	8.78	8.58	40
41	9.78	9.55	9.34	9.23	9.13	8.92	8.72	8.53	8.35	8.17	8.00	7.84	41
42	8.61	8.43	8.26	8.18	8.10	7.93	7.78	7.63	7.48	7.34	7.20	7.07	42
43	7.46	7.33	7.20	7.13	7.07	6.95	6.83	6.71	6.60	6.49	6.38	6.28	43
44	6.33	6.24	6.14	6.10	6.05	5.96	5.87	5.78	5.70	5.62	5.54	5.46	44
45	5.23	5.16	5.10	5.06	5.03	4.97	4.91	4.85	4.79	4.73	4.68	4.62	45
46	4.14	4.10	4.06	4.04	4.02	3.98	3.94	3.90	3.86	3.83	3.79	3.75	46
47	3.08	3.06	3.03	3.02	3.01	2.99	2.97	2.94	2.92	2.90	2.88	2.86	47
48	2.03	2.02	2.01	2.01	2.00	1.99	1.98	1.97	1.96	1.96	1.95	1.94	48
49	1.01	1.01	1.00	1.00	1.00	1.00	1.00	0.99	0.99	0.99	0.99	0.98	49

Table 4: Multipliers for loss of earnings to pension age 50 (females)

Age at date of trial	\-	\-	\-	Multiplier calculated with allowance for projected mortality from the 2008–based population projections and rate of return of	\-	\-	\-	\-	\-	\-	\-	\-	Age at date of trial
	–2.0%	*–1.5%*	*–1.0%*	*–0.75%*	*–0.5%*	*0.0%*	*0.5%*	*1.0%*	*1.5%*	*2.0%*	*2.5%*	*3.0%*	
16	48.58	44.19	40.30	38.53	36.87	33.82	31.12	28.71	26.56	24.63	22.91	21.36	16
17	46.62	42.53	38.91	37.25	35.69	32.82	30.27	27.99	25.95	24.12	22.47	20.99	17
18	44.71	40.91	37.53	35.98	34.52	31.83	29.42	27.27	25.33	23.59	22.02	20.60	18
19	42.83	39.30	36.16	34.72	33.35	30.83	28.57	26.54	24.71	23.06	21.56	20.21	19
20	40.98	37.73	34.81	33.46	32.19	29.83	27.72	25.80	24.08	22.51	21.09	19.80	20
21	39.18	36.17	33.47	32.22	31.03	28.84	26.85	25.06	23.43	21.96	20.61	19.39	21
22	37.41	34.64	32.14	30.99	29.89	27.84	25.99	24.31	22.78	21.39	20.12	18.96	22
23	35.68	33.13	30.83	29.76	28.74	26.85	25.12	23.55	22.12	20.81	19.61	18.51	23
24	33.98	31.65	29.53	28.54	27.60	25.85	24.25	22.78	21.44	20.22	19.09	18.06	24
25	32.31	30.18	28.24	27.34	26.47	24.85	23.37	22.01	20.76	19.61	18.56	17.59	25
26	30.68	28.74	26.97	26.14	25.35	23.86	22.49	21.23	20.07	19.00	18.01	17.10	26
27	29.08	27.33	25.71	24.95	24.23	22.86	21.60	20.44	19.37	18.37	17.45	16.60	27
28	27.52	25.93	24.46	23.78	23.11	21.87	20.71	19.64	18.65	17.74	16.88	16.09	28
29	25.98	24.55	23.23	22.61	22.01	20.87	19.82	18.84	17.93	17.08	16.30	15.56	29
30	24.48	23.20	22.01	21.45	20.90	19.88	18.92	18.03	17.20	16.42	15.70	15.02	30
31	23.01	21.86	20.80	20.30	19.81	18.88	18.02	17.21	16.45	15.74	15.08	14.46	31
32	21.56	20.55	19.60	19.15	18.72	17.89	17.11	16.38	15.70	15.05	14.45	13.88	32
33	20.15	19.26	18.42	18.02	17.63	16.89	16.20	15.55	14.93	14.35	13.80	13.29	33
34	18.76	17.98	17.25	16.90	16.55	15.90	15.28	14.70	14.15	13.63	13.14	12.68	34
35	17.41	16.73	16.09	15.78	15.48	14.91	14.37	13.85	13.36	12.90	12.46	12.05	35
36	16.08	15.49	14.94	14.67	14.41	13.92	13.44	12.99	12.56	12.16	11.77	11.40	36
37	14.77	14.28	13.80	13.57	13.35	12.92	12.51	12.12	11.75	11.40	11.06	10.73	37
38	13.50	13.08	12.68	12.48	12.30	11.93	11.58	11.25	10.93	10.62	10.33	10.05	38
39	12.25	11.90	11.56	11.40	11.24	10.94	10.64	10.36	10.09	9.83	9.58	9.34	39
40	11.02	10.73	10.46	10.33	10.20	9.95	9.70	9.47	9.24	9.02	8.82	8.61	40
41	9.82	9.59	9.37	9.26	9.16	8.95	8.76	8.56	8.38	8.20	8.03	7.86	41
42	8.64	8.46	8.29	8.20	8.12	7.96	7.80	7.65	7.51	7.36	7.22	7.09	42
43	7.48	7.35	7.22	7.15	7.09	6.97	6.85	6.73	6.62	6.51	6.40	6.29	43
44	6.35	6.25	6.16	6.11	6.06	5.97	5.89	5.80	5.72	5.63	5.55	5.48	44
45	5.24	5.17	5.11	5.08	5.04	4.98	4.92	4.86	4.80	4.74	4.69	4.63	45
46	4.15	4.11	4.07	4.05	4.03	3.99	3.95	3.91	3.87	3.83	3.80	3.76	46
47	3.08	3.06	3.04	3.03	3.01	2.99	2.97	2.95	2.93	2.90	2.88	2.86	47
48	2.04	2.03	2.02	2.01	2.01	2.00	1.99	1.98	1.97	1.96	1.95	1.94	48
49	1.01	1.01	1.00	1.00	1.00	1.00	1.00	0.99	0.99	0.99	0.99	0.98	49

A8: The Ogden Tables

Table 5: Multipliers for loss of earnings to pension age 55 (males)

Age at date of trial	\-2.0%	\-1.5%	\-1.0%	\-0.75%	\-0.5%	0.0%	0.5%	1.0%	1.5%	2.0%	2.5%	3.0%	Age at date of trial
16	58.33	52.26	47.00	44.63	42.43	38.44	34.96	31.90	29.22	26.85	24.76	22.90	16
17	56.17	50.49	45.54	43.31	41.22	37.44	34.13	31.22	28.65	26.38	24.37	22.58	17
18	54.07	48.74	44.09	41.99	40.02	36.45	33.30	30.53	28.08	25.90	23.97	22.24	18
19	52.00	47.03	42.67	40.69	38.83	35.46	32.48	29.84	27.50	25.42	23.56	21.90	19
20	49.99	45.34	41.26	39.40	37.65	34.47	31.65	29.14	26.91	24.92	23.14	21.55	20
21	48.01	43.68	39.86	38.12	36.48	33.48	30.81	28.44	26.31	24.42	22.72	21.19	21
22	46.07	42.04	38.47	36.84	35.31	32.49	29.97	27.72	25.71	23.90	22.28	20.82	22
23	44.17	40.43	37.11	35.58	34.14	31.49	29.13	27.00	25.10	23.38	21.83	20.43	23
24	42.31	38.84	35.75	34.33	32.98	30.50	28.28	26.28	24.47	22.85	21.37	20.04	24
25	40.49	37.28	34.41	33.09	31.83	29.52	27.43	25.54	23.84	22.30	20.90	19.63	25
26	38.70	35.74	33.08	31.85	30.69	28.53	26.57	24.81	23.20	21.75	20.42	19.21	26
27	36.95	34.23	31.77	30.63	29.55	27.54	25.71	24.06	22.55	21.18	19.93	18.78	27
28	35.24	32.74	30.47	29.42	28.42	26.55	24.85	23.30	21.89	20.60	19.42	18.34	28
29	33.56	31.27	29.18	28.21	27.29	25.56	23.98	22.54	21.22	20.01	18.91	17.89	29
30	31.91	29.82	27.91	27.02	26.17	24.57	23.11	21.78	20.55	19.42	18.38	17.42	30
31	30.30	28.40	26.66	25.84	25.06	23.59	22.24	21.00	19.86	18.81	17.83	16.94	31
32	28.73	27.00	25.41	24.67	23.95	22.61	21.37	20.22	19.17	18.19	17.28	16.44	32
33	27.19	25.63	24.19	23.51	22.86	21.63	20.49	19.44	18.46	17.56	16.72	15.94	33
34	25.68	24.27	22.97	22.36	21.76	20.65	19.61	18.65	17.75	16.92	16.14	15.41	34
35	24.20	22.94	21.77	21.21	20.68	19.67	18.72	17.85	17.03	16.26	15.55	14.88	35
36	22.75	21.63	20.58	20.08	19.60	18.69	17.83	17.04	16.29	15.59	14.94	14.32	36
37	21.33	20.33	19.40	18.95	18.52	17.71	16.94	16.22	15.55	14.91	14.32	13.76	37
38	19.94	19.06	18.23	17.84	17.46	16.73	16.04	15.40	14.79	14.22	13.68	13.17	38
39	18.57	17.80	17.07	16.73	16.39	15.75	15.14	14.56	14.02	13.51	13.02	12.56	39
40	17.23	16.56	15.93	15.63	15.33	14.76	14.23	13.72	13.24	12.79	12.35	11.94	40
41	15.92	15.34	14.79	14.53	14.28	13.78	13.32	12.87	12.45	12.05	11.67	11.30	41
42	14.63	14.14	13.67	13.45	13.23	12.80	12.40	12.01	11.65	11.30	10.96	10.64	42
43	13.37	12.96	12.56	12.37	12.18	11.82	11.48	11.15	10.83	10.53	10.24	9.96	43
44	12.13	11.79	11.46	11.30	11.14	10.84	10.55	10.27	10.01	9.75	9.50	9.26	44
45	10.92	10.64	10.37	10.24	10.11	9.86	9.62	9.39	9.17	8.95	8.74	8.54	45
46	9.73	9.51	9.29	9.19	9.08	8.88	8.68	8.50	8.31	8.14	7.97	7.80	46
47	8.57	8.39	8.22	8.14	8.06	7.90	7.74	7.59	7.45	7.31	7.17	7.04	47
48	7.43	7.29	7.17	7.10	7.04	6.92	6.80	6.68	6.57	6.46	6.35	6.25	48
49	6.31	6.21	6.12	6.07	6.02	5.93	5.85	5.76	5.68	5.60	5.52	5.44	49
50	5.21	5.14	5.08	5.05	5.01	4.95	4.89	4.83	4.77	4.72	4.66	4.60	50
51	4.13	4.09	4.05	4.03	4.01	3.97	3.93	3.89	3.85	3.81	3.78	3.74	51
52	3.07	3.05	3.03	3.01	3.00	2.98	2.96	2.94	2.91	2.89	2.87	2.85	52
53	2.03	2.02	2.01	2.01	2.00	1.99	1.98	1.97	1.96	1.95	1.94	1.93	53
54	1.01	1.01	1.00	1.00	1.00	1.00	1.00	0.99	0.99	0.99	0.99	0.98	54

A8: The Ogden Tables

Table 6: Multipliers for loss of earnings to pension age 55 (females)

Age at date of trial	-2.0%	-1.5%	-1.0%	-0.75%	-0.5%	0.0%	0.5%	1.0%	1.5%	2.0%	2.5%	3.0%	Age at date of trial
16	58.83	52.69	47.37	44.98	42.75	38.72	35.20	32.11	29.40	27.01	24.90	23.03	16
17	56.66	50.91	45.90	43.65	41.54	37.72	34.37	31.43	28.84	26.54	24.51	22.70	17
18	54.54	49.15	44.45	42.33	40.34	36.72	33.55	30.74	28.26	26.07	24.11	22.37	18
19	52.46	47.43	43.02	41.02	39.14	35.73	32.71	30.05	27.68	25.58	23.71	22.03	19
20	50.43	45.73	41.60	39.72	37.95	34.73	31.88	29.35	27.09	25.09	23.29	21.68	20
21	48.43	44.05	40.19	38.43	36.77	33.73	31.04	28.64	26.50	24.58	22.86	21.32	21
22	46.48	42.41	38.80	37.15	35.59	32.74	30.20	27.92	25.89	24.06	22.42	20.95	22
23	44.56	40.78	37.42	35.87	34.42	31.74	29.35	27.20	25.27	23.54	21.97	20.56	23
24	42.69	39.18	36.05	34.61	33.25	30.74	28.49	26.47	24.65	23.00	21.51	20.17	24
25	40.85	37.60	34.70	33.36	32.09	29.75	27.64	25.73	24.01	22.46	21.04	19.76	25
26	39.04	36.05	33.36	32.12	30.94	28.75	26.78	24.99	23.37	21.90	20.56	19.34	26
27	37.28	34.52	32.04	30.89	29.79	27.76	25.91	24.24	22.72	21.33	20.06	18.91	27
28	35.55	33.02	30.73	29.66	28.65	26.76	25.04	23.48	22.05	20.75	19.56	18.46	28
29	33.86	31.54	29.43	28.45	27.51	25.77	24.17	22.72	21.38	20.16	19.04	18.01	29
30	32.20	30.08	28.15	27.25	26.38	24.77	23.30	21.94	20.70	19.56	18.51	17.54	30
31	30.57	28.64	26.88	26.05	25.26	23.78	22.42	21.16	20.01	18.94	17.96	17.05	31
32	28.98	27.23	25.62	24.87	24.15	22.79	21.53	20.38	19.31	18.32	17.40	16.56	32
33	27.42	25.84	24.38	23.69	23.03	21.79	20.64	19.58	18.60	17.68	16.83	16.04	33
34	25.89	24.46	23.15	22.53	21.93	20.80	19.75	18.78	17.87	17.03	16.25	15.52	34
35	24.39	23.11	21.93	21.37	20.83	19.81	18.86	17.97	17.14	16.37	15.65	14.97	35
36	22.92	21.78	20.73	20.22	19.74	18.82	17.96	17.15	16.40	15.69	15.03	14.41	36
37	21.48	20.48	19.53	19.09	18.65	17.83	17.05	16.33	15.65	15.01	14.40	13.84	37
38	20.07	19.19	18.35	17.96	17.57	16.84	16.14	15.49	14.88	14.30	13.76	13.25	38
39	18.69	17.92	17.19	16.84	16.50	15.85	15.23	14.65	14.11	13.59	13.10	12.64	39
40	17.34	16.67	16.03	15.72	15.43	14.86	14.32	13.80	13.32	12.86	12.42	12.01	40
41	16.02	15.44	14.89	14.62	14.36	13.87	13.40	12.95	12.52	12.12	11.73	11.36	41
42	14.72	14.22	13.75	13.53	13.30	12.88	12.47	12.08	11.71	11.36	11.02	10.70	42
43	13.45	13.03	12.63	12.44	12.25	11.89	11.54	11.21	10.89	10.59	10.29	10.01	43
44	12.20	11.85	11.52	11.36	11.20	10.90	10.61	10.33	10.06	9.80	9.55	9.31	44
45	10.98	10.70	10.42	10.29	10.16	9.91	9.67	9.43	9.21	8.99	8.79	8.58	45
46	9.78	9.56	9.34	9.23	9.13	8.92	8.73	8.54	8.35	8.17	8.00	7.84	46
47	8.61	8.43	8.26	8.18	8.09	7.93	7.78	7.63	7.48	7.34	7.20	7.07	47
48	7.46	7.33	7.20	7.13	7.07	6.95	6.83	6.71	6.60	6.49	6.38	6.28	48
49	6.33	6.24	6.14	6.09	6.05	5.96	5.87	5.78	5.70	5.62	5.54	5.46	49
50	5.23	5.16	5.10	5.06	5.03	4.97	4.91	4.85	4.79	4.73	4.68	4.62	50
51	4.14	4.10	4.06	4.04	4.02	3.98	3.94	3.90	3.86	3.83	3.79	3.75	51
52	3.08	3.06	3.03	3.02	3.01	2.99	2.97	2.94	2.92	2.90	2.88	2.86	52
53	2.03	2.02	2.01	2.01	2.00	1.99	1.98	1.97	1.96	1.96	1.95	1.94	53
54	1.01	1.01	1.00	1.00	1.00	1.00	1.00	0.99	0.99	0.99	0.99	0.98	54

Multiplier calculated with allowance for projected mortality from the 2008–based population projections and rate of return of

Table 7: Multipliers for loss of earnings to pension age 60 (males)

Age at date of trial	-2.0%	-1.5%	-1.0%	-0.75%	-0.5%	0.0%	0.5%	1.0%	1.5%	2.0%	2.5%	3.0%	Age at date of trial
16	69.28	61.13	54.18	51.10	48.26	43.18	38.81	35.03	31.77	28.93	26.46	24.29	16
17	66.90	59.22	52.65	49.73	47.02	42.18	38.00	34.38	31.24	28.50	26.11	24.01	17
18	64.58	57.34	51.13	48.36	45.79	41.18	37.19	33.73	30.71	28.07	25.75	23.72	18
19	62.30	55.49	49.63	47.01	44.57	40.19	36.38	33.06	30.17	27.62	25.39	23.42	19
20	60.08	53.68	48.15	45.67	43.36	39.20	35.57	32.40	29.62	27.17	25.02	23.11	20
21	57.90	51.89	46.68	44.34	42.15	38.21	34.75	31.72	29.06	26.71	24.64	22.80	21
22	55.76	50.13	45.23	43.02	40.95	37.21	33.93	31.04	28.50	26.25	24.25	22.47	22
23	53.66	48.40	43.79	41.71	39.76	36.22	33.11	30.36	27.93	25.77	23.85	22.14	23
24	51.61	46.69	42.37	40.41	38.57	35.23	32.28	29.66	27.35	25.28	23.44	21.80	24
25	49.60	45.01	40.96	39.12	37.40	34.24	31.45	28.97	26.76	24.79	23.02	21.44	25
26	47.64	43.35	39.57	37.85	36.22	33.25	30.61	28.26	26.16	24.28	22.59	21.08	26
27	45.71	41.72	38.19	36.58	35.06	32.27	29.77	27.55	25.56	23.77	22.16	20.71	27
28	43.82	40.12	36.83	35.32	33.90	31.28	28.93	26.83	24.94	23.24	21.71	20.32	28
29	41.97	38.54	35.48	34.07	32.74	30.29	28.09	26.10	24.32	22.70	21.25	19.92	29
30	40.15	36.99	34.14	32.84	31.59	29.30	27.24	25.37	23.69	22.16	20.78	19.52	30
31	38.38	35.46	32.83	31.61	30.46	28.32	26.39	24.64	23.05	21.61	20.29	19.10	31
32	36.65	33.96	31.53	30.40	29.33	27.34	25.53	23.89	22.40	21.04	19.80	18.67	32
33	34.96	32.48	30.24	29.20	28.21	26.36	24.68	23.15	21.75	20.47	19.30	18.23	33
34	33.30	31.03	28.97	28.01	27.09	25.38	23.82	22.39	21.09	19.89	18.79	17.78	34
35	31.67	29.60	27.71	26.83	25.98	24.40	22.96	21.63	20.42	19.30	18.27	17.32	35
36	30.07	28.19	26.46	25.65	24.88	23.43	22.09	20.87	19.74	18.69	17.73	16.84	36
37	28.51	26.80	25.23	24.49	23.78	22.45	21.22	20.09	19.04	18.08	17.18	16.35	37
38	26.98	25.43	24.01	23.34	22.69	21.48	20.35	19.31	18.34	17.45	16.61	15.84	38
39	25.48	24.08	22.80	22.19	21.60	20.50	19.47	18.52	17.63	16.81	16.04	15.32	39
40	24.00	22.76	21.60	21.05	20.52	19.52	18.59	17.72	16.91	16.15	15.44	14.78	40
41	22.56	21.45	20.41	19.92	19.45	18.54	17.70	16.91	16.17	15.48	14.84	14.23	41
42	21.15	20.16	19.24	18.80	18.38	17.57	16.81	16.10	15.43	14.80	14.21	13.66	42
43	19.76	18.90	18.08	17.69	17.31	16.59	15.92	15.28	14.68	14.11	13.58	13.07	43
44	18.41	17.65	16.93	16.59	16.26	15.62	15.02	14.45	13.91	13.41	12.93	12.47	44
45	17.08	16.42	15.79	15.49	15.20	14.64	14.12	13.61	13.14	12.69	12.26	11.85	45
46	15.78	15.21	14.67	14.41	14.16	13.67	13.21	12.77	12.35	11.95	11.58	11.22	46
47	14.50	14.02	13.56	13.33	13.12	12.70	12.30	11.92	11.55	11.21	10.88	10.56	47
48	13.26	12.85	12.46	12.27	12.08	11.73	11.38	11.06	10.75	10.45	10.16	9.89	48
49	12.03	11.69	11.37	11.21	11.05	10.75	10.47	10.19	9.93	9.67	9.43	9.19	49
50	10.83	10.56	10.29	10.16	10.03	9.78	9.55	9.32	9.10	8.88	8.68	8.48	50
51	9.66	9.44	9.22	9.12	9.01	8.81	8.62	8.43	8.25	8.08	7.91	7.75	51
52	8.51	8.34	8.17	8.08	8.00	7.84	7.69	7.54	7.40	7.26	7.12	6.99	52
53	7.38	7.25	7.12	7.06	7.00	6.87	6.76	6.64	6.53	6.42	6.32	6.21	53
54	6.27	6.18	6.08	6.04	5.99	5.90	5.82	5.73	5.65	5.57	5.49	5.41	54
55	5.18	5.12	5.05	5.02	4.99	4.93	4.87	4.81	4.75	4.69	4.64	4.58	55
56	4.12	4.07	4.03	4.01	3.99	3.95	3.91	3.87	3.84	3.80	3.76	3.73	56
57	3.06	3.04	3.02	3.01	2.99	2.97	2.95	2.93	2.91	2.89	2.86	2.84	57
58	2.03	2.02	2.01	2.00	2.00	1.99	1.98	1.97	1.96	1.95	1.94	1.93	58
59	1.01	1.00	1.00	1.00	1.00	1.00	0.99	0.99	0.99	0.99	0.98	0.98	59

Table 8: Multipliers for loss of earnings to pension age 60 (females)

Age at date of trial	−2.0%	−1.5%	−1.0%	−0.75%	−0.5%	0.0%	0.5%	1.0%	1.5%	2.0%	2.5%	3.0%	Age at date of trial
16	70.04	61.77	54.73	51.60	48.72	43.57	39.14	35.32	32.02	29.14	26.64	24.45	16
17	67.65	59.85	53.18	50.22	47.48	42.57	38.33	34.67	31.49	28.72	26.29	24.17	17
18	65.30	57.96	51.66	48.85	46.24	41.57	37.52	34.01	30.96	28.28	25.94	23.88	18
19	63.01	56.10	50.15	47.49	45.02	40.57	36.71	33.35	30.41	27.84	25.58	23.59	19
20	60.76	54.27	48.66	46.14	43.80	39.57	35.90	32.68	29.87	27.39	25.21	23.28	20
21	58.56	52.46	47.18	44.80	42.58	38.58	35.08	32.01	29.31	26.93	24.83	22.97	21
22	56.40	50.69	45.71	43.47	41.37	37.58	34.25	31.32	28.74	26.46	24.44	22.64	22
23	54.29	48.94	44.26	42.15	40.17	36.58	33.42	30.64	28.17	25.98	24.04	22.31	23
24	52.21	47.21	42.83	40.84	38.98	35.58	32.59	29.94	27.59	25.50	23.63	21.97	24
25	50.18	45.51	41.41	39.54	37.79	34.59	31.75	29.24	27.00	25.00	23.21	21.61	25
26	48.19	43.84	40.00	38.25	36.60	33.59	30.91	28.53	26.40	24.49	22.78	21.25	26
27	46.24	42.20	38.61	36.97	35.43	32.59	30.07	27.81	25.79	23.98	22.34	20.87	27
28	44.33	40.58	37.24	35.70	34.26	31.60	29.22	27.09	25.17	23.45	21.89	20.49	28
29	42.46	38.98	35.87	34.45	33.09	30.60	28.37	26.36	24.55	22.91	21.43	20.09	29
30	40.63	37.41	34.53	33.20	31.94	29.61	27.51	25.62	23.91	22.37	20.96	19.69	30
31	38.83	35.86	33.19	31.96	30.79	28.62	26.65	24.88	23.27	21.81	20.48	19.27	31
32	37.08	34.34	31.87	30.73	29.64	27.62	25.79	24.13	22.62	21.24	19.98	18.83	32
33	35.35	32.84	30.57	29.51	28.50	26.63	24.93	23.37	21.96	20.66	19.48	18.39	33
34	33.67	31.37	29.28	28.30	27.37	25.64	24.06	22.61	21.29	20.07	18.96	17.93	34
35	32.01	29.91	28.00	27.10	26.25	24.65	23.18	21.84	20.60	19.47	18.43	17.46	35
36	30.40	28.48	26.73	25.91	25.13	23.66	22.30	21.06	19.91	18.86	17.88	16.98	36
37	28.81	27.08	25.48	24.73	24.02	22.67	21.42	20.28	19.21	18.23	17.32	16.48	37
38	27.26	25.69	24.24	23.56	22.91	21.68	20.54	19.48	18.50	17.60	16.75	15.97	38
39	25.73	24.32	23.02	22.40	21.81	20.69	19.65	18.68	17.78	16.95	16.17	15.44	39
40	24.24	22.98	21.81	21.25	20.72	19.70	18.76	17.88	17.05	16.29	15.57	14.90	40
41	22.78	21.66	20.61	20.11	19.63	18.71	17.86	17.06	16.31	15.61	14.96	14.34	41
42	21.35	20.35	19.42	18.98	18.55	17.73	16.96	16.24	15.56	14.93	14.33	13.77	42
43	19.95	19.07	18.24	17.85	17.47	16.74	16.05	15.41	14.80	14.23	13.69	13.18	43
44	18.58	17.81	17.08	16.74	16.40	15.75	15.15	14.57	14.03	13.52	13.03	12.57	44
45	17.24	16.57	15.93	15.63	15.33	14.77	14.23	13.73	13.25	12.79	12.36	11.95	45
46	15.92	15.34	14.80	14.53	14.28	13.79	13.32	12.87	12.45	12.05	11.67	11.30	46
47	14.63	14.14	13.67	13.45	13.23	12.80	12.40	12.01	11.65	11.30	10.96	10.64	47
48	13.37	12.95	12.56	12.37	12.18	11.82	11.48	11.15	10.83	10.53	10.24	9.96	48
49	12.13	11.79	11.46	11.30	11.14	10.84	10.55	10.27	10.00	9.75	9.50	9.26	49
50	10.92	10.64	10.37	10.24	10.11	9.86	9.62	9.39	9.17	8.95	8.74	8.54	50
51	9.73	9.51	9.29	9.19	9.08	8.88	8.69	8.50	8.31	8.14	7.97	7.80	51
52	8.57	8.39	8.22	8.14	8.06	7.90	7.75	7.60	7.45	7.31	7.17	7.04	52
53	7.43	7.30	7.17	7.10	7.04	6.92	6.80	6.68	6.57	6.46	6.36	6.25	53
54	6.31	6.21	6.12	6.07	6.03	5.94	5.85	5.76	5.68	5.60	5.52	5.44	54
55	5.21	5.14	5.08	5.05	5.02	4.95	4.89	4.83	4.77	4.72	4.66	4.61	55
56	4.13	4.09	4.05	4.03	4.01	3.97	3.93	3.89	3.85	3.82	3.78	3.74	56
57	3.07	3.05	3.03	3.02	3.00	2.98	2.96	2.94	2.92	2.89	2.87	2.85	57
58	2.03	2.02	2.01	2.01	2.00	1.99	1.98	1.97	1.96	1.95	1.94	1.93	58
59	1.01	1.01	1.00	1.00	1.00	1.00	1.00	0.99	0.99	0.99	0.99	0.98	59

Table 9: Multipliers for loss of earnings to pension age 65 (males)

Age at date of trial	\-2.0%	\-1.5%	\-1.0%	\-0.75%	\-0.5%	0.0%	0.5%	1.0%	1.5%	2.0%	2.5%	3.0%	Age at date of trial
16	81.11	70.46	61.56	57.67	54.09	47.80	42.47	37.95	34.08	30.77	27.92	25.46	16
17	78.49	68.41	59.95	56.23	52.82	46.80	41.68	37.32	33.59	30.38	27.61	25.21	17
18	75.93	66.39	58.35	54.82	51.56	45.80	40.89	36.69	33.09	29.98	27.29	24.96	18
19	73.42	64.40	56.78	53.41	50.31	44.80	40.10	36.06	32.58	29.58	26.97	24.70	19
20	70.97	62.45	55.22	52.02	49.07	43.81	39.30	35.42	32.07	29.16	26.64	24.43	20
21	68.57	60.53	53.68	50.64	47.83	42.82	38.50	34.78	31.55	28.74	26.30	24.15	21
22	66.21	58.63	52.16	49.27	46.60	41.82	37.70	34.13	31.02	28.31	25.95	23.87	22
23	63.90	56.77	50.65	47.92	45.38	40.83	36.89	33.47	30.49	27.88	25.59	23.57	23
24	61.64	54.93	49.15	46.57	44.16	39.84	36.08	32.81	29.94	27.43	25.22	23.27	24
25	59.43	53.12	47.68	45.23	42.95	38.85	35.27	32.14	29.39	26.98	24.85	22.96	25
26	57.26	51.35	46.22	43.91	41.75	37.86	34.45	31.46	28.84	26.52	24.47	22.65	26
27	55.14	49.60	44.77	42.59	40.56	36.87	33.63	30.78	28.27	26.05	24.07	22.32	27
28	53.06	47.87	43.34	41.29	39.37	35.88	32.81	30.10	27.70	25.57	23.67	21.98	28
29	51.02	46.17	41.92	39.99	38.18	34.89	31.98	29.40	27.11	25.08	23.26	21.63	29
30	49.03	44.50	40.52	38.71	37.01	33.90	31.15	28.70	26.52	24.58	22.84	21.28	30
31	47.08	42.86	39.14	37.44	35.84	32.92	30.32	28.00	25.93	24.07	22.41	20.91	31
32	45.17	41.25	37.78	36.19	34.69	31.94	29.49	27.29	25.33	23.56	21.97	20.54	32
33	43.31	39.67	36.43	34.95	33.54	30.96	28.65	26.58	24.72	23.04	21.53	20.16	33
34	41.48	38.11	35.10	33.71	32.40	29.99	27.81	25.86	24.10	22.51	21.07	19.77	34
35	39.69	36.57	33.78	32.49	31.27	29.01	26.97	25.14	23.48	21.97	20.60	19.36	35
36	37.94	35.06	32.47	31.28	30.14	28.03	26.13	24.41	22.84	21.42	20.13	18.95	36
37	36.22	33.57	31.18	30.07	29.02	27.06	25.28	23.67	22.20	20.86	19.64	18.52	37
38	34.54	32.11	29.90	28.88	27.90	26.08	24.43	22.92	21.55	20.29	19.13	18.08	38
39	32.89	30.66	28.64	27.69	26.79	25.11	23.57	22.17	20.88	19.70	18.62	17.62	39
40	31.27	29.24	27.38	26.52	25.69	24.13	22.71	21.41	20.21	19.11	18.09	17.16	40
41	29.69	27.84	26.14	25.35	24.59	23.16	21.85	20.64	19.53	18.50	17.55	16.68	41
42	28.14	26.46	24.92	24.19	23.50	22.19	20.98	19.87	18.84	17.88	17.00	16.18	42
43	26.62	25.10	23.70	23.04	22.41	21.22	20.11	19.09	18.14	17.26	16.44	15.68	43
44	25.13	23.77	22.50	21.91	21.33	20.25	19.24	18.30	17.43	16.62	15.86	15.16	44
45	23.68	22.45	21.32	20.78	20.26	19.28	18.36	17.51	16.71	15.97	15.27	14.62	45
46	22.25	21.16	20.14	19.66	19.19	18.31	17.48	16.71	15.98	15.30	14.67	14.07	46
47	20.86	19.89	18.98	18.55	18.14	17.34	16.60	15.90	15.24	14.63	14.05	13.50	47
48	19.49	18.64	17.84	17.45	17.08	16.38	15.71	15.09	14.50	13.94	13.42	12.92	48
49	18.15	17.41	16.70	16.37	16.04	15.41	14.82	14.27	13.74	13.24	12.77	12.33	49
50	16.85	16.20	15.58	15.29	15.00	14.46	13.94	13.44	12.98	12.53	12.11	11.71	50
51	15.57	15.01	14.48	14.22	13.98	13.50	13.04	12.61	12.20	11.81	11.44	11.09	51
52	14.32	13.84	13.39	13.17	12.95	12.54	12.15	11.77	11.42	11.08	10.75	10.44	52
53	13.09	12.69	12.30	12.12	11.94	11.59	11.25	10.93	10.62	10.33	10.05	9.78	53
54	11.89	11.56	11.24	11.08	10.93	10.63	10.35	10.08	9.82	9.57	9.33	9.10	54
55	10.71	10.44	10.18	10.05	9.92	9.68	9.45	9.22	9.00	8.79	8.59	8.40	55
56	9.56	9.34	9.13	9.03	8.93	8.73	8.54	8.35	8.17	8.00	7.84	7.67	56
57	8.43	8.26	8.09	8.01	7.93	7.77	7.62	7.47	7.33	7.19	7.06	6.93	57
58	7.32	7.19	7.06	7.00	6.94	6.82	6.70	6.59	6.48	6.37	6.26	6.16	58
59	6.22	6.13	6.03	5.99	5.94	5.85	5.77	5.68	5.60	5.52	5.45	5.37	59
60	5.14	5.08	5.01	4.98	4.95	4.89	4.83	4.77	4.71	4.66	4.60	4.55	60
61	4.09	4.04	4.00	3.98	3.96	3.92	3.89	3.85	3.81	3.77	3.74	3.70	61
62	3.04	3.02	3.00	2.99	2.98	2.95	2.93	2.91	2.89	2.87	2.85	2.83	62
63	2.02	2.01	2.00	1.99	1.99	1.98	1.97	1.96	1.95	1.94	1.93	1.92	63
64	1.00	1.00	1.00	1.00	1.00	0.99	0.99	0.99	0.99	0.98	0.98	0.98	64

A8: The Ogden Tables

Table 10: Multipliers for loss of earnings to pension age 65 (females)

Age at date of trial	\-2.0%	\-1.5%	\-1.0%	\-0.75%	\-0.5%	0.0%	0.5%	1.0%	1.5%	2.0%	2.5%	3.0%	Age at date of trial
16	82.26	71.41	62.34	58.38	54.74	48.34	42.93	38.33	34.41	31.05	28.16	25.66	16
17	79.62	69.34	60.72	56.94	53.47	47.34	42.14	37.71	33.91	30.66	27.85	25.41	17
18	77.03	67.31	59.12	55.52	52.20	46.34	41.35	37.08	33.42	30.26	27.53	25.16	18
19	74.50	65.30	57.53	54.11	50.95	45.34	40.55	36.45	32.91	29.86	27.21	24.91	19
20	72.02	63.33	55.96	52.71	49.70	44.34	39.75	35.81	32.40	29.45	26.88	24.64	20
21	69.59	61.39	54.41	51.32	48.45	43.34	38.95	35.16	31.88	29.03	26.54	24.37	21
22	67.20	59.48	52.87	49.93	47.21	42.34	38.15	34.51	31.35	28.60	26.20	24.08	22
23	64.87	57.59	51.35	48.56	45.98	41.35	37.33	33.85	30.82	28.16	25.84	23.79	23
24	62.58	55.73	49.84	47.20	44.75	40.35	36.52	33.19	30.27	27.72	25.47	23.49	24
25	60.34	53.91	48.35	45.85	43.53	39.35	35.70	32.51	29.72	27.27	25.10	23.19	25
26	58.14	52.11	46.87	44.52	42.32	38.35	34.88	31.84	29.16	26.80	24.72	22.87	26
27	55.99	50.33	45.41	43.19	41.11	37.35	34.05	31.15	28.60	26.33	24.33	22.54	27
28	53.88	48.59	43.96	41.87	39.91	36.36	33.23	30.46	28.02	25.85	23.93	22.21	28
29	51.82	46.87	42.53	40.56	38.72	35.36	32.39	29.77	27.44	25.36	23.51	21.86	29
30	49.80	45.18	41.12	39.27	37.53	34.36	31.56	29.06	26.84	24.87	23.09	21.51	30
31	47.82	43.52	39.72	37.98	36.35	33.37	30.72	28.35	26.25	24.36	22.66	21.14	31
32	45.88	41.88	38.33	36.71	35.18	32.38	29.87	27.64	25.64	23.84	22.22	20.77	32
33	43.98	40.27	36.96	35.45	34.01	31.38	29.03	26.92	25.02	23.31	21.77	20.38	33
34	42.12	38.68	35.60	34.19	32.85	30.39	28.18	26.19	24.39	22.78	21.31	19.98	34
35	40.30	37.11	34.26	32.95	31.70	29.40	27.32	25.45	23.76	22.23	20.84	19.57	35
36	38.51	35.58	32.93	31.71	30.56	28.41	26.47	24.71	23.12	21.67	20.35	19.15	36
37	36.76	34.06	31.62	30.49	29.42	27.42	25.61	23.96	22.47	21.10	19.86	18.72	37
38	35.05	32.57	30.32	29.28	28.28	26.43	24.74	23.21	21.81	20.52	19.35	18.28	38
39	33.38	31.10	29.04	28.07	27.16	25.44	23.88	22.44	21.14	19.93	18.83	17.82	39
40	31.73	29.66	27.76	26.88	26.04	24.45	23.00	21.68	20.46	19.33	18.30	17.35	40
41	30.12	28.24	26.51	25.70	24.92	23.47	22.13	20.90	19.77	18.72	17.76	16.86	41
42	28.55	26.84	25.26	24.52	23.81	22.48	21.25	20.12	19.07	18.10	17.20	16.37	42
43	27.01	25.46	24.03	23.36	22.71	21.50	20.37	19.33	18.36	17.46	16.63	15.85	43
44	25.49	24.10	22.81	22.20	21.62	20.51	19.48	18.53	17.64	16.82	16.05	15.33	44
45	24.02	22.77	21.61	21.06	20.53	19.53	18.60	17.73	16.92	16.16	15.45	14.79	45
46	22.57	21.46	20.42	19.93	19.45	18.55	17.71	16.92	16.18	15.49	14.84	14.23	46
47	21.15	20.17	19.24	18.80	18.38	17.57	16.81	16.10	15.43	14.81	14.22	13.66	47
48	19.77	18.90	18.08	17.69	17.31	16.59	15.92	15.28	14.68	14.11	13.58	13.08	48
49	18.41	17.65	16.93	16.59	16.26	15.62	15.02	14.45	13.91	13.41	12.93	12.47	49
50	17.08	16.42	15.80	15.50	15.21	14.65	14.12	13.62	13.14	12.69	12.26	11.85	50
51	15.78	15.21	14.67	14.41	14.16	13.67	13.21	12.77	12.35	11.96	11.58	11.22	51
52	14.51	14.02	13.56	13.34	13.12	12.70	12.30	11.92	11.56	11.21	10.88	10.56	52
53	13.26	12.85	12.46	12.27	12.09	11.73	11.39	11.06	10.75	10.45	10.17	9.89	53
54	12.04	11.70	11.37	11.22	11.06	10.76	10.47	10.20	9.93	9.68	9.43	9.20	54
55	10.84	10.56	10.30	10.17	10.04	9.79	9.55	9.32	9.10	8.89	8.68	8.49	55
56	9.67	9.44	9.23	9.12	9.02	8.82	8.63	8.44	8.26	8.09	7.92	7.75	56
57	8.52	8.34	8.17	8.09	8.01	7.85	7.70	7.55	7.40	7.26	7.13	7.00	57
58	7.39	7.25	7.13	7.06	7.00	6.88	6.76	6.65	6.53	6.43	6.32	6.22	58
59	6.28	6.18	6.09	6.04	5.99	5.91	5.82	5.73	5.65	5.57	5.49	5.41	59
60	5.19	5.12	5.05	5.02	4.99	4.93	4.87	4.81	4.75	4.69	4.64	4.58	60
61	4.11	4.07	4.03	4.01	3.99	3.95	3.91	3.87	3.84	3.80	3.76	3.73	61
62	3.06	3.04	3.02	3.00	2.99	2.97	2.95	2.93	2.91	2.88	2.86	2.84	62
63	2.03	2.02	2.01	2.00	2.00	1.99	1.98	1.97	1.96	1.95	1.94	1.93	63
64	1.01	1.00	1.00	1.00	1.00	1.00	0.99	0.99	0.99	0.99	0.98	0.98	64

A8: The Ogden Tables

Table 11: Multipliers for loss of earnings to pension age 70 (males)

Age at date of trial	\-2.0%	\-1.5%	\-1.0%	\-0.75%	\-0.5%	0.0%	0.5%	1.0%	1.5%	2.0%	2.5%	3.0%	Age at date of trial
16	93.75	80.18	69.05	64.24	59.87	52.26	45.93	40.62	36.16	32.38	29.18	26.44	16
17	90.86	77.97	67.35	62.75	58.57	51.26	45.15	40.02	35.69	32.02	28.89	26.22	17
18	88.04	75.80	65.68	61.28	57.27	50.25	44.37	39.41	35.22	31.65	28.61	25.99	18
19	85.28	73.67	64.03	59.83	55.99	49.26	43.59	38.81	34.74	31.28	28.31	25.76	19
20	82.58	71.57	62.39	58.38	54.71	48.26	42.81	38.19	34.26	30.90	28.01	25.52	20
21	79.94	69.50	60.78	56.95	53.44	47.26	42.03	37.58	33.78	30.52	27.71	25.28	21
22	77.35	67.47	59.17	55.53	52.18	46.27	41.24	36.95	33.28	30.12	27.39	25.03	22
23	74.81	65.46	57.59	54.12	50.93	45.27	40.45	36.32	32.78	29.72	27.07	24.77	23
24	72.32	63.49	56.02	52.72	49.68	44.27	39.65	35.68	32.26	29.31	26.74	24.50	24
25	69.89	61.55	54.47	51.33	48.44	43.28	38.85	35.04	31.75	28.89	26.40	24.23	25
26	67.50	59.64	52.93	49.96	47.20	42.29	38.05	34.39	31.22	28.47	26.06	23.95	26
27	65.17	57.76	51.42	48.60	45.98	41.29	37.25	33.74	30.69	28.03	25.70	23.66	27
28	62.88	55.91	49.92	47.24	44.76	40.30	36.44	33.08	30.15	27.59	25.34	23.36	28
29	60.64	54.08	48.43	45.90	43.54	39.31	35.63	32.41	29.61	27.14	24.97	23.05	29
30	58.45	52.29	46.96	44.57	42.34	38.32	34.81	31.74	29.05	26.68	24.59	22.74	30
31	56.31	50.53	45.51	43.25	41.14	37.33	34.00	31.07	28.49	26.22	24.20	22.42	31
32	54.21	48.80	44.08	41.95	39.96	36.35	33.18	30.39	27.93	25.75	23.81	22.09	32
33	52.17	47.10	42.67	40.67	38.79	35.37	32.37	29.71	27.36	25.27	23.41	21.75	33
34	50.16	45.43	41.28	39.39	37.62	34.40	31.55	29.02	26.78	24.79	23.00	21.41	34
35	48.20	43.78	39.89	38.12	36.46	33.42	30.73	28.33	26.20	24.29	22.58	21.05	35
36	46.28	42.16	38.53	36.87	35.31	32.45	29.90	27.63	25.60	23.79	22.15	20.69	36
37	44.39	40.57	37.18	35.62	34.16	31.47	29.07	26.93	25.00	23.27	21.72	20.31	37
38	42.55	39.00	35.84	34.39	33.02	30.50	28.24	26.21	24.39	22.75	21.27	19.93	38
39	40.74	37.45	34.51	33.16	31.88	29.52	27.40	25.49	23.77	22.21	20.80	19.53	39
40	38.96	35.92	33.20	31.94	30.75	28.55	26.56	24.76	23.14	21.67	20.33	19.12	40
41	37.23	34.42	31.90	30.73	29.63	27.57	25.71	24.03	22.50	21.11	19.85	18.70	41
42	35.53	32.95	30.62	29.54	28.51	26.60	24.87	23.29	21.86	20.55	19.36	18.26	42
43	33.86	31.50	29.35	28.35	27.40	25.63	24.02	22.55	21.20	19.98	18.85	17.82	43
44	32.23	30.07	28.10	27.18	26.30	24.66	23.17	21.80	20.54	19.39	18.34	17.36	44
45	30.64	28.66	26.86	26.01	25.21	23.70	22.31	21.04	19.87	18.80	17.81	16.90	45
46	29.08	27.28	25.63	24.86	24.12	22.73	21.45	20.28	19.19	18.19	17.27	16.41	46
47	27.55	25.92	24.42	23.72	23.04	21.77	20.59	19.51	18.51	17.58	16.72	15.92	47
48	26.06	24.58	23.22	22.58	21.97	20.81	19.73	18.74	17.81	16.95	16.16	15.41	48
49	24.60	23.27	22.04	21.46	20.91	19.85	18.87	17.96	17.11	16.32	15.58	14.90	49
50	23.17	21.98	20.88	20.36	19.85	18.90	18.01	17.18	16.40	15.68	15.00	14.37	50
51	21.78	20.72	19.73	19.26	18.81	17.95	17.14	16.39	15.69	15.02	14.40	13.82	51
52	20.42	19.48	18.60	18.18	17.78	17.00	16.28	15.60	14.96	14.36	13.80	13.27	52
53	19.09	18.26	17.48	17.11	16.75	16.06	15.41	14.81	14.23	13.69	13.18	12.70	53
54	17.79	17.06	16.38	16.05	15.73	15.12	14.55	14.01	13.49	13.01	12.55	12.11	54
55	16.51	15.88	15.29	15.00	14.72	14.19	13.68	13.20	12.75	12.31	11.90	11.52	55
56	15.27	14.73	14.21	13.96	13.72	13.25	12.81	12.39	11.99	11.61	11.25	10.90	56
57	14.05	13.59	13.14	12.93	12.72	12.32	11.94	11.57	11.22	10.89	10.57	10.27	57
58	12.85	12.46	12.09	11.91	11.73	11.39	11.06	10.75	10.45	10.16	9.88	9.62	58
59	11.68	11.35	11.04	10.89	10.74	10.45	10.17	9.91	9.66	9.41	9.18	8.95	59
60	10.52	10.26	10.00	9.87	9.75	9.51	9.28	9.06	8.85	8.65	8.45	8.26	60
61	9.39	9.18	8.97	8.87	8.77	8.58	8.39	8.21	8.04	7.87	7.71	7.55	61
62	8.28	8.11	7.95	7.87	7.79	7.64	7.49	7.35	7.21	7.07	6.94	6.82	62
63	7.19	7.06	6.94	6.88	6.82	6.70	6.59	6.48	6.37	6.27	6.16	6.06	63
64	6.12	6.03	5.94	5.90	5.85	5.77	5.68	5.60	5.52	5.44	5.36	5.29	64
65	5.07	5.01	4.95	4.92	4.89	4.83	4.77	4.71	4.65	4.60	4.54	4.49	65
66	4.04	4.00	3.96	3.94	3.92	3.88	3.84	3.81	3.77	3.73	3.70	3.66	66
67	3.02	3.00	2.97	2.96	2.95	2.93	2.91	2.89	2.86	2.84	2.82	2.80	67
68	2.01	2.00	1.99	1.98	1.98	1.97	1.96	1.95	1.94	1.93	1.92	1.91	68
69	1.00	1.00	1.00	0.99	0.99	0.99	0.99	0.99	0.98	0.98	0.98	0.98	69

Multiplier calculated with allowance for projected mortality from the 2008–based population projections and rate of return of

A8: The Ogden Tables

Table 12: Multipliers for loss of earnings to pension age 70 (females)

Age at date of trial	\multicolumn{12}{c}{Multiplier calculated with allowance for projected mortality from the 2008–based population projections and rate of return of}	Age at date of trial
	-2.0%	-1.5%	-1.0%	-0.75%	-0.5%	0.0%	0.5%	1.0%	1.5%	2.0%	2.5%	3.0%	
16	95.47	81.58	70.18	65.26	60.79	53.01	46.54	41.12	36.57	32.73	29.47	26.68	16
17	92.56	79.35	68.47	63.77	59.48	52.01	45.76	40.53	36.11	32.37	29.19	26.46	17
18	89.71	77.16	66.79	62.29	58.18	51.00	44.99	39.93	35.65	32.01	28.91	26.24	18
19	86.92	75.00	65.12	60.82	56.89	50.00	44.21	39.32	35.18	31.64	28.62	26.02	19
20	84.18	72.88	63.47	59.37	55.61	49.00	43.43	38.71	34.70	31.27	28.32	25.79	20
21	81.50	70.79	61.84	57.92	54.33	48.00	42.64	38.09	34.21	30.88	28.02	25.55	21
22	78.87	68.73	60.22	56.49	53.06	47.00	41.85	37.47	33.72	30.49	27.71	25.30	22
23	76.30	66.70	58.62	55.06	51.79	46.00	41.06	36.84	33.22	30.09	27.39	25.04	23
24	73.77	64.70	57.04	53.65	50.53	44.99	40.26	36.20	32.71	29.68	27.06	24.78	24
25	71.30	62.73	55.47	52.25	49.28	43.99	39.46	35.56	32.19	29.27	26.73	24.51	25
26	68.88	60.80	53.91	50.86	48.03	42.99	38.65	34.91	31.67	28.85	26.39	24.23	26
27	66.51	58.89	52.38	49.48	46.80	41.99	37.85	34.26	31.13	28.41	26.03	23.95	27
28	64.19	57.01	50.86	48.11	45.56	40.99	37.03	33.59	30.60	27.98	25.68	23.65	28
29	61.91	55.17	49.36	46.76	44.34	39.99	36.22	32.93	30.05	27.53	25.31	23.35	29
30	59.68	53.35	47.87	45.41	43.12	39.00	35.40	32.25	29.50	27.07	24.93	23.04	30
31	57.50	51.56	46.40	44.08	41.91	38.00	34.58	31.58	28.94	26.61	24.55	22.72	31
32	55.37	49.79	44.94	42.76	40.71	37.01	33.75	30.89	28.37	26.13	24.15	22.39	32
33	53.27	48.06	43.51	41.44	39.52	36.01	32.92	30.20	27.79	25.65	23.75	22.05	33
34	51.22	46.35	42.08	40.14	38.33	35.02	32.09	29.50	27.21	25.16	23.34	21.70	34
35	49.22	44.67	40.67	38.85	37.14	34.02	31.26	28.80	26.61	24.66	22.91	21.35	35
36	47.25	43.02	39.28	37.57	35.97	33.03	30.42	28.09	26.01	24.15	22.48	20.98	36
37	45.32	41.39	37.90	36.30	34.80	32.04	29.58	27.37	25.40	23.63	22.04	20.60	37
38	43.44	39.79	36.54	35.05	33.64	31.05	28.73	26.65	24.78	23.10	21.58	20.21	38
39	41.59	38.21	35.19	33.80	32.48	30.06	27.88	25.92	24.16	22.56	21.12	19.81	39
40	39.78	36.66	33.85	32.56	31.34	29.07	27.03	25.19	23.52	22.01	20.65	19.40	40
41	38.01	35.13	32.53	31.33	30.20	28.08	26.18	24.45	22.88	21.46	20.16	18.98	41
42	36.28	33.62	31.23	30.12	29.06	27.10	25.32	23.70	22.23	20.89	19.66	18.54	42
43	34.58	32.14	29.94	28.91	27.93	26.11	24.46	22.95	21.57	20.31	19.15	18.10	43
44	32.92	30.69	28.66	27.72	26.81	25.13	23.59	22.19	20.90	19.72	18.63	17.64	44
45	31.29	29.26	27.40	26.53	25.70	24.15	22.73	21.42	20.22	19.12	18.10	17.17	45
46	29.70	27.85	26.15	25.36	24.60	23.17	21.86	20.65	19.54	18.51	17.56	16.68	46
47	28.15	26.47	24.92	24.20	23.50	22.19	20.99	19.87	18.84	17.89	17.01	16.19	47
48	26.63	25.11	23.71	23.05	22.41	21.22	20.11	19.09	18.14	17.26	16.44	15.68	48
49	25.14	23.77	22.51	21.91	21.34	20.25	19.24	18.30	17.43	16.62	15.86	15.16	49
50	23.68	22.46	21.32	20.78	20.27	19.28	18.36	17.51	16.71	15.97	15.27	14.62	50
51	22.26	21.17	20.15	19.67	19.20	18.31	17.49	16.71	15.99	15.31	14.67	14.07	51
52	20.87	19.90	18.99	18.56	18.14	17.35	16.60	15.91	15.25	14.63	14.05	13.51	52
53	19.50	18.65	17.85	17.46	17.09	16.39	15.72	15.09	14.50	13.95	13.42	12.93	53
54	18.17	17.42	16.72	16.38	16.05	15.43	14.83	14.28	13.75	13.25	12.78	12.33	54
55	16.86	16.21	15.60	15.30	15.02	14.47	13.95	13.45	12.99	12.54	12.12	11.72	55
56	15.58	15.02	14.49	14.24	13.99	13.51	13.05	12.62	12.21	11.82	11.45	11.09	56
57	14.33	13.85	13.40	13.18	12.96	12.55	12.16	11.78	11.43	11.09	10.76	10.45	57
58	13.10	12.70	12.31	12.13	11.95	11.59	11.26	10.94	10.63	10.34	10.05	9.78	58
59	11.89	11.56	11.24	11.08	10.93	10.64	10.35	10.08	9.82	9.57	9.33	9.10	59
60	10.71	10.44	10.18	10.05	9.92	9.68	9.44	9.22	9.00	8.79	8.59	8.39	60
61	9.55	9.33	9.12	9.02	8.92	8.72	8.53	8.35	8.17	8.00	7.83	7.67	61
62	8.42	8.25	8.08	8.00	7.92	7.76	7.61	7.46	7.32	7.18	7.05	6.92	62
63	7.30	7.17	7.05	6.98	6.92	6.80	6.69	6.57	6.47	6.36	6.25	6.15	63
64	6.21	6.12	6.02	5.98	5.93	5.85	5.76	5.68	5.59	5.51	5.44	5.36	64
65	5.14	5.07	5.01	4.98	4.95	4.89	4.83	4.77	4.71	4.65	4.60	4.54	65
66	4.08	4.04	4.00	3.98	3.96	3.92	3.88	3.85	3.81	3.77	3.74	3.70	66
67	3.04	3.02	3.00	2.99	2.98	2.95	2.93	2.91	2.89	2.87	2.85	2.83	67
68	2.02	2.01	2.00	1.99	1.99	1.98	1.97	1.96	1.95	1.94	1.93	1.92	68
69	1.00	1.00	1.00	1.00	1.00	0.99	0.99	0.99	0.99	0.98	0.98	0.98	69

Table 13: Multipliers for loss of earnings to pension age 75 (males)

Age at date of trial	-2.0%	-1.5%	-1.0%	-0.75%	-0.5%	0.0%	0.5%	1.0%	1.5%	2.0%	2.5%	3.0%	Age at date of trial
16	107.05	90.16	76.55	70.74	65.51	56.51	49.13	43.04	37.99	33.77	30.23	27.24	16
17	103.88	87.79	74.76	69.20	64.17	55.50	48.37	42.46	37.55	33.44	29.97	27.04	17
18	100.78	85.45	73.01	67.67	62.84	54.49	47.60	41.88	37.10	33.10	29.71	26.84	18
19	97.75	83.16	71.27	66.16	61.52	53.49	46.83	41.29	36.65	32.75	29.44	26.63	19
20	94.79	80.91	69.55	64.66	60.21	52.48	46.06	40.70	36.20	32.40	29.17	26.42	20
21	91.89	78.69	67.86	63.17	58.91	51.48	45.29	40.11	35.74	32.04	28.89	26.20	21
22	89.04	76.51	66.17	61.69	57.61	50.48	44.52	39.50	35.27	31.67	28.61	25.98	22
23	86.25	74.36	64.51	60.23	56.32	49.48	43.74	38.89	34.79	31.30	28.31	25.74	23
24	83.52	72.24	62.86	58.77	55.04	48.48	42.95	38.28	34.31	30.92	28.01	25.51	24
25	80.85	70.15	61.23	57.33	53.76	47.48	42.17	37.66	33.82	30.53	27.70	25.26	25
26	78.23	68.10	59.63	55.91	52.50	46.48	41.38	37.04	33.32	30.14	27.39	25.01	26
27	75.67	66.09	58.03	54.49	51.24	45.48	40.59	36.41	32.82	29.74	27.07	24.75	27
28	73.16	64.10	56.46	53.09	49.99	44.48	39.79	35.77	32.31	29.32	26.74	24.48	28
29	70.70	62.14	54.90	51.69	48.74	43.49	38.99	35.13	31.79	28.91	26.40	24.21	29
30	68.29	60.22	53.35	50.31	47.50	42.49	38.19	34.48	31.27	28.48	26.05	23.93	30
31	65.95	58.33	51.84	48.95	46.28	41.50	37.39	33.83	30.74	28.05	25.70	23.64	31
32	63.65	56.48	50.34	47.60	45.06	40.52	36.59	33.18	30.21	27.62	25.35	23.35	32
33	61.41	54.66	48.86	46.27	43.86	39.54	35.79	32.52	29.67	27.18	24.98	23.05	33
34	59.22	52.87	47.40	44.95	42.66	38.56	34.98	31.86	29.13	26.73	24.61	22.74	34
35	57.06	51.11	45.95	43.63	41.47	37.58	34.17	31.19	28.58	26.27	24.23	22.43	35
36	54.96	49.37	44.52	42.33	40.29	36.60	33.36	30.52	28.02	25.80	23.84	22.10	36
37	52.90	47.67	43.11	41.05	39.12	35.62	32.55	29.84	27.45	25.33	23.45	21.77	37
38	50.87	45.98	41.70	39.76	37.95	34.64	31.73	29.16	26.87	24.85	23.04	21.42	38
39	48.89	44.33	40.31	38.49	36.78	33.67	30.91	28.46	26.29	24.35	22.62	21.07	39
40	46.95	42.69	38.94	37.23	35.62	32.69	30.08	27.76	25.70	23.85	22.19	20.70	40
41	45.05	41.09	37.58	35.98	34.47	31.71	29.25	27.06	25.10	23.34	21.75	20.33	41
42	43.19	39.51	36.24	34.74	33.33	30.74	28.42	26.35	24.49	22.81	21.31	19.95	42
43	41.37	37.96	34.91	33.52	32.20	29.77	27.59	25.63	23.87	22.29	20.85	19.55	43
44	39.59	36.43	33.60	32.30	31.07	28.80	26.76	24.91	23.25	21.75	20.39	19.15	44
45	37.85	34.93	32.31	31.10	29.95	27.83	25.92	24.19	22.62	21.20	19.91	18.73	45
46	36.14	33.45	31.03	29.91	28.84	26.87	25.08	23.46	21.98	20.64	19.42	18.31	46
47	34.47	32.00	29.76	28.73	27.74	25.90	24.24	22.72	21.34	20.08	18.93	17.87	47
48	32.84	30.58	28.52	27.56	26.65	24.95	23.39	21.98	20.69	19.50	18.42	17.42	48
49	31.25	29.18	27.29	26.41	25.56	23.99	22.55	21.24	20.03	18.92	17.90	16.97	49
50	29.70	27.81	26.07	25.27	24.49	23.04	21.71	20.49	19.37	18.33	17.38	16.50	50
51	28.18	26.46	24.88	24.14	23.43	22.10	20.87	19.74	18.70	17.74	16.85	16.03	51
52	26.70	25.14	23.70	23.03	22.38	21.16	20.03	18.99	18.03	17.13	16.31	15.54	52
53	25.26	23.85	22.54	21.93	21.34	20.23	19.19	18.24	17.35	16.52	15.76	15.04	53
54	23.85	22.58	21.40	20.85	20.31	19.30	18.35	17.48	16.66	15.90	15.20	14.53	54
55	22.48	21.34	20.28	19.78	19.29	18.37	17.52	16.72	15.98	15.28	14.63	14.02	55
56	21.13	20.12	19.17	18.72	18.28	17.46	16.68	15.96	15.28	14.64	14.05	13.49	56
57	19.82	18.92	18.07	17.67	17.28	16.54	15.85	15.19	14.58	14.00	13.46	12.95	57
58	18.53	17.74	16.99	16.63	16.29	15.63	15.00	14.42	13.86	13.34	12.85	12.39	58
59	17.27	16.57	15.91	15.60	15.29	14.71	14.16	13.63	13.14	12.67	12.23	11.81	59
60	16.03	15.42	14.85	14.57	14.30	13.79	13.30	12.84	12.40	11.99	11.60	11.22	60
61	14.81	14.29	13.79	13.55	13.32	12.87	12.45	12.04	11.66	11.29	10.95	10.61	61
62	13.62	13.18	12.75	12.55	12.35	11.96	11.59	11.24	10.91	10.59	10.28	9.99	62
63	12.46	12.09	11.73	11.55	11.38	11.05	10.74	10.44	10.15	9.88	9.61	9.36	63
64	11.33	11.02	10.72	10.57	10.43	10.15	9.89	9.63	9.39	9.15	8.93	8.71	64
65	10.22	9.97	9.72	9.60	9.48	9.25	9.03	8.82	8.61	8.42	8.23	8.04	65
66	9.14	8.93	8.73	8.64	8.54	8.36	8.18	8.00	7.83	7.67	7.52	7.36	66
67	8.08	7.92	7.76	7.68	7.61	7.46	7.32	7.18	7.04	6.91	6.79	6.66	67
68	7.04	6.91	6.79	6.73	6.67	6.56	6.45	6.34	6.24	6.14	6.04	5.94	68
69	6.01	5.92	5.83	5.78	5.74	5.66	5.58	5.50	5.42	5.34	5.27	5.19	69
70	4.99	4.93	4.87	4.84	4.81	4.75	4.69	4.63	4.58	4.52	4.47	4.42	70
71	3.98	3.94	3.90	3.88	3.86	3.83	3.79	3.75	3.72	3.68	3.65	3.61	71
72	2.98	2.96	2.94	2.93	2.92	2.89	2.87	2.85	2.83	2.81	2.79	2.77	72
73	1.99	1.98	1.97	1.96	1.96	1.95	1.94	1.93	1.92	1.91	1.90	1.89	73
74	1.00	0.99	0.99	0.99	0.99	0.99	0.98	0.98	0.98	0.98	0.97	0.97	74

A8: The Ogden Tables

Table 14: Multipliers for loss of earnings to pension age 75 (females)

Age at date of trial	\-2.0%	\-1.5%	\-1.0%	\-0.75%	\-0.5%	0.0%	0.5%	1.0%	1.5%	2.0%	2.5%	3.0%	Age at date of trial
16	109.63	92.19	78.15	72.17	66.79	57.53	49.95	43.70	38.52	34.21	30.59	27.53	16
17	106.42	89.80	76.36	70.62	65.44	56.52	49.19	43.13	38.09	33.88	30.34	27.34	17
18	103.28	87.44	74.59	69.09	64.11	55.51	48.43	42.55	37.65	33.55	30.08	27.15	18
19	100.20	85.12	72.84	67.56	62.78	54.51	47.66	41.97	37.21	33.21	29.82	26.95	19
20	97.19	82.84	71.11	66.05	61.47	53.50	46.90	41.38	36.76	32.86	29.56	26.74	20
21	94.24	80.59	69.39	64.55	60.15	52.50	46.13	40.79	36.30	32.51	29.28	26.53	21
22	91.35	78.38	67.69	63.06	58.85	51.49	45.35	40.19	35.84	32.15	29.00	26.31	22
23	88.51	76.19	66.01	61.58	57.55	50.49	44.57	39.58	35.37	31.78	28.71	26.08	23
24	85.73	74.04	64.34	60.12	56.25	49.48	43.79	38.97	34.89	31.40	28.42	25.85	24
25	83.01	71.93	62.69	58.66	54.97	48.48	43.00	38.35	34.40	31.02	28.12	25.61	25
26	80.34	69.84	61.06	57.22	53.69	47.47	42.21	37.73	33.91	30.63	27.81	25.37	26
27	77.73	67.79	59.45	55.78	52.42	46.47	41.41	37.10	33.41	30.23	27.49	25.11	27
28	75.17	65.77	57.85	54.36	51.15	45.46	40.62	36.47	32.90	29.83	27.17	24.85	28
29	72.67	63.79	56.27	52.96	49.90	44.46	39.82	35.83	32.39	29.42	26.84	24.59	29
30	70.22	61.83	54.71	51.56	48.65	43.46	39.01	35.18	31.87	29.00	26.50	24.31	30
31	67.82	59.91	53.17	50.17	47.40	42.46	38.20	34.53	31.34	28.57	26.15	24.03	31
32	65.47	58.01	51.64	48.80	46.17	41.46	37.40	33.87	30.81	28.13	25.79	23.74	32
33	63.16	56.15	50.13	47.44	44.94	40.46	36.58	33.21	30.26	27.69	25.43	23.44	33
34	60.91	54.31	48.63	46.09	43.72	39.47	35.77	32.54	29.72	27.24	25.06	23.13	34
35	58.70	52.51	47.15	44.75	42.51	38.47	34.95	31.86	29.16	26.78	24.68	22.82	35
36	56.54	50.73	45.69	43.42	41.30	37.47	34.12	31.18	28.59	26.31	24.29	22.49	36
37	54.42	48.98	44.24	42.10	40.10	36.48	33.30	30.49	28.02	25.83	23.89	22.16	37
38	52.35	47.26	42.81	40.80	38.91	35.49	32.47	29.80	27.44	25.34	23.48	21.81	38
39	50.32	45.57	41.40	39.50	37.73	34.49	31.64	29.10	26.85	24.85	23.06	21.46	39
40	48.33	43.90	40.00	38.22	36.55	33.50	30.80	28.40	26.26	24.35	22.63	21.10	40
41	46.38	42.26	38.61	36.95	35.38	32.51	29.96	27.69	25.65	23.83	22.20	20.73	41
42	44.48	40.64	37.24	35.69	34.22	31.53	29.12	26.97	25.04	23.31	21.75	20.34	42
43	42.61	39.06	35.89	34.44	33.06	30.54	28.28	26.25	24.42	22.78	21.29	19.95	43
44	40.79	37.49	34.55	33.20	31.92	29.55	27.43	25.52	23.79	22.24	20.82	19.55	44
45	39.00	35.96	33.23	31.97	30.78	28.57	26.58	24.79	23.16	21.69	20.35	19.13	45
46	37.26	34.45	31.93	30.76	29.65	27.59	25.73	24.05	22.52	21.13	19.86	18.71	46
47	35.55	32.97	30.64	29.56	28.53	26.62	24.88	23.30	21.87	20.56	19.36	18.27	47
48	33.88	31.51	29.37	28.37	27.42	25.64	24.03	22.56	21.21	19.98	18.86	17.83	48
49	32.25	30.08	28.11	27.19	26.31	24.67	23.18	21.81	20.55	19.40	18.34	17.37	49
50	30.66	28.68	26.87	26.03	25.22	23.71	22.32	21.05	19.88	18.81	17.82	16.90	50
51	29.10	27.30	25.65	24.88	24.14	22.75	21.47	20.29	19.20	18.20	17.28	16.42	51
52	27.58	25.94	24.44	23.73	23.06	21.78	20.61	19.52	18.52	17.59	16.73	15.93	52
53	26.08	24.61	23.25	22.61	21.99	20.83	19.75	18.75	17.83	16.97	16.17	15.43	53
54	24.63	23.30	22.07	21.49	20.93	19.87	18.89	17.98	17.13	16.34	15.60	14.91	54
55	23.20	22.01	20.91	20.38	19.88	18.92	18.03	17.20	16.42	15.69	15.02	14.38	55
56	21.81	20.75	19.76	19.29	18.83	17.97	17.16	16.41	15.70	15.04	14.42	13.84	56
57	20.45	19.50	18.62	18.20	17.80	17.02	16.30	15.62	14.98	14.38	13.81	13.28	57
58	19.11	18.28	17.50	17.13	16.77	16.08	15.43	14.82	14.25	13.70	13.19	12.71	58
59	17.80	17.07	16.39	16.06	15.74	15.13	14.56	14.02	13.50	13.02	12.56	12.12	59
60	16.52	15.88	15.29	15.00	14.72	14.19	13.68	13.20	12.75	12.32	11.91	11.52	60
61	15.26	14.71	14.20	13.95	13.71	13.24	12.80	12.38	11.98	11.60	11.24	10.89	61
62	14.03	13.56	13.12	12.91	12.70	12.30	11.92	11.56	11.21	10.88	10.56	10.26	62
63	12.83	12.43	12.06	11.88	11.70	11.36	11.04	10.72	10.42	10.14	9.86	9.60	63
64	11.65	11.33	11.01	10.86	10.71	10.43	10.15	9.89	9.63	9.39	9.16	8.93	64
65	10.50	10.24	9.98	9.86	9.73	9.50	9.27	9.05	8.84	8.63	8.43	8.24	65
66	9.38	9.16	8.96	8.86	8.76	8.57	8.38	8.20	8.03	7.86	7.70	7.54	66
67	8.28	8.11	7.95	7.87	7.79	7.64	7.49	7.35	7.21	7.07	6.94	6.81	67
68	7.19	7.07	6.94	6.88	6.82	6.70	6.59	6.48	6.37	6.27	6.17	6.07	68
69	6.13	6.04	5.95	5.90	5.86	5.77	5.69	5.60	5.52	5.44	5.37	5.29	69
70	5.08	5.01	4.95	4.92	4.89	4.83	4.77	4.71	4.66	4.60	4.55	4.49	70
71	4.04	4.00	3.96	3.94	3.92	3.88	3.85	3.81	3.77	3.73	3.70	3.66	71
72	3.02	3.00	2.97	2.96	2.95	2.93	2.91	2.89	2.86	2.84	2.82	2.80	72
73	2.01	2.00	1.99	1.98	1.98	1.97	1.96	1.95	1.94	1.93	1.92	1.91	73
74	1.00	1.00	1.00	0.99	0.99	0.99	0.99	0.99	0.98	0.98	0.98	0.98	74

Table 15: Multipliers for loss of pension commencing age 50 (males)

Multiplier calculated with allowance for projected mortality from the 2008-based population projections and rate of return of

Age at date of trial	-2.0%	-1.5%	-1.0%	-0.75%	-0.5%	0.0%	0.5%	1.0%	1.5%	2.0%	2.5%	3.0%	Age at date of trial
0	179.64	121.70	83.09	68.85	57.16	39.61	27.64	19.42	13.74	9.78	7.00	5.04	0
1	176.24	120.05	82.40	68.47	56.99	39.70	27.85	19.67	13.99	10.01	7.20	5.21	1
2	172.05	117.83	81.32	67.74	56.54	39.59	27.92	19.83	14.17	10.19	7.37	5.36	2
3	167.93	115.64	80.24	67.02	56.09	39.49	27.99	19.98	14.35	10.37	7.54	5.51	3
4	163.90	113.48	79.16	66.30	55.63	39.37	28.06	20.13	14.53	10.56	7.72	5.67	4
5	159.97	111.36	78.10	65.59	55.18	39.26	28.12	20.28	14.72	10.75	7.89	5.83	5
6	156.12	109.27	77.05	64.88	54.73	39.14	28.19	20.43	14.91	10.94	8.08	5.99	6
7	152.36	107.22	76.01	64.18	54.28	39.03	28.25	20.59	15.10	11.14	8.26	6.16	7
8	148.69	105.21	74.99	63.48	53.83	38.91	28.32	20.74	15.29	11.33	8.45	6.34	8
9	145.10	103.23	73.98	62.79	53.39	38.80	28.38	20.90	15.48	11.54	8.65	6.52	9
10	141.59	101.28	72.97	62.10	52.95	38.68	28.44	21.05	15.68	11.74	8.84	6.70	10
11	138.17	99.37	71.98	61.42	52.51	38.56	28.51	21.21	15.87	11.95	9.05	6.89	11
12	134.83	97.50	71.01	60.75	52.07	38.44	28.57	21.36	16.07	12.16	9.26	7.08	12
13	131.57	95.66	70.04	60.09	51.64	38.33	28.63	21.52	16.28	12.38	9.47	7.28	13
14	128.40	93.86	69.10	59.44	51.21	38.21	28.70	21.68	16.48	12.60	9.69	7.48	14
15	125.31	92.10	68.16	58.79	50.79	38.10	28.76	21.85	16.69	12.82	9.91	7.69	15
16	122.29	90.37	67.24	58.15	50.38	37.99	28.83	22.01	16.90	13.05	10.14	7.91	16
17	119.35	88.68	66.34	57.53	49.96	37.88	28.89	22.17	17.12	13.29	10.37	8.13	17
18	116.49	87.02	65.46	56.91	49.56	37.77	28.96	22.34	17.34	13.53	10.61	8.36	18
19	113.71	85.41	64.59	56.30	49.16	37.67	29.03	22.52	17.56	13.77	10.86	8.60	19
20	111.01	83.83	63.74	55.71	48.78	37.57	29.11	22.69	17.79	14.02	11.11	8.85	20
21	108.37	82.28	62.90	55.12	48.39	37.46	29.18	22.87	18.02	14.28	11.37	9.10	21
22	105.78	80.76	62.06	54.54	48.00	37.36	29.26	23.04	18.25	14.53	11.63	9.36	22
23	103.25	79.25	61.24	53.96	47.62	37.26	29.33	23.22	18.49	14.80	11.90	9.62	23
24	100.79	77.78	60.42	53.38	47.24	37.16	29.40	23.40	18.73	15.06	12.18	9.90	24
25	98.39	76.35	59.63	52.82	46.86	37.06	29.48	23.58	18.97	15.34	12.46	10.18	25
26	96.06	74.95	58.85	52.27	46.50	36.96	29.56	23.77	19.22	15.62	12.76	10.47	26
27	93.80	73.57	58.08	51.73	46.14	36.87	29.64	23.96	19.47	15.90	13.06	10.77	27
28	91.57	72.22	57.32	51.18	45.77	36.77	29.71	24.14	19.72	16.19	13.36	11.08	28
29	89.39	70.88	56.56	50.64	45.41	36.68	29.79	24.33	19.98	16.49	13.67	11.39	29
30	87.27	69.58	55.82	50.11	45.06	36.58	29.87	24.52	20.24	16.79	13.99	11.72	30
31	85.23	68.32	55.10	49.60	44.71	36.50	29.96	24.72	20.51	17.10	14.33	12.05	31
32	83.24	67.09	54.41	49.10	44.38	36.42	30.05	24.93	20.79	17.42	14.67	12.40	32
33	81.32	65.90	53.73	48.62	44.06	36.35	30.15	25.14	21.07	17.75	15.02	12.77	33
34	79.44	64.72	53.05	48.14	43.74	36.27	30.24	25.35	21.36	18.08	15.38	13.14	34
35	77.60	63.57	52.39	47.66	43.42	36.20	30.34	25.56	21.65	18.42	15.75	13.52	35
36	75.82	62.44	51.74	47.19	43.11	36.13	30.44	25.78	21.95	18.77	16.13	13.92	36
37	74.08	61.34	51.09	46.73	42.81	36.06	30.54	26.00	22.25	19.12	16.51	14.32	37
38	72.37	60.25	50.46	46.28	42.50	35.99	30.64	26.22	22.55	19.49	16.91	14.74	38
39	70.70	59.18	49.83	45.82	42.19	35.92	30.74	26.45	22.86	19.85	17.32	15.17	39
40	69.07	58.13	49.21	45.37	41.89	35.85	30.85	26.67	23.18	20.23	17.74	15.62	40
41	67.49	57.11	48.61	44.93	41.60	35.79	30.96	26.91	23.50	20.62	18.17	16.08	41
42	65.95	56.11	48.01	44.51	41.31	35.73	31.07	27.14	23.83	21.01	18.61	16.55	42
43	64.46	55.14	47.44	44.09	41.03	35.68	31.18	27.39	24.16	21.42	19.07	17.04	43
44	63.01	54.19	46.87	43.68	40.76	35.63	31.30	27.63	24.51	21.84	19.54	17.55	44
45	61.60	53.26	46.32	43.28	40.49	35.58	31.42	27.89	24.86	22.26	20.02	18.07	45
46	60.22	52.36	45.77	42.88	40.23	35.54	31.55	28.14	25.22	22.70	20.52	18.62	46
47	58.88	51.47	45.24	42.50	39.98	35.50	31.68	28.41	25.59	23.15	21.03	19.18	47
48	57.59	50.62	44.73	42.13	39.73	35.47	31.83	28.69	25.97	23.62	21.56	19.76	48
49	56.34	49.79	44.23	41.78	39.50	35.46	31.98	28.97	26.37	24.10	22.11	20.37	49
50	55.14	48.99	43.76	41.44	39.29	35.45	32.14	29.27	26.78	24.60	22.69	21.01	50

Table 16: Multipliers for loss of pension commencing age 50 (females)

Age at date of trial	-2.0%	-1.5%	-1.0%	-0.75%	-0.5%	0.0%	0.5%	1.0%	1.5%	2.0%	2.5%	3.0%	Age at date of trial
0	199.59	134.37	91.19	75.34	62.37	42.98	29.85	20.87	14.70	10.42	7.43	5.33	0
1	195.74	132.49	90.40	74.89	62.16	43.07	30.06	21.13	14.95	10.65	7.64	5.51	1
2	191.18	130.11	89.25	74.13	61.69	42.97	30.15	21.30	15.16	10.85	7.82	5.67	2
3	186.71	127.75	88.10	73.38	61.23	42.87	30.24	21.48	15.36	11.05	8.00	5.83	3
4	182.34	125.44	86.97	72.63	60.76	42.77	30.32	21.65	15.56	11.26	8.19	6.00	4
5	178.06	123.16	85.85	71.88	60.30	42.67	30.41	21.82	15.77	11.46	8.39	6.17	5
6	173.88	120.92	84.74	71.14	59.84	42.56	30.49	22.00	15.97	11.67	8.58	6.35	6
7	169.79	118.72	83.65	70.41	59.38	42.46	30.58	22.17	16.18	11.89	8.78	6.53	7
8	165.80	116.55	82.56	69.68	58.92	42.36	30.66	22.35	16.40	12.10	8.99	6.72	8
9	161.89	114.43	81.49	68.96	58.47	42.25	30.75	22.53	16.61	12.33	9.20	6.91	9
10	158.08	112.34	80.43	68.25	58.02	42.15	30.83	22.70	16.83	12.55	9.42	7.11	10
11	154.36	110.29	79.39	67.54	57.57	42.04	30.92	22.89	17.05	12.78	9.64	7.31	11
12	150.73	108.28	78.36	66.84	57.12	41.94	31.00	23.07	17.27	13.01	9.86	7.52	12
13	147.17	106.30	77.34	66.15	56.68	41.83	31.08	23.25	17.50	13.25	10.09	7.73	13
14	143.71	104.36	76.34	65.47	56.24	41.73	31.17	23.43	17.73	13.49	10.33	7.95	14
15	140.33	102.45	75.35	64.79	55.81	41.62	31.25	23.62	17.96	13.74	10.57	8.18	15
16	137.02	100.58	74.37	64.12	55.38	41.52	31.34	23.81	18.20	13.99	10.82	8.41	16
17	133.80	98.75	73.41	63.46	54.95	41.42	31.42	24.00	18.44	14.25	11.07	8.65	17
18	130.66	96.95	72.46	62.80	54.53	41.32	31.51	24.19	18.68	14.51	11.33	8.90	18
19	127.60	95.19	71.52	62.16	54.11	41.22	31.60	24.38	18.92	14.78	11.60	9.16	19
20	124.61	93.47	70.61	61.53	53.70	41.12	31.69	24.58	19.18	15.05	11.87	9.42	20
21	121.70	91.78	69.70	60.90	53.30	41.03	31.78	24.78	19.43	15.32	12.15	9.69	21
22	118.85	90.11	68.80	60.27	52.89	40.93	31.87	24.97	19.69	15.61	12.44	9.97	22
23	116.05	88.47	67.91	59.65	52.48	40.82	31.96	25.17	19.94	15.89	12.73	10.25	23
24	113.32	86.85	67.03	59.03	52.08	40.72	32.05	25.37	20.21	16.18	13.03	10.54	24
25	110.66	85.27	66.16	58.43	51.68	40.62	32.14	25.57	20.47	16.48	13.33	10.85	25
26	108.06	83.73	65.31	57.83	51.28	40.53	32.23	25.78	20.74	16.78	13.65	11.16	26
27	105.53	82.21	64.47	57.24	50.89	40.43	32.32	25.99	21.02	17.09	13.97	11.48	27
28	103.06	80.72	63.64	56.65	50.50	40.33	32.41	26.19	21.29	17.40	14.30	11.81	28
29	100.65	79.26	62.82	56.07	50.12	40.24	32.50	26.41	21.58	17.72	14.64	12.14	29
30	98.30	77.82	62.02	55.50	49.74	40.15	32.60	26.62	21.86	18.05	14.98	12.49	30
31	96.01	76.42	61.23	54.94	49.37	40.06	32.69	26.84	22.15	18.38	15.33	12.85	31
32	93.78	75.05	60.46	54.39	49.00	39.97	32.79	27.06	22.45	18.73	15.70	13.22	32
33	91.61	73.71	59.69	53.84	48.64	39.88	32.89	27.28	22.75	19.07	16.07	13.61	33
34	89.48	72.38	58.93	53.30	48.28	39.79	32.99	27.50	23.05	19.43	16.45	14.00	34
35	87.39	71.08	58.18	52.76	47.92	39.70	33.09	27.73	23.36	19.79	16.84	14.40	35
36	85.37	69.81	57.45	52.24	47.57	39.62	33.19	27.96	23.68	20.16	17.24	14.82	36
37	83.40	68.57	56.73	51.72	47.22	39.54	33.29	28.19	24.00	20.53	17.65	15.25	37
38	81.47	67.35	56.02	51.20	46.87	39.45	33.40	28.43	24.32	20.92	18.07	15.69	38
39	79.59	66.15	55.31	50.70	46.53	39.37	33.50	28.66	24.65	21.31	18.50	16.14	39
40	77.75	64.97	54.62	50.19	46.19	39.29	33.61	28.90	24.99	21.71	18.95	16.61	40
41	75.96	63.82	53.94	49.70	45.86	39.22	33.72	29.15	25.33	22.11	19.40	17.10	41
42	74.22	62.69	53.27	49.22	45.54	39.14	33.83	29.40	25.67	22.53	19.87	17.60	42
43	72.53	61.59	52.62	48.74	45.22	39.07	33.95	29.65	26.03	22.96	20.35	18.11	43
44	70.88	60.52	51.98	48.28	44.90	39.01	34.07	29.91	26.39	23.40	20.84	18.64	44
45	69.28	59.47	51.35	47.82	44.60	38.94	34.19	30.17	26.76	23.85	21.35	19.19	45
46	67.72	58.45	50.74	47.38	44.30	38.89	34.32	30.44	27.14	24.31	21.87	19.76	46
47	66.20	57.45	50.14	46.94	44.01	38.83	34.45	30.72	27.53	24.78	22.41	20.35	47
48	64.73	56.48	49.56	46.52	43.73	38.79	34.59	31.01	27.93	25.27	22.97	20.96	48
49	63.31	55.54	48.99	46.11	43.46	38.76	34.74	31.30	28.34	25.77	23.54	21.59	49
50	61.93	54.62	48.44	45.71	43.20	38.73	34.90	31.61	28.76	26.29	24.14	22.25	50

Table 17: Multipliers for loss of pension commencing age 55 (males)

Age at date of trial	\-2.0%	\-1.5%	\-1.0%	\-0.75%	\-0.5%	0.0%	0.5%	1.0%	1.5%	2.0%	2.5%	3.0%	Age at date of trial
	Multiplier calculated with allowance for projected mortality from the 2008–based population projections and rate of return of												
0	165.74	111.07	74.94	61.71	50.90	34.80	23.94	16.57	11.54	8.08	5.69	4.02	0
1	162.56	109.52	74.30	61.34	50.73	34.87	24.11	16.78	11.74	8.26	5.85	4.16	1
2	158.64	107.46	73.29	60.68	50.31	34.76	24.17	16.90	11.89	8.41	5.98	4.27	2
3	154.79	105.43	72.29	60.01	49.89	34.65	24.22	17.02	12.04	8.56	6.12	4.39	3
4	151.03	103.43	71.30	59.34	49.47	34.54	24.27	17.15	12.19	8.71	6.26	4.52	4
5	147.35	101.46	70.32	58.68	49.05	34.43	24.31	17.27	12.34	8.86	6.40	4.64	5
6	143.76	99.52	69.35	58.03	48.63	34.32	24.36	17.39	12.49	9.02	6.54	4.77	6
7	140.25	97.62	68.39	57.38	48.22	34.20	24.41	17.52	12.64	9.17	6.69	4.90	7
8	136.83	95.76	67.44	56.74	47.80	34.09	24.45	17.64	12.80	9.33	6.84	5.04	8
9	133.48	93.92	66.51	56.10	47.39	33.97	24.50	17.77	12.96	9.50	7.00	5.18	9
10	130.21	92.11	65.58	55.46	46.98	33.86	24.54	17.89	13.11	9.66	7.15	5.32	10
11	127.02	90.34	64.67	54.84	46.57	33.74	24.59	18.02	13.27	9.83	7.32	5.47	11
12	123.91	88.61	63.77	54.22	46.17	33.63	24.63	18.14	13.44	10.00	7.48	5.62	12
13	120.87	86.91	62.88	53.61	45.77	33.51	24.68	18.27	13.60	10.18	7.65	5.78	13
14	117.91	85.24	62.00	53.00	45.37	33.40	24.72	18.40	13.77	10.35	7.82	5.94	14
15	115.03	83.61	61.14	52.41	44.98	33.29	24.77	18.53	13.94	10.53	8.00	6.10	15
16	112.22	82.01	60.30	51.82	44.60	33.17	24.81	18.66	14.11	10.72	8.18	6.27	16
17	109.49	80.45	59.47	51.24	44.22	33.06	24.86	18.79	14.28	10.90	8.37	6.45	17
18	106.83	78.92	58.65	50.67	43.84	32.96	24.91	18.93	14.46	11.10	8.56	6.63	18
19	104.24	77.42	57.85	50.11	43.47	32.85	24.96	19.07	14.64	11.29	8.75	6.81	19
20	101.73	75.97	57.07	49.57	43.11	32.75	25.02	19.21	14.82	11.49	8.95	7.00	20
21	99.28	74.54	56.29	49.02	42.76	32.65	25.07	19.35	15.01	11.70	9.16	7.20	21
22	96.87	73.13	55.52	48.48	42.40	32.55	25.12	19.49	15.19	11.90	9.37	7.40	22
23	94.52	71.74	54.76	47.95	42.04	32.45	25.17	19.63	15.38	12.11	9.58	7.61	23
24	92.23	70.38	54.02	47.42	41.69	32.34	25.23	19.77	15.58	12.33	9.80	7.82	24
25	90.00	69.05	53.28	46.90	41.34	32.24	25.28	19.92	15.77	12.54	10.02	8.04	25
26	87.84	67.76	52.56	46.39	41.00	32.15	25.34	20.07	15.97	12.77	10.25	8.27	26
27	85.73	66.49	51.86	45.89	40.67	32.06	25.40	20.22	16.17	13.00	10.49	8.50	27
28	83.67	65.24	51.16	45.39	40.33	31.96	25.45	20.37	16.38	13.23	10.73	8.74	28
29	81.64	64.01	50.46	44.89	39.99	31.86	25.51	20.52	16.58	13.46	10.97	8.98	29
30	79.68	62.81	49.78	44.41	39.66	31.76	25.56	20.67	16.79	13.70	11.23	9.24	30
31	77.78	61.65	49.12	43.93	39.35	31.68	25.63	20.83	17.01	13.95	11.49	9.50	31
32	75.95	60.52	48.48	43.48	39.04	31.60	25.69	20.99	17.23	14.20	11.76	9.77	32
33	74.17	59.42	47.86	43.03	38.74	31.52	25.77	21.16	17.46	14.46	12.03	10.05	33
34	72.42	58.34	47.24	42.59	38.44	31.44	25.84	21.33	17.69	14.73	12.32	10.34	34
35	70.72	57.27	46.62	42.15	38.15	31.36	25.91	21.50	17.92	15.00	12.61	10.64	35
36	69.07	56.24	46.03	41.72	37.86	31.29	25.98	21.68	18.16	15.28	12.90	10.94	36
37	67.45	55.22	45.44	41.29	37.57	31.22	26.06	21.85	18.40	15.56	13.21	11.26	37
38	65.87	54.22	44.85	40.87	37.29	31.14	26.13	22.03	18.65	15.85	13.52	11.58	38
39	64.33	53.23	44.27	40.45	37.00	31.07	26.21	22.21	18.89	16.14	13.84	11.91	39
40	62.82	52.27	43.70	40.04	36.72	31.00	26.28	22.38	19.14	16.44	14.17	12.26	40
41	61.36	51.33	43.15	39.63	36.45	30.93	26.36	22.57	19.40	16.74	14.50	12.61	41
42	59.93	50.41	42.60	39.24	36.18	30.86	26.45	22.76	19.66	17.06	14.85	12.98	42
43	58.55	49.51	42.07	38.85	35.92	30.80	26.53	22.95	19.93	17.38	15.21	13.36	43
44	57.21	48.64	41.55	38.47	35.66	30.74	26.62	23.15	20.21	17.71	15.57	13.75	44
45	55.90	47.78	41.04	38.10	35.41	30.69	26.71	23.35	20.49	18.04	15.95	14.15	45
46	54.63	46.95	40.54	37.74	35.16	30.64	26.81	23.55	20.77	18.39	16.34	14.57	46
47	53.39	46.14	40.05	37.38	34.93	30.59	26.91	23.76	21.06	18.74	16.74	15.00	47
48	52.20	45.35	39.58	37.04	34.70	30.55	27.01	23.98	21.37	19.11	17.15	15.45	48
49	51.04	44.58	39.12	36.71	34.48	30.52	27.12	24.20	21.68	19.49	17.58	15.92	49
50	49.93	43.85	38.68	36.39	34.27	30.50	27.25	24.44	22.00	19.88	18.03	16.40	50
51	48.86	43.14	38.26	36.09	34.08	30.49	27.38	24.69	22.34	20.29	18.49	16.91	51
52	47.83	42.46	37.86	35.81	33.91	30.49	27.53	24.95	22.69	20.72	18.98	17.44	52
53	46.84	41.81	37.48	35.55	33.74	30.50	27.68	25.22	23.06	21.16	19.48	17.99	53
54	45.90	41.19	37.12	35.30	33.60	30.53	27.86	25.51	23.44	21.62	20.01	18.57	54
55	44.99	40.60	36.79	35.07	33.47	30.58	28.04	25.81	23.85	22.11	20.56	19.18	55

A8: The Ogden Tables

Table 18: Multipliers for loss of pension commencing age 55 (females)

Age at date of trial	\-2.0%	\-1.5%	\-1.0%	\-0.75%	\-0.5%	0.0%	0.5%	1.0%	1.5%	2.0%	2.5%	3.0%	Age at date of trial
0	185.47	123.56	82.90	68.08	56.01	38.10	26.08	17.97	12.46	8.69	6.09	4.30	0
1	181.85	121.80	82.16	67.66	55.81	38.16	26.26	18.19	12.68	8.88	6.26	4.44	1
2	177.57	119.58	81.09	66.95	55.37	38.06	26.33	18.33	12.84	9.05	6.41	4.57	2
3	173.37	117.38	80.03	66.25	54.94	37.96	26.40	18.48	13.01	9.21	6.56	4.69	3
4	169.26	115.23	78.98	65.56	54.51	37.86	26.47	18.62	13.18	9.38	6.71	4.83	4
5	165.25	113.10	77.94	64.87	54.08	37.76	26.54	18.76	13.35	9.55	6.87	4.97	5
6	161.33	111.01	76.92	64.18	53.65	37.66	26.60	18.91	13.52	9.72	7.03	5.11	6
7	157.49	108.96	75.90	63.50	53.22	37.56	26.67	19.05	13.69	9.89	7.19	5.25	7
8	153.74	106.95	74.89	62.83	52.79	37.45	26.73	19.20	13.87	10.07	7.36	5.40	8
9	150.08	104.96	73.90	62.16	52.37	37.35	26.80	19.35	14.04	10.25	7.53	5.55	9
10	146.51	103.02	72.92	61.50	51.95	37.24	26.86	19.49	14.22	10.44	7.70	5.71	10
11	143.02	101.11	71.95	60.85	51.53	37.14	26.93	19.64	14.41	10.63	7.88	5.87	11
12	139.61	99.24	71.00	60.20	51.12	37.04	26.99	19.79	14.59	10.82	8.06	6.04	12
13	136.29	97.39	70.05	59.55	50.71	36.93	27.06	19.94	14.78	11.01	8.25	6.21	13
14	133.04	95.59	69.12	58.92	50.30	36.83	27.12	20.09	14.97	11.21	8.44	6.38	14
15	129.87	93.82	68.21	58.29	49.90	36.72	27.19	20.25	15.16	11.41	8.63	6.56	15
16	126.78	92.08	67.30	57.67	49.50	36.62	27.26	20.40	15.35	11.61	8.83	6.75	16
17	123.76	90.37	66.41	57.06	49.10	36.52	27.32	20.55	15.55	11.82	9.03	6.94	17
18	120.82	88.70	65.53	56.45	48.71	36.42	27.39	20.71	15.75	12.03	9.24	7.13	18
19	117.96	87.07	64.67	55.86	48.32	36.32	27.46	20.87	15.95	12.25	9.46	7.34	19
20	115.17	85.47	63.82	55.27	47.94	36.23	27.53	21.03	16.16	12.47	9.68	7.54	20
21	112.45	83.90	62.98	54.69	47.56	36.13	27.60	21.20	16.37	12.70	9.90	7.76	21
22	109.78	82.35	62.15	54.11	47.19	36.03	27.67	21.36	16.58	12.93	10.13	7.98	22
23	107.16	80.82	61.33	53.54	46.81	35.93	27.73	21.52	16.79	13.16	10.37	8.20	23
24	104.61	79.32	60.51	52.97	46.43	35.83	27.80	21.68	17.00	13.40	10.61	8.43	24
25	102.12	77.86	59.71	52.40	46.06	35.73	27.87	21.85	17.22	13.64	10.85	8.67	25
26	99.70	76.42	58.92	51.85	45.69	35.63	27.94	22.02	17.44	13.88	11.10	8.92	26
27	97.34	75.01	58.15	51.30	45.33	35.54	28.01	22.19	17.67	14.13	11.36	9.17	27
28	95.02	73.63	57.38	50.76	44.97	35.44	28.08	22.36	17.89	14.39	11.62	9.43	28
29	92.77	72.27	56.62	50.23	44.61	35.34	28.15	22.53	18.12	14.65	11.89	9.70	29
30	90.58	70.94	55.88	49.70	44.26	35.25	28.22	22.71	18.36	14.91	12.17	9.97	30
31	88.45	69.65	55.15	49.18	43.92	35.16	28.29	22.88	18.60	15.18	12.45	10.26	31
32	86.37	68.38	54.44	48.67	43.58	35.07	28.37	23.06	18.84	15.46	12.74	10.55	32
33	84.34	67.13	53.73	48.17	43.24	34.98	28.45	23.24	19.09	15.74	13.04	10.85	33
34	82.35	65.90	53.03	47.67	42.90	34.89	28.52	23.43	19.33	16.03	13.35	11.16	34
35	80.41	64.70	52.34	47.17	42.57	34.80	28.60	23.61	19.59	16.32	13.66	11.48	35
36	78.53	63.52	51.66	46.68	42.24	34.72	28.67	23.80	19.84	16.62	13.98	11.80	36
37	76.69	62.37	51.00	46.20	41.92	34.63	28.75	23.99	20.10	16.92	14.30	12.14	37
38	74.89	61.24	50.34	45.73	41.60	34.55	28.83	24.18	20.37	17.23	14.64	12.49	38
39	73.14	60.13	49.69	45.26	41.28	34.46	28.91	24.37	20.64	17.55	14.98	12.85	39
40	71.43	59.04	49.05	44.80	40.97	34.38	29.00	24.57	20.91	17.87	15.34	13.22	40
41	69.76	57.97	48.43	44.34	40.66	34.30	29.08	24.77	21.19	18.20	15.70	13.60	41
42	68.14	56.93	47.81	43.90	40.35	34.23	29.17	24.97	21.47	18.54	16.07	13.99	42
43	66.56	55.91	47.21	43.46	40.05	34.15	29.25	25.17	21.76	18.88	16.45	14.39	43
44	65.03	54.92	46.62	43.03	39.76	34.08	29.35	25.38	22.05	19.23	16.84	14.81	44
45	63.54	53.95	46.04	42.61	39.48	34.02	29.44	25.60	22.35	19.60	17.25	15.24	45
46	62.09	53.00	45.47	42.19	39.20	33.95	29.54	25.82	22.66	19.97	17.66	15.68	46
47	60.68	52.07	44.91	41.79	38.93	33.89	29.64	26.04	22.97	20.35	18.09	16.14	47
48	59.31	51.18	44.38	41.40	38.66	33.84	29.75	26.27	23.30	20.74	18.53	16.62	48
49	57.99	50.31	43.85	41.02	38.41	33.80	29.87	26.51	23.63	21.14	18.99	17.12	49
50	56.70	49.46	43.35	40.65	38.17	33.76	29.99	26.76	23.97	21.56	19.46	17.63	50
51	55.46	48.63	42.85	40.29	37.93	33.73	30.12	27.01	24.32	21.99	19.95	18.16	51
52	54.25	47.83	42.37	39.94	37.70	33.70	30.25	27.27	24.68	22.43	20.45	18.71	52
53	53.08	47.05	41.90	39.61	37.49	33.68	30.40	27.54	25.06	22.88	20.97	19.29	53
54	51.95	46.30	41.45	39.29	37.28	33.68	30.55	27.83	25.44	23.35	21.51	19.88	54
55	50.86	45.57	41.02	38.99	37.09	33.68	30.71	28.12	25.84	23.84	22.07	20.51	55

Table 19: Multipliers for loss of pension commencing age 60 (males)

Age at date of trial	-2.0%	-1.5%	-1.0%	-0.75%	-0.5%	0.0%	0.5%	1.0%	1.5%	2.0%	2.5%	3.0%	Age at date of trial
0	150.59	99.76	66.49	54.40	44.58	30.06	20.38	13.89	9.52	6.56	4.54	3.16	0
1	147.63	98.33	65.89	54.05	44.41	30.10	20.52	14.06	9.69	6.70	4.66	3.26	1
2	144.02	96.44	64.97	53.44	44.02	30.00	20.55	14.16	9.80	6.82	4.77	3.35	2
3	140.47	94.58	64.06	52.83	43.63	29.89	20.59	14.26	9.92	6.94	4.88	3.44	3
4	137.00	92.74	63.15	52.22	43.25	29.78	20.62	14.35	10.04	7.06	4.98	3.54	4
5	133.61	90.93	62.25	51.62	42.86	29.67	20.65	14.45	10.16	7.18	5.10	3.63	5
6	130.29	89.16	61.36	51.02	42.47	29.56	20.68	14.54	10.28	7.30	5.21	3.73	6
7	127.06	87.42	60.49	50.42	42.09	29.45	20.71	14.64	10.40	7.42	5.32	3.83	7
8	123.91	85.71	59.63	49.84	41.71	29.34	20.74	14.74	10.52	7.55	5.44	3.94	8
9	120.82	84.03	58.77	49.25	41.33	29.22	20.77	14.84	10.65	7.68	5.56	4.05	9
10	117.81	82.38	57.93	48.67	40.95	29.11	20.80	14.93	10.77	7.81	5.68	4.16	10
11	114.87	80.76	57.09	48.10	40.58	29.00	20.82	15.03	10.90	7.94	5.81	4.27	11
12	112.01	79.17	56.27	47.54	40.21	28.88	20.85	15.13	11.03	8.07	5.94	4.39	12
13	109.22	77.62	55.46	46.98	39.84	28.77	20.88	15.23	11.16	8.21	6.07	4.50	13
14	106.50	76.10	54.67	46.43	39.48	28.66	20.91	15.33	11.29	8.35	6.20	4.63	14
15	103.85	74.61	53.88	45.88	39.12	28.55	20.94	15.43	11.42	8.49	6.34	4.75	15
16	101.27	73.15	53.11	45.35	38.77	28.44	20.96	15.53	11.55	8.63	6.48	4.88	16
17	98.76	71.72	52.36	44.82	38.42	28.33	20.99	15.63	11.69	8.78	6.62	5.02	17
18	96.32	70.32	51.61	44.30	38.07	28.23	21.03	15.74	11.83	8.93	6.77	5.15	18
19	93.94	68.96	50.88	43.79	37.74	28.12	21.06	15.84	11.97	9.08	6.92	5.30	19
20	91.64	67.63	50.17	43.29	37.41	28.02	21.09	15.95	12.11	9.24	7.08	5.44	20
21	89.39	66.33	49.47	42.80	37.08	27.92	21.13	16.06	12.26	9.40	7.23	5.59	21
22	87.18	65.04	48.77	42.31	36.75	27.82	21.16	16.17	12.41	9.56	7.40	5.74	22
23	85.02	63.77	48.08	41.82	36.42	27.72	21.19	16.28	12.55	9.72	7.56	5.90	23
24	82.92	62.54	47.40	41.34	36.09	27.62	21.23	16.39	12.70	9.89	7.73	6.06	24
25	80.88	61.33	46.73	40.86	35.78	27.52	21.26	16.50	12.86	10.06	7.90	6.23	25
26	78.91	60.15	46.08	40.40	35.46	27.42	21.30	16.61	13.01	10.23	8.08	6.40	26
27	76.98	59.00	45.44	39.95	35.16	27.33	21.34	16.73	13.17	10.41	8.26	6.58	27
28	75.09	57.86	44.80	39.49	34.85	27.23	21.37	16.84	13.33	10.59	8.45	6.76	28
29	73.23	56.74	44.17	39.03	34.54	27.13	21.41	16.96	13.49	10.77	8.63	6.95	29
30	71.44	55.65	43.55	38.59	34.24	27.04	21.44	17.08	13.65	10.96	8.83	7.14	30
31	69.70	54.59	42.95	38.16	33.95	26.95	21.48	17.20	13.82	11.15	9.03	7.34	31
32	68.02	53.56	42.37	37.74	33.66	26.86	21.53	17.32	13.99	11.35	9.23	7.54	32
33	66.40	52.56	41.80	37.34	33.39	26.79	21.58	17.45	14.17	11.55	9.45	7.75	33
34	64.81	51.58	41.24	36.93	33.12	26.71	21.63	17.58	14.35	11.76	9.66	7.97	34
35	63.25	50.61	40.68	36.53	32.84	26.63	21.67	17.71	14.53	11.96	9.89	8.20	35
36	61.74	49.67	40.14	36.14	32.58	26.55	21.72	17.85	14.72	12.18	10.11	8.43	36
37	60.27	48.75	39.60	35.75	32.31	26.47	21.78	17.98	14.90	12.40	10.35	8.66	37
38	58.83	47.84	39.07	35.37	32.05	26.40	21.83	18.12	15.09	12.62	10.58	8.91	38
39	57.42	46.95	38.55	34.99	31.79	26.32	21.88	18.25	15.28	12.84	10.83	9.16	39
40	56.04	46.07	38.03	34.61	31.53	26.24	21.93	18.39	15.48	13.07	11.08	9.42	40
41	54.71	45.22	37.53	34.24	31.28	26.17	21.98	18.53	15.68	13.31	11.33	9.68	41
42	53.42	44.38	37.04	33.88	31.03	26.10	22.03	18.67	15.88	13.55	11.60	9.96	42
43	52.16	43.57	36.55	33.53	30.79	26.03	22.09	18.82	16.09	13.80	11.87	10.24	43
44	50.93	42.78	36.08	33.18	30.55	25.97	22.15	18.97	16.30	14.05	12.15	10.54	44
45	49.74	42.01	35.62	32.85	30.32	25.91	22.22	19.12	16.51	14.31	12.44	10.84	45
46	48.58	41.25	35.16	32.51	30.09	25.85	22.28	19.28	16.73	14.57	12.73	11.15	46
47	47.46	40.51	34.72	32.19	29.87	25.79	22.35	19.44	16.96	14.84	13.03	11.48	47
48	46.37	39.80	34.29	31.87	29.65	25.74	22.42	19.60	17.19	15.12	13.35	11.81	48
49	45.32	39.10	33.87	31.57	29.45	25.70	22.50	19.77	17.43	15.41	13.67	12.16	49
50	44.30	38.43	33.47	31.28	29.26	25.66	22.59	19.95	17.68	15.71	14.01	12.52	50
51	43.33	37.79	33.09	31.00	29.07	25.64	22.69	20.14	17.94	16.03	14.36	12.90	51
52	42.39	37.17	32.72	30.74	28.91	25.62	22.79	20.34	18.21	16.35	14.72	13.30	52
53	41.49	36.58	32.37	30.49	28.75	25.62	22.91	20.55	18.49	16.69	15.11	13.71	53
54	40.63	36.01	32.04	30.26	28.61	25.63	23.04	20.77	18.79	17.04	15.50	14.14	54

Table 19: Multipliers for loss of pension commencing age 60 (males) *continued*

Age at date of trial	\-2.0%	\-1.5%	\-1.0%	\-0.75%	\-0.5%	0.0%	0.5%	1.0%	1.5%	2.0%	2.5%	3.0%	Age at date of trial
55	39.81	35.48	31.73	30.05	28.48	25.65	23.18	21.01	19.10	17.41	15.92	14.60	55
56	39.03	34.97	31.45	29.86	28.37	25.69	23.33	21.26	19.43	17.80	16.36	15.07	56
57	38.29	34.49	31.18	29.68	28.28	25.74	23.50	21.52	19.77	18.21	16.82	15.57	57
58	37.56	34.02	30.92	29.51	28.20	25.80	23.68	21.79	20.12	18.63	17.29	16.09	58
59	36.86	33.56	30.67	29.35	28.12	25.86	23.86	22.07	20.49	19.06	17.79	16.64	59
60	36.17	33.12	30.42	29.19	28.04	25.92	24.04	22.36	20.86	19.51	18.30	17.20	60

Multiplier calculated with allowance for projected mortality from the 2008–based population projections and rate of return of

Table 20: Multipliers for loss of pension commencing age 60 (females)

Age at date of trial	-2.0%	-1.5%	-1.0%	-0.75%	-0.5%	0.0%	0.5%	1.0%	1.5%	2.0%	2.5%	3.0%	Age at date of trial
0	169.99	112.01	74.27	60.62	49.55	33.26	22.45	15.24	10.40	7.14	4.92	3.41	0
1	166.62	110.38	73.58	60.22	49.35	33.30	22.59	15.42	10.58	7.30	5.06	3.52	1
2	162.64	108.33	72.60	59.57	48.95	33.20	22.65	15.53	10.71	7.43	5.17	3.62	2
3	158.74	106.30	71.62	58.93	48.55	33.10	22.70	15.65	10.85	7.56	5.29	3.72	3
4	154.93	104.31	70.66	58.29	48.15	33.00	22.75	15.77	10.98	7.69	5.41	3.83	4
5	151.21	102.36	69.71	57.65	47.75	32.90	22.80	15.88	11.12	7.83	5.54	3.93	5
6	147.57	100.43	68.76	57.02	47.36	32.80	22.85	16.00	11.26	7.97	5.66	4.04	6
7	144.01	98.54	67.83	56.40	46.96	32.70	22.89	16.11	11.40	8.11	5.79	4.16	7
8	140.54	96.68	66.91	55.78	46.57	32.60	22.94	16.23	11.54	8.25	5.92	4.27	8
9	137.14	94.85	65.99	55.16	46.18	32.49	22.99	16.35	11.69	8.39	6.06	4.39	9
10	133.83	93.06	65.09	54.56	45.79	32.39	23.03	16.47	11.83	8.54	6.20	4.51	10
11	130.60	91.31	64.21	53.96	45.41	32.29	23.08	16.59	11.98	8.69	6.34	4.64	11
12	127.45	89.58	63.33	53.36	45.02	32.18	23.13	16.71	12.13	8.84	6.48	4.77	12
13	124.36	87.89	62.47	52.77	44.65	32.08	23.17	16.83	12.28	9.00	6.63	4.90	13
14	121.36	86.23	61.62	52.19	44.27	31.98	23.22	16.95	12.43	9.16	6.78	5.04	14
15	118.43	84.60	60.77	51.62	43.90	31.88	23.27	17.07	12.58	9.32	6.93	5.18	15
16	115.57	83.00	59.95	51.05	43.53	31.78	23.31	17.19	12.74	9.48	7.09	5.32	16
17	112.78	81.44	59.13	50.49	43.16	31.67	23.36	17.32	12.90	9.65	7.25	5.47	17
18	110.06	79.90	58.33	49.93	42.80	31.58	23.41	17.44	13.06	9.82	7.42	5.62	18
19	107.41	78.40	57.53	49.39	42.45	31.48	23.46	17.57	13.22	9.99	7.58	5.78	19
20	104.83	76.93	56.76	48.85	42.10	31.38	23.51	17.70	13.38	10.17	7.76	5.94	20
21	102.32	75.49	55.99	48.32	41.75	31.29	23.56	17.83	13.55	10.35	7.93	6.11	21
22	99.85	74.07	55.23	47.79	41.40	31.19	23.61	17.96	13.72	10.53	8.12	6.28	22
23	97.44	72.67	54.48	47.26	41.05	31.09	23.66	18.09	13.89	10.71	8.30	6.45	23
24	95.08	71.29	53.73	46.74	40.70	30.99	23.70	18.22	14.06	10.90	8.49	6.63	24
25	92.79	69.95	53.00	46.22	40.36	30.89	23.75	18.35	14.24	11.09	8.68	6.82	25
26	90.55	68.63	52.28	45.72	40.03	30.79	23.80	18.48	14.41	11.29	8.88	7.01	26
27	88.37	67.34	51.57	45.22	39.69	30.70	23.85	18.62	14.59	11.49	9.08	7.20	27
28	86.24	66.07	50.87	44.72	39.36	30.60	23.90	18.75	14.77	11.69	9.29	7.41	28
29	84.17	64.83	50.18	44.23	39.03	30.51	23.95	18.89	14.96	11.90	9.50	7.61	29
30	82.15	63.61	49.50	43.75	38.71	30.41	24.00	19.03	15.15	12.11	9.71	7.83	30
31	80.18	62.43	48.84	43.28	38.39	30.32	24.05	19.17	15.34	12.32	9.94	8.04	31
32	78.27	61.26	48.19	42.81	38.08	30.23	24.11	19.31	15.53	12.54	10.16	8.27	32
33	76.40	60.12	47.54	42.35	37.77	30.14	24.16	19.45	15.72	12.76	10.40	8.50	33
34	74.57	59.00	46.90	41.89	37.46	30.05	24.22	19.60	15.92	12.99	10.64	8.74	34
35	72.79	57.90	46.27	41.44	37.15	29.96	24.27	19.74	16.12	13.22	10.88	8.99	35
36	71.05	56.82	45.66	40.99	36.85	29.88	24.33	19.89	16.33	13.45	11.13	9.24	36
37	69.36	55.77	45.05	40.56	36.55	29.79	24.38	20.04	16.53	13.69	11.38	9.50	37
38	67.71	54.73	44.45	40.12	36.26	29.71	24.44	20.19	16.74	13.94	11.65	9.77	38
39	66.10	53.72	43.86	39.70	35.97	29.62	24.50	20.34	16.96	14.19	11.92	10.04	39
40	64.53	52.73	43.28	39.27	35.68	29.54	24.56	20.50	17.17	14.44	12.19	10.32	40
41	63.00	51.75	42.70	38.86	35.39	29.46	24.62	20.65	17.39	14.70	12.47	10.62	41
42	61.51	50.80	42.14	38.45	35.11	29.38	24.68	20.81	17.62	14.97	12.76	10.92	42
43	60.06	49.87	41.59	38.05	34.84	29.30	24.74	20.97	17.85	15.24	13.06	11.23	43
44	58.65	48.97	41.06	37.65	34.57	29.23	24.81	21.14	18.08	15.52	13.36	11.55	44
45	57.28	48.08	40.53	37.27	34.31	29.16	24.88	21.31	18.32	15.80	13.68	11.88	45
46	55.95	47.21	40.01	36.89	34.05	29.09	24.95	21.48	18.56	16.09	14.00	12.22	46
47	54.65	46.37	39.50	36.52	33.79	29.02	25.02	21.65	18.81	16.39	14.33	12.57	47
48	53.40	45.55	39.01	36.16	33.55	28.97	25.10	21.84	19.06	16.70	14.67	12.94	48
49	52.19	44.75	38.54	35.81	33.32	28.92	25.19	22.03	19.33	17.01	15.03	13.32	49
50	51.01	43.98	38.07	35.47	33.09	28.87	25.28	22.22	19.60	17.34	15.39	13.71	50
51	49.86	43.22	37.62	35.14	32.87	28.83	25.38	22.42	19.87	17.67	15.77	14.11	51
52	48.76	42.49	37.17	34.82	32.65	28.79	25.47	22.62	20.16	18.02	16.16	14.53	52
53	47.68	41.78	36.75	34.52	32.45	28.76	25.58	22.83	20.45	18.38	16.56	14.97	53
54	46.65	41.09	36.34	34.22	32.26	28.74	25.70	23.06	20.76	18.74	16.98	15.43	54

A8: The Ogden Tables

Table 20: Multipliers for loss of pension commencing age 60 (females) *continued*

Age at date of trial	\multicolumn{12}{c}{Multiplier calculated with allowance for projected mortality from the 2008–based population projections and rate of return of}	Age at date of trial
	-2.0%	*-1.5%*	*-1.0%*	*-0.75%*	*-0.5%*	*0.0%*	*0.5%*	*1.0%*	*1.5%*	*2.0%*	*2.5%*	*3.0%*	
55	45.65	40.43	35.94	33.94	32.08	28.73	25.82	23.29	21.07	19.13	17.41	15.90	55
56	44.69	39.79	35.57	33.67	31.91	28.73	25.95	23.53	21.40	19.52	17.86	16.39	56
57	43.76	39.18	35.20	33.41	31.75	28.73	26.09	23.78	21.74	19.93	18.33	16.91	57
58	42.86	38.57	34.85	33.16	31.59	28.74	26.24	24.04	22.09	20.35	18.81	17.44	58
59	41.98	37.99	34.50	32.92	31.44	28.76	26.39	24.30	22.44	20.79	19.31	17.99	59
60	41.12	37.41	34.16	32.68	31.30	28.78	26.55	24.57	22.81	21.24	19.83	18.57	60

A8: The Ogden Tables

Table 21: Multipliers for loss of pension commencing age 65 (males)

Multiplier calculated with allowance for projected mortality from the 2008–based population projections and rate of return of

Age at date of trial	-2.0%	-1.5%	-1.0%	-0.75%	-0.5%	0.0%	0.5%	1.0%	1.5%	2.0%	2.5%	3.0%	Age at date of trial
0	134.16	87.81	57.78	46.96	38.22	25.41	16.98	11.40	7.69	5.21	3.54	2.42	0
1	131.46	86.50	57.23	46.64	38.06	25.44	17.08	11.53	7.82	5.32	3.64	2.50	1
2	128.17	84.80	56.40	46.08	37.70	25.33	17.10	11.60	7.91	5.41	3.72	2.57	2
3	124.95	83.11	55.57	45.53	37.35	25.23	17.12	11.67	8.00	5.50	3.80	2.64	3
4	121.80	81.45	54.76	44.98	37.00	25.12	17.14	11.75	8.09	5.59	3.88	2.71	4
5	118.72	79.82	53.95	44.43	36.64	25.01	17.15	11.82	8.18	5.68	3.97	2.78	5
6	115.71	78.22	53.15	43.89	36.29	24.90	17.17	11.89	8.27	5.78	4.05	2.85	6
7	112.78	76.65	52.36	43.36	35.95	24.80	17.18	11.96	8.36	5.87	4.14	2.93	7
8	109.92	75.11	51.59	42.83	35.60	24.69	17.20	12.03	8.46	5.97	4.23	3.01	8
9	107.13	73.60	50.82	42.30	35.26	24.58	17.21	12.11	8.55	6.07	4.32	3.09	9
10	104.40	72.11	50.06	41.78	34.91	24.47	17.22	12.18	8.65	6.17	4.41	3.17	10
11	101.74	70.65	49.31	41.26	34.57	24.36	17.23	12.25	8.74	6.27	4.51	3.26	11
12	99.15	69.23	48.57	40.76	34.24	24.25	17.25	12.32	8.84	6.37	4.60	3.34	12
13	96.62	67.83	47.84	40.25	33.91	24.14	17.26	12.39	8.94	6.47	4.70	3.43	13
14	94.16	66.46	47.13	39.76	33.58	24.03	17.27	12.47	9.04	6.58	4.80	3.52	14
15	91.77	65.12	46.43	39.27	33.25	23.92	17.28	12.54	9.14	6.68	4.91	3.62	15
16	89.44	63.81	45.74	38.79	32.93	23.82	17.30	12.62	9.24	6.79	5.01	3.71	16
17	87.17	62.53	45.06	38.31	32.61	23.71	17.31	12.69	9.34	6.90	5.12	3.81	17
18	84.97	61.27	44.39	37.85	32.30	23.61	17.33	12.77	9.45	7.02	5.23	3.91	18
19	82.83	60.05	43.74	37.39	32.00	23.51	17.34	12.85	9.55	7.13	5.34	4.02	19
20	80.75	58.86	43.10	36.94	31.70	23.41	17.36	12.93	9.66	7.25	5.46	4.13	20
21	78.72	57.69	42.47	36.50	31.40	23.31	17.38	13.01	9.77	7.37	5.58	4.24	21
22	76.73	56.54	41.84	36.05	31.10	23.21	17.39	13.09	9.88	7.49	5.70	4.35	22
23	74.79	55.40	41.22	35.61	30.80	23.11	17.41	13.17	9.99	7.61	5.82	4.47	23
24	72.90	54.29	40.61	35.18	30.51	23.01	17.42	13.25	10.11	7.74	5.95	4.59	24
25	71.06	53.21	40.01	34.76	30.22	22.91	17.44	13.33	10.22	7.87	6.08	4.71	25
26	69.28	52.16	39.43	34.34	29.94	22.82	17.46	13.41	10.34	8.00	6.21	4.83	26
27	67.55	51.13	38.86	33.93	29.66	22.73	17.48	13.50	10.46	8.13	6.34	4.97	27
28	65.85	50.11	38.29	33.52	29.38	22.63	17.50	13.58	10.58	8.26	6.48	5.10	28
29	64.18	49.10	37.72	33.11	29.10	22.53	17.51	13.66	10.69	8.40	6.62	5.23	29
30	62.57	48.13	37.17	32.72	28.82	22.44	17.53	13.75	10.82	8.54	6.76	5.38	30
31	61.01	47.18	36.64	32.33	28.56	22.35	17.55	13.83	10.94	8.68	6.91	5.52	31
32	59.50	46.27	36.12	31.96	28.30	22.26	17.58	13.93	11.07	8.83	7.07	5.67	32
33	58.05	45.38	35.61	31.59	28.06	22.18	17.61	14.02	11.20	8.98	7.22	5.83	33
34	56.62	44.50	35.11	31.23	27.81	22.10	17.63	14.12	11.34	9.14	7.38	5.99	34
35	55.23	43.64	34.61	30.87	27.56	22.02	17.66	14.21	11.47	9.29	7.55	6.15	35
36	53.87	42.80	34.13	30.52	27.32	21.94	17.69	14.31	11.61	9.45	7.72	6.32	36
37	52.56	41.97	33.65	30.17	27.08	21.87	17.72	14.41	11.75	9.61	7.89	6.49	37
38	51.26	41.16	33.18	29.83	26.84	21.79	17.75	14.50	11.89	9.78	8.07	6.67	38
39	50.00	40.37	32.71	29.48	26.60	21.71	17.77	14.60	12.03	9.95	8.24	6.85	39
40	48.77	39.59	32.25	29.15	26.36	21.63	17.80	14.70	12.18	10.12	8.43	7.04	40
41	47.58	38.83	31.80	28.82	26.13	21.55	17.83	14.80	12.32	10.29	8.62	7.24	41
42	46.42	38.09	31.36	28.49	25.91	21.48	17.86	14.90	12.47	10.47	8.81	7.44	42
43	45.30	37.36	30.93	28.18	25.69	21.41	17.90	15.01	12.63	10.65	9.01	7.64	43
44	44.21	36.66	30.51	27.87	25.47	21.34	17.93	15.12	12.78	10.84	9.21	7.86	44
45	43.15	35.97	30.09	27.56	25.26	21.27	17.97	15.23	12.94	11.03	9.43	8.08	45
46	42.11	35.30	29.69	27.26	25.05	21.21	18.01	15.34	13.10	11.22	9.64	8.30	46
47	41.11	34.64	29.29	26.97	24.85	21.15	18.05	15.46	13.27	11.42	9.86	8.54	47
48	40.14	34.01	28.91	26.68	24.65	21.09	18.10	15.57	13.44	11.63	10.09	8.78	48
49	39.20	33.39	28.53	26.41	24.46	21.04	18.15	15.70	13.62	11.84	10.33	9.03	49
50	38.29	32.79	28.18	26.15	24.28	20.99	18.20	15.83	13.80	12.07	10.58	9.29	50
51	37.42	32.22	27.83	25.90	24.11	20.96	18.27	15.97	13.99	12.29	10.83	9.56	51
52	36.58	31.67	27.50	25.66	23.96	20.93	18.34	16.11	14.19	12.53	11.10	9.85	52
53	35.78	31.14	27.19	25.43	23.81	20.91	18.41	16.26	14.40	12.78	11.37	10.15	53
54	35.01	30.64	26.89	25.22	23.67	20.90	18.50	16.42	14.62	13.04	11.66	10.46	54

Sweet & Maxwell

A8: The Ogden Tables

Table 21: Multipliers for loss of pension commencing age 65 (males) *continued*

Age at date of trial	Multiplier calculated with allowance for projected mortality from the 2008–based population projections and rate of return of												Age at date of trial
	-2.0%	-1.5%	-1.0%	-0.75%	-0.5%	0.0%	0.5%	1.0%	1.5%	2.0%	2.5%	3.0%	
55	34.28	30.15	26.61	25.02	23.55	20.90	18.60	16.59	14.85	13.31	11.97	10.78	55
56	33.59	29.70	26.35	24.84	23.44	20.91	18.71	16.78	15.09	13.60	12.29	11.13	56
57	32.92	29.27	26.10	24.68	23.35	20.94	18.83	16.97	15.34	13.90	12.62	11.49	57
58	32.28	28.85	25.87	24.52	23.26	20.97	18.95	17.18	15.60	14.21	12.97	11.86	58
59	31.65	28.44	25.64	24.36	23.17	21.00	19.08	17.38	15.87	14.53	13.32	12.25	59
60	31.03	28.04	25.41	24.21	23.09	21.03	19.21	17.59	16.14	14.85	13.69	12.65	60
61	30.43	27.65	25.19	24.06	23.01	21.07	19.35	17.81	16.43	15.19	14.08	13.07	61
62	29.87	27.28	24.99	23.94	22.94	21.12	19.50	18.04	16.73	15.55	14.48	13.51	62
63	29.34	26.94	24.81	23.83	22.90	21.20	19.67	18.29	17.05	15.93	14.91	13.98	63
64	28.85	26.63	24.65	23.74	22.88	21.29	19.86	18.56	17.39	16.33	15.37	14.49	64
65	28.40	26.37	24.54	23.70	22.90	21.42	20.08	18.87	17.77	16.77	15.86	15.03	65

Table 22: Multipliers for loss of pension commencing age 65 (females)

Multiplier calculated with allowance for projected mortality from the 2008–based population projections and rate of return of

Age at date of trial	-2.0%	-1.5%	-1.0%	-0.75%	-0.5%	0.0%	0.5%	1.0%	1.5%	2.0%	2.5%	3.0%	Age at date of trial
0	153.09	99.71	65.31	52.96	43.01	28.47	18.95	12.67	8.52	5.75	3.90	2.66	0
1	149.98	98.22	64.68	52.59	42.82	28.50	19.06	12.81	8.66	5.87	4.00	2.74	1
2	146.34	96.35	63.78	52.00	42.45	28.40	19.10	12.90	8.76	5.98	4.09	2.82	2
3	142.77	94.51	62.90	51.42	42.08	28.30	19.13	12.99	8.87	6.08	4.19	2.90	3
4	139.29	92.70	62.02	50.84	41.72	28.21	19.16	13.08	8.98	6.18	4.28	2.98	4
5	135.88	90.92	61.16	50.26	41.36	28.11	19.20	13.17	9.08	6.29	4.38	3.06	5
6	132.55	89.17	60.30	49.69	40.99	28.01	19.23	13.26	9.19	6.40	4.47	3.14	6
7	129.30	87.45	59.46	49.12	40.63	27.91	19.26	13.35	9.30	6.51	4.57	3.23	7
8	126.13	85.76	58.62	48.56	40.27	27.81	19.29	13.45	9.41	6.62	4.68	3.32	8
9	123.03	84.10	57.80	48.00	39.92	27.70	19.32	13.54	9.53	6.73	4.78	3.41	9
10	120.00	82.48	56.98	47.45	39.56	27.60	19.35	13.63	9.64	6.85	4.89	3.50	10
11	117.06	80.89	56.18	46.91	39.21	27.50	19.38	13.72	9.75	6.97	4.99	3.60	11
12	114.18	79.32	55.39	46.37	38.87	27.40	19.41	13.81	9.87	7.08	5.11	3.69	12
13	111.37	77.79	54.61	45.83	38.52	27.30	19.44	13.90	9.99	7.20	5.22	3.79	13
14	108.63	76.28	53.84	45.31	38.18	27.20	19.47	14.00	10.11	7.33	5.33	3.90	14
15	105.96	74.81	53.08	44.79	37.84	27.10	19.50	14.09	10.23	7.45	5.45	4.00	15
16	103.35	73.36	52.33	44.27	37.50	27.00	19.53	14.19	10.35	7.58	5.57	4.11	16
17	100.81	71.94	51.59	43.76	37.17	26.90	19.56	14.28	10.47	7.71	5.70	4.23	17
18	98.33	70.55	50.86	43.26	36.84	26.80	19.59	14.38	10.60	7.84	5.82	4.34	18
19	95.92	69.19	50.15	42.77	36.52	26.71	19.62	14.47	10.72	7.97	5.95	4.46	19
20	93.58	67.87	49.45	42.28	36.20	26.61	19.65	14.57	10.85	8.11	6.09	4.58	20
21	91.29	66.56	48.76	41.80	35.88	26.52	19.69	14.67	10.98	8.25	6.22	4.71	21
22	89.05	65.28	48.07	41.33	35.56	26.42	19.72	14.77	11.11	8.39	6.36	4.84	22
23	86.86	64.01	47.39	40.85	35.24	26.32	19.74	14.87	11.24	8.53	6.50	4.97	23
24	84.71	62.77	46.72	40.37	34.93	26.23	19.77	14.97	11.38	8.68	6.65	5.11	24
25	82.63	61.55	46.06	39.91	34.62	26.13	19.80	15.07	11.51	8.83	6.79	5.25	25
26	80.60	60.37	45.41	39.45	34.31	26.03	19.83	15.17	11.65	8.98	6.94	5.39	26
27	78.62	59.20	44.77	39.00	34.01	25.94	19.86	15.27	11.79	9.13	7.10	5.54	27
28	76.69	58.06	44.14	38.55	33.71	25.84	19.89	15.38	11.93	9.29	7.26	5.69	28
29	74.81	56.94	43.52	38.11	33.41	25.75	19.93	15.48	12.07	9.44	7.42	5.84	29
30	72.98	55.84	42.91	37.68	33.12	25.66	19.96	15.58	12.21	9.61	7.58	6.00	30
31	71.20	54.77	42.32	37.25	32.83	25.57	19.99	15.69	12.36	9.77	7.75	6.17	31
32	69.46	53.73	41.73	36.83	32.54	25.48	20.03	15.80	12.51	9.94	7.92	6.34	32
33	67.77	52.70	41.15	36.42	32.26	25.39	20.06	15.91	12.66	10.11	8.10	6.51	33
34	66.12	51.69	40.58	36.00	31.98	25.30	20.09	16.02	12.81	10.28	8.28	6.69	34
35	64.50	50.70	40.01	35.60	31.70	25.21	20.13	16.13	12.97	10.46	8.47	6.88	35
36	62.93	49.73	39.45	35.19	31.43	25.13	20.16	16.24	13.12	10.64	8.66	7.06	36
37	61.41	48.78	38.91	34.80	31.15	25.04	20.20	16.35	13.28	10.83	8.85	7.26	37
38	59.91	47.85	38.37	34.41	30.89	24.95	20.23	16.47	13.44	11.01	9.05	7.46	38
39	58.46	46.94	37.84	34.02	30.62	24.87	20.27	16.58	13.61	11.20	9.25	7.67	39
40	57.04	46.05	37.32	33.64	30.36	24.79	20.31	16.70	13.77	11.40	9.46	7.88	40
41	55.66	45.17	36.80	33.27	30.10	24.70	20.35	16.81	13.94	11.60	9.67	8.10	41
42	54.31	44.32	36.30	32.90	29.84	24.62	20.38	16.93	14.11	11.80	9.89	8.32	42
43	53.01	43.48	35.81	32.54	29.59	24.54	20.43	17.05	14.29	12.00	10.12	8.55	43
44	51.74	42.67	35.33	32.18	29.35	24.47	20.47	17.18	14.46	12.22	10.35	8.79	44
45	50.50	41.88	34.85	31.84	29.11	24.40	20.51	17.31	14.65	12.43	10.58	9.04	45
46	49.30	41.10	34.39	31.50	28.87	24.32	20.56	17.44	14.83	12.65	10.83	9.29	46
47	48.13	40.34	33.93	31.16	28.64	24.26	20.61	17.57	15.02	12.88	11.08	9.55	47
48	47.00	39.61	33.49	30.84	28.42	24.19	20.66	17.70	15.22	13.11	11.33	9.82	48
49	45.91	38.89	33.06	30.52	28.20	24.14	20.72	17.85	15.42	13.35	11.60	10.10	49
50	44.85	38.20	32.64	30.22	27.99	24.08	20.78	17.99	15.62	13.60	11.88	10.40	50
51	43.82	37.52	32.23	29.92	27.79	24.03	20.85	18.14	15.83	13.85	12.16	10.70	51
52	42.82	36.86	31.84	29.63	27.59	23.99	20.92	18.29	16.05	14.12	12.45	11.01	52
53	41.85	36.22	31.45	29.35	27.40	23.95	20.99	18.45	16.27	14.38	12.75	11.33	53
54	40.92	35.60	31.08	29.08	27.22	23.91	21.07	18.62	16.50	14.66	13.06	11.67	54

Table 22: Multipliers for loss of pension commencing age 65 (females) *continued*

Age at date of trial	\-2.0%	\-1.5%	\-1.0%	\-0.75%	\-0.5%	0.0%	0.5%	1.0%	1.5%	2.0%	2.5%	3.0%	Age at date of trial
55	40.02	35.01	30.73	28.82	27.05	23.89	21.16	18.80	16.74	14.95	13.39	12.02	55
56	39.16	34.44	30.38	28.57	26.89	23.87	21.26	18.98	16.99	15.25	13.73	12.38	56
57	38.32	33.88	30.05	28.34	26.74	23.86	21.36	19.17	17.25	15.56	14.08	12.76	57
58	37.51	33.34	29.73	28.11	26.59	23.86	21.46	19.36	17.51	15.88	14.44	13.16	58
59	36.72	32.81	29.42	27.88	26.45	23.85	21.57	19.56	17.78	16.21	14.81	13.56	59
60	35.94	32.29	29.10	27.66	26.31	23.85	21.68	19.76	18.06	16.54	15.19	13.98	60
61	35.18	31.78	28.80	27.44	26.17	23.85	21.79	19.97	18.34	16.89	15.59	14.42	61
62	34.46	31.29	28.51	27.24	26.04	23.86	21.91	20.18	18.63	17.25	16.00	14.87	62
63	33.76	30.83	28.23	27.04	25.93	23.88	22.05	20.41	18.94	17.62	16.43	15.35	63
64	33.10	30.39	27.98	26.88	25.83	23.92	22.20	20.66	19.27	18.02	16.89	15.86	64
65	32.50	29.99	27.76	26.74	25.77	23.98	22.38	20.93	19.63	18.45	17.38	16.40	65

Table 23: Multipliers for loss of pension commencing age 70 (males)

Age at date of trial	-2.0%	-1.5%	-1.0%	-0.75%	-0.5%	0.0%	0.5%	1.0%	1.5%	2.0%	2.5%	3.0%	Age at date of trial
0	116.52	75.30	48.89	39.47	31.89	20.90	13.76	9.09	6.04	4.02	2.69	1.81	0
1	114.10	74.13	48.39	39.17	31.74	20.91	13.83	9.19	6.13	4.11	2.76	1.87	1
2	111.17	72.62	47.66	38.67	31.42	20.81	13.84	9.24	6.20	4.17	2.82	1.91	2
3	108.30	71.12	46.93	38.18	31.10	20.70	13.84	9.29	6.27	4.24	2.88	1.96	3
4	105.50	69.65	46.20	37.69	30.78	20.60	13.85	9.34	6.33	4.31	2.94	2.02	4
5	102.76	68.21	45.49	37.21	30.47	20.50	13.85	9.39	6.40	4.37	3.00	2.07	5
6	100.08	66.80	44.78	36.73	30.16	20.39	13.85	9.44	6.46	4.44	3.06	2.12	6
7	97.48	65.41	44.09	36.25	29.84	20.29	13.85	9.49	6.53	4.51	3.13	2.18	7
8	94.95	64.05	43.40	35.79	29.54	20.19	13.85	9.54	6.60	4.58	3.19	2.23	8
9	92.47	62.71	42.72	35.32	29.23	20.08	13.85	9.59	6.67	4.65	3.26	2.29	9
10	90.04	61.40	42.05	34.86	28.92	19.97	13.85	9.64	6.74	4.73	3.33	2.35	10
11	87.69	60.11	41.39	34.40	28.62	19.87	13.85	9.69	6.81	4.80	3.39	2.41	11
12	85.39	58.86	40.74	33.95	28.32	19.76	13.85	9.74	6.88	4.87	3.46	2.47	12
13	83.16	57.63	40.10	33.51	28.02	19.66	13.85	9.79	6.95	4.95	3.54	2.54	13
14	80.98	56.42	39.47	33.07	27.73	19.56	13.85	9.84	7.02	5.02	3.61	2.60	14
15	78.87	55.24	38.85	32.64	27.44	19.45	13.85	9.89	7.09	5.10	3.68	2.67	15
16	76.81	54.09	38.25	32.21	27.15	19.35	13.85	9.94	7.16	5.18	3.76	2.74	16
17	74.80	52.96	37.65	31.79	26.87	19.25	13.85	9.99	7.24	5.26	3.84	2.81	17
18	72.86	51.86	37.06	31.38	26.59	19.15	13.85	10.05	7.31	5.34	3.92	2.88	18
19	70.97	50.79	36.49	30.98	26.32	19.06	13.85	10.10	7.39	5.43	4.00	2.95	19
20	69.13	49.74	35.93	30.58	26.05	18.96	13.85	10.15	7.47	5.51	4.08	3.03	20
21	67.34	48.71	35.38	30.19	25.79	18.87	13.85	10.21	7.55	5.60	4.17	3.11	21
22	65.59	47.70	34.82	29.80	25.52	18.77	13.85	10.26	7.63	5.69	4.25	3.19	22
23	63.88	46.71	34.28	29.41	25.25	18.67	13.85	10.31	7.70	5.77	4.34	3.27	23
24	62.22	45.74	33.75	29.03	24.99	18.58	13.85	10.37	7.78	5.86	4.43	3.36	24
25	60.60	44.79	33.22	28.65	24.74	18.48	13.86	10.42	7.87	5.96	4.52	3.44	25
26	59.04	43.87	32.71	28.29	24.48	18.39	13.86	10.48	7.95	6.05	4.62	3.53	26
27	57.52	42.97	32.21	27.93	24.24	18.30	13.86	10.54	8.03	6.14	4.71	3.63	27
28	56.02	42.07	31.71	27.57	23.99	18.21	13.86	10.59	8.12	6.24	4.81	3.72	28
29	54.56	41.20	31.22	27.21	23.74	18.11	13.86	10.65	8.20	6.34	4.91	3.82	29
30	53.15	40.34	30.73	26.86	23.49	18.02	13.87	10.70	8.29	6.44	5.01	3.92	30
31	51.78	39.52	30.27	26.52	23.26	17.93	13.87	10.76	8.38	6.54	5.12	4.02	31
32	50.46	38.72	29.81	26.19	23.03	17.85	13.88	10.82	8.47	6.64	5.23	4.12	32
33	49.19	37.94	29.37	25.87	22.81	17.77	13.89	10.89	8.56	6.75	5.34	4.23	33
34	47.94	37.18	28.93	25.55	22.59	17.69	13.90	10.95	8.66	6.86	5.45	4.35	34
35	46.72	36.43	28.50	25.24	22.37	17.61	13.91	11.02	8.75	6.97	5.57	4.46	35
36	45.54	35.70	28.08	24.93	22.15	17.53	13.92	11.08	8.85	7.08	5.69	4.58	36
37	44.39	34.98	27.66	24.62	21.94	17.45	13.93	11.15	8.95	7.20	5.81	4.70	37
38	43.26	34.27	27.24	24.32	21.72	17.37	13.94	11.21	9.04	7.32	5.93	4.82	38
39	42.16	33.58	26.84	24.02	21.51	17.30	13.95	11.28	9.14	7.43	6.06	4.95	39
40	41.09	32.90	26.43	23.72	21.30	17.22	13.95	11.34	9.24	7.55	6.19	5.08	40
41	40.05	32.24	26.04	23.43	21.10	17.14	13.97	11.41	9.35	7.68	6.32	5.22	41
42	39.04	31.60	25.66	23.15	20.90	17.07	13.98	11.48	9.45	7.80	6.46	5.36	42
43	38.06	30.97	25.28	22.87	20.70	16.99	13.99	11.55	9.56	7.93	6.60	5.50	43
44	37.11	30.36	24.92	22.60	20.51	16.92	14.01	11.62	9.67	8.06	6.74	5.65	44
45	36.18	29.76	24.56	22.33	20.32	16.85	14.02	11.69	9.78	8.20	6.89	5.80	45
46	35.28	29.18	24.20	22.06	20.13	16.79	14.04	11.77	9.89	8.33	7.04	5.96	46
47	34.41	28.61	23.86	21.81	19.95	16.72	14.06	11.85	10.01	8.47	7.19	6.12	47
48	33.57	28.06	23.52	21.56	19.77	16.66	14.08	11.92	10.13	8.62	7.35	6.29	48
49	32.75	27.52	23.19	21.31	19.60	16.60	14.10	12.01	10.25	8.77	7.52	6.46	49
50	31.96	27.01	22.88	21.08	19.43	16.55	14.13	12.09	10.38	8.92	7.69	6.64	50
51	31.21	26.51	22.58	20.86	19.28	16.51	14.17	12.19	10.51	9.08	7.87	6.83	51
52	30.48	26.03	22.29	20.64	19.13	16.47	14.21	12.28	10.65	9.25	8.05	7.02	52
53	29.79	25.57	22.01	20.44	19.00	16.43	14.25	12.39	10.79	9.42	8.24	7.23	53
54	29.12	25.13	21.75	20.25	18.87	16.41	14.30	12.50	10.94	9.60	8.44	7.44	54

Table 23: Multipliers for loss of pension commencing age 70 (males) *continued*

Age at date of trial	\-2.0%	\-1.5%	\-1.0%	\-0.75%	\-0.5%	0.0%	0.5%	1.0%	1.5%	2.0%	2.5%	3.0%	Age at date of trial
55	28.48	24.71	21.50	20.07	18.75	16.39	14.36	12.61	11.10	9.79	8.65	7.66	55
56	27.88	24.32	21.27	19.91	18.65	16.39	14.43	12.74	11.27	9.99	8.88	7.90	56
57	27.30	23.94	21.05	19.76	18.55	16.39	14.51	12.88	11.45	10.20	9.11	8.15	57
58	26.74	23.58	20.84	19.61	18.46	16.40	14.59	13.02	11.63	10.42	9.35	8.40	58
59	26.19	23.22	20.63	19.47	18.38	16.40	14.68	13.16	11.82	10.64	9.59	8.67	59
60	25.65	22.86	20.42	19.32	18.29	16.41	14.76	13.30	12.01	10.86	9.85	8.94	60
61	25.13	22.52	20.22	19.18	18.20	16.42	14.84	13.44	12.20	11.10	10.11	9.23	61
62	24.63	22.19	20.03	19.05	18.13	16.44	14.94	13.60	12.41	11.34	10.38	9.52	62
63	24.16	21.88	19.86	18.94	18.07	16.47	15.04	13.77	12.63	11.60	10.67	9.84	63
64	23.72	21.60	19.71	18.84	18.03	16.52	15.17	13.95	12.86	11.87	10.98	10.18	64
65	23.33	21.35	19.59	18.78	18.01	16.59	15.31	14.16	13.12	12.17	11.32	10.54	65
66	22.97	21.14	19.50	18.74	18.02	16.69	15.48	14.39	13.40	12.50	11.68	10.93	66
67	22.66	20.96	19.44	18.73	18.06	16.81	15.68	14.65	13.71	12.86	12.07	11.36	67
68	22.38	20.82	19.40	18.75	18.12	16.96	15.90	14.93	14.05	13.24	12.50	11.82	68
69	22.13	20.70	19.40	18.79	18.21	17.13	16.15	15.24	14.42	13.66	12.96	12.31	69
70	21.91	20.60	19.41	18.85	18.32	17.32	16.41	15.58	14.81	14.10	13.44	12.84	70

Multiplier calculated with allowance for projected mortality from the 2008–based population projections and rate of return of

Table 24: Multipliers for loss of pension commencing age 70 (females)

Age at date of trial	\-2.0%	\-1.5%	\-1.0%	\-0.75%	\-0.5%	0.0%	0.5%	1.0%	1.5%	2.0%	2.5%	3.0%	Age at date of trial
	Multiplier calculated with allowance for projected mortality from the 2008–based population projections and rate of return of												
0	134.74	86.70	56.06	45.17	36.43	23.78	15.60	10.28	6.80	4.52	3.01	2.02	0
1	131.93	85.35	55.49	44.82	36.25	23.79	15.68	10.38	6.91	4.61	3.09	2.08	1
2	128.66	83.68	54.69	44.29	35.92	23.69	15.70	10.45	6.99	4.69	3.16	2.14	2
3	125.45	82.03	53.90	43.77	35.58	23.60	15.72	10.52	7.07	4.77	3.23	2.20	3
4	122.32	80.42	53.12	43.25	35.25	23.50	15.74	10.58	7.15	4.85	3.30	2.25	4
5	119.26	78.83	52.35	42.74	34.93	23.41	15.76	10.65	7.23	4.93	3.37	2.32	5
6	116.28	77.27	51.59	42.22	34.60	23.31	15.77	10.72	7.31	5.01	3.44	2.38	6
7	113.36	75.74	50.83	41.72	34.27	23.21	15.79	10.78	7.39	5.09	3.52	2.44	7
8	110.51	74.23	50.09	41.22	33.95	23.11	15.80	10.85	7.48	5.18	3.59	2.51	8
9	107.73	72.75	49.35	40.72	33.63	23.01	15.82	10.92	7.56	5.26	3.67	2.57	9
10	105.03	71.30	48.63	40.23	33.31	22.92	15.83	10.98	7.65	5.35	3.75	2.64	10
11	102.39	69.89	47.92	39.74	33.00	22.82	15.85	11.05	7.73	5.43	3.83	2.71	11
12	99.81	68.49	47.21	39.26	32.68	22.72	15.86	11.12	7.82	5.52	3.92	2.79	12
13	97.30	67.13	46.52	38.78	32.37	22.62	15.87	11.18	7.91	5.61	4.00	2.86	13
14	94.85	65.79	45.83	38.32	32.07	22.53	15.89	11.25	8.00	5.71	4.09	2.94	14
15	92.46	64.48	45.16	37.85	31.76	22.43	15.90	11.32	8.09	5.80	4.17	3.01	15
16	90.13	63.19	44.49	37.39	31.46	22.33	15.92	11.39	8.18	5.89	4.26	3.09	16
17	87.86	61.93	43.84	36.94	31.16	22.24	15.93	11.46	8.27	5.99	4.36	3.18	17
18	85.65	60.70	43.19	36.49	30.86	22.14	15.95	11.53	8.36	6.09	4.45	3.26	18
19	83.51	59.49	42.56	36.05	30.57	22.05	15.96	11.60	8.46	6.19	4.55	3.35	19
20	81.42	58.32	41.94	35.62	30.29	21.96	15.98	11.67	8.55	6.29	4.64	3.44	20
21	79.38	57.16	41.33	35.20	30.00	21.86	15.99	11.74	8.65	6.40	4.74	3.53	21
22	77.38	56.02	40.72	34.77	29.72	21.77	16.01	11.81	8.75	6.50	4.85	3.62	22
23	75.43	54.90	40.12	34.35	29.43	21.67	16.02	11.88	8.85	6.61	4.95	3.72	23
24	73.52	53.80	39.52	33.93	29.15	21.58	16.03	11.95	8.94	6.71	5.06	3.82	24
25	71.67	52.72	38.94	33.51	28.87	21.48	16.05	12.03	9.04	6.82	5.16	3.92	25
26	69.86	51.67	38.37	33.11	28.60	21.39	16.06	12.10	9.14	6.93	5.28	4.03	26
27	68.11	50.64	37.80	32.71	28.32	21.30	16.07	12.17	9.25	7.05	5.39	4.13	27
28	66.39	49.63	37.25	32.31	28.05	21.21	16.09	12.24	9.35	7.16	5.50	4.24	28
29	64.72	48.64	36.70	31.92	27.79	21.11	16.10	12.32	9.46	7.28	5.62	4.36	29
30	63.09	47.68	36.16	31.53	27.52	21.03	16.12	12.39	9.56	7.40	5.74	4.47	30
31	61.51	46.73	35.63	31.16	27.27	20.94	16.13	12.47	9.67	7.52	5.87	4.59	31
32	59.98	45.81	35.11	30.78	27.01	20.85	16.15	12.55	9.78	7.65	6.00	4.72	32
33	58.48	44.91	34.60	30.42	26.76	20.76	16.16	12.62	9.89	7.77	6.13	4.84	33
34	57.02	44.02	34.10	30.05	26.51	20.68	16.18	12.70	10.00	7.90	6.26	4.97	34
35	55.59	43.14	33.60	29.69	26.26	20.59	16.20	12.78	10.12	8.03	6.39	5.10	35
36	54.20	42.29	33.11	29.34	26.01	20.50	16.21	12.86	10.23	8.16	6.53	5.24	36
37	52.85	41.45	32.63	28.99	25.77	20.42	16.23	12.94	10.35	8.30	6.67	5.38	37
38	51.53	40.64	32.16	28.64	25.53	20.33	16.25	13.02	10.46	8.44	6.82	5.53	38
39	50.24	39.83	31.69	28.30	25.29	20.25	16.26	13.10	10.58	8.57	6.97	5.67	39
40	48.99	39.05	31.23	27.96	25.06	20.17	16.28	13.18	10.70	8.72	7.12	5.83	40
41	47.77	38.28	30.78	27.63	24.82	20.08	16.30	13.27	10.83	8.86	7.27	5.98	41
42	46.58	37.53	30.34	27.31	24.60	20.00	16.32	13.35	10.95	9.01	7.43	6.14	42
43	45.43	36.80	29.90	26.99	24.37	19.93	16.34	13.44	11.08	9.16	7.59	6.31	43
44	44.31	36.08	29.48	26.67	24.15	19.85	16.36	13.52	11.21	9.31	7.76	6.48	44
45	43.23	35.39	29.06	26.37	23.94	19.78	16.39	13.61	11.34	9.47	7.93	6.66	45
46	42.17	34.70	28.65	26.06	23.73	19.70	16.41	13.70	11.47	9.63	8.11	6.84	46
47	41.14	34.04	28.25	25.77	23.52	19.63	16.44	13.80	11.61	9.80	8.29	7.03	47
48	40.14	33.39	27.86	25.48	23.32	19.57	16.47	13.89	11.75	9.97	8.47	7.22	48
49	39.18	32.77	27.49	25.20	23.12	19.51	16.50	13.99	11.90	10.14	8.67	7.42	49
50	38.25	32.16	27.12	24.93	22.93	19.45	16.54	14.10	12.05	10.32	8.86	7.63	50
51	37.34	31.56	26.76	24.66	22.75	19.39	16.57	14.20	12.20	10.51	9.07	7.84	51
52	36.46	30.99	26.41	24.40	22.57	19.34	16.62	14.31	12.36	10.69	9.28	8.06	52
53	35.61	30.43	26.07	24.15	22.40	19.29	16.66	14.42	12.52	10.89	9.49	8.30	53
54	34.79	29.89	25.74	23.91	22.23	19.25	16.71	14.54	12.69	11.09	9.72	8.53	54

Table 24: Multipliers for loss of pension commencing age 70 (females) *continued*

Age at date of trial	\-2.0%	\-1.5%	\-1.0%	\-0.75%	\-0.5%	0.0%	0.5%	1.0%	1.5%	2.0%	2.5%	3.0%	Age at date of trial
55	34.00	29.36	25.43	23.68	22.08	19.21	16.77	14.67	12.86	11.30	9.95	8.78	55
56	33.24	28.86	25.12	23.46	21.93	19.19	16.83	14.80	13.04	11.52	10.19	9.04	56
57	32.51	28.37	24.83	23.25	21.79	19.16	16.89	14.93	13.23	11.74	10.44	9.31	57
58	31.79	27.90	24.54	23.04	21.65	19.14	16.96	15.07	13.42	11.97	10.70	9.59	58
59	31.10	27.43	24.26	22.84	21.51	19.12	17.03	15.21	13.61	12.21	10.97	9.88	59
60	30.41	26.97	23.98	22.63	21.37	19.10	17.10	15.35	13.81	12.44	11.24	10.17	60
61	29.74	26.52	23.71	22.43	21.24	19.08	17.17	15.49	14.01	12.69	11.52	10.48	61
62	29.10	26.09	23.44	22.24	21.11	19.06	17.25	15.64	14.22	12.94	11.81	10.80	62
63	28.48	25.67	23.19	22.06	21.00	19.06	17.33	15.80	14.43	13.21	12.11	11.13	63
64	27.90	25.28	22.96	21.90	20.90	19.07	17.43	15.97	14.67	13.49	12.43	11.48	64
65	27.36	24.92	22.75	21.76	20.82	19.10	17.55	16.17	14.92	13.79	12.78	11.86	65
66	26.86	24.60	22.58	21.65	20.77	19.15	17.69	16.38	15.19	14.12	13.15	12.26	66
67	26.40	24.30	22.43	21.56	20.74	19.22	17.85	16.61	15.49	14.47	13.54	12.69	67
68	25.97	24.04	22.30	21.50	20.73	19.32	18.03	16.87	15.81	14.84	13.96	13.15	68
69	25.57	23.79	22.19	21.45	20.74	19.43	18.23	17.14	16.15	15.24	14.40	13.64	69
70	25.19	23.57	22.10	21.41	20.76	19.55	18.44	17.43	16.50	15.65	14.87	14.15	70

Multiplier calculated with allowance for projected mortality from the 2008–based population projections and rate of return of

Table 25: Multipliers for loss of pension commencing age 75 (males)

Multiplier calculated with allowance for projected mortality from the 2008–based population projections and rate of return of

Age at date of trial	-2.0%	-1.5%	-1.0%	-0.75%	-0.5%	0.0%	0.5%	1.0%	1.5%	2.0%	2.5%	3.0%	Age at date of trial
0	97.81	62.36	39.93	32.00	25.68	16.58	10.74	6.99	4.57	2.99	1.97	1.30	0
1	95.69	61.34	39.49	31.73	25.52	16.56	10.79	7.06	4.63	3.05	2.02	1.34	1
2	93.15	60.03	38.85	31.30	25.24	16.47	10.79	7.09	4.68	3.10	2.06	1.37	2
3	90.66	58.74	38.22	30.87	24.97	16.37	10.78	7.12	4.73	3.15	2.10	1.41	3
4	88.23	57.47	37.59	30.45	24.69	16.28	10.77	7.16	4.77	3.19	2.14	1.44	4
5	85.86	56.23	36.98	30.03	24.41	16.18	10.76	7.19	4.82	3.24	2.19	1.48	5
6	83.55	55.01	36.37	29.61	24.14	16.08	10.75	7.22	4.86	3.29	2.23	1.52	6
7	81.31	53.82	35.77	29.20	23.86	15.98	10.74	7.25	4.91	3.33	2.27	1.55	7
8	79.12	52.65	35.18	28.80	23.59	15.88	10.73	7.28	4.95	3.38	2.32	1.59	8
9	76.97	51.50	34.59	28.39	23.32	15.79	10.72	7.31	5.00	3.43	2.36	1.63	9
10	74.89	50.37	34.02	27.99	23.06	15.69	10.71	7.34	5.05	3.48	2.41	1.67	10
11	72.85	49.27	33.45	27.60	22.79	15.59	10.70	7.37	5.09	3.53	2.46	1.71	11
12	70.88	48.19	32.89	27.21	22.53	15.49	10.69	7.40	5.14	3.58	2.50	1.76	12
13	68.96	47.14	32.34	26.83	22.27	15.39	10.67	7.43	5.19	3.63	2.55	1.80	13
14	67.09	46.10	31.80	26.45	22.02	15.29	10.66	7.46	5.23	3.68	2.60	1.84	14
15	65.27	45.10	31.27	26.08	21.76	15.20	10.65	7.49	5.28	3.74	2.65	1.89	15
16	63.50	44.11	30.75	25.71	21.51	15.10	10.64	7.52	5.33	3.79	2.71	1.94	16
17	61.78	43.15	30.24	25.35	21.27	15.01	10.63	7.55	5.38	3.85	2.76	1.98	17
18	60.12	42.21	29.74	24.99	21.03	14.92	10.62	7.58	5.43	3.90	2.81	2.03	18
19	58.50	41.29	29.25	24.65	20.79	14.82	10.61	7.61	5.48	3.96	2.87	2.08	19
20	56.93	40.40	28.77	24.31	20.55	14.74	10.60	7.65	5.53	4.02	2.92	2.13	20
21	55.40	39.52	28.29	23.97	20.32	14.65	10.59	7.68	5.59	4.08	2.98	2.19	21
22	53.90	38.66	27.82	23.63	20.09	14.55	10.58	7.71	5.64	4.13	3.04	2.24	22
23	52.44	37.81	27.36	23.30	19.86	14.46	10.57	7.74	5.69	4.19	3.10	2.30	23
24	51.02	36.99	26.90	22.97	19.63	14.37	10.55	7.77	5.74	4.25	3.16	2.35	24
25	49.64	36.18	26.46	22.65	19.41	14.28	10.54	7.81	5.80	4.31	3.22	2.41	25
26	48.31	35.40	26.02	22.34	19.19	14.20	10.53	7.84	5.85	4.38	3.29	2.47	26
27	47.02	34.64	25.60	22.03	18.98	14.11	10.52	7.87	5.91	4.44	3.35	2.53	27
28	45.74	33.88	25.17	21.72	18.76	14.02	10.51	7.90	5.96	4.51	3.42	2.60	28
29	44.50	33.14	24.75	21.41	18.54	13.93	10.50	7.94	6.01	4.57	3.48	2.66	29
30	43.30	32.41	24.34	21.11	18.33	13.85	10.49	7.97	6.07	4.64	3.55	2.73	30
31	42.14	31.71	23.94	20.82	18.13	13.76	10.48	8.00	6.13	4.70	3.62	2.79	31
32	41.02	31.04	23.56	20.54	17.93	13.69	10.48	8.04	6.19	4.77	3.69	2.86	32
33	39.94	30.38	23.18	20.27	17.74	13.61	10.47	8.08	6.25	4.85	3.77	2.94	33
34	38.89	29.74	22.81	20.00	17.54	13.53	10.47	8.12	6.31	4.92	3.84	3.01	34
35	37.86	29.10	22.44	19.73	17.35	13.45	10.46	8.15	6.37	4.99	3.92	3.09	35
36	36.86	28.49	22.08	19.46	17.16	13.38	10.46	8.19	6.43	5.07	4.00	3.16	36
37	35.88	27.88	21.73	19.20	16.98	13.30	10.45	8.23	6.50	5.14	4.08	3.24	37
38	34.93	27.29	21.38	18.94	16.79	13.23	10.44	8.27	6.56	5.22	4.16	3.33	38
39	34.00	26.71	21.03	18.68	16.61	13.15	10.44	8.31	6.62	5.30	4.24	3.41	39
40	33.10	26.14	20.69	18.43	16.43	13.07	10.43	8.34	6.69	5.38	4.33	3.49	40
41	32.22	25.58	20.36	18.18	16.25	13.00	10.43	8.38	6.75	5.46	4.42	3.58	41
42	31.38	25.04	20.04	17.94	16.07	12.93	10.42	8.42	6.82	5.54	4.51	3.67	42
43	30.55	24.51	19.72	17.70	15.90	12.86	10.42	8.46	6.89	5.62	4.60	3.77	43
44	29.75	24.00	19.41	17.47	15.73	12.79	10.42	8.50	6.96	5.71	4.69	3.86	44
45	28.98	23.50	19.10	17.24	15.57	12.72	10.41	8.55	7.03	5.79	4.79	3.96	45
46	28.22	23.01	18.80	17.01	15.41	12.65	10.41	8.59	7.10	5.88	4.88	4.06	46
47	27.49	22.53	18.51	16.79	15.25	12.59	10.41	8.63	7.17	5.97	4.99	4.17	47
48	26.78	22.07	18.23	16.58	15.09	12.52	10.41	8.68	7.25	6.07	5.09	4.28	48
49	26.10	21.62	17.95	16.37	14.94	12.46	10.42	8.73	7.33	6.16	5.20	4.39	49
50	25.44	21.18	17.68	16.17	14.80	12.41	10.43	8.78	7.41	6.26	5.31	4.50	50
51	24.80	20.77	17.43	15.98	14.66	12.36	10.44	8.83	7.49	6.37	5.42	4.62	51
52	24.20	20.37	17.18	15.80	14.53	12.31	10.45	8.89	7.58	6.48	5.54	4.75	52
53	23.61	19.98	16.95	15.62	14.41	12.27	10.47	8.96	7.67	6.59	5.67	4.88	53
54	23.05	19.61	16.72	15.45	14.29	12.23	10.50	9.02	7.77	6.70	5.80	5.02	54

Table 25: Multipliers for loss of pension commencing age 75 (males) *continued*

Age at date of trial	\-2.0%	\-1.5%	\-1.0%	\-0.75%	\-0.5%	0.0%	0.5%	1.0%	1.5%	2.0%	2.5%	3.0%	Age at date of trial
55	22.52	19.26	16.51	15.30	14.18	12.20	10.53	9.09	7.87	6.83	5.93	5.16	55
56	22.01	18.93	16.31	15.15	14.08	12.18	10.56	9.17	7.98	6.96	6.08	5.31	56
57	21.53	18.61	16.12	15.02	13.99	12.17	10.60	9.26	8.10	7.09	6.23	5.47	57
58	21.06	18.30	15.94	14.88	13.91	12.16	10.65	9.34	8.21	7.23	6.38	5.64	58
59	20.60	18.00	15.76	14.75	13.82	12.15	10.69	9.43	8.33	7.38	6.54	5.81	59
60	20.15	17.70	15.58	14.62	13.73	12.13	10.74	9.52	8.45	7.52	6.70	5.98	60
61	19.71	17.41	15.40	14.49	13.65	12.12	10.78	9.61	8.58	7.67	6.87	6.16	61
62	19.29	17.13	15.23	14.38	13.57	12.12	10.84	9.71	8.71	7.83	7.04	6.35	62
63	18.89	16.86	15.08	14.27	13.51	12.12	10.89	9.81	8.85	7.99	7.23	6.55	63
64	18.52	16.62	14.94	14.17	13.45	12.13	10.96	9.92	8.99	8.16	7.42	6.76	64
65	18.18	16.40	14.82	14.10	13.41	12.16	11.05	10.05	9.16	8.35	7.63	6.99	65
66	17.87	16.21	14.73	14.04	13.40	12.21	11.15	10.20	9.34	8.56	7.86	7.23	66
67	17.60	16.04	14.65	14.01	13.40	12.28	11.27	10.36	9.53	8.79	8.11	7.50	67
68	17.35	15.90	14.60	14.00	13.42	12.37	11.41	10.54	9.75	9.03	8.38	7.78	68
69	17.12	15.78	14.56	14.00	13.46	12.47	11.56	10.73	9.98	9.30	8.67	8.09	69
70	16.92	15.67	14.54	14.02	13.51	12.58	11.72	10.94	10.23	9.58	8.97	8.42	70
71	16.72	15.57	14.53	14.04	13.57	12.70	11.90	11.17	10.49	9.87	9.30	8.77	71
72	16.53	15.48	14.52	14.07	13.64	12.83	12.08	11.40	10.77	10.18	9.64	9.14	72
73	16.36	15.40	14.52	14.11	13.71	12.97	12.28	11.64	11.05	10.51	10.00	9.53	73
74	16.19	15.33	14.53	14.16	13.80	13.12	12.49	11.90	11.36	10.86	10.39	9.95	74
75	16.04	15.27	14.56	14.22	13.90	13.29	12.72	12.19	11.70	11.24	10.81	10.40	75

Multiplier calculated with allowance for projected mortality from the 2008-based population projections and rate of return of

Table 26: Multipliers for loss of pension commencing age 75 (females)

Age at date of trial	-2.0%	-1.5%	-1.0%	-0.75%	-0.5%	0.0%	0.5%	1.0%	1.5%	2.0%	2.5%	3.0%	Age at date of trial
0	114.99	73.05	46.61	37.29	29.87	19.22	12.42	8.06	5.25	3.43	2.25	1.48	0
1	112.51	71.86	46.09	36.97	29.69	19.21	12.48	8.13	5.33	3.50	2.31	1.53	1
2	109.64	70.40	45.40	36.51	29.40	19.12	12.48	8.18	5.38	3.56	2.36	1.57	2
3	106.83	68.96	44.71	36.05	29.10	19.02	12.49	8.23	5.44	3.61	2.41	1.61	3
4	104.08	67.55	44.02	35.60	28.81	18.93	12.49	8.27	5.50	3.67	2.46	1.65	4
5	101.41	66.16	43.35	35.15	28.52	18.84	12.49	8.32	5.56	3.73	2.51	1.69	5
6	98.79	64.80	42.69	34.70	28.23	18.75	12.50	8.36	5.62	3.79	2.56	1.74	6
7	96.24	63.47	42.03	34.25	27.94	18.65	12.50	8.41	5.67	3.84	2.61	1.78	7
8	93.75	62.16	41.38	33.81	27.66	18.56	12.50	8.45	5.73	3.90	2.67	1.83	8
9	91.32	60.87	40.74	33.38	27.37	18.46	12.50	8.50	5.79	3.97	2.72	1.88	9
10	88.95	59.61	40.11	32.95	27.09	18.37	12.50	8.54	5.85	4.03	2.78	1.92	10
11	86.65	58.38	39.49	32.53	26.82	18.28	12.50	8.59	5.92	4.09	2.84	1.97	11
12	84.41	57.17	38.88	32.11	26.54	18.18	12.51	8.63	5.98	4.15	2.90	2.03	12
13	82.21	55.99	38.27	31.69	26.26	18.09	12.51	8.68	6.04	4.22	2.96	2.08	13
14	80.08	54.83	37.68	31.28	25.99	18.00	12.51	8.72	6.10	4.28	3.02	2.13	14
15	78.00	53.69	37.09	30.88	25.73	17.91	12.51	8.77	6.16	4.35	3.08	2.19	15
16	75.98	52.58	36.52	30.48	25.46	17.81	12.51	8.81	6.23	4.42	3.14	2.24	16
17	74.00	51.48	35.95	30.08	25.20	17.72	12.51	8.86	6.29	4.49	3.21	2.30	17
18	72.08	50.42	35.39	29.69	24.94	17.63	12.51	8.90	6.36	4.55	3.27	2.36	18
19	70.22	49.37	34.84	29.31	24.68	17.54	12.51	8.95	6.42	4.63	3.34	2.42	19
20	68.41	48.36	34.31	28.94	24.43	17.45	12.51	9.00	6.49	4.70	3.41	2.48	20
21	66.64	47.36	33.78	28.57	24.18	17.36	12.51	9.05	6.56	4.77	3.48	2.55	21
22	64.91	46.38	33.26	28.20	23.93	17.27	12.51	9.09	6.63	4.85	3.55	2.61	22
23	63.22	45.41	32.73	27.83	23.68	17.18	12.51	9.14	6.69	4.92	3.63	2.68	23
24	61.56	44.46	32.22	27.46	23.43	17.09	12.51	9.18	6.76	4.99	3.70	2.75	24
25	59.96	43.53	31.71	27.10	23.18	17.00	12.51	9.23	6.83	5.07	3.78	2.82	25
26	58.40	42.63	31.22	26.75	22.94	16.91	12.51	9.28	6.90	5.15	3.85	2.89	26
27	56.88	41.74	30.73	26.40	22.70	16.82	12.51	9.32	6.97	5.23	3.93	2.97	27
28	55.40	40.87	30.25	26.06	22.47	16.74	12.50	9.37	7.04	5.31	4.01	3.04	28
29	53.96	40.02	29.78	25.72	22.23	16.65	12.50	9.42	7.12	5.39	4.10	3.12	29
30	52.56	39.19	29.32	25.39	22.00	16.56	12.50	9.47	7.19	5.47	4.18	3.20	30
31	51.20	38.38	28.86	25.06	21.78	16.48	12.50	9.52	7.26	5.56	4.27	3.28	31
32	49.88	37.59	28.42	24.74	21.55	16.39	12.51	9.57	7.34	5.65	4.35	3.37	32
33	48.59	36.82	27.98	24.42	21.33	16.31	12.51	9.62	7.42	5.73	4.44	3.45	33
34	47.33	36.05	27.55	24.11	21.11	16.23	12.51	9.67	7.49	5.82	4.54	3.54	34
35	46.10	35.30	27.12	23.79	20.89	16.14	12.51	9.72	7.57	5.91	4.63	3.63	35
36	44.91	34.57	26.70	23.49	20.68	16.06	12.51	9.77	7.65	6.00	4.73	3.73	36
37	43.75	33.86	26.29	23.19	20.47	15.98	12.51	9.82	7.73	6.10	4.82	3.82	37
38	42.62	33.16	25.88	22.89	20.26	15.90	12.51	9.87	7.81	6.19	4.92	3.92	38
39	41.52	32.48	25.48	22.59	20.05	15.82	12.51	9.92	7.89	6.29	5.02	4.02	39
40	40.44	31.81	25.09	22.30	19.84	15.73	12.51	9.97	7.97	6.39	5.13	4.13	40
41	39.40	31.15	24.70	22.02	19.64	15.66	12.51	10.03	8.05	6.49	5.23	4.23	41
42	38.38	30.51	24.32	21.74	19.44	15.58	12.52	10.08	8.14	6.59	5.34	4.34	42
43	37.40	29.89	23.95	21.46	19.24	15.50	12.52	10.13	8.22	6.69	5.45	4.46	43
44	36.44	29.28	23.59	21.19	19.05	15.43	12.52	10.19	8.31	6.80	5.57	4.57	44
45	35.52	28.69	23.23	20.93	18.86	15.35	12.53	10.25	8.40	6.90	5.69	4.69	45
46	34.61	28.10	22.88	20.66	18.68	15.28	12.53	10.31	8.49	7.01	5.81	4.82	46
47	33.73	27.54	22.54	20.41	18.49	15.21	12.54	10.36	8.58	7.13	5.93	4.94	47
48	32.89	26.99	22.21	20.16	18.32	15.14	12.55	10.43	8.68	7.24	6.06	5.07	48
49	32.07	26.46	21.88	19.92	18.15	15.08	12.56	10.49	8.78	7.36	6.19	5.21	49
50	31.27	25.94	21.57	19.69	17.98	15.02	12.58	10.56	8.88	7.48	6.32	5.35	50
51	30.50	25.43	21.26	19.45	17.81	14.96	12.59	10.62	8.98	7.61	6.46	5.49	51
52	29.75	24.94	20.96	19.23	17.65	14.90	12.61	10.69	9.09	7.74	6.60	5.64	52
53	29.03	24.47	20.67	19.01	17.50	14.85	12.63	10.77	9.20	7.87	6.75	5.80	53
54	28.33	24.01	20.39	18.80	17.35	14.80	12.66	10.84	9.31	8.01	6.90	5.96	54

A8: The Ogden Tables

Table 26: Multipliers for loss of pension commencing age 75 (females) *continued*

Age at date of trial	−2.0%	−1.5%	−1.0%	−0.75%	−0.5%	0.0%	0.5%	1.0%	1.5%	2.0%	2.5%	3.0%	Age at date of trial
55	27.66	23.56	20.12	18.60	17.21	14.76	12.69	10.92	9.43	8.15	7.06	6.12	55
56	27.02	23.14	19.86	18.41	17.08	14.72	12.72	11.01	9.55	8.30	7.22	6.30	56
57	26.39	22.72	19.60	18.22	16.95	14.69	12.75	11.10	9.67	8.45	7.39	6.48	57
58	25.78	22.32	19.36	18.04	16.83	14.66	12.79	11.19	9.80	8.60	7.56	6.66	58
59	25.19	21.92	19.11	17.86	16.70	14.62	12.83	11.28	9.93	8.76	7.74	6.85	59
60	24.61	21.53	18.87	17.68	16.57	14.59	12.86	11.37	10.06	8.92	7.92	7.05	60
61	24.04	21.14	18.63	17.50	16.45	14.55	12.90	11.46	10.19	9.08	8.11	7.25	61
62	23.49	20.77	18.40	17.33	16.33	14.52	12.94	11.55	10.33	9.25	8.30	7.46	62
63	22.96	20.41	18.17	17.16	16.22	14.50	12.99	11.65	10.47	9.43	8.50	7.68	63
64	22.46	20.07	17.97	17.01	16.12	14.48	13.04	11.76	10.63	9.62	8.71	7.91	64
65	22.00	19.76	17.78	16.88	16.04	14.49	13.11	11.89	10.79	9.82	8.94	8.16	65
66	21.56	19.48	17.62	16.77	15.97	14.51	13.20	12.03	10.98	10.03	9.19	8.42	66
67	21.16	19.22	17.48	16.68	15.93	14.54	13.30	12.18	11.17	10.27	9.45	8.71	67
68	20.79	18.98	17.36	16.61	15.90	14.59	13.41	12.35	11.39	10.51	9.72	9.01	68
69	20.44	18.76	17.25	16.55	15.88	14.65	13.54	12.53	11.61	10.78	10.02	9.33	69
70	20.11	18.55	17.15	16.49	15.87	14.72	13.67	12.72	11.85	11.05	10.33	9.66	70
71	19.78	18.35	17.05	16.44	15.87	14.79	13.81	12.91	12.09	11.34	10.65	10.01	71
72	19.46	18.14	16.95	16.39	15.86	14.86	13.95	13.11	12.34	11.63	10.98	10.38	72
73	19.13	17.93	16.84	16.33	15.84	14.93	14.08	13.31	12.59	11.93	11.32	10.75	73
74	18.80	17.72	16.74	16.28	15.83	15.00	14.23	13.51	12.86	12.24	11.68	11.15	74
75	18.48	17.53	16.64	16.23	15.83	15.08	14.38	13.74	13.14	12.58	12.06	11.58	75

Multiplier calculated with allowance for projected mortality from the 2008–based population projections and rate of return of

Table 27: Discounting factors for term certain

Term	\-2.0%	\-1.5%	\-1.0%	\-0.75%	\-0.5%	0.0%	0.5%	1.0%	1.5%	2.0%	2.5%	3.0%	Term
1	1.0204	1.0152	1.0101	1.0076	1.0050	1.0000	0.9950	0.9901	0.9852	0.9804	0.9756	0.9709	1
2	1.0412	1.0307	1.0203	1.0152	1.0101	1.0000	0.9901	0.9803	0.9707	0.9612	0.9518	0.9426	2
3	1.0625	1.0464	1.0306	1.0228	1.0152	1.0000	0.9851	0.9706	0.9563	0.9423	0.9286	0.9151	3
4	1.0842	1.0623	1.0410	1.0306	1.0203	1.0000	0.9802	0.9610	0.9422	0.9238	0.9060	0.8885	4
5	1.1063	1.0785	1.0515	1.0384	1.0254	1.0000	0.9754	0.9515	0.9283	0.9057	0.8839	0.8626	5
6	1.1289	1.0949	1.0622	1.0462	1.0305	1.0000	0.9705	0.9420	0.9145	0.8880	0.8623	0.8375	6
7	1.1519	1.1116	1.0729	1.0541	1.0357	1.0000	0.9657	0.9327	0.9010	0.8706	0.8413	0.8131	7
8	1.1754	1.1285	1.0837	1.0621	1.0409	1.0000	0.9609	0.9235	0.8877	0.8535	0.8207	0.7894	8
9	1.1994	1.1457	1.0947	1.0701	1.0461	1.0000	0.9561	0.9143	0.8746	0.8368	0.8007	0.7664	9
10	1.2239	1.1632	1.1057	1.0782	1.0514	1.0000	0.9513	0.9053	0.8617	0.8203	0.7812	0.7441	10
11	1.2489	1.1809	1.1169	1.0863	1.0567	1.0000	0.9466	0.8963	0.8489	0.8043	0.7621	0.7224	11
12	1.2743	1.1989	1.1282	1.0945	1.0620	1.0000	0.9419	0.8874	0.8364	0.7885	0.7436	0.7014	12
13	1.3004	1.2171	1.1396	1.1028	1.0673	1.0000	0.9372	0.8787	0.8240	0.7730	0.7254	0.6810	13
14	1.3269	1.2356	1.1511	1.1112	1.0727	1.0000	0.9326	0.8700	0.8118	0.7579	0.7077	0.6611	14
15	1.3540	1.2545	1.1627	1.1195	1.0781	1.0000	0.9279	0.8613	0.7999	0.7430	0.6905	0.6419	15
16	1.3816	1.2736	1.1745	1.1280	1.0835	1.0000	0.9233	0.8528	0.7880	0.7284	0.6736	0.6232	16
17	1.4098	1.2930	1.1863	1.1365	1.0889	1.0000	0.9187	0.8444	0.7764	0.7142	0.6572	0.6050	17
18	1.4386	1.3126	1.1983	1.1451	1.0944	1.0000	0.9141	0.8360	0.7649	0.7002	0.6412	0.5874	18
19	1.4679	1.3326	1.2104	1.1538	1.0999	1.0000	0.9096	0.8277	0.7536	0.6864	0.6255	0.5703	19
20	1.4979	1.3529	1.2226	1.1625	1.1054	1.0000	0.9051	0.8195	0.7425	0.6730	0.6103	0.5537	20
21	1.5285	1.3735	1.2350	1.1713	1.1110	1.0000	0.9006	0.8114	0.7315	0.6598	0.5954	0.5375	21
22	1.5596	1.3944	1.2475	1.1801	1.1166	1.0000	0.8961	0.8034	0.7207	0.6468	0.5809	0.5219	22
23	1.5915	1.4157	1.2601	1.1890	1.1222	1.0000	0.8916	0.7954	0.7100	0.6342	0.5667	0.5067	23
24	1.6240	1.4372	1.2728	1.1980	1.1278	1.0000	0.8872	0.7876	0.6995	0.6217	0.5529	0.4919	24
25	1.6571	1.4591	1.2856	1.2071	1.1335	1.0000	0.8828	0.7798	0.6892	0.6095	0.5394	0.4776	25
26	1.6909	1.4814	1.2986	1.2162	1.1392	1.0000	0.8784	0.7720	0.6790	0.5976	0.5262	0.4637	26
27	1.7254	1.5039	1.3117	1.2254	1.1449	1.0000	0.8740	0.7644	0.6690	0.5859	0.5134	0.4502	27
28	1.7606	1.5268	1.3250	1.2347	1.1507	1.0000	0.8697	0.7568	0.6591	0.5744	0.5009	0.4371	28
29	1.7966	1.5501	1.3384	1.2440	1.1565	1.0000	0.8653	0.7493	0.6494	0.5631	0.4887	0.4243	29
30	1.8332	1.5737	1.3519	1.2534	1.1623	1.0000	0.8610	0.7419	0.6398	0.5521	0.4767	0.4120	30
31	1.8706	1.5976	1.3656	1.2629	1.1681	1.0000	0.8567	0.7346	0.6303	0.5412	0.4651	0.4000	31
32	1.9088	1.6220	1.3793	1.2724	1.1740	1.0000	0.8525	0.7273	0.6210	0.5306	0.4538	0.3883	32
33	1.9478	1.6467	1.3933	1.2820	1.1799	1.0000	0.8482	0.7201	0.6118	0.5202	0.4427	0.3770	33
34	1.9875	1.6717	1.4074	1.2917	1.1858	1.0000	0.8440	0.7130	0.6028	0.5100	0.4319	0.3660	34
35	2.0281	1.6972	1.4216	1.3015	1.1918	1.0000	0.8398	0.7059	0.5939	0.5000	0.4214	0.3554	35
36	2.0695	1.7230	1.4359	1.3113	1.1978	1.0000	0.8356	0.6989	0.5851	0.4902	0.4111	0.3450	36
37	2.1117	1.7493	1.4504	1.3212	1.2038	1.0000	0.8315	0.6920	0.5764	0.4806	0.4011	0.3350	37
38	2.1548	1.7759	1.4651	1.3312	1.2098	1.0000	0.8274	0.6852	0.5679	0.4712	0.3913	0.3252	38
39	2.1988	1.8030	1.4799	1.3413	1.2159	1.0000	0.8232	0.6784	0.5595	0.4619	0.3817	0.3158	39
40	2.2437	1.8304	1.4948	1.3514	1.2220	1.0000	0.8191	0.6717	0.5513	0.4529	0.3724	0.3066	40
41	2.2894	1.8583	1.5099	1.3616	1.2282	1.0000	0.8151	0.6650	0.5431	0.4440	0.3633	0.2976	41
42	2.3362	1.8866	1.5252	1.3719	1.2343	1.0000	0.8110	0.6584	0.5351	0.4353	0.3545	0.2890	42
43	2.3838	1.9153	1.5406	1.3823	1.2405	1.0000	0.8070	0.6519	0.5272	0.4268	0.3458	0.2805	43
44	2.4325	1.9445	1.5561	1.3927	1.2468	1.0000	0.8030	0.6454	0.5194	0.4184	0.3374	0.2724	44
45	2.4821	1.9741	1.5719	1.4032	1.2530	1.0000	0.7990	0.6391	0.5117	0.4102	0.3292	0.2644	45
46	2.5328	2.0042	1.5877	1.4138	1.2593	1.0000	0.7950	0.6327	0.5042	0.4022	0.3211	0.2567	46
47	2.5845	2.0347	1.6038	1.4245	1.2657	1.0000	0.7910	0.6265	0.4967	0.3943	0.3133	0.2493	47
48	2.6372	2.0657	1.6200	1.4353	1.2720	1.0000	0.7871	0.6203	0.4894	0.3865	0.3057	0.2420	48
49	2.6911	2.0971	1.6363	1.4461	1.2784	1.0000	0.7832	0.6141	0.4821	0.3790	0.2982	0.2350	49
50	2.7460	2.1291	1.6529	1.4570	1.2848	1.0000	0.7793	0.6080	0.4750	0.3715	0.2909	0.2281	50
51	2.8020	2.1615	1.6696	1.4681	1.2913	1.0000	0.7754	0.6020	0.4680	0.3642	0.2838	0.2215	51
52	2.8592	2.1944	1.6864	1.4792	1.2978	1.0000	0.7716	0.5961	0.4611	0.3571	0.2769	0.2150	52
53	2.9175	2.2278	1.7035	1.4903	1.3043	1.0000	0.7677	0.5902	0.4543	0.3501	0.2702	0.2088	53
54	2.9771	2.2617	1.7207	1.5016	1.3109	1.0000	0.7639	0.5843	0.4475	0.3432	0.2636	0.2027	54
55	3.0378	2.2962	1.7381	1.5129	1.3174	1.0000	0.7601	0.5785	0.4409	0.3365	0.2572	0.1968	55

Table 27: Discounting factors for term certain *continued*

Term	-2.0%	-1.5%	-1.0%	-0.75%	-0.5%	0.0%	0.5%	1.0%	1.5%	2.0%	2.5%	3.0%	Term
56	3.0998	2.3312	1.7556	1.5244	1.3241	1.0000	0.7563	0.5728	0.4344	0.3299	0.2509	0.1910	56
57	3.1631	2.3667	1.7733	1.5359	1.3307	1.0000	0.7525	0.5671	0.4280	0.3234	0.2448	0.1855	57
58	3.2277	2.4027	1.7913	1.5475	1.3374	1.0000	0.7488	0.5615	0.4217	0.3171	0.2388	0.1801	58
59	3.2935	2.4393	1.8094	1.5592	1.3441	1.0000	0.7451	0.5560	0.4154	0.3109	0.2330	0.1748	59
60	3.3607	2.4764	1.8276	1.5710	1.3509	1.0000	0.7414	0.5504	0.4093	0.3048	0.2273	0.1697	60
61	3.4293	2.5141	1.8461	1.5828	1.3577	1.0000	0.7377	0.5450	0.4032	0.2988	0.2217	0.1648	61
62	3.4993	2.5524	1.8647	1.5948	1.3645	1.0000	0.7340	0.5396	0.3973	0.2929	0.2163	0.1600	62
63	3.5707	2.5913	1.8836	1.6069	1.3713	1.0000	0.7304	0.5343	0.3914	0.2872	0.2111	0.1553	63
64	3.6436	2.6308	1.9026	1.6190	1.3782	1.0000	0.7267	0.5290	0.3856	0.2816	0.2059	0.1508	64
65	3.7180	2.6708	1.9218	1.6312	1.3852	1.0000	0.7231	0.5237	0.3799	0.2761	0.2009	0.1464	65
66	3.7938	2.7115	1.9412	1.6436	1.3921	1.0000	0.7195	0.5185	0.3743	0.2706	0.1960	0.1421	66
67	3.8713	2.7528	1.9608	1.6560	1.3991	1.0000	0.7159	0.5134	0.3688	0.2653	0.1912	0.1380	67
68	3.9503	2.7947	1.9806	1.6685	1.4061	1.0000	0.7124	0.5083	0.3633	0.2601	0.1865	0.1340	68
69	4.0309	2.8373	2.0007	1.6811	1.4132	1.0000	0.7088	0.5033	0.3580	0.2550	0.1820	0.1301	69
70	4.1132	2.8805	2.0209	1.6938	1.4203	1.0000	0.7053	0.4983	0.3527	0.2500	0.1776	0.1263	70
71	4.1971	2.9243	2.0413	1.7066	1.4275	1.0000	0.7018	0.4934	0.3475	0.2451	0.1732	0.1226	71
72	4.2827	2.9689	2.0619	1.7195	1.4346	1.0000	0.6983	0.4885	0.3423	0.2403	0.1690	0.1190	72
73	4.3702	3.0141	2.0827	1.7325	1.4418	1.0000	0.6948	0.4837	0.3373	0.2356	0.1649	0.1156	73
74	4.4593	3.0600	2.1038	1.7456	1.4491	1.0000	0.6914	0.4789	0.3323	0.2310	0.1609	0.1122	74
75	4.5503	3.1066	2.1250	1.7588	1.4564	1.0000	0.6879	0.4741	0.3274	0.2265	0.1569	0.1089	75
76	4.6432	3.1539	2.1465	1.7721	1.4637	1.0000	0.6845	0.4694	0.3225	0.2220	0.1531	0.1058	76
77	4.7380	3.2019	2.1682	1.7855	1.4710	1.0000	0.6811	0.4648	0.3178	0.2177	0.1494	0.1027	77
78	4.8347	3.2507	2.1901	1.7990	1.4784	1.0000	0.6777	0.4602	0.3131	0.2134	0.1457	0.0997	78
79	4.9333	3.3002	2.2122	1.8125	1.4859	1.0000	0.6743	0.4556	0.3084	0.2092	0.1422	0.0968	79
80	5.0340	3.3504	2.2345	1.8262	1.4933	1.0000	0.6710	0.4511	0.3039	0.2051	0.1387	0.0940	80

Table 28: Multipliers for pecuniary loss for term certain

Term	−2.0%	−1.5%	−1.0%	−0.75%	−0.5%	0.0%	0.5%	1.0%	1.5%	2.0%	2.5%	3.0%	Term
1	1.01	1.01	1.01	1.00	1.00	1.00	1.00	1.00	0.99	0.99	0.99	0.99	1
2	2.04	2.03	2.02	2.02	2.01	2.00	1.99	1.98	1.97	1.96	1.95	1.94	2
3	3.09	3.07	3.05	3.03	3.02	3.00	2.98	2.96	2.93	2.91	2.89	2.87	3
4	4.17	4.12	4.08	4.06	4.04	4.00	3.96	3.92	3.88	3.85	3.81	3.77	4
5	5.26	5.19	5.13	5.10	5.06	5.00	4.94	4.88	4.82	4.76	4.70	4.65	5
6	6.38	6.28	6.18	6.14	6.09	6.00	5.91	5.82	5.74	5.66	5.58	5.50	6
7	7.52	7.38	7.25	7.19	7.12	7.00	6.88	6.76	6.65	6.54	6.43	6.32	7
8	8.68	8.50	8.33	8.25	8.16	8.00	7.84	7.69	7.54	7.40	7.26	7.12	8
9	9.87	9.64	9.42	9.31	9.21	9.00	8.80	8.61	8.42	8.24	8.07	7.90	9
10	11.08	10.80	10.52	10.39	10.25	10.00	9.75	9.52	9.29	9.07	8.86	8.66	10
11	12.32	11.97	11.63	11.47	11.31	11.00	10.70	10.42	10.15	9.88	9.63	9.39	11
12	13.58	13.16	12.75	12.56	12.37	12.00	11.65	11.31	10.99	10.68	10.39	10.10	12
13	14.87	14.37	13.89	13.66	13.43	13.00	12.59	12.19	11.82	11.46	11.12	10.79	13
14	16.18	15.59	15.03	14.76	14.50	14.00	13.52	13.07	12.64	12.23	11.84	11.46	14
15	17.52	16.84	16.19	15.88	15.58	15.00	14.45	13.93	13.44	12.98	12.54	12.12	15
16	18.89	18.10	17.36	17.00	16.66	16.00	15.38	14.79	14.24	13.71	13.22	12.75	16
17	20.28	19.38	18.54	18.14	17.75	17.00	16.30	15.64	15.02	14.43	13.88	13.36	17
18	21.71	20.69	19.73	19.28	18.84	18.00	17.22	16.48	15.79	15.14	14.53	13.96	18
19	23.16	22.01	20.94	20.43	19.93	19.00	18.13	17.31	16.55	15.83	15.17	14.54	19
20	24.64	23.35	22.15	21.58	21.04	20.00	19.03	18.14	17.30	16.51	15.78	15.10	20
21	26.16	24.71	23.38	22.75	22.15	21.00	19.94	18.95	18.03	17.18	16.39	15.65	21
22	27.70	26.10	24.62	23.93	23.26	22.00	20.84	19.76	18.76	17.83	16.97	16.17	22
23	29.28	27.50	25.88	25.11	24.38	23.00	21.73	20.56	19.48	18.47	17.55	16.69	23
24	30.88	28.93	27.14	26.30	25.50	24.00	22.62	21.35	20.18	19.10	18.11	17.19	24
25	32.53	30.38	28.42	27.51	26.63	25.00	23.50	22.13	20.87	19.72	18.65	17.67	25
26	34.20	31.85	29.71	28.72	27.77	26.00	24.38	22.91	21.56	20.32	19.19	18.14	26
27	35.91	33.34	31.02	29.94	28.91	27.00	25.26	23.68	22.23	20.91	19.71	18.60	27
28	37.65	34.86	32.34	31.17	30.06	28.00	26.13	24.44	22.90	21.49	20.21	19.04	28
29	39.43	36.40	33.67	32.41	31.21	29.00	27.00	25.19	23.55	22.06	20.71	19.47	29
30	41.24	37.96	35.01	33.66	32.37	30.00	27.86	25.94	24.20	22.62	21.19	19.89	30
31	43.10	39.54	36.37	34.92	33.54	31.00	28.72	26.67	24.83	23.17	21.66	20.30	31
32	44.99	41.15	37.74	36.18	34.71	32.00	29.58	27.41	25.46	23.70	22.12	20.69	32
33	46.91	42.79	39.13	37.46	35.89	33.00	30.43	28.13	26.07	24.23	22.57	21.08	33
34	48.88	44.45	40.53	38.75	37.07	34.00	31.27	28.85	26.68	24.74	23.01	21.45	34
35	50.89	46.13	41.95	40.04	38.26	35.00	32.12	29.56	27.28	25.25	23.43	21.81	35
36	52.94	47.84	43.37	41.35	39.45	36.00	32.95	30.26	27.87	25.74	23.85	22.16	36
37	55.03	49.58	44.82	42.67	40.65	37.00	33.79	30.95	28.45	26.23	24.26	22.50	37
38	57.16	51.34	46.28	43.99	41.86	38.00	34.62	31.64	29.02	26.70	24.65	22.83	38
39	59.34	53.13	47.75	45.33	43.07	39.00	35.44	32.32	29.58	27.17	25.04	23.15	39
40	61.56	54.95	49.24	46.68	44.29	40.00	36.26	33.00	30.14	27.63	25.42	23.46	40
41	63.83	56.79	50.74	48.03	45.52	41.00	37.08	33.67	30.69	28.08	25.78	23.76	41
42	66.14	58.66	52.26	49.40	46.75	42.00	37.89	34.33	31.23	28.52	26.14	24.06	42
43	68.50	60.56	53.79	50.78	47.99	43.00	38.70	34.98	31.76	28.95	26.49	24.34	43
44	70.91	62.49	55.34	52.16	49.23	44.00	39.51	35.63	32.28	29.37	26.83	24.62	44
45	73.36	64.45	56.90	53.56	50.48	45.00	40.31	36.27	32.80	29.78	27.17	24.88	45
46	75.87	66.44	58.48	54.97	51.74	46.00	41.10	36.91	33.30	30.19	27.49	25.15	46
47	78.43	68.46	60.08	56.39	53.00	47.00	41.90	37.54	33.80	30.59	27.81	25.40	47
48	81.04	70.51	61.69	57.82	54.27	48.00	42.69	38.16	34.30	30.98	28.12	25.64	48
49	83.70	72.59	63.32	59.26	55.54	49.00	43.47	38.78	34.78	31.36	28.42	25.88	49
50	86.42	74.70	64.96	60.71	56.82	50.00	44.25	39.39	35.26	31.74	28.72	26.11	50
51	89.20	76.85	66.62	62.17	58.11	51.00	45.03	40.00	35.73	32.10	29.00	26.34	51
52	92.03	79.03	68.30	63.65	59.41	52.00	45.80	40.60	36.20	32.47	29.28	26.56	52
53	94.92	81.24	69.99	65.13	60.71	53.00	46.57	41.19	36.66	32.82	29.56	26.77	53
54	97.86	83.48	71.71	66.63	62.01	54.00	47.34	41.78	37.11	33.17	29.82	26.97	54
55	100.87	85.76	73.44	68.14	63.33	55.00	48.10	42.36	37.55	33.51	30.08	27.17	55

A8: The Ogden Tables

Table 28: Multipliers for pecuniary loss for term certain *continued*

Term	\-2.0%	\-1.5%	\-1.0%	\-0.75%	\-0.5%	0.0%	0.5%	1.0%	1.5%	2.0%	2.5%	3.0%	Term
56	103.94	88.08	75.18	69.65	64.65	56.00	48.86	42.93	37.99	33.84	30.34	27.37	56
57	107.07	90.43	76.95	71.18	65.98	57.00	49.61	43.50	38.42	34.17	30.59	27.56	57
58	110.27	92.81	78.73	72.73	67.31	58.00	50.36	44.07	38.84	34.49	30.83	27.74	58
59	113.53	95.23	80.53	74.28	68.65	59.00	51.11	44.63	39.26	34.80	31.06	27.92	59
60	116.85	97.69	82.35	75.84	70.00	60.00	51.85	45.18	39.67	35.11	31.29	28.09	60
61	120.25	100.18	84.19	77.42	71.35	61.00	52.59	45.73	40.08	35.41	31.52	28.26	61
62	123.71	102.72	86.04	79.01	72.71	62.00	53.33	46.27	40.48	35.70	31.74	28.42	62
63	127.25	105.29	87.91	80.61	74.08	63.00	54.06	46.81	40.88	36.00	31.95	28.58	63
64	130.85	107.90	89.81	82.22	75.46	64.00	54.79	47.34	41.26	36.28	32.16	28.73	64
65	134.53	110.55	91.72	83.85	76.84	65.00	55.52	47.86	41.65	36.56	32.36	28.88	65
66	138.29	113.24	93.65	85.49	78.23	66.00	56.24	48.39	42.02	36.83	32.56	29.02	66
67	142.12	115.97	95.60	87.14	79.62	67.00	56.95	48.90	42.40	37.10	32.75	29.16	67
68	146.03	118.75	97.57	88.80	81.03	68.00	57.67	49.41	42.76	37.36	32.94	29.30	68
69	150.02	121.56	99.56	90.47	82.44	69.00	58.38	49.92	43.12	37.62	33.13	29.43	69
70	154.10	124.42	101.57	92.16	83.85	70.00	59.09	50.42	43.48	37.87	33.31	29.56	70
71	158.25	127.32	103.61	93.86	85.28	71.00	59.79	50.91	43.83	38.12	33.48	29.68	71
72	162.49	130.27	105.66	95.57	86.71	72.00	60.49	51.41	44.17	38.36	33.65	29.80	72
73	166.82	133.26	107.73	97.30	88.15	73.00	61.19	51.89	44.51	38.60	33.82	29.92	73
74	171.23	136.30	109.82	99.04	89.59	74.00	61.88	52.37	44.85	38.83	33.98	30.03	74
75	175.74	139.38	111.94	100.79	91.04	75.00	62.57	52.85	45.18	39.06	34.14	30.15	75
76	180.33	142.51	114.07	102.56	92.50	76.00	63.26	53.32	45.50	39.29	34.30	30.25	76
77	185.02	145.69	116.23	104.33	93.97	77.00	63.94	53.79	45.82	39.51	34.45	30.36	77
78	189.81	148.92	118.41	106.13	95.45	78.00	64.62	54.25	46.14	39.72	34.60	30.46	78
79	194.69	152.19	120.61	107.93	96.93	79.00	65.29	54.71	46.45	39.93	34.74	30.56	79
80	199.68	155.52	122.83	109.75	98.42	80.00	65.97	55.16	46.75	40.14	34.88	30.65	80

ACTUARIAL FORMULAE AND BASIS

The functions tabulated are:

Tables 1 and 2	$\bar{a}_x$	Tables 17 and 18	$_{(55-x)|}\bar{a}_x$
Tables 3 and 4	$\bar{a}_{x:\,\overline{50-x|}}$	Tables 19 and 20	$_{(60-x)|}\bar{a}_x$
Tables 5 and 6	$\bar{a}_{x:\,\overline{55-x|}}$	Tables 21 and 22	$_{(65-x)|}\bar{a}_x$
Tables 7 and 8	$\bar{a}_{x:\,\overline{60-x|}}$	Tables 23 and 24	$_{(70-x)|}\bar{a}_x$
Tables 9 and 10	$\bar{a}_{x:\,\overline{65-x|}}$	Tables 25 and 26	$_{(75-x)|}\bar{a}_x$
Tables 11 and 12	$\bar{a}_{x:\,\overline{70-x|}}$	Table 27	$1/(1+i)^n$
Tables 13 and 14	$\bar{a}_{x:\,\overline{75-x|}}$	Table 28	$\bar{a}_{\overline{n|}}$
Tables 15 and 16	$_{(50-x)|}\bar{a}_x$		

- Mortality assumptions for 2008-based official population projections for the United Kingdom.
- Loadings: None.
- Rate of return: As stated in the tables.

A9: The Lord Chancellor's statement, 27 February 2017

Discount rate: statement placed by The Rt Hon Elizabeth Truss MP, Lord Chancellor, in the libraries of the Houses of Parliament on 27 February 2017

1. As Lord Chancellor, I have power pursuant to section 1 of the Damages Act 1996 from time to time to set the discount rate applied to personal injury awards covering future pecuniary losses. In November 2010 my predecessors began a review of the discount rate for personal injury damages awards. On 27 January this year I indicated my intention to complete the review in February 2017.

2. In the course of my review, I have considered all the material available to me, including the responses to a Ministry of Justice public consultation in 2012, the report of an expert panel in 2015 (which reached majority and minority conclusions) and the responses of statutory consultees, HM Treasury and the Government Actuary. The process of review has been lengthy, and extraordinarily thorough. That process reflects the complexity and importance of the subject matter.

3. This statement sets out the decision I have reached as a result of this exercise and a summary of my reasons for that decision. I am also separately publishing today the Response to the 2012 public consultation.

Decision

4. I have concluded that a discount rate of minus 0.75% is the appropriate rate.

Reasons

5. I emphasise at the outset that the approach to the exercise of setting the discount rate is inevitably relatively broad brush. It is not a simple arithmetical exercise leading to a single, correct answer. It involves making judgements at various stages of the consideration of the issues, some of which are finely balanced and some of which involve making predictions about the future which are inherently uncertain.

6. I have noted the object of the award of damages set out by the House of Lords in *Wells v Wells* [1999] 1 AC 34, per Lord Hope of Craighead (page 390A-B):

" . . . the object of the award of damages for future expenditure is to place the injured party as nearly as possible in the same financial position he or she would have been in but for the accident. The aim is to award such a sum of money as will amount to no more, and at the same time no less, than the net loss . . . "

7. I have approached the setting of the discount rate on the basis that the governing principle is as identified by Lord Hope in that case: "*[The discount rate]* is the rate of interest to be expected where the investment is without risk, there being no question about the availability of the money when the investor requires repayment of the capital and there being no question of loss due to inflation."

8. The principles in *Wells v Wells* lead me to base the discount rate on the investment portfolio that offers the least risk to investors in protecting an award of damages against inflation and against

A9: The Lord Chancellor's statement, 27 February 2017

market risk. I take the view that a portfolio that contains 100% index-linked gilts (ILGs) best meets this criterion at the current time. A portfolio of ILGs, comprising stocks spread across a range of redemption dates guarantees the investor an inflation-adjusted income, known with certainty at the time of the award. Basing the discount rate on the real redemption yield of ILGs is consistent with the approach taken by the House of Lords in *Wells v Wells* and by the then Lord Chancellor, Lord Irvine, when he last set the rate in the Damages (Personal Injury) Order 2001 (S.I. 2001/2301).

9. I am aware that issues have been raised as to whether ILGs (or a portfolio containing 100% ILGs) continues to represent a realistic or the appropriate basis for arriving at the discount rate, in part because changed economic circumstances have had an impact on the demand for ILGs. In particular, the case has been made by a number of respondents to the consultation exercises that it might be more appropriate and realistic to use a 'mixed portfolio' approach (in which other securities feature). I acknowledge that those arguments have some merit. However, I am not persuaded by them. I consider that a faithful application of the principles in *Wells v Wells* leads to the 100% ILGs approach as the best way, in the current markets, of ensuring that there is "*no question about the availability of the money when the investor requires repayment of the capital and there being no question of loss due to inflation.*" The mixed portfolio approach in contrast runs counter to these principles by requiring the assumption by the investor of a greater degree of risk.

10. I have specifically considered whether the 100% ILGs approach might create different risks such as the risk of not being able to meet unexpected capital needs. I recognise that point. However, I consider that those risks should be capable of effective management and that they are outweighed by the risks associated with the 'mixed portfolio' approach.

11. In a statement laid before Parliament on 27 July 2001, Lord Irvine recommended that the approach to setting the discount rate should respect the following general principles, which I have adopted.

    a. There should be a single, fixed rate to cover all cases. This accords with the solution adopted by the House of Lords in *Wells v Wells*. It eliminates argument about the applicable rate at court and avoids the complexity and extra costs that a formula would entail.

    b. The rate should be one which is easy for all parties and their lawyers to apply in practice and which reflects the fact that the rate is bound to be applied in a range of different circumstances over a period of time. Given the uncertainties and imprecisions involved in the process of setting the discount rate, a rounded rate is preferable. Accordingly, I have decided to round to the nearest 0.25%. Ogden tables, applied by the courts to adjust awards according to a given discount rate, are currently published for rates at intervals of 0.5%. However, they can readily and swiftly be adapted to an intermediate rate.

12. In his 2001 decision, Lord Irvine obtained a discount rate by taking the average gross real redemption yields on ILGs across all maturity dates. He averaged real yield over the previous three years and rounded after making allowances for various factors. Lord Irvine noted that Lord Hope in *Wells v Wells* had regard to an average of gross redemption yields on ILGs with more than five years to maturity. Lord Irvine decided, however, to include all stocks in his calculations on the basis that some claimants, whose losses extend over periods of about 5 years or less, would have to purchase all or most of their ILGs in this category of stock. However, real yields on ILGs vary according to the maturity dates of stocks. I consider that it is the real yields of long-dated stocks that should be given more weighting when setting the discount rate according to real ILGs yields. This is because awards intended to cover the longest periods are most sensitive to any discrepancy

between the discount rate set and the real yield obtained at the date of the award. Indeed, many awards are for the long term, quite often decades.

13. To weight long term stocks in a simple and transparent way, I have taken a simple average of gross real redemption yields across all ILGs and, in line with *Wells v Wells*, have excluded stocks with less than five years to maturity. This is not to deny the need for some or, indeed, all claimants to receive an income in the first few years of their award but to account, in a simple way, for the effect that short-dated stocks can have on real redemption yield as a representative discount rate for claimants as a whole. The real yield data on which I have obtained an average are those published by the Debt Management Office (DMO).

14. Regarding the period over which the real redemption yield is averaged, I have followed the majority view from *Wells v Wells* and the practice adopted by Lord Irvine in 2001, namely to average over the three years to a convenient date (in this instance, 30 December, the last trading day of 2016). I note that real yields have witnessed steady decline since 2001 and there may be a case for changing the averaging period to limit the influence of historical trends. However, I am reluctant to depart from earlier practice on this occasion.

15. The three year simple average gross real redemption yield on ILGs is minus 0.83% as of 30 December 2016 excluding ILGs with less than 5 years to maturity. As noted above, it would be appropriate to round this figure to acknowledge the inherent uncertainties and imprecisions involved in setting a representative discount rate and I am persuaded that rounding to the nearest 0.25% points is adequate. This would lead to a discount rate of minus 0.75%. The only reason to round down to minus 1.00% would be to account for claimant costs, in particular taxation and management fees. However, the case for such adjustment is not strong and has weakened in recent years. Because of the steady issuance of new ILGs with lower coupons (and, therefore lower taxation), it is not unreasonable that an adjustment for tax should be lower now than when Lord Irvine determined the discount rate in 2001; and investment management costs are relatively modest for ILGs.

16. For all of these reasons, I have decided that the discount rate should be minus 0.75%.

The Rt Hon Elizabeth Truss MP
Lord Chancellor
27 February 2017

A9: The Lord Chancellor's statement, 27 February 2017

Written statement to Parliament

Change to personal injury discount rate

Published 27 February 2017

From: Ministry of Justice and The Rt Hon Elizabeth Truss MP

Delivered on: 27 February 2017

Earlier today, I notified the market via the London Stock Exchange group that I would today lay a Statutory Instrument to change the discount rate applicable to personal injury lump sum compensation payments, to minus 0.75%.

Under the Damages Act 1996, I, as Lord Chancellor, have the power to set a discount rate which courts must consider when awarding compensation for future financial losses in the form of a lump sum in personal injury cases.

The current legal framework makes clear that claimants must be treated as risk averse investors, reflecting the fact that they may be financially dependent on this lump sum, often for long periods or the duration of their life.

The discount rate was last set in 2001, when the then-Lord Chancellor, Lord Irvine of Lairg, set the rate at 2.5%. This was based on a three year average of real yields on index-linked gilts.

Since 2001, the real yields on index-linked gilts has fallen, so I have decided to take action.

Having completed the process of statutory consultation, I am satisfied that the rate should be based on a three year average of real returns on index-linked gilts. Therefore I am setting it at minus 0.75%. A full statement of reasons, explaining how I have decided upon this rate, will be placed in the Libraries of both Houses. The Statutory Instrument to effect this change has been laid today, and will become effective on 20 March 2017.

There will clearly be significant implications across the public and private sector. The government has committed to ensuring that the NHS Litigation Authority has appropriate funding to cover changes to hospitals' clinical negligence costs. The Department of Health will also work closely with General Practitioners (GPs) and Medical Defence Organisations to ensure that appropriate funding is available to meet additional costs to GPs, recognising the crucial role they play in the delivery of NHS care.

The government will review the framework under which I have set the rate today to ensure that it remains fit for purpose in the future. I will bring forward a consultation before Easter that will consider options for reform including: whether the rate should in future be set by an independent body; whether more frequent reviews would improve predictability and certainty for all parties; and whether the methodology—which in effect assumes that claimants would invest only in index-linked gilts—is appropriate for the future. Following the consultation, which will consider whether there is a better or fairer framework for claimants and defendants, the government will bring forward any necessary legislation at an early stage.

I recognise the impacts this decision will have on the insurance industry. My Rt. Hon. Friend the Chancellor will meet with insurance industry representatives to discuss the situation.

Published 27 February 2017

Group B
Damages

B1: General damages table following *Heil v Rankin* and *Simmons v Castle*

B2: Bereavement damages

B3: *Auty v National Coal Board* (pension claims)

B4: *Roberts v Johnstone* (accommodation claims)

B5: Periodical payments

B6: Step-by-step guide to finding the annual estimates for hourly pay in ASHE SOC 2000 6115

B1: General damages table following *Heil v Rankin* and *Simmons v Castle*

General introduction

1. These tables are for updating awards of general damages in the light of *Heil v Rankin*[1] and *Simmons v Castle*[2]. At Tables E1 and E2 there are a Retail Prices Index and an inflation table.

2. While the Court of Appeal in *Heil* said that it did not intend to lay down a mathematical formula, a graph which is a shallow curve was annexed to the judgment. That curve approximately represents an uplift on an original award of £A of

$$£A\text{-}10{,}000/420{,}000 \times £A$$

3. In *Simmons v Castle* the Court of Appeal increased awards for general damages by 10 per cent, unless the claimant fell within s.44(6) of the Legal Aid, Sentencing and Punishment of Offenders Act 2012[3].

4. For example:

    a. The claimant in *Chan v Chan* was awarded £75,000 in January 1988.

    b. Update £75,000 to 23 March 2000 in line with the Retail Prices Index, giving £122,250.

    c. Subtract £10,000 (giving £112,250), and divide by £420,000 (giving an uplift factor of 0.27).

    d. Apply this to the original award giving [0.27 × £122,250] = 33,008.

    e. The original award was therefore worth [122,250 + 33,008] = £155,258 on 23.3.2000.

    f. Update from 23.3.2000 to the present and, unless s.44(6) applies, increase by 10 per cent. That is, multiply by [present RPI × 1.10 / RPI on 23.3.2000}.

5. Note that because the degree of uplift varies with the size of the original award, it is inaccurate to apply the *Heil* uplift to a figure already adjusted for inflation to a date later than 23 March 2000.

TO UPDATE A PRE-*HEIL v RANKIN* AWARD

The table which follows shows the factor to allow for inflation from an earlier date to 23 March 2000. The second table shows, at £1,000 intervals, the figure uplifted following *Heil*. Update award as follows:

Damages awarded, say, January 1990 x inflation increase to 23 March 2000 (from first table).

Award uplifted under *Heil* (from second table).

Uplift for inflation from 23 March 2000 to date of trial; and add 10 per cent (unless s.44(6) applies).

---

[1] [2000] 2 W.L.R. 1173.
[2] [2012] EWCA Civ 1039 and [2012] EWCA Civ 1288.
[3] In *Summers v Bundy* [2016] EWCA Civ 126, the Court held that cases within s.44(6) are the only exception and the judge has no discretion to dispense with the uplift in other cases.

B1: General damages table following *Heil v Rankin* and *Simmons v Castle*

TABLE TO UPDATE FOR INFLATION TO MARCH 2000

	J	F	M	A	M	J	J	A	S	O	N	D	
1980	2.708	2.670	2.634	2.547	2.524	2.500	2.480	2.474	2.459	2.443	2.424	2.411	1980
1981	2.396	2.374	2.339	2.274	2.259	2.246	2.236	2.220	2.207	2.187	2.165	2.151	1981
1982	2.139	2.138	2.120	2.078	2.063	2.057	2.057	2.056	2.057	2.047	2.037	2.041	1982
1983	2.038	2.030	2.026	1.998	1.990	1.985	1.974	1.965	1.957	1.950	1.943	1.938	1983
1984	1.939	1.931	1.925	1.900	1.893	1.888	1.890	1.872	1.869	1.857	1.852	1.853	1984
1985	1.846	1.832	1.815	1.777	1.769	1.765	1.768	1.764	1.765	1.762	1.756	1.753	1985
1986	1.750	1.743	1.741	1.724	1.721	1.722	1.727	1.722	1.713	1.710	1.696	1.690	1986
1987	1.684	1.677	1.674	1.654	1.653	1.653	1.654	1.649	1.645	1.637	1.629	1.630	1987
1988	1.630	1.624	1.618	1.592	1.586	1.580	1.578	1.561	1.554	1.538	1.531	1.527	1988
1989	1.517	1.506	1.500	1.473	1.464	1.459	1.458	1.454	1.444	1.433	1.421	1.418	1989
1990	1.409	1.401	1.387	1.346	1.334	1.329	1.328	1.315	1.302	1.292	1.295	1.296	1990
1991	1.293	1.286	1.282	1.265	1.261	1.256	1.259	1.256	1.251	1.246	1.242	1.241	1991
1992	1.242	1.236	1.232	1.213	1.209	1.209	1.213	1.212	1.208	1.204	1.205	1.210	1992
1993	1.221	1.213	1.209	1.198	1.193	1.194	1.197	1.192	1.187	1.188	1.189	1.187	1993
1994	1.192	1.185	1.182	1.168	1.164	1.164	1.169	1.164	1.161	1.160	1.159	1.153	1994
1995	1.153	1.146	1.142	1.130	1.126	1.124	1.129	1.123	1.118	1.124	1.124	1.117	1995
1996	1.121	1.116	1.112	1.104	1.101	1.101	1.105	1.100	1.095	1.095	1.094	1.091	1996
1997	1.091	1.086	1.084	1.077	1.073	1.069	1.069	1.062	1.057	1.056	1.055	1.053	1997
1998	1.056	1.051	1.047	1.036	1.030	1.031	1.033	1.029	1.024	1.024	1.024	1.024	1998
1999	1.031	1.029	1.026	1.019	1.017	1.017	1.020	1.018	1.013	1.011	1.010	1.007	1999
2000	1.011	1.005											2000
	J	F	M	A	M	J	J	A	S	O	N	D	

TABLE OF UPLIFTS FOLLOWING *HEIL v RANKIN*

Old	New	Old	New	Old	New	Old	New
0–10,000	No change	45,000	48,750	80,000	93,333	115,000	143,750
11,000	11,026	46,000	49,942	81,000	94,693	116,000	142,276
12,000	12,057	47,000	51,140	82,000	96,057	117,000	146,807
13,000	13,092	48,000	52,342	83,000	97,426	118,000	148,343
14,000	14,133	49,000	53,549	84,000	98,800	119,000	149,883
15,000	15,178	50,000	54,761	85,000	100,179	120,000	151,428
16,000	16,228	51,000	55,978	86,000	101,562	121,000	152,979
17,000	17,283	52,000	57,200	87,000	102,945	122,000	154,533
18,000	18,342	53,000	58,426	88,000	104,343	123,000	156,093
19,000	19,407	54,000	59,657	89,000	105,740	124,000	157,657
20,000	20,476	55,000	60,892	90,000	107,142	125,000	159,226
21,000	21,549	56,000	62,133	91,000	108,549	126,000	160,800
22,000	22,628	57,000	63,378	92,000	109,961	127,000	162,379
23,000	23,711	58,000	64,628	93,000	111,378	128,000	163,962
24,000	24,799	59,000	65,883	94,000	112,800	129,000	165,549
25,000	25,892	60,000	67,142	95,000	114,226	130,000	167,143
26,000	26,990	61,000	68,407	96,000	115,657	131,000	168,740
27,000	28,092	62,000	69,676	97,000	117,092	132,000	170,343
28,000	29,199	63,000	70,949	98,000	118,533	133,000	171,950
29,000	30,311	64,000	72,228	99,000	119,978	134,000	173,562
30,000	31,428	65,000	73,511	100,000	121,428	135,000	175,179
31,000	32,550	66,000	74,799	101,000	122,883	136,000	176,800
32,000	33,676	67,000	76,092	102,000	124,342	137,000	178,426
33,000	34,807	68,000	77,390	103,000	125,807	138,000	180,057

B1: General damages table following *Heil v Rankin* and *Simmons v Castle*

TABLE OF UPLIFTS FOLLOWING *HEIL v RANKIN* continued

Old	New	Old	New	Old	New	Old	New
34,000	35,942	69,000	78,692	104,000	127,276	139,000	181,692
35,000	37,083	70,000	79,999	105,000	128,745	140,000	183,333
36,000	38,228	71,000	81,311	106,000	130,229	141,000	184,978
37,000	39,378	72,000	82,628	107,000	131,712	142,000	186,628
38,000	40,533	73,000	83,950	108,000	133,200	143,000	188,283
39,000	41,692	74,000	85,276	109,000	134,693	144,000	189,942
40,000	42,857	75,000	86,607	110,000	136,190	145,000	191,607
41,000	44,026	76,000	87,942	111,000	137,693	146,000	193,276
42,000	45,199	77,000	89,283	112,000	139,200	147,000	194,949
43,000	46,378	78,000	90,629	113,000	140,712	148,000	196,628
44,000	47,561	79,000	91,979	114,000	142,229	149,000	198,311
						150,000	200,000

UPLIFT FOR INFLATION, AND *SIMMONS v CASTLE*, FROM MARCH 2000 TO TRIAL

The Retail Prices Index on 23 March 2000 was 168.4. 168.4 ÷ 110% = 153.1. In April 2018 the RPI was 279.7.

The uplift for inflation from March 2000 is calculated as follows:

£award × (RPI at date of trial) / 153.1. (Note that using the figure of 153.1 already takes account of the *Simmons v Castle* 10 per cent uplift.)

For an award that was worth £5,000 in March 2000, this would give at April 2018:

£5,000 × 279.7 / 153.1 = £9,135.

TO UPDATE A POST-*HEIL v RANKIN*, BUT PRE-*SIMMONS v CASTLE*, AWARD

Awards since *Heil* but before the *Simmons* uplift should be updated in this way:

£award × 1.1 × (RPI at date of trial)/(RPI at date of award)

For an award that was worth £5,000 in June 2008, this gives at April 2018 (unless s.44(6) applies):

£5,000 × 1.1 × 279.7 / 216.8 = £6,451

TO UPDATE A POST-*SIMMONS v CASTLE* AWARD

Awards which already include the *Simmons v Castle* uplift (generally awards since 1 April 2013 unless s.44(6) applied to them), should be updated in this way:

£award × (RPI at date of trial)/(RPI at date of award).

For an award that was worth £5,000 in June 2013, this would give at April 2018:

£5,000 × 279.7 / 249.7 = £5,601

B2: Bereavement damages

1. Damages for bereavement are awarded under s.1A of the Fatal Accidents Act 1976. This is a fixed sum, set by statute as amended (see below).

2. The claim for bereavement damages can only be brought by:

    (i) a bereaved spouse, or

    (ii) where the deceased was a minor who never married, by:
    (a) either of his parents if the deceased was legitimate; or
    (b) the mother if the deceased was illegitimate.

3. Where there is a claim for damages for bereavement for the benefit of the parents of the deceased, s.1A(4) of the Fatal Accidents Act 1976 provides that:

    "The sum awarded shall be divided equally between them (subject to any deduction falling to be made in respect of costs not recovered from the defendant)."

    Where the parents are divorced or separated and only one parent makes the claim, that parent will hold half of the bereavement damages on trust for the other parent.

4. The Administration of Justice Act 1982 contains a provision (at s.1A(5)) for the Lord Chancellor to vary the statutory sum. The original statute fixed the sum at £3,500, and that was raised by four subsequent statutory instruments (SI 1990/2575, SI 2002/644, SI 2007/3488 and SI 2013/510). Hence the relevant dates and statutory sums are as follows:

– if the death was before 1 January 1983, the award is	**nil**
– if the death was between 1 January 1983 and 31 March 1991, the award is	**£3,500**
– if the death was between 1 April 1991 and 31 March 2002, the award is	**£7,500**
– if the death was between 1 April 2002 and 31 December 2007, the award is	**£10,000**
– if the death was between 1 January 2008 and 31 March 2013, the award is	**£11,800**
– if the death was on or after 1 April 2013, the award is	**£12,980**

5. The claimant is entitled to interest on bereavement damages from the date of death to the date of trial or settlement of the action—see *Prior v Hastie*.[1]

---

[1] [1987] C.L.Y. 1219.

B3: *Auty v National Coal Board* (pension claims)

In *Wells v Wells*, the House of Lords made only passing reference to the calculation of future pension losses. The implication is that the multipliers for such losses are to be taken from the Ogden Tables, as are those for pecuniary losses for life and for loss of earnings. There is no justification for adopting a different approach. Since the mid-1980s, pension claims have often been based on the principles set out in *Auty v National Coal Board*.[1] This analysis is a guide to those principles, but is included with the caution that the method of selecting multipliers and discount factors has been superseded by *Wells v Wells* and the availability of suitable post-retirement factors at different discount rates in Tables 15 to 26 of the Ogden Tables. Further guidance on how to make the pension loss calculation is given in H3.

It is important to remember that the trial judge in *Auty* was not working from the Ogden Tables, but from a period table of expectation of life in the early 1980s. Here is the calculation carried out by the judge in *Auty*:

1. The net annual pension loss after tax: £443.

2. The claimant and his wife were both aged 34 at the date of trial.

3. The life tables showed that the claimant's expectation of life beyond the age of 65 was 6.68 years, and his wife's expectation of life beyond the age of 65 was 12.26 years[2]. She was therefore expected to survive him by 5.58 years. She was entitled to a two-thirds widow's pension, so the judge added two-thirds of 5.58 years (i.e. 3.72 years) to the claimant's life expectancy beyond 65 of 6.68 to give a total period of loss of 10.4 years.

4. **First step**: the judge considered an appropriate multiplier (at a 5 per cent discount rate) for 10.4 years to be seven. This is the equivalent of the discounting calculation that would now be performed (at -0.75 per cent) by using the Ogden Tables.

5. The basic pension loss at 65 was therefore [7 × £443] = £3,101.

6. Loss of lump sum gratuity: £1,899.

7. Total capital value of loss at retirement age [£3,101 + £1,899] = £5,000.

8. **Second step**: Mr Auty was 34 years old. He was therefore being compensated for his pension loss 31 years prematurely. The judge discounted the sum of £5,000 at 5 per cent over 31 years, leaving £1,100. This discount would now be performed using Ogden Table 27 at -0.75 per cent.[3]

9. **Third step**: The judge discounted the pension claim by a further 27 per cent for contingencies. This brought the sum of £1,100 down to £800. Of this step the Court of Appeal said[4]:

    "The discount for imponderables which the judge made in Auty's case was 27 per cent. The judge said that the imponderables included voluntary wastage, redundancy, dismissal, supervening ill-health, disablement or death before 65, and said that death was the major discount."

10. Add value of loss of death in service benefit (£200).

11. Total value of award: **£1,000**.

[1] [1985] 1 All E.R. 930.
[2] We consider this to have been a mistake as these figures were derived by subtracting 65 years from the period expectation of life at birth of 71.68 for males and 77.26 for females. The true expectations of life for 34-year-olds would have been significantly higher, but the difference between the male and female expectations would not have been too far different. Using the Ogden Tables (which include allowance for future mortality improvement) the figures from Tables 21 and 22 at 0.0 per cent are 22.10 and 25.30 respectively for the expected number of years the individuals would live beyond 65.
[3] The calculation using the Ogden Tables in 2017 would take the age 34 figures at -0.75% p.a. from Table 21.
[4] Waller LJ in *Auty*, at 937.

Note: The three steps bring the annual pension element alone (ignoring the lump sum and the death in service benefit) down to below £500. If one simply applied Table 21 of the Ogden Tables and a -0.75 per cent discount rate to the above annual pension loss, the claimant would receive [31.23 × £443] = £13,835 for the man's pension alone, before any adjustment for contingencies other than mortality. It should be noted that, when using the Ogden Tables (other than Tables 27 and 28), no further discount should be made in the contingencies deduction for Ogden Tables, so applying a further contingency discount would amount to a "double discount".

Employment tribunals have developed a different approach to the calculation of pension loss. Those interested are referred to the guidelines in Sneath, Sara, Daykin and Gallop, *Industrial Tribunals: Compensation for loss of pension rights* (3rd edn, HMSO, 2003), approved by the Employment Appeal Tribunal in *Benson v Dairy Crest*.[5] A new set of guidelines "Principles for Compensating Pension Loss" was published in August 2017 by the Tribunals Judiciary and Employment Tribunals (Scotland).

Auty has many critics but it has not been overruled. In practice, for many lower value cases, the *Auty* approach will probably be agreed by both parties and it provides a comparatively simple means of assessing pension loss.

However, in some cases, the pension loss may be the biggest single head of claim. This can apply, for example, in military claims if the claimant has lost an army career but found alternative employment in the private sector. In those circumstances, the earnings may be comparable, but the pension will probably not be.

We suggest that in a case of this type, the parties may wish to instruct experts to analyse the financial loss which will include calculation of the pension loss. The more accurately the loss can be calculated, the less discount for uncertainty will be applied. However, the Court will always have to contend with some uncertainty, especially for younger claimants. It would be a great help for practitioners if the Court of Appeal were to re-visit pension claim calculations, bearing in mind that *Auty* is now well over 30 years old. Unless and until that happens, contending methods of dealing with pension claims will be considered in the legal press. Readers who wish to look at possible solutions may consult the textbooks and journals which offer a variety of potential answers.

---

[5] (EAT/192/89).

B4: *Roberts v Johnstone* (accommodation claims)

1. An injured claimant may require special accommodation because of an acquired disability. Common examples are amputees and wheelchair users.

2. In many cases, the claimant will be advised to buy and adapt a house. Insofar as the costs of adaptation do not increase the value of the property, they can be claimed as "costs thrown away" and recovered in full.

3. The claimant can also recover in full the costs of a move that would not otherwise have occurred (stamp duty, legal costs, solicitors' fees etc.) and any additional annual running costs which arise because of the need to live in bigger or adapted premises.

4. A more difficult problem arises in relation to the extra capital cost of buying the more expensive house (and in relation to those adaptations which do increase the value of the house). In *Roberts v Johnstone*[1], the Court of Appeal held that the full additional capital costs could not be recovered. Instead, the claimant was awarded a notional sum to reflect the loss of investment opportunity. Once the discount rate became standardised, this became the basis for the *Roberts* compensation. Hence, with a discount rate of 2.5 per cent, additional capital expenditure of, say, £200,000 and a life multiplier of, say, 30, the *Roberts* claim would have been:

   £200,000 × 2.5% × 30 = £150,000

5. However, now the discount rate is fixed at -0.75 per cent which means that the deemed return on capital is negative; this discloses an argument that the claimant has not lost any investment opportunity and therefore the *Roberts* claim must be nil—irrespective of the additional capital commitment and multiplier. This was the approach adopted in May 2017 by William Davis J in *JR v Sheffield Teaching Hospitals Foundation NHS Trust*[2].

6. The Court of Appeal was due to hear the claimant's appeal in *JR* in October 2017. Shortly before the hearing, the defendant NHSR agreed to pay the full capital costs of buying a suitable home. The resulting settlement of the claim was then approved by the Court of Appeal. It should be borne in mind that the Court's approval of the settlement, which was favourable to the claimant, does not necessarily mean that the Court of Appeal would have ruled in the claimant's favour had the case been heard. The settlement (and its approval) does, however, offer some ammunition to the contention that the capital claim survives the negative discount rate.

7. An alternative view (which was unsuccessfully advanced by representatives of the claimant in the *JR* case) is that the 2.5 per cent figure is not truly derived from the discount rate but it is a conventional and pragmatic means of assessing a capital loss. On this analysis, the *Roberts v Johnstone* award would survive with the caveat that no *Roberts* claim could exceed the capital cost of purchase (as was conceded by the claimant in *JR*). This is a possibility because the lower discount rates mean that multipliers may easily exceed 40 so that if 2.5 per cent were adopted as the right figure for annual loss of capital, the claim would have to be capped at 100 per cent of the price of the house.

8. The position as of May 2018 is therefore unclear. The Court of Appeal authority of *Roberts* is still good law but its interpretation is a matter of debate. Practitioners will await further rulings from the courts and, of course, any revision of the discount rate and the implications of that.

[1] [1989] QB 878.
[2] [2017] EWHC Civ 1245.

B5: Periodical payments

The circumstances in which a periodical payment should be made

The Damages Act 1996 as amended now empowers the Court to order Periodical Payments for future losses. Provisions dealing with the making of a periodical payments order are contained in CPR rr.41.4 to 41.10 and the attendant Practice Directions. Rule 41.7 provides that:

> "When considering–
>
> (a) its indication as to whether periodical payments or a lump sum is likely to be the more appropriate form for all or part of an award of damages under rule 41.6; or
>
> (b) whether to make an order under section 2(1)(a) of the 1996 Act,
>
> the court shall have regard to all the circumstances of the case and in particular the form of award which best meets the claimant's needs, having regard to the factors set out in Practice Direction 41B."

The factors involved are derived from the Practice Direction supplementing Part 41 which provides that:

> "The factors which the court shall have regard to under rule 41.7 include–
>
> (1) the scale of the annual payments taking into account any deduction for contributory negligence;
>
> (2) the form of award preferred by the claimant including–
>
>   (a) the reasons for the claimant's preference; and
>
>   (b) the nature of any financial advice received by the claimant when considering the form of award; and
>
> (3) the form of award preferred by the defendant including the reasons for the defendant's preference."

Practitioners representing claimants may wish to obtain financial advice in order to decide whether or not to ask the Court to make an award for Periodical Payments. Such advice will be particularly useful in difficult cases such as those involving incomplete recovery (contributory negligence or agreed reduction of damages for litigation risk in a clinical negligence claim).

Circumstances in which periodical payments are not available

Section 2(3) of the 1996 Act provides that:

> "(3) A court may not make an order for periodical payments unless satisfied that the continuity of payment under the order is reasonably secure."

Continuity of payment will only be secure in three situations, each dignified by its own sub-clause in subsection 2(4):

> "(4) For the purposes of subsection (3) the continuity of payment under an order is reasonably secure if–

(a) it is protected by a guarantee given under section 6 of or the Schedule to this Act,

(b) it is protected by a scheme under section 213 of the Financial Services and Markets Act 2000 (compensation) (whether or not as modified by section 4 of this Act), or

(c) the source of payment is a government or health service body."

The effect of this is that Periodical Payments will not be available unless the defendant is either a government body (such as the NHSLA) or a UK insurer within one of the two statutory schemes. Hence practitioners must ascertain whether or not the defendant is within those schemes well before the matter comes to trial or settlement meeting.

The indexation of periodical payments

Section 2(8) of the Damages Act 1996 (as amended) provides that orders for periodical payments are to be treated as providing for the amount of the payment ordered to vary with the Retail Prices Index ("RPI"). However, section 2(9) of the Damages Act 1996 then stipulates that an order for periodical payments may include provision disapplying section 2(8) or modifying its effect.

In *Thompstone v Tameside and Glossop NHS Trust*[1], the Court of Appeal held that the appropriate means of indexation of future costs of care and case management would be by reference to ASHE 6115 (see next section of *Facts & Figures*) which was the most reliable way of "tracking" changes to these costs.

Consequently, the ASHE 6115 indexation will apply to periodical payments in respect of future care and case management. The Retail Prices Index will be used for future losses which are goods-based (such as future equipment and assistive technology). In *Sarwar v Ali and Motor Insurers Bureau*[2], Lloyd Jones J awarded a periodical payment for future losses of earnings and index-linked the loss by reference to the ASHE aggregated earnings data for male full-time employees. Theoretically, it would be possible for a party to contend for another means of indexation, although to our knowledge this has not been successfully attempted in a reported case.

"Model Order" for periodical payments

The leading case is now *RH v University Hospitals Bristol NHS Foundation Trust*[3]. Swift J held that since there had been a change in statistical methodology used to generate the ASHE 6115 indexation, there was a need to adapt the previous model order made by Sir Christopher Holland on 2 December 2008[4]. The model order approved in *RH* may be used for periodical payments and it deals with the complex issues of indexation and changes to payments caused by that indexation. The NHSLA continues to uprate indexed payments on 15 December each year although other defendants and insurers may have different preferences. Clearly, the starting date must be set at sufficient distance to allow its satisfactory introduction; this is likely to be more protracted if the claimant has a deputy.

Is the claimant still alive?

In *Long v Norwich Union*[5], Mackay J held that a claimant was not entitled to recover the costs of proving that he was still alive at the date of periodical payment. The court held that this cost would be covered by the award for the costs of deputyship; alternatively, it might be said that the modest costs of this type borne by the claimant would be covered by the interest generated on the advance payments to be made under the order.

[1] [2008] AER 72.
[2] [2007] LS Law Med 375.
[3] [2013] EWHC 229.
[4] [2009] P.I.Q.R. P153.
[5] [2009] EWHC 715 QB.

B6: Step-by-step guide to finding the annual estimates for hourly pay in ASHE SOC 2000 6115

The data collection point for the Annual Survey of Hours and Earnings (ASHE) is April each year. The data are collected over the summer and the first release of estimates takes place in November/December of that year. These are provisional estimates which are revised and published as final estimates the following October/November/December. The following estimates were published for ASHE SOC2000 on 22 October/November 2012, 12 December 2013, 19 November 2014, 18 November 2015, 26 October 2016 and 26 October 2017. Estimates for 2017 are provisional and will be replaced by final estimates in October/November/December 2018.

ASHE SOC 2000 6115 Centile estimates for hourly earnings £ for UK employees 2011–2017

Centile	10	20	25	30	40	50	60	70	75	80	90
ASHE 6115 2011 Final release	6.05	6.44	6.65	6.87	7.28	7.83	8.45	9.17	9.67	10.22	11.92
ASHE 6115 2012 Final release	6.21	6.57	6.80	7.00	7.44	7.92	8.51	9.21	9.69	10.25	11.97
ASHE 6115 2013 Final release	6.30	6.61	6.80	7.00	7.40	7.91	8.50	9.22	9.73	10.29	12.02
ASHE 6115 2014 Final release	6.41	6.74	6.94	7.12	7.53	8.00	8.55	9.23	9.72	10.21	11.95
ASHE 6115 2015 Final release	6.63	6.98	7.10	7.29	7.72	8.18	8.73	9.44	9.88	10.38	12.21
ASHE 6115 2016 Final release	7.20	7.36	7.50	7.70	8.08	8.50	9.02	9.76	10.18	10.75	12.50
ASHE 6115 2017 First release	7.50	7.76	7.93	8.07	8.42	8.85	9.36	10.05	10.50	11.04	12.91

Source: ONS, ASHE

ASHE estimates are only available online. They can be found on the website of the Office for National Statistics (ONS). This website was redesigned and launched on 25 February 2016. Step-by-step instructions to locate estimates for ASHE SOC 2000 6115 are provided. You need not follow all these instructions each time you consult the tables as you can either download the tables as an Excel file or you can save the web link to the tables in Bookmarks.

Reclassification of occupational categories occurs every 10 years. Estimates from 2011 final are based on the Standard Occupational Classification (SOC) 2010 weights. When calculating a growth rate, care must be taken that estimates in different years are made on the basis of the same occupational weights. When comparing earnings in any year from 2011 onwards with 2011, use the 2011 final release. When comparing earnings in any year before 2011, use the 2011 first release.

The classification for carers changed in SOC 2010 to include two separate categories, ASHE 6145 care workers and home carers and ASHE 6146 senior care workers. For the purposes of the indexation of future care, the new classification for carers should be ignored and the older classification based on SOC 2000 6115 used instead. The occupational earnings tables for SOC 2000 6115 can be found at Table 26. The title for this table is Care Workers (SOC) - ASHE: Table 26.

1. Find the home page of the Office for National Statistics (ONS) at *www.ons.gov.uk*
2. Type in ASHE Care Workers in the search box at the top of this page and click Search.
3. Refine the search using the menu on the left hand side by checking the box for Datasets.
4. The title for this Table is Care Workers (SOC) - ASHE: Table 26.

B6: Step-by-step guide to finding the annual estimates for hourly pay in ASHE SOC 2000 6115

5. Clicking on the table title opens a new menu containing tables for care workers from 2011 to 2017. Clicking on the table title for each year will open a .zip file.

6. Opening the .zip file will produce a contents list of Excel files each of which contain a different set of earnings estimates for carers.

7. Hourly pay for carers is in Care Workers (SOC 6145 and 6146 - equiv. to SOC 2000 6115) Table 26.5a Hourly Pay - Gross. A double-click on the table title will take you to a worksheet in an Excel file. If you are sure that you have located the file that you want, save it using File → Save in Excel.

8. Once in the Excel file, check the bottom tab. "All" refers to all employees (male and female, part- and full-time).

9. Read across the centile estimates. Shading indicates the reliability of the estimate. Where the estimate of the error is less than five per cent (reliable), there is no shading. ASHE 6115 estimates are normally reliable due to a large sample size. The key to the shading can be found at the bottom and at the right hand side of the table.

10. If you have not already saved this file at step 7 above, this table can be saved now, either in part or in full. If the file is saved before the final release in October/November/December 2018, make a note that the 2017 estimates are provisional.

This guide has been prepared by Dr Victoria Wass, Cardiff Business School, November 2017.

Group C
Interest Rates

C1: Interest base rates

C2: Real and nominal interest rates and price inflation

C3: Special investment account rates

C4: Special and general damages interest

C5: Base rate + 10 per cent

C6: Number of days between two dates

C7: Decimal years

C8: Judgment debt interest rates (England and Wales)

C9: Judicial rates of interest (Scotland)

C1: Interest base rates

Introductory note

1. The data for this table are obtained from retail banks Barclays, Lloyds TSB, HSBC and National Westminster. Since 3 August 2006, these retail banks' base rates have been identical to the Bank of England's Official Bank Rate.

Date	New rate (%)	Date	New rate (%)	Date	New rate (%)
1987		22 September	9.00	5 April	5.50
10 March	10.50	16 October	8.00	10 May	5.25
19 March	10.00	13 November	7.00	2 August	5.00
29 April	9.50			18 September	4.75
11 May	9.00	**1993**		4 October	4.50
7 August	10.00	26 January	6.00	8 November	4.00
26 October	9.50	23 November	5.50		
5 November	9.00			**2003**	
4 December	8.50	**1994**		7 February	3.75
		8 February	5.25	10 July	3.50
1988		12 September	5.75	6 November	3.75
2 February	9.00	7 December	6.25		
17 March	8.50			**2004**	
11 April	8.00	**1995**		5 February	4.00
18 May	7.50	2 February	6.75	6 May	4.25
3 June	8.00	13 December	6.50	10 June	4.50
6 June	8.25*			5 August	4.75
7 June	8.50	**1996**			
22 June	9.00	18 January	6.25	**2005**	
29 June	9.50	8 March	6.00	4 August	4.50
5 July	10.00	6 June	5.75		
19 July	10.50	30 October	6.00	**2006**	
8 August	10.75*			3 August	4.75
9 August	11.00	**1997**		9 November	5.00
25 August	11.50	7 May	6.25		
26 August	12.00	9 June	6.50	**2007**	
25 November	13.00	11 July	6.75	11 January	5.25
		8 August	7.00	10 May	5.50
1989		7 November	7.25	5 July	5.75
24 May	14.00			6 December	5.50
5 October	15.00	**1998**			
		5 June	7.50	**2008**	
1990		9 October	7.25	7 February	5.25
8 October	14.00	6 November	6.75	10 April	5.00
		11 December	6.25	8 October	4.50
1991				6 November	3.00
13 February	13.50	**1999**		4 December	2.00
27 February	13.00	8 January	6.00		
25 March	12.50	5 February	5.50	**2009**	
12 April	12.00	8 April	5.25	8 January	1.50
24 May	11.50	10 June	5.00	5 February	1.00
12 July	11.00	8 September	5.25	5 March	0.50
4 September	10.50	4 November	5.50		
				2016	
1992		**2000**		4 August	0.25
5 May	10.00	13 January	5.75		
16 September	12.00	10 February	6.00	**2017**	
17 September	10.00			2 November	0.50
		2001			
		8 February	5.75		

C2: Real and nominal interest rates and price inflation

Introductory notes

1. Price inflation is calculated as the rate of change of the Retail Prices Index.
2. The nominal interest rate is based on the rate on 20-year British Government Securities.
3. No account has been taken of tax in these figures.

	Price Inflation %	Nominal Interest Rate %	Real Interest Rate %
1995	3.41	8.26	4.85
1996	2.44	8.10	5.66
1997	3.12	7.09	3.97
1998	3.42	5.45	2.03
1999	1.56	4.70	3.14
2000	2.93	4.70	1.77
2001	1.84	4.78	2.94
2002	1.62	4.83	3.21
2003	2.91	4.64	1.73
2004	2.96	4.78	1.82
2005	2.84	4.39	1.55
2006	3.20	4.29	1.09
2007	4.26	4.73	0.47
2008	4.00	4.68	0.68
2009	(0.53)	4.25	4.78
2010	4.61	4.24	(0.37)
2011	5.21	3.83	(1.38)
2012	3.22	2.86	(0.36)
2013	3.05	3.19	0.14
2014	2.38	3.10	0.72
2015	0.98	2.41	1.43
2016	1.74	1.91	0.17
2017	3.58	1.82	(1.76)
Averages:			
1980–89	7.44	11.18	3.74
1990–99	3.71	7.96	4.25
2000–09	2.60	4.61	2.01
2010–17	3.10	2.92	(0.18)

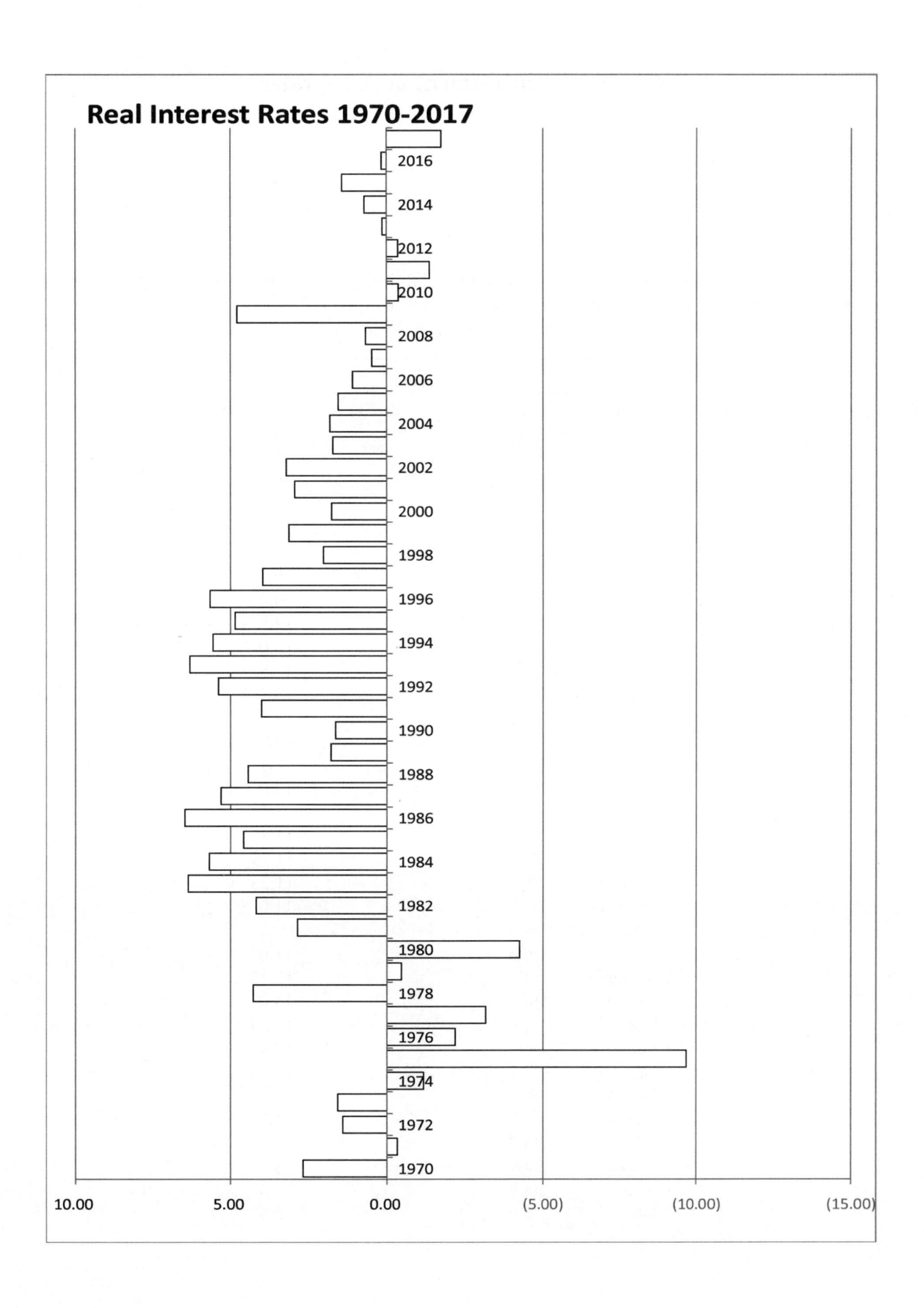

Real Interest Rates 1970-2017

C3: Special investment account rates

Introductory notes

This is a composite table including both the Short-term Investment Account rate and the succeeding High Court Special Investment Account rate.

The manner of crediting interest is set out in Court Fund Rules 1987 r.27. Interest accruing to a special investment account is credited without the deduction of income tax.

From:		%
1 October	1965	5.0
1 September	1966	5.5
1 March	1968	6.0
1 March	1969	6.5
1 March	1970	7.0
1 March	1971	7.5
1 March	1973	8.0
1 March	1974	9.0
1 February	1977	10.0
1 March	1979	12.5
1 January	1980	15.0
1 January	1981	12.5
1 December	1981	15.0
1 March	1982	14.0
1 July	1982	13.0
1 April	1983	12.5
1 April	1984	12.0
1 August	1986	11.5
1 January	1987	12.25
1 April	1987	11.75
1 November	1987	11.25
1 December	1987	11.0
1 May	1988	9.5
1 August	1988	11.0
1 November	1988	12.25
1 January	1989	13.0
1 November	1989	14.25
1 April	1991	12.0
1 October	1991	10.25
1 February	1993	8.0
1 August	1999	7.0
1 February	2002	6.0
1 February	2009	3.0
1 June	2009	1.5
1 July	2009	0.5

C4: Special and general damages interest

Introductory notes

Special damages

The appropriate rate of interest for special damages is the rate, over the period for which the interest is awarded, which is payable on the court special account. This rate was reduced to 0.5 per cent on 1 July 2009. Interest since June 1987 has been paid daily on a 1/365th basis, even in a leap year such as 2016.

In cases of continuing special damages, half the appropriate rate from the date of injury to the date of trial is awarded. In cases where the special damages have ceased and are thus limited to a finite period, there are conflicting Court of Appeal decisions as to whether the award should be half the appropriate rate from injury to trial (*Dexter v Courtaulds*[1]) or the full special account rate from a date within the period to which the special damages are limited (*Prokop v DHSS*[2]).

The relevant rates since 1965 are set out in Table C3.

The table on the next page records the total of these rates from January 1981. In the left-hand column is shown the month from the first day of which interest is assumed to run. The right-hand column shows the percentage interest accumulated from the first day of each month to 30 June 2018 (including both of those days).

Continued use may be made of this table by adding to the figures in it 1/365th of the special account rate for each day from 1 July 2018 onwards, using Table C6, which records the number of days between two dates in a two-year period.

Suppose that interest runs from 1 January 2001 to 13 October 2018. The total to 30 June 2018 is 55.24 per cent (see Table C4). From Table C6, July 1 to October 13 is 286–182 days = 104 days, but add 1 day as both days are to be included = 105 days. If the rate remains at 0.5 per cent p.a., the appropriate addition will be 0.5 per cent × 105/365 = 0.14 per cent. Thus the grand total from 1 January 2001 to 13 October 2018 will be 55.24 + 0.14 = 55.38 per cent.

General damages

In personal injury cases, the normal rate of interest on general damages for pain, suffering and loss of amenity was by convention two per cent per annum. In *Lawrence v Chief Constable of Staffordshire*[3] the Court of Appeal held that in spite of *Wells v Wells*,[4] the rate should remain at two per cent. Interest runs from the date of service of proceedings.

Scotland

The notes above and the tables on the next page apply in England and Wales. For interest on damages in Scotland please refer to table **C9: Judicial rates of interest (Scotland).**

[1] [1984] 1 All E.R. 70.
[2] [1985] C.L.Y. 1037.
[3] CA, transcript 29 June 2000.
[4] [1999] A.C. 345.

C4: Special and general damages interest

Table of cumulative interest at the special account rate from the first day of each month to 30 June 2018.

	1981	1982	1983	1984	1985	1986	1987	1988	1989	1990
Jan	265.47	252.76	239.10	226.48	214.32	202.32	190.53	178.76	167.90	154.69
Feb	264.41	251.49	238.00	225.42	213.30	201.30	189.49	177.83	166.80	153.48
Mar	263.45	250.34	237.00	224.43	212.38	200.38	188.55	176.96	165.80	152.39
Apr	262.39	249.15	235.90	223.36	211.36	199.36	187.51	176.02	164.70	151.18
May	261.36	248.00	234.87	222.38	210.38	198.38	186.55	175.12	163.63	150.01
Jun	260.30	246.81	233.81	221.36	209.36	197.36	185.55	174.31	162.53	148.80
Jul	259.28	245.66	232.78	220.37	208.37	196.37	184.58	173.53	161.46	147.63
Aug	258.21	244.55	231.72	219.35	207.35	195.35	183.58	172.72	160.35	146.42
Sep	257.15	243.45	230.66	218.33	206.33	194.38	182.59	171.79	159.25	145.21
Oct	256.12	242.38	229.63	217.35	205.35	193.43	181.62	170.88	158.18	144.04
Nov	255.06	241.28	228.57	216.33	204.33	192.45	180.62	169.95	157.08	142.83
Dec	254.04	240.21	227.54	215.34	203.34	191.51	179.70	168.94	155.90	141.65

	1991	1992	1993	1994	1995	1996	1997	1998	1999	2000
Jan	140.44	128.33	118.05	109.86	101.86	93.86	85.84	77.84	69.84	62.26
Feb	139.23	127.46	117.18	109.18	101.18	93.18	85.16	77.16	69.16	61.66
Mar	138.14	126.65	116.57	108.57	100.57	92.55	84.55	76.55	68.55	61.11
Apr	136.93	125.78	115.89	107.89	99.89	91.87	83.87	75.87	67.87	60.51
May	135.94	124.93	115.23	107.23	99.23	91.21	83.21	75.21	67.21	59.94
Jun	134.93	124.06	114.55	106.55	98.55	90.53	82.53	74.53	66.53	59.34
Jul	133.94	123.22	113.89	105.89	97.89	89.87	81.87	73.87	65.87	58.77
Aug	132.92	122.35	113.22	105.22	97.22	89.19	81.19	73.19	65.19	58.17
Sep	131.90	121.48	112.54	104.54	96.54	88.51	80.51	72.51	64.60	57.58
Oct	130.91	120.64	111.88	103.88	95.88	87.86	79.86	71.86	64.02	57.00
Nov	130.04	119.77	111.20	103.20	95.20	87.18	79.18	71.18	63.43	56.41
Dec	129.20	118.92	110.54	102.54	94.54	86.52	78.52	70.52	62.85	55.83

	2001	2002	2003	2004	2005	2006	2007	2008	2009	2010
Jan	55.24	48.24	42.15	36.15	30.14	24.14	18.14	12.14	6.12	4.25
Feb	54.65	47.65	41.65	35.65	29.63	23.63	17.63	11.63	5.61	4.21
Mar	54.11	47.18	41.18	35.17	29.17	23.17	17.17	11.15	5.38	4.17
Apr	53.51	46.68	40.68	34.66	28.66	22.66	16.66	10.64	5.13	4.13
May	52.94	46.18	40.18	34.17	28.17	22.17	16.17	10.15	4.88	4.09
Jun	52.34	45.67	39.67	33.66	27.66	21.66	15.66	9.64	4.63	4.04
Jul	51.77	45.18	39.18	33.16	27.16	21.16	15.16	9.15	4.50	4.00
Aug	51.17	44.67	38.67	32.65	26.65	20.65	14.65	8.64	4.46	3.96
Sep	50.58	44.16	38.16	32.14	26.14	20.14	14.14	8.13	4.42	3.92
Oct	50.00	43.67	37.67	31.65	25.65	19.65	13.65	7.63	4.38	3.88
Nov	49.41	43.16	37.16	31.14	25.14	19.14	13.14	7.12	4.33	3.83
Dec	48.83	42.66	36.66	30.65	24.65	18.65	12.65	6.63	4.29	3.79

	2011	2012	2013	2014	2015	2016	2017	2018
Jan	3.75	3.25	2.75	2.25	1.75	1.25	0.75	0.25
Feb	3.71	3.21	2.71	2.21	1.71	1.21	0.71	0.21
Mar	3.67	3.17	2.67	2.17	1.67	1.17	0.67	0.17
Apr	3.63	3.13	2.63	2.13	1.63	1.12	0.62	0.12
May	3.59	3.08	2.58	2.08	1.58	1.08	0.58	0.08
Jun	3.54	3.04	2.54	2.04	1.54	1.04	0.54	0.04
Jul	3.50	3.00	2.50	2.00	1.50	1.00	0.50	
Aug	3.46	2.96	2.46	1.96	1.46	0.96	0.46	
Sep	3.42	2.92	2.42	1.92	1.42	0.92	0.42	
Oct	3.38	2.88	2.38	1.88	1.38	0.87	0.37	
Nov	3.33	2.83	2.33	1.83	1.33	0.83	0.33	
Dec	3.29	2.79	2.29	1.79	1.29	0.79	0.29	

If the rate remains at 0.5%, interest to the last day of successive later months can be found to a date after 30 June 2018 by adding the figure from the following table:

	2018	2019
Jan		0.29
Feb		0.33
Mar		0.38
Apr		0.42
May		0.46
Jun		0.50
Jul	0.04	
Aug	0.08	
Sep	0.13	
Oct	0.17	
Nov	0.21	
Dec	0.25	

C5: Base rate + 10 per cent

Introductory notes

1. Under the Civil Procedure Rules 1998 r.36.17, where the judgment is more advantageous to the claimant than the proposals in a claimant's Part 36 offer, the court may order interest on the sums awarded and on the costs, for some or all of the period starting with the latest date on which the defendant could have accepted the Part 36 offer without needing the permission of the court, at a rate not exceeding 10 per cent above base rate. Where the rule applies, the court will make those orders unless it considers it unjust to do so.

2. Since August 2005 base rates plus 10 per cent have been as follows. For base rates from 1997 to 2005 see the 2016/17 edition of *Facts and Figures*.

		Rate + 10%			Rate + 10%			Rate + 10%
2005	4 August	14.50%	2007	6 December	15.50%	2009	8 January	11.50%
2006	3 August	14.75%	2008	7 February	15.25%		5 February	11.00%
	9 November	15.00%		10 April	15.00%		5 March	10.50%
2007	11 January	15.25%		8 October	14.50%	2016	4 August	10.25%
	10 May	15.50%		6 November	13.00%	2017	2 November	10.50%
	5 July	15.75%		4 December	12.00%			

The following table shows cumulative interest at 10 per cent above base rate from the first day of each month until 30 June 2018 (including both dates). Interest for parts of a month can be found by following the method in the notes to Table C4.

	2008	2009	2010	2011	2012	2013	2014	2015	2016	2017	2018
January	114.02	99.60	88.95	78.45	67.95	57.42	46.92	36.42	25.92	15.50	5.21
February	112.80	98.61	88.06	77.56	67.06	56.53	46.03	35.53	25.03	14.63	4.32
March	111.51	97.76	87.26	76.76	66.23	55.73	45.23	34.73	24.20	13.84	3.51
April	110.27	96.86	86.36	75.86	65.33	54.83	44.33	33.83	23.31	12.97	2.62
May	109.00	96.00	85.50	75.00	64.47	53.97	43.47	32.97	22.44	12.13	1.75
June	107.76	95.11	84.61	74.11	63.58	53.08	42.58	32.08	21.55	11.26	0.86
July	106.49	94.25	83.75	73.25	62.72	52.22	41.72	31.22	20.69	10.42	
August	105.21	93.35	82.85	72.35	61.83	51.33	40.83	30.33	19.80	9.54	
September	103.98	92.46	81.96	71.46	60.93	50.43	39.93	29.43	18.92	8.67	
October	102.74	91.60	81.10	70.60	60.07	49.57	39.07	28.57	18.08	7.83	
November	101.65	90.71	80.21	69.71	59.18	48.68	38.18	27.68	17.21	6.96	
December	100.62	89.84	79.34	68.84	58.32	47.82	37.32	26.82	16.37	6.10	

Interest to the last day of successive later months can be found to a date after 30 June 2018 by adding the figure from the following table:

July 2018	0.89	November 2018	4.40	March 2019	7.88
August 2018	1.78	December 2018	5.29	April 2019	8.75
September 2018	2.65	January 2019	6.18	May 2019	9.64
October 2018	3.54	February 2019	6.99	June 2019	10.50

C6: Number of days between two dates

Introductory notes

Deduct the number of the opening date from the number of the closing date (where necessary adding a day for 29 February).
Example: 14 October–19 March (where the February is not a leap year) is 443 − 287 = 156 days.
Note that the calculation produces the *interval* between the two dates; so that it includes the first date and excludes the last date. For example, 1 January to 31 January is calculated as 31 − 1 = 30 days, not 31. If the last date is to be included then "add 1" to the number of days.

Day numbers

Day of month	Jan	Feb	Mar	Apr	May	Jun	Jul	Aug	Sep	Oct	Nov	Dec	Jan	Feb	Mar	Apr	May	Jun	Jul	Aug	Sep	Oct	Nov	Dec	Day of month
1	1	32	60	91	121	152	182	213	244	274	305	335	366	397	425	456	486	517	547	578	609	639	670	700	1
2	2	33	61	92	122	153	183	214	245	275	306	336	367	398	426	457	487	518	548	579	610	640	671	701	2
3	3	34	62	93	123	154	184	215	246	276	307	337	368	399	427	458	488	519	549	580	611	641	672	702	3
4	4	35	63	94	124	155	185	216	247	277	308	338	369	400	428	459	489	520	550	581	612	642	673	703	4
5	5	36	64	95	125	156	186	217	248	278	309	339	370	401	429	460	490	521	551	582	613	643	674	704	5
6	6	37	65	96	126	157	187	218	249	279	310	340	371	402	430	461	491	522	552	583	614	644	675	705	6
7	7	38	66	97	127	158	188	219	250	280	311	341	372	403	431	462	492	523	553	584	615	645	676	706	7
8	8	39	67	98	128	159	189	220	251	281	312	342	373	404	432	463	493	524	554	585	616	646	677	707	8
9	9	40	68	99	129	160	190	221	252	282	313	343	374	405	433	464	494	525	555	586	617	647	678	708	9
10	10	41	69	100	130	161	191	222	253	283	314	344	375	406	434	465	495	526	556	587	618	648	679	709	10
11	11	42	70	101	131	162	192	223	254	284	315	345	376	407	435	466	496	527	557	588	619	649	680	710	11
12	12	43	71	102	132	163	193	224	255	285	316	346	377	408	436	467	497	528	558	589	620	650	681	711	12
13	13	44	72	103	133	164	194	225	256	286	317	347	378	409	437	468	498	529	559	590	621	651	682	712	13
14	14	45	73	104	134	165	195	226	257	287	318	348	379	410	438	469	499	530	560	591	622	652	683	713	14
15	15	46	74	105	135	166	196	227	258	288	319	349	380	411	439	470	500	531	561	592	623	653	684	714	15
16	16	47	75	106	136	167	197	228	259	289	320	350	381	412	440	471	501	532	562	593	624	654	685	715	16
17	17	48	76	107	137	168	198	229	260	290	321	351	382	413	441	472	502	533	563	594	625	655	686	716	17
18	18	49	77	108	138	169	199	230	261	291	322	352	383	414	442	473	503	534	564	595	626	656	687	717	18
19	19	50	78	109	139	170	200	231	262	292	323	353	384	415	443	474	504	535	565	596	627	657	688	718	19
20	20	51	79	110	140	171	201	232	263	293	324	354	385	416	444	475	505	536	566	597	628	658	689	719	20
21	21	52	80	111	141	172	202	233	264	294	325	355	386	417	445	476	506	537	567	598	629	659	690	720	21
22	22	53	81	112	142	173	203	234	265	295	326	356	387	418	446	477	507	538	568	599	630	660	691	721	22
23	23	54	82	113	143	174	204	235	266	296	327	357	388	419	447	478	508	539	569	600	631	661	692	722	23
24	24	55	83	114	144	175	205	236	267	297	328	358	389	420	448	479	509	540	570	601	632	662	693	723	24
25	25	56	84	115	145	176	206	237	268	298	329	359	390	421	449	480	510	541	571	602	633	663	694	724	25
26	26	57	85	116	146	177	207	238	269	299	330	360	391	422	450	481	511	542	572	603	634	664	695	725	26
27	27	58	86	117	147	178	208	239	270	300	331	361	392	423	451	482	512	543	573	604	635	665	696	726	27
28	28	59	87	118	148	179	209	240	271	301	332	362	393	424	452	483	513	544	574	605	636	666	697	727	28
29	29		88	119	149	180	210	241	272	302	333	363	394		453	484	514	545	575	606	637	667	698	728	29
30	30		89	120	150	181	211	242	273	303	334	364	395		454	485	515	546	576	607	638	668	699	729	30
31	31		90		151		212	243		304		365	396		455		516		577	608		669		730	31

C7: Decimal years

An alternative way of calculating interest is with a table expressing intervals as decimals of a year. It is in some respects simpler than using Table C6 (Number of Days) as it avoids the need to divide by 365.

The first table below gives days, weeks and months as decimals of a year.

The second table gives the period between corresponding days of two months, with the earlier month down the left-hand side and the later month across the top. Thus from the two figures in bold one sees that from 1 April–1 June is 0.167 years; from 1 June to the next 1 April is 0.833 years. The calculation again produces the *interval* between the dates: 1 January to 1 February is 31 days (not 32).

Days, weeks and months expressed as decimals of a year

Days

1	0.003	2	0.005	3	0.008	4	0.011	5	0.014	6	0.016	7	0.019	8	0.022	9	0.025	10	0.027
11	0.030	12	0.033	13	0.036	14	0.038	15	0.041	16	0.044	17	0.047	18	0.049	19	0.052	20	0.055
21	0.058	22	0.060	23	0.063	24	0.066	25	0.068	26	0.071	27	0.074	28	0.077	29	0.079	30	0.082

Weeks

1	0.019	2	0.038	3	0.058	4	0.077	5	0.096	6	0.115	7	0.134	8	0.153	9	0.173	10	0.192

Months

28 days	0.077	29 days	0.079	30 days	0.082	31 days	0.085

Intervals between corresponding days of months as decimals of a year

Later month

Earlier month	Jan	Feb	Mar	Apr	May	Jun
Jan	1.000	0.085	0.162	0.247	0.329	0.414
Feb	0.915	1.000	0.077	0.162	0.244	0.329
Mar	0.838	0.923	1.000	0.085	0.167	0.252
Apr	0.753	0.838	0.915	1.000	0.082	**0.167**
May	0.671	0.756	0.833	0.918	1.000	0.085
Jun	0.586	0.671	0.748	**0.833**	0.915	1.000
Jul	0.504	0.589	0.666	0.751	0.833	0.918
Aug	0.419	0.504	0.581	0.666	0.748	0.833
Sept	0.334	0.419	0.496	0.581	0.663	0.748
Oct	0.252	0.337	0.414	0.499	0.581	0.666
Nov	0.167	0.252	0.329	0.414	0.496	0.581
Dec	0.085	0.170	0.247	0.332	0.414	0.499

Earlier month	Jul	Aug	Sept	Oct	Nov	Dec
Jan	0.496	0.581	0.666	0.748	0.833	0.915
Feb	0.411	0.496	0.581	0.663	0.748	0.830
Mar	0.334	0.419	0.504	0.586	0.671	0.753
Apr	0.249	0.334	0.419	0.501	0.586	0.668
May	0.167	0.252	0.337	0.419	0.504	0.586
Jun	0.082	0.167	0.252	0.334	0.419	0.501
Jul	1.000	0.085	0.170	0.252	0.337	0.419
Aug	0.915	1.000	0.085	0.167	0.252	0.334
Sept	0.830	0.915	1.000	0.082	0.167	0.249
Oct	0.748	0.833	0.918	1.000	0.085	0.167
Nov	0.663	0.748	0.833	0.915	1.000	0.082
Dec	0.581	0.666	0.751	0.833	0.918	1.000

Example: to calculate interest at eight per cent from 3 June 2018 to 15 April 2019

3 June to 15 June	= 12 days	= 0.033 years	
15 June to 15 April the following year		= 0.833	
Total 3.6.18 to 15.4.19		= 0.866 years	
Interest at 8% from 3.6.18 to 15.4.19		= 0.866 × 8	= 6.928%

Sweet & Maxwell

C8: Judgment debt interest rates (England and Wales)

Introductory notes

Interest rates under the Judgments Act 1838 s.17.

This table sets out the interest rates as determined by the Judgment Debts (Rate of Interest) Orders. Such orders are made under the Administration of Justice Act 1970 s.44.

By virtue of The County Courts (Interest on Judgment Debts) Order 1991, the general rule is that every judgment debt of not less than £5,000 carries interest from the date on which it was given, at the same rate as that payable on High Court judgments.

From	At %	Order
20 April 1971	7.5	SI 1971/491
1 March 1977	10	SI 1977/141
3 December 1979	12.5	SI 1979/1382
9 June 1980	15	SI 1980/672
8 June 1982	14	SI 1982/696
10 November 1982	12	SI 1982/1427
16 April 1985	15	SI 1985/437
1 April 1993 to date	8	SI 1993/564

C9: Judicial rates of interest (Scotland)

From	At %	Act of Sederunt
4 May 1965	5	SI 1965/321
6 January 1970	7	SI 1969/1819
7 January 1975	11	SI 1974/2090
5 April 1983	12	SI 1983/398
16 August 1985	15	SI 1985/1178
1 April 1993 to date	8	SI 1993/770 and SI 1994/1443

The courts have, and exercise, a discretion to adopt a different rate in any particular case—*Farstad Supply AS v Enviroco Ltd.*[1] The Scottish Law Commission—Report on Interest on Debt and Damages (Scot Law Com No 203)—was of the view that there was uncertainty as to when interest started to run on particular heads of damage, and that the current 8% judicial rate of interest was uncommercial and not truly compensatory. It recommended reform but its proposals were not implemented.

[1] [2013] CSIH 9

Group D
Investment

D1: Share price index (FTSE 100)

D2: Graph of share price index

D3: Index-linked stock

Group D

D1: Share price index (FTSE 100)

FTSE® 100 (on last day of month)

	1987	1988	1989	1990	1991	1992	1993	1994
January	1808.3	1790.8	2051.8	2337.3	2170.3	2571.2	2807.2	3491.8
February	1979.2	1768.8	2002.4	2255.4	2380.9	2562.1	2868.0	3328.1
March	1997.6	1742.5	2075.0	2247.9	2456.5	2440.1	2878.7	3086.4
April	2050.5	1802.2	2118.0	2103.4	2486.2	2654.1	2813.1	3125.3
May	2203.0	1784.5	2114.4	2345.1	2499.5	2707.6	2840.7	2970.5
June	2284.1	1857.6	2151.0	2374.6	2414.8	2521.2	2900.0	2919.2
July	2360.9	1853.6	2297.0	2326.2	2588.8	2399.6	2926.5	3082.6
August	2249.7	1753.6	2387.9	2162.8	2645.7	2312.6	3100.0	3251.3
September	2366.0	1826.5	2299.4	1990.2	2621.7	2553.0	3037.5	3026.3
October	1749.8	1852.4	2142.6	2050.3	2566.0	2658.3	3171.0	3097.4
November	1579.9	1792.4	2276.8	2149.4	2420.2	2778.8	3166.9	3081.4
December	1713.9	1793.1	2422.7	2143.5	2493.1	2846.5	3418.4	3065.5

	1995	1996	1997	1998	1999	200	2001	2002
January	2991.6	3759.3	4275.8	5458.5	5896.0	6268.5	6297.5	5164.8
February	3009.3	3727.6	4308.3	5767.3	6175.1	6232.6	5917.9	5101.0
March	3137.9	3699.7	4312.9	5932.2	6295.3	6540.2	5633.7	5271.8
April	3216.7	3817.9	4436.0	5928.4	6552.2	6327.4	5967.0	5165.6
May	3319.4	3747.8	4621.3	5870.7	6226.2	6359.4	5796.2	5085.1
June	3314.6	3711.0	4604.6	5832.6	6318.5	6312.7	5642.5	4656.4
July	3463.3	3703.2	4907.5	5837.1	6231.9	6365.3	5529.1	4246.2
August	3477.8	3867.6	4817.5	5249.4	6246.4	6672.7	5345.0	4227.3
September	3508.2	3953.7	5244.2	5064.4	6029.8	6294.2	4903.4	3721.8
October	3529.1	3979.1	4842.3	5438.4	6255.7	6438.4	5039.7	4039.7
November	3664.3	4058.0	4831.8	5743.9	6597.2	6142.2	5203.6	4169.4
December	3689.3	4118.5	5135.5	5882.6	6930.2	6222.5	5217.4	3940.4

	2003	2004	2005	2006	2007	2008	2009	2010
January	3567.4	4390.7	4852.3	5760.3	6203.1	5879.8	4149.6	5188.5
February	3655.6	4492.2	4968.5	5791.5	6171.5	5884.3	3830.1	5354.5
March	3613.3	4385.7	4894.4	5964.6	6308.0	5702.1	3926.1	5679.6
April	3926.0	4489.7	4801.7	6023.1	6449.2	6087.3	4243.7	5553.5
May	4048.1	4430.7	4964.0	5723.8	6621.5	6053.5	4417.9	5188.4
June	4031.2	4464.1	5113.2	5833.4	6607.9	5625.9	4249.2	4916.9
July	4157.0	4413.1	5282.3	5928.3	6360.1	5411.9	4608.4	5258.0
August	4161.1	4459.3	5296.9	5906.1	6303.3	5636.6	4908.9	5225.2
September	4091.3	4570.8	5477.7	5960.8	6466.8	4902.5	5133.9	5548.6
October	4287.6	4624.2	5317.3	6129.2	6721.6	4377.3	5044.6	5675.2
November	4342.6	4703.2	5423.2	6048.8	6432.5	4288.0	5190.7	5528.3
December	4476.9	4814.3	5618.8	6220.8	6456.9	4434.2	5412.9	5899.9

	2011	2012	2013	2014	2015	2016	2017	2018
January	5862.9	5681.6	6276.9	6510.4	6749.4	6083.8	7099.2	7533.6
February	5994.0	5871.5	6360.8	6809.7	6946.7	6097.1	7263.4	7231.9
March	5908.8	5768.5	6411.7	6598.4	6773.0	6174.9	7322.9	7533.6
April	6069.9	5737.8	6430.1	6780.0	6960.6	6241.9	7203.9	7056.6
May	5990.0	5320.9	6583.1	6844.5	6984.4	6230.8	7520.0	7059.3
June	5945.7	5571.2	6215.5	6743.9	6521.0	6504.3	7312.7	
July	5815.2	5635.3	6621.1	6730.1	6696.3	6724.4	7372.0	
August	5394.5	5711.5	6412.9	6819.8	6247.9	6781.5	7430.6	
September	5128.5	5742.1	6462.2	6622.7	6061.6	6899.3	7372.8	
October	5544.2	5782.7	6731.4	6546.5	6361.1	6954.2	7493.7	
November	5505.4	5866.8	6650.6	6722.6	6356.1	6783.8	7326.7	
December	5572.3	5897.8	6749.1	6566.1	6242.3	7142.8	7687.8	

Source: https://uk.investing.com/indices/uk-100-historical-data

D2: Graph of share price index

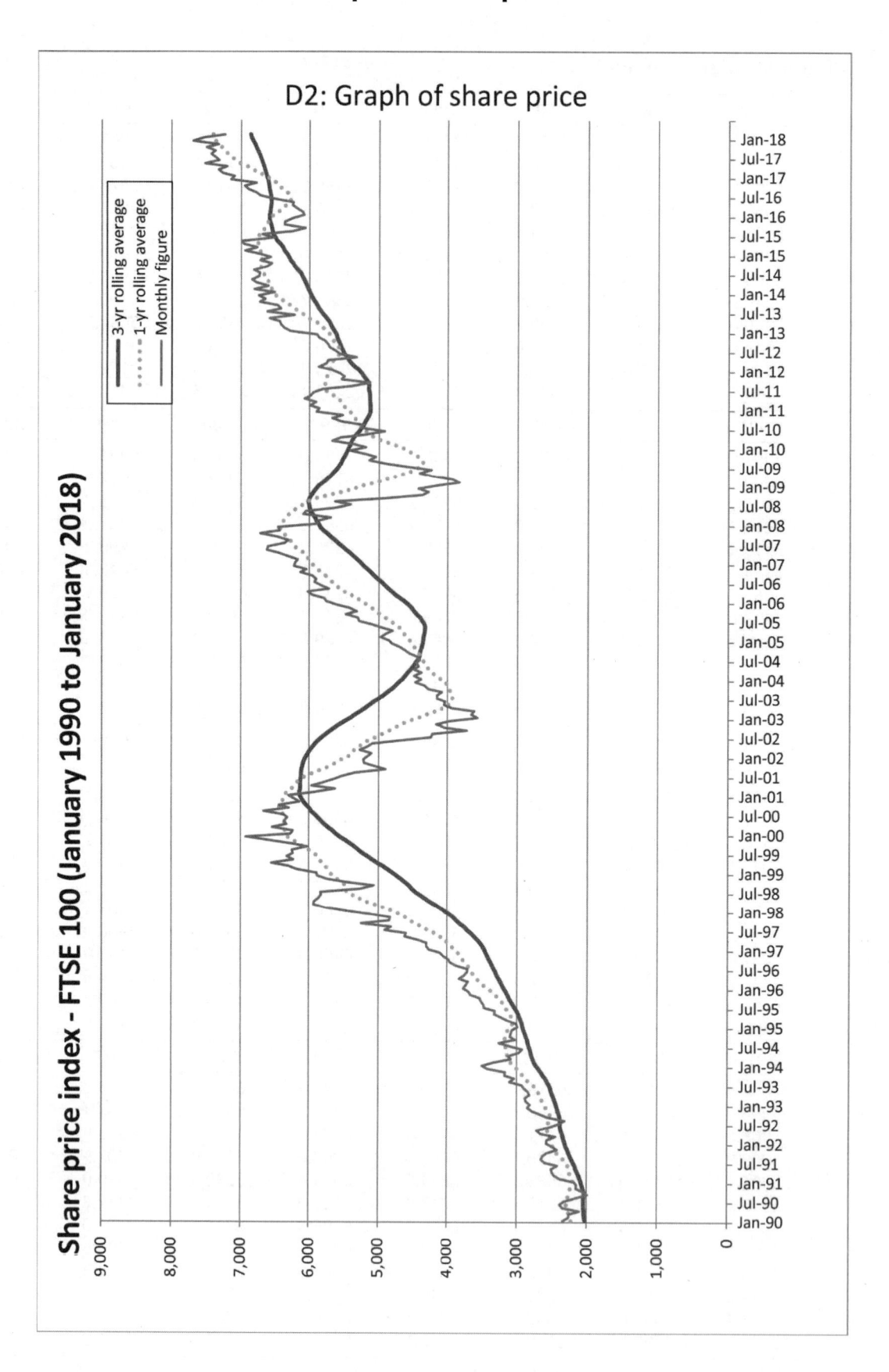

D3: Index-linked stock

Return on index-linked government securities

	2004 Gross %	2004 Net %	2005 Gross %	2005 Net %	2006 Gross %	2006 Net %	2007 Gross %	2007 Net %	2008 Gross %	2008 Net %
January	1.96%	1.66%	1.72%	1.47%	1.13%	0.88%	1.55%	1.30%	1.02%	0.77%
February	1.83%	1.55%	1.69%	1.44%	1.11%	0.86%	1.33%	1.08%	1.00%	0.75%
March	1.75%	1.48%	1.71%	1.46%	1.32%	1.07%	1.47%	1.22%	0.88%	0.63%
April	1.92%	1.63%	1.66%	1.41%	1.47%	1.22%	1.55%	1.30%	1.04%	0.79%
May	1.99%	1.69%	1.63%	1.38%	1.45%	1.20%	1.72%	1.47%	1.11%	0.86%
June	1.97%	1.67%	1.49%	1.24%	1.55%	1.30%	1.78%	1.53%	0.99%	0.74%
July	2.00%	1.70%	1.60%	1.35%	1.38%	1.13%	1.61%	1.36%	1.10%	0.85%
August	1.84%	1.57%	1.41%	1.16%	1.22%	0.97%	1.47%	1.22%	0.71%	0.46%
September	1.80%	1.53%	1.40%	1.15%	1.27%	1.02%	1.46%	1.21%	1.06%	0.81%
October	1.78%	1.51%	1.40%	1.15%	1.16%	0.91%	1.43%	1.18%	1.66%	1.41%
November	1.71%	1.45%	1.33%	1.08%	1.18%	0.93%	1.20%	0.95%	1.85%	1.60%
December	1.63%	1.39%	1.19%	0.94%	1.36%	1.11%	1.10%	0.85%	1.13%	0.88%

	2009 Gross %	2009 Net %	2010 Gross %	2010 Net %	2011 Gross %	2011 Net %	2012 Gross %	2012 Net %	2013 Gross %	2013 Net %
January	1.15%	1.00%	0.75%	0.60%	0.64%	0.49%	−0.32%	−0.47%	−0.38%	−0.53%
February	1.33%	1.18%	0.81%	0.66%	0.57%	0.42%	−0.22%	−0.37%	−0.37%	−0.52%
March	1.06%	0.91%	0.65%	0.50%	0.58%	0.43%	−0.23%	−0.38%	−0.61%	−0.76%
April	1.12%	0.97%	0.67%	0.52%	0.48%	0.33%	−0.17%	−0.32%	−0.59%	−0.74%
May	1.01%	0.86%	0.71%	0.56%	0.44%	0.29%	−0.35%	−0.50%	−0.42%	−0.57%
June	0.91%	0.76%	0.66%	0.51%	0.45%	0.30%	−0.20%	−0.35%	−0.07%	−0.22%
July	1.01%	0.86%	0.81%	0.66%	0.28%	0.13%	−0.21%	−0.36%	−0.10%	−0.25%
August	0.79%	0.64%	0.48%	0.33%	0.31%	0.16%	−0.26%	−0.41%	−0.12%	−0.27%
September	0.74%	0.59%	0.46%	0.31%	0.06%	−0.09%	−0.04%	−0.19%	−0.13%	−0.28%
October	0.61%	0.46%	0.55%	0.40%	0.13%	−0.02%	−0.04%	−0.19%	−0.19%	−0.34%
November	0.53%	0.38%	0.60%	0.45%	−0.16%	−0.31%	−0.13%	−0.28%	−0.13%	−0.28%
December	0.73%	0.58%	0.47%	0.32%	−0.31%	−0.46%	−0.16%	−0.31%	−0.01%	−0.16%

	2014 Gross %	2014 Net %	2015 Gross %	2015 Net %	2016 Gross %	2016 Net %	2017 Gross %	2017 Net %	2018 Gross %	2018 Net %
January	−0.11%	−0.26%	−0.98%	−1.13%	−0.90%	−1.05%	−1.73%	−1.88%	−1.56%	−1.71%
February	−0.09%	−0.24%	−0.75%	−0.90%	−0.92%	−1.07%	−1.78%	−1.93%	−1.55%	−1.70%
March	−0.18%	−0.33%	−0.95%	−1.10%	−0.99%	−1.14%	−1.82%	−1.97%		
April	−0.20%	−0.35%	−0.87%	−1.02%	−0.85%	−1.00%	−1.88%	−2.03%		
May	−0.25%	−0.40%	−0.88%	−1.03%	−0.93%	−1.08%	−1.81%	−1.96%		
June	−0.17%	−0.32%	−0.74%	−0.89%	−1.41%	−1.56%	−1.65%	−1.80%		
July	−0.23%	−0.38%	−0.85%	−1.00%	−1.50%	−1.65%	−1.60%	−1.75%		
August	−0.48%	−0.63%	−0.81%	−0.96%	−1.89%	−2.04%	−1.81%	−1.96%		
September	−0.42%	−0.57%	−0.82%	−0.97%	−1.86%	−2.01%	−1.60%	−1.75%		
October	−0.49%	−0.64%	−0.76%	−0.91%	−1.81%	−1.96%	−1.61%	−1.76%		
November	−0.72%	−0.87%	−0.82%	−0.97%	−1.57%	−1.72%	−1.61%	−1.76%		
December	−0.79%	−0.94%	−0.66%	−0.81%	−1.74%	−1.89%	−1.71%	−1.86%		

Notes:

1. The above table shows the month end gross redemption yields of British Government index-linked stocks with over five years to maturity.

2. The net percentage yield shown above up to and including 2004 is stated after deducting tax at 15% (this was the assumption used in *Wells v Wells* and by the Lord Chancellor when he set the discount rate in 2001).

3. From 2005 to 2008 (inclusive) a fixed deduction of 0.25% has been allowed for tax instead of a percentage. This is because, in spite of reducing yields in this period, taxable interest remained

D3: Index-linked stock

high in this period so that applying a percentage to the combined gross yield would understate the deduction for tax. The actual average tax rate will vary depending on the size of the award.

4. From 2009 a fixed deduction of 0.15% has been allowed for tax. The average Income Tax deduction on taxable interest has been calculated by expert accountants as ranging from 0% to 0.30% depending on the size of the award, so 0.15% is adopted as the midpoint of the range.

D3: Index-linked stock

Index-linked stock (January 2007 to February 2018)

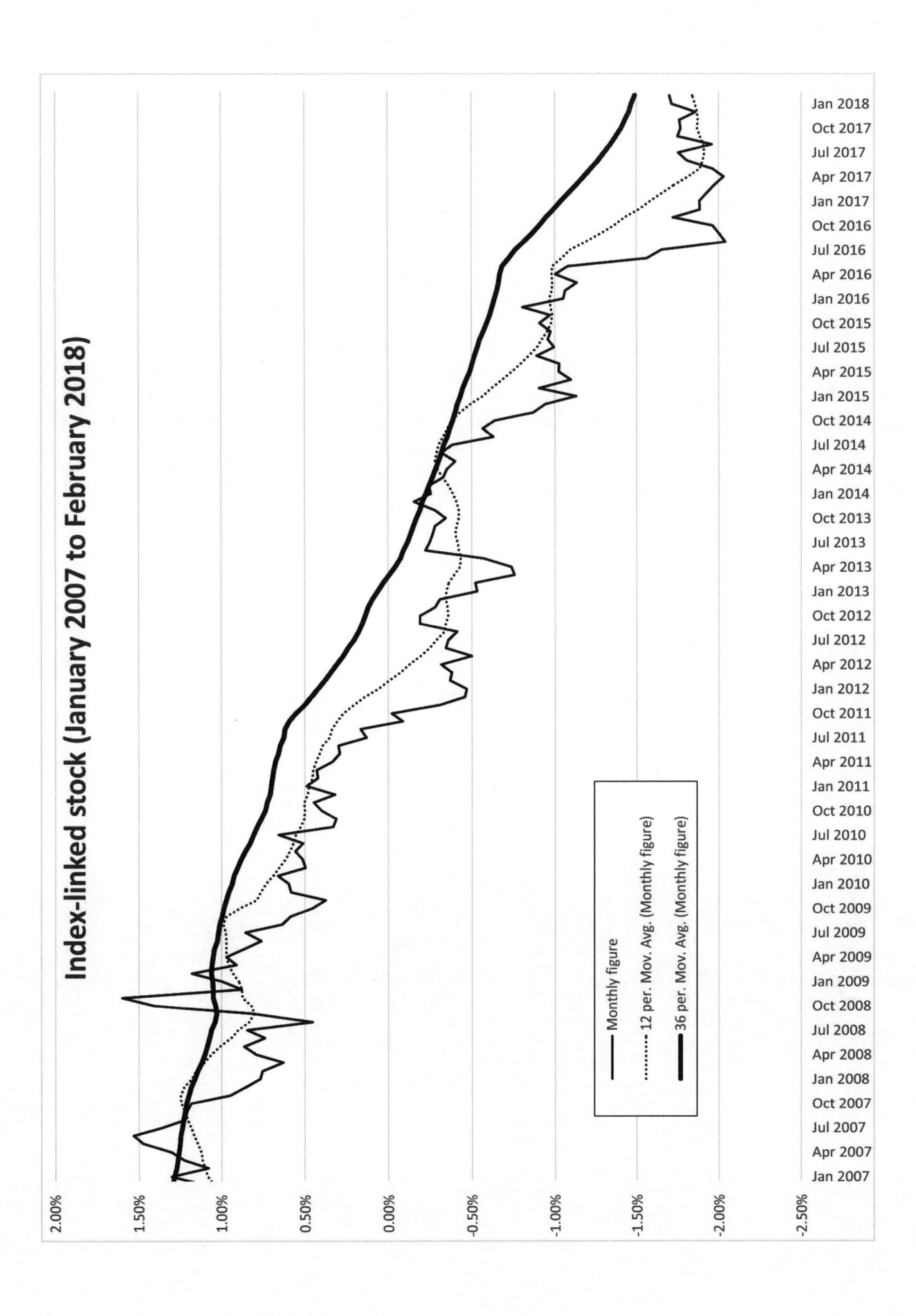

Group E
Prices

E1: **Retail Prices Index**

E2: **Inflation table**

E3: **House price indices**

E4: **Average semi-detached house prices by region**

E5: **How prices have changed over 12 years**

E1: Retail Prices Index

	Jan	Feb	Mar	Apr	May	June	July	Aug	Sept	Oct	Nov	Dec	
2018	276.0	278.1	278.3	279.7	271.7	272.3	272.9	274.7	275.1	275.3	275.8	278.1	2018
2017	265.5	268.4	269.3	270.6	262.1	263.1	263.4	264.4	264.9	264.8	265.5	267.1	2017
2016	258.8	260.0	261.1	261.4	258.5	258.9	258.6	259.8	259.6	259.5	259.8	260.6	2016
2015	255.4	256.7	257.1	258.0	255.9	256.3	256.0	257.0	257.6	257.7	257.1	257.5	2015
2014	252.6	254.2	254.8	255.7	255.9	256.3	256.0	257.0	257.6	257.7	257.1	257.5	2014
2013	245.8	247.6	248.7	249.5	250.0	249.7	249.7	251.0	251.9	251.9	252.1	253.4	2013
2012	238.0	239.9	240.8	242.5	242.4	241.8	242.1	243.0	244.2	245.6	245.6	246.8	2012
2011	229.0	231.3	232.5	234.4	235.2	235.2	234.7	236.1	237.9	238.0	238.5	239.4	2011
2010	217.9	219.2	220.7	222.8	223.6	224.1	223.6	224.5	225.3	225.8	226.8	228.4	2010
2009	210.1	211.4	211.3	211.5	212.8	213.4	213.4	214.4	215.3	216.0	216.6	218.0	2009
2008	209.8	211.4	212.1	214.0	215.1	216.8	216.5	217.2	218.4	217.7	216.0	212.9	2008
2007	201.6	203.1	204.4	205.4	206.2	207.3	206.1	207.3	208.0	208.9	209.7	210.9	2007
2006	193.4	194.2	195.0	196.5	197.7	198.5	198.5	199.2	200.1	200.4	201.1	202.7	2006
2005	188.9	189.6	190.5	191.6	192.0	192.2	192.2	192.6	193.1	193.3	193.6	194.1	2005
2004	183.1	183.8	184.6	185.7	186.5	186.8	186.8	187.4	188.1	188.6	189.0	189.9	2004
2003	178.4	179.3	179.9	181.2	181.5	181.3	181.3	181.6	182.5	182.6	182.7	183.5	2003
2002	173.3	173.8	174.5	175.7	176.2	176.2	175.9	176.4	177.6	177.9	178.2	178.5	2002
2001	171.1	172.0	172.2	173.1	174.2	174.4	173.3	174.0	174.6	174.3	173.6	173.4	2001
2000	166.6	167.5	168.4	170.1	170.7	171.1	170.5	170.5	171.7	171.6	172.1	172.2	2000
1999	163.4	163.7	164.1	165.2	165.6	165.6	165.1	165.5	166.2	166.5	166.7	167.3	1999
1998	159.5	160.3	160.8	162.6	163.5	163.4	163.0	163.7	164.4	164.5	164.4	164.4	1998
1997	154.4	155.0	155.4	156.3	156.9	157.5	157.5	158.5	159.3	159.5	159.6	160.0	1997
1996	150.2	150.9	151.5	152.6	152.9	153.0	152.4	153.1	153.8	153.8	153.9	154.4	1996
1995	146.0	146.9	147.5	149.0	149.6	149.8	149.1	149.9	150.6	149.8	149.8	150.7	1995
1994	141.3	142.1	142.5	144.2	144.7	144.7	144.0	144.7	145.0	145.2	145.3	146.0	1994
1993	137.9	138.8	139.3	140.6	141.1	141.0	140.7	141.3	141.9	141.8	141.6	141.9	1993
1992	135.6	136.3	136.7	138.8	139.3	139.3	138.8	138.9	139.4	139.9	139.7	139.2	1992
1991	130.2	130.9	131.4	133.1	133.5	134.1	133.8	134.1	134.6	135.1	135.6	135.7	1991
1990	119.5	120.2	121.4	125.1	126.2	126.7	126.8	128.1	129.3	130.3	130.0	129.9	1990
1989	111.0	111.8	112.3	114.3	115.0	115.4	115.5	115.8	116.6	117.5	118.5	118.8	1989
1988	103.3	103.7	104.1	105.8	106.2	106.6	106.7	107.9	108.4	109.5	110.0	110.3	1988
1987	100.0	100.4	100.6	101.8	101.9	101.9	101.8	102.1	102.4	102.9	103.4	103.3	1987
1986	96.25	96.60	96.73	97.67	97.85	97.79	97.52	97.82	98.30	98.45	99.29	99.62	1986
1985	91.20	91.94	92.80	94.78	95.21	95.41	95.23	95.49	95.44	95.59	95.92	96.05	1985
1984	86.84	87.20	87.48	88.64	88.97	89.20	89.10	89.94	90.11	90.67	90.95	90.87	1984
1983	82.61	82.97	83.12	84.28	84.64	84.84	85.30	85.68	86.06	86.36	86.67	86.89	1983
1982	78.73	78.76	79.44	81.04	81.62	81.85	81.88	81.90	81.85	82.26	82.66	82.51	1982
1981	70.29	70.93	71.99	74.07	74.55	74.98	75.31	75.87	76.30	76.98	77.79	78.28	1981
1980	62.18	63.07	63.93	66.11	66.72	67.35	67.91	68.06	68.49	68.92	69.48	69.86	1980
1979	52.52	52.95	53.38	54.30	54.73	55.67	58.07	58.53	59.11	59.72	60.25	60.68	1979
1978	48.04	48.31	48.62	49.33	49.61	49.99	50.22	50.54	50.75	50.98	51.33	51.76	1978
1977	43.70	44.13	44.56	45.70	46.06	46.54	46.59	46.82	47.07	47.28	47.50	47.76	1977
	Jan	Feb	Mar	Apr	May	June	July	Aug	Sept	Oct	Nov	Dec	

E1: Retail Prices Index

	Jan	Feb	Mar	Apr	May	June	July	Aug	Sept	Oct	Nov	Dec	
1976	37.49	37.97	38.17	38.91	39.34	39.54	39.62	40.18	40.71	41.44	42.03	42.59	1976
1975	30.39	30.90	31.51	32.72	34.09	34.75	35.11	35.31	35.61	36.12	36.55	37.01	1975
1974	25.35	25.78	26.01	26.89	27.28	27.55	27.81	27.83	28.14	28.69	29.20	29.63	1974
1973	22.64	22.78	22.92	23.35	23.52	23.64	23.75	23.82	24.03	24.50	24.69	24.87	1973
1972	21.01	21.12	21.19	21.38	21.49	21.63	21.70	21.87	21.99	22.30	22.37	22.49	1972
1971	19.43	19.53	19.69	20.11	20.25	20.39	20.51	20.52	20.55	20.67	20.79	20.89	1971
1970	17.91	18.00	18.11	18.38	18.44	18.49	18.62	18.61	18.70	18.90	19.03	19.16	1970
1969	17.06	17.15	17.22	17.41	17.38	17.46	17.46	17.42	17.47	17.60	17.64	17.76	1969
1968	16.07	16.15	16.20	16.49	16.51	16.57	16.59	16.61	16.63	16.71	16.74	16.97	1968
1967	15.66	15.67	15.67	15.79	15.78	15.85	15.75	15.71	15.70	15.82	15.91	16.02	1967
1966	15.11	15.12	15.15	15.33	15.44	15.48	15.41	15.50	15.48	15.52	15.61	15.63	1966
1965	14.47	14.47	14.52	14.80	14.85	14.89	14.89	14.92	14.93	14.95	15.01	15.08	1965
1964	13.84	13.85	13.90	14.02	14.14	14.19	14.19	14.25	14.25	14.26	14.38	14.43	1964
1963	13.57	13.69	13.71	13.74	13.73	13.73	13.65	13.61	13.65	13.71	13.74	13.77	1963
1962	13.22	13.23	13.28	13.47	13.51	13.60	13.55	13.43	13.41	13.40	13.45	13.52	1962
1961	12.63	12.63	12.68	12.74	12.78	12.89	12.89	13.01	12.99	13.01	13.15	13.17	1961
1960	12.36	12.36	12.34	12.41	12.41	12.47	12.50	12.42	12.43	12.53	12.59	12.62	1960
1959	12.42	12.41	12.41	12.32	12.27	12.29	12.26	12.29	12.23	12.28	12.37	12.40	1959
1958	12.16	12.10	12.19	12.33	12.28	12.40	12.20	12.18	12.19	12.31	12.35	12.40	1958
1957	11.74	11.73	11.71	11.75	11.77	11.89	11.99	11.97	11.93	12.05	12.11	12.17	1957
1956	11.25	11.25	11.39	11.55	11.53	11.52	11.47	11.51	11.48	11.55	11.60	11.63	1956
1955	10.70	10.70	10.70	10.76	10.74	10.97	11.00	10.93	11.00	11.11	11.29	11.29	1955
1954	10.28	10.26	10.35	10.39	10.36	10.42	10.60	10.53	10.51	10.56	10.61	10.66	1954
1953	10.14	10.17	10.24	10.33	10.30	10.35	10.35	10.29	10.27	10.27	10.30	10.26	1953
1952	9.71	9.72	9.77	9.93	9.93	10.09	10.08	10.02	10.00	10.09	10.08	10.15	1952
1951	8.60	8.68	8.74	8.88	9.10	9.13	9.27	9.31	9.38	9.44	9.48	9.54	1951
1950	8.28	8.30	8.32	8.35	8.37	8.33	8.33	8.30	8.35	8.44	8.47	8.52	1950
1949	7.99	8.01	7.98	7.96	8.11	8.14	8.15	8.16	8.19	8.23	8.23	8.25	1949
1948	7.64	7.78	7.80	7.91	7.90	8.04	7.92	7.92	7.93	7.95	7.97	7.98	1948
1947	–	–	–	–	–	7.33	7.38	7.34	7.37	7.43	7.58	7.60	1947
	Jan	Feb	Mar	Apr	May	June	July	Aug	Sept	Oct	Nov	Dec	

Source: Office for National Statistics licensed under the Open Government Licence V.I.O.

Note:

To calculate the equivalent value of a lump sum, divide by the RPI at the time and multiply the result by the current RPI. Thus £460 in June 1981 would be calculated as:

$$\left(\frac{460}{74.98}\right) \times \text{current RPI}$$

to show the relative value of that amount in "today's money".

E2: Inflation table

Introductory notes

The table shows the value each January in earlier years equivalent to £1 in January 2018, after taking account of inflation over time.

Price inflation is measured by reference to the Retail Prices Index.

Year	Multiplier	Year	Multiplier
1948	36.13	1983	3.34
1949	34.54	1984	3.18
1950	33.33	1985	3.03
1951	32.09	1986	2.87
1952	28.42	1987	2.76
1953	27.22	1988	2.67
1954	26.85	1989	2.49
1955	25.79	1990	2.31
1956	24.53	1991	2.12
1957	23.51	1992	2.04
1958	22.70	1993	2.00
1959	22.22	1994	1.95
1960	22.33	1995	1.89
1961	21.85	1996	1.84
1962	20.88	1997	1.79
1963	20.34	1998	1.73
1964	19.94	1999	1.69
1965	19.07	2000	1.66
1966	18.27	2001	1.61
1967	17.62	2002	1.59
1968	17.17	2003	1.55
1969	16.18	2004	1.51
1970	15.41	2005	1.46
1971	14.20	2006	1.43
1972	13.14	2007	1.37
1973	12.19	2008	1.32
1974	10.89	2009	1.31
1975	9.08	2010	1.27
1976	7.36	2011	1.21
1977	6.32	2012	1.16
1978	5.75	2013	1.12
1979	5.26	2014	1.09
1980	4.44	2015	1.08
1981	3.93	2016	1.07
1982	3.51	2017	1.04
		2018	1.00

E3: House price indices

Introductory notes

1. There are several price indices available in April 2018. These include the Halifax, Nationwide, the Financial Times, the Royal Institute of Chartered Surveyors, Hometrack, Rightmove, the Government Index and the Land Registry index.

2. The editors of *Facts & Figures* have used the Halifax table in previous editions and continue to do so. The Index Year for the Halifax table is 1983. In certain circumstances, the data offered by other indices may be useful. For example the Land Registry figures are broken down regionally and contain information about the numbers of first-time buyers. However, they exclude cash purchases which account for about a quarter of all transactions. Each table has strengths and weaknesses of this sort.

3. None of the indices should be treated as definitive. They can only be used as guides to the movement of prices over longer periods of time. Readers should be cautious about over-interpreting the analysis of short-term price changes.

All Houses

Year	Index (U.K.)	%	Average Price £
1992	208.1	−5.6	64,309
1993	202.1	−2.9	62,455
1994	203.1	0.5	62,750
1995	199.6	−1.7	61,666
1996	208.6	4.5	64,441
1997	221.7	6.3	68,504
1998	233.7	5.4	72,196
1999	250.5	7.2	77,405
2000	275.1	9.8	85,005
2001	298.6	8.5	92,256
2002	350.6	17.4	108,342
2003	429.1	22.4	132,589
2004	507.6	18.3	156,831
2005	536.6	5.7	165,807
2006	581.3	8.3	179,601
2007	635.9	9.4	196,478
2008	585.9	−7.9	181,032
2009	524.6	−10.5	162,085
2010	539.6	2.9	166,739
2011	525.4	−2.6	162,322
2012	522.1	−0.6	161,308
2013	547.0	4.77	169,003
2014	593.5	8.51	183,391
2015	648.4	9.2	200,329
2016	686.8	9.2	212,204
2017	707.1	2.6	218,477
2018	726.1	1.8	224,353

E3: House price indices

Year	North Index	%	Yorks/Humb Index	%	N. West Index	%	E. Midlands Index	%
1992	210.1	−1.6	231.9	−3.6	226.1	−4.3	214.4	−5.9
1993	206.3	−1.8	228.3	−1.6	219.3	−3.0	208.3	−2.8
1994	203.6	−1.3	226.3	−0.9	215.8	−1.6	209.1	0.4
1995	195.9	−3.8	219.2	−3.1	207.8	−3.7	203.9	−2.5
1996	201.9	3.1	224.5	2.4	210.7	1.4	209.4	2.7
1997	206.5	2.3	228.5	1.8	216.7	2.9	221.5	5.8
1998	211.2	2.3	229.8	0.5	220.4	1.7	229.9	3.8
1999	220.1	4.2	236.5	2.9	231.0	4.8	244.8	6.5
2000	221.9	0.8	243.9	3.2	242.6	5.0	265.0	8.2
2001	234.0	5.5	257.5	5.6	255.7	5.4	287.3	8.4
2002	271.4	16.0	297.7	15.6	292.8	14.5	361.7	25.9
2003	370.6	36.5	395.6	32.9	366.3	25.1	457.5	26.5
2004	490.3	32.3	495.0	25.1	472.8	29.1	541.4	18.3
2005	533.3	8.8	549.3	11.0	523.7	10.8	564.9	4.3
2006	567.3	6.4	602.4	9.7	565.1	7.9	599.4	6.1
2007	601.8	6.1	640.5	6.3	596.8	5.6	632.4	5.5
2008	547.2	−9.1	580.0	−9.5	558.3	−6.5	582.0	−8.0
2009	500.2	−8.6	526.3	−9.3	492.8	−11.7	518.2	−11.0
2010	511.5	2.3	538.2	2.3	486.7	−1.3	541.7	4.5
2011	483.1	−5.6	513.2	−4.6	485.0	−0.4	517.9	−4.4
2012	478.1	−1.0	509.1	−0.8	468.6	−3.4	523.1	1.0
2013	496.8	3.9	527.3	3.6	501.9	7.1	539.2	3.1
2014	507.7	2.2	562.1	6.6	540.4	7.7	584.3	8.4
2015	548.0	7.9	615.6	9.5	573.4	6.1	633.3	8.4
2016	548.0	7.9	615.6	9.5	573.4	6.1	633.3	8.4
2017	572.9	2.8	673.7	4.5	627.0	3.5	718.2	8.0

Year	W. Midlands Index	%	E. Anglia Index	%	S. West Index	%	S. East Index	%
1992	229.4	−4.6	198.5	−7.4	193.9	−7.8	192.8	−8.5
1993	219.1	−4.5	193.2	−2.7	185.9	−4.1	186.4	−3.3
1994	218.3	−0.4	195.8	1.3	186.6	1.5	189.8	1.8
1995	215.6	−1.2	193.5	−1.1	186.1	−1.3	190.3	0.3
1996	224.6	4.2	197.7	2.1	195.1	4.8	199.9	5.0
1997	237.3	5.6	211.0	6.7	209.7	7.5	221.2	10.7
1998	250.0	5.4	224.4	6.4	226.4	8.0	244.2	10.4
1999	254.7	1.9	241.1	7.5	248.8	9.9	271.2	11.0
2000	282.2	10.8	279.7	16.0	291.0	17.0	318.3	17.4
2001	301.5	6.8	322.6	15.4	327.8	12.6	354.7	11.4
2002	363.7	20.7	386.0	19.6	403.4	23.0	413.7	16.6
2003	460.7	26.7	465.0	20.5	477.7	18.4	483.8	17.0
2004	540.5	17.3	522.3	12.3	545.4	14.2	528.8	9.3
2005	565.4	4.6	536.0	2.6	552.6	1.3	537.0	1.5
2006	602.8	6.6	581.1	8.4	587.5	6.3	571.2	6.4
2007	640.4	6.2	637.3	9.7	641.9	9.3	636.9	11.5
2008	591.9	−7.6	600.8	−5.7	583.2	−9.1	588.6	−7.6
2009	534.1	−9.8	520.2	−13.4	540.0	−7.4	532.1	−9.6
2010	549.5	2.9	540.9	4.0	568.5	5.3	561.4	5.5
2011	530.9	−3.4	544.1	0.6	547.3	−3.7	553.1	−1.5
2012	528.8	−0.4	540.7	−0.6	553.1	1.1	558.8	1.0
2013	540.7	2.3	551.1	1.9	565.8	2.3	591	5.8
2014	574.3	6.2	601.2	9.1	610.5	7.9	654.6	10.8
2015	624.9	8.8	682.4	13.5	646.5	5.9	725.2	10.8
2016	624.9	8.8	682.4	13.5	646.5	5.9	725.2	10.8
2017	702.6	5.0	777.0	4.5	731.9	4.9	840.5	3.6

Year	Gr. London Index	%	Wales Index	%	Scotland Index	%	N. Ireland Index	%
1992	202.0	−9.4	207.7	−4.3	193.2	0.2	145.5	−1.0
1993	192.0	−4.9	204.5	−1.6	196.4	1.6	151.7	4.3
1994	195.5	1.8	201.9	−1.2	199.4	1.6	162.1	6.9
1995	194.9	−0.4	194.2	−3.8	199.4	0.0	172.8	6.6
1996	212.4	9.0	205.5	5.9	204.9	2.8	204.5	18.3
1997	246.3	16.0	212.0	3.1	204.7	0.1	210.6	3.0
1998	272.3	10.5	220.2	3.8	209.8	2.5	235.6	11.9
1999	317.9	16.8	232.3	5.5	212.8	1.4	248.8	5.6
2000	373.6	17.5	245.0	5.5	214.2	0.7	264.4	6.3
2001	428.3	14.7	263.6	7.7	220.0	2.7	296.8	12.2
2002	499.4	16.6	299.8	13.6	238.5	8.4	307.4	3.6
2003	563.3	12.8	397.2	32.5	274.5	15.1	340.3	10.7
2004	608.5	8.0	516.3	30.0	330.6	20.4	397.9	16.9
2005	621.4	2.1	553.7	7.3	375.7	13.6	486.0	22.1
2006	680.9	9.6	589.7	6.5	421.7	12.2	581.3	32.6
2007	777.6	14.2	640.7	8.7	488.2	15.8	844.5	31.1
2008	705.3	−9.3	579.4	−9.6	478.2	−2.1	679.2	−19.6
2009	622.0	−11.8	512.0	−11.6	426.6	−10.8	563.7	−17.0
2010	659.9	6.1	530.3	3.6	421.4	−1.2	506.2	−10.2
2011	659.6	0.0	521.5	−1.7	406.8	−3.5	444.1	−12.3
2012	674.4	2.2	505.6	−3.0	384.3	−5.5	405.4	−8.7
2013	737.3	9.3	557.3	10.2	400.5	4.2	368.9	−9.0
2014	855.2	16.0	572.8	2.8	430.2	7.4	430.8	16.8
2015	995.1	16.4	585.9	2.3	463.3	7.7	452.0	4.9
2016	995.1	16.4	585.9	2.3	463.3	7.7	452.0	4.9
2017	1126.1	1.0	632.7	8.0	473.2	−0.2	480.5	−5.6

E4: Average semi-detached house prices by region

Prices are as of first quarter of 2018.

Region	£
England	£245,955
Scotland	£138,603
Wales	£156,916
East Midlands	£190,927
East of England	£294,340
London	£479,451
North East	£129,565
North West	£157,960
South East	£322,754
South West	£253,420
West Midlands	£189,542
Yorkshire and The Humber	£159,458

E5: How prices have changed over 13 years

PRICE COMPARISON 2005–2018

Item	2005	2018	% change	Source
Milk (pint)	35p	49p	+40%	ONS
Loaf of white sliced bread (800g)	65p	£1.07	+65%	ONS
Eggs (a dozen)	£1.55	£2.04	+32%	ONS
Sugar (kg)	74p	69p	−7%	ONS
Draught lager (pint)	£2.33	£3.63	+56%	ONS
Cigarettes (20)	£4.39	£9.94	+126%	ONS
Unleaded petrol per litre	81.49p	£1.22	+50%	ONS
House prices (All UK)[1]	£150,633	£226,756	+51%	ONS
Weekly State Pension	£82.05	£122.30	+49%	Royal London
Price of gold (per ounce)	£230.26	£957.15	+316%	Goldprice.org
Price of oil (per barrel)	$61.65	$65.28	+6%	Inflationdata.com
McDonald's Big Mac	£2.23	£3.19	+43%	Big-mac-index.com

Note: The ONS statistics are averages taken over a wide range of sources.

[1] These prices are for semi-detached houses.

Group F
Earnings

F1: **Earnings losses in personal injury and fatal accident cases**

F2: **Lost years**

F3: **Payroll documents**

F4: **National minimum wage**

F5: **Regional unemployment statistics**

F6: **Average weekly earnings index**

F7: **Average weekly earnings**

F8: **Average earnings statistics**

F9: **Public sector comparable earnings**

F1: Earnings losses in personal injury and fatal accident cases

1. **Purpose of note**

    The purpose of this note is to provide some basic guidance on what information to request from a claimant in order to make an initial assessment as to whether an earnings loss is likely to arise.

2. **Nature of occupation**

    Identify at an early stage into which category of occupation the claimant falls:

    Employment
    — Employee without ownership rights.
    — Director/shareholder (of private company).

    Self-employment
    — Sole trader.
    — Partner.

3. **Relevant dates**

    For the purposes of proposing the periods for which information should be requested, relevant dates will be identified as follows:

    For an individual in employment
    (References here are to tax years ending on 5 April although the tax for many salaried employees will often effectively run from 1 April to 31 March.)

    D1   6 April three years before D2
    D2   5 April immediately preceding D3
    D3   Incident date
    D4   5 April immediately preceding D5
    D5   Present time

    For business accounts
    D6   Date of beginning of accounting period three years before D7
    D7   Date of end of accounting period immediately preceding D3
    D8   Date of end of accounting period immediately preceding D5

    A full three years' pre-accident financial information should often be sufficient (having regard to the need for proportionality), although documentation for a longer period may be appropriate if it emerges that business results have been volatile.

    For an individual in employment

D1			D2	D3 [Incident]		D4		D5
6 April 5 April	6 April 5 April	6 April 5 April	6 April 5 April	6 April 5 April	6 April 5 April	6 April 5 April	6 April	Present time
Tax year −3	Tax year −2	Tax year −1	Tax year 0	Tax year +1		Current tax year −1	Current tax year

Sweet & Maxwell

F1: Earnings losses in personal injury and fatal accident cases

For business accounts

D6		D7	D3 Incident		D8		D5
Beginning End	Beginning End	Beginning End	Beginning End	Beginning End	Beginning	End	Beginning Present time
Accounts year −3	Accounts year −2	Accounts year −1	Accounts year 0	Accounts year +1	Current accounts year −1		Current accounts year

4. **Employment: Employee without ownership rights**

   This is the likely category for most employees—but excluding in particular those who are directors and/or shareholders with a degree of control over private companies.

   In the absence of detailed representations from the employer, or from an employment expert, the earnings history may be the only useful guide to potential earnings but for the incident giving rise to the claim.

   The most useful documentation will usually be a comprehensive set of pay advices (monthly, sometimes four-weekly, or weekly) because these may be expected to show:

   - basic pay level (and dates/amounts of periodic increases),
   - overtime (if paid) and any other regular or periodic enhancements,
   - bonuses (and dates/amounts paid),
   - sick pay (and dates), and
   - employee pension contributions.

   Request:

   - **Pay advices (whether from employment or subsequent pension) from D1 to D5.**
   - **Details of benefits other than pay for each tax year between D1 and D2 and for each tax year since D2.**

5. **Employment: Director/shareholders**

   This category relates mainly to those individuals who have a degree of ownership or control, probably in a private company, and whose remuneration as such may not be a fair reflection of the personal reward available from the business.

   For instance:

   - profits may have been drawn by way of dividend for reasons of tax efficiency; or
   - profits (which the claimant could have drawn) have been re-invested in the business.

   It may well be appropriate to assess loss along the lines that would be adopted in relation to a sole trader or partner, that is:

   - first to identify whether a business loss has occurred that is attributable to the claim incident, and
   - if so, go on to identify the share of the business loss suffered personally by the claimant.

   In such a case, it will often be appropriate to review not only the remuneration history of the individual but also the dividend history. Benefits history may also be important.

F1: Earnings losses in personal injury and fatal accident cases

Request:

Regarding the business

- **full accounts (including detailed profit and loss accounts) from D6 to D8,**

  and consider requesting

- **figures for monthly (preferably) or quarterly sales from D6 to D5.**
  (Important if the claimant's role is likely to have influenced sales levels; the figures should show trends and seasonality, etc.)

Regarding the claimant

- **pay advices (whether from employment or pension) from D1 to D5, and**
- **tax returns from D1 to D4.**
  (Mainly to check remuneration and dividends received in each tax year, but also benefits and any personal pension contributions, etc.)

6. **Self-employment: Sole trader**

Request:

- **full accounts from D6 to D8,**
- **figures for monthly or quarterly sales from D6 to D5, and**
- **tax returns from D1 to D4.**
  (Mainly to check private usage deductions from business expenses, capital allowances, personal pension contributions, etc.)

7. **Self-employment: Partner**

Approach will be:

- first to identify whether a business loss has occurred that is attributable to the claim incident, and
- if so, go on to identify the share of the business loss suffered personally by the claimant.

Request:

Regarding the business

- **full partnership accounts from D6 to D8, and**
- **figures for monthly (preferably) or quarterly sales from D6 to D5.**

Regarding the claimant

- **personal tax returns from D1 to D4.**
  (Mainly to check personal pension contributions, etc.)

8. **Benefits other than pay (employees)**

In the first instance, it is probably sufficient simply to ask, in relation to any employee (including a company director), for:

- **details of any non-pecuniary benefits in employment, and any pension benefits.**

Sweet & Maxwell

9. **Other points**

- **Company searches**

Searches of small UK limited companies seldom yield helpful results as regards accounts because the contents of the accounts to be filed are invariably in abbreviated form, sometimes only a balance sheet.

In cases where there are doubts about full disclosure, a search may be useful in identifying whether a claimant has more directorships than advised, or possibly a history of connections with insolvent companies.

- **Permanent Health Insurance income**

Where a claimant receives insurance money through his employer, this will usually be evident from review of the pay advices.

As to whether credit needs to be given by the claimant for such insurance money for claim purposes will probably depend on the nature of the underlying policy. See *Gaca v Pirelli General plc*.[1]

- **Ill-health pension**

Where a claimant receives an ill-health pension following an incident, this should again be evident from review of the pay advices.

Generally, no credit is to be given for actual pension in a loss of earnings claim: *Parry v Cleaver*.[2]

- **Partnerships**

There may be cases where the profit-sharing arrangements do not reflect the realistic commercial input of the respective partners. This issue may arise particularly where spouses are business partners. The court may be prepared to put aside the historic arrangements in assessing loss: *Ward v Newalls Insulation Co Ltd*.[3]

---

[1] [2004] 1 W.L.R. 2683.
[2] [1970] A.C. 1.
[3] [1998] 1 W.L.R. 1722.

F2: Lost years

Introductory

1. Where a living adult[1] claimant's life expectancy has been reduced by reason of the defendant's tort, the claimant may suffer financial losses during his or her "lost years", i.e. the years after his or her death but before the date he or she was expected to have passed away in the absence of the injury.[2] Take for example a claimant who had a normal life expectancy before developing mesothelioma due to the defendant's negligence. If the claimant's life expectancy is now reduced to age 50 years, he will have "lost years" claims for loss of earnings from age 50 to his normal retirement age and for loss of pension from his retirement age until the date he would have died (calculated by reference to normal life expectancy in the absence of any pre-existing condition).[3]

Approach to Assessment

2. A detailed analysis of types of lost years claim that can be made and the applicable principles for assessing damages for lost years is beyond the scope of this book.[4]

3. Where the reduction in life expectancy is modest instead of making a detailed calculation, the judge may simply decide to make a small upwards adjustment to the loss of earnings multiplier.[5]

4. However, where the court decides to adopt an accurate multiplier and multiplicand method for assessing lost years the approach is as follows:

   - Calculate the net annual multiplicand (whether loss of earnings, loss of pension etc.).

   - Apply the applicable percentage deduction for living expenses.[6]

   - Calculate the multiplier for the lost years.

   - Apply any applicable discount for contingencies other than mortality.

---

[1] Claims for lost years cannot be made on behalf of young children: *Croke v Wiseman* [1982] 1 WLR 71. However, note that this decision is inconsistent with two previous House of Lords authorities. It seems illogical and discriminatory that there is a pecuniary head of loss which cannot be claimed by some claimants merely because of their age: see further *Iqbal v Whipps Cross University NHS Trust* [2007] EWCA Civ 1190; and *Totham v King's College Hospitals NHS Foundation Trust* [2015] EWHC 97 (QB).

[2] In *Pickett v BRE* [1980] AC 136 the House of Lords held that an adult claimant is entitled to recover damages for loss of financial expectations during the lost years. Such losses are deemed to be the claimant's own pecuniary losses. Importantly, it is not necessary for the claimant to have dependants before being able to claim such losses.

[3] For calculating normal life expectancy based upon projected life expectancy data from the ONS, please see the tables at A3 or use the 0% column of Table 1 for men or Table 2 for women.

[4] See further *McGregor on Damages* (20th edition, Sweet & Maxwell, 2017), *Kemp & Kemp on Damages* (looseleaf, Sweet and Maxwell); and *Schedules of Loss: Calculating Damages* (4th edition, Bloomsbury Publishing, 2018).

[5] For example, in *Hunt v Severs* [1993] QB 815 the Court of Appeal upheld the trial judge's calculation of lost years reached by adding 0.5 to the claimant multiplier for loss of earnings. A similar approach was adopted in *Sarwar (1) Ali (2) MIB* [2007] EWHC 1225 (Admin) to reflect loss of pension during the lost years.

[6] Different deductions for living expenses are made depending upon the circumstances of the claimant. Unfortunately, there is limited judicial guidance regarding the meaning or calculation of living expenses. However, percentage discounts for living expenses in the region of 50% might be expected for married claimants with no dependants (*Phipps v Brooks Dry Cleaning Services Ltd* [1996] PIQR Q100); 25–50% for married claimants with children; and 50–75% for unmarried claimants.

F2: Lost years

- Multiply the adjusted annual loss by the adjusted multiplier.

A Worked Example

5. The claimant is married with no dependants. She is aged 50 at trial. She obtained a degree at university and has a job earning £30,000 net p.a. But for her injury, the claimant would have worked to a normal retirement age of 68. Thereafter, at present day values, she would have had a private pension of £7,500 net p.a. and a full state pension of £8,296.60 p.a. By reason of the defendant's negligence she is expected to live to 55.

Loss of Earnings During the Lost Years

Annual net earnings multiplicand is £30,000 p.a.

The discount for living expenses is 50%.

The adjusted multiplicand is £30,000 × 50% = £15,000.

The multiplier from age 55 to 68 is calculated by deducting the multiplier to age 55 of 5.06 (Table 6) from the multiplier to age 68 of 18.66 (interpolated from Tables 10 and 12). The multiplier is therefore 18.66 minus 5.06 = 13.60.

A discount for contingencies of 0.86 is applied (Table C).

The adjusted multiplier is 13.60 × 0.86 = 11.70.

Subtotal loss of earnings during the lost years is therefore £15,000 × 11.70 = £175,500.

Loss of Pension During the Lost Years

Annual pension multiplicand is £7,500, plus £8,296.60 = £15,796.60. Income tax is payable at 20% beyond £11,500. This reduces the net multiplicand to £14,937.28.

The discount for living expenses is 50%.

The adjusted multiplicand is £14,937.28 × 50% = £7,468.64.

The multiplier from age 68 is calculated by deducting the earnings multiplier to age 68 of 18.66 (interpolated from Tables 10 and 12) from the lifetime multiplier of 45.71 (Table 2). The multiplier is therefore 45.71 minus 18.66 = 27.05.

A discount for contingencies of 0.86 is applied (Table C).[7]

The adjusted multiplier is 27.05 × 0.86 = 23.26.

Subtotal loss of pension during the lost years is therefore £7,468.64 × 23.26 = £173,720.57.

6. Therefore the total claim for lost years is £175,500 + £173,720.57 = £349,220.57.

---

[7] In the absence of specific discount factors for contingencies other than mortality in respect of pension loss claims, many practitioners apply the same discount for contingencies suggested for loss of earnings claims as set out in Tables A–D of the Ogden Guidance notes. However, arguably a different (lower) discount factor may be appropriate, especially if the claimant has an entitlement to an ill-health retirement pension.

F3: Payroll documents

SPECIMEN PAY ADVICE

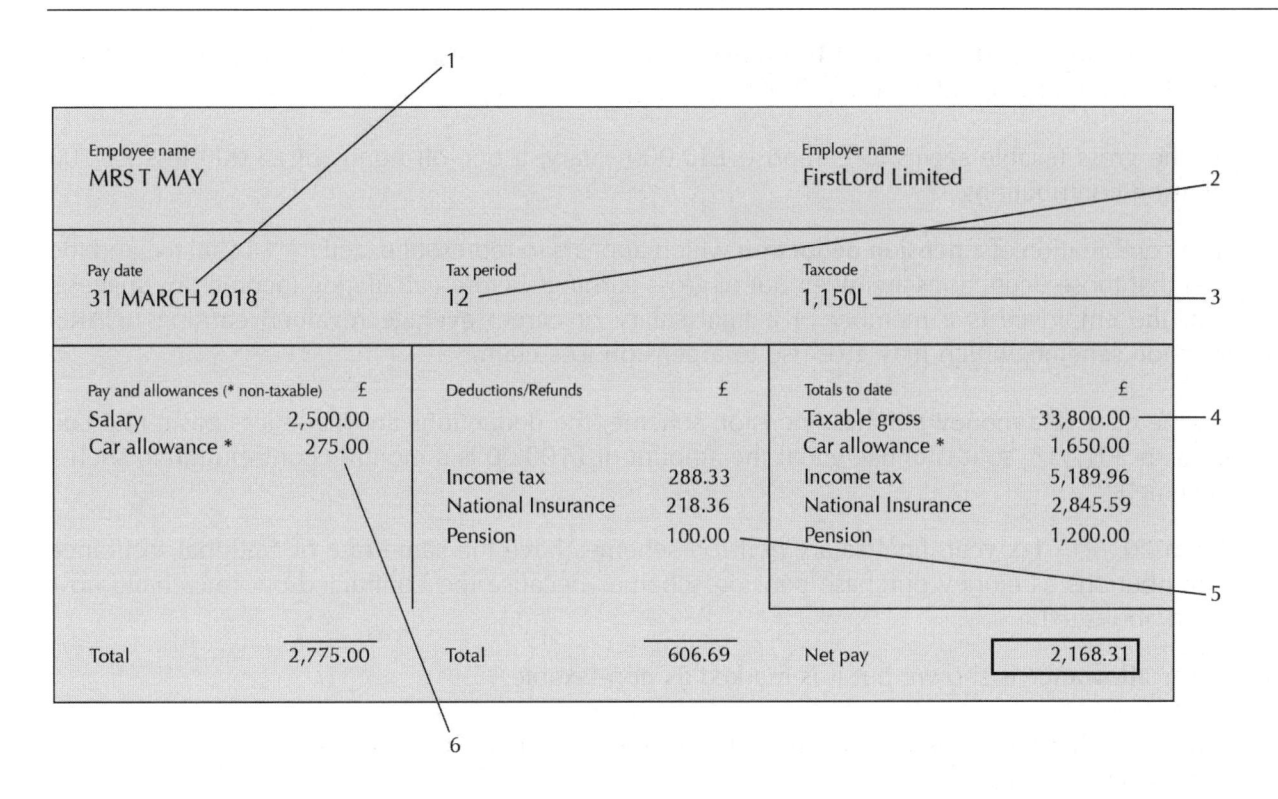

Employee name			Employer name	
MRS T MAY			FirstLord Limited	
Pay date	Tax period		Taxcode	
31 MARCH 2018	12		1,150L	

Pay and allowances (* non-taxable)	£	Deductions/Refunds	£	Totals to date	£
Salary	2,500.00			Taxable gross	33,800.00
Car allowance *	275.00			Car allowance *	1,650.00
		Income tax	288.33	Income tax	5,189.96
		National Insurance	218.36	National Insurance	2,845.59
		Pension	100.00	Pension	1,200.00
Total	2,775.00	Total	606.69	Net pay	2,168.31

Points to note

1. As good a starting point as any is usually a pay advice at the end of the **last full tax year**, but try also to obtain all subsequent pay advices whether to date of trial in a personal injury case or to date of death if a fatal accident.

2. It is worth bearing in mind that some employers pay every four weeks, and on rare occasions every two weeks, rather than necessarily monthly or weekly. The tax period should help to identify payment frequency.

3. The tax code, **1150L**, represents the basic tax allowance of £11,500. This indicates that the tax inspector has no reason to make any adjustment to the standard code to collect additional tax due in the year.

    This in turn implies that the employee has no taxable benefits from the employer.

    The most common taxable benefits are probably health insurance cover and those related to private use of motor vehicles.

    By way of example, were the employee enjoying taxable benefits to a value of £1,000 p.a., the code could be expected to be 1050L. Application of this code would result in the tax due on the benefit being collected under PAYE over the course of the tax year.

4. In the illustration shown above, the **gross taxable income** figure requires some reconciliation to other figures.

The year-end figures suggest that salary has probably been running consistently at £2,500 per month (i.e. £30,000 per annum), with a £100 per month pension contribution. That would produce a taxable total of £28,800 in the year, suggesting that there has been additional pay of £5,000 in arriving at the taxable gross figure of £33,800.

The figure for the total **National Insurance** for the year is consistent with a salary of £2,500 per month, with a single addition of £5,000.

So the gross taxable seems to comprise £30,000 salary, a one-off bonus of £5,000 less £1,200 pension contributions.

5. The combination of a **pension deduction** which appears to represent exactly 4% of salary, and the fact that those deductions are taken out of gross earnings before calculating income tax, suggests that the employee is a member of a final salary or career average revalued earnings (CARE) pension scheme, which may give rise to a pension loss claim.

   (In the case of a money purchase pension scheme, the deductions are made less basic rate tax, 20% in 2017/18, so it is unlikely that the amount of £100.00 is a monthly contribution to such a scheme.)

   From 2016/17 tax year, final salary pension schemes have the same rate of National Insurance contributions as money purchase pension schemes because the contracted-out rates have now been abolished.

6. A **car allowance** is shown, but it is marked as non-taxable.

   Note also that the totals to date suggest that the allowance has been in payment for only six months in the year.

   Generally, if an allowance is non-taxable, it is unlikely to represent a valuable benefit. Perhaps the car allowance in this case is a fixed level reimbursement of business costs on a prescribed formula, which will be adjusted after the year-end in accordance with actual business mileage or the like.

   Nevertheless it would be worth establishing why the car allowance was not in payment throughout the year.

F4: National Minimum Wage and National Living Wage

Introductory notes

1. The National Minimum Wage became law on 1 April 1999 and the National Living Wage became law on 1 April 2016.

2. The National Minimum Wage and National Living Wage are the minimum amount of pay to which workers over a specified age are entitled. Up to 30 September 2004, the minimum age for the National Minimum Wage was 18. Since 1 October 2004 a new rate has been available to workers under 18 who are no longer of compulsory school age. The National Living Wage was introduced on 1 April 2016 for workers aged 25 and older. The National Minimum Wage still applies for workers aged under 25.

3. Most adult workers who are resident in the UK, who have a written, oral or implied contract and who are not genuinely self-employed, are entitled to the National Minimum Wage or National Living Wage.

4. The National Minimum Wage and National Living Wage are enforced by HM Revenue and Customs.

5. There are currently four levels of National Minimum Wage: a development rate for those aged between 18 and 20; a main rate for workers aged between 21 and 24; from 1 October 2004, a rate for workers under 18 who are no longer of compulsory school age; and, from 1 October 2010, an apprentice minimum wage (see note 8, below).

6. The main rate was extended to workers aged 21 or over from October 2010. Prior to that the qualifying age for the main rate was 22. Correspondingly the development rate has been available to those aged between 18 and 20 from October 2010. Prior to that it was available to those aged between 18 and 21.

7. A development rate is available, subject to various conditions, to workers aged 22 or over who started a new job with a new employer and did accredited training, being a course approved by the UK government to obtain a vocational qualification, was abolished for pay reference periods starting on or after 1 October 2006. When applicable, the accredited training rate could only be paid for the first six months of the new job, after which the National Minimum Wage main rate applied.

8. A new apprentice minimum wage was introduced with effect from 1 October 2010, available to apprentices aged under 19, or apprentices aged 19 or over but in the first year of their apprenticeship.

9. The government has announced that they will align the National Minimum Wage and National Living Wages cycles so that both rates are amended in April each year. This took place with effect from April 2017.

F4: National Minimum Wage and National Living Wage

National Minimum Wage

Pay reference periods starting on or after	1 October							1 April	
	2010 £/hr	2011 £/hr	2012 £/hr	2013 £/hr	2014 £/hr	2015 £/hr	2016 £/hr	2017 £/hr	2018 £/hr
Workers under 18 who are no longer of compulsory school age (notes 2 and 5)	3.64	3.68	3.68	3.72	3.79	3.87	4.00	4.05	4.20
Development rate for workers aged 18 to 20 years (from October 2010) (notes 5 and 6)	4.92	4.98	4.98	5.03	5.13	5.30	5.55	5.60	5.90
Rate for apprentices aged under 19, or 19 or over but in the first year of their apprenticeship (note 8)	2.50	2.60	2.65	2.68	2.73	3.30	3.40	3.50	3.70
Main rate for workers aged 21 or over from October 2010 and for workers aged 21 to 24 years from April 2016 (notes 2, 5, and 9)	5.93	6.08	6.19	6.31	6.50	6.70	6.95	7.05	7.38

National Living Wage

Pay reference periods starting on or after	1 April		
	2016 £/hr	2017 £/hr	2018 £/hr
For workers aged 25 or over from April 2016 (see note 2)	7.20	7.50	7.83

F5: Regional unemployment statistics

In previous years, tables showing the average duration of claims for Jobseeker's Allowance have been drawn from the Office of National Statistics Economic and Labour Market Review. This is no longer being produced.

The tables below have been based on data available on the Nomis website for January 2018.

North East
Median duration (weeks)

Age	Female	Male	All
Under 17	0.0	0.0	0.0
17	7.0	8.0	7.3
18	9.4	9.0	9.2
19	12.5	10.7	11.9
20–24	29.8	24.9	27.6
25–29	37.6	26.4	32.5
30–34	33.5	27.6	30.9
35–39	39.0	30.8	35.3
40–44	42.7	32.9	38.2
45–49	50.0	34.7	43.3
50–54	51.6	33.3	44.5
55–59	51.9	36.4	45.6
60+	50.7	35.9	44.5

North West
Median duration (weeks)

Age	Female	Male	All
Under 17	0.0	0.0	0.0
17	7.3	8.0	7.6
18	9.2	8.0	8.6
19	11.4	11.5	11.5
20–24	21.5	20.7	21.2
25–29	26.6	21.4	24.5
30–34	27.1	20.6	24.1
35–39	28.9	22.7	25.6
40–44	29.9	25.6	28.1
45–49	37.7	30.0	34.5
50–54	41.9	28.0	36.0
55–59	45.4	30.1	38.1
60+	43.9	31.5	38.3

Yorkshire and the Humber
Median duration (weeks)

Age	Female	Male	All
Under 17	0.0	0.0	0.0
17	5.5	5.0	5.3
18	9.4	8.0	8.9
19	11.6	11.5	11.6
20–24	23.6	19.9	22.2
25–29	26.6	23.5	25.1
30–34	25.9	22.8	24.4
35–39	27.1	24.7	25.7
40–44	33.5	27.9	31.0
45–49	38.7	31.0	35.2
50–54	45.7	31.8	38.9
55–59	43.4	30.0	37.2
60+	44.0	28.7	37.9

East Midlands
Median duration (weeks)

Age	Female	Male	All
Under 17	0.0	0.0	0.0
17	5.0	3.3	4.4
18	7.2	8.8	8.0
19	12.0	11.6	11.9
20–24	24.1	18.3	21.7
25–29	29.3	20.7	24.7
30–34	27.2	22.5	24.8
35–39	27.1	22.3	24.6
40–44	32.4	22.6	27.0
45–49	32.4	25.4	29.2
50–54	36.1	24.7	30.8
55–59	36.9	25.4	32.1
60+	35.2	25.2	31.4

F5: Regional unemployment statistics

West Midlands
Median duration (weeks)

Age	Female	Male	All
Under 17	1.0	6.0	4.0
17	5.2	8.0	5.6
18	9.9	8.1	9.0
19	17.0	13.8	15.7
20–24	28.8	22.9	25.8
25–29	37.9	29.0	33.8
30–34	40.9	29.6	35.2
35–39	40.9	32.8	37.0
40–44	44.0	34.8	39.3
45–49	50.6	40.3	46.2
50–54	55.8	37.7	47.6
55–59	62.2	39.5	51.2
60+	51.5	38.3	46.5

East
Median duration (weeks)

Age	Female	Male	All
Under 17	0.0	0.0	0.0
17	5.5	6.7	6.5
18	9.2	7.7	8.6
19	10.7	12.0	11.3
20–24	18.8	17.4	18.2
25–29	24.8	20.2	22.4
30–34	22.9	20.1	21.3
35–39	25.1	17.3	21.2
40–44	28.2	21.7	24.5
45–49	29.5	22.9	25.7
50–54	32.8	22.5	27.4
55–59	33.2	24.5	29.5
60+	37.1	25.3	32.0

London
Median duration (weeks)

Age	Female	Male	All
Under 17	0.0	0.0	0.0
17	1.0	4.0	4.0
18	8.6	7.8	8.3
19	11.8	10.2	11.1
20–24	19.7	15.8	18.0
25–29	25.0	21.2	23.2
30–34	26.0	20.8	23.3
35–39	29.1	22.2	25.1
40–44	30.1	28.1	29.1
45–49	36.8	30.9	34.0
50–54	44.6	34.7	39.4
55–59	49.0	38.9	44.5
60+	49.6	38.0	45.0

South East
Median duration (weeks)

Age	Female	Male	All
Under 17	0.0	0.0	0.0
17	8.0	11.3	9.7
18	8.2	8.5	8.4
19	12.1	10.6	11.4
20–24	20.0	16.0	18.3
25–29	23.3	20.2	21.8
30–34	22.8	18.9	20.7
35–39	23.3	18.5	20.9
40–44	24.6	21.8	23.2
45–49	25.3	22.6	24.0
50–54	28.8	22.7	25.8
55–59	33.3	24.5	29.4
60+	32.3	24.7	29.0

South West
Median duration (weeks)

Age	Female	Male	All
Under 17	2.0	0.0	2.0
17	10.0	4.0	8.8
18	7.8	6.7	7.3
19	11.1	11.4	11.3
20–24	23.0	20.2	22.0
25–29	25.9	19.3	22.5
30–34	22.5	16.9	19.8
35–39	22.0	18.6	20.2
40–44	30.3	21.8	26.1
45–49	32.0	21.1	26.6
50–54	33.1	22.2	27.7
55–59	36.2	24.2	31.3
60+	36.6	25.2	32.1

England
Median duration (weeks)

Age	Female	Male	All
Under 17	4.0	6.0	6.0
17	6.9	6.5	6.7
18	8.9	8.1	8.6
19	12.1	11.4	11.8
20–24	23.0	19.4	21.5
25–29	28.6	22.7	25.4
30–34	28.1	22.2	24.9
35–39	29.7	23.2	25.9
40–44	32.7	26.3	29.7
45–49	37.1	29.1	33.5
50–54	41.5	29.7	36.0
55–59	44.0	31.7	38.1
60+	43.1	31.4	38.0

F5: Regional unemployment statistics

Wales
Median duration (weeks)

Age	Female	Male	All
Under 17	0.0	0.0	0.0
17	6.0	1.0	6.0
18	10.4	9.9	10.1
19	11.5	13.6	12.3
20–24	27.5	21.9	25.0
25–29	32.9	24.8	29.0
30–34	29.8	26.1	28.1
35–39	31.1	27.8	29.6
40–44	37.3	29.2	33.9
45–49	45.8	31.1	39.1
50–54	49.4	32.5	41.6
55–59	53.0	33.8	45.5
60+	45.1	33.4	39.9

Scotland
Median duration (weeks)

Age	Female	Male	All
Under 17	3.7	3.3	3.5
17	7.8	7.3	7.6
18	11.3	14.0	12.4
19	14.1	12.8	13.7
20–24	21.1	17.2	19.7
25–29	25.4	20.4	23.4
30–34	24.8	21.4	23.3
35–39	27.5	22.4	25.1
40–44	31.3	23.3	27.1
45–49	37.3	24.9	32.3
50–54	41.4	23.5	33.6
55–59	38.2	25.5	33.2
60+	39.0	29.4	35.3

Northern Ireland
Median duration (weeks)

Age	Female	Male	All
Under 17	1.0	0.0	1.0
17	11.3	17.3	13.0
18	8.6	9.2	8.9
19	12.1	12.7	12.3
20–24	21.8	18.3	20.7
25–29	25.3	20.9	23.7
30–34	26.7	22.6	24.8
35–39	32.2	25.1	28.9
40–44	34.3	28.2	31.5
45–49	45.5	31.3	39.2
50–54	42.7	32.3	38.3
55–59	48.3	35.0	42.4
60+	52.0	39.3	47.8

United Kingdom
Median duration (weeks)

Age	Female	Male	All
Under 17	3.5	3.7	3.7
17	7.4	7.0	7.2
18	9.1	8.8	8.9
19	12.2	11.8	12.0
20–24	22.8	19.2	21.4
25–29	28.1	22.5	25.2
30–34	27.6	22.4	24.8
35–39	29.7	23.4	26.1
40–44	32.9	26.1	29.8
45–49	37.9	28.9	33.9
50–54	41.9	29.4	36.2
55–59	44.1	31.4	38.1
60+	43.3	31.7	38.2

F5: Regional unemployment statistics

Labour Force Survey (August–November 2017)

Thousands, seasonally adjusted

	Total aged 16-64	Economically active							Employment									Unemployment						
	Total	Total		Men		Women		Total		Men		Women			Total		Men			Women				
	Level	Level	Rate (%)*	Level	Rate(%)*	Level	Rate (%)*	Level	Rate (%)*	Level	Rate (%)*	Level	Rate (%)**		Level	Rate (%)**	Level	Rate (%)**		Level	Rate (%)**			
	1	2	3	4	5	6	7	8	9	10	11	12	13		14	15	16	17		18	19			
North East	1,645	1,271	77.3	658	81.0	613	73.6	1,194	72.6	617	76.0	577	69.3		77	6.0	41	6.2		36	5.9			
North West	4,479	3,455	77.1	1,806	81.2	1,649	73.2	3,307	73.8	1,720	77.3	1,587	70.4		148	4.3	86	4.8		62	3.7			
Yorkshire & the Humber	3,378	2,582	76.4	1,372	81.5	1,209	71.4	2,452	72.6	1,300	77.2	1,152	68.0		130	5.0	72	5.2		58	4.8			
East Midlands	2,920	2,267	77.6	1,207	83.1	1,060	72.2	2,171	74.3	1,156	79.6	1,015	69.1		97	4.3	51	4.2		46	4.3			
West Midlands	3,573	2,745	76.8	1,458	81.6	1,287	72.0	2,596	72.7	1,386	77.6	1,210	67.7		148	5.4	72	4.9		77	6.0			
East	3,758	3,041	80.9	1,592	85.3	1,449	76.6	2,927	77.9	1,524	81.7	1,403	74.1		114	3.7	67	4.2		46	3.2			
London	6,074	4,763	78.4	2,584	84.7	2,180	72.1	4,526	74.5	2,457	80.5	2,070	68.5		237	5.0	127	4.9		110	5.0			
South East	5,551	4,566	82.3	2,396	87.0	2,170	77.6	4,424	79.7	2,318	84.1	2,106	75.3		142	3.1	78	3.3		64	2.9			
South West	3,311	2,674	80.8	1,392	84.6	1,283	77.0	2,570	77.6	1,345	81.7	1,226	73.6		104	3.9	47	3.4		57	4.5			
England	34,690	27,364	78.9	14,464	83.7	12,900	74.1	26,169	75.4	13,823	80.0	12,345	70.9		1,195	4.4	640	4.4		554	4.3			
Wales	1,898	1,451	76.4	756	80.1	694	72.9	1,382	72.8	722	76.4	660	69.3		68	4.7	35	4.6		34	4.9			
Scotland	34,100	2,665	78.2	1,366	82.0	1,300	74.5	2,555	74.9	1,295	77.7	1,261	72.3		110	4.1	71	5.2		39	3.0			
United Kingdom[1]	41,169	32,311	78.5	17,023	83.2	15,288	73.8	30,904	75.1	16,255	79.4	14,649	70.8		1,407	4.4	768	4.5		639	4.2			

Relationship between columns: 2 = 4+6 = 8+14; 8 = 10+12; 14 = 16+18

[1] Due to slight methodological differences between the way the national and regional LFS estimates have been interim adjusted for the 2001 Census, there may be small differences between the UK totals and the sum of the regional components.
* Denominator = all persons of working age
** Denominator = Total economically active

Data source: Labour Force Survey
Labour market statistics enquiries: labour.market@ons.gov.uk

Labour Force Survey

The table reports headline labour market indicators for the UK and its constituent regions and nations. These are reported for the working age population (16–64 years) and include the number economically active in the working age population, the number in employment or self-employment (or government employment scheme) and the number unemployed. The statistics are derived from the Labour Force Survey (LFS) for August to October 2017. Updated statistics are available on NOMIS (*www.nomisweb.co.uk*). The UK statistics are reported in Table A02 and the regional statistics are reported in Tables HI01 to HI11.

Unemployment is defined using the ILO definition and includes those who were without work during the reference week but who are currently available for work and who were either actively seeking work in the past four weeks or who had already found a job to start within the next three months. This definition of unemployment is independent of whether or not the individual is eligible to claim benefit.

Those who are either employed or unemployed (and looking for work) are defined as economically active. The economically inactive are calculated by the difference between the estimate in column 1, the working age population and the estimate in column 2, the economically active working age population. Many people who are disabled will be inactive rather than unemployed.

Non-employment includes unemployment and inactivity. It is the difference between column 1 and column 8.

Claimant Count v ILO Unemployment

Along with a large number of other countries, the United Kingdom publishes two defined measures of unemployment that complement each other.

One comes from a monthly count of those claiming unemployment-related benefits. This administrative measure is known as the "Claimant Count".

The other comes from a quarterly survey of households, the Labour Force Survey (LFS). This survey measure is accepted as an international standard because it is based on methods recommended by the International Labour Organisation (ILO). It is known as the p and is used by the European Union (EU) and the Organisation for Economic Co-operation and Development (OECD).

Both measures have their advantages and disadvantages.

The advantage of the Claimant Count is that it is available quickly and monthly and because it is a 100 per cent count, it also provides precise information on very small areas.

The ILO measure on the other hand, as well as being internationally standard, springs from a data source (the Labour Force Survey) which allows unemployment to be analysed in the context of other labour market information and a variety of demographic characteristics.

A disadvantage of the Claimant Count is that it can be affected if there are changes to the benefit system from which it is derived.

Although changes in the benefit system may also affect the labour market behaviour of respondents to the LFS, the ILO definition itself is entirely independent of the benefit system. Comparatively the LFS results, based on the ILO measure, are not reliable for areas smaller than counties or the larger local authority districts, because of sample size restrictions. Estimates of less than 10,000 persons unemployed (after grossing up) are not shown in published tables because they are subject to unacceptably high sampling error and are, therefore, unreliable.

This said, government statistics apply recognised statistical procedures in order to minimise these disadvantages and maintain the relevance of both measures as accurate labour market indicators.

F5: Regional unemployment statistics

Claimant Count Rates

Area	2007	2008	2009	2010	2011	2012	2013	2014	2015	2016	2017
North East	4.1	4.5	6.9	6.7	4.7	5.4	5.4	4.2	4.0	3.9	3.3
North West	3.2	3.4	5.4	5.2	4.0	4.4	4.2	3.2	2.2	2.7	2.5
Yorkshire and the Humber	3.1	3.4	5.7	5.6	4.2	4.7	4.7	3.8	3.2	2.6	2.3
East Midlands	2.6	2.8	4.9	4.6	3.4	3.7	3.6	2.7	2.2	1.7	1.6
West Midlands	3.8	3.9	6.3	5.9	4.6	4.7	4.5	3.6	3.0	2.8	2.4
East	2.1	2.2	4.0	3.8	2.9	3.0	3.0	2.2	1.6	1.4	1.4
London	3.0	2.8	4.3	4.5	4.0	4.1	3.9	2.9	2.1	1.9	2.1
South East	1.6	1.7	3.3	3.1	2.5	2.5	2.4	1.8	1.3	1.2	1.2
South West	1.6	1.7	3.4	3.1	2.5	2.6	2.5	1.9	1.3	1.3	1.4
England	2.7	2.8	4.7	4.5	3.7	3.9	3.7	2.9	2.1	2.0	1.9
Wales	2.9	3.3	5.5	5.2	3.8	4.0	4.0	3.4	3.2	2.6	2.0
Scotland	2.8	2.9	4.6	4.9	4.0	4.2	4.0	3.2	2.9	2.7	2.3
Northern Ireland	2.8	3.1	5.5	6.4	6.1	5.3	5.5	4.9	5.1	3.5	2.5
United Kingdom	**2.7**	**2.8**	**4.7**	**4.6**	**3.7**	**3.9**	**3.7**	**2.9**	**2.3**	**2.1**	**2.0**

Percentages, seasonally adjusted annual averages

ILO Unemployment Rates

Area	2007	2008	2009	2010	2011	2012	2013	2014	2015	2016	2017
North East	5.8	8.6	9.5	10.2	9.8	10.8	10.0	9.7	7.7	6.8	5.4
North West	5.9	7.7	8.5	7.7	8.5	9.5	8.2	8.3	6.2	4.9	4.2
Yorkshire and the Humber	5.5	7.1	9.6	9.3	8.7	9.7	9.3	8.8	6.0	5.3	5.1
East Midlands	5.7	6.4	7.8	8.0	7.9	8.3	8.0	7.2	5.0	4.3	4.1
West Midlands	6.3	7.9	9.5	9.9	8.7	8.5	9.5	8.4	6.5	5.6	5.9
East	5.0	5.5	6.6	6.2	6.7	6.6	6.9	5.9	5.1	4.4	4.1
London	6.4	7.5	8.9	9.4	9.4	8.9	8.7	8.2	6.2	5.6	6
South East	4.6	4.8	6.4	6.3	5.7	6.3	6.8	5.3	4.5	3.5	3.5
South West	3.9	5.1	6.4	6.3	5.7	5.9	6.4	6.0	4.5	3.6	3.4
England	5.4	6.6	8.0	7.9	7.8	8.1	8.0	7.3	5.6	4.7	4.6
Wales	5.1	7.6	6.4	8.7	7.9	9.0	8.3	6.9	6.2	4.4	4.8
Scotland	4.6	5.1	7.8	8.1	7.7	7.9	7.5	7.1	5.9	4.7	4
Northern Ireland	4.0	5.7	6.4	8.0	7.1	6.9	8.3	7.7	6.0	5.7	5.4
United Kingdom	**5.3**	**6.5**	**8.0**	**8.0**	**7.8**	**8.1**	**8.0**	**7.3**	**5.6**	**4.7**	**4.6**

Percentages, Spring each year, seasonally adjusted

F6: Average weekly earnings index

Average weekly earnings index

Whole economy, excluding bonuses and arrears of pay, and seasonally adjusted.

	2001	2002	2003	2004	2005	2006
January	102.5	107.1	110.8	114.6	119.3	124.2
February	102.5	107.9	111.1	114.7	119.5	124.6
March	103.2	108.1	111.3	115.1	120.2	124.8
April	104.0	108.4	111.7	115.6	120.6	125.0
May	104.1	108.4	112.0	116.0	120.8	125.7
June	104.3	109.1	112.2	116.3	121.2	126.3
July	105.0	109.3	112.5	116.7	121.9	126.3
August	105.7	109.0	112.9	117.2	122.4	126.5
September	105.8	109.3	113.3	117.4	122.8	127.1
October	106.2	109.5	113.6	118.0	123.0	127.9
November	106.6	109.8	114.0	118.3	123.3	128.2
December	106.7	109.8	114.5	119.1	123.6	128.7
Yearly Average	104.7	108.8	112.5	116.6	121.6	126.3

	2007	2008	2009	2010	2011	2012
January	128.9	134.2	138.0	140.5	143.6	145.0
February	129.4	134.8	138.3	140.4	143.3	145.8
March	130.0	135.3	138.2	141.1	143.4	146.2
April	130.1	136.3	138.7	140.7	143.6	146.0
May	131.0	135.9	138.9	140.6	143.8	146.3
June	131.6	136.3	139.0	141.0	143.8	146.6
July	132.1	136.7	138.6	141.6	144.0	146.6
August	132.7	137.0	138.8	141.9	144.1	147.2
September	132.9	137.3	139.1	142.2	144.6	146.8
October	132.9	137.8	139.2	142.3	144.9	146.8
November	133.6	137.9	139.3	142.6	145.2	147.3
December	133.8	138.0	139.8	142.5	145.2	147.0
Yearly Average	131.6	136.5	138.8	141.5	144.1	146.5

	2013	2014	2015	2016	2017	2018
January	146.6	149.2	151.5	155.0	158.1	162.4
February	146.8	148.6	152.1	155.6	158.3	162.9
March	147.0	148.5	152.7	155.4	158.6	163.3
April	148.0	148.7	152.9	156.7	159.2	
May	147.9	148.9	153.1	156.2	159.7	
June	147.9	149.2	153.4	156.7	159.9	
July	148.1	149.3	153.6	156.9	160.2	
August	148.1	149.7	153.6	157.2	160.8	
September	148.0	150.7	153.5	157.7	161.1	
October	148.3	151.2	153.7	157.8	161.5	
November	148.3	150.9	154.2	158.4	161.8	
December	148.9	151.3	154.5	158.1	162.3	
Yearly Average	147.8	149.7	153.2	156.8	162.3	

ONS index reference: K54L

F7: Average weekly earnings

These figures are the average (mean) gross weekly earnings of full-time employees on adult rates whose pay was not affected by absence.

	Men	Women
	£	£
1985	192.4	126.4
1986	207.5	137.2
1987	224.0	148.1
1988	245.8	164.2
1989	269.5	182.3
1990	295.6	201.5
1991	318.9	222.4
1992	340.1	241.1
1993	353.5	252.6
1994	362.1	261.5
1995	374.6	269.8
1996	391.6	283.0
1997	408.7	297.2
1998	427.1	309.6
1999	442.4	326.5
2000	453.3	337.6
2001	490.3	366.9
2002	513.8	383.2
2003	525.0	396.0
2004	556.8	420.2
2005	569.0	435.2
2006	589.8	450.0
2007	605.0	463.8
2008	634.0	484.4
2009	643.0	501.2
2010	653.3	513.1
2011	658.4	515.5
2012	660.7	525.1
2013	677.0	533.0
2014	674.0	539.3
2015	680.0	547.1
2016	697.7	562.1
2017	717.9	578.0

Until 2004 these figures were taken from the New Earnings Survey.
In 2004 the Annual Survey of Hours and Earnings (ASHE) was developed to replace the New Earnings Survey.
The above ASHE figures are taken from 14.1a revised tables other than the latest year which is provisional (p).
Both the New Earnings Survey and ASHE are published by HMSO.

F8: Average Earnings Statistics

Introductory notes

1. It will usually be possible to obtain agreement, or a direction, that the earnings shown in the Annual Survey of Hours and Earnings (ASHE) may be adduced in evidence without formal proof but occasionally it may be necessary to adduce formal proof. This is done by calling a witness from the Office for National Statistics (ONS).

2. ASHE provides information about the levels, distribution and make-up of earnings and hours of paid work for employees. The data are collected and published by the ONS. ASHE replaced the New Earnings Survey (NES) in 2004.

3. ASHE is based upon a one per cent sample of employees taken from HM Revenue and Customs PAYE records. ASHE does not cover the self-employed nor employees not paid in the reference period.

4. ASHE is collected in April of each year and is published as a first release the following October/November/December. A second and final release is published in October/November/December a year later and includes any revisions to the estimates which may be required. The revisions are usually small.

5. The tables reproduced here relate to a sample restricted to full-time employees on adult rates of pay whose pay was not affected by absence. The estimates are disaggregated by sex and by a four-digit occupational classification. They are first release estimates for 2017. They were published by the ONS on 26 October 2017.

6. The earnings information relates to weekly and annual gross pay before tax, national insurance or other deductions and excludes payments in kind. Earnings are reported for full-time employees who are defined as those who work more than 30 paid hours per week.

7. Two measures of typical earnings are reported, the mean and median. The median is ONS's preferred measure of average earnings as it is less affected by the relatively small number of very high earners which skews the distribution of earnings. The median provides a better indication of typical earnings than does the mean.

8. It is helpful to understand the Standard Occupational Classification (SOC) as an ordered taxonomy of jobs in which narrowly defined jobs at the four-digit level (unit groups) are included within a wider definition at the three-digit level which in turn are included within a wider category at the two-digit level and a still wider category at the one-digit level. The hierarchy is based upon the concepts of the type of job and on the level of skill. There are 369 four-digit occupational unit groups in SOC 2010 which cluster to form 90 minor groups, 25 sub-major groups and nine major groups. As an example, Rail Travel Assistants, 6215, are included within the three-digit group Leisure and Travel Services (621) and at the two-digit level, within Leisure, Travel and Related Personal Service Occupations (62), and, at the one-digit level, within Caring, Leisure and other Personal Service Occupations (6). The abbreviation "n.e.c." stands for "not elsewhere classified".

9. Reclassification of occupational categories occurs every 10 years and occurred in ASHE 2011 released in March 2012. For 2011 there is a dual set of tables, one using the SOC 2000 and the second using the SOC 2010.

10. Statistics derived from samples are called "estimates" because they estimate the population parameters that we are interested in. All sample estimates are subject to a degree of unreliability due

F8: Average Earnings Statistics

to sampling variation. This is measured by ONS in the form of the coefficient of variation (CV) and is published in the series of Tables b which accompany the sample estimates in the series of Tables a. The CV is the ratio of the standard error of the estimate to the estimate itself. The smaller is the CV, the higher the precision (or quality) of the estimate. The ONS define four standards of reliability in relation to the size of the CV: less than five per cent, 5–10 per cent, 10–20 per cent, and greater than 20 per cent. An estimate with a CV of less than five per cent is the most reliable. Estimates with CVs of greater than 20 per cent are considered insufficiently reliable and are not published. Those in between are shaded in the ONS publication, though not in the reproduction here.

11. Tables of ASHE estimates are published online where alternative breakdowns can be found, for example by region, age group, industrial sector etc. and at 10 points across the earnings distribution. In October/November/December 2018, the estimates published online for 2017 will be the revised final release ones. A further advantage of the online source is the shading according to the levels of reliability referred to in 10 above. The tables can be found on the website of the ONS. Step-by-step instructions to find the estimates produced here are provided below. You need not follow these step-by-step instructions each time you consult the tables as you can either download the tables as an Excel file or you can save the web link to bookmarks/favourites.

12. Find the home page of the ONS at *www.ons.gov.uk*

13. Type ASHE in the search box at the top of this page and click Search.

14. Refine the search using the menu on the left-hand side by checking the box for Datasets.

15. Scroll down the list of tables to the table title "Occupation (4 digit SOC) - ASHE: Table 14". Clicking on the table title will open a .zip file.

16. Opening the .zip file will produce a contents list of Excel files, each of which contains different tables of earnings estimates.

17. Weekly pay by occupational group is in Table 14.1a Weekly Pay - Gross. A double-click on the table title will take you to a worksheet in an Excel file. If you are sure that you have located the file that you want, save it using File → Save in Excel. Weekly pay is measured for the reference week in April 2017.

18. Annual pay by occupational group is in Table 14.7a Annual Pay - Gross. A double-click on the table title will take you to a worksheet in an Excel file. Annual estimates are provided for the tax year that ended in April 2017.

19. Note that all files marked with a file extension "b" report the coefficient of variation on the estimate (see 10 above)

20. Once in the Excel file, check the bottom tabs. Choose "Male Full-time" or "Female Full-time" to view the tables reproduced here. The median is reported in column 3 and the mean in column 5.

20. The shading indicates the reliability of the estimate. Where the estimate of the error is less than five per cent, there is no shading. The key to the shading can be found at the bottom and at the right-hand side of the table. The shading is not reproduced here.

21. If you have not already saved this file at step 17 above, this table can be saved now either in part or in full. If the file is saved prior to the final release, make a note that the 2017 estimates are provisional. They will be replaced in the final release in October/November/December 2018 under the same title.

This guide has been prepared by Dr Victoria Wass, Cardiff Business School, November 2017.

F8: Average Earnings Statistics

Full-time male employees on adult rates (where pay was not affected by absence) in UK

n.e.c. = not elsewhere classified
X = n/a, nil, disclosive

Occupation SOC 2010	SOC Code	Gross Weekly Pay in April 2017 Number of jobs (thousand)	Median £	Mean £	Gross Annual Pay April 2016-2017 Number of jobs (thousand)	Median £	Mean £
All employees		11,405	591.5	717.9	9,683	31,103	39,003
Managers, directors and senior officials	1	1,586	879.7	1,103.3	1,399	45,900	64,465
Corporate managers and directors	11	1,378	942.5	1,159.8	1,223	48,951	68,105
Chief executives and senior officials	111	56	1,807.5	2,088.8	49	93,690	136,378
Chief executives and senior officials	1115	53	1,820.7	2,169.9	47	98,059	142,409
Elected officers and representatives	1116	x	x	542.2	x	x	27,470
Production managers and directors	112	466	918.9	1,080.4	418	47,536	59,416
Production managers and directors in manufacturing	1121	362	944.1	1,111.8	332	49,198	61,125
Production managers and directors in construction	1122	98	837.2	955.6	80	43,369	52,316
Production managers and directors in mining and energy	1123	6	932.5	1,223.2	x	46,984	59,401
Functional managers and directors	113	441	1,281.0	1,462.5	386	68,718	90,276
Financial managers and directors	1131	162	1,346.6	1,610.1	140	76,241	105,206
Marketing and sales directors	1132	131	1,477.5	1,588.7	113	81,667	97,755
Purchasing managers and directors	1133	42	927.8	1,062.1	38	48,411	56,204
Advertising and public relations directors	1134	x	1,035.1	1,166.5	x	x	63,621
Human resource managers and directors	1135	41	919.9	1,056.4	35	51,540	61,774
Information technology and telecommunications directors	1136	28	1,326.5	1,365.2	26	70,346	79,438
Functional managers and directors n.e.c.	1139	32	1,185.2	1,374.8	29	63,591	81,469
Financial institution managers and directors	115	45	1,105.8	1,427.8	43	58,056	96,969
Financial institution managers and directors	1150	45	1,105.8	1,427.8	43	58,056	96,969
Managers and directors in transport and logistics	116	160	620.6	698.3	147	33,418	37,634
Managers and directors in transport and distribution	1161	60	715.8	824.3	56	38,754	44,535
Managers and directors in storage and warehousing	1162	100	570.6	622.4	91	30,389	33,430
Senior officers in protective services	117	13	1,098.0	1,183.6	x	x	59,221
Officers in armed forces	1171	x	x	x	x	x	x
Senior police officers	1172	8	1,168.7	1,258.6	8	61,956	63,472
Senior officers in fire, ambulance, prison and related services	1173	x	976.5	1,077.1	x	x	52,708
Health and social services managers and directors	118	22	898.4	988.8	18	45,907	51,345
Health services and public health managers and directors	1181	17	925.8	1,004.2	14	47,995	51,984
Social services managers and directors	1184	x	773.5	931.4	x	x	48,982
Managers and directors in retail and wholesale	119	174	574.9	681.2	149	30,621	37,164
Managers and directors in retail and wholesale	1190	174	574.9	681.2	149	30,621	37,164
Other managers and proprietors	12	209	599.5	730.4	176	32,224	39,149
Managers and proprietors in agriculture related services	121	13	582.1	635.8	10	29,623	32,656
Managers and proprietors in agriculture and horticulture	1211	10	570.4	640.1	9	29,561	32,678
Managers and proprietors in forestry, fishing and related services	1213	x	x	615.6	x	x	32,539
Managers and proprietors in hospitality and leisure services	122	66	491.2	592.5	52	27,437	33,243
Hotel and accommodation managers and proprietors	1221	9	480.1	601.0	8	29,753	31,775
Restaurant and catering establishment managers and proprietors	1223	26	474.5	529.8	x	25,084	29,659
Publicans and managers of licensed premises	1224	8	480.8	554.4	x	x	32,349
Leisure and sports managers	1225	22	561.1	667.9	19	28,947	37,191
Travel agency managers and proprietors	1226	x	x	x	x	x	37,720
Managers and proprietors in health and care services	124	10	659.2	689.7	8	31,475	34,134
Health care practice managers	1241	x	x	847.4	x	x	x
Residential, day and domiciliary care managers and proprietors	1242	8	641.6	647.7	x	30,494	31,742

F8: Average Earnings Statistics

Full-time male employees on adult rates (where pay was not affected by absence) in UK

n.e.c. = not elsewhere classified
X = n/a, nil, disclosive

Occupation SOC 2010	SOC Code	Gross Weekly Pay in April 2017 Number of jobs (thousand)	Median £	Mean £	Gross Annual Pay April 2016-2017 Number of jobs (thousand)	Median £	Mean £
Managers and proprietors in other services	125	120	678.7	820.5	106	35,275	43,002
Property, housing and estate managers	1251	60	725.9	854.7	52	38,756	44,189
Garage managers and proprietors	1252	6	634.5	852.2	x	34,148	39,794
Hairdressing and beauty salon managers and proprietors	1253	x	x	506.8	x	x	x
Shopkeepers and proprietors – wholesale and retail	1254	x	x	983.6	x	x	x
Waste disposal and environmental services managers	1255	x	x	882.1	x	x	42,460
Managers and proprietors in other services n.e.c.	1259	44	619.8	754.0	39	32,227	39,788
Professional occupations	2	2,464	793.6	899.8	2,056	41,543	48,055
Science, research, engineering and technology professionals	21	1,001	804.9	865.3	849	42,286	46,564
Natural and social science professionals	211	81	728.1	804.8	68	39,451	44,516
Chemical scientists	2111	9	705.5	735.4	8	35,866	39,805
Biological scientists and biochemists	2112	24	767.0	837.9	21	40,387	46,967
Physical scientists	2113	10	773.5	877.8	8	40,048	48,362
Social and humanities scientists	2114	7	653.0	663.9	x	34,896	39,115
Natural and social science professionals n.e.c.	2119	32	731.8	805.3	27	39,339	43,595
Engineering professionals	212	336	803.8	839.8	288	41,898	44,065
Civil engineers	2121	40	788.6	846.7	35	40,350	43,689
Mechanical engineers	2122	30	833.8	892.7	26	42,353	47,296
Electrical engineers	2123	19	897.2	892.7	17	47,619	48,637
Electronics engineers	2124	x	765.5	838.6	x	44,383	45,669
Design and development engineers	2126	71	785.4	814.4	61	40,157	42,411
Production and process engineers	2127	40	763.7	818.5	37	40,688	42,614
Engineering professionals n.e.c.	2129	132	801.6	838.2	109	42,300	44,080
Information technology and telecommunications professionals	213	528	828.0	891.5	441	43,619	48,585
IT specialist managers	2133	128	930.2	996.6	112	48,444	54,458
IT project and programme managers	2134	12	1,000.5	1,036.1	11	51,753	54,876
IT business analysts, architects and systems designers	2135	89	893.9	973.2	76	46,406	51,271
Programmers and software development professionals	2136	190	790.9	841.7	155	41,698	45,695
Web design and development professionals	2137	32	589.3	623.8	25	31,412	33,680
Information technology and telecommunications professionals n.e.c.	2139	77	766.6	833.5	63	40,917	46,875
Conservation and environment professionals	214	27	653.5	705.5	25	34,317	36,288
Conservation professionals	2141	x	733.2	770.4	x	36,331	36,834
Environment professionals	2142	22	648.1	690.1	20	33,982	36,142
Research and development managers	215	29	897.8	1,002.1	28	47,034	54,595
Research and development managers	2150	29	897.8	1,002.1	28	47,034	54,595
Health professionals	22	298	813.2	1,065.0	236	41,234	55,788
Health professionals	221	175	1,106.8	1,331.4	130	60,847	73,956
Medical practitioners	2211	122	1,382.3	1,553.1	86	88,904	89,709
Psychologists	2212	7	831.2	883.2	x	x	42,799
Pharmacists	2213	14	881.3	899.1	11	46,375	48,557
Ophthalmic opticians	2214	x	837.0	817.0	x	45,672	45,519
Dental practitioners	2215	x	x	1,216.6	x	x	x
Veterinarians	2216	6	708.6	827.8	x	35,937	40,229
Medical radiographers	2217	10	655.7	719.8	8	32,986	36,860
Podiatrists	2218	x	663.3	679.6	x	35,225	35,565
Health professionals n.e.c.	2219	9	675.1	696.6	8	35,186	36,680
Therapy professionals	222	19	616.4	634.9	17	31,668	32,793
Physiotherapists	2221	12	595.9	630.0	11	30,788	32,816
Occupational therapists	2222	x	631.9	613.0	x	31,730	31,406

F8: Average Earnings Statistics

Full-time male employees on adult rates (where pay was not affected by absence) in UK

n.e.c. = not elsewhere classified
X = n/a, nil, disclosive

Occupation SOC 2010	SOC Code	Gross Weekly Pay in April 2017 Number of jobs (thousand)	Median £	Mean £	Gross Annual Pay April 2016-2017 Number of jobs (thousand)	Median £	Mean £
Speech and language therapists	2223	x	x	x	x	x	x
Therapy professionals n.e.c.	2229	x	657.4	636.7	x	28,957	32,033
Nursing and midwifery professionals	223	104	648.5	695.6	89	33,231	33,835
Nurses	2231	102	648.3	694.4	88	33,191	33,745
Midwives	2232	x	672.1	787.1	x	36,182	40,741
Teaching and educational professionals	23	405	790.1	855.2	349	40,720	43,865
Teaching and educational professionals	231	405	790.1	855.2	349	40,720	43,865
Higher education teaching professionals	2311	81	1,016.4	1,090.1	73	52,195	56,389
Further education teaching professionals	2312	50	730.7	738.1	44	36,479	37,100
Secondary education teaching professionals	2314	146	772.0	788.5	124	39,822	40,032
Primary and nursery education teaching professionals	2315	73	707.0	722.9	59	36,648	36,379
Special needs education teaching professionals	2316	7	690.9	710.1	x	37,293	36,559
Senior professionals of educational establishments	2317	30	1,135.8	1,234.0	26	60,026	64,440
Education advisers and school inspectors	2318	x	831.9	842.8	x	37,540	40,633
Teaching and other educational professionals n.e.c.	2319	16	572.0	614.9	x	x	30,479
Business, media and public service professionals	24	759	769.4	904.2	622	41,000	49,510
Legal professionals	241	54	996.6	1,430.1	45	59,122	74,771
Barristers and judges	2412	x	x	998.2	x	x	x
Solicitors	2413	32	862.4	x	26	45,223	60,086
Legal professionals n.e.c.	2419	18	1,534.7	1,742.2	16	84,761	104,192
Business, research and administrative professionals	242	390	824.1	932.2	308	44,332	52,515
Chartered and certified accountants	2421	42	766.6	834.2	35	40,753	46,585
Management consultants and business analysts	2423	101	806.0	907.4	77	45,146	52,249
Business and financial project management professionals	2424	151	967.1	1,048.6	120	50,624	57,952
Actuaries, economists and statisticians	2425	16	964.0	1,246.8	12	53,397	x
Business and related research professionals	2426	55	650.5	685.1	42	34,266	37,016
Business, research and administrative professionals n.e.c.	2429	25	841.9	838.6	22	44,040	43,805
Architects, town planners and surveyors	243	125	747.4	815.7	106	38,642	44,068
Architects	2431	26	764.9	911.3	22	39,757	50,857
Town planning officers	2432	x	755.2	902.6	x	x	48,931
Quantity surveyors	2433	28	821.1	839.0	23	43,557	44,359
Chartered surveyors	2434	50	709.4	762.7	43	36,001	40,898
Chartered architectural technologists	2435	x	602.4	664.1	x	x	35,196
Construction project managers and related professionals	2436	15	687.0	792.1	13	37,941	42,742
Welfare professionals	244	47	575.2	588.9	41	28,336	30,360
Social workers	2442	20	680.2	693.1	17	34,866	35,628
Probation officers	2443	x	511.9	508.3	x	26,270	26,322
Clergy	2444	21	465.6	497.3	20	25,333	26,143
Welfare professionals n.e.c.	2449	x	595.6	599.4	x	29,048	30,568
Librarians and related professionals	245	x	533.1	595.8	x	x	30,019
Librarians	2451	x	552.5	602.5	x	x	30,684
Archivists and curators	2452	x	522.7	585.0	x	26,453	28,938
Quality and regulatory professionals	246	82	754.0	855.2	71	40,308	45,746
Quality control and planning engineers	2461	33	729.6	759.1	28	37,649	38,928
Quality assurance and regulatory professionals	2462	45	804.9	940.1	39	43,227	51,463
Environmental health professionals	2463	x	681.3	697.0	x	36,135	37,167
Media professionals	247	56	685.1	768.2	46	36,123	41,894
Journalists, newspaper and periodical editors	2471	27	674.1	757.9	22	36,138	41,743
Public relations professionals	2472	16	638.9	752.3	13	32,552	41,464
Advertising accounts managers and creative directors	2473	14	766.0	806.0	x	39,841	42,693
Associate professional and technical occupations	3	2,054	651.6	751.3	1,737	34,925	41,340

F8: Average Earnings Statistics

Full-time male employees on adult rates (where pay was not affected by absence) in UK

n.e.c. = not elsewhere classified
X = n/a, nil, disclosive

		Gross Weekly Pay in April 2017			Gross Annual Pay April 2016-2017		
Occupation SOC 2010	SOC Code	Number of jobs (thousand)	Median £	Mean £	Number of jobs (thousand)	Median £	Mean £
Science, engineering and technology associate professionals	31	500	571.4	611.8	419	30,011	32,194
Science, engineering and production technicians	311	272	570.0	610.7	231	29,850	31,881
Laboratory technicians	3111	25	431.6	484.5	20	23,456	27,305
Electrical and electronics technicians	3112	8	666.1	719.6	7	33,438	35,213
Engineering technicians	3113	70	694.6	710.0	62	35,895	36,599
Building and civil engineering technicians	3114	x	514.8	584.8	x	28,140	31,086
Quality assurance technicians	3115	19	493.9	549.7	18	26,651	28,607
Planning, process and production technicians	3116	23	630.2	660.5	21	34,525	35,153
Science, engineering and production technicians n.e.c.	3119	123	536.6	573.3	101	27,992	29,597
Draughtspersons and related architectural technicians	312	40	574.9	602.7	34	29,668	31,533
Architectural and town planning technicians	3121	11	566.4	597.1	8	29,367	30,608
Draughtspersons	3122	29	574.9	604.7	26	29,750	31,832
Information technology technicians	313	188	571.4	615.4	154	30,328	32,811
IT operations technicians	3131	82	572.0	627.0	68	30,966	33,843
IT user support technicians	3132	106	568.4	606.5	85	30,186	31,988
Health and social care associate professionals	32	79	522.8	550.0	65	26,721	28,555
Health associate professionals	321	28	632.2	641.2	25	32,484	32,916
Paramedics	3213	12	712.1	747.3	11	37,710	38,162
Dispensing opticians	3216	x	x	x	x	x	x
Pharmaceutical technicians	3217	x	451.3	503.0	x	23,045	24,392
Medical and dental technicians	3218	12	558.7	577.9	10	28,571	30,262
Health associate professionals n.e.c.	3219	x	458.8	526.0	x	23,940	27,581
Welfare and housing associate professionals	323	52	481.6	501.1	40	24,999	25,805
Youth and community workers	3231	17	487.3	505.1	13	25,248	25,743
Child and early years officers	3233	7	467.9	491.5	x	24,288	24,971
Housing officers	3234	12	527.3	529.9	9	26,767	27,251
Counsellors	3235	x	403.2	446.9	x	21,954	23,756
Welfare and housing associate professionals n.e.c.	3239	15	448.1	484.9	11	23,176	25,430
Protective service occupations	33	285	746.3	760.5	268	39,129	38,841
Protective service occupations	331	285	746.3	760.5	268	39,129	38,841
NCOs and other ranks	3311	x	x	x	x	x	x
Police officers (sergeant and below)	3312	191	798.0	822.5	180	41,947	42,132
Fire service officers (watch manager and below)	3313	44	653.8	671.3	42	34,037	34,547
Prison service officers (below principal officer)	3314	28	564.8	570.5	28	28,632	28,116
Police community support officers	3315	9	522.8	526.4	8	27,274	27,012
Protective service associate professionals n.e.c.	3319	12	664.3	725.2	10	32,616	36,659
Culture, media and sports occupations	34	100	533.2	847.1	86	28,739	x
Artistic, literary and media occupations	341	37	602.8	667.4	33	31,872	35,356
Artists	3411	x	533.0	564.0	x	x	28,270
Authors, writers and translators	3412	6	613.3	706.6	x	x	x
Actors, entertainers and presenters	3413	x	x	x	x	x	x
Dancers and choreographers	3414	x	x	x	x	x	x
Musicians	3415	x	793.3	764.3	x	41,482	39,417
Arts officers, producers and directors	3416	11	672.4	761.3	10	39,044	41,494
Photographers, audio-visual and broadcasting equipment operators	3417	14	544.5	591.4	13	27,904	30,684
Design occupations	342	41	524.4	571.4	35	28,000	30,943
Graphic designers	3421	28	499.0	542.5	24	26,085	28,744
Product, clothing and related designers	3422	13	581.9	632.2	11	32,395	35,613
Sports and fitness occupations	344	22	459.8	x	19	23,880	x
Sports players	3441	7	x	x	x	x	x
Sports coaches, instructors and officials	3442	12	452.0	515.3	10	23,254	26,555
Fitness instructors	3443	x	404.8	385.7	x	18,807	19,022

F8: Average Earnings Statistics

Full-time male employees on adult rates (where pay was not affected by absence) in UK

n.e.c. = not elsewhere classified
X = n/a, nil, disclosive

Occupation SOC 2010	SOC Code	Gross Weekly Pay in April 2017 Number of jobs (thousand)	Median £	Mean £	Gross Annual Pay April 2016-2017 Number of jobs (thousand)	Median £	Mean £
Business and public service associate professionals	35	1,090	689.9	818.7	899	37,612	46,410
Transport associate professionals	351	12	1,573.5	1,576.6	11	80,514	78,710
Air traffic controllers	3511	x	1,696.1	1,814.5	x	90,015	90,295
Aircraft pilots and flight engineers	3512	7	1,848.2	1,783.0	x	85,569	88,633
Ship and hovercraft officers	3513	x	x	843.0	x	x	42,434
Legal associate professionals	352	20	574.9	670.3	16	30,519	38,023
Legal associate professionals	3520	20	574.9	670.3	16	30,519	38,023
Business, finance and related associate professionals	353	268	687.5	824.0	222	37,085	48,842
Estimators, valuers and assessors	3531	29	605.6	686.0	26	31,335	36,836
Brokers	3532	8	1,284.1	1,931.1	x	x	x
Insurance underwriters	3533	12	653.1	804.9	11	32,967	46,513
Finance and investment analysts and advisers	3534	71	673.5	797.8	56	36,511	47,041
Taxation experts	3535	7	874.4	951.6	x	45,159	53,014
Importers and exporters	3536	x	478.8	574.3	x	27,703	29,563
Financial and accounting technicians	3537	16	853.2	905.9	12	45,232	49,515
Financial accounts managers	3538	50	804.9	959.6	45	43,436	56,424
Business and related associate professionals n.e.c.	3539	74	603.7	671.5	58	31,793	36,933
Sales, marketing and related associate professionals	354	589	751.3	869.8	481	41,000	49,141
Buyers and procurement officers	3541	25	582.2	660.7	23	32,474	35,654
Business sales executives	3542	155	613.3	708.4	125	34,545	40,433
Marketing associate professionals	3543	50	541.1	656.6	37	29,168	x
Estate agents and auctioneers	3544	8	496.1	577.0	x	25,877	29,927
Sales accounts and business development managers	3545	342	881.8	1,003.8	283	48,768	55,976
Conference and exhibition managers and organisers	3546	9	529.0	581.1	x	26,343	30,197
Conservation and environmental associate professionals	355	x	438.5	523.6	x	23,343	27,654
Conservation and environmental associate professionals	3550	x	438.5	523.6	x	23,343	27,654
Public services and other associate professionals	356	198	579.8	635.1	165	31,522	34,279
Public services associate professionals	3561	59	591.8	629.2	53	31,459	33,489
Human resources and industrial relations officers	3562	51	557.3	625.3	37	31,508	35,756
Vocational and industrial trainers and instructors	3563	50	574.9	615.3	41	30,512	32,677
Careers advisers and vocational guidance specialists	3564	x	480.5	537.8	x	24,922	27,998
Inspectors of standards and regulations	3565	13	570.2	620.5	12	28,879	32,108
Health and safety officers	3567	21	695.3	744.6	19	37,460	39,406
Administrative and secretarial occupations	4	631	465.3	530.1	507	24,500	27,793
Administrative occupations	41	595	471.5	534.3	480	24,730	28,013
Administrative occupations: Government and related organisations	411	83	484.0	523.6	73	26,238	27,748
National government administrative occupations	4112	61	472.7	514.5	53	25,801	27,517
Local government administrative occupations	4113	20	520.6	540.6	18	26,947	27,925
Officers of non-governmental organisations	4114	x	532.6	666.4	x	29,718	34,386
Administrative occupations: Finance	412	131	462.8	526.7	107	24,378	28,271
Credit controllers	4121	6	437.4	506.6	5	23,481	27,214
Book-keepers, payroll managers and wages clerks	4122	63	498.6	561.1	51	25,866	29,627
Bank and post office clerks	4123	30	428.4	466.8	26	22,882	25,261
Finance officers	4124	5	533.4	754.7	x	26,538	x
Financial administrative occupations n.e.c.	4129	28	433.3	479.4	21	22,963	26,325
Administrative occupations: Records	413	129	452.6	485.2	107	23,533	25,440
Records clerks and assistants	4131	28	459.9	497.5	22	24,342	26,603
Pensions and insurance clerks and assistants	4132	14	408.0	447.3	12	21,656	23,434
Stock control clerks and assistants	4133	43	433.7	465.5	37	22,091	24,071
Transport and distribution clerks and assistants	4134	38	495.0	524.1	32	25,801	27,573
Library clerks and assistants	4135	3	386.1	405.7	x	19,579	19,805
Human resources administrative occupations	4138	x	395.4	389.5	x	18,887	20,608
Other administrative occupations	415	188	443.0	524.5	139	22,815	26,736

F8: Average Earnings Statistics

Full-time male employees on adult rates (where pay was not affected by absence) in UK

n.e.c. = not elsewhere classified
X = n/a, nil , disclosive

Occupation SOC 2010	SOC Code	Gross Weekly Pay in April 2017 Number of jobs (thousand)	Median £	Mean £	Gross Annual Pay April 2016-2017 Number of jobs (thousand)	Median £	Mean £
Sales administrators	4151	15	440.0	455.8	12	22,889	22,860
Other administrative occupations n.e.c.	4159	173	443.3	530.3	127	22,803	27,100
Administrative occupations: Office managers and supervisors	416	64	633.5	690.5	54	32,775	36,283
Office managers	4161	50	689.2	728.0	42	36,288	38,412
Office supervisors	4162	14	534.8	557.8	12	27,251	28,626
Secretarial and related occupations	42	35	390.4	458.8	27	20,286	23,908
Secretarial and related occupations	421	35	390.4	458.8	27	20,286	23,908
Medical secretaries	4211	x	376.5	405.7	x	19,706	20,677
Legal secretaries	4212	x	328.1	334.5	x	16,581	18,147
School secretaries	4213	x	409.8	421.2	x	20,830	21,622
Company secretaries	4214	x	x	x	x	x	x
Personal assistants and other secretaries	4215	8	538.5	617.3	7	27,809	32,203
Receptionists	4216	19	356.7	382.2	x	x	18,803
Typists and related keyboard occupations	4217	5	400.3	413.7	x	20,606	21,507
Skilled trades occupations	5	1,598	523.0	564.0	1,395	27,092	28,946
Skilled agricultural and related trades	51	86	379.9	413.1	75	19,783	21,700
Agricultural and related trades	511	86	379.9	413.1	75	19,783	21,700
Farmers	5111	x	498.1	608.2	x	x	29,755
Horticultural trades	5112	x	365.3	406.5	x	18,056	20,956
Gardeners and landscape gardeners	5113	35	382.1	405.1	31	19,925	20,833
Groundsmen and greenkeepers	5114	37	367.7	396.3	32	19,086	21,486
Agricultural and fishing trades n.e.c.	5119	7	424.4	444.3	x	22,547	22,828
Skilled metal, electrical and electronic trades	52	947	576.9	615.1	845	30,015	31,358
Metal forming, welding and related trades	521	66	517.3	554.6	60	25,877	27,336
Smiths and forge workers	5211	x	391.4	443.4	x	x	x
Moulders, core makers and die casters	5212	x	491.1	507.7	x	x	x
Sheet metal workers	5213	10	518.5	578.3	11	26,311	28,075
Metal plate workers, and riveters	5214	x	583.6	627.6	x	26,967	29,876
Welding trades	5215	46	493.9	528.4	40	24,716	26,591
Pipe fitters	5216	x	676.6	773.3	x	33,447	34,305
Metal machining, fitting and instrument making trades	522	381	585.6	627.7	343	30,034	31,654
Metal machining setters and setter-operators	5221	54	539.4	568.4	51	26,843	28,562
Tool makers, tool fitters and markers-out	5222	7	539.8	612.1	7	28,076	30,737
Metal working production and maintenance fitters	5223	303	601.5	639.1	269	30,671	32,286
Precision instrument makers and repairers	5224	9	467.5	542.3	9	24,927	28,595
Air-conditioning and refrigeration engineers	5225	7	666.0	717.1	x	33,258	34,694
Vehicle trades	523	162	520.0	557.7	145	27,221	28,657
Vehicle technicians, mechanics and electricians	5231	119	508.4	537.7	107	26,892	27,650
Vehicle body builders and repairers	5232	20	529.7	534.4	18	26,005	27,661
Vehicle paint technicians	5234	8	471.3	484.5	x	24,194	25,929
Aircraft maintenance and related trades	5235	9	686.2	805.4	8	34,930	38,660
Boat and ship builders and repairers	5236	x	529.3	556.8	x	26,629	28,004
Rail and rolling stock builders and repairers	5237	x	921.9	921.2	x	45,976	48,123
Electrical and electronic trades	524	299	604.9	629.6	260	31,743	32,592
Electricians and electrical fitters	5241	128	600.9	617.6	112	30,886	31,664
Telecommunications engineers	5242	29	624.3	663.9	28	33,244	34,944
TV, video and audio engineers	5244	x	629.2	623.3	x	32,630	32,408
IT engineers	5245	14	536.6	619.0	12	29,049	31,761
Electrical and electronic trades n.e.c.	5249	123	604.0	635.3	104	32,000	33,055
Skilled metal, electrical and electronic trades supervisors	525	39	661.1	719.7	36	33,325	37,108
Skilled metal, electrical and electronic trades supervisors	5250	39	661.1	719.7	36	33,325	37,108
Skilled construction and building trades	53	285	519.8	556.2	255	26,725	28,406

F8: Average Earnings Statistics

Full-time male employees on adult rates (where pay was not affected by absence) in UK

n.e.c. = not elsewhere classified
X = n/a, nil , disclosive

		Gross Weekly Pay in April 2017			Gross Annual Pay April 2016-2017		
Occupation SOC 2010	SOC Code	Number of jobs (thousand)	Median £	Mean £	Number of jobs (thousand)	Median £	Mean £
Construction and building trades	531	208	506.6	538.0	187	26,160	27,433
Steel erectors	5311	x	499.6	540.1	x	26,395	28,188
Bricklayers and masons	5312	16	477.9	482.5	15	25,249	25,252
Roofers, roof tilers and slaters	5313	15	495.5	517.8	13	24,439	25,495
Plumbers and heating and ventilating engineers	5314	50	587.6	613.3	44	29,840	31,761
Carpenters and joiners	5315	78	510.0	534.4	69	26,416	26,893
Glaziers, window fabricators and fitters	5316	19	403.8	425.7	20	20,917	21,500
Construction and building trades n.e.c.	5319	26	485.5	533.0	22	25,721	28,469
Building finishing trades	532	37	479.0	490.2	34	24,984	25,354
Plasterers	5321	7	487.8	487.9	x	25,007	25,019
Floorers and wall tilers	5322	9	500.5	517.4	8	25,964	26,886
Painters and decorators	5323	21	461.2	479.3	19	24,203	24,792
Construction and building trades supervisors	533	41	660.6	709.1	35	34,661	36,602
Construction and building trades supervisors	5330	41	660.6	709.1	35	34,661	36,602
Textiles, printing and other skilled trades	54	280	418.1	445.6	220	21,678	22,777
Textiles and garments trades	541	13	432.9	512.6	11	23,266	24,528
Weavers and knitters	5411	x	465.4	461.0	x	23,233	23,809
Upholsterers	5412	6	440.2	488.2	x	22,785	22,886
Footwear and leather working trades	5413	x	403.2	546.1	x	x	25,239
Tailors and dressmakers	5414	x	x	419.5	x	x	x
Textiles, garments and related trades n.e.c.	5419	x	x	585.9	x	28,922	29,167
Printing trades	542	26	476.8	492.4	26	24,215	25,646
Pre-press technicians	5421	x	498.1	512.9	x	26,292	26,773
Printers	5422	14	496.0	524.0	14	26,454	27,544
Print finishing and binding workers	5423	10	417.2	441.6	9	21,538	22,550
Food preparation and hospitality trades	543	217	406.0	431.8	160	20,778	21,916
Butchers	5431	24	372.7	403.5	21	20,270	21,027
Bakers and flour confectioners	5432	14	378.3	408.6	13	19,527	21,044
Fishmongers and poultry dressers	5433	x	360.2	366.1	x	16,807	17,224
Chefs	5434	149	412.2	437.1	102	21,056	21,826
Cooks	5435	6	360.0	377.1	x	19,767	20,255
Catering and bar managers	5436	22	415.9	466.6	18	23,027	25,189
Other skilled trades	544	24	442.8	485.2	23	23,463	24,700
Glass and ceramics makers, decorators and finishers	5441	x	417.6	434.6	x	20,401	20,484
Furniture makers and other craft woodworkers	5442	8	433.7	458.2	8	23,454	23,461
Florists	5443	x	x	x	x	x	x
Other skilled trades n.e.c.	5449	12	451.5	519.5	12	24,766	26,793
Caring, leisure and other service occupations	6	303	396.9	433.8	252	20,477	21,830
Caring personal service occupations	61	200	388.1	412.7	160	19,913	20,385
Childcare and related personal services	612	29	345.4	367.4	21	17,323	18,634
Nursery nurses and assistants	6121	5	320.1	370.1	x	x	19,904
Childminders and related occupations	6122	x	x	x	x	x	x
Playworkers	6123	x	x	x	x	x	x
Teaching assistants	6125	16	343.6	365.0	11	16,959	18,269
Educational support assistants	6126	8	346.4	375.1	7	17,611	19,196
Animal care and control services	613	8	392.2	416.1	6	21,775	22,256
Veterinary nurses	6131	x	x	x	x	x	x
Pest control officers	6132	x	435.2	441.4	x	23,206	23,479
Animal care services occupations n.e.c.	6139	5	375.0	401.2	x	19,243	21,422
Caring personal services	614	163	397.0	420.5	133	20,104	20,570
Nursing auxiliaries and assistants	6141	62	392.9	422.9	52	20,103	20,549
Ambulance staff (excluding paramedics)	6142	9	485.5	472.7	x	22,261	23,639
Dental nurses	6143	x	331.1	341.6	x	x	x
Houseparents and residential wardens	6144	x	530.6	529.5	x	27,168	27,620
Care workers and home carers	6145	76	385.6	404.3	61	18,777	19,573
Senior care workers	6146	7	391.9	422.0	6	20,379	21,634

F8: Average Earnings Statistics

Full-time male employees on adult rates (where pay was not affected by absence) in UK

n.e.c. = not elsewhere classified
X = n/a, nil, disclosive

Occupation SOC 2010	SOC Code	Gross Weekly Pay in April 2017 Number of jobs (thousand)	Median £	Mean £	Gross Annual Pay April 2016-2017 Number of jobs (thousand)	Median £	Mean £
Care escorts	6147	x	326.7	364.5	x	20,716	19,730
Undertakers, mortuary and crematorium assistants	6148	6	452.4	476.5	x	22,792	24,307
Leisure, travel and related personal service occupations	62	103	425.3	474.8	92	22,431	24,345
Leisure and travel services	621	50	482.7	543.3	45	26,145	27,647
Sports and leisure assistants	6211	16	351.2	380.0	13	18,392	18,614
Travel agents	6212	5	427.1	463.9	x	23,246	24,372
Air travel assistants	6214	10	478.4	587.8	x	x	29,879
Rail travel assistants	6215	17	676.9	710.4	17	33,873	35,122
Leisure and travel service occupations n.e.c.	6219	x	425.9	435.0	x	18,515	20,477
Hairdressers and related services	622	x	303.0	344.4	x	x	17,386
Hairdressers and barbers	6221	x	293.7	319.6	x	x	15,939
Beauticians and related occupations	6222	x	411.2	452.2	x	x	24,189
Housekeeping and related services	623	40	391.3	413.8	35	20,500	21,265
Housekeepers and related occupations	6231	x	340.2	373.1	x	17,967	19,409
Caretakers	6232	36	393.3	417.7	33	20,900	21,413
Cleaning and housekeeping managers and supervisors	624	9	396.6	420.3	x	x	22,088
Cleaning and housekeeping managers and supervisors	6240	9	396.6	420.3	x	x	22,088
Sales and customer service occupations	7	485	386.6	441.0	411	19,969	22,557
Sales occupations	71	306	373.7	420.0	267	19,066	21,172
Sales assistants and retail cashiers	711	236	361.4	412.0	207	18,333	20,536
Sales and retail assistants	7111	199	356.4	404.1	175	18,111	20,333
Retail cashiers and check-out operators	7112	10	315.0	328.7	11	16,100	16,548
Telephone salespersons	7113	8	403.4	429.1	7	21,677	22,706
Pharmacy and other dispensing assistants	7114	4	325.8	357.6	x	16,965	18,090
Vehicle and parts salespersons and advisers	7115	14	450.1	584.5	x	x	26,942
Sales related occupations	712	28	398.4	443.4	23	20,814	23,565
Collector salespersons and credit agents	7121	x	356.7	390.5	x	x	21,677
Debt, rent and other cash collectors	7122	8	345.5	370.7	7	18,779	19,160
Roundspersons and van salespersons	7123	4	410.2	418.7	x	20,843	21,377
Market and street traders and assistants	7124	x	x	x	x	x	x
Merchandisers and window dressers	7125	5	455.5	506.2	x	23,693	26,476
Sales related occupations n.e.c.	7129	10	413.4	487.3	7	22,061	27,508
Sales supervisors	713	42	419.2	450.0	37	21,436	23,243
Sales supervisors	7130	42	419.2	450.0	37	21,436	23,243
Customer service occupations	72	179	413.5	476.8	144	21,788	25,128
Customer service occupations	721	143	388.9	432.7	113	20,598	22,366
Call and contact centre occupations	7211	18	358.1	385.0	14	18,277	20,082
Telephonists	7213	x	331.1	369.5	x	18,861	19,158
Communication operators	7214	5	532.4	568.7	5	28,493	28,938
Market research interviewers	7215	x	420.5	437.8	x	19,250	22,351
Customer service occupations n.e.c.	7219	117	391.7	434.9	92	20,659	22,409
Customer service managers and supervisors	722	36	597.7	652.5	31	32,401	35,317
Customer service managers and supervisors	7220	36	597.7	652.5	31	32,401	35,317
Process, plant and machine operatives	8	1,204	489.2	530.5	1,047	25,464	27,176
Process, plant and machine operatives	81	542	463.2	505.1	471	24,305	26,288
Process operatives	811	156	428.0	467.4	137	22,059	24,140
Food, drink and tobacco process operatives	8111	91	398.0	423.4	78	19,769	21,212
Glass and ceramics process operatives	8112	x	422.3	458.7	x	21,856	24,848
Textile process operatives	8113	7	432.3	482.3	x	x	x
Chemical and related process operatives	8114	19	561.7	612.2	17	30,637	32,911
Rubber process operatives	8115	x	509.7	541.5	x	30,629	30,680
Plastics process operatives	8116	11	450.5	493.0	x	x	26,503

Full-time male employees on adult rates (where pay was not affected by absence) in UK

n.e.c. = not elsewhere classified
X = n/a, nil , disclosive

Occupation SOC 2010	SOC Code	Gross Weekly Pay in April 2017 Number of jobs (thousand)	Median £	Mean £	Gross Annual Pay April 2016-2017 Number of jobs (thousand)	Median £	Mean £
Metal making and treating process operatives	8117	9	493.0	520.2	9	25,146	26,720
Electroplaters	8118	6	471.3	479.3	x	23,008	23,812
Process operatives n.e.c.	8119	7	445.1	490.9	6	23,044	26,162
Plant and machine operatives	812	75	467.3	505.1	68	23,837	25,933
Paper and wood machine operatives	8121	15	408.6	453.0	14	19,557	21,690
Coal mine operatives	8122	x	x	x	x	x	x
Quarry workers and related operatives	8123	x	576.1	603.8	x	x	x
Energy plant operatives	8124	5	586.0	663.3	x	31,739	35,674
Metal working machine operatives	8125	17	440.6	477.2	16	23,214	24,624
Water and sewerage plant operatives	8126	10	531.8	547.6	9	28,273	29,878
Printing machine assistants	8127	13	416.4	449.9	13	22,316	23,405
Plant and machine operatives n.e.c.	8129	11	473.9	548.8	9	23,383	27,201
Assemblers and routine operatives	813	172	484.7	534.7	160	25,656	27,906
Assemblers (electrical and electronic products)	8131	9	447.7	471.8	9	22,811	23,894
Assemblers (vehicles and metal goods)	8132	51	655.6	668.8	51	34,913	34,668
Routine inspectors and testers	8133	34	517.6	543.3	31	26,704	27,783
Weighers, graders and sorters	8134	x	466.4	478.9	x	22,651	23,875
Tyre, exhaust and windscreen fitters	8135	15	377.8	404.8	13	19,556	20,490
Sewing machinists	8137	x	339.9	364.9	x	18,347	17,998
Assemblers and routine operatives n.e.c.	8139	57	432.7	465.6	51	22,520	24,482
Construction operatives	814	141	482.7	510.5	105	26,132	26,857
Scaffolders, stagers and riggers	8141	16	673.8	693.4	13	32,835	34,597
Road construction operatives	8142	22	534.0	552.0	19	27,304	28,750
Rail construction and maintenance operatives	8143	6	545.4	636.7	x	26,522	27,538
Construction operatives n.e.c.	8149	97	438.9	464.0	69	24,219	24,864
Transport and mobile machine drivers and operatives	82	662	508.7	551.4	576	26,268	27,902
Road transport drivers	821	534	497.5	524.2	461	25,480	26,165
Large goods vehicle drivers	8211	201	564.6	587.6	173	28,805	28,823
Van drivers	8212	226	432.5	465.2	190	21,897	23,397
Bus and coach drivers	8213	96	490.3	528.4	88	25,328	26,651
Taxi and cab drivers and chauffeurs	8214	9	523.4	507.0	8	26,843	26,868
Driving instructors	8215	x	x	684.1	x	x	37,635
Mobile machine drivers and operatives	822	73	501.0	549.3	65	26,796	28,194
Crane drivers	8221	8	677.6	779.1	7	38,856	40,190
Fork-lift truck drivers	8222	25	415.9	452.7	21	21,315	22,728
Agricultural machinery drivers	8223	x	x	491.1	x	25,802	26,647
Mobile machine drivers and operatives n.e.c.	8229	38	532.0	571.1	35	28,247	29,071
Other drivers and transport operatives	823	55	838.8	820.6	50	46,061	43,428
Train and tram drivers	8231	26	1,031.2	1,027.6	26	52,885	52,793
Marine and waterways transport operatives	8232	x	678.6	693.7	x	33,165	35,350
Air transport operatives	8233	12	477.7	520.9	10	27,743	28,915
Rail transport operatives	8234	9	724.8	781.7	8	39,062	40,223
Other drivers and transport operatives n.e.c.	8239	5	596.7	609.8	x	31,299	31,618
Elementary occupations	9	1,081	392.8	424.2	880	20,509	21,831
Elementary trades and related occupations	91	235	400.0	431.4	184	20,708	22,567
Elementary agricultural occupations	911	33	395.1	423.8	27	20,803	21,818
Farm workers	9111	23	416.3	442.4	18	22,190	22,696
Forestry workers	9112	x	392.8	403.8	x	20,620	22,036
Fishing and other elementary agriculture occupations n.e.c.	9119	8	363.1	377.7	7	19,407	19,492
Elementary construction occupations	912	58	418.9	454.2	43	22,072	24,166
Elementary construction occupations	9120	57	418.8	454.1	42	22,055	24,168
Elementary process plant occupations	913	145	392.2	424.2	115	20,295	22,151
Industrial cleaning process occupations	9132	8	366.0	385.5	x	x	x

F8: Average Earnings Statistics

Full-time male employees on adult rates (where pay was not affected by absence) in UK

n.e.c. = not elsewhere classified
X = n/a, nil , disclosive

Occupation SOC 2010	SOC Code	Gross Weekly Pay in April 2017 Number of jobs (thousand)	Median £	Mean £	Gross Annual Pay April 2016-2017 Number of jobs (thousand)	Median £	Mean £
Packers, bottlers, canners and fillers	9134	49	389.0	421.0	41	19,489	20,972
Elementary process plant occupations n.e.c.	9139	88	400.0	429.5	67	20,800	23,255
Elementary administration and service occupations	92	845	390.5	422.2	696	20,455	21,636
Elementary administration occupations	921	101	443.3	468.4	90	26,061	26,676
Postal workers, mail sorters, messengers and couriers	9211	87	459.3	485.3	84	26,517	27,193
Elementary administration occupations n.e.c.	9219	13	339.6	356.8	6	18,485	19,024
Elementary cleaning occupations	923	91	350.4	375.8	75	18,022	18,603
Window cleaners	9231	X	372.6	448.6	X	X	X
Street cleaners	9232	7	346.4	369.3	X	17,987	18,165
Cleaners and domestics	9233	51	340.0	364.6	41	17,225	17,885
Launderers, dry cleaners and pressers	9234	X	327.5	347.9	X	16,434	17,125
Refuse and salvage occupations	9235	21	382.7	407.6	19	19,523	20,430
Vehicle valeters and cleaners	9236	7	339.0	344.7	5	16,622	17,120
Elementary cleaning occupations n.e.c.	9239	X	460.9	486.4	X	19,686	22,449
Elementary security occupations	924	104	439.9	466.4	89	22,776	23,631
Security guards and related occupations	9241	92	445.2	470.7	80	23,009	23,820
Parking and civil enforcement occupations	9242	8	401.1	411.5	7	20,395	20,902
School midday and crossing patrol occupations	9244	X	X	X	X	X	X
Elementary security occupations n.e.c.	9249	4	458.9	474.6	X	24,582	24,865
Elementary sales occupations	925	8	306.8	345.4	9	16,242	17,494
Shelf fillers	9251	7	301.9	344.2	8	16,045	17,446
Elementary sales occupations n.e.c.	9259	X	319.5	351.8	X	16,614	17,762
Elementary storage occupations	926	396	402.4	442.6	345	20,714	22,057
Elementary storage occupations	9260	396	402.4	442.6	345	20,714	22,057
Other elementary services occupations	927	146	318.8	336.8	87	15,811	15,800
Hospital porters	9271	3	376.9	386.4	X	18,879	19,354
Kitchen and catering assistants	9272	93	322.4	338.1	59	16,001	16,080
Waiters and waitresses	9273	19	306.8	317.7	9	15,713	15,449
Bar staff	9274	22	308.5	327.0	11	15,422	15,701
Leisure and theme park attendants	9275	X	299.8	337.0	X	13,375	15,715
Other elementary services occupations n.e.c.	9279	7	337.7	386.6	X	X	X
Not Classified		X	X	X	X	X	X

Source: *Annual Survey of Hours and Earnings, Office for National Statistics*, Tables 14.1a and 14.7a.

F8: Average Earnings Statistics

Full-time female employees on adult rates (where pay was not affected by absence) in UK

n.e.c. = not elsewhere classified
X = n/a, nil , disclosive

Occupation SOC 2010	SOC Code	Gross Weekly Pay in April 2017 Number of jobs (thousand)	Median £	Mean £	Gross Annual Pay April 2016-2017 Number of jobs (thousand)	Median £	Mean £
All employees		7,490	493.6	578.0	6,265	25,308	29,891
Managers, directors and senior officials	1	749	725.4	871.4	650	37,304	46,809
Corporate managers and directors	11	582	800.1	948.1	510	40,999	50,927
Chief executives and senior officials	111	21	1,341.6	1,526.3	20	70,000	87,627
Chief executives and senior officials	1115	20	1,354.0	1,561.3	19	70,663	90,591
Elected officers and representatives	1116	x	x	x	x	x	x
Production managers and directors	112	89	774.8	940.1	79	40,488	50,220
Production managers and directors in manufacturing	1121	83	777.2	947.1	73	40,830	50,945
Production managers and directors in construction	1122	5	698.7	862.1	x	36,407	40,783
Production managers and directors in mining and energy	1123	x	x	713.8	x	x	x
Functional managers and directors	113	261	981.6	1,113.6	223	50,545	60,361
Financial managers and directors	1131	95	996.6	1,136.5	82	51,013	60,714
Marketing and sales directors	1132	44	1,230.3	1,380.6	35	x	81,749
Purchasing managers and directors	1133	20	876.8	943.5	17	43,655	49,341
Advertising and public relations directors	1134	x	1,149.9	1,207.7	x	59,746	60,120
Human resource managers and directors	1135	74	920.3	965.9	63	47,267	52,115
Information technology and telecommunications directors	1136	x	1,368.4	1,475.8	x	x	72,554
Functional managers and directors n.e.c.	1139	21	970.0	1,057.8	19	48,158	54,146
Financial institution managers and directors	115	30	794.7	1,002.2	29	41,566	53,065
Financial institution managers and directors	1150	30	794.7	1,002.2	29	41,566	53,065
Managers and directors in transport and logistics	116	37	521.3	624.2	32	28,551	34,300
Managers and directors in transport and distribution	1161	7	668.5	871.3	x	35,399	x
Managers and directors in storage and warehousing	1162	30	480.6	565.0	26	25,948	30,704
Senior officers in protective services	117	x	1,077.6	1,065.8	x	53,201	53,185
Officers in armed forces	1171	x		x			
Senior police officers	1172	x	1,097.1	1,131.3	x	57,100	54,570
Senior officers in fire, ambulance, prison and related services	1173	x	801.9	914.3	x	43,455	49,155
Health and social services managers and directors	118	30	803.8	934.5	28	41,303	47,224
Health services and public health managers and directors	1181	20	893.0	994.4	18	43,463	50,961
Social services managers and directors	1184	11	766.4	822.7	10	39,662	40,890
Managers and directors in retail and wholesale	119	111	453.6	550.0	97	23,658	28,379
Managers and directors in retail and wholesale	1190	111	453.6	550.0	97	23,658	28,379
Other managers and proprietors	12	167	547.1	604.2	140	29,021	31,839
Managers and proprietors in agriculture related services	121	x	436.2	525.0	x	x	26,211
Managers and proprietors in agriculture and horticulture	1211	x	553.8	593.9	x	x	29,287
Managers and proprietors in forestry, fishing and related services	1213	x	362.3	383.4	x	18,440	19,886
Managers and proprietors in hospitality and leisure services	122	51	452.4	498.7	38	24,537	26,425
Hotel and accommodation managers and proprietors	1221	8	468.1	531.5	x	28,613	30,098
Restaurant and catering establishment managers and proprietors	1223	23	421.8	453.1	17	22,008	22,977
Publicans and managers of licensed premises	1224	x	465.2	526.3	x	x	x
Leisure and sports managers	1225	14	502.8	529.8	11	26,500	28,258
Travel agency managers and proprietors	1226	x	531.4	591.6	x	x	31,150
Managers and proprietors in health and care services	124	46	643.9	676.1	40	32,355	34,101
Health care practice managers	1241	9	666.0	649.8	8	34,980	35,312
Residential, day and domiciliarycare managers and proprietors	1242	36	643.4	682.9	32	31,691	33,781

F8: Average Earnings Statistics

Full-time female employees on adult rates (where pay was not affected by absence) in UK

n.e.c. = not elsewhere classified
X = n/a, nil , disclosive

Occupation SOC 2010	SOC Code	Gross Weekly Pay in April 2017 Number of jobs (thousand)	Median £	Mean £	Gross Annual Pay April 2016-2017 Number of jobs (thousand)	Median £	Mean £
Managers and proprietors in other services	125	68	563.0	637.3	60	29,454	33,990
Property, housing and estate managers	1251	34	569.7	637.0	29	30,162	33,627
Garage managers and proprietors	1252	x	x	x	x	x	x
Hairdressing and beauty salon managers and proprietors	1253	x	539.9	529.4	x	21,833	25,199
Shopkeepers and proprietors – wholesale and retail	1254	x	x	x	x	x	x
Waste disposal and environmental services managers	1255	x	x	977.5	x	x	x
Managers and proprietors in other services n.e.c.	1259	29	525.1	634.8	27	27,780	34,471
Professional occupations	2	2,013	681.1	733.2	1,694	35,000	37,422
Science, research, engineering and technology professionals	21	209	701.6	757.5	172	37,025	40,288
Natural and social science professionals	211	48	674.3	705.7	40	35,045	37,230
Chemical scientists	2111	x	533.9	605.8	x	x	31,335
Biological scientists and biochemists	2112	24	685.3	742.1	22	35,592	38,576
Physical scientists	2113	x	677.1	690.5	x	36,176	36,599
Social and humanities scientists	2114	x	x	561.4	x	x	x
Natural and social science professionals n.e.c.	2119	18	668.2	679.5	14	34,505	35,851
Engineering professionals	212	36	710.8	750.0	29	37,416	39,322
Civil engineers	2121	5	668.7	732.1	x	39,635	39,405
Mechanical engineers	2122	x	799.4	851.2	x	38,103	41,759
Electrical engineers	2123	x	704.4	863.3	x	x	35,206
Electronics engineers	2124	x	x	x	x	x	x
Design and development engineers	2126	5	698.3	748.6	x	38,379	40,215
Production and process engineers	2127	x	655.4	663.2	x	33,387	33,868
Engineering professionals n.e.c.	2129	18	717.6	760.2	15	37,234	40,373
Information technology and telecommunications professionals	213	99	728.3	783.2	81	37,921	42,115
IT specialist managers	2133	28	792.8	847.5	25	41,790	44,816
IT project and programme managers	2134	x	940.0	988.8	x	47,918	53,738
IT business analysts, architects and systems designers	2135	16	687.2	785.5	13	37,573	43,158
Programmers and software development professionals	2136	24	731.8	778.6	19	36,679	40,679
Web design and development professionals	2137	10	574.7	600.5	x	27,961	30,353
Information technology and telecommunications professionals n.e.c.	2139	16	687.8	729.5	13	35,931	41,265
Conservation and environment professionals	214	11	595.8	622.9	10	29,128	31,569
Conservation professionals	2141	x	562.6	570.8	x	x	25,700
Environment professionals	2142	8	607.8	644.6	7	30,211	33,365
Research and development managers	215	15	842.5	870.2	12	43,758	47,507
Research and development managers	2150	15	842.5	870.2	12	43,758	47,507
Health professionals	22	716	652.2	719.8	604	33,152	35,907
Health professionals	221	165	819.5	962.1	125	41,373	50,145
Medical practitioners	2211	83	1,074.9	1,202.8	59	55,142	63,870
Psychologists	2212	13	739.7	791.0	11	40,993	42,243
Pharmacists	2213	20	741.5	725.4	15	39,212	38,022
Ophthalmic opticians	2214	x	700.2	688.0	x	x	37,034
Dental practitioners	2215	x	x	1,009.3	x	x	57,151
Veterinarians	2216	6	696.2	753.0	x	38,396	41,574
Medical radiographers	2217	19	659.6	696.0	17	34,896	36,617
Podiatrists	2218	x	639.6	625.2	x	x	x
Health professionals n.e.c.	2219	15	561.1	611.6	13	28,696	31,572
Therapy professionals	222	50	588.2	623.9	42	29,942	32,100
Physiotherapists	2221	19	619.2	636.8	16	32,159	33,021
Occupational therapists	2222	19	570.9	611.1	15	28,846	31,415

Full-time female employees on adult rates (where pay was not affected by absence) in UK

n.e.c. = not elsewhere classified
X = n/a, nil , disclosive

Occupation SOC 2010	SOC Code	Gross Weekly Pay in April 2017 Number of jobs (thousand)	Median £	Mean £	Gross Annual Pay April 2016-2017 Number of jobs (thousand)	Median £	Mean £
Speech and language therapists	2223	6	555.8	593.5	x	28,133	29,471
Therapy professionals n.e.c.	2229	6	644.5	652.9	x	32,670	33,621
Nursing and midwifery professionals	223	502	627.2	649.8	437	31,777	32,191
Nurses	2231	477	624.5	648.3	415	31,606	32,040
Midwives	2232	24	680.0	679.4	22	36,128	35,064
Teaching and educational professionals	23	621	689.4	716.8	538	35,763	36,477
Teaching and educational professionals	231	621	689.4	716.8	538	35,763	36,477
Higher education teaching professionals	2311	52	899.3	894.7	46	45,091	46,151
Further education teaching professionals	2312	41	675.1	688.1	35	34,433	35,110
Secondary education teaching professionals	2314	192	712.7	717.4	165	36,660	36,512
Primary and nursery education teaching professionals	2315	233	677.6	666.2	197	34,252	33,730
Special needs education teaching professionals	2316	22	648.2	638.1	x	35,151	33,283
Senior professionals of educational establishments	2317	44	957.8	956.5	41	49,248	47,577
Education advisers and school inspectors	2318	10	756.3	749.4	8	35,366	37,163
Teaching and other educational professionals n.e.c.	2319	28	479.1	518.3	25	24,366	25,994
Business, media and public service professionals	24	467	689.9	764.9	382	35,458	39,860
Legal professionals	241	56	838.0	974.9	45	44,843	52,546
Barristers and judges	2412	x	756.3	843.6	x	x	x
Solicitors	2413	34	742.4	836.7	26	39,995	46,189
Legal professionals n.e.c.	2419	17	1,250.5	1,299.8	x	64,041	69,474
Business, research and administrative professionals	242	214	709.1	787.6	170	36,646	41,101
Chartered and certified accountants	2421	31	717.9	755.1	28	35,412	37,970
Management consultants and business analysts	2423	56	728.0	807.4	44	38,499	43,464
Business and financial project management professionals	2424	71	803.6	864.7	56	41,159	43,851
Actuaries, economists and statisticians	2425	5	766.6	809.8	x	40,187	45,026
Business and related research professionals	2426	35	631.6	625.1	24	32,828	33,342
Business, research and administrative professionals n.e.c.	2429	16	711.7	784.2	15	37,534	41,128
Architects, town planners and surveyors	243	27	661.0	695.3	23	33,819	35,468
Architects	2431	10	690.6	713.6	8	35,092	35,529
Town planning officers	2432	x	480.7	568.4	x	26,554	28,608
Quantity surveyors	2433	x	712.9	759.7	x	x	41,474
Chartered surveyors	2434	8	612.2	706.8	8	32,295	35,829
Chartered architectural technologists	2435	x	x	x	x	x	x
Construction project managers and related professionals	2436	x	629.3	638.1	x	x	31,379
Welfare professionals	244	76	647.4	650.8	65	33,018	32,874
Social workers	2442	61	661.9	669.9	54	33,359	33,619
Probation officers	2443	x	478.1	530.5	x	x	28,729
Clergy	2444	6	444.3	492.6	x	23,184	25,142
Welfare professionals n.e.c.	2449	8	663.9	636.9	x	34,171	32,922
Librarians and related professionals	245	11	514.5	574.0	9	25,482	29,266
Librarians	2451	7	481.5	556.3	x	24,689	28,407
Archivists and curators	2452	x	572.0	604.2	x	29,362	31,014
Quality and regulatory professionals	246	39	739.3	779.3	35	37,459	41,182
Quality control and planning engineers	2461	6	680.0	694.4	x	35,027	36,673
Quality assurance and regulatory professionals	2462	28	766.6	807.7	25	38,384	42,926
Environmental health professionals	2463	x	681.6	718.3	x	34,516	36,355
Media professionals	247	45	593.2	666.6	34	30,468	35,061
Journalists, newspaper and periodical editors	2471	18	592.6	679.4	13	30,205	34,282
Public relations professionals	2472	17	574.9	620.1	13	28,996	34,222
Advertising accounts managers and creative directors	2473	10	665.0	724.9	7	33,758	37,974

F8: Average Earnings Statistics

Full-time female employees on adult rates (where pay was not affected by absence) in UK

n.e.c. = not elsewhere classified
X = n/a, nil, disclosive

Occupation SOC 2010	SOC Code	Gross Weekly Pay in April 2017 Number of jobs (thousand)	Median £	Mean £	Gross Annual Pay April 2016-2017 Number of jobs (thousand)	Median £	Mean £
Associate professional and technical occupations	3	1,294	546.2	610.3	1,063	28,660	32,519
Science, engineering and technology associate professionals	31	139	478.5	508.1	116	24,216	26,172
Science, engineering and production technicians	311	72	435.4	477.7	61	21,891	24,321
Laboratory technicians	3111	26	368.3	421.3	22	18,973	21,336
Electrical and electronics technicians	3112	x	x	595.0	x	x	x
Engineering technicians	3113	9	584.7	648.5	7	31,998	34,702
Building and civil engineering technicians	3114	x	565.8	637.5	x	x	34,200
Quality assurance technicians	3115	10	464.6	506.5	7	24,476	25,673
Planning, process and production technicians	3116	9	518.7	526.1	7	25,552	25,911
Science, engineering and production technicians n.e.c.	3119	18	393.5	430.7	16	19,680	21,846
Draughtspersons and related architectural technicians	312	9	498.3	513.2	x	26,462	27,081
Architectural and town planning technicians	3121	5	514.9	526.5	x	26,917	28,140
Draughtspersons	3122	x	481.5	493.3	x	25,480	25,433
Information technology technicians	313	58	513.4	545.1	49	26,808	28,349
IT operations technicians	3131	28	530.2	566.8	24	28,198	29,922
IT user support technicians	3132	30	488.9	524.5	25	25,378	26,808
Health and social care associate professionals	32	157	478.5	496.4	132	24,455	25,452
Health associate professionals	321	36	490.7	524.2	32	23,968	26,580
Paramedics	3213	6	672.6	678.6	x	33,644	33,807
Dispensing opticians	3216	x	492.5	508.2	x	24,108	23,281
Pharmaceutical technicians	3217	14	439.3	454.6	12	22,607	23,347
Medical and dental technicians	3218	9	504.1	530.9	8	23,630	26,962
Health associate professionals n.e.c.	3219	6	471.4	535.3	x	x	27,646
Welfare and housing associate professionals	323	121	478.4	488.3	100	24,620	25,095
Youth and community workers	3231	33	488.2	508.2	30	25,382	26,223
Child and early years officers	3233	18	478.4	483.5	15	23,831	24,178
Housing officers	3234	24	510.5	511.6	20	25,977	26,184
Counsellors	3235	x	499.2	526.3	x	25,206	26,381
Welfare and housing associate professionals n.e.c.	3239	42	439.8	458.1	32	22,805	23,678
Protective service occupations	33	99	693.6	685.3	91	35,486	35,258
Protective service occupations	331	99	693.6	685.3	91	35,486	35,258
NCOs and other ranks	3311	x	x	x	x	x	x
Police officers (sergeant and below)	3312	68	734.6	738.2	64	38,439	37,848
Fire service officers (watch manager and below)	3313	6	613.7	633.1	x	31,819	32,927
Prison service officers (below principal officer)	3314	11	473.5	500.0	10	24,730	25,549
Police community support officers	3315	7	506.6	513.6	x	26,212	26,078
Protective service associate professionals n.e.c.	3319	7	610.4	665.0	x	32,344	35,262
Culture, media and sports occupations	34	54	488.7	542.8	44	26,269	28,931
Artistic, literary and media occupations	341	22	517.5	612.2	19	27,710	32,921
Artists	3411	x	533.1	530.7	x	25,070	26,279
Authors, writers and translators	3412	7	486.9	577.1	x	25,407	29,695
Actors, entertainers and presenters	3413	x	x	x	x	x	x
Dancers and choreographers	3414	x	x	x	x	x	x
Musicians	3415	x	525.7	550.4	x	27,027	26,151
Arts officers, producers and directors	3416	7	635.4	697.8	x	36,459	39,830
Photographers, audio-visual and broadcasting equipment operators	3417	x	413.5	438.8	x	20,989	22,913
Design occupations	342	26	487.6	511.0	21	25,888	26,601
Graphic designers	3421	13	457.0	468.2	10	23,881	24,534
Product, clothing and related designers	3422	13	527.8	553.6	11	27,000	28,427
Sports and fitness occupations	344	7	421.0	437.8	x	22,267	23,454
Sports players	3441	x	x	x	x	x	x
Sports coaches, instructors and officials	3442	x	439.8	460.7	x	23,496	24,542

F8: Average Earnings Statistics

Full-time female employees on adult rates (where pay was not affected by absence) in UK

n.e.c. = not elsewhere classified
X = n/a, nil , disclosive

Occupation SOC 2010	SOC Code	Gross Weekly Pay in April 2017 Number of jobs (thousand)	Median £	Mean £	Gross Annual Pay April 2016-2017 Number of jobs (thousand)	Median £	Mean £
Fitness instructors	3443	x	368.9	380.5	x	x	20,458
Business and public service associate professionals	35	845	574.9	643.9	680	30,025	34,834
Transport associate professionals	351	x	x	1,202.3	x	x	x
Air traffic controllers	3511	x	x	x	x	x	x
Aircraft pilots and flight engineers	3512	x	x	x	x	x	x
Ship and hovercraft officers	3513	x	x	x	x	x	x
Legal associate professionals	352	34	502.5	553.6	27	26,749	29,234
Legal associate professionals	3520	34	502.5	553.6	27	26,749	29,234
Business, finance and related associate professionals	353	216	580.2	646.0	184	30,000	35,013
Estimators, valuers and assessors	3531	13	516.3	554.4	11	26,793	29,349
Brokers	3532	x	x	x	x	x	x
Insurance underwriters	3533	11	590.9	685.3	10	31,424	36,486
Finance and investment analysts and advisers	3534	43	632.4	713.5	36	31,714	38,686
Taxation experts	3535	7	849.8	974.5	x	45,582	53,804
Importers and exporters	3536	x	477.1	510.1	x	24,291	26,058
Financial and accounting technicians	3537	11	727.7	799.7	10	37,401	41,858
Financial accounts managers	3538	49	633.4	680.4	44	33,003	35,742
Business and related associate professionals n.e.c.	3539	80	492.0	536.2	64	25,451	27,624
Sales, marketing and related associate professionals	354	375	607.5	694.4	293	32,500	38,179
Buyers and procurement officers	3541	25	574.6	623.0	21	30,157	32,951
Business sales executives	3542	64	514.1	565.6	51	26,634	31,035
Marketing associate professionals	3543	77	502.3	536.8	55	26,787	29,443
Estate agents and auctioneers	3544	7	411.5	464.3	x	22,810	26,601
Sales accounts and business development managers	3545	183	747.4	837.8	147	39,749	45,788
Conference and exhibition managers and organisers	3546	19	494.8	567.3	14	27,324	31,216
Conservation and environmental associate professionals	355	x	425.5	444.6	x	22,172	23,113
Conservation and environmental associate professionals	3550	x	425.5	444.6	x	22,172	23,113
Public services and other associate professionals	356	217	529.4	566.3	175	28,011	29,739
Public services associate professionals	3561	61	535.7	569.7	54	28,732	29,991
Human resources and industrial relations officers	3562	86	532.8	571.2	65	27,901	29,841
Vocational and industrial trainers and instructors	3563	53	514.0	547.5	42	27,333	28,853
Careers advisers and vocational guidance specialists	3564	5	500.7	550.0	x	25,255	28,516
Inspectors of standards and regulations	3565	x	499.8	551.4	x	28,096	29,422
Health and safety officers	3567	8	572.9	632.8	x	29,715	33,169
Administrative and secretarial occupations	4	1,319	419.9	463.3	1,111	21,681	23,800
Administrative occupations	41	1,033	423.2	467.0	867	21,920	23,936
Administrative occupations: Government and related organisations	411	111	440.2	467.5	97	23,194	24,339
National government administrative occupations	4112	73	438.1	468.1	63	23,180	24,553
Local government administrative occupations	4113	35	443.7	463.3	31	23,277	23,916
Officers of non-governmental organisations	4114	4	447.0	496.3	x	22,159	24,175
Administrative occupations: Finance	412	246	441.6	478.9	210	22,816	24,948
Credit controllers	4121	17	434.6	443.8	14	22,559	23,260
Book-keepers, payroll managers and wages clerks	4122	129	459.9	503.2	108	23,325	26,147
Bank and post office clerks	4123	40	424.6	450.5	36	22,315	23,491
Finance officers	4124	10	457.6	492.7	9	23,553	24,908
Financial administrative occupations n.e.c.	4129	51	421.3	448.8	43	21,810	23,706
Administrative occupations: Records	413	146	403.2	427.7	124	20,607	21,873
Records clerks and assistants	4131	71	402.3	430.4	60	20,380	21,741
Pensions and insurance clerks and assistants	4132	17	393.0	413.9	13	20,732	21,834
Stock control clerks and assistants	4133	23	404.5	427.1	21	20,373	21,851
Transport and distribution clerks and assistants	4134	17	426.3	442.8	x	21,810	22,722
Library clerks and assistants	4135	6	382.9	390.5	5	19,505	19,695
Human resources administrative occupations	4138	13	406.7	428.7	11	21,445	22,602

F8: Average Earnings Statistics

Full-time female employees on adult rates (where pay was not affected by absence) in UK

n.e.c. = not elsewhere classified
X = n/a, nil, disclosive

Occupation SOC 2010	SOC Code	Gross Weekly Pay in April 2017 Number of jobs (thousand)	Median £	Mean £	Gross Annual Pay April 2016-2017 Number of jobs (thousand)	Median £	Mean £
Other administrative occupations	415	411	387.0	437.5	329	19,960	21,817
Sales administrators	4151	46	383.4	415.6	36	20,348	21,911
Other administrative occupations n.e.c.	4159	365	387.4	440.2	294	19,931	21,805
Administrative occupations: Office managers and supervisors	416	119	545.5	591.4	106	28,462	30,532
Office managers	4161	104	562.2	603.9	93	29,030	31,220
Office supervisors	4162	15	479.9	506.7	13	24,730	25,668
Secretarial and related occupations	42	286	402.5	450.2	244	20,713	23,313
Secretarial and related occupations	421	286	402.5	450.2	244	20,713	23,313
Medical secretaries	4211	25	417.3	411.9	23	20,948	20,902
Legal secretaries	4212	18	402.5	439.3	14	21,427	23,168
School secretaries	4213	11	356.4	390.4	10	18,305	20,256
Company secretaries	4214	x	549.6	601.7	x	28,118	31,782
Personal assistants and other secretaries	4215	116	518.2	551.3	102	26,934	28,522
Receptionists	4216	104	333.9	353.0	85	17,002	17,652
Typists and related keyboard occupations	4217	9	359.1	419.7	7	19,007	24,553
Skilled trades occupations	5	139	378.7	412.5	114	18,854	20,845
Skilled agricultural and related trades	51	6	357.8	396.2	x	18,536	20,070
Agricultural and related trades	511	6	357.8	396.2	x	18,536	20,070
Farmers	5111	x	323.1	411.1	x	x	21,256
Horticultural trades	5112	x	377.8	404.5	x	16,730	18,738
Gardeners and landscape gardeners	5113	x	396.9	410.7	x	20,055	21,166
Groundsmen and greenkeepers	5114	x	329.3	366.3	x	17,986	19,103
Agricultural and fishing trades n.e.c.	5119	x	x	x	x	x	x
Skilled metal, electrical and electronic trades	52	27	492.8	545.7	23	26,074	28,331
Metal forming, welding and related trades	521	x	x	x	x	x	x
Smiths and forge workers	5211	x	x	x	x	x	x
Moulders, core makers and die casters	5212	x	x	x	x	x	x
Sheet metal workers	5213	x	x	x	x	x	x
Metal plate workers, and riveters	5214	x	x	x	x	x	x
Welding trades	5215	x	x	x	x	x	x
Pipe fitters	5216	x	x	x	x	x	x
Metal machining, fitting and instrument making trades	522	11	421.3	505.6	10	22,724	25,561
Metal machining setters and setter-operators	5221	x	x	426.3	x	x	x
Tool makers, tool fitters and markers-out	5222	x	x	x	x	x	x
Metal working production and maintenance fitters	5223	9	417.4	515.7	x	23,693	26,561
Precision instrument makers and repairers	5224	x	469.0	536.2	x	25,117	25,980
Air-conditioning and refrigeration engineers	5225	x	x	x	x	x	x
Vehicle trades	523	x	427.0	474.2	x	21,570	23,889
Vehicle technicians, mechanics and electricians	5231	x	387.0	445.4	x	20,559	21,783
Vehicle body builders and repairers	5232	x	x	x	x	x	x
Vehicle paint technicians	5234	x	x	x	x	x	x
Aircraft maintenance and related trades	5235	x	x	x	x	x	x
Boat and ship builders and repairers	5236	x	x	x	x	x	x
Rail and rolling stock builders and repairers	5237	x	x	x	x	x	x
Electrical and electronic trades	524	10	523.8	584.2	x	28,355	32,143
Electricians and electrical fitters	5241	x	x	509.1	x	x	28,137
Telecommunications engineers	5242	x	570.3	567.5	x	29,678	30,456
TV, video and audio engineers	5244	x	x	x	x	x	x
IT engineers	5245	x	484.4	575.5	x	x	x
Electrical and electronic trades n.e.c.	5249	x	535.8	618.8	x	x	33,310
Skilled metal, electrical and electronic trades supervisors	525	x	642.7	697.9	x	33,062	35,502
Skilled metal, electrical and electronic trades supervisors	5250	x	642.7	697.9	x	33,062	35,502

F8: Average Earnings Statistics

Full-time female employees on adult rates (where pay was not affected by absence) in UK

n.e.c. = not elsewhere classified
X = n/a, nil, disclosive

Occupation SOC 2010	SOC Code	Gross Weekly Pay in April 2017 Number of jobs (thousand)	Median £	Mean £	Gross Annual Pay April 2016-2017 Number of jobs (thousand)	Median £	Mean £
Skilled construction and building trades	53	x	419.2	418.2	x	x	18,515
Construction and building trades	531	x	412.4	414.5	x	19,555	20,872
Steel erectors	5311	x	x	x	x	x	x
Bricklayers and masons	5312	x	x	x	x	x	x
Roofers, roof tilers and slaters	5313	x	x	x	x	x	x
Plumbers and heating and ventilating engineers	5314	x	x	x	x	x	x
Carpenters and joiners	5315	x	339.6	415.2	x	x	x
Glaziers, window fabricators and fitters	5316	x	x	x	x	x	x
Construction and building trades n.e.c.	5319	x	444.9	440.1	x	19,555	20,787
Building finishing trades	532	x	x	380.5	x	x	16,242
Plasterers	5321	x	x	x	x	x	x
Floorers and wall tilers	5322	x	x	x	x	x	x
Painters and decorators	5323	x	x	380.5	x	x	16,242
Construction and building trades supervisors	533	x	508.4	471.8	x	x	x
Construction and building trades supervisors	5330	x	508.4	471.8	x	x	x
Textiles, printing and other skilled trades	54	100	360.1	377.0	81	17,993	18,876
Textiles and garments trades	541	x	324.7	351.6	x	16,237	16,795
Weavers and knitters	5411	x	x	x	x	x	x
Upholsterers	5412	x	280.3	311.9	x	15,011	15,554
Footwear and leather working trades	5413	x	321.1	344.6	x	x	15,940
Tailors and dressmakers	5414	x	314.3	366.0	x	x	16,887
Textiles, garments and related trades n.e.c.	5419	x	x	x	x	x	x
Printing trades	542	x	341.2	356.8	x	18,342	18,681
Pre-press technicians	5421	x	x	x	x	x	x
Printers	5422	x	335.3	378.8	x	17,957	19,508
Print finishing and binding workers	5423	x	341.0	345.1	x	18,176	18,195
Food preparation and hospitality trades	543	86	360.6	377.0	68	17,953	18,825
Butchers	5431	x	367.7	388.9	x	x	x
Bakers and flour confectioners	5432	x	308.5	334.3	x	16,438	17,826
Fishmongers and poultry dressers	5433	x	310.4	331.5	x	x	14,916
Chefs	5434	39	377.8	388.3	27	18,411	19,221
Cooks	5435	18	309.0	318.0	x	15,865	16,072
Catering and bar managers	5436	22	391.3	413.7	19	19,676	20,905
Other skilled trades	544	6	380.8	409.4	x	19,030	20,767
Glass and ceramics makers, decorators and finishers	5441	x	337.2	358.6	x	17,395	18,208
Furniture makers and other craft woodworkers	5442	x	331.6	392.9	x	21,204	22,787
Florists	5443	x	365.1	386.2	x	14,866	17,539
Other skilled trades n.e.c.	5449	x	418.0	475.4	x	x	23,866
Caring, leisure and other service occupations	6	941	350.8	376.0	786	17,437	18,221
Caring personal service occupations	61	818	350.8	373.7	682	17,292	17,950
Childcare and related personal services	612	267	324.1	339.6	233	15,928	16,547
Nursery nurses and assistants	6121	95	317.0	327.7	82	15,600	16,085
Childminders and related occupations	6122	12	424.6	427.9	8	20,758	21,478
Playworkers	6123	5	321.1	343.4	x	15,503	15,856
Teaching assistants	6125	111	327.8	340.5	98	16,083	16,645
Educational support assistants	6126	44	322.8	339.2	40	15,831	16,287
Animal care and control services	613	20	352.2	372.5	16	17,438	18,454
Veterinary nurses	6131	9	395.2	404.5	6	19,970	19,696
Pest control officers	6132	x	x	x	x	x	x
Animal care services occupations n.e.c.	6139	12	320.3	348.7	9	16,548	17,631
Caring personal services	614	531	368.3	390.9	434	18,081	18,684
Nursing auxiliaries and assistants	6141	199	378.4	401.6	162	18,887	19,174
Ambulance staff (excluding paramedics)	6142	6	426.4	443.7	5	22,708	22,963
Dental nurses	6143	22	359.1	369.6	20	17,748	18,425
Houseparents and residential wardens	6144	9	413.9	465.9	7	20,180	23,756
Care workers and home carers	6145	256	352.3	378.6	207	17,138	17,869

F8: Average Earnings Statistics

Full-time female employees on adult rates (where pay was not affected by absence) in UK

n.e.c. = not elsewhere classified
X = n/a, nil , disclosive

Occupation SOC 2010	SOC Code	Gross Weekly Pay in April 2017			Gross Annual Pay April 2016-2017		
		Number of jobs (thousand)	Median £	Mean £	Number of jobs (thousand)	Median £	Mean £
Senior care workers	6146	34	376.7	398.9	30	18,295	19,318
Care escorts	6147	x	312.3	318.2	x	15,419	15,593
Undertakers, mortuary and crematorium assistants	6148	x	471.3	485.7	x	24,967	26,088
Leisure, travel and related personal service occupations	62	124	350.3	390.9	104	18,242	19,999
Leisure and travel services	621	47	404.1	457.8	43	21,945	23,521
Sports and leisure assistants	6211	8	361.0	403.7	7	18,268	20,920
Travel agents	6212	15	354.4	391.8	13	19,174	20,542
Air travel assistants	6214	17	420.0	482.2	15	22,566	24,506
Rail travel assistants	6215	6	625.8	646.3	6	31,339	32,229
Leisure and travel service occupations n.e.c.	6219	x	355.7	429.8	x	x	19,751
Hairdressers and related services	622	35	308.5	324.0	27	14,921	15,937
Hairdressers and barbers	6221	22	294.3	310.0	17	14,693	15,353
Beauticians and related occupations	6222	13	327.9	346.8	10	15,576	16,946
Housekeeping and related services	623	23	339.8	366.1	18	17,461	18,900
Housekeepers and related occupations	6231	16	326.6	352.4	13	17,002	18,302
Caretakers	6232	6	378.1	402.3	5	19,221	20,288
Cleaning and housekeeping managers and supervisors	624	19	359.4	378.1	17	17,889	18,627
Cleaning and housekeeping managers and supervisors	6240	19	359.4	378.1	17	17,889	18,627
Sales and customer service occupations	7	482	355.6	391.1	413	17,949	19,461
Sales occupations	71	282	327.0	360.8	249	16,260	17,636
Sales assistants and retail cashiers	711	228	317.4	349.3	202	15,647	16,800
Sales and retail assistants	7111	184	317.6	353.0	162	15,504	16,849
Retail cashiers and check-out operators	7112	15	296.8	308.9	16	15,082	15,224
Telephone salespersons	7113	6	350.2	378.7	6	19,291	20,646
Pharmacy and other dispensing assistants	7114	21	317.7	324.1	18	16,018	16,099
Vehicle and parts salespersons and advisers	7115	x	x	631.2	x	24,183	25,269
Sales related occupations	712	18	393.5	424.1	14	20,797	22,859
Collector salespersons and credit agents	7121	x	x	x	x	x	x
Debt, rent and other cash collectors	7122	4	348.2	386.6	x	19,366	20,698
Roundspersons and van salespersons	7123	x	x	x	x	x	x
Market and street traders and assistants	7124	x	x	x	x	x	x
Merchandisers and window dressers	7125	7	421.6	450.1	6	21,156	22,815
Sales related occupations n.e.c.	7129	7	390.9	422.5	5	23,141	24,508
Sales supervisors	713	37	377.9	401.8	33	19,224	20,571
Sales supervisors	7130	37	377.9	401.8	33	19,224	20,571
Customer service occupations	72	200	397.3	433.9	164	20,639	22,241
Customer service occupations	721	160	380.8	407.5	130	19,778	20,732
Call and contact centre occupations	7211	20	345.4	361.8	16	18,165	18,646
Telephonists	7213	x	340.7	383.2	x	20,431	20,394
Communication operators	7214	6	543.3	545.4	5	28,800	28,096
Market research interviewers	7215	x	x	386.4	x	x	x
Customer service occupations n.e.c.	7219	132	383.3	408.8	107	19,849	20,702
Customer service managers and supervisors	722	39	505.5	541.5	34	26,781	28,017
Customer service managers and supervisors	7220	39	505.5	541.5	34	26,781	28,017
Process, plant and machine operatives	8	139	354.4	396.3	114	17,950	19,784
Process, plant and machine operatives	81	119	342.2	379.4	97	17,454	18,955
Process operatives	811	42	329.4	364.5	35	17,389	18,401
Food, drink and tobacco process operatives	8111	36	322.1	361.5	29	17,156	18,266
Glass and ceramics process operatives	8112	x	x	408.1	x	17,718	19,044
Textile process operatives	8113	x	350.5	351.4	x	18,675	18,893
Chemical and related process operatives	8114	x	373.4	426.6	x	19,361	20,353
Rubber process operatives	8115	x	x	x	x	x	x

Full-time female employees on adult rates (where pay was not affected by absence) in UK

n.e.c. = not elsewhere classified
X = n/a, nil , disclosive

Occupation SOC 2010	SOC Code	Gross Weekly Pay in April 2017 Number of jobs (thousand)	Median £	Mean £	Gross Annual Pay April 2016-2017 Number of jobs (thousand)	Median £	Mean £
Plastics process operatives	8116	x	x	x	x	x	x
Metal making and treating process operatives	8117	x	x	x	x	x	x
Electroplaters	8118	x	x	x	x	x	x
Process operatives n.e.c.	8119	x	309.8	322.9	x	16,826	16,768
Plant and machine operatives	812	10	366.3	389.7	x	x	x
Paper and wood machine operatives	8121	x	337.7	358.9	x	15,122	16,471
Coal mine operatives	8122	x	x	x	x	x	x
Quarry workers and related operatives	8123	x	x	x	x	x	x
Energy plant operatives	8124	x	x	x	x	x	x
Metal working machine operatives	8125	x	334.0	379.6	x	18,859	19,664
Water and sewerage plant operatives	8126	x	393.9	438.5	x	x	x
Printing machine assistants	8127	x	348.1	382.8	x	17,829	19,526
Plant and machine operatives n.e.c.	8129	x	328.3	367.8	x	17,483	18,747
Assemblers and routine operatives	813	54	356.2	392.0	49	17,631	19,336
Assemblers (electrical and electronic products)	8131	x	352.9	393.7	x	16,550	18,274
Assemblers (vehicles and metal goods)	8132	x	423.9	505.2	x	20,745	24,889
Routine inspectors and testers	8133	14	392.3	434.1	12	20,041	21,781
Weighers, graders and sorters	8134	x	344.7	416.1	x	x	x
Tyre, exhaust and windscreen fitters	8135	x	x	x	x	x	x
Sewing machinists	8137	9	319.5	347.5	9	16,230	16,762
Assemblers and routine operatives n.e.c.	8139	23	338.6	364.2	19	17,243	18,385
Construction operatives	814	13	325.7	366.5	x	x	19,595
Scaffolders, stagers and riggers	8141	x	x	x	x	x	x
Road construction operatives	8142	x	x	x	x	x	x
Rail construction and maintenance operatives	8143	x	732.3	773.7	x	x	35,132
Construction operatives n.e.c.	8149	12	323.8	354.5	x	x	18,165
Transport and mobile machine drivers and operatives	82	20	425.0	496.3	17	21,699	24,446
Road transport drivers	821	15	423.6	447.5	12	21,110	21,726
Large goods vehicle drivers	8211	x	x	497.3	x	22,740	24,152
Van drivers	8212	8	368.2	401.7	6	17,700	19,512
Bus and coach drivers	8213	5	450.6	505.0	x	23,519	24,337
Taxi and cab drivers and chauffeurs	8214	x	x	378.9	x	x	20,092
Driving instructors	8215	x	x	x	x	x	x
Mobile machine drivers and operatives	822	x	394.5	418.5	x	19,919	21,355
Crane drivers	8221	x	x	x	x	x	x
Fork-lift truck drivers	8222	x	367.5	379.4	x	x	x
Agricultural machinery drivers	8223	x	x	x	x	x	x
Mobile machine drivers and operatives n.e.c.	8229	x	399.9	438.2	x	19,919	21,756
Other drivers and transport operatives	823	x	954.2	825.4	x	x	x
Train and tram drivers	8231	x	1,048.5	1,037.4	x	48,816	47,598
Marine and waterways transport operatives	8232	x		x			
Air transport operatives	8233	x		x			
Rail transport operatives	8234	x		x	29,717	35,175	
Other drivers and transport operatives n.e.c.	8239	x	x	346.2	x	x	x
Elementary occupations	9	413	323.6	349.0	320	16,192	17,017
Elementary trades and related occupations	91	70	336.2	358.0	55	16,881	17,425
Elementary agricultural occupations	911	7	369.3	361.6	x	16,477	17,255
Farm workers	9111	x	383.3	379.5	x	18,395	18,100
Forestry workers	9112	x	x	x	x	x	x
Fishing and other elementary agriculture occupations n.e.c.	9119	x	342.7	342.9	x	15,983	16,599
Elementary construction occupations	912	x	335.2	382.0	x	17,113	19,796
Elementary construction occupations	9120	x	335.2	382.0	x	17,113	19,796
Elementary process plant occupations	913	63	331.9	357.3	50	16,764	17,406
Industrial cleaning process occupations	9132	4	346.1	352.7	x	17,907	17,914

F8: Average Earnings Statistics

Full-time female employees on adult rates (where pay was not affected by absence) in UK

n.e.c. = not elsewhere classified
X = n/a, nil , disclosive

Occupation SOC 2010	SOC Code	Gross Weekly Pay in April 2017 Number of jobs (thousand)	Median £	Mean £	Gross Annual Pay April 2016-2017 Number of jobs (thousand)	Median £	Mean £
Packers, bottlers, canners and fillers	9134	40	328.7	356.1	34	16,741	17,411
Elementary process plant occupations n.e.c.	9139	18	328.5	360.9	13	16,635	17,248
Elementary administration and service occupations	92	343	322.2	347.2	265	16,002	16,932
Elementary administration occupations	921	25	365.4	405.0	22	21,163	21,818
Postal workers, mail sorters, messengers and couriers	9211	17	431.6	446.1	16	23,686	23,787
Elementary administration occupations n.e.c.	9219	8	313.8	322.2	6	15,884	16,322
Elementary cleaning occupations	923	74	306.9	325.5	63	15,152	15,411
Window cleaners	9231	x	x	x	x	x	x
Street cleaners	9232	x	x	x	x	x	x
Cleaners and domestics	9233	65	307.0	325.3	55	15,032	15,292
Launderers, dry cleaners and pressers	9234	8	299.9	315.6	6	15,189	15,653
Refuse and salvage occupations	9235	x	339.7	342.3	x	16,197	17,463
Vehicle valeters and cleaners	9236	x	x	431.7	x	x	23,041
Elementary cleaning occupations n.e.c.	9239	x	x	x	x	x	x
Elementary security occupations	924	19	430.2	461.7	16	22,040	23,780
Security guards and related occupations	9241	15	442.7	475.0	13	23,724	24,546
Parking and civil enforcement occupations	9242	x	466.7	476.1	x	22,949	24,143
School midday and crossing patrol occupations	9244	x	308.8	331.5	x	15,743	16,525
Elementary security occupations n.e.c.	9249	x	413.5	437.1	x	x	22,158
Elementary sales occupations	925	4	309.6	323.5	5	15,943	16,830
Shelf fillers	9251	4	303.0	320.9	4	15,735	16,807
Elementary sales occupations n.e.c.	9259	x	323.4	336.1	x	16,546	16,951
Elementary storage occupations	926	75	351.0	391.2	64	17,230	18,546
Elementary storage occupations	9260	75	351.0	391.2	64	17,230	18,546
Other elementary services occupations	927	146	301.9	311.5	96	14,680	14,632
Hospital porters	9271	x	343.3	400.7	x	17,855	19,418
Kitchen and catering assistants	9272	94	304.6	316.0	70	14,991	14,984
Waiters and waitresses	9273	28	300.0	300.2	13	14,356	13,747
Bar staff	9274	18	290.1	299.6	9	12,946	12,763
Leisure and theme park attendants	9275	x	299.1	320.8	x	x	x
Other elementary services occupations n.e.c.	9279	x	308.5	313.6	x	15,015	15,003
Not Classified		x	x	x	x	x	x

Source: *Annual Survey of Hours and Earnings, Office for National Statistics*, Tables 14.1a and 14.7a.

F9: Public sector comparable earnings

In the table below we show gross salary ranges and compare with equivalent gross salaries in the public sector

Gross salary range From (£)	To (£)	Comparable gross salaries
£10,000	£19,999	National Minimum Wage (37.5 hours pw) £14,391; Soldier (new entrant) (B) £15,080; National Living Wage (37.5 hours pw) £15,269; Clinical Support Worker (B) £17,138*; Army Private (B) £18,673*; Nurse Associate Practitioner (B) £19,603*; Clinical Support Worker (T) £20,051*
£20,000	£24,999	Nurse (B) £22,349*; Teacher (newly qualified) (B) £22,917; Nurse Associate Practitioner (T) £22,910*
£25,000	£29,999	Lance Corporal (B) £25,779*; Officer (new entrant) (B) £26,244*; Nurse Specialist (B) £26,831*; Trainee Doctor (B) £26,880*; Nurse (T) £29,034*; Corporal (B) £30,066*
£30,000	£34,999	Trainee Doctor (T) £31,113*; Lieutenant (B) £32,651*; Teacher (main scale) (T) £33,824; Sergeant (B) £33,825*; Assistant Bishop £35,260
£35,000	£39,999	Teacher (upper scale) (B) £35,927; Nurse Specialist (T) £35,933*; Dean £36,210; Staff Sergeant (B) £38,074*; Teacher (upper scale) (T) £38,633; Head Teacher (B) £39,374
£40,000	£44,999	Captain (B) £40,425*; Warrant Officer (Class 2) (B) £41,412*; Diocesan Bishop £44,380
£45,000	£59,999	Warrant Officer (Class 1) (B) £47,962*; Major (B) £50,921*; Teacher (advanced skills) (T) £59,857
£60,000	£74,999	Bishop of London £64,230; Archbishop of York £70,070; Lt Colonel (B) £71,468*
£75,000	£89,999	Member of Parliament £77,379; Consultant (B) £77,529*; Archbishop of Canterbury £81,760; Colonel (B) £86,583*
£90,000	£119,999	General Practitioner £85,298; Brigadier (B) £103,180*; Consultant (T) £104,525*; District Judges £108,171; Head Teacher (T) £109,366; Major General (B) £112,683
£120,000	£149,999	Major General (T) £124,143; Deputy Senior District Judge £126,946; Lieutenant General (B) £131,109; Circuit Judges £134,841; Senior Circuit Judges £145,614; Chancellor of the Exchequer £147,223
£150,000	£199,999	Prime Minister £155,275; Lieutenant General (T) £158,929; Chief Exec—HSE £167,500; General (B) £171,995; High Court Judge £181,566; Government Actuary (M) £192,500; General (T) £192,703
£200,000	£249,999	Lord Justice of Appeal £206,742; Director Public Prosecutions (M) £207,500; General Counsel—Department for Work & Pensions (M) £212,500; Chief Executive—Department for Communities & Local Government (M) £212,500; Chancellor of the High Court £217,409
£250,000	and over	Master of the Rolls £252,079; Lord Chief Justice £252,079; Chief of the Defence Staff (M) £257,500; Chief Executive—Civil Aviation Authority (M) £297,500; Chief Executive—Nuclear Decommissioning Authority (M) £367,500; Chief Executive—Network Rail (M) £747,500

Notes: All categories are subject to varying terms and conditions. (A), (B) and (T) indicate average, bottom and top of range or seniority for post or rank. (M) indicates midpoint of published £5,000 pay band, including taxable benefits and allowances.

* Salaries marked with an asterix are estimated. The pay review for the Armed Forces and the NHS has been delayed. Under the Agenda For Change (AFC) increases in Public Services are capped at 1%. Hence the estimates are based on the salaries for 2017/18 plus 1%. However, the Government is coming under increasing pressure to lift the 1% cap on public pay increases, so the actual salaries for 2018/19 may end up being higher than indicated.

Group G
Tax and National Insurance

G1: **Net equivalents to a range of gross annual income figures**

G2: **Illustrative net earnings calculations**

G3: **Income tax reliefs and rates**

G4: **National Insurance contributions**

G5: **VAT registration thresholds and rates**

G1: Net equivalents to a range of gross annual income figures

Gross income £pa	2006/07 Net equivalent income Employed £pa	2006/07 Net equivalent income Self-employed £pa	2007/08 Net equivalent income Employed £pa	2007/08 Net equivalent income Self-employed £pa	2008/09 Net equivalent income Employed £pa	2008/09 Net equivalent income Self-employed £pa
1,000	1,000	1,000	1,000	1,000	1,000	1,000
2,000	2,000	2,000	2,000	2,000	2,000	2,000
3,000	3,000	3,000	3,000	3,000	3,000	3,000
4,000	4,000	4,000	4,000	4,000	4,000	4,000
5,000	5,000	4,891	5,000	4,886	5,000	4,880
6,000	5,797	5,717	5,837	5,747	5,938	5,835
7,000	6,587	6,537	6,627	6,567	6,635	6,562
8,000	7,280	7,260	7,352	7,321	7,325	7,282
9,000	7,950	7,960	8,022	8,021	8,015	8,002
10,000	8,620	8,660	8,692	8,721	8,705	8,722
11,000	9,290	9,360	9,362	9,421	9,395	9,442
12,000	9,960	10,060	10,032	10,121	10,085	10,162
13,000	10,630	10,760	10,702	10,821	10,775	10,882
14,000	11,300	11,460	11,372	11,521	11,465	11,602
15,000	11,970	12,160	12,042	12,221	12,155	12,322
16,000	12,640	12,860	12,712	12,921	12,845	13,042
17,000	13,310	13,560	13,382	13,621	13,535	13,762
18,000	13,980	14,260	14,052	14,321	14,225	14,482
19,000	14,650	14,960	14,722	15,021	14,915	15,202
20,000	15,320	15,660	15,392	15,721	15,605	15,922
21,000	15,990	16,360	16,062	16,421	16,295	16,642
22,000	16,660	17,060	16,732	17,121	16,985	17,362
23,000	17,330	17,760	17,402	17,821	17,675	18,082
24,000	18,000	18,460	18,072	18,521	18,365	18,802
25,000	18,670	19,160	18,742	19,221	19,055	19,522
26,000	19,340	19,860	19,412	19,921	19,745	20,242
27,000	20,010	20,560	20,082	20,621	20,435	20,962
28,000	20,680	21,260	20,752	21,321	21,125	21,682
29,000	21,350	21,960	21,422	22,021	21,815	22,402
30,000	22,020	22,660	22,092	22,721	22,505	23,122
31,000	22,690	23,360	22,762	23,421	23,195	23,842
32,000	23,360	24,060	23,432	24,121	23,885	24,562
33,000	24,030	24,760	24,102	24,821	24,575	25,282
34,000	24,746	25,492	24,772	25,521	25,265	26,002
35,000	25,516	26,262	25,458	26,233	25,955	26,722
40,000	29,066	29,812	29,276	30,051	29,405	30,322
45,000	32,016	32,762	32,226	33,001	32,518	33,436
50,000	34,966	35,712	35,176	35,951	35,468	36,386
55,000	37,916	38,662	38,126	38,901	38,418	39,336
60,000	40,866	41,612	41,076	41,851	41,368	42,286
65,000	43,816	44,562	44,026	44,801	44,138	45,236
70,000	46,766	47,512	46,976	47,751	47,268	48,186
75,000	49,716	50,462	49,926	50,701	50,218	51,136
80,000	52,666	53,412	52,876	53,651	53,168	54,086
85,000	55,616	56,362	55,826	56,601	56,118	57,036
90,000	58,566	59,312	58,776	59,551	59,068	59,986
95,000	61,516	62,262	61,726	62,501	62,018	62,936
100,000	64,466	65,212	64,676	65,451	64,968	65,886
150,000	93,966	94,712	94,176	94,951	94,468	95,386
200,000	123,466	124,212	123,676	124,451	123,968	124,886
250,000	152,966	153,712	153,176	153,951	153,468	154,386
300,000	182,466	183,212	182,676	183,451	182,968	183,886

G1: Net equivalents to a range of gross annual income figures

	2009/10 Employed				2009/10 Self-employed			
Gross income £pa	Net equivalent income £pa	Net per £100 extra £pa	Reason		Gross income £pa	Net equivalent income £pa	Net per £100 extra £pa	Reason
1,000	1,000	100			1,000	1,000	100	
2,000	2,000	100			2,000	2,000	100	
3,000	3,000	100			3,000	3,000	100	
4,000	4,000	100			4,000	4,000	100	
5,000	5,000	100			5,075	5,075	*	← £125 NIC Class 2 payable
5,715	5,715	89	← 11% NIC Class 1 payable		5,715	5,590	92	← 8% NIC Class 4 payable
6,000	5,969	89			6,000	5,852	92	
6,475	6,391	69	← 20% tax payable		6,475	6,289	72	← 20% tax payable
7,000	6,754	69			7,000	6,667	72	
8,000	7,444	69			8,000	7,387	72	
9,000	8,134	69			9,000	8,107	72	* £2.40 x 52 weeks = £125 pa fixed for any level of income in excess of £5,075 pa. So net equivalent of £5,100 gross is £4,975.
10,000	8,824	69			10,000	8,827	72	
11,000	9,514	69			11,000	9,547	72	
12,000	10,204	69			12,000	10,267	72	
13,000	10,894	69			13,000	10,987	72	
14,000	11,584	69			14,000	11,707	72	
15,000	12,274	69			15,000	12,427	72	
16,000	12,964	69			16,000	13,147	72	
17,000	13,654	69			17,000	13,867	72	
18,000	14,344	69			18,000	14,587	72	
19,000	15,034	69			19,000	15,307	72	
20,000	15,724	69			20,000	16,027	72	
21,000	16,414	69			21,000	16,747	72	
22,000	17,104	69			22,000	17,467	72	
23,000	17,794	69			23,000	18,187	72	
24,000	18,484	69			24,000	18,907	72	
25,000	19,174	69			25,000	19,627	72	
26,000	19,864	69			26,000	20,347	72	
27,000	20,554	69			27,000	21,067	72	
28,000	21,244	69			28,000	21,787	72	
29,000	21,934	69			29,000	22,507	72	
30,000	22,624	69			30,000	23,227	72	
31,000	23,314	69			31,000	23,947	72	
32,000	24,004	69			32,000	24,667	72	
33,000	24,694	69			33,000	25,387	72	
34,000	25,384	69			34,000	26,107	72	
35,000	26,074	69			35,000	26,827	72	
37,500	27,799	69			37,500	28,627	72	
40,000	29,524	69			40,000	30,427	72	
43,875	32,197	59	← NIC Class 1 reduced to 1% and 40% tax payable		43,875	33,217	59	← NIC Class 4 reduced to 1% and 40% tax payable
45,000	32,861	59			45,000	33,881	59	
50,000	35,811	59			50,000	36,831	59	
55,000	38,761	59			55,000	39,781	59	
60,000	41,711	59			60,000	42,731	59	
65,000	44,661	59			65,000	45,681	59	
70,000	47,611	59			70,000	48,631	59	
75,000	50,561	59			75,000	51,581	59	
80,000	53,511	59			80,000	54,531	59	
85,000	56,461	59			85,000	57,481	59	
90,000	59,411	59			90,000	60,431	59	
95,000	62,361	59			95,000	63,381	59	
100,000	65,311	59			100,000	66,331	59	
150,000	94,811	59			150,000	95,831	59	
200,000	124,311	59			200,000	125,331	59	
250,000	153,811	59			250,000	154,831	59	
300,000	183,311	59			300,000	184,331	59	

Note: please refer to the earlier editions of *Facts and Figures* for data before 2008/09.

G1: Net equivalents to a range of gross annual income figures

	2010/11 Employed				2010/11 Self–employed		
Gross income £pa	Net equivalent income £pa	Net per £100 extra £pa	Reason	Gross income £pa	Net equivalent income £pa	Net per £100 extra £pa	Reason
1,000	1,000	100		1,000	1,000	100	
2,000	2,000	100		2,000	2,000	100	
3,000	3,000	100		3,000	3,000	100	
4,000	4,000	100		4,000	4,000	100	
5,000	5,000	100		5,075	5,075	*	← £125 NIC Class 2 payable
5,715	5,715	89	← 11% NIC Class 1 payable	5,715	5,590	92	← 8% NIC Class 4 payable
6,000	5,969	89		6,000	5,852	92	
6,475	6,391	69	← 20% tax payable	6,475	6,289	72	← 20% tax payable
7,000	6,754	69		7,000	6,667	72	
8,000	7,444	69		8,000	7,387	72	
9,000	8,134	69		9,000	8,107	72	* £2.40 x 52 weeks
10,000	8,824	69		10,000	8,827	72	= £125 pa fixed for any
11,000	9,514	69		11,000	9,547	72	level of income in excess of
12,000	10,204	69		12,000	10,267	72	£5,075 pa. So net
13,000	10,894	69		13,000	10,987	72	equivalent of £5,100
14,000	11,584	69		14,000	11,707	72	gross is £4,975.
15,000	12,274	69		15,000	12,427	72	
16,000	12,964	69		16,000	13,147	72	
17,000	13,654	69		17,000	13,867	72	
18,000	14,344	69		18,000	14,587	72	
19,000	15,034	69		19,000	15,307	72	
20,000	15,724	69		20,000	16,027	72	
21,000	16,414	69		21,000	16,747	72	
22,000	17,104	69		22,000	17,467	72	
23,000	17,794	69		23,000	18,187	72	
24,000	18,484	69		24,000	18,907	72	
25,000	19,174	69		25,000	19,627	72	
26,000	19,864	69		26,000	20,347	72	
27,000	20,554	69		27,000	21,067	72	
28,000	21,244	69		28,000	21,787	72	
29,000	21,934	69		29,000	22,507	72	
30,000	22,624	69		30,000	23,227	72	
31,000	23,314	69		31,000	23,947	72	
32,000	24,004	69		32,000	24,667	72	
33,000	24,694	69		33,000	25,387	72	
34,000	25,384	69		34,000	26,107	72	
35,000	26,074	69		35,000	26,827	72	
37,500	27,799	69		37,500	28,627	72	
40,000	29,524	69		40,000	30,427	72	
43,875	32,197	59	← NIC Class 1 reduced to 1% and 40% tax payable	43,875	33,217	59	← NIC Class 4 reduced to 1% and 40% tax payable
45,000	32,861	59		45,000	33,881	59	
50,000	35,811	59		50,000	36,831	59	
55,000	38,761	59		55,000	39,781	59	
60,000	41,711	59		60,000	42,731	59	
65,000	44,661	59		65,000	45,681	59	
70,000	47,611	59		70,000	48,631	59	
75,000	50,561	59		75,000	51,581	59	
80,000	53,511	59		80,000	54,531	59	
85,000	56,461	59		85,000	57,481	59	
90,000	59,411	59		90,000	60,431	59	
95,000	62,361	59		95,000	63,381	59	
100,000	65,311	39	← PA reduces here	100,000	66,331	39	← PA reduces here
112,950	70,362	59	← PA reduced to zero	112,950	71,381	59	← PA reduced to zero
150,000	92,221	49	← 50% tax payable	150,000	93,241	49	← 50% tax payable
200,000	116,721	49		200,000	117,741	49	
250,000	141,221	49		250,000	142,241	49	
300,000	165,721	49		300,000	166,741	49	

G1: Net equivalents to a range of gross annual income figures

	2011/12 Employed				2011/12 Self–employed		
Gross income £pa	Net equivalent income £pa	Net per £100 extra £pa	Reason	Gross income £pa	Net equivalent income £pa	Net per £100 extra £pa	Reason
1,000	1,000	100		1,000	1,000	100	
2,000	2,000	100		2,000	2,000	100	
3,000	3,000	100		3,000	3,000	100	
4,000	4,000	100		4,000	4,000	100	
5,000	5,000	100		5,315	5,315	*	← £130 NIC Class 2 payable
6,000	6,000	100		6,000	5,870	*	
7,000	7,000	100		7,000	6,870	*	
7,225	7,225	88	← 12% NIC Class 1 payable	7,225	7,095	91	← 9% NIC Class 4 payable
7,475	7,445	68	← 20% tax payable	7,475	7,322	71	← 20% tax payable
8,000	7,802	68		8,000	7,695	71	
9,000	8,482	68		9,000	8,405	71	* £2.50 x 52 weeks
10,000	9,162	68		10,000	9,115	71	= £130 pa fixed for any
11,000	9,842	68		11,000	9,825	71	level of income in excess of
12,000	10,522	68		12,000	10,535	71	£5,315 pa. So net
13,000	11,202	68		13,000	11,245	71	equivalent of £5,400
14,000	11,882	68		14,000	11,955	71	gross is £5,270.
15,000	12,562	68		15,000	12,665	71	
16,000	13,242	68		16,000	13,375	71	
17,000	13,922	68		17,000	14,085	71	
18,000	14,602	68		18,000	14,795	71	
19,000	15,282	68		19,000	15,505	71	
20,000	15,962	68		20,000	16,215	71	
21,000	16,642	68		21,000	16,925	71	
22,000	17,322	68		22,000	17,635	71	
23,000	18,002	68		23,000	18,345	71	
24,000	18,682	68		24,000	19,055	71	
25,000	19,362	68		25,000	19,765	71	
26,000	20,042	68		26,000	20,475	71	
27,000	20,722	68		27,000	21,185	71	
28,000	21,402	68		28,000	21,895	71	
29,000	22,082	68		29,000	22,605	71	
30,000	22,762	68		30,000	23,315	71	
31,000	23,442	68		31,000	24,025	71	
32,000	24,122	68		32,000	24,735	71	
33,000	24,802	68		33,000	25,445	71	
34,000	25,482	68		34,000	26,155	71	
35,000	26,162	68		35,000	26,865	71	
37,500	27,862	68		37,500	28,640	71	
40,000	29,562	68		40,000	30,415	71	
42,475	31,245	58	← NIC Class 1 reduced to 2% and 40% tax payable	42,475	32,172	58	← NIC Class 4 reduced to 2% and 40% tax payable
45,000	32,709	58		45,000	33,636	58	
50,000	35,609	58		50,000	36,536	58	
55,000	38,509	58		55,000	39,436	58	
60,000	41,409	58		60,000	42,336	58	
65,000	44,309	58		65,000	45,236	58	
70,000	47,209	58		70,000	48,136	58	
75,000	50,109	58		75,000	51,036	58	
80,000	53,009	58		80,000	53,936	58	
85,000	55,909	58		85,000	56,836	58	
90,000	58,809	58		90,000	59,736	58	
95,000	61,709	58		95,000	62,636	58	
100,000	64,609	38	← PA reduces here	100,000	65,536	38	← PA reduces here
114,950	70,290	58	← PA reduced to zero	114,950	71,217	58	← PA reduced to zero
150,000	90,619	48	← 50% tax payable	150,000	91,546	48	← 50% tax payable
200,000	114,619	48		200,000	115,546	48	
250,000	138,619	48		250,000	139,546	48	
300,000	162,619	48		300,000	163,546	48	

G1: Net equivalents to a range of gross annual income figures

	2012/13 Employed				2012/13 Self-employed		
Gross income £pa	Net equivalent income £pa	Net per £100 extra £pa	Reason	Gross income £pa	Net equivalent income £pa	Net per £100 extra £pa	Reason
1,000	1,000	100		1,000	1,000	100	
2,000	2,000	100		2,000	2,000	100	
3,000	3,000	100		3,000	3,000	100	
4,000	4,000	100		4,000	4,000	100	
5,000	5,000	100		5,595	5,595	*	← £130 NIC Class 2 payable
6,000	6,000	100		6,000	5,862	*	
7,000	7,000	100		7,000	6,862	*	
7,605	7,605	88	← 12% NIC Class 1 payable	7,605	7,467	91	← 9% NIC Class 4 payable
8,000	7,953	88		8,000	7,826	91	
8,105	8,045	68	← 20% tax payable	8,105	7,922	71	← 20% tax payable
9,000	8,654	68		9,000	8,557	71	* £2.65 x 52 weeks
10,000	9,334	68		10,000	9,267	71	= £138 pa fixed for any level of income in excess of £5,595 pa. So net equivalent of £5,600 gross is £5,462.
11,000	10,014	68		11,000	9,977	71	
12,000	10,694	68		12,000	10,687	71	
13,000	11,374	68		13,000	11,397	71	
14,000	12,054	68		14,000	12,107	71	
15,000	12,734	68		15,000	12,817	71	
16,000	13,414	68		16,000	13,527	71	
17,000	14,094	68		17,000	14,237	71	
18,000	14,774	68		18,000	14,947	71	
19,000	15,454	68		19,000	15,657	71	
20,000	16,134	68		20,000	16,367	71	
21,000	16,814	68		21,000	17,077	71	
22,000	17,494	68		22,000	17,787	71	
23,000	18,174	68		23,000	18,497	71	
24,000	18,854	68		24,000	19,207	71	
25,000	19,534	68		25,000	19,917	71	
26,000	20,214	68		26,000	20,627	71	
27,000	20,894	68		27,000	21,337	71	
28,000	21,574	68		28,000	22,047	71	
29,000	22,254	68		29,000	22,757	71	
30,000	22,934	68		30,000	23,467	71	
31,000	23,614	68		31,000	24,177	71	
32,000	24,294	68		32,000	24,887	71	
33,000	24,974	68		33,000	25,597	71	
34,000	25,654	68		34,000	26,307	71	
35,000	26,334	68		35,000	27,017	71	
37,500	28,034	68		37,500	28,792	71	
40,000	29,734	68		40,000	30,567	71	
42,475	31,417	58	← NIC Class 1 reduced to 2% and 40% tax payable	42,475	32,325	58	← NIC Class 4 reduced to 2% and 40% tax payable
45,000	32,881	58		45,000	33,789	58	
50,000	35,781	58		50,000	36,689	58	
55,000	38,681	58		55,000	39,589	58	
60,000	41,581	58		60,000	42,489	58	
65,000	44,481	58		65,000	45,389	58	
70,000	47,381	58		70,000	48,289	58	
75,000	50,281	58		75,000	51,189	58	
80,000	53,181	58		80,000	54,089	58	
85,000	56,081	58		85,000	56,989	58	
90,000	58,981	58		90,000	59,889	58	
95,000	61,881	58		95,000	62,789	58	
100,000	64,781	38	← PA reduces here	100,000	65,689	38	← PA reduces here
116,210	70,941	58	← PA reduced to zero	116,210	70,610	58	← PA reduced to zero
150,000	90,539	48	← 50% tax payable	150,000	91,447	48	← 50% tax payable
200,000	114,539	48		200,000	115,447	48	
250,000	138,539	48		250,000	139,447	48	
300,000	162,539	48		300,000	163,447	48	

G1: Net equivalents to a range of gross annual income figures

	2013/14 Employed				2013/14 Self-employed		
Gross income £pa	Net equivalent income £pa	Net per £100 extra £pa	Reason	Gross income £pa	Net equivalent income £pa	Net per £100 extra £pa	Reason
1,000	1,000	100		1,000	1,000	100	
2,000	2,000	100		2,000	2,000	100	
3,000	3,000	100		3,000	3,000	100	
4,000	4,000	100		4,000	4,000	100	
5,000	5,000	100		5,725	5,725	*	← £140 NIC Class 2 payable
6,000	6,000	100		6,000	5,860	*	
7,000	7,000	100		7,000	6,860	*	
7,755	7,755	88	← 12% NIC Class 1 payable	7,755	7,615	91	← 9% NIC Class 4 payable
8,000	7,971	88		8,000	7,838	91	
9,000	8,851	88		9,000	8,748	91	
9,440	9,238	68	← 20% tax payable	9,440	9,148	71	← 20% tax payable
10,000	9,619	68		10,000	9,546	71	* £2.70 x 52 weeks
11,000	10,299	68		11,000	10,256	71	= £140 pa fixed for any
12,000	10,979	68		12,000	10,966	71	level of income in excess of
13,000	11,659	68		13,000	11,676	71	£5,725 pa. So net
14,000	12,339	68		14,000	12,386	71	equivalent of £6,100
15,000	13,019	68		15,000	13,096	71	gross is £5,960.
16,000	13,699	68		16,000	13,806	71	
17,000	14,379	68		17,000	14,516	71	
18,000	15,059	68		18,000	15,226	71	
19,000	15,739	68		19,000	15,936	71	
20,000	16,419	68		20,000	16,646	71	
21,000	17,099	68		21,000	17,356	71	
22,000	17,779	68		22,000	18,066	71	
23,000	18,459	68		23,000	18,776	71	
24,000	19,139	68		24,000	19,486	71	
25,000	19,819	68		25,000	20,196	71	
26,000	20,499	68		26,000	20,906	71	
27,000	21,179	68		27,000	21,616	71	
28,000	21,859	68		28,000	22,326	71	
29,000	22,539	68		29,000	23,036	71	
30,000	23,219	68		30,000	23,746	71	
31,000	23,899	68		31,000	24,456	71	
32,000	24,579	68		32,000	25,166	71	
33,000	25,259	68		33,000	25,876	71	
34,000	25,939	68		34,000	26,586	71	
35,000	26,619	68		35,000	27,296	71	
37,500	28,319	68		37,500	29,071	71	
40,000	30,019	68		40,000	30,846	71	
41,450	31,005	58	← NIC Class 1 reduced	41,450	31,875	58	← NIC Class 4 reduced to
45,000	33,064	58	to 2% and 40% tax	45,000	33,934	58	2% and 40% tax payable
50,000	35,964	58	payable	50,000	36,834	58	
55,000	38,864	58		55,000	39,734	58	
60,000	41,764	58		60,000	42,634	58	
65,000	44,664	58		65,000	45,534	58	
70,000	47,564	58		70,000	48,434	58	
75,000	50,464	58		75,000	51,334	58	
80,000	53,364	58		80,000	54,234	58	
85,000	56,264	58		85,000	57,134	58	
90,000	59,164	58		90,000	60,034	58	
95,000	62,064	58		95,000	62,934	58	
100,000	64,964	38	← PA reduces here	100,000	65,834	38	← PA reduces here
118,880	72,138	58	← PA reduced to zero	118,880	73,008	58	← PA reduced to zero
150,000	90,188	53	← 45% tax payable	150,000	91,058	53	← 45% tax payable
200,000	116,688	53		200,000	117,558	53	
250,000	143,188	53		250,000	144,058	53	
300,000	169,688	53		300,000	170,558	53	

G1: Net equivalents to a range of gross annual income figures

	2014/15 Employed				2014/15 Self-employed		
Gross income £pa	Net equivalent income £pa	Net per £100 extra £pa	Reason	Gross income £pa	Net equivalent income £pa	Net per £100 extra £pa	Reason
1,000	1,000	100		1,000	1,000	100	
2,000	2,000	100		2,000	2,000	100	
3,000	3,000	100		3,000	3,000	100	
4,000	4,000	100		4,000	4,000	100	
5,000	5,000	100		5,885	5,885	*	← £143 NIC Class 2 payable
6,000	6,000	100		6,000	5,857	*	
7,000	7,000	100		7,000	6,857	*	
7,956	7,956	88	← 12% NIC Class 1 payable	7,956	7,813	91	← 9% NIC Class 4 payable
8,000	7,995	88		8,000	7,853	91	
9,000	8,875	88		9,000	8,763	91	
10,000	9,755	68	← 20% tax payable	10,000	9,673	71	← 20% tax payable
11,000	10,435	68		11,000	10,383	71	* £2.75 x 52 weeks
12,000	11,115	68		12,000	11,093	71	= £143 pa fixed for any
13,000	11,795	68		13,000	11,803	71	level of income in excess of
14,000	12,475	68		14,000	12,513	71	£5,885 pa. So net
15,000	13,155	68		15,000	13,223	71	equivalent of £6,100
16,000	13,835	68		16,000	13,933	71	gross is £5,957.
17,000	14,515	68		17,000	14,643	71	
18,000	15,195	68		18,000	15,353	71	
19,000	15,875	68		19,000	16,063	71	
20,000	16,555	68		20,000	16,773	71	
21,000	17,235	68		21,000	17,483	71	
22,000	17,915	68		22,000	18,193	71	
23,000	18,595	68		23,000	18,903	71	
24,000	19,275	68		24,000	19,613	71	
25,000	19,955	68		25,000	20,323	71	
26,000	20,635	68		26,000	21,033	71	
27,000	21,315	68		27,000	21,743	71	
28,000	21,995	68		28,000	22,453	71	
29,000	22,675	68		29,000	23,163	71	
30,000	23,355	68		30,000	23,873	71	
31,000	24,035	68		31,000	24,583	71	
32,000	24,715	68		32,000	25,293	71	
33,000	25,395	68		33,000	26,003	71	
34,000	26,075	68		34,000	26,713	71	
35,000	26,755	68		35,000	27,423	71	
37,500	28,455	68		37,500	29,198	71	
40,000	30,155	68		40,000	30,973	71	
41,865	31,423	58	← NIC Class 1 reduced to 2% and 40% tax payable	41,865	32,297	58	← NIC Class 4 reduced to 2% and 40% tax payable
45,000	33,241	58		45,000	34,115	58	
50,000	36,141	58		50,000	37,015	58	
55,000	39,041	58		55,000	39,915	58	
60,000	41,941	58		60,000	42,815	58	
65,000	44,841	58		65,000	45,715	58	
70,000	47,741	58		70,000	48,615	58	
75,000	50,641	58		75,000	51,515	58	
80,000	53,541	58		80,000	54,415	58	
85,000	56,441	58		85,000	57,315	58	
90,000	59,341	58		90,000	60,215	58	
95,000	62,241	58		95,000	63,115	58	
100,000	65,141	38	← PA reduces here	100,000	66,015	38	← PA reduces here
120,000	72,741	58	← PA reduced to zero	120,000	73,615	58	← PA reduced to zero
150,000	90,141	53	← 45% tax payable	150,000	91,015	53	← 45% tax payable
200,000	116,641	53		200,000	117,515	53	
250,000	143,141	53		250,000	144,015	53	
300,000	169,641	53		300,000	170,515	53	

G1: Net equivalents to a range of gross annual income figures

	2015/16 Employed				2015/16 Self-employed		
Gross income £pa	Net equivalent income £pa	Net per £100 extra £pa	Reason	Gross income £pa	Net equivalent income £pa	Net per £100 extra £pa	Reason
1,000	1,000	100		1,000	1,000	100	
2,000	2,000	100		2,000	2,000	100	
3,000	3,000	100		3,000	3,000	100	
4,000	4,000	100		4,000	4,000	100	
5,000	5,000	100		5,965	5,965	*	← £146 NIC Class 2 payable
6,000	6,000	100		6,000	5,854	*	
7,000	7,000	100		7,000	6,854	*	
8,000	8,000	100		8,000	7,854	*	
8,060	8,060	88	← 12% NIC Class 1 payable	8,060	7,914	91	← 9% NIC Class 4 payable
9,000	8,887	88		9,000	8,769	91	
10,000	9,767	68	← 20% tax payable	10,000	9,679	91	
10,600	10,295	68		10,600	10,225	71	← 20% tax payable
11,000	10,567	68		11,000	10,509	71	* £2.80 x 52 weeks
12,000	11,247	68		12,000	11,219	71	= £146 pa fixed for any
13,000	11,927	68		13,000	11,929	71	level of income in excess of
14,000	12,607	68		14,000	12,639	71	£5,965 pa. So net
15,000	13,287	68		15,000	13,349	71	equivalent of £6,100
16,000	13,967	68		16,000	14,059	71	gross is £5,954.
17,000	14,647	68		17,000	14,769	71	
18,000	15,327	68		18,000	15,479	71	
19,000	16,007	68		19,000	16,189	71	
20,000	16,687	68		20,000	16,899	71	
21,000	17,367	68		21,000	17,609	71	
22,000	18,047	68		22,000	18,319	71	
23,000	18,727	68		23,000	19,029	71	
24,000	19,407	68		24,000	19,739	71	
25,000	20,087	68		25,000	20,449	71	
26,000	20,767	68		26,000	21,159	71	
27,000	21,447	68		27,000	21,869	71	
28,000	22,127	68		28,000	22,579	71	
29,000	22,807	68		29,000	23,289	71	
30,000	23,487	68		30,000	23,999	71	
31,000	24,167	68		31,000	24,709	71	
32,000	24,847	68		32,000	25,419	71	
33,000	25,527	68		33,000	26,129	71	
34,000	26,207	68		34,000	26,839	71	
35,000	26,887	68		35,000	27,549	71	
37,500	28,587	68		37,500	29,324	71	
40,000	30,287	68		40,000	31,099	71	
42,385	31,909	58	← NIC Class 1 reduced to 2% and 40% tax payable	42,385	32,793	58	← NIC Class 4 reduced to 2% and 40% tax payable
45,000	33,426	58		45,000	34,310	58	
50,000	36,326	58		50,000	37,210	58	
55,000	39,226	58		55,000	40,110	58	
60,000	42,126	58		60,000	43,010	58	
65,000	45,026	58		65,000	45,910	58	
70,000	47,926	58		70,000	48,810	58	
75,000	50,826	58		75,000	51,710	58	
80,000	53,726	58		80,000	54,610	58	
85,000	56,626	58		85,000	57,510	58	
90,000	59,526	58		90,000	60,410	58	
95,000	62,426	58		95,000	63,310	58	
100,000	65,326	38	← PA reduces here	100,000	66,210	38	← PA reduces here
121,200	73,382	53	← PA reduced to zero	121,200	74,266	58	← PA reduced to zero
150,000	90,086	53	← 45% tax payable	150,000	90,970	53	← 45% tax payable
200,000	116,586	53		200,000	117,470	53	
250,000	143,086	53		250,000	143,970	53	
300,000	169,586	53		300,000	170,470	53	

G1: Net equivalents to a range of gross annual income figures

	2016/17 Employed				2016/17 Self-employed		
Gross income £pa	Net equivalent income £pa	Net per £100 extra £pa	Reason	Gross income £pa	Net equivalent income £pa	Net per £100 extra £pa	Reason
1,000	1,000	100		1,000	1,000	100	
2,000	2,000	100		2,000	2,000	100	
3,000	3,000	100		3,000	3,000	100	
4,000	4,000	100		4,000	4,000	100	← £146 NIC Class 2 payable
5,000	5,000	100		5,965	5,965	*	
6,000	6,000	100		6,000	5,854	*	
7,000	7,000	100		7,000	6,854	*	
8,000	8,000	100		8,000	7,854	*	← 9% NIC Class 4 payable
8,060	*8,060*	*88*	← 12% NIC Class 1 payable	*8,060*	*7,914*	*91*	
9,000	8,887	88		9,000	8,769	91	
10,000	9,767	88		10,000	9,679	91	
11,000	10,647	68	← 20% tax payable	11,000	10,589	71	← 20% tax payable
12,000	11,327	68		12,000	11,299	71	* £2.80 x 52 weeks
13,000	12,007	68		13,000	12,009	71	= £146 pa fixed for any
14,000	12,687	68		14,000	12,719	71	level of income in excess of
15,000	13,367	68		15,000	13,429	71	£5,965 pa. So net
16,000	14,047	68		16,000	14,139	71	equivalent of £6,100
17,000	14,727	68		17,000	14,849	71	gross is £5,954.
18,000	15,407	68		18,000	15,559	71	
19,000	16,087	68		19,000	16,269	71	
20,000	16,767	68		20,000	16,979	71	
21,000	17,447	68		21,000	17,689	71	
22,000	18,127	68		22,000	18,399	71	
23,000	18,807	68		23,000	19,109	71	
24,000	19,487	68		24,000	19,819	71	
25,000	20,167	68		25,000	20,529	71	
26,000	20,847	68		26,000	21,239	71	
27,000	21,527	68		27,000	21,949	71	
28,000	22,207	68		28,000	22,659	71	
29,000	22,887	68		29,000	23,369	71	
30,000	23,567	68		30,000	24,079	71	
31,000	24,247	68		31,000	24,789	71	
32,000	24,927	68		32,000	25,499	71	
33,000	25,607	68		33,000	26,209	71	
34,000	26,287	68		34,000	26,919	71	
35,000	26,967	68		35,000	27,629	71	
37,500	28,667	68		37,500	29,404	71	
40,000	30,367	68		40,000	31,179	71	
43,000	*32,407*	*58*	← NIC Class 1 reduced to 2% and 40% tax payable	*43,000*	*33,309*	*58*	← NIC Class 4 reduced to 2% and 40% tax payable
45,000	33,567	58		45,000	34,469	58	
50,000	36,467	58		50,000	37,369	58	
55,000	39,367	58		55,000	40,269	58	
60,000	42,267	58		60,000	43,169	58	
65,000	45,167	58		65,000	46,069	58	
70,000	48,067	58		70,000	48,969	58	
75,000	50,967	58		75,000	51,869	58	
80,000	53,867	58		80,000	54,769	58	
85,000	56,767	58		85,000	57,669	58	
90,000	59,667	58		90,000	60,569	58	
95,000	62,567	58		95,000	63,469	58	
100,000	65,467	38	← PA reduces here	100,000	66,369	38	← PA reduces here
122,000	*73,827*	*58*	← PA reduced to zero	*122,000*	*74,729*	*58*	← PA reduced to zero
150,000	90,067	53	← 45% tax payable	150,000	90,969	53	← 45% tax payable
200,000	116,567	53		200,000	117,469	53	
250,000	143,067	53		250,000	143,969	53	
300,000	169,567	53		300,000	170,469	53	

G1: Net equivalents to a range of gross annual income figures

	2017/18 Employed				2017/18 Self-employed		
Gross income £pa	Net equivalent income £pa	Net per £100 extra £pa	Reason	Gross income £pa	Net equivalent income £pa	Net per £100 extra £pa	Reason
1,000	1,000	100		1,000	1,000	100	
2,000	2,000	100		2,000	2,000	100	
3,000	3,000	100		3,000	3,000	100	
4,000	4,000	100		4,000	4,000	100	
5,000	5,000	100		5,000	5,000	*	
6,000	6,000	100		6,025	5,877	*	← Class 2 NI payable at £2.85 a week
7,000	7,000	100		7,000	6,852	100	
8,000	8,000	100		8,000	7,852	100	
8,164	8,164	88	← Class 1 NI payable at 12%	8,164	8,016	91	← Class 4 NI payable at 9%
9,000	8,900	88		9,000	8,777	91	
10,000	9,780	88		10,000	9,687	91	
11,000	10,660	78		11,000	10,597	81	
11,500	11,100	68	← Income tax payable at 20%	11,500	11,052	71	← Income tax payable at 20%
12,000	11,440	68		12,000	11,407	71	
13,000	12,120	68		13,000	12,117	71	
14,000	12,800	68		14,000	12,827	71	
15,000	13,480	68		15,000	13,537	71	
16,000	14,160	68		16,000	14,247	71	
17,000	14,840	68		17,000	14,957	71	
18,000	15,520	68		18,000	15,667	71	
19,000	16,200	68		19,000	16,377	71	
20,000	16,880	68		20,000	17,087	71	
21,000	17,560	68		21,000	17,797	71	
22,000	18,240	68		22,000	18,507	71	
23,000	18,920	68		23,000	19,217	71	
24,000	19,600	68		24,000	19,927	71	
25,000	20,280	68		25,000	20,637	71	
26,000	20,960	68		26,000	21,347	71	
27,000	21,640	68		27,000	22,057	71	
28,000	22,320	68		28,000	22,767	71	
29,000	23,000	68		29,000	23,477	71	
30,000	23,680	68		30,000	24,187	71	
31,000	24,360	68		31,000	24,897	71	
32,000	25,040	68		32,000	25,607	71	
33,000	25,720	68		33,000	26,317	71	
34,000	26,400	68		34,000	27,027	71	
35,000	27,080	68		35,000	27,737	71	
37,500	28,780	68		37,500	29,512	71	
40,000	30,480	68		40,000	31,287	71	
42,500	32,180	68		42,500	33,062	71	
45,000	33,880	*	← Income tax payable at 40%	45,000	34,837	58	← Income tax payable at 40% and NI payable at 2%
45,032	33,895	58	← NI payable at 2%	47,500	36,287	58	
50,000	36,776	58		50,000	37,737	58	
55,000	39,676	58		55,000	40,637	58	
60,000	42,576	58		60,000	43,537	58	
65,000	45,476	58		65,000	46,437	58	
70,000	48,376	58		70,000	49,337	58	
75,000	51,276	58		75,000	52,237	58	
80,000	54,176	58		80,000	55,137	58	
85,000	57,076	58		85,000	58,037	58	
90,000	59,976	58		90,000	60,937	58	
95,000	62,876	58		95,000	63,837	58	
100,000	65,776	38	← PA reduces here	100,000	66,737	38	← PA reduces here
123,000	74,516	58	← PA reduced to zero	123,000	75,477	58	← PA reduced to zero
150,000	90,176	53	← Income tax payable at 45%	150,000	91,137	53	← Income tax payable at 45%
200,000	116,676	53		200,000	117,637	53	
250,000	143,176	53		250,000	144,137	53	
300,000	169,676	53		300,000	170,637	53	

G1: Net equivalents to a range of gross annual income figures

	2018/19 Employed				2018/19 Self-employed		
Gross income £pa	Net equivalent income £pa	Net per £100 extra £pa	Reason	Gross income £pa	Net equivalent income £pa	Net per £100 extra £pa	Reason
1,000	1,000	100		1,000	1,000	100	
2,000	2,000	100		2,000	2,000	100	
3,000	3,000	100		3,000	3,000	100	
4,000	4,000	100		4,000	4,000	100	
5,000	5,000	100		5,000	5,000	*	
6,000	6,000	100		6,205	6,052	100	← Class 2 NI payable at £2.95 a week
7,000	7,000	100		7,000	6,852	100	
8,000	8,000	100		8,000	7,847	100	
8,424	8,424	88	← Class 1 NI payable at 12%	8,424	8,271	91	← Class 4 NI payable at 9%
9,000	8,931	88		9,000	8,795	91	
10,000	9,811	88		10,000	9,705	91	
11,000	10,691	88		11,000	10,615	91	
11,850	11,439	68	← Income tax payable at 20%	11,850	11,388	71	← Income tax payable at 20%
12,000	11,541	68		12,000	11,495	71	
13,000	12,221	68		13,000	12,205	71	
14,000	12,901	68		14,000	12,915	71	
15,000	13,581	68		15,000	13,625	71	
16,000	14,261	68		16,000	14,335	71	
17,000	14,941	68		17,000	15,045	71	
18,000	15,621	68		18,000	15,755	71	
19,000	16,301	68		19,000	16,465	71	
20,000	16,981	68		20,000	17,175	71	
21,000	17,661	68		21,000	17,885	71	
22,000	18,341	68		22,000	18,595	71	
23,000	19,021	68		23,000	19,305	71	
24,000	19,701	68		24,000	20,015	71	
25,000	20,381	68		25,000	20,725	71	
26,000	21,061	68		26,000	21,435	71	
27,000	21,741	68		27,000	22,145	71	
28,000	22,421	68		28,000	22,855	71	
29,000	23,101	68		29,000	23,565	71	
30,000	23,781	68		30,000	24,275	71	
31,000	24,461	68		31,000	24,985	71	
32,000	25,141	68		32,000	25,695	71	
33,000	25,821	68		33,000	26,405	71	
34,000	26,501	68		34,000	27,115	71	
35,000	27,181	68		35,000	27,825	71	
37,500	28,881	68		37,500	29,600	71	
40,000	30,581	68		40,000	31,375	71	
42,500	32,281	68		42,500	33,150	71	
45,000	33,981	68		45,000	34,925	71	
46,350	34,899	*	← Income tax payable at 40%	46,350	35,883	58	← Income tax payable at 40% and NI payable at 2%
46,384	34,915	58	← NI payable at 2%	47,500	36,550	58	
50,000	37,012	58		50,000	38,000	58	
55,000	39,912	58		55,000	40,900	58	
60,000	42,812	58		60,000	43,800	58	
65,000	45,712	58		65,000	46,700	58	
70,000	48,612	58		70,000	49,600	58	
75,000	51,512	58		75,000	52,500	58	
80,000	54,412	58		80,000	55,400	58	
85,000	57,312	58		85,000	58,300	58	
90,000	60,212	58		90,000	61,200	58	
95,000	63,112	58		95,000	64,100	58	
100,000	66,012	38	← PA reduces here	100,000	67,000	38	← PA reduces here
123,700	75,018	58	← PA reduced to zero	123,700	76,006	58	← PA reduced to zero
150,000	90,272	53	← Income tax payable at 45%	150,000	91,260	53	← Income tax payable at 45%
200,000	116,772	53		200,000	117,760	53	
250,000	143,272	53		250,000	144,260	53	
300,000	169,772	53		300,000	170,760	53	

G2: Illustrative net earnings calculations

Man under 65 at 2018/19 tax rates

		Employed person						Self-employed person			
		£pa	£pa	£pa	£pa	£pa	£pa	£pa	£pa	£pa	£pa
Gross income	[a]	15,000	35,000	50,000	110,000	160,000		15,000	35,000	50,000	110,000	160,000
Income tax												
Gross		15,000	35,000	50,000	110,000	160,000		15,000	35,000	50,000	110,000	160,000
Personal allowance (note 1)		(11,850)	(11,850)	(11,850)	(6,850)	–		(11,850)	(11,850)	(11,850)	(6,850)	–
Taxable		3,150	23,150	38,150	103,150	160,000		3,150	23,150	38,150	103,150	160,000
Tax payable												
– At 20%		600	4,630	6,900	6,900	6,900		630	4,630	6,900	6,900	6,900
– At 40%				1,460	27,460	46,200				1,460	27,460	46,200
– At 45%						4,500						4,500
	[b]	630	4,630	8,360	34,360	57,600		630	4,630	8,360	34,360	57,600
National insurance												
Class 1												
– At 12%		789	3,189	4,555	4,555	4,555						
– At 2%		0	0	72	1,272	2,272						
Class 2								153	153	153	153	153
Class 4												
– At 9%								592	2,392	3,413	3,413	3,413
– At 2%								0	0	73	1,273	2,273
	[c]	789	3,189	4,628	5,828	6,828		745	2,545	3,640	4,840	5,840
Net income	[a–b–c]	13,581	27,181	37,012	69,812	95,572		13,625	27,825	38,000	70,800	96,560
Note 1: personal allowance												
Personal allowance		11,850	11,850	11,850	11,850	11,850		11,850	11,850	11,850	11,850	11,850
Restriction for excess of income over limit*		–	–	–	(5,000)	(11,850)		–	–	–	(5,000)	(11,850)
Net allowance		11,850	11,850	11,850	6,850	0		11,850	11,850	11,850	6,850	0

*If gross income does not exceed £100,000, no restriction.
If gross income does exceed £100,000, restriction is the lower of:
(a) (gross pay–£100,000)/2, and
(b) £11,850

G3: Income tax reliefs and rates

Introductory notes

Personal allowance

Every taxpayer resident in the UK (as well as certain non-UK residents) is entitled to a personal allowance.

From 2010/11, the personal allowance has been subject to an income limit of £100,000. Where total income exceeds this limit, the personal allowance is reduced by 50 per cent of the excess. Accordingly, no personal allowance is available on incomes in excess of £123,700 in 2018/19.

Age-related personal allowance

The age-related personal allowance has been frozen from 2012/13 onwards and from 2016/17 onwards all individuals are entitled to the same personal allowance, regardless of the individuals' date of birth.

Age-related married couple's allowance

Where a couple was married before 5 December 2005, live together and at least one spouse was born before 6 April 1935, the husband can claim married couple's allowance.

Where a couple married or entered into a civil partnership on or after 5 December 2005, live together and at least one spouse or partner was born before 6 April 1935, the person with the higher income can claim married couple's allowance.

For 2018/19 the allowance is £8,695 and the rate of tax relief is 10 per cent, subject to an income limit—£28,900 for 2018/19.

Where the claimant's income exceeds the income limit, the married couple's allowance is reduced by 50 per cent of the excess less any reduction of the personal allowance (as above), until the allowance is equal to the following amounts:

Tax year	Minimum allowance	Tax relief
Tax year 2006/07	Minimum allowance £2,350	Tax relief £235
Tax year 2007/08	Minimum allowance £2,440	Tax relief £244
Tax year 2008/09	Minimum allowance £2,540	Tax relief £254
Tax year 2009/10	Minimum allowance £2,670	Tax relief £267
Tax year 2010/11	Minimum allowance £2,670	Tax relief £267
Tax year 2011/12	Minimum allowance £2,800	Tax relief £280
Tax year 2012/13	Minimum allowance £2,960	Tax relief £296
Tax year 2013/14	Minimum allowance £3,040	Tax relief £304
Tax year 2014/15	Minimum allowance £3,140	Tax relief £314
Tax year 2015/16	Minimum allowance £3,220	Tax relief £322
Tax year 2016/17	Minimum allowance £3,220	Tax relief £322
Tax year 2017/18	Minimum allowance £3,260	Tax relief £326
Tax year 2018/19	Minimum allowance £3,360	Tax relief £336

Child Tax Credit

Child tax credits can top up income for those who are responsible for at least one child or young person. The claimant does not have to be working.

G3: Income tax reliefs and rates

Child tax credits are made up of a number of different payments (called "elements"). How much received depends on the claimant's income, the number of children they have, and whether any of the children are disabled.

To get the maximum amount of child tax credit, which is £3,325, annual income must be £16,105 or less in the tax year 2018/19. If the claimant earns more than this then the amount of child credit reduces. For every £1 of income over this threshold you earn per year, the amount of tax credits paid decreases by 41p. At an income level of £24,215 the child tax credit is reduced to £0.

Some additional child tax credit is available for those with disabled or severely disabled children.

Child Benefit

From January 2013, if an individual's income is more than £50,000 and they, or their partner, choose to carry on getting Child Benefit payments, they will need to declare these payments by registering for Self Assessment and filling in a tax return as they may be liable for a High Income Benefit charge, being one per cent of the Child Benefit for each £100 of income between £50,000 and £60,000.

Taxation of Dividends

Savings income is subdivided into dividends and other savings income, with dividends treated as the top slice of savings income.

Prior to 2016/17 dividends were "grossed up" by the Dividend Tax Credit and tax was payable on dividend income (prior to deducting the Dividend Tax Credit) at the dividend ordinary rate of 10 per cent up to the basic rate limit, and at the dividend upper rate of 32.5 per cent thereafter up to the higher rate limit. From 2010/11 to 2015/16, in addition to these rates, tax is payable on dividend income falling into the additional rate band at the dividend additional rate, as follows:

Tax year 2010/11	42.5 per cent
Tax year 2011/12	42.5 per cent
Tax year 2012/13	42.5 per cent
Tax year 2013/14	37.5 per cent
Tax year 2014/15	37.5 per cent
Tax year 2015/16	37.5 per cent

From 2016/17 that whole methodology of taxing dividends has been changed. The Dividend Tax Credit has been replaced by a tax-free Dividend Allowance. There is no tax payable on the Dividend Allowance, no matter what non-dividend income is received. The Dividend Allowance is as follows:

Tax year 2016/17	£ 5,000
Tax year 2017/18	£ 5,000
Tax year 2018/19	£ 2,000

Tax is payable on any dividend income in excess of the Dividend Allowance at the following rates:

- 7.5 per cent on dividend income within the basic rate band
- 32.5 per cent on dividend income within the higher rate band
- 38.1 per cent on dividend income within the additional rate band

Taxation of Savings

Tax is payable on other savings income at 10 per cent on income in the starting rate band, at 20 per cent on income in the basic rate band, and at 40 per cent thereafter up to the higher rate limit. From

2010/11, in addition to these rates, tax is payable on other savings income falling into the additional rate band at the following rates:

Tax year 2010/11	50 per cent
Tax year 2011/12	50 per cent
Tax year 2012/13	50 per cent
Tax year 2013/14	45 per cent
Tax year 2014/15	45 per cent
Tax year 2015/16	45 per cent
Tax year 2016/17	45 per cent
Tax year 2017/18	45 per cent
Tax year 2018/19	45 per cent

Between 2008/09 and 2014/15 there was a 10 per cent starting rate for savings income only. From 2015/16 there is a 0 per cent starting rate for savings only, so the following rates and limits apply:

	Rate	Limit
Tax year 2008/09	10 per cent	£2,320
Tax year 2009/10	10 per cent	£2,440
Tax year 2010/11	10 per cent	£2,440
Tax year 2011/12	10 per cent	£2,560
Tax year 2012/13	10 per cent	£2,710
Tax year 2013/14	10 per cent	£2,790
Tax year 2014/15	10 per cent	£2,880
Tax year 2015/16	0 per cent	£5,000
Tax year 2016/17	0 per cent	£5,000
Tax year 2017/18	0 per cent	£5,000
Tax year 2018/19	0 per cent	£5,000

If the taxpayer's non-savings income exceeds these limits, the savings rate does not apply.

From 2016/17 a new Personal Savings Allowance was introduced which means that basic rate taxpayers will not have to pay tax on the first £1,000 of savings income they receive and higher rate taxpayers will not have to pay tax on their first £500 of savings income.

2010/11 to 2018/19

Fiscal year:	2010/11 £	2011/12 £	2012/13 £	2013/14 £	2014/15 £	2015/16 £	2016/17 £	2017/18 £	2018/19 £
Income tax reliefs									
Personal allowance	6,475*	7,475*	8,105*	9,440*	10,000*	10,600*	11,000*	11,500*	11,850*
Income tax rates									
Basic rate band – Payable at 20%	37,400	35,000	34,370	32,010	31,865	31,785	32,000	33,500	34,500
Higher rate band – Payable at 40%	112,600	115,000	115,630	117,990	118,135	118,215	118,000	116,500	115,500
Additional rate band – Payable at 45%	–	–	–	Balance	Balance	Balance	Balance	Balance	Balance
Additional rate band – Payable at 50%	Balance	Balance	Balance	–	–	–	–	–	–

* Please refer to the preceding note on personal allowance for possible restriction.

G4: National Insurance contributions

Introductory notes

1. Married women and widows have been able to elect to pay a reduced contribution as follows:

   - 4.85 per cent on earnings between primary threshold and upper earnings limit, and one per cent on earnings above upper earnings limit from 2003/04 to 2010/11.

   - 5.85 per cent on earnings between primary threshold and upper earnings limit, and two per cent on earnings above upper earnings limit in 2011/12 to 2018/19.

2. Class 1 employee contributions and Class 2 contributions cease to be payable when an individual reaches State pension age.

3. Class 4 contributions are not payable in respect of any fiscal year that starts after State pension age has been reached.

4. Class 3 contributions are voluntary at a flat weekly rate (£14.65pw in 2018/19).

5. From 6 April 2009 an Upper Accrual Point (UAP) was introduced at a frozen rate of £770.00 per week for the calculation of the State Second Pension (S2P) and Class 1 National Insurance rebates under contracted-out schemes. From the same date the Upper Earnings Limit (UEL) previously used for these purposes was aligned with the higher rate threshold for income tax.

6. Employment allowance will reduce employers' Class 1 National Insurance each time the payroll is run until the £3,000 allowance (2018/19 rates) has been fully utilised or the tax year ends (whichever is sooner). Claims are only against employers' Class 1 National Insurance paid, up to a maximum of £3,000 each tax year. The employment allowance was £2,000 in 2014/15 and 2015/16, and has been £3,000 since 2016/17.

   Employment Allowance can be claimed by businesses or charities (including community amateur sports clubs) paying employers' Class 1 National Insurance. Claims can also be made by individuals that employ a care or support worker.

   Claims can not be made if:

   - you are the director and only paid employee in your company;

   - you employ someone for personal, household or domestic work (e.g. a nanny or gardener) —unless they are a care or support worker;

   - you are a public body or business doing more than half your work in the public sector (e.g. local councils and NHS services)—unless you are a charity;

   - you are a service company with only deemed payments of employment income under "IR35 rules".

7. On 6 April 2016 the current basic State pension and S2P were abolished and replaced by a single-tier State pension. The abolition of S2P also meant the end of contracting-out. The measures that implemented the single-tier State pension and abolition of contracting-out are contained in the Pensions Act 2014.

8. For those retiring on or after 6 April 2016, a New State Pension was introduced. The weekly amount of the New State Pension is as follows:

	Monthly	Annual
Tax year 2016/17	£155.65	£8,094
Tax year 2017/18	£159.55	£8,297
Tax year 2018/19	£164.35	£8,546

G4: National Insurance contributions

2010/11 to 2014/15

Fiscal year:	2011/12 £	2012/13 £	2013/14 £	2014/15 £
Class 1 contributions (Employees)				
Lower earnings limit (LEL) (pa)	5,304	5,564	5,668	5,772
Primary threshold (PT) (pa)	7,225	7,605	7,755	7,956
Upper Accrual Point (UAP) (pa)	40,040	40,040	40,040	40,040
Upper earnings limit (UEL) (pa)	42,475	42,475	41,450	41,865
Standard rate				
If earnings below LEL:	Nil	Nil	Nil	Nil
If earnings at or above LEL: – Contribution rate on earnings up to PT	Nil	Nil	Nil	Nil
– Contribution rate on earnings between PT and UEL	12%	12%	12%	12%
– Contribution rate on earnings above UEL	2%	2%	2%	2%
Maximum contribution (pa)	4,230 +2% of excess over UEL	4,184 +2% of excess over UEL	4,043 +2% of excess over UEL	4,069 +2% of excess over UEL
Contracted-out rate				
As standard rate except – Contribution rate on earnings between PT and UEL				
– Contribution rate on earnings between PT and UAP	10.4%	10.6%	10.6%	10.6%
– Contribution rate on earnings between UAP and UEL	12.0%	12.0%	12.0%	12.0%
Maximum contribution (pa)	3,705 +2% of excess over UEL	3,730 +2% of excess over UEL	3,591 +2% of excess over UEL	3,620 +2% of excess over UEL
Class 2 contributions (Self-employed)				
Small earnings exception limit	5,315	5,595	5,725	5,885
Fixed weekly contributions (pw)	2.50	2.65	2.70	2.75
Class 4 contributions (Self-employed)				
Lower profits limit (LPL) (pa)	7,225	7,605	7,755	7,956
Upper profits limit (UPL) (pa)	42,475	42,475	41,450	41,865
Contribution rate on profits between LPL and UPL	9.0%	9.0%	9.0%	9.0%
Contribution rate on profits above UPL	2.0%	2.0%	2.0%	2.0%
Maximum contribution (pa)	3,173 +2% of excess over UPL	3,138 +2% of excess over UPL	3,033 +2% of excess over UPL	3,052 +2% of excess over UPL

2015/16 to 2018/19

Fiscal year:	2015/16 £	2016/17 £	2017/18 £	2018/19 £
Class 1 contributions (Employees)				
Lower earnings limit (LEL) (pa)	5,824	5,824	5,876	6,032
Primary threshold (PT) (pa)	8,060	8,060	8,164	8,424
Upper Accrual Point (UAP) (pa)	40,040	40,040	40,040	40,040
Upper earnings limit (UEL) (pa)	42,385	43,000	45,032	46,384
Standard rate				
If earnings below LEL:	Nil	Nil	Nil	Nil
If earnings at or above LEL: – Contribution rate on earnings up to PT	Nil	Nil	Nil	Nil
– Contribution rate on earnings between PT and UEL	12%	12%	12%	12%
– Contribution rate on earnings above UEL	2%	2%	2%	2%
Maximum contribution (pa)	4,119 +2% of excess over UEL	4,193 +2% of excess over UEL	4,424 +2% of excess over UEL	4,555 +2% of excess over UEL
Contracted-out rate				
As standard rate except – Contribution rate on earnings between PT and UEL				
– Contribution rate on earnings between PT and UAP	10.6%	n/a	n/a	n/a
– Contribution rate on earnings between UAP and UEL	12.0%	n/a	n/a	n/a
Maximum contribution (pa)	3,671 +2% of excess over UEL	n/a	n/a	n/a
Class 2 contributions (Self-employed)				
Small earnings exception limit				
Small profits threshold	5,965	5,965	6,025	6,205
Fixed weekly contributions (pw)	2.80	2.80	2.85	2.95
Class 4 contributions (Self-employed)				
Lower profits limit (LPL) (pa)	8,060	8,060	8,164	8,424
Upper profits limit (UPL) (pa)	42,385	43,000	45,000	46,350
Contribution rate on profits between LPL and UPL	9.0%	9.0%	9.0%	9.0%
Contribution rate on profits above UPL	2.0%	2.0%	2.0%	2.0%
Maximum contribution (pa)	3,089 +2% of excess over UPL	3,145 +2% of excess over UPL	3,315 +2% of excess over UPL	3,413 +2% of excess over UPL

G5: VAT registration thresholds and rates

Registration is required when a person's turnover (taxable supplies from all the person's businesses) exceeds prescribed limits.

Past and future turnover limits apply (looking one year back and one year forward).

Registration is also required if a turnover limit is to be exceeded in a period of 30 days.

The registration levels are:

	Past turnover		Future turnover
	1 year	Unless turnover for next year will not exceed	30 days
	£	£	£
1 April 2004 to 31 March 2005	58,000	56,000	58,000
1 April 2005 to 31 March 2006	60,000	58,000	60,000
1 April 2006 to 31 March 2007	61,000	59,000	61,000
1 April 2007 to 31 March 2008	64,000	62,000	64,000
1 April 2008 to 30 April 2009	67,000	65,000	67,000
1 May 2009 to 31 March 2010	68,000	66,000	68,000
1 April 2010 to 31 March 2011	70,000	68,000	70,000
1 April 2011 to 31 March 2012	73,000	71,000	73,000
1 April 2012 to 31 March 2013	77,000	75,000	77,000
1 April 2013 to 31 March 2014	79,000	77,000	79,000
1 April 2014 to 31 March 2015	81,000	79,000	81,000
1 April 2015 to 31 March 2016	82,000	80,000	82,000
1 April 2016 to 31 March 2017	83,000	81,000	83,000
1 April 2017 to 31 March 2018	85,000	83,000	85,000
From 1 April 2018	85,000	83,000	85,000

De-registration depends on satisfying HM Revenue & Customs that the future annual limit (being the same as the "unless turnover for next year will not exceed" in the table above, e.g. £83,000 since 1 April 2017) will not be exceeded.

Note:

These registration and de-registration limits can be of particular relevance in considering likely turnover levels for businesses such as taxis and driving schools, where VAT registration may render charges uncompetitive (because most such businesses operate below the registration limits).

VAT Rates

Date	VAT Rate
From 1 April 1991 to 30 November 2008	17.5%
1 December 2008 to 31 December 2009	15.0%
1 January 2010 to 3 January 2011	17.5%
4 January 2011	20.0%

Group H
Pension

H1: Net equivalents to a range of gross annual pension figures

H2: Illustrative net pension calculations

H3: Note on pension losses

H4: State pension age timetables

H1: Net equivalents to a range of gross annual pension figures

Introductory notes

1. The following table sets out the net equivalents to a range of annual pension figures in 2018/19, distinguishing between a single person and a married person.

2. The table is followed by illustrative net pension calculations for each marital status and age category, at income levels of £15,000, £20,000, £30,000, £50,000, £110,000 and £160,000 per annum.

3. Since pensions are not subject to National Insurance contributions, the net equivalent figures represent the gross pension less income tax. Given that liability to primary Class 1 National Insurance contributions falls away when the earner has reached State pension age [note 2 of G4], it follows that the net equivalent figures for those of State pension age or over apply equally to earnings from employment and pensions.

4. Similarly, given that Class 4 contributions are not payable in respect of any fiscal year that starts after State pension age has been reached [note 3 of G4], it follows that the net equivalent figures for those of State pension age or over apply also to earnings from self-employment where State pension age has been reached in a prior fiscal year.

H1: Net equivalents to a range of gross annual pension figures

	2018/19 Net equivalent pension				
	Single, or married where neither spouse was born before 6.4.35		Married, where either spouse was born before 6.4.35		Reason
Gross pension £pa	£pa	Net per £100 extra	£pa	Net per £100 extra	
1,000	1,000	100	1,000	100	
2,000	2,000	100	2,000	100	
3,000	3,000	100	3,000	100	
4,000	4,000	100	4,000	100	
5,000	5,000	100	5,000	100	
6,000	6,000	100	6,000	100	
7,000	7,000	100	7,000	100	
8,000	8,000	100	8,000	100	
8,546	8,546	100	8,546	100	← State pension amount
9,000	9,000	100	9,000	100	
10,000	10,000	100	10,000	100	
11,000	11,000	100	11,000	100	
11,850	11,850	80	11,850	90	← Income tax payable at 20%
12,000	11,970	80	11,985	90	
13,000	12,770	80	12,885	90	
14,000	13,570	80	13,785	90	
15,000	14,370	80	14,685	90	
16,000	15,170	80	15,585	90	
17,000	15,970	80	16,485	90	
18,000	16,770	80	17,385	90	
19,000	17,570	80	18,285	90	
20,000	18,370	80	19,185	*	
20,195	18,526	80	19,361	90	← Maximum Married Couple's allowance
21,000	19,170	80	20,040	80	
22,000	19,970	80	20,840	80	
23,000	20,770	80	21,640	80	
24,000	21,570	80	22,440	80	
25,000	22,370	80	23,240	80	
26,000	23,170	80	24,040	80	
27,000	23,970	80	24,840	80	
28,000	24,770	80	25,640	80	
29,000	25,570	80	26,440	80	
30,000	26,370	80	27,240	80	
31,000	27,170	80	28,040	80	
32,000	27,970	80	28,840	80	
33,000	28,770	80	29,640	80	
34,000	29,570	80	30,440	80	
35,000	30,370	80	31,240	80	
40,000	34,370	80	35,240	80	
46,350	39,450	60	40,320	60	← Income tax payable at 40%
50,000	41,640	60	42,510	60	
55,000	44,640	60	45,510	60	
60,000	47,640	60	48,510	60	
65,000	50,640	60	51,510	60	
70,000	53,640	60	54,510	60	
75,000	56,640	60	57,510	60	
80,000	59,640	60	60,510	60	
85,000	62,640	60	63,510	60	
90,000	65,640	60	66,510	60	
95,000	68,640	60	69,510	60	
100,000	71,640	40	72,510	40	← PA reduces here
123,700	81,120	60	81,990	60	← PA reduced to zero
150,000	96,900	55	97,770	55	← Income tax payable at 45%
200,000	124,400	55	125,270	55	
250,000	151,900	55	152,770	55	
300,000	179,400	55	180,270	55	

H2: Illustrative net pension calculations

Single person* at 2018/19 rates

		£pa	£pa	£pa	£pa	£pa	£pa
Gross pension	[a]	15,000	20,000	30,000	50,000	110,000	160,000
Income tax							
Gross		15,000	20,000	30,000	50,000	110,000	160,000
Personal allowance (see note 1 below)		(11,850)	(11,850)	(11,850)	(11,850)	(6,850)	–
Taxable		3,150	8,150	18,150	38,150	103,150	160,000
Tax payable							
– At 20%		630	1,630	3,630	6,900	6,900	6,900
– At 40%		–	–	–	1,4600	27,460	46,200
– At 45%		–	–	–	–	–	4,500
	[b]	630	1,630	3,630	8,360	34,360	57,600
Net income	[a–b]	14,370	18,370	26,370	41,640	75,640	102,400
Net % of gross		95.8%	91.9%	87.9%	83.3%	68.8%	64.0%
Note 1: personal allowance							
Personal allowance		11,850	11,850	11,850	11,850	11,850	11,850
Restriction for excess of income over limit#		–	–	–	–	(5,000)	(11,850)
Net allowance		11,850	11,850	11,850	11,850	6,850	–

#If gross pay does not exceed £100,000, no restriction.
If gross pay does exceed £100,000, restriction is the lower of:
(a) (gross pay–£100,000)/2, and
(b) £11,850.

* = and married persons that do not meet the criteria shown in the married persons' calculations on the next page

H2: Illustrative net pension calculations

Married person at 2018/19 rates

(But only applies if at least one spouse born before 6 April 1935 and full married couple's allowance allocated to pensioner in this calculation)*

		£pa	£pa	£pa	£pa	£pa	£pa
Gross pension	[a]	15,000	20,000	30,000	50,000	110,000	160,000
Income tax							
Gross		15,000	20,000	30,000	50,000	110,000	160,000
Personal allowance (see note 1 below)		(11,850)	(11,850)	(11,850)	(11,850)	(6,850)	–
Taxable		3,150	8,150	18,150	38,150	103,150	160,000
Tax payable							
– At 20%		630	1,630	3,630	6,900	6,900	6,900
– At 40%		–	–	–	1,460	27,460	46,200
– At 45%		–	–	–	–	–	4,500
		630	1,630	3,630	8,360	34,360	57,600
Relief for married couple's allowance (note 2)		(870)	(870)	(815)	(336)	(336)	(336)
	[b]	–	760	2,815	8,024	34,024	57,264
Net income	[a–b]	15,000	19,240	27,185	41,976	75,976	102,736
Net % of gross		100.0%	96.2%	90.6%	84.0%	69.1%	64.2%
Note 1: personal allowance							
Personal allowance		11,850	11,850	11,850	11,850	11,850	11,850
Restriction for excess of income over limits#		–	–	–	–	(5,000)	(11,850)
Net allowance		11,850	11,850	11,850	11,850	6,850	–

#If gross pay does not exceed £100,000, no restriction.
If gross pay does exceed £100,000, restriction is the lower of:
(a) (gross pay–£100,000)/2; and
(b) £11,850

Note 2: married couple's allowance

Married couple's allowance		8,695	8,695	8,695	8,695	8,695	8,695
Restriction for excess of income over limit^		–	–	(550)	(5,335)	(5,335)	(5,335)
Net allowance		8,695	8,695	8,145	3,360	3,360	3,360
Relief at 10%		870	870	815	336	336	336

^ If gross pension does not exceed £28,900, no restriction.
If gross pension does exceed £28,900, restriction is the lower of:
(a) [(gross pension–£28,900)/2] **less** restriction of personal allowance, and
(b) £8,695 – £3,360 = £5,335

* If these criteria are not met, use Single Person calculator shown on previous page

H3: Note on pension losses

1. Purpose of note

The purpose of this note is to provide some basic guidance to practitioners who need to consider whether a pension loss is likely to arise in any specific case. Where the loss is significant consideration should be given to appointing an actuary or forensic accountant with appropriate experience in order to quantify the loss.

2. "Defined Benefit" or "Defined Contribution" scheme?

Ascertain of which type of scheme the claimant was a member.
There are two types of Defined Benefit schemes:

1) Final Salary schemes

- benefits are defined in advance, usually in terms of:

  - final salary (averaged over the last year or last few years of service before retirement);
  - number of years of pensionable service; and
  - a factor (often 1/60th or 1/80th for each year of pensionable service),

- contributions are usually deducted from the salary of active members still accruing benefits, and

- the financial risk of ensuring that benefits are paid lies with the employer, who will be expected to make additional contributions as necessary.

2) Career Average Revalued Earnings schemes (also known as CARE schemes)

- benefits depend on a combination of:

  - each year's pensionable earnings throughout the member's career;
  - the scheme's accrual rate; and
  - annual revaluation of accrued pension entitlement for the period up to retirement age;

- contributions are usually deducted from the salary of active members still accruing benefits, and

- the financial risk of ensuring that benefits are paid lies with the employer, who will be expected to make additional contributions as necessary.

There are also **Defined Contribution schemes** (also known as Personal Pensions or Money Purchase schemes).

- benefits depend on a combination of:

  - the amounts paid in by the member (if any),
  - the amounts paid in by the employer (if there is one),
  - the investment returns (net of charges) achieved up to retirement,
  - the annuity rates available on retirement if an annuity is selected rather than cash, uncrystallised funds pension lump sum or a drawdown contract, and

H3: Note on pension losses

- the financial risk lies with the member.

All employers are now required to auto-enrol their employees earning over £10,000 a year into a **Workplace Pension** if they are aged between 22 and state pension age (on earnings up to £46,350 a year).

These are defined contribution schemes, under which:

- the employer must contribute two per cent of earnings from 1 April 2018, rising to three per cent from 1 April 2019;
- the employee must contribute three per cent of earnings from 1 April 2018, rising to five per cent from 1 April 2019;
- the employee contributions are paid from gross earnings but are eligible for tax relief at the employee's marginal rate;
- employers and/or employees may opt to contribute at a higher level than the minimum required under auto-enrolment; and
- employees may opt out but the employer is obliged to contribute for as long as the employee chooses to remain a member.

By definition, a self-employed person will have no employer contributions and there is no requirement to auto-enrol.

3. Is there likely to be a loss?

Start by assuming that there will be a loss to be evaluated, if:

- the claimant (and/or the employer) was contributing to a pension scheme, or the claimant was due to join the employer's workplace pension scheme, and/or
- there is a claim for loss of earnings.

There may be an off-setting pension benefit associated with any earnings mitigation, at least at the auto-enrolment minimum contribution level.

4. Final salary scheme member

Potential pension:

- Obtain a copy of the members' guide (which will often be in simple terms).

- Obtain a copy of the most recent statement of the individual member's scheme benefits (an estimate of pension at normal retirement age based on current salary).

- With these documents, and the projection of final salary being used for evaluating loss of earnings, it should be possible to calculate the expected pension at retirement date (at its present-day value).

Actual pension:

- Establish the actual (reduced) pension that will be payable at normal retirement date (at its present-day value).

Proceed by:

- Applying *Wells v Wells*[1] principles. Follow the step-by-step guide at Table B3.

[1] [1999] 1 A.C. 345.

H3: Note on pension losses

- Calculating loss of annual pension (after tax). Table H1 will assist.

- Applying an appropriate multiplier drawn from the Ogden tables for the relevant retirement age. Tables A1 and A8 refer.

Defined benefit pension loss calculations are generally complex and consideration should be given to taking advice from an actuary or a forensic accountant expert in pension matters.

5. Career Average Revalued Earnings scheme member

Potential pension:

- Obtain a copy of the members' guide (which will often be in simple terms).

- Obtain a copy of the most recent statement of the individual member's scheme benefit (an estimate of pension at normal retirement age based on current salary). Note: this may include estimated future inflation to normal retirement age, which must be ignored.

- With these documents, and the projection of annual salary being used for evaluating loss of earnings, it should be possible to calculate pension at retirement date (at its present-day value), by following the step-by-step guide at Table B3.

Actual pension:

- Establish the actual (reduced) pension that will be payable at normal retirement date (at its present-day value).

Proceed by:

- Applying *Wells v Wells*[2] principles.

- Follow the step-by-step guide at Table B3.

- Calculating loss of annual pension (after tax). Table H1 will assist.

- Applying an appropriate multiplier drawn from the Ogden Tables for the relevant retirement age. Tables A1 and A8 refer.

Defined benefit pension loss calculations are generally complex and consideration should be given to taking advice from an actuary or a forensic accountant expert in pension matters.

6. Defined contribution scheme member (including Workplace Pension)

The main loss in respect of a defined contribution scheme member is the loss of the future contributions by the employer. This can readily be taken into account as part of the calculation of loss of earnings, by adding the employer pension contributions to the earnings assumed to be lost. Deductions from earnings for the employee's own contributions should be ignored in the earnings loss calculation.

Unlike the loss of earnings, 25 per cent of the loss of employer contributions is not subject to tax. Furthermore, whilst the loss of the employee's own contributions is ignored (since it is both a cost

[2] [1999] 1 A.C. 345.

and a benefit), allowance may be made for the fact that 25 per cent of the employee's own contributions is also completely free of tax, however, the benefit is taken.

Care is needed to make appropriate allowance for tax reliefs in the case of higher rate taxpayers and advice should generally be sought from a forensic accountant in such cases.

Since the introduction of "pension freedoms" in the 2015 Budget, the benefits from a defined contribution scheme can generally be assumed to be available in cash, rather than having to purchase an annuity. Twenty-five per cent of the accumulated amount is entirely free of tax and the rest is taxable, whether it is taken as immediate cash, through a drawdown contract, an uncrystallised funds pension lump sum or indeed as an annuity.

However, in fatal accident cases the assumption about availability of cash does not apply and an approach assuming annuitisation will usually be appropriate.

It is important to recognise that pension loss calculations can be quite complex and the advice of a forensic accountant or an actuary is recommended in cases where the pension loss is material.

7. Important cases

Have regard to:

- *Parry v Cleaver*[3]:

    Briefly: pension loss only runs from anticipated retirement age.

    So that: no credit need be given against earnings losses for an early/ill health pension

- *Longden v British Coal Corporation*[4]:

    Briefly: explains how to apportion an actual tax-free lump sum received ahead of expected retirement age between pre- and post-retirement periods.

    So that: treatment of the actual lump sum is brought into line with *Parry v Cleaver* principles.

- *Aboul-Hosn v Trustees of the Italian Hospital*[5]:

    Briefly: allows for a simple calculation in which pension loss is based on the tax relief forgone on the claimant's potential personal pension contributions.

8. Further points

- Do not rely on quotations from pension providers; they invariably incorporate inflation and are not therefore compatible with conventional multipliers.

- Keep in mind the reality of life expectancy. If life expectancy is impaired, pension loss will be reduced.

[3] [1970] A.C. 1.
[4] [1998] A.C. 653.
[5] (1987) (unreported).

H3: Note on pension losses

- That said, do not overlook the possibility of a "lost years" claim in respect of pension losses between the end of the post-accident life expectancy and the end of the pre-accident life expectancy.

- Do not assume that individuals necessarily retire at State pension age.

- Consider possible pension losses in cases where a claimant has missed out on the opportunity of joining the employer's recently established workplace pension.

- It is possible for there to be a pension loss claim without a loss of earnings claim, e.g. in cases where the claimant has moved from the public sector (with a final salary/CARE scheme) to the private sector.

- Bear in mind that, between April 2010 and November 2018, the State pension age for women is gradually increasing from 60 to 65. The State pension age for men and women will then, based on current legislation, increase from 65 to 66 between March 2019 and October 2020 and then from 66 to 67 between April 2026 and April 2028. On 19 July 2017 the Government announced that the increase in the State pension age from 67 to 68 would be phased in between 2037 and 2039. More information about future increases in State pension age is provided at Table H4.

- Claims for loss of State pension may also need to be considered, following the above principles.

H4: State pension age timetables

Introductory notes

The following tables show how the legislated increases in State pension age will be phased in. A State pension age calculator is provided on the Gov.uk website: *www.gov.uk/state-pension-age*. This calculator tells people when they will reach their State pension age, under current legislation, based on their gender and date of birth.

The Pensions Act 2014 provides for a regular review of the State pension age, at least once every five years. The Government is not planning to revise the existing timetables for the equalisation of State pension age to 65 or the rise in the State pension age to 66 or 67. However, the timetable for the increase in the State pension age from 67 to 68 is expected to change from the current legislated position. The Government announced on 19 July 2017 that the increase in the State pension age from 67 to 68 would be phased in between 2037 and 2039 (instead of between 2044 and 2046). Those born in the 1980s may expect to have a State pension age of 69 and those born in the 1990s a State pension age of 70. Before any future changes could become law Parliament would need to approve the plans.

Changes under the Pensions Act 2011

Under the Pensions Act 2011, women's State pension age will increase more quickly to 65 between April 2016 and November 2018. From March 2019 the State pension age for both men and women will start to increase to reach 66 by October 2020.

Women's State pension age under the Pensions Act 2011

Date of birth	Date State pension age reached
6 April 1953 – 5 May 1953	6 July 2016
6 May 1953 – 5 June 1953	6 November 2016
6 June 1953 – 5 July 1953	6 March 2017
6 July 1953 – 5 August 1953	6 July 2017
6 August 1953 – 5 September 1953	6 November 2017
6 September 1953 – 5 October 1953	6 March 2018
6 October 1953 – 5 November 1953	6 July 2018
6 November 1953 – 5 December 1953	6 November 2018

Increase in State pension age from 65 to 66, men and women

Date of birth	Date State pension age reached
6 December 1953 – 5 January 1954	6 March 2019
6 January 1954 – 5 February 1954	6 May 2019
6 February 1954 – 5 March 1954	6 July 2019
6 March 1954 – 5 April 1954	6 September 2019
6 April 1954 – 5 May 1954	6 November 2019
6 May 1954 – 5 June 1954	6 January 2020
6 June 1954 – 5 July 1954	6 March 2020
6 July 1954 – 5 August 1954	6 May 2020
6 August 1954 – 5 September 1954	6 July 2020
6 September 1954 – 5 October 1954	6 September 2020
6 October 1954 – 5 April 1960	66th birthday

H4: State pension age timetables

Increase in State pension age from 66 to 67 under the Pensions Act 2014

The Pensions Act 2014 brought the increase in the State pension age from 66 to 67 forward by eight years. The State pension age for men and women will now increase to 67 between 2026 and 2028. The Government also changed the way in which the increase in State pension age is phased so that rather than reaching State pension age on a specific date, people born between 6 April 1960 and 5 March 1961 will reach their State pension age at 66 years and the specified number of months.

Increase in State pension age from 66 to 67, men and women

Date of birth	Date State pension age reached
6 April 1960 – 5 May 1960	66 years and 1 month
6 May 1960 – 5 June 1960	66 years and 2 months
6 June 1960 – 5 July 1960	66 years and 3 months
6 July 1960 – 5 August 1960	66 years and 4 months*
6 August 1960 – 5 September 1960	66 years and 5 months
6 September 1960 – 5 October 1960	66 years and 6 months
6 October 1960 – 5 November 1960	66 years and 7 months
6 November 1960 – 5 December 1960	66 years and 8 months
6 December 1960 – 5 January 1961	66 years and 9 months#
6 January 1961 – 5 February 1961	66 years and 10 months^
6 February 1961 – 5 March 1961	66 years and 11 months
6 March 1961 – 5 April 1977~	67 years

* = A person born on 31 July 1960 is considered to reach the age of 66 years and 4 months on 30 November 2026.
# = A person born on 31 December 1960 is considered to reach the age of 66 years and 9 months on 30 September 2027.
^ = A person born on 31 January 1961 is considered to reach the age of 66 years and 10 months on 30 November 2027.
~ = For people born after 5 April 1969 but before 6 April 1977, under the Pensions Act 2007, State pension age was already 67.

Increase in State pension age from 67 to 68

Under the Pensions Act 2007 the State pension age for men and women is planned to increase from 67 to 68 between 2044 and 2046.

In the Autumn Statement on 5 December 2013, the Chancellor announced that the Government believed that future generations should spend up to a third of their adult life in retirement. This principle implied that State pension age should rise to 68 by the 2030s, and 69 by the 2040s.

The Pensions Act 2014 provided for a regular review of the State pension age, at least once every five years. The reviews would be based around the idea that people should be able to spend a certain proportion of their adult life drawing a State pension. As well as life expectancy, they would take into account a range of factors relevant to setting the pension age. The first review was completed in July 2017, following a report from the Government Actuary[1] and an independent review by Sir John Cridland[2], both published in March 2017. The Government announced on 19 July 2017[3] that the increase in the State pension age from 67 to 68 would be phased in between 2037 and 2039 (instead of between 2044 and 2046). However, this proposal still requires primary legislation.

---

[1] Periodic review of rules about State Pension Age: Report by the Government Actuary.
[2] Independent Review of the State Pension Age: Smoothing the Transition. Sir John Cridland.
[3] State pension age review. July 2017.

H4: State pension age timetables

The information in the table below is based on the current law (Pensions Act 2007).

Increase in State pension age from 67 to 68, men and women

Date of birth	Date State pension age reached
6 April 1977 – 5 May 1977	6 May 2044
6 May 1977 – 5 June 1977	6 July 2044
6 June 1977 – 5 July 1977	6 September 2044
6 July 1977 – 5 August 1977	6 November 2044
6 August 1977 – 5 September 1977	6 January 2045
6 September 1977 – 5 October 1977	6 March 2045
6 October 1977 – 5 November 1977	6 May 2045
6 November 1977 – 5 December 1977	6 July 2045
6 December 1977 – 5 January 1978	6 September 2045
6 January 1978 – 5 February 1978	6 November 2045
6 February 1978 – 5 March 1978	6 January 2046
6 March 1978 – 5 April 1978	6 March 2046
6 April 1978 onwards	68th birthday

If a similar phasing were adopted for the proposed increase in State pension age from 67 to 68 between 2037 and 2039, the impact of the change in retirement age would be as follows:

Date of birth	Date State pension age reached
6 April 1970 – 5 May 1970	6 May 2037
6 May 1970 – 5 June 1970	6 July 2037
6 June 1970 – 5 July 1970	6 September 2037
6 July 1970 – 5 August 1970	6 November 2037
6 August 1970 – 5 September 1970	6 January 2038
6 September 1970 – 5 October 1970	6 March 2038
6 October 1970 – 5 November 1970	6 May 2038
6 November 1970 – 5 December 1970	6 July 2038
6 December 1977 – 5 January 1971	6 September 2038
6 January 1971 – 5 February 1971	6 November 2038
6 February 1971 – 5 March 1971	6 January 2039
6 March 1971 – 5 April 1971	6 March 2039
6 April 1971 onwards	68th birthday

Group I
Benefits, Allowances, Charges

I1: **Social security benefits (non-means-tested)**

I2: **Social security benefits and tax credits (means-tested)**

I3: **Personal injury trusts**

I4: **Claims for loss of earnings and maintenance at public expense**

I5: **Foster care allowances**

I1: Social security benefits (non-means-tested)

How they work

Generally, all of these benefits may be claimed independently of each other. However, there are overlapping benefit rules which prevent more than one income replacement benefit being payable. If the claimant is entitled to more than one income replacement benefit, then the amount of the highest will be payable.

Many benefits are contributory, entitlement being dependent on satisfying conditions as to amount of national insurance contributions paid.

Until April 2003, increases were payable for many benefits for dependent children, subject to an earnings limit. The increases have now been replaced by Child Tax Credit and latterly Universal Credit (see section I2) but people in receipt of the increases on 5 April 2003 have transitional protection.

Entitlement to some non-means-tested benefits is affected if claimants are in hospital or in full-time care.

Claims for all benefits must be made in writing. Claims can be backdated only to a limited extent (varying according to the type of benefit).

Most benefits are affected by the claimant's immigration status and/or length of residence in UK. Seek advice from a CAB if this is an issue—*https://www.citizensadvice.org.uk/*.

A. Income replacement

1. Retirement

Retirement Pension if retired before 6 April 2016)   **2018–2019**
Claimant (Category A or B)   £125.95
    (Category B—lower basic pension)   £75.50

A person may qualify in their own right (Category A) or on death of spouse/civil partner (Category B) or as a spouse or civil partner who is a dependent of a category A recipient (Category B—lower). Special rules apply for parents, carers, divorced people, widows and widowers. Women's State pension age is gradually increasing to 65 by November 2018, and for men and women to 66 by March 2020.

New State Pension (retiring after 6 April 2016)   £164.35
No additions for dependents or transfer of pension rights in cases of bereavement.
Both old-style and new-style pensions can be highly variable according to contribution history as well any additional pensions earned e.g. State Earnings Related Pension or if receipt is deferred beyond pension age.
Contributory and taxable.

For information for Form E submit Form BR20 (for valuation of additional State pension); or Form BR19(for benefit forecast): downloadable at *http://www.direct.gov.uk*

2. Ill Health

i. Statutory Sick Pay   **2018–2019**
Standard rate   £92.05

Paid by the employer for up to 168 days (28 six-day weeks), to employees earning not less than £116 gross p.w. Taxable.

ii. Employment and Support Allowance (ESA)   **2018–2019**
Single person under 25:   £57.90
Single person 25 or over: £73.10
Lone parent under 18:   £57.90
Lone parent 18 or over: £73.10
Couple, both under 18:   £57.90
Couple, both under 18, with a child: £87.50
Couple, both over 18:   £114.85

Single people with work-related activity component: £29.05
Single people with the support group component: £37.65
Single people with no component (assessment rate in first 13 weeks)—age 25 or over: £73.10
Single people with no component (assessment rate in first 13 weeks)—age 16-24   £57.90

Premiums (part of IRESA)
Enhanced disability (single)   £16.40
Enhanced disability (couple)   £23.55
Severe disability (single)   £64.30
Severe disability (couple—one qualifies)   £64.30
Severe disability (couple—both qualify)   £128.60
Carers   £36.00

Includes both contributory and "income-related" (means-tested) benefit, based on either limited capability for work (placed in "work-related activity group", helped to prepare for suitable work) or limited capability for work-related activity (not expected to work, placed in support group). Anyone making new claim for ESA after 1 April 2017 will only get basic rate of £73.10 (single) or £114.85 (couple) if placed in work-related activity group.

Benefit paid at basic rate during 13-week assessment phase. Lower rates for under 25s during assessment period; Contributory ESA (CESA): time-limited to one year for those in work-related activity group; also no age or spouse's additions, and no housing costs allowances. Income related ESA (IRESA): assessment,

---

Entitlement to contributory benefits depends on payment of National Insurance Contributions. Amounts are per week.

housing costs and capital rules modelled on IS (Table 29). Child maintenance disregarded for IRESA. Earnings of up to £120 p.w. for less than 16 hours a week now allowed indefinitely on CESA and IRESA as "permitted work"). Occupational pension counts in full against IRESA. First £85 per week of occupational pension ignored for CESA, then CESA reduced by 50p for every £1 received above £85. Passport to other benefits including full HB and CTB (HB & CTB: Table 29) if on IRESA. May be due full HB and CTB if on CESA depending on other or partners income.
Contributory ESA taxable: IRESA not. IRESA being phased out and replaced by universal credit (2016–2022).

iii. Carer's Allowance   **2018–2019**
Claimant   £64.60

Paid to people 16 or over (no upper age limit) who spend at least 35 hours p.w. caring for recipient of higher or middle rates
Care Component of Disability Living Allowance, either rate of Attendance Allowance or Personal Independence Payment (daily living element), or Constant Attendance Allowance at or above the normal rate with a related pension. Claimant can earn no more than £116 p.w. net and must not be in full-time education; however, entitled to offset against earnings up to half any sums paid to someone else (not close relative) to care for either recipient of allowances or carer's children under 16. Not dependent on national insurance but can't be paid in addition to any other N.I. benefit. May still be worth claiming however, in order to get an "underlying entitlement" to it, as this can lead to increase in most means-tested benefits.

Claimant's benefit and adult dependency increases are taxable; child dependency increases are not.

3. UNEMPLOYMENT—JOBSEEKER'S ALLOWANCE (JSA)

i. Contribution-based JSA   **2018–2019**
Claimant   18–24   £57.90
           25 and over   £73.10

ii. Income-based JSA (IBJSA)   **2018–2019**
Claimant   16–24   £57.90
           25 and over   £73.10
Couple Both over 18   £114.85

Premiums: as for IS (Table 29)

Contributory JSA is age-related flat-rate payment; without dependant allowances: paid for up to 26 weeks. IBJSA is paid with, or from expiry of, contributory JSA, with IS-style rules for income, capital, premiums and mortgage interest.
Personal allowance payments and premiums for children are being phased out (replaced initially by Child Tax Credit and now by Universal Credit). Child maintenance is disregarded. Claimants must be under State pension age, available for and actively seeking work, and have a current Claimant Commitment: IBJSA is a passport to other benefits including full HB & CTB. Main rates only given. Not usually available for those under 18 or those working 16+ hours p.w. Only main rates shown.
Personal allowance taxable.

4. MATERNITY/PATERNITY/ADOPTION

i. Statutory Maternity Pay (SMP)   **2018–2019**
Payable to employees earning on average at least £116 a week.
Higher rate (first 6 weeks)   90 per cent of average weekly wage
Lower rate (for up to next 33 weeks)   £145.18[2]
Paid by employer for a maximum of 39 weeks. Taxable.

ii. Statutory Paternity Pay (SPP)   **2018–2019**
Rate   £145.18[2]

Payable for up to two weeks. Additional SPP at same rate if upon mother's return to work, baby 20 weeks old and she would otherwise still be entitled to SMP, SAP or MA. Not payable beyond mother's 39-week maternity period. Taxable.

iii. Maternity Allowance   **2018–2019**
Average earnings threshold   £30.00
Standard rate   £145.18[2]

Paid to claimants not entitled to SMP but employed or self-employed for at least 26 weeks in 66 weeks before due date, and average pay over earnings threshold. Maximum 39 weeks (during which may work up to 10 days). Adult dependency increases no longer paid. Non-taxable.

iv. Statutory Adoption Pay[1]   **2018–2019**
Standard rate   £145.18

Paid by employer for a maximum of 39 weeks. Taxable.

v. Surestart Maternity Grant   **2018–2019**
Standard one-off payment   £500.00

Subject to complex conditions, related to receipt of "qualifying benefit". Available only for first child.

5. BEREAVEMENT

i. Bereavement Benefit (if bereaved before 6 April 2017)   **2018–2019**
Lump sum   £2,000.00
Eligible age 16 to pension age.

[1] *Qualifying conditions based on length of service and average earnings*
[2] *Or (if less) 90 per cent of the parent's weekly average earnings*

Entitlement to contributory benefits depends on payment of National Insurance Contributions. Amounts are per week.

ii. Bereavement Allowance (if bereaved before 6 April 2017)
(age-related) £35.13 to £117.10

Available to bereaved spouses/civil partners of either sex, aged 45 or over but under State pension age who do not remarry or cohabit and who are not bringing up children. Standard rate £117.10 for those 55 and over, then reduces by £7.10 for every year the person is below that age when bereaved. Not payable to those under 45 unless they have children (see WPA below).
Payable for up to 52 weeks from date of bereavement.

iii. Widowed Parent's Allowance (WPA)—if bereaved before 6 April 2017 £117.10

Available to bereaved spouses/civil partners under State pension age and in receipt of child benefit who do not remarry or cohabit.
Widowed Parent's Allowance and Bereavement Allowance cannot be claimed together.
Can be paid in addition to wages and not affected by any occupational pension that is received. Counts as income when means-tested benefits are calculated.
All benefits are contributory (unless caused by industrial injury or accident) and (save lump sum) taxable.

iv. Bereavement Support Payment for deaths occurring on or after 6 April 2017

Standard Rate (bereaved without children) lump sum £2500
Standard Rate monthly payment £100 for maximum of 18 months
Higher Rate (bereaved with children) lump sum £3500
Higher Rate monthly payment £350 for maximum of 18 months
Based on N.I. record of the deceased (unless industrial injury or disease). Still paid if spouse/civil partner remarries or cohabits. Does not count as income when means-tested benefits are calculated. Can be claimed from age 16 to pension age

B. Special needs

1. PERSONAL INDEPENDENCE PAYMENT (PIP)

		2018–2019
Care Component	Enhanced	£85.60
	Standard	£57.30
Mobility Component	Enhanced	£59.75
	Standard	£22.65

The claimant must qualify before reaching 65 (if older, see Attendance Allowance) but can continue in payment beyond 65 if awarded beforehand. Not available to under-16s (see Disability Living Allowance).

2. ATTENDANCE ALLOWANCE

	2018–2019
Higher rate	£85.60
Lower rate	£57.30

Paid for care needs of those over 65 or over.

3. DISABILITY LIVING ALLOWANCE

	2018–2019
Care—higher rate	£85.60
Care—middle rate	£57.30
Care—lower rate	£22.65
Mobility—higher rate	£59.75
Mobility—Lower rate	£22.65

DLA is being phased out for all aged 16 or over and replaced by PIP after a fresh assessment.
All of above allowances are based on need and a medical assessment, but there are no restrictions on how they are used. All are non-contributory, non-means-tested, non-taxable and are ignored as income for means-tested benefits. There are complicated rules in place if people are in residential or nursing care or hospital and are not fully self-funding—notify DWP if this occurs.

C. Children

1. CHILD BENEFIT (CB)

	2018–2019
Only/elder/eldest child	£20.70
Each subsequent child	£13.70

A child must be under 16, or under 20 and in full-time secondary education, or under 18 and registered for work or work-based training. There is a tax liability if claimant or partner earns over £50,000 a year, which reaches 100% of the benefit at £60,000. Otherwise non-taxable. Non-contributory. Administered by HMRC.
Administered by HMRC.

2. GUARDIAN'S ALLOWANCE

	2018–2019
Guardian's allowance	£17.20

Payable with child benefit to those raising the children of deceased (or, sometimes, unavailable) parents. Non-contributory, non-taxable. Administered by HMRC.

Entitlement to contributory benefits depends on payment of National Insurance Contributions.
Amounts are per week except for the Surestart Maternity Grant payment and Bereavement Benefit lump sum.

12: Social security benefits and tax credits (means-tested)

Housing Benefit (HB) and Council Tax Support (CTS)

HB meets rent costs up to a certain level. It can be paid whether the person is in or out of work, with the amount of help given towards the rent being based on a comparison of their actual income with what they would get if out of work. The higher the income, the more the tenant is expected to pay (generally 65p for every £1 earned above the out-of-work level of income).

HB may not meet the full cost of the rent in some circumstances e.g. if a private rent is deemed to be too high for the area; if there are spare bedrooms in the property; if a non-dependent lives with the claimant; if the total benefit income is above a benefit cap figure; if the rent includes costs such as food, fuel, supervision (see below).

HB is administered at present by local councils but will be incorporated into the DWP's universal credit system for working age claimants during 2016–2022 period. See *https://www.gov.uk/apply-housing-benefit-from-council*.

HB is assessed using income support figures as the baseline—see below.

Council Tax Support (CTS) is also known as Council Tax Reduction and was formerly known as council tax benefit. This is means-tested support for tenants and owner-occupiers who have a council tax bill. Although the national framework of CTS is fairly standard, local councils can make variations. It is generally, but not totally, based on the same income support figures used in the HB calculation.

CTS will **not** be incorporated into universal credit and people getting UC will need to make a separate claim for it.

CTS is separate to the system of discounts, exemptions and reductions that are available on a non-means-tested basis e.g. for a single person, or in cases of severe mental impairment, or for an empty property. See *https://www.gov.uk/council-tax*.

Income Support (IS) 2018–2019

For those under pension age on low income, who are working less than 16 hrs per week (e.g. lone parents of young children, carers, some disabled people who are not on ESA, foster carers and some students). Not for the unemployed (see JSA: Table 28) or claimants who are sick/disabled (see ESA: Table 28) or most childless people under 18. Children remain dependent while CB (Table 28) is payable, but replacement of allowances by CTC (and now universal credit) continues.

Entitlement for lone parents ceases once youngest child reaches five, unless they also have responsibilities as a carer for a disabled person. At that point, the lone parent would switch to income-based JSA or (increasingly) universal credit.

Main rates only are shown.

IS brings automatic entitlement on income grounds to other benefits including maximum HB and CTC.

A need level is established from the allowances and premiums shown below. Mortgage interest will not be included from 1 April 2018 onwards, except as an interest-bearing loan repayable to the DWP on death or resale. These loans are also limited to mortgages of up to £200,000. IS is then paid to supplement other income to the need level. There are detailed rules on the application of premiums and disregarded income. Spousal maintenance counts as income but all child maintenance disregarded. No disregard for childcare costs (but see tax credits and universal credit below).

Capital up to £6,000 is disregarded (£10,000 for those in residential/nursing homes; £3,000 for child). Capital between £6,000 and £16,000 is deemed to produce tariff income of £1 for each £250 (or part) over £6,000. There is no entitlement to IS if capital exceeds £16,000, disregarding value of home. "Notional capital" rules penalise deliberate deprivation of capital to obtain IS.

Non-contributory.

Personal allowances

		p.w.
Single person	16–24	57.90
	25 or over	73.10
Lone parent	Under 18	57.90
	Over 18	73.10
Couple	Both over 18	114.85

Main Premiums

Carer	36.00
Disability (single)	33.55
Disability (couple)	47.80
Enhanced disability	
Single	16.40
Couple	23.35
Severe disability	
Single (or one of couple)	64.30
Couple (both qualifying)	128.60

Pension Credit (PC) 2018–2019

PC comprises two elements: Guarantee Credit (GC) for those of qualifying age whose income is below the "standard minimum guarantee"; and Savings Credit for those 65 and over with modest savings or income. Either or both are claimable.

Age at which GC available is rising gradually in line with increases in State pension age; this is key date for other benefits and retirement age-related provisions: for current law see Pensions Act 1995 Sch.4.

Means-tested, some income disregarded. No upper capital limit. £10,000 disregarded; thereafter tariff income is £1 for every £500 (or part).

Not a tax credit. State pension is not affected. Administered by the DWP's Pension Service. Child maintenance disregarded; No provision for childcare costs. Housing costs as for IS, including mortgage interest being paid only as a loan from April 2018. Guarantee Credit is a passport to maximum HB and CTB.

Non-contributory. Not taxable.

Standard Minimum Guarantee

	p.w.
Single	163.00
Couple	248.80
Additional amount for severe disability	
Single	64.30
Couple (both qualify)	28.60
Additional amount for carers	36.00

Savings Credit

Threshold	Single	140.67
	Couple	223.82
Maximum	Single	13.40
	Couple	14.99

No new savings credit claims being accepted, except from people who reached pension age before 1 April 2016. Pension credit is based on age of oldest partner if a couples. It is not immediately affected by the introduction of universal credit. At some point, couples who are not on pension credit where one is below pension age will be advised to claim universal credit and not pension credit.

Working Tax Credit (WTC) 2018–2019

	p.a.
First Income threshold	6,420.00
Withdrawal rate (41%)	
Basic element	1,960.00
Additional couple's/lone parent element	2,010.00
30 hours element	810.00
Disabled worker element	3,090.00
Severe disability element	1,330.00

Childcare element

	p.w.
Percentage of eligible costs covered (70%)	
Maximum eligible cost for two or more children (maximum payable £210 p.w.)	300.00
Maximum eligible cost for one child (maximum payable £122.50 p.w.)	175.00

Based on gross annual income: in-work support for families with child/children where lone parent works at least 16 hours p.w., or couple's combined work hours total 24 hours p.w., with one parent working at least 16 hours p.w. Extra payment for working at least 30 hours p.w. Also in-work support for some households without child, including those aged 25 and over working at least 30 hours p.w., and those aged 60 and over or with disability working at least 16 hours p.w. Up to first threshold, claimants receive the maximum. Credit then tapers by 41p per £1 of income as income rises. Above first threshold, claimant loses main element of WTC first, then childcare element, then child element of any CTC.

Elements are cumulative. Complex assessment rules. Maintenance ignored. Assessment on annual income, joint incomes for couples (disregarding £300 of certain types of unearned income).

Awards provisional until end of year notice identifies under/overpayments. Disregard of £2,500 before in-year falls or rises in income affect entitlement; Administered by HMRC.

Child Tax Credit (CTC) 2018–2019

	p.a.
First Income threshold for those entitled to CTC only	16,105.00
Withdrawal rate (41%)	

Family elements

Family element (only if child born before 6 April 2017)	545.00

Child elements

Child element (per child)	2,780.00
Disabled child additional element (includes child element)	3,175.00
Severely disabled child additional element (includes child element)	4,600

Based on gross annual income. First the per-child element then the family element tapered by 41p per £1 of income once income above £16,105.00 (WTC abated first).

One family element per family. Paid to nominated main carer. Replaces most benefit additions for children but in turn is being replaced by universal credit (2016–2022).

Administered by HMRC.

NB: Since 6 April 2017, no new basic child elements will be added for children born after that date, except in specific circumstances (conceived due to rape or due to a controlling or coercive relationship, or multiple birth or adoption/special guardianship). See *https://www.gov.uk/guidance/claiming-benefits-for-2-or-more-children*

NB: There is also an additional benefit cap in place, which limits an individual claim to a maximum of £20,000 a year outside London and £23,000 inside London. It includes housing benefit, child benefit and all means-tested or N.I. based benefits. It generally affects people with children and/or high rents. Families that include a disabled person or a carer or where a parent is working above certain a certain amount are exempt from being capped. See *https://www.gov.uk/benefit-cap*

Universal Credit (UC)

Administered solely by DWP. Means-tested. Generally not taxable. Paid to people of working age only (although could include some couples where only one person is below pension age).

This new benefit has been trialled since 2013. The main roll-out however started in 2016 and is due to be completed for all new claims by February 2019. From July 2019 to March 2022, the DWP will manage the migration of all existing customers of legacy benefits to UC. If people move across to UC before then, they may get less benefit. If they move as part of "managed migration".

The legacy benefits that will eventually disappear for people of a working-age are income support, child and working tax credits, housing benefit and the income-related versions of ESA and JSA.

Although UC shares many characteristics of these benefits (capital limit of £16,000; requirement to look for work or be covered by a medical certificate or be a carer etc; private rents met only up to certain levels; benefit cap/two-child policy/bedroom tax all still applying), it also has its own rules. Some of the amounts are substantially different especially for people with disabilities or a disabled child. UC is also paid monthly in arrears, and the rent element is normally paid to the claimant to pass to the landlord (except in cases of arrears or vulnerability). See *www.universalcreditinfo.net* for more information.

I2: Social security benefits and tax credits (means-tested)

The perceived advantage of UC is that a person would be entitled to the maximum whilst out of work but will remain on UC, but at a reduced rate, as they move into work. It is supposed to be more flexible and adaptable than having to stop claiming JSA/income support/ESA and start claiming in-work benefits.

Universal Credit (monthly amounts)

Single under 25	251.77
Single 25 or over	317.82
Joint claimants both under 25	395.20
Joint claimants, one or both 25 or over	498.89
First child (born prior to 6 April 2017)	277.08
Second/ subsequent child (born on or after 6 April 2017)	231.67
Lower rate addition for disabled child	126.11
Higher rate addition for disabled child	383.86
Limited Capability for Work amount	126.11
Limited Capability for Work and Work-Related Activity amount	328.32
Carer amount	156.45
Maximum child care costs for one child	646.35
Maximum child care costs for two or more children	1108.04

13: Personal injury trusts

Introduction

Following a serious personal injury a client may receive substantial sums of money, be they from a claim for damages, personal accident insurance payouts, charitable gifts, or other sources.

Such clients often have to live for many years, if not the rest of their lives, with the personal, social and financial repercussions that arise because of their injury. They may be left unable to work, their family members may give up jobs to provide care, and they may have expensive ongoing costs to pay for, such as the costs of private care, case management, specialist aids and equipment. They will also continue to have their regular living costs to meet, including the maintenance of any children or dependant relatives.

Therefore, it is important to ensure that each client is provided with proper and complete advice, and practical support where required, to ensure that:

- they get the best possible award from their personal injury claim;
- they are able to claim all of the state benefits they are entitled to and statutory care and support they need, both now and in years to come; and
- they have a suitable structure in place to properly manage and invest their award in the future.

It is, of course, important for any legal advisor to ensure that they have given each and every client the proper advice with regard to each of these matters. To fail to do so has in the past led to a number of personal injury lawyers being found to have been negligent because they have not provided their clients with proper advice about the possible use of personal injury trusts.

What is a personal injury trust?

A personal injury trust is a formal structure in which to hold and manage any funds which the client has received as a consequence of their personal injury.

A formal trust deed should be put in place, which sets out the rules for the management of the funds. It is important that it is the right kind of trust, that best suits the client's requirements in their particular circumstances.

The trust deed should specify the trustees—two or more people, or a trust corporation, who are then in charge of the trust. The trustees should together make decisions about the management of the trust funds, including any payments made out of those funds, and are under an obligation to exercise their powers for the benefit of those named as beneficiaries. In most cases there will only be one beneficiary, the injured person.

The benefits of a personal injury trust

There are several benefits of having a personal injury trust in place, which include the following (albeit not an exhaustive list):

13: Personal injury trusts

- If held in a personal injury trust, capital derived from a payment made in consequence of any personal injury to the claimant or the claimant's partner is disregarded for the purpose of many means-tested state benefits and services.

    Therefore, a client (and their partner if they claim benefits together) can continue to receive these benefits, despite having funds within the trust which, if held by them personally, would have left them with too much capital to remain entitled.

    These means-tested state benefits include Income Support, Income Related Employment Support Allowance, Income Based Job Seekers Allowance, Universal Credit, Housing Benefit and Council Tax Support. A personal injury trust exempts capital from means testing for a disabled facilities grant. A trust also protects entitlement to Local Authority funding for care.

- The trust structure can help to protect the interests of young, older, disabled or otherwise vulnerable clients.

    Because of the requirement to have trustees in place who must each authorise all transactions within the trust, a client can be protected if their trustees are vigilant to any inappropriate proposals for the use of the funds.

    A steadfast trustee, be they a solicitor, interested family friend or parent, can exercise their effective veto against the use of trust funds to ensure that the funds are only applied in the client's best interests. The balance of power will depend on the type of trust chosen, and clients who fear that they may need extra safeguards should be advised carefully about this.

- A client can benefit from the knowledge, experience and wisdom of their trustees.

    Having appropriate trustees appointed can provide a client with important advice and support when making big decisions. Particularly when dealing with a large lump sum, this can be invaluable to ensure that decisions are appropriate to protect and ensure the long-term interests of the client.

    Some clients prefer to have an appropriately experienced solicitor appointed as one of their trustees, so that they can give advice on matters such as investment decisions, budgeting, and large items of capital expenditure.

- The personal injury trust helps to define and "ring fence" the funds that arise as a consequence of the client's personal injury, keeping them separate from other assets that may belong to the client.

    This can be of help if the client's circumstances change in the future and they suddenly find that they may be eligible for means-tested benefits or care funding; for example, if they have to go in to a care home, or if they separate from a working partner.

    The personal injury trust "wrapper" can also help to define what funds were awarded for their future needs. This can help to differentiate the funds if the client goes through a divorce or any other process where their personal finances are taken into consideration.

The basic rules for entitlement to means-tested benefits

As you may imagine, the rules for assessing a client's entitlement to means-tested benefits are detailed and complex.

However, when considering how personal injury funds may affect a client's entitlement to means-tested benefits, the key principles for Income Support, Income Related Employment Support Allowance, Income Based Job Seeker's Allowance, Universal Credit, Housing Benefit and Council Tax Support are, broadly speaking, as follows:

- When considering a client's capital, it is important to consider both the personal injury funds that they are due to receive, as well as any savings or investments that they already hold.
- The first payment of any money derived from a personal injury will be ignored for 52 weeks from the date of receipt. An interim payment, or indeed any other payment received as a consequence of the injury, will qualify as the first payment. The rules under the Universal Credit Regulations are

more generous and exempt each payment for 52 weeks. The intention of this disregard is that the claimant will have an appropriate period to seek advice and set up the trust.
- If a client has capital below £6,000, then their capital will not affect their entitlement. This lower threshold is £10,000 for those living in a care home or independent hospital.
- If a client has capital between £6,000 and £16,000, then their entitlement will be reduced. For capital between those two thresholds they will be treated as having income of £1 for every £250 or part thereof above £6,000.
- If a client has capital over £16,000 they will be excluded from entitlement altogether.
- A client and their partner (with whom they live) will share a capital allowance, so it is important to look at their capital together. They should ideally have less than £6,000 between them both, if they are to maintain full entitlement.
- Certain assets, such as the value of the home a client lives in and their personal possessions, are disregarded when calculating capital.
- Any income received by the client, including that received by their partner, is deducted from the amount of benefits payable, albeit subject to some personal disregards and allowances.

The basic rules for entitlement to means-tested benefits for elderly clients

For Pension Credit (currently available for female claimants after the age of 62 years and 9 months, and for male claimants after the age of 65 years, pension ages go up, which will increase gradually to 66 by October 2020), the lower capital threshold is £10,000, and above that amount tariff income from a client's capital is assumed at a rate of £1 for every £500, or part thereof. There is no upper capital threshold. Income derived from a personal injury settlement is ignored, whether paid from a trust or otherwise. Actual capital is ignored, except to the extent that it creates assumed tariff income.

If a person receives Pension Credit Guarantee Credit then personal injury monies are ignored completely, whether in a trust or not, both in respect of capital and income. Due to the vagaries of the rules, there is a concern that growth on capital assets may not be disregarded. In addition, in order to access the disregard for residential care funding a trust will be required and so it is best to advise clients to consider a trust even if it appears their damages will be disregarded at the moment.

Welfare reform

Since the implementation of the Welfare Reform Act 2012 in March 2013, Council Tax Benefit was abolished from 31 March 2013 and replaced by a discretionary scheme designed by local authorities. Each local authority has its own scheme although there is a national precedent scheme which local authorities can adopt. Ten per cent less money is available to reduce people's Council Tax than was previously available under the Council Tax Benefit scheme. Local authorities have to protect the position of pensioners. The net result is that in many local authority areas, people of working age are having to pay a proportion of their Council Tax even if they would previously have been entitled to full Council Tax Benefit. A number of people have been caught out by this in the belief that they are entitled to full Council Tax Support and so have not paid a great deal of attention to the Council Tax statement which comes once a year until they receive a summons for non-payment.

The primary income related benefits are being replaced by Universal Credit for new claims. That has been going on for some years and is still in progress. The intention was that there would be no new claims for Income Support, Income Related Employment Support Allowance and Income Based Job Seeker's Allowance after April 2016. However, the timetable is running rather behind.

Readers will be aware that benefits have been a very hot topic in recent years and it is fair to say that we may not yet have seen the full effects of the reforms. It also remains to be seen how far this will have

13: Personal injury trusts

a knock-on effect on social care funding, the calculation of which is closely tied to the existing income-related benefits regulations.

Care funding

Adult funding in England

The Care Act 2014 was implemented on April 1, 2015. It applies in England only. It has applied to all cases since 1 April 2016, regardless of whether they have been reassessed under the Act.

There are some significant differences to the treatment of domiciliary care and in particular the treatment of periodical payments to which disregards now apply in some circumstances. Where no reassessment of means has been carried out under the Care Act, some individuals could be due repayments of charges unlawfully made.

The Care and Support (Charging and Assessment of Resources) Regulations 2014 (CSCAR) now apply to all cases.

Capital placed in a personal injury trust is disregarded for means assessment purposes, both for home and residential care. The arguments previously raised by local authorities that they had discretion to take account of the care element of such assets in domiciliary care cases have no arguable basis under the CSCAR.

For the year 2018–19 there is an upper capital limit for assessable capital of £23,250. There is a lower capital limit of £14,250. These limits have been in place since April 2010. Between these two limits, the resident is treated as having tariff income of £1 for every £250 or part of £250. Amendments to the upper capital limit will appear in regulation 12 of the charging regulations and to the lower limit in regulation 25.

Investment income paid to a deputy or trustee of a PI trust is disregarded.

Periodical payments placed in a personal injury trust are also disregarded as income but an issue may arise if this was done to avoid care fees.

The question of whether periodical payments made to the claimant in person for meeting care needs are disregarded is subject to some debate. The position taken here is that periodical payments to the claimant from the trust by the trustees (or otherwise direct to the claimant) are disregarded subject to a cap of £20 unless they are to pay for care.

If the periodical payments made direct to the claimant are for care they should be disregarded if they are awarded for care which the council accepts is a genuine need but does not fit within the new statutory eligibility criteria. Although the regulation is ambiguous, the position taken here is that this disregard is not capped. We consider that the aim is to allow such payments to be used for topping up care. There is a further condition that they are actually used for that purpose.

If periodical payments to the claimant in person are unused after the relevant period and accumulate as capital in the hands of the claimant to a sum exceeding the lower capital limit, they will be taken into account under the general capital limits.

Payments made by trustees directly to a domiciliary care provider are disregarded. It is possible that regular payments made by trustees to a residential care provider may be treated as the income of the resident.

Means testing reform

Section 15 of the Care Act provides that the cost to an adult of their care and support other than for daily living costs may be capped.

In a statement made on 7 December 2017 the care minister stated that the government was not going ahead with its previous plans to implement s.15 in April 2020.

On 17 November 2017, the government announced that it would publish a green paper on the future of care funding in the summer of 2018. This followed an apparently hastily drafted and equally hastily withdrawn proposal from the Conservative Party, appearing in the middle of the 2017 general election campaign, that the absolute disregard of a person's own home in respect of the means testing of domiciliary care would be amended so that its value would be taken into account to an extent to be specified. This shows that the government has been willing to consider radical changes to the means testing regime and that the current arrangements cannot necessarily be relied upon to persist into the future.

Care funding for minors in England

The provision of care support for minors in England continues to be provided under ss.17 & 18 of the Children Act 1989 and under s.2 of the Chronically Sick and Disabled Persons Act 1970.

Section 29 sets out that a local authority may charge for these services except where they are for advice, guidance or counselling. There are no regulations made under this section.

The section also states that where the child is under 16, the person to be charged is the "parent". Where the child is over 16, it is the child.

The means testing position is complicated by the fact that s.17(8) states that:

> "Before giving any assistance or imposing any conditions, a local authority shall have regard to the means of the child concerned and of each of his parents."

There is no case law deciding how this relates to s.29. It is submitted that if the two provisions are to work together in a sensible manner, s.29 should qualify the generality of s.17(8).

The Social Services and Well-Being (Wales) Act 2014

This Act was implemented on 5 April 2016. A major difference between this Act and the Care Act in England, is that the Welsh Act incorporates care and support provision for minors and so replaces the Children Act 1989 and the Chronically Sick & Disabled Persons Act 1970.

Part 5 of the Act deals with charging and financial assessment. Section 59 permits a local authority to make a charge for providing the service. Section 60 states that a charge for a service provided to a child may be imposed upon an adult with parental responsibility for that child.

The Care and Support (Financial Assessment) (Wales) Regulations 2015 and the Care and Support (Charging) (Wales) Regulations 2015 provide a unified scheme for the means testing of domiciliary and residential support. This scheme of charging does not apply to looked after and accommodated children under Pt.6.

There is a capital limit which for the year 2018–19 is £40,000 for residential care means assessment and £24,000 for domiciliary care assessment. Revised limits are specified from time to time in reg.11 of the Care and Support (Charging) (Wales) Regulations 2015. There is no tariff income scheme in Wales and so there is no lower limit for capital below which tariff income does not apply.

The disregards for personal injury trust capital and the first capital payment to the claimant in person in consequence of a personal injury, are the same as those now applying in England under the Care Act 2014.

Investment income paid to a trustee of a PI trust is disregarded

As in England, periodical payments are defined as income (para.16(6) 2015 financial assessment regulations). Otherwise, periodical payments are treated differently in Wales. In practice they are disregarded because contributions from income to the cost of domiciliary support are in any event limited to £80 per week (2018–19) and this cap also applies to income in the form of periodical payments. Revised income cap limits are specified from time to time in reg.7 of the Care and Support (Charging) (Wales) Regulations 2015.

Paragraph 14 of schedule 1 of the 2015 financial assessment regulations suggests that income type payments made out of a trust by the trustees to the claimant or periodical payments made to the claimant direct from the insurer are disregarded unless they are to pay for care. Periodical payments made direct to the claimant should be disregarded if they are awarded for care which the council accepts is a genuine need but does not fit within the new statutory eligibility criteria. There is a further condition that they are actually used for that purpose. The aim is to allow such payments to be used for topping up care. However even if all these conditions are met, they are then subject to a cap of £20. The complexity of this regulation seems unnecessary having regard to the overall income cap.

Where it is proposed that periodical payments are paid into a personal injury trust, they should be disregarded in full. An issue may arise if this was done to avoid care fees but the impact of any such argument may be limited by the effect of the overall income cap.

If periodical payments to the claimant in person are unused and accumulate as capital in the hands of the claimant to a sum exceeding the capital limit, they will be taken into account under the general capital limits.

Payments made by trustees directly to a domiciliary care provider are disregarded. It is possible that regular payments made by trustees to a residential care provider may be treated as the income of the resident.

There are no proposals for care capping contained in the Welsh Care Act.

What funds can go into a personal injury trust?

The benefits regulations for most benefits take a wide definition, allowing any sums of capital to be disregarded if they are "derived from a payment made in consequence of any personal injury to the claimant or the claimant's partner". However, the Universal Credit regulations refer to "compensation" in the title to the disregard section. The effect of that may be to narrow the types of funds which can be protected in a personal injury trust for injured people who are claiming Universal Credit. Some clients may find that they are in a dual system where certain funds within a trust might be disregarded for care purposes for example but not for Universal Credit. For most benefits however the wider definition means that the use of personal injury trusts are not just limited to awards of damages, and can include:

- A personal injury award, including interim payments received during the course of a claim.
- A Criminal Injuries Compensation Authority award.
- A Motor Insurers' Bureau award.
- Payments from the Armed Forces Compensation Scheme, and similar schemes.
- Payments from various "no fault" schemes, sometimes set up by government bodies both here and abroad, such as payments from the Irish Residential Institutions Redress Board.
- Funds received from a Periodical Payment or Structured Settlement.
- Charitable or public donations following an accident.
- Funds received from accident or travel insurance.
- Funds received from a professional negligence claim paid to compensate for an undervalued or negligently pursued personal injury claim.

It is vitally important to remember that, although the capital disregard is quite wide, the income disregard is rather more restricted. Where a person receives income from, for example, a personal accident policy or an occupational ill health pension, it is unlikely that those funds would be able to be disregarded, even if they are placed in to a personal injury trust.

When to set up a personal injury trust

It is important that, if at all possible, a personal injury trust is set up before a client receives their funds.

Lawyers should be aware that any client funds held on their Client Account may be treated as the client's money by the benefits agency and local authority. Therefore, any funds held on Client Account can jeopardise a client's benefit entitlement and consideration should be given to the suitability of a personal injury trust straight away.

Lawyers also run the risk that if funds remain on their client account, and they are aware that the client has not notified the benefits agency, they could find their firm obliged to report the client's non-disclosure as defrauding the benefits agency. Furthermore, they run the risk that they may be construed as aiding and abetting the client in a possible benefits fraud.

While it is usually best advice that a personal injury trust should be set up sooner rather than later, it is possible to set up a trust after the funds have been received and held personally by the client for some time. There is no restriction upon when personal injury funds must be placed into a trust, so funds can be held for months, or years, before a client arranges to place them in a trust. This does not allow the client to claim retrospectively for any benefits that they have missed out on prior to the trust being set up.

However, a client will have to demonstrate to the satisfaction of the benefits agency, or local authority, that the funds placed into the trust are purely those arising from their personal injury. There is a risk that the funds may over time have been mixed up with, or diluted by, other income or capital belonging to the client. For example, if personal injury money and personal injury money only has been used to purchase a house, that would be much more straightforward to add to the trust than money that has been put in the client's own bank account and used for all sorts of things. Therefore, clients may find that they have some difficulty persuading the authorities that all of the funds should be disregarded.

Setting up a personal injury trust

It will be necessary to appoint appropriate trustees. There should be at least two trustees, and no more than four. They must be over 18 years of age and mentally capable of acting as a trustee. It is usually best to avoid trustees whose health and age might make them incapable of fulfilling their obligations in the foreseeable future.

The choice of trustees is an important one, as they will for all intents and purposes have full control over the personal injury trust and the assets held within it. It is important to consider whether they will be able to work well together and continue to act in the best interests of the beneficiaries. For this reason, some caution should be exercised before appointing partners, spouses, or other family members as trustees, if there is a risk of the relationship breaking down in the future. Often partners or spouses will shy away from wanting to be involved in a personal injury trust, particularly if they have appeared on the scene after the injury and are concerned that people might question their motives.

Some clients may prefer to have an appropriately experienced solicitor appointed as one of their trustees. This allows an impartial and professional person to assist in the trustees' deliberations and decision making. It can help to ensure that the trustees are making decisions together which are appropriate to the needs of the beneficiaries, as well as providing the professional expertise and experience that can be invaluable when making difficult decisions.

It is also important that a client receives the correct advice about the right kind of trust to put in place. Consideration needs to be given to the client's particular circumstances, their potential liability to tax and the provision that they may wish to make for their family in the future. This will in turn affect whether the client is named as the sole beneficiary of the trust, or whether other beneficiaries are named and, if so, whether the trustees have any discretion in how they apply funds for their benefit.

The client being advised about Personal Injury Trusts should be advised about wills at the same time.

Once the advice is given, and the necessary decisions are made, the trust deed will need to be prepared by the instructed lawyer, before being signed in the presence of witnesses, and dated. The personal injury trust will usually have a suitable title, such as the "John Smith Personal Injury Trust."

Once a personal injury trust is set up

Once a personal injury trust is set up, the trustees' first act will usually be to open a bank or building society account to hold the trust funds. The account should be suitably named, such as the "Josephine Anne Bloggs Personal Injury Trust". The account should usually require that each and every one of the trustees is required to sign to authorise all transactions on account, including all cheques. Some financial institutions are happy to operate a single signature system provided all of the trustees have given their instructions and that can be helpful when trustees are geographically dispersed.

Once the trustees have set up the trust bank account, the personal injury lawyer can confidently arrange for a cheque to be issued for the personal injury funds, ensuring that the cheque is made payable to the trust, i.e. payable to the "Josephine Anne Bloggs Personal Injury Trust", and not to the client personally.

The trustees will need to keep to certain rules in order to be able to use funds from the trust without affecting the client's benefit entitlement, namely:

- Any income arising from the funds in the trust, such as interest or dividends, should be paid into a trust account, and not paid to the client personally.

- The trustees can transfer funds into the client's own personal account, but should take care to ensure that the client's capital (including the capital held by their partner if they are claiming benefits as a couple) stays below £6,000 at all times, which is the lower capital threshold for most means-tested benefits.

- Possibly the simplest way to use funds from the trust is to make direct payments from the trust to third parties. This way the funds go directly from the trust account, to the third party and do not go through the client's hands in any way.

- Any further assets set up to be held by the trustees, be they bank accounts, investments or property, should be set up with the same restrictions as the original trust bank account, namely:

- in the name of the trust, or trustees; and

- with the restriction that each and every one of the trustees is required to sign all transactions with regard to that asset unless an alternative system has been agreed for convenience but the consent of all the trustees will always be needed.

Is a client likely to benefit from a personal injury trust in the future?

For many clients it is easy to determine that they are entitled to means-tested benefits, or care funding, at the time that they receive their funds, and so it makes sense to protect their entitlement straight away by setting up a personal injury trust.

However, some clients may at the time have no entitlement to means-tested benefits, and so a personal injury trust may not seem immediately relevant. In such cases careful consideration should be given to the client's potential to claim means-tested benefits in the future.

A client may become entitled to means-tested benefits in the future if their relevant circumstance change, which may include:

- If they need to move to live in a residential care home.

- If they move out of the family home to live on their own.

- If they leave full or part-time education.

- If they are discharged from hospital or residential care.

- If they and their spouse divorce or separate.

- When they reach a significant age for benefits purposes, such as 16, 18 or 60 years of age or state pension age, gradually increasing to 66 by 2020. There is a helpful online calculator at *gov.uk*

- If they or their partner lose their job, retire or are medically unable to continue to work.

- If they, or their partner, lose their entitlement to another benefit or source of income.

- If they, or their partner, find their health deteriorates and they become entitled to higher rates of disability benefits, which in turn have a knock-on effect for some means-tested benefits.

- If they, or their partner, find that they have used up their pre-existing savings (those which have not arisen from the personal injury claim and which have previously prevented them claiming means-tested benefits) and so find that they would become entitled to means-tested benefits if their personal injury funds were disregarded as capital.

In such cases clients should be advised to use up their pre-existing savings with some caution. The benefits agency or local authority can ask to look at a person's history of expenditure, and any gifts made, to see if the client has in the opinion of the authority, deliberately depleted their estate in order to gain entitlement to means-tested benefits or services. If the authority feels that a client has deliberately depleted their estate in such a manner, they can decide to treat the spent funds as "notional capital", essentially treating the client as if they still have the funds and leaving them with no entitlement to the means-tested benefit or service which they have applied for. Therefore, it is important that clients keep a careful record of their expenditure to demonstrate that their use of funds has been reasonable and not a deliberate attempt to deplete their estate.

The 52-week rule

Payments received as a consequence of a personal injury are disregarded for the purpose of assessing entitlement to means tested benefits for the first 52 weeks after they are received.

However, that disregard applies only to the first payment received as a consequence of that personal injury, which may often be the client's first interim payment. It is also important to check to see a client has received other earlier payments, which may count as their "first payment", such as payments from an accident insurance policy or even a capital payment from a charity.

Any later payments, including further interim payments, are not protected by this disregard after the expiry of the original 52-week period.

Under the Universal Credit regulations there is a disregard of 52 weeks for every payment. That may be helpful for some clients who receive smaller awards but if they decide not to set up a trust they will need to be extremely careful in monitoring the various 52 week disregard periods. Establishing which funds form part of which interim and when the disregard therefore runs out could be quite tricky and the client would be caught out.

Therefore, when receiving a first payment as a consequence of a personal injury, a client may choose not to set up a trust if they anticipate spending enough of that sum to bring their capital below the relevant threshold by the end of the 52-week period. However, they should be advised to hold that payment in a bank account separate from any other funds. That way, if towards the end of period they find that they unexpectedly have funds remaining, they can still arrange to place them into a personal injury trust safe in the knowledge that the funds have not become mixed up with other capital in any way. Clients do need to be advised that the deprivation rules will still apply. If they deliberately use their capital in ways which are designed to mean that they keep their benefits then the benefits authorities could still treat them as owning it.

However, in many cases it will be appropriate to set up a personal injury trust as soon as any funds are received, regardless of the 52-week rule. Where the amount of funds due to the client overall are almost certainly going to last longer than that period, there is little if no benefit in delaying the setting up of a personal injury trust which is likely to remain in place to manage the client's funds for many years to come.

Personal injury trusts for children and protected parties

In most cases the decision as to whether or not to set up a personal injury trust is one for the client to make for themselves, albeit with the benefit of good advice from a lawyer. The matter does not require court approval in any way.

However, if a client is unable to make their own decision it will be necessary to obtain approval from the appropriate court with authority to make a decision on behalf of the client (CPR r.21.11 and supplementary Practice Direction), namely:

- The High Court will need to approve the establishment of a personal injury trust to manage an infant's funds until the infant reaches 18 years of age.
- In cases involving mentally incapable people, the Court of Protection will need to approve the establishment of a personal injury trust, in preference to the appointment of a Deputy for Property and Affairs. Following the case of *Re HM*,[4] the court is likely to approve the establishment of trusts in limited circumstances only. The recent case of *OH v Craven* has said that there is not a preference for deputyship as such, as was widely thought to be the case after *HM*. The Court is still highly likely to prefer a deputyship to a trust in most cases.

---

[4] (2011) C.O.P. 11875043 April 11, 2011.

14: Claims for loss of earnings and maintenance at public expense

Section 5 of the Administration of Justice Act 1980 provides:

Maintenance at public expense to be taken into account in assessment of damages.

In an action under the law of England and Wales or the law of Northern Ireland for damages for personal injuries (including any such action arising out of a contract) any saving to the injured person which is attributable to his maintenance wholly or partly at public expense in a hospital, nursing home or other institution shall be set off against any income lost by him as a result of his injuries.

This deduction is comparable to (but not the same as) the common law principle that where a Claimant is in a private hospital or home (in respect of which damages are claimed from the Defendant), credit must be given for the domestic expenses thereby saved. This is the "domestic element" which was discussed in *Fairhurst v St Helens and Knowsley Health Authority*.[5] The principle is clear, but there is a dearth of authority on how to value such maintenance.

It is worth looking at the House of Lords' decision in *O'Brien v Independent Assessor*,[6] in which it held (in the context of statutory compensation for miscarriages of justice), that living expenses are deductible from the claim of a wrongly-convicted defendant for loss of the earnings that he would have received had he not been wrongfully imprisoned. The Assessor had awarded the three appellants:

- O'Brien: £143,497 for past loss of earnings, less £37,158 saved living expenses.
- Michael and Vincent Hickey: "A substantial figure for loss of earnings" less 25 per cent saved living expenses

In upholding these deductions, the House of Lords did not give any guidance on how to assess them, but said:

23 It is in my opinion inapt and understandably offensive to the appellants to regard or treat their imprisonment as a benefit conferred on them by the state.... [However, the] assessor's task, in relation to the appellants' loss of earnings claim, was to assess what they had really lost . . .

30 . . . the appropriate deduction is a highly judgmental matter . . .

15: Foster care allowances

Introductory notes:

Every April the Fostering Network publishes the cost of bringing up a child in its own home for the next 12 months. Contact Fostering Network Publications, 87 Blackfriars Road, London SE1 8HA (tel: 020 7620 6400; *http://www.fostering.net*).

The Fostering Network publishes Foster Care Finance, with recommended minimum weekly allowances for fostering in the UK and a full survey of allowances paid by each local authority. The Fostering

---

[5] [1995] P.I.Q.R. Q1.
[6] [2007] UKHL 10, [2007] 2 A.C. 312. Not to be confused with the more saintly protagonist of O'Brien v Ministry of Justice [2017] UKSC 46.

Network's recommended minimum allowance depends on the age of the child and whether or not the placement is in London. The allowances do not include any form of reward for carers themselves. The Fostering Network recommends four extra weeks' payment, to cover the cost of birthdays, holidays and a religious festival. It encourages local authorities to pay allowances to all carers at least in line with its recommended rates. Despite such encouragement the majority of local authorities give foster carers less than the Fostering Network's recommended minimum allowances for spending on the care of fostered children. From a survey published by the Fostering Network in September 2003, 53 per cent of local authorities in England and 87 per cent of local authorities in Wales paid below the Fostering Network's recommended minimum allowance.

Fostering Network recommended costs of bringing up a child in its own home for the year beginning 6 April 2018

Foster Care Allowances

Age of child (years)	London (£ per week)	South East (£ per week)	Rest of the UK (£ per week)
Babies	144.00	136.00	128.00
Pre Primary	147.00	142.00	138.00
Primary	165.00	158.00	141.00
11 to 15	187.00	179.00	161.00
16 to 17	218.00	211.00	188.00

In *Spittle v Bunney*[2] it was said that the cost of fostering services is not an appropriate measure for the value of the loss of a (deceased) mother's services, but the case is not uncontroversial.

---

[2] [1988] 1 W.L.R. 847.

Group J
Court of Protection

J1: **Note on the Court of Protection**

J2: **The incidence of deputyship costs over a claimant's life**

J3: **Deputyship costs**

J1: Note on the Court of Protection

1. **Introduction: The Mental Capacity Act 2005**
   The Mental Capacity Act 2005 ("the Act") came into force on 1 October 2007. At the time of its inception, the Act was considered a fundamental change in the law. It is intended to empower incapacitated adults and provide a framework for those who work with, and for, them.

   The Act as amended and its accompanying Code of Practice ("the Code") govern all dealings with those who lack capacity to make decisions about some or all aspects of their property and affairs or their health and welfare.

   Capacity is time and function specific—in other words, is someone capable of making a decision or carrying out an action *at the time that the decision or action is needed*? A person may be capable of making many decisions or very few and that may change over time or with circumstances.

   It is important to remember that there is no general level below which a claimant lacks capacity and above which they do not. The statement that a person "lacks capacity" in itself is meaningless. Clearly some claimants will lack the capacity needed to deal with all or any of their financial affairs but others will retain some capacity.

   In order to determine whether someone has capacity to make a decision we must adhere to the principles set out in s.1 of the Act:

   1. A person must be assumed to have capacity unless it is established that he lacks capacity.
   2. A person is not to be treated as unable to make that decision unless all practicable steps to help him to do so have been taken without success.
   3. A person is not to be treated as unable to make a decision merely because he makes an unwise decision.
   4. An act done, or decision made, under the Act for or on behalf of a person who lacks capacity must be done, or made, in his best interests.
   5. Before the act is done, or the decision is made, regard must be had to whether the purpose for which it is needed can be as effectively achieved in a way that is less restrictive of the person's rights and freedom of action.

   The Act says that a person lacks capacity in relation to a matter if at the material time he is unable to make a decision for himself because of an impairment of, or a disturbance in the functioning of, the mind. It goes on to say that it doesn't matter whether the impairment or disturbance is permanent or temporary and that a lack of capacity should not be established by mere reference to a person's age or appearance or an aspect of his behaviour which might lead to unjustified assumptions about his capacity.

   The test for establishing whether someone lacks capacity is based upon the balance of probabilities and not beyond all reasonable doubt.

   The Act says that a person is unable to make a decision for himself if he is unable:

   1. To understand the information relevant to the decision.

      A person must not be regarded as unable to understand the relevant information if he can understand an explanation of it given in a way which is appropriate to his circumstances; this may involve the explanation being delivered using simple language, visual aids or other means. Information relevant to the decision includes information about the reasonably foreseeable consequences of deciding one way or another or failing to make the decision at all.

2. To retain that information.

> The fact that someone can only retain relevant information for a short period of time doesn't mean that they should be regarded as unable to make the decision.

3. To use or weigh that information as part of the process of making the decision.
4. To communicate their decision by whatever means.

Failing to meet any one of the first three tests will establish a lack of capacity on a specific decision. However, someone who passes the first three tests but is unable to communicate their decision will be deemed to lack capacity, even though medically they may have full capacity. It is therefore important to ensure that a Claimant's ability to communicate is maximised.

2. **The scope and authority of the Court of Protection**

If a claimant lacks capacity to make a decision, the Court of Protection is there to help. The Act established a new court (albeit with the same name). This new court is a superior court of record with authority equivalent to that of the High Court. Its powers extend to health and welfare issues, and financial matters.

Those empowered to act on the orders of the court are known as deputies, and claimants who fall within the court's jurisdiction are referred to as "P". The Office of the Public Guardian (OPG) supervises deputies. The court now publishes its judgments which is of assistance to practitioners as are the Practice Notes issued by the OPG and the Court. Professional deputies must also adhere to a set of professional deputyship standards. The Act has greatly changed the role of the deputy; it is an increasingly specialist field of practice.

3. **The appointment of a property and affairs deputy**

The court will confer on a deputy powers which should be as limited in scope and duration as is reasonably practicable in the circumstances. For a claimant with a head injury the court is more likely to make an order which gives the deputy wide powers given the number of decisions that will need to be made on P's behalf. However, despite these wide powers, there is an ongoing duty on the deputy to make only the decisions that P is unable to make. This goes to the heart of the Act and its underlying aim, which is to empower, rather than limit, the decision-making capabilities of a person living with a mental impairment. Despite these wide powers the deputy may still need to return to the court for further authority, or satisfy the court on certain issues.

4. **When to make an application**

Whilst a deputy is not needed until there are funds available that the claimant cannot manage, it can take six months for a deputy to be appointed, sometimes longer. It will be prudent to make the application in good time.

Rule 14.5 of the Solicitors' Accounts Rules provides that a deputy must not provide banking facilities through a client account. The management of an interim payment through a client account may give rise to a breach of this rule.

5. **Invoking the court's jurisdiction**

The court must have evidence to show that a person has a mental impairment that brings them within the scope of the Act and that they are unable to make or take decisions and actions which are needed. This is provided in the form COP3 Assessment of Capacity.

The practitioner giving instructions for the capacity assessment will set out in Part A of the COP3 form:

- the matters that the court is being asked to decide,
- the order sought,

- the reasons why the claimant will benefit from the order, and
- any other relevant information.

The capacity assessor will then use this information in their assessment. Where there is conflicting medical evidence, within the litigation, as to the claimant's capacity, there has been a recent but important change in the Court of Protection's approach to the appointment of a deputy. In *Loughlin v Singh* [2013] EWHC 1641 (QB) Kenneth Parker J made it clear that when an application is made for the appointment of a deputy the Court of Protection must have "all the material which, on proper reflection, is necessary for a just and accurate decision", this being a direct reference to material relating to P's mental capacity. Historically, where there has been conflicting evidence in relation to the claimant's capacity to manage aspects of their finances, the Court of Protection has often appointed a deputy, albeit that the order may be time limited and require further directions to be sought on conclusion of the litigation. This approach was taken against a background of the deputy being bound by the Mental Capacity Act 2005 and empowered only to make decisions that P is unable to make.

The Court of Protection has recently changed its approach to cases where there is ongoing litigation coupled with conflicting evidence on the issue of mental capacity and it will no longer appoint a deputy until the issue of capacity has been addressed by the Court having conduct of the personal injury litigation. At the time of publication this is not incorporated within a Practice Direction or judgment but is the Court's stated practice.

6. Surety bonds for deputies

For the deputy to act, the court requires that a surety be put in place to safeguard the claimant's assets. The level of security is set by the court, and can be based on a number of factors, including the size of the claimant's estate and the extent to which the deputy will have access to it. The bond safeguards the claimant's assets from any financial loss suffered as a result of the failure of the deputy to perform their duties. The surety bond is required even though the deputy has professional indemnity insurance.

Although Judge Hazel Marshall laid down in the case of *Re H*[1] clear guidelines to be followed when calculating a suitable level of surety, the level of surety remains in the discretion of the judiciary.

The fee for the bond will depend upon the level of surety that the court sets. Sureties can be obtained from a provider of the deputy's choice, but the court and OPG have from time to time identified preferred providers, following completion of a tendering process. The current preferred provider has introduced a charging structure which is significantly different from its predecessors, who charged an annual premium throughout the claimant's lifetime. The new structure provides for the payment of an initial premium, and four further premiums which fall due on the anniversary of the first order. The premiums reduce in years three and four, and after that no further fees are payable unless the value of the surety changes or a new deputy is appointed.

Sureties are typically set at £200,000—£350,000 for solicitors acting as professional deputies in high value personal injury and clinical negligence claims. Such a surety will attract bond premiums of:

- between £150 and £262.50 on the appointment of the deputy, and on the first and second anniversaries, and
- between £100 and £175 on the third and fourth anniversaries;
- thereafter no further premiums will be due.

[1] [2009] EWHC 1331 (COP).

The position is a little more complex if the court directs that the surety level should increase, which is often the case following the making of a large interim payment and on a final award.

A full table of bond premiums with some worked examples can be found at:

htttps://www.howdendeputybonds.co.uk/upload/224/bond_premium_facts_jan2017.pdf

This charging structure is fairly new, and it is not certain whether it will be sustainable in the long term. Given the uncertainty, practitioners may consider it prudent to allow for annual premiums over the claimant's lifetime.

7. **Professional or lay deputy?**
There is no prescribed limit above or below which a professional appointment is deemed appropriate. But in cases involving large awards (exceeding, say, £500,000), a professional is often preferred by the court and it can remove tensions that can arise when a family member is appointed. In high value, complex cases (such as multi-million-pound cerebral palsy cases), the court is unlikely to allow a lay deputy to be appointed as a sole deputy but may consider a joint appointment with a professional.

8. **Decision-making by deputies**
When a deputy makes a decision on behalf of a person, it must be one which is in their best interests. The Act does not define "best interests" but in s.4 of the Act it sets out some guidelines. The overriding rule is that the deputy or any other decision-maker must consider all relevant circumstances and "so far as is reasonably practicable" also permit and encourage the claimant to be involved as far as possible in the decision-making process. If it is practicable and appropriate the deputy should also consult others, e.g. family and carers, before making a decision.

The deputy must also consider whether the claimant might have capacity in the future; if so, decisions may have to be deferred.

9. **The role of the financial deputy**
With high-value awards, deputyship can be likened to running a small business. There are some legal and technical elements of deputyship work, sometimes requiring the input of other professionals. These can include:

- Instructing solicitors to deal with employment issues, especially regarding support workers;
- Instructing a property finder to locate a suitable property (or a plot on which a suitable property can be built) and negotiating a purchase of the property, arranging surveys etc.;
- Instructing solicitors to act in the purchase;
- Commissioning architects, structural engineers and quantity surveyors.

Routine, day to day management tasks for deputies include:

- Applications to the Court of Protection and liaising with the OPG and the court visitor where necessary;
- Preparation of an annual account and report to the OPG, including the provision of a cost budget;
- Arranging and funding the deputyship bond;
- Completion of tax returns and making payments to HMRC;
- Dealing with requests for capital expenditure;
- Setting budgets;
- Considering and approving investment proposals;
- Liaising with case managers and their assistants;
- Paying household bills;

- Arranging payroll services and ensuring that funds are available in order to pay wages, national insurance, pension contributions etc.;
- Meeting the cost of staff training;
- Contracting with treating therapists;
- Liaising with P and, wherever possible, taking all practical steps to enable them to make their own decisions;
- Ensuring that P receives the correct state funding, tax exemptions, etc;
- Buying aids and equipment;
- Buying vehicles and arranging for their maintenance, licensing, etc.;
- Contributing to the arrangements for holidays and funding them;
- Arranging and paying for household support, cleaning and gardening;
- Liaising with a financial advisor regarding the investment of funds;
- Approving an activity budget for the client;
- Arranging all necessary maintenance contracts and insurance policies including employer's liability insurance, employer's protection insurance, equipment insurance, house and contents insurance, vehicle insurance and breakdown cover. Obtaining insurance disclosure declarations from employees where relevant.

10. Visiting the Client

The deputy (or an appropriately qualified person acting on their behalf) must visit the claimant at least once a year. There may be other ways to stay in touch, such as Skype or FaceTime, but a visit to a client's home can be extremely informative and an annual visit should be undertaken whenever possible.

It may be necessary for more frequent visits in the early years, particularly after settlement, or during a house adaptation. A time of crisis may generate the need for more direct contact.

11. Approval of damages awards by the Court of Protection

The Court of Protection is no longer required to approve a personal injury settlement: Civil Procedure (Amendment) Rules 2007. However, if the court appoints a deputy while litigation is ongoing it is highly likely that the order appointing them will require the deputy to return to the court to seek further directions on the making of an interim payment or at the time of a final settlement.

12. Welfare deputies

Very few welfare deputies have been appointed. If court assistance is needed, matters are often dealt with by way of one-off declarations. Welfare deputyships are only for the most severely disabled, whose circumstances call for frequent and regular welfare decisions to be made for them.

13. Remuneration of the deputy and the deputy's staff

The deputy is entitled to be paid. Deputyship orders will usually give the deputy the option of taking fixed costs or having costs assessed on the basis of the hourly rates set by the SCCO.

14. Fixed costs in the Court of Protection

In low cost cases, fixed costs provide an alternative to an assessment. A Practice Direction dealing with Court of Protection costs was issued on 1 December 2017. The fixed costs and the date from which they apply are set out below. (Different rates apply to public authority deputies.)

Costs on appointment of a property and affairs deputy

For work up to and including the date upon which the court makes an order appointing the deputy, an amount not exceeding £950 + VAT can be claimed for all orders made on or after 1 April 2017.

J1: Note on the Court of Protection

Annual general management costs for a professional property and affairs deputy

The following will be payable on the anniversary of the court order for those matters where the anniversary falls on or after 1 January 2017:

a) For the first year: an amount not exceeding £1,670 + VAT.
b) For the second and subsequent years: an amount not exceeding £1,320 + VAT.
c) If P's net assets are below £16,000, - an annual management fee not exceeding 4.5 per cent of P's net assets on the anniversary of the court order appointing the deputy.
d) If P's net assets are below £16,000 the option for detailed assessment will only arise if the court makes a specific order for detailed assessment.

Where the period for which an annual management fee claimed is less than one year, for example where the deputyship comes to an end before the anniversary of the appointment, the amount claimed must be the same proportion of the applicable fee as the period bears to one year.

The deputy's annual report or account

For work undertaken in the preparation and lodgement of a report to the Public Guardian on or after 1 April 2017: an amount not exceeding £265 + VAT.

Tax returns made on or after 1 April 2017

For the preparation of a basic HMRC income tax return (bank or NS&I interest and taxable benefits, discretionary trust or estate income): an amount not exceeding £250 + VAT.

For the preparation of a complex HMRC income tax return (bank or NS&I interest, multiple investment portfolios, taxable benefits, one or more rental properties): an amount not exceeding £600 + VAT.

Conveyancing costs

Where a deputy or other person authorised by the court is selling or purchasing a property on behalf of the claimant, the following fixed rates apply for the legal cost of conveying the property, except where the sale or purchase is by trustees (in which case the costs should be agreed with the trustees).

- A value element of 0.15 per cent of the consideration with a minimum sum of £400 and a maximum sum of £1,670 plus disbursements.

15. Assessed costs in the Court of Protection

In large value damages claims it is rarely appropriate to take fixed costs, and in most cases the deputy's costs will need to be assessed. The guideline hourly rates are reviewed from time to time. They were last published on 19 April 2010 and can be downloaded at: *https://www.gov.uk/guidance/solicitors-guideline-hourly-rates*

Where a detailed assessment is to be undertaken, a professional deputy can, where the period covered by the remuneration ends on or after 1 April 2017, take a sum not exceeding 75 per cent on account of their estimated annual fees; before that date the sum was 60 per cent. A bill is sent for assessment at the end of the deputyship year in the usual way. If the quarterly "on account" bills exceed that which is subsequently allowed on assessment, the claimant must be credited with the overpayment.

Work within the deputyship team will be undertaken by various fee earners falling within the categories below:

- Grade A—solicitor or fellow of the Institute of Legal Executives (Chartered Legal Executive or CILEX) with over eight years' post-qualifications experience.

- Grade B—solicitors and Chartered Legal Executives with over four years' post-qualifications experience.
- Grade C—other solicitors, Chartered Legal Executives and other fee earners of equivalent experience with less than four years' post-qualifications experience.
- Grade D—trainee solicitors, paralegals and fee earners.

If work is undertaken at an inappropriate grade, the higher-grade fee earner will only recover the lower grade hourly rate. The SCCO will also look carefully at the proportionality of charges. The OPG and the SCCO have issued a joint guidance statement on deputyship costs which can be found at:

https://www.gov.uk/government/uploads/system/uploads/attachment_data/file/538901/19_07_16_Professional_deputy_costs__FINAL.pdf

Charges for the appointment of professional deputies and general management undertaken by them

It is important to cost carefully for the claim for future deputyship as it can be a significant head of loss. An independent expert's statement or report is usually preferable over an "in-house" report, in order to establish objectivity.

The introduction of the Act and the Code has undoubtedly led to an increase in the time, and therefore the costs, incurred by deputies. The ongoing need to assess capacity in all areas of financial decision-making, and the need to consult with the claimant or others before best interest decisions are made, all add to the time spent.

The initial application

This and most other applications will generally be dealt with on the papers and without a hearing, but nonetheless the initial application may take at least six months, as may an application for appointment of a new deputy.

Further applications

A deputy may need to make further applications to the court from time to time if there is a limited order, a conflict of interest or a breakdown in their relationship with the claimant. There may be also be limitations in the order due to the prognosis in relation to capacity, or because the claimant is a child approaching adulthood. Some orders contain restrictions on property sales and acquisitions; sometimes orders are time-limited because they are made before a claim has settled, or when a large interim payment was made. Such events can trigger a need to seek further orders. Whilst many orders will contain standard provisions, they should be individually tailored to the claimant's needs.

Wills and statutory Wills

No one under the age of 18 can make a Will.

The *Banks v Goodfellow*[2] criteria provide that in order to give instructions for a Will a person over the age of 18 must be able to understand:

    a) What they are doing when they make a Will and the effect of that
    b) The extent of their property and estate.
    c) The nature of the claims of those they propose to benefit or exclude from the Will.
And
    d) They must be suffering from no disorder of the mind or insane delusion that would result in an unwanted distribution of their estate.

---

[2] (1870) L.R. 5 Q.B.

Clients with testamentary capacity

If the deputy obtains a capacity report which confirms the claimant has testamentary capacity, the claimant can give instructions for and execute a Will in the usual way.

In calculating the likely costs associated with the making of a Will, regard should be given to any factor which may add to the time that will be taken in preparation to take account of cognitive issues such as slowness of processing or communication issues which require the use of e.g. specialist equipment or translation services.

Clients who lack testamentary capacity

If it is established that the claimant lacks testamentary capacity, an application can be made to the court for a statutory Will to be approved on their behalf.

Practice Direction 9E, which supplements the Court of Protection Rules 2017, sets out the detailed procedure to be followed. Consideration must be given to what the claimant would do if they were able to make a Will for themselves, their beliefs and personal values, how they have acted and made decisions for themselves in the past, and the content of any Wills made prior to their incapacity. If the claimant is able to participate in the process and contribute to the content of the proposed Will they should be supported to do so. Again, this may take extra time and involve additional cost.

The cost of an application to make a statutory Will can be significant. The procedure requires the involvement of the Official Solicitor, who will be invited to represent the claimant. Others who are adversely or materially affected by the application—e.g. those who might lose their entitlement under the intestacy rules if there is no existing will, or whose entitlement may be changed by the making of a new Will—may be represented.

A capacity assessment in the court's form COP3 will be needed. This may require input from a specialist practitioner rather than the claimant's GP. The fee could be £1,000.00 or more if the litigation is not ongoing and the GP is reluctant to assist, which is often the case. The assessor will need to read the client's medical history and may need to visit them on more than one occasion.

A court fee of £400 is payable on making the application, and a further £500 for an attended hearing. Hearings are usually only required if there is a serious dispute over the proposed Will. In the simplest cases, costs can amount to a few thousand pounds; in the most difficult of cases they can be tens of thousands of pounds. The usual rule is that all parties' costs are paid out of the claimant's estate, but the court can order costs against any party who it believes has acted unreasonably. Regard should be had to the particular circumstances of the client's family, and the possibility of the future breakdown of relationships. It is reasonable to make provision for two or three wills over the lifetime of a young person with a normal life expectancy.

Contingency for the unexpected or times of crisis

It is very difficult to weigh up accurately how head-injured claimants will behave in the long term. It is prudent to include a contingency fund for unexpected events. Sometimes there is talk of cases "settling down" after the early post-settlement years, but some clients will never fall within this description, due to the nature of their brain injury or premorbid personality. These cases frequently result in high general management costs. This should be recognised in the annual provision, rather than within the contingency.

The financial consequences of relationship breakdown

In the case of claimants who are likely to form relationships it may be prudent to ensure that steps are taken to protect their funds in the event of relationship breakdown, whether that be by way of prenuptial or cohabitation agreements. If the claimant lacks capacity to enter into these agreements, court approval may be needed.

16. **Fees of the Court, the OPG and the SCCO**
    The current fees are:

    - For the appointment of a deputy: £400

    - For an attended hearing (in addition to the application fee): £500
    - On the appointment of a deputy: £100
    - Supervision fee: £320 p.a. unless (which is unlikely) there is minimal supervision (when the fee is £35 per annum)
    - The fee on the submission of a bill of costs for assessment is £225 per bill. Costs below £3,000 excluding VAT and disbursements attract a lower fee of £115.

    Fee remissions and exemptions

    These are available for both Court of Protection and OPG fees, and are based on the claimant's financial circumstances. Further details can be found at:

    https://www.gov.uk/government/uploads/system/uploads/attachment_data/file/601084/OPG120-deputy-fees.pdf

17. **Keeping up to date**
    Information about the OPG can be found in the DIRECTGOV site; information about the Court of Protection is on the HMCS website.

SOME IMPORTANT INFORMATION ABOUT BENEFITS RELEVANT TO DEPUTIES

1. Income Support Regulations 1987 (as amended)

52-week disregard

There is a period of 52 weeks running from the day of receipt of the first payment (no matter how small) in consequence of a personal injury claim, during which the capital received will be disregarded. However, you do not receive a separate 52-week period on the occasion of future payments.

e.g.
- £10,000 interim payment received on 1 January 2018.
- £100,000 final compensation received 1 July 2018.
- The 52-week period of disregard starts on the date of the first payment; so that the disregard for the £100,000 will expire on 1st January 2019.

In most cases, interim payments are received over a much longer period; this may mean that the disregard will run out well before the interim payment is exhausted. As a result, the funds received have to be disclosed. However, if the funds are held by the deputy under a deputyship order, they are disregarded regardless of the 52-week period.

2. Funds held in a trust or subject to the order or direction of the Court of Protection

Under the Regulations, funds received as a consequence of a personal injury are disregarded entirely if they are either held in trust or are under the control of the Court of Protection.

As a result of SI 593/2008, funds held "to the Order of the court" are disregarded. Accordingly, there is no need to contemplate personal injury trusts where there is a deputyship in order to preserve an entitlement to statutory benefits.

J2: The incidence of deputyship costs over a claimant's life

1. The appointment of a deputy is likely to arise during a personal injury or clinical negligence claim, when a claimant lacks capacity to manage their financial affairs.

2. Deputyship costs are a recoverable head of loss:

    a. if the incapacity preceded the index injury,
    b. but it is only in consequence of that injury that the claimant has financial affairs and property of sufficient size and complexity to warrant the appointment of a deputy, and
    c. where the incapacity is a direct consequence of the injury.

3. The Court of Protection will appoint a deputy for infants where the damages are significant and the probability is that the infant will not acquire legal capacity on attaining their majority.

4. On an admission of liability or judgment, an application should be made without delay so that the deputyship can be put in place as soon as possible, and interim funds can be applied for the claimant's benefit.

5. The order appointing a deputy will provide authority for the professional deputy to be paid for the work undertaken.

6. On appointment the court will require the deputy to enter into a surety. The figure provided in the accompanying cost breakdown is an estimate in a typical high-value case. The surety is usually arranged by way of a bond, which will be renewed on an annual basis.

7. An OPG annual supervision fee will be payable. Some cases are deemed not to require supervision, but that will not be the case for clients with a damages award.

8. The management of the claimant's affairs will proceed in annual stages, known as deputyship years. In the earlier years of a deputyship, costs are likely to be higher than they will be later. Costs are given in the accompanying breakdown for the first two deputyship years, within which it is contemplated that significant structural issues will be addressed including:

    - acquisition and/or adaptation of accommodation,
    - the major/initial investment decisions, and
    - the establishment, through case managers or otherwise, of care and other support regimes.

    These could be post-settlement or on receipt of a significant interim payment.

9. The impact of continuing litigation should be factored in. Litigation will inevitably increase costs because:

    - long-term/annual budgeting will not generally be possible while the deputyship is in its infancy and the claimant is dependent upon interim payments;
    - liaison with the litigation team will be needed, to consider the claimant's requirements for interim funding and the adequacy of offers;
    - stresses will occur to the claimant and the claimant's family. These can be expected to extend beyond the conclusion of the litigation. The first two or three years after litigation are likely to be unsettled.

10. Caution: the cost of work undertaken by the deputy or the deputy's team which could properly be claimed within the context of ongoing litigation (e.g. interim payments on account of damages, or providing information for the purpose of conducting the litigation) will be disallowed by the SCCO if it is included within the deputyship general management bill. If the deputy or the deputy's team are asked to undertake this work, this time should be billed to the firm having conduct of the litigation.

J2: The incidence of Deputyship costs over a claimant's life

11. The general management costs identified for "the first two deputyship years" are for a case of medium level complexity. Such costs will vary from case to case. General management costs might amount to £12,000–£30,000+. They assume that in the first year a property is found and adaptation works are begun, and that in the second year the adaptation works are all but completed and the care and treatment regimes are put in place. The third (and possibly the fourth) year allow for the family to settle down.

12. Matters usually settle down to a general routine after that period. In a typical case of catastrophic injury, general management costs of £10,000–£14,000 are not uncommon.

13. A claimant will often need face-to-face meetings, so that the deputy can provide appropriate explanations for decisions; the cost for this should be included in the claim. If the claimant has special communication needs (e.g. the use of assistive technology) additional provision should be made for the time spent in preparing for and conducting those meetings. If the claimant cannot be consulted, time will be spent in consulting with others.

14. Some claimants have behavioural problems which can be difficult to overcome, which require greater than usual time to manage. Additional costs should be included to allow for this where appropriate. It is not unusual in such cases to see annual costs well in excess of £30,000 + VAT and disbursements. *Robshaw v United Lincolnshire Hospitals NHS Trust*[3] acknowledges that there is no "one cap fits all" approach to deputyship costs. The annual cost will principally depend upon how active the deputy has been, which in turn will depend upon a large number of factors. These include the size and complexity of the deputyship; the number of carers, treating clinicians and therapists involved; the claimant's behaviour; and the family dynamics.

15. Issues will arise periodically during the claimant's lifetime which are impossible to foresee, including changes in family circumstances, such as the death of a close family member, the birth of a child or the breakdown in a relationship. A contingency sum has been allowed in the accompanying schedule; however this should be adjusted to reflect various factors including the claimant's capacity and life expectancy.

16. On the application for a new deputy much of the information will readily available so the costs incurred are likely to be lower. A capacity report will be required and the cost for that may be significantly more than one completed at the time of the litigation. The schedule below reflects this.

17. The deputyship will come to an end on the claimant recovering their capacity or on their death. There will be winding-up costs associated with accounting to the claimant or to the representatives of the claimant's estate. An application for discharge requires a court application and a supportive capacity assessment.

18. No provision has been made in the accompanying breakdown for incidental applications for additional or special authority, but each will cost £400 in terms of an application fee, with a further £500 payable in the event of an attended hearing.

19. A professional deputy's annual management costs are assessed by the Senior Court Costs Office (SCCO) on the anniversary of each deputyship year. The bill will need to be prepared by a Costs Draftsman whose fees will be between 5.5 per cent and 6.5 per cent of the profit costs claimed plus VAT. In addition there will be an SCCO assessment fee of £225, unless the bill has a value of £3,000 or less, in which case the fee will be £115.

20. Bills are also submitted for assessment on the appointment of the first deputy and on completion of a statutory will application.

---

[3] [2015] EWHC 923 (QB).

J3: Deputyship costs

One-off cost of application for a deputy to be appointed

1	Solicitors' costs	£4,000
2	Cost Draftsman's fees—6% of item 1	£240
3	+ VAT @ 20%	£848
4	Capacity report—assumes an expert within the litigation can provide the report	£600 including VAT
5	Court of Protection Application fee	£400
6	OPG fee	£100
7	Security Bond Premium—assumes use of the current preferred provider at a bond level of £300,000	£225
8	SCCO Assessment Fee	£225
	Total set up cost	£6,638

Estimated annual costs for the first deputyship year during which funds become available for the purchase of a property and the commencement of adaptations

9	General management costs	£25,000
10	Cost Draftsman's fees—6% of item 12	£1,500
11	+ VAT @ 20%	£5,300
12	SCCO Annual Assessment fee	£225
13	Security Bond Premium—assumes use of the current preferred provider at a bond level of £300,000	£225
14	OPG Annual Supervision fee	£320
	Total first year	£32,570

J3: Deputyship costs

Estimated annual costs for the second deputyship year, during which property adaptations are completed and a care regime implemented

15	General management costs	£18,000
16	Cost Draftsman's fees—6% of item 15	£1,080
17	+ VAT @ 20%	£3,816
18	SCCO Annual Assessment fee	£225
19	Security Bond Premium—assumes use of the current preferred provider at a bond level of £300,000	£225
20	OPG Annual Supervision fee	£320
	Total second year	£23,666

Estimated annual costs for year 3 (and possibly year 4, depending on progress made during the first two years). Costs per year.

21	General management costs	£15,000
22	Cost Draftsman's fees—6% of item 21	£900
23	+ VAT @ 20%	£3,180
24	SCCO Annual Assessment fee	£225
25	Security Bond Premium—assumes use of the current preferred provider at a bond level of £300,000	£150
26	OPG Annual Supervision fee	£320
	Total each year	£19,775

Ongoing years

27	General management costs	£12,000
28	Cost Draftsman's fees—6% of item 27	£720
29	+ VAT @ 20%	£2,544
30	SCCO Annual Assessment fee	£225
31	Assumes use of the current preferred provider at a bond level of £300,000*	£150
32	OPG Annual Supervision fee	£320
	Total each year	£15,959

* Under the current provisions this fee will cease after the fourth anniversary of the appointment of the deputy unless there is a change in security—see earlier text.

Other future costs

Applications for the appointment of a new deputy—per application

33	Professional fees	£2,000
34	Cost Draftsman's fees—6.0% of item 33	£120
35	+ VAT @ 20%	£424.00
36	COP application fee	£400
37	OPG Assessment fee	£100
38	Capacity Report	£1,000.00
	Total	£4,044.00

Statutory will (non-contentious), per application

39	Professional fees	£5,500
40	Official Solicitor's Costs for general management	£1,440.00–£2,880.00*
41	Costs of others to be notified	£2,000
42	+ VAT @ 20%	£2,076.00
43	Application fee	£400
44	Medical Report	£1,000.00
45	Costs draftsman fee—6% of items 39, 40 (at the higher end), and 41	£622.80
46	+ VAT @ 20%	£124.56
47	SCCO detailed assessment fees: two short form bills @ £115 and one full bill @ £225	£455
	Total	£13,618.36–£15,058.36

* The average costs of an uncontested statutory will application can be glimpsed from the OS client care letter which says "applications for authority to execute a statutory will or statutory codicil can take between 6 and 12 hours of the Official Solicitors time. This is equivalent to £1,440–£2,880 plus VAT and any disbursements"

The OS has suggested that their costs for an uncontested Statutory Will at the lower end would be £1,440.00 plus VAT and disbursements.

Contingency for additional deputy input or crisis, per crisis

48	Professional fees for general management costs	£5,000
49	Costs draftsman fee—6.0% of item 48	£300
50	+ VAT @ 20%	£1,060.00
	Total	£6,360

Preparation of tax returns and associated work: cost per annum

51	Professional fees	£500
52	+ VAT @ 20%	£100
	Total	£600

Winding up: single payment

53	Winding up costs	£1,500
54	+ VAT @ 20%	£300
	Total	£1,800

Group K
Carer Rates and Rehabilitation

K1: **Care and attendance**

K2: **Nannies, cleaners and school fees**

K3: **DIY, gardening and housekeeping**

K4: **Hospital self-pay (uninsured) charges**

K5: **NHS charges**

K6: **The Rehabilitation Code 2015**

K7: **APIL/FOIL Serious Injury Guide**

K1: Care and attendance

Introduction

1. A series of cases since 2005 involving injuries of the utmost severity has led to highly developed claims for care and attendance, including case management.[1] This section aims to be a source of practical assistance to practitioners and courts setting about the task of assessing damages for care and attendance.

Past non-commercial care

2. Damages awarded in respect of non-commercial care, usually by family members, are governed by the following rules/practical advice.
3. The aim is to award the reasonable value of/proper recompense for gratuitous services rendered—*Hunt v Severs*.[2]
4. Accordingly, a claimant holds the damages on trust for those who provided the care.[3]
5. If a tortfeasor has himself provided the care, there can be no recovery of damages on that score.[4]
6. If a claimant has fallen out with the care provider so that the recovery on trust will not be honoured, again there will be no award in damages.[5]
7. There is no threshold requirement to be satisfied before an award can be made, whether in terms of severity of injury or level of care.[6] Extra domestic services are sufficient.[7]
8. While there is no threshold to satisfy, there must be actual care. So, when a claimant is still in hospital, damages are not to be awarded for mere visiting—only for any periods of care given during the course of the visit.[8]

---

[1] Readers interested in the finer detail of big cases can find it set out in the updated paper by James Rowley QC "Serious PI litigation—a Quantum Update" with the accompanying tables at: *www.byromstreet.com*.

[2] [1994] 2 A.C. 350 at 363A ff. These are special damages. While not referred to expressly in the speeches, the rationale in *Daly v General Steam Navigation Co Ltd* [1981] 1 WLR 120 CA—awarding general damages in respect of past non-commercial domestic services—was overruled by the House of Lords through the result in *Hunt v Severs*.

[3] *Hunt v Severs* above also expressly over-ruled the line of authority derived from *Donnelly v Joyce* [1974] QB 454 in favour of that derived from Lord Denning's judgment in *Cunningham v Harrison* [1973] QB 942. No longer is an award for services considered as a claimant's damages (based on his need for the care) for him then to make a present to the carer. Rather it is recompense to the carer and only held by a claimant on trust.

[4] *Hunt v Severs* at 363D. This is a common occurrence when passengers are suing a member of the family who was the negligent driver. Where liability is split, there is no known authority but no reason in principle why a tortfeasor carer cannot recover to the extent of another tortfeasor's share of the blame.

[5] See *ATH v MS* [2003] PIQR Q1 at [30] as to the principle; but in this case of fatal accident, the court was already ordering damages to be paid into court for investment on behalf of dependent children and felt able to enforce the trust through the investment control of the court. It would be otherwise if the monies were simply to be paid over to a claimant and the court really felt the trust would not be honoured.

[6] The Court of Appeal in *Giambrone v Sunworld Holidays Ltd* [2004] PIQR Q4 at Q36 decided that dicta in *Mills v British Rail Engineering Ltd* [1992] PIQR Q130 to the effect that there was a threshold of devoted care or care well beyond the ordinary call of duty (and similar phrases) were obiter and not to be followed.

[7] The Court of Appeal in *Mills* had overlooked a passage from Lord Denning in *Cunningham v Harrison*—quoted with apparent approval by Lord Bridge in *Hunt v Severs* above at 360E—"Even though she had not been doing paid work but only domestic duties in the house, nevertheless all extra attendance on him certainly calls for compensation." [1973] QB 942 at 952B-C.

[8] *Havenhand v Jeffrey* (unreported, 24 February 1997 CA); *Tagg v Countess of Chester Hospital Foundation NHS Trust* [2007] EWHC 509 (QB) at [85]; *Huntley v Simmons* [2009] EWHC 405 (QB) at [65].

K1: Care and attendance

9. Compensable care must relate to the person—the claimant himself or, under the rule in *Lowe v Guise*[9], another disabled member of the same household, usually cared for by the claimant but who, because of the claimant's injury, is cared for by another. So, where the provision spreads out into non-commercial cover for the claimant in his business, different considerations apply; there is no compensable claim here for the hours provided by analogy with real care.[10]

10. Claims are rarely put on the following footing but where a carer has lost earnings in the provision of services, the value can be assessed as the lost net earnings up to a ceiling of the commercial value of the care provided.[11] The usual reduction for the non-commercial element still stands to be applied from the ceiling: a submission to opposite effect was rejected in *Mehmetemin v Farrell*—it would amount to an artificial inflation and include an element that could never be paid to a relative.[12]

11. In the majority of cases the exercise is to examine the care and make a fair assessment of the number of hours in fact provided. (In doing this, one will in passing register if care has been given at anti-social hours or has been particularly demanding.) The assessment is easy in respect of discrete blocks of care; but calls for more subtle evidence/judgment when care is given in multiple short bursts over the course of day and night or constitutes more general supervision/support in the home while daily life continues.

12. Hourly rates are then applied to the determined number of hours.

13. Many different scales have been used in the past; but now there is uniformity in taking rates derived from Local Authority Spinal Point 8.

14. The suggested starting points are the basic (daytime weekday) rate or the enhanced aggregate rate (which takes into account care in the evenings, at night and at weekends). Both are set out in the table below.

15. The aggregate rate balances all the hours of the week by their relative number and appropriate rate. It is logically entirely apt only when care is spread out evenly through the whole week and the hours of the day and night. The odd hour here and there in the evening will not justify an aggregate rate; but intensive care given only at night and not by day, seven days a week (for example when commercial daytime care has been purchased but a relative left to care at night), would logically justify more than the aggregate rate. Where a spouse has risen early to provide care before going to work and then carried on in the evenings on returning home, no care has been given when the daytime weekday rate is applicable.

16. There is no reason in principle why different rates cannot be used in different periods—the aggregate rate during more intensive care in early convalescence and the basic rate afterwards; or a rate over the whole period averaged somewhere between the two. No doubt the exercise would have to be relatively broad brush but it may be none the worse for that.[13] The overarching aim is to attach a reasonable value to the actual care and award proper recompense.

17. Notwithstanding the logical attraction, however, of choosing a rate close to the circumstances of

---

[9] [2002] QB 1369 at [38]. The ratio of this case (and how widely or narrowly the rule established should be construed) is a fertile area for argument. Is it really confined to care of a disabled member or will care of a baby or child suffice? Is the element of provision being within the same household essential to the legal rule? Is it an important difference if a disabled mother has come to rely on her daughter's care while living in the next street; or in a self-contained granny-flat within the curtilage of the daughter's house; or in the spare room of her house?

[10] *Hardwick v Hudson* [1999] 1 WLR 1770.

[11] *Housecroft v Burnett* [1986] 1 All ER 332 O'Connor LJ at 343e, albeit his view of the *Cunningham v Harrison* and *Donnelly v Joyce* debate was over-ruled in *Hunt v Severs*. The ceiling of the commercial rate has sometimes been criticised on the basis that it would have been enough simply to apply a wider test of reasonableness to the evaluation of the mother's claim for care of her daughter. However, that evaluation was at the very heart of the appeal and it would be difficult to contend that the invocation of the commercial ceiling was not part of the ratio.

[12] [2017] EWHC 103 (QB) Sir Robert Nelson at [33].

[13] Averaging things with a broad brush appealed to Stuart-Smith J in *Ali v Caton & MIB* [2013] EWHC 1730 (QB) at [323b–d] and he effectively reached a rate between the aggregate and basic ones. He took the starting point of the claimant's expert's figures and discounted them by 25 per cent on account of arguments over both rates and the number of hours. " . . . Adoption of a basic rate throughout would lead to under-compensation while adoption of the enhanced rate would have the opposite effect." See below for more about this case.

the actual provision, following *Fairhurst v St Helens & Knowsley Health Authority*[14] the basic rate was used for over a decade in reported cases, even those of maximum severity when the care was of an onerous nature and much of it provided at nights and at weekends.[15]

18. Notwithstanding *Wells v Wells*[16] and modernisation of the assessment of damages for personal injuries, it took until *Massey v Tameside*[17] for there to be a reported case at the aggregate rate. Since then there has been a move away from using the basic rate as the universal starting point.

19. The position on choice of rate now stands as follows:
    a) In very serious cases involving long-term, high quality care of a grievously injured claimant including care at anti-social hours (the *Massey* type case), nothing less than the full aggregate rate will provide reasonable value/proper recompense.[18]
    b) Where care is found *not* to include a significant element at anti-social hours, the basic rate still forms the basis of reasonable value/proper recompense.[19]
    c) The area of interest lies in the hinterland where there is indeed some care at anti-social hours but the case is not at the most serious end of the spectrum. Here there is no uniformity of approach and the matter calls for judgment.[20]

20. It is increasingly common for experts in very valuable cases to break the past down into many periods with minor fluctuations in hours and annual increases in rates. It may be fine in that type of case, albeit use of properly considered averages would surely simplify things considerably at no significant cost in overall accuracy. In cases without experts, practical experience suggests focussing on fewer distinct periods of care and taking into account minor fluctuations through the reasoned choice of an average number of hours or average rate[21] rather than embarking on over-elaborate calculation. Where cases involve gradually diminishing care from a point on hospital discharge to recovery or a plateau of continuing need, looking to the level of care midway through that period has much to commend it as a starting point in picking an overall average.

---

[14] [1995] PIQR Q.1.
[15] Many settlements were negotiated with an enhancement for a higher rate, but there was no reported case until *Massey v Tameside* [2007] EWHC 317 (QB).
[16] [1999] 1 AC 345.
[17] [2007] EWHC 317 (QB).
[18] This line started with *Massey* and moved through numerous cases including the landmark decision in *Whiten v St George's Healthcare NHS Trust* [2011] EWHC 2066 (QB), Swift J at [141] and [144], and is most recently exemplified in *AB v Royal Devon & Exeter NHS Foundation Trust* [2016] EWHC 1024 (QB), Irwin J as he then was at [129]—care of a paraplegic at various times of the day and sometimes including travel. The *full aggregate rate* used in these cases includes attendance at night. It is to be contrasted with a new *aggregate day rate* i.e. 7-day care without significant input at night, calculated in the tables below for the first time last year.
[19] Recent examples of use of the basic rate include three chronic pain cases: *Hayden v Maidstone & Tunbridge Wells NHS Trust* [2016] EWHC 3276 (QB), Jay J (general damages £37,500); *Maguire v Carillion Services Limited* HHJ Main QC, Manchester County Court 31 March 2017 (unreported) at [154] (general damages £26,500), where the Judge referred to the *Massey* line as reflecting cases of an exceptional nature with extraordinary commitment; *Karapetianas v Kent and Sussex Loft Conversions Limited* [2017] EWHC 859 (QB), Mr Jonathan Swift QC sitting as a Judge of the High Court at [51] (general damages £29,000) with a finding that care was not needed at nights or weekends. In *Thorburn v South Warwickshire NHS Foundation Trust* [2017] EWHC 1791 (QB), a case of failed knee replacement surgery, HHJ Pearce sitting as a High Court Judge awarded [126] the basic rate with a 25% reduction, not the 33% argued for the defendant.
[20] Examples can be given of Courts taking both the aggregate and basic rates in this group of cases, often without much in the way of detailed argument or reasoning, so reference is no longer made to them. The key is a finding as to what would constitute reasonable value/proper recompense in all the circumstances of the case. It will likely balance the severity of the disability, the commitment of the relative, the period required, the relative proportion of the care at anti-social hours. Having made that effort, a broad brush finding amounting to compensation somewhere between the 2 rates may well commend itself in this type of case. For those who prefer greater apparent accuracy, the newly calculated aggregate *day* rate might be suggested.
[21] See also *Ali v Caton & MIB*, above.

K1: Care and attendance

21. Since personal injury damages are awarded net of tax and NI, there is invariably an appropriate reduction in respect of past non-commercial care.[22] It is now almost always 25 per cent[23] but the bracket appears historically to have been between 20 per cent and 33 per cent.[24]
22. A sum equivalent to any Carer's Allowance received is to be deducted from an award for non-commercial care.[25]

Example schedule[26]

Care while an in-patient—2 weeks
Average of 2 hours actual care at the bedside each evening (including Saturday and Sunday):
2 hours × 14 days @ the aggregate rate (£10.38)　　　　　　　　　　291

Care during 4 weeks intensive convalescence at home:
6 hours provided daily, including weekends and evenings:
6 hours × 28 days @ the aggregate rate (£10.38)　　　　　　　　　　1,744

---

[22] At a time when the basic rate was being used as the universal starting point, a few very serious cases emerged where it was felt that a deduction from such a low rate would leave a carer with inadequate recompense; and some Courts refused to make a deduction. Now that the quality and difficulty of care is beginning to be reflected through higher rates, this method of achieving a fair result is no longer required. Choose the appropriate rate for the quality/intensity of care; but then make the principled deduction for tax and NI. As with any rule, however, there is the odd reasoned departure to be found: in *AC v Farooq & MIB* [2012] EWHC 1484 QB) King J did not make deduction from the £7.11 rate used by one of the nursing experts since it already represented a compromise over what was the appropriate commercial rate [131].

Recently in *Totham v King's College Hospital NHS Foundation Trust* [2015] EWHC 97 (QB), the parties agreed the rate and the hours. Nevertheless, the claimant submitted that Mrs Totham had given up highly paid work and consequently there should be no discount at all for the non-commercial element. The submission was rejected by Laing J at [25]–[28]: the argument in respect of Mrs Totham's work did not go to the correct non-commercial reduction (principally to do with tax and NI), rather it went to the correct rate to be allowed for the hours (which had already been compromised.) The moral of the tale is to take the advice in the earlier part of this footnote to heart and to choose the right rate to start with to provide proper recompense.

[23] This was the considered reduction in *Whiten* above from the already chosen aggregate rate—see [144]. It was described by Stuart-Smith J in *Ali v Caton & MIB* above, footnote 12, as the "conventional 25% discount" and he refused to make more adjustment [323c]. 25 per cent has been the reduction in *Loughlin v Singh* [2013] EWHC 1641 (QB); *Farrugia* [2014] EWHC 1036 (QB); *Tate v Ryder Holdings* [2014] EWHC 4256 (QB); *Ellison v University Hospitals of Morecambe Bay NHS Foundation* Trust [2015] EWHC 366 (QB); *Totham* above; *Robshaw v United Lincolnshire Hospitals NHS Trust* [2015] EWHC 923 (QB), *AB v Devon & Exeter*, above; *Mehmetemin* above and other cases too numerous to specify.

[24] *Evans v Pontypridd Roofing Limited* [2002] PIQR Q5 is the leading general authority on the non-commercial reduction. In *Zambarda v Shipbreaking (Queenborough) Ltd* [2013] EWHC 2263 (QB), John Leighton Williams QC (sitting as a Deputy High Court Judge) made only a 20 per cent discount [64] because the sum was so small that income tax would not be paid. It is a very long time since an argued and reported decision at 33 per cent: *Nash v Southmead Health Authority* [1993] P.I.Q.R. Q.156, decided in late 1992, is the case usually cited.

[25] Teare J in *Massey* above at [52]:

> "To the extent that the carer has received benefits in respect of his or her voluntary care the claimant does not need a sum of money to give proper recompense for that care. It therefore seems to me that the Defendant's contention is right in principle."

Where there has been a discount on liability for litigation risk, carers might well argue that the Carers Allowance should be considered as filling in for that reduction and not taken off their already reduced claims for non-commercial care.

[26] The example will pick up the threads of the "logical" approach as outlined in the text. No doubt a counter schedule, as well as attempting to reduce the number of hours, would take a point that the basic rate only should be allowed in a case beneath that of maximum severity. The multipliers have been increased from previous years to reflect a -0.75 per cent discount rate at the time of writing.

K1: Care and attendance

Further 6 months of care gradually diminishing from 6 hours a day to nil, more during the evenings and weekends at the beginning than at the end:
Average of 3 hours a day care × 365/2 × the average of the basic and aggregate rates (£9.14)   5,004

                                                                                                                                              7,039
Non-commercial discount   ×0.75
                                                                                                                                                        5,279

No continuing personal care but assistance still required in respect of heavier DIY, gardening etc. chores
Making allowance from £1,500 p.a.[27] for the chores still possible:
£750 pa × 15 (discounted lifetime multiplier to say 70):
                                                                                                                                                       11,250

Total   £16,529

Past commercial care

23. Where there has been actual expenditure in the past on commercial care, it should be capable of easy proof (or reasonably accurate estimation if records have not been kept.)
24. It will usually be awarded in full unless the defendant raises issues of unreasonable provision (or elements of separate causation leading to unrelated provision.)[28]

---

[27] Mackay J in *Fleet v Fleet* [2009] EWHC 3166 (QB):
"25. This is claimed based on a multiplicand of £1500 p.a. I do not understand the multiplier to be controversial. The defendant contends for between £750 and £1,000 per annum as a 'more conventional sum' than the £1500 sought by the Claimant. The evidence on this issue is that Mr Fleet did all the DIY in the house and had in the past installed a new bathroom according to his wife. He was a skilled man albeit he was busy and worked long days and sometimes long weeks. He also said that he had plans to redecorate the house, and Mrs Fleet said that the living room now needs redecoration; though she could do some of the preparatory work, and did do so when her husband did the work, she could not in my judgement be reasonably expected to fill the gap left by him.
26. Equally, there is considerable garden at the house which Mrs Fleet tends but she cannot manage the trimming of the trees a screen of which separates the house from its neighbours and which has to be kept in order, or cut the grass.
27. I believe I am justified in saying that I can take into account the general level of awards under this head of damage from past experience. It would be dismal if experts had to be called to say how much it costs to mow a lawn or paint a room; after all judges do have some experience of that kind of activity and what it cost to buy it in the market place.
28. I see nothing wrong with the figure of £1,500 per annum claimed by the plaintiff and I think that is the right sum."
John Leighton Williams QC (sitting as a High Court Judge) allowed £1,250 p.a. to age 77 in *Zambarda v Shipbreaking (Queenborough) Ltd* above at [88]. Contrast Stuart-Smith J in *Ali v Caton & MIB* above and below at [337] where he awarded £250 p.a. to a young man with no track record for DIY, decorating and gardening. In *McGinty v Pipe* [2012] EWHC 506 (QB) HHJ Foster QC (sitting as a High Court Judge) awarded a woman of 51 £750 p.a. for gardening and DIY with a multiplier of 16 (to just beyond 70.) Kenneth Parker J in *Tate v Ryder Holdings* above discounted the claim for a 24-year-old man heavily to a lump sum award of £15,000 because of the considerable uncertainty over whether he would have carried out such activities. HHJ McKenna (sitting as a High Court Judge) awarded [96] £900 p.a. between the ages of 25 and 70 in *FM v Ipswich Hospital NHS Trust* [2015] EWHC 775 (QB). Foskett J [421] awarded £1,500 p.a. in *Robshaw* above from age 25 when life expectancy was reduced to 63.
[28] In *O'Brien v Harris* (Transcript 22 February 2001) the BIRT rehabilitation costs (£21,860) significantly exceeded those originally estimated (£13,700) [191]. There was no evidence from BIRT explaining the difference or resiling from the estimate [192]. The case manager was not called to justify the additional case management costs (£10,834 v £6,461) [193]. Some increased costs were allowed based on inferences from the invoices to the effect that a higher quality of support worker had been provided than in the estimate [195]. There had, however, been inadequate management of cost [194] (but by whom?—see below) and Pitchford J made an overall award of £18,500 [196].
In the case of *Loughlin v Singh* above, Kenneth Parker J was invited [62] to disallow the costs of past care and case management on the basis that "the standard of such care and management fell significantly below that which could reasonably be expected to meet the exigencies of the claimant's condition and circumstances". The full submission was rejected as "wholly disproportionate and unjust"; but the claim was reduced by 20 per cent with a broad brush on account

K1: Care and attendance

25. The primary measure of damage against which to judge the claimed level of provision is one of reasonable care to meet a claimant's needs.[29]
26. If, at first blush, the claim in the past appears to exceed the primary measure of damage, principles of mitigation of loss may yet come to a claimant's aid if some evidence is adduced to explain the apparent over-spend. Once a claimant raises such arguments, the burden of proof lies on a defendant to prove a failure in mitigation; and the standard against which to judge a claimant's actions is not a harsh one.[30]
27. The value of direct payments stands to be deducted.[31] There is no loss to the extent that there is NHS continuing care.

Future non-commercial care

28. If non-commercial care is to be carried on long into the future, the potential break down of the package is a contingency to be assessed. Where there is detailed expert evidence, there will often be an alternative package laid out drawing on greater commercial care. It will then be a matter for

---

of the case manager's failure to address the claimant's need for a specific and effective sleep hygiene regime in timely fashion. Kenneth Parker J made a finding that

"the efforts made on this fundamental aspect of the rehabilitation were simply not adequate [61]. . . . Principle requires that I should take due account of the fact, that I have found, that the standard of the care and case management services did, in an important respect, fall significantly below the standard that could reasonably have been expected. In other words, the objective value of what the Claimant received was less than the amount of the charges made for the relevant services" [62].

There was no finding in *Loughlin* that the claimant through his Financial Deputy had knowingly appointed an incompetent case manager. Kenneth Parker J made no finding of failure to mitigate against the claimant/Financial Deputy in the handling/funding of the case manager (although this may have been an under-current in the case). As long as Kenneth Parker J's findings amounted to *gross* negligence on the part of the case manager, his observations can be squared with wider principles of *novus actus* under *Rahman v Arearose Ltd* [2001] QB 351 and *Webb v Barclays Bank* [2001] EWCA Civ 1141: insofar as the increased costs of failing to implement a sleep hygiene regime were caused by the gross negligence of a third party, they were separately caused. It is difficult to see, however, why a finding of mere as against gross negligence in the past on the part of a case manager should break the chain of causation and lead to the dis-allowance of part of the claim.

In the more recent case of *Ali v Caton & MIB* above and below, Stuart-Smith J awarded the full claim for past support workers, the regime having been set up in accordance with apparently competent third party advice.

"The position of a significantly brain-damaged claimant who acts on the basis of apparently reasonable advice is strong, though not always impregnable, when seeking to recover the costs of doing so from a tortfeasor. On this item, the balance of the argument strongly favours the claimant" [323f–h].

This approach is in keeping with the writer's understanding of the real legal issue set out in the previous paragraph.

Laing J in *Totham* above conveniently ignored deciding whether the poor case management had been grossly negligent or merely negligent and awarded the whole claim on the basis that Mrs Totham "had acted reasonably in appointing [the case management company] in the first place, and in continuing to employ, and pay, them until they walked off the job." [39]

[29] The principle was put succinctly by Lord Lloyd in *Wells v Wells* [1999] 1 AC 345 at 377F in just 17 words: "Plaintiffs are entitled to a reasonable standard of care to meet their requirements, but that is all." Stephenson LJ traced in *Rialis v Mitchell* (Court of Appeal transcript, 6 July 1984) how the 100 per cent principle was finessed through a series of Victorian cases involving fatal accidents on the railways to reflect the recovery of reasonable rather than perfect compensation. Reasonable compensation is now 100 per cent compensation since it is the primary measure of damage. Professor Andrew Burrows, writing Chapter 28 of the leading practitioner's textbook *Clerk & Lindsell*, 22nd Edition, clearly espouses what this Chapter has considered the orthodox line: see §28-23. For an alternative view, see the late Dr Harvey McGregor in *McGregor on Damages*, 20th Edition (London: Sweet & Maxwell, 2018) at 38-056 (but his line ignores *Rialis* and Lord Lloyd in *Wells* above, as well as practice over decades and the other decisions mentioned in footnote 206 within his own section). This paragraph now appears at 40-057 of the 20th edition, without revision after Dr McGregor's death.

Recently, claimants and defendants are jousting, the one using the language of "full compensation" and the other "proportionality". It is far from clear what these ideas add if the primary measure of damage is "reasonable compensation": this test is infinitely flexible and requires no gloss; all the decisions are ultimately explicable applying a simple test of *reasonableness* to the very specific facts. Readers interested in seeing the development of this trend can look to *Whiten* above at [4]-[5]; *Totham* above at [12]; *Ellison* above at [9]; *Robshaw* above at [161]-[167].

[30] The topic is beyond the scope of this chapter; an obvious source of assistance lies in *McGregor on Damages*, 20th edition, para. 9-079 and in the surrounding paragraphs.

[31] *Crofton v NHS Litigation Authority* [2007] 1WLR 923.

the judge to reach a fair balanced assumption in monetary terms between two or more packages, weighting the award according to the available evidence.[32]

29. Where the evidence is not so detailed and there is no provision elsewhere in the calculations for a break down in the non-commercial care package, it may well be appropriate to reflect adverse contingencies by refusing to apply the usual non-commercial discount. In this way some allowance is made with a broad brush for the possibility of more expensive commercial care on separation/ill health/death in the family member who is to supply the care.[33]

Future commercial care

Care—hourly rates

30. There is no "conventional" hourly rate for future commercial care, whether recruited through direct employment or an agency. All depends on the nature/difficulty of the required care; the level of need for continuity in carers; the prevailing rates local to a claimant's home (probably the biggest factor). Evidence on all three scores is highly desirable.[34] The most recent cases have not often involved argument over the hourly rate; compromised cases in 2017/18 suggest that 50p to £1 an hour can be added to the later cases in the table below. Examples in the biggest cases (direct employment not agency rates) are as follows:

Case[35]	Weekday—£	Weekend—£	Location
Manna[36] (determined—July 2015)	10.50	11.50	Bolton suburbs
Robshaw (agreed—March 2015)	10	11	Lincs.
Farrugia[37] (determined—March 2014)	11.50	14	Hants.
Streeter[38] (determined—Sept. 2013)	9	10	Aylesbury
Whiten (agreed—mid-2011)	13	15	"Good" London rates
Sklair (agreed—late 2009)	11	13	Beckenham, Kent

---

[32] In *C v Dixon* [2009] EWHC 708 (QB) King J assessed damages where the relationship between the claimant and his partner was far from assured in the long run. He took an assumed period of 10 years before break up as a fair reflection of the chances and proceeded to do the arithmetic from that starting point.

[33] See *Willbye v Gibbons* [2004] PIQR P15 at [12] and [16] in which, on a quality of evidence which was insufficient to warrant fine alternative contingency calculations in the event of breakdown in the non-commercial package, Kennedy LJ varied the sum awarded by removing the non-commercial discount allowed by the Recorder.

[34] Jack J bewailed the lack of evidence of decent quality in *XXX* [2008] EWHC 2727 (QB) at [16].

[35] Full case references can be found in the wider text of this Chapter and footnotes if not given explicitly.

[36] *Manna v Central Manchester University Hospitals NHS Foundation Trust* [2015] EWHC 2279 (QB) at [214].

[37] [2014] EWHC 1036 (QB) Jay J at [102].

[38] [2013] EWHC 2841 (QB): the judgment at [209] did not articulate the figures beyond the annual multiplicands but the accepted rates were as set out in Mrs Gough's evidence in the Joint Statement. This was a tetraplegia case and Mrs Gough adduced evidence of actual research into local rates.

K1: Care and attendance

Case[35]	Weekday—£	Weekend—£	Location
C v Dixon (determined—evidence as at mid-2008)	10	11	Barnsley
Huntley (determined—aggregate rate for late 2008)	9.50	9.50	Portsmouth Cosham/ Hillsea
XXX (agreed—late 2008)	12	14	Guildford
Smith[39] (determined—mid-2008)	10	12	Herts.
Crofts (agreed composite rate—summer 2008)	12	12	Herts.

Case management—hourly rates

31. As with support worker rates there is no "conventional" hourly rate for case management; but the rate for this (as against the number of hours required) is mostly uncontroversial. The rate has crept up gradually and £90 an hour + travel time (£45 an hour plus mileage) was agreed in *Whiten*. £95 an hour was awarded in *Ali v Caton* [332], *Streeter* [217] (noting the agreement of Mrs Gough's costing) and *Farrugia* at [107], all above. £98 an hour was the rate allowed in *Tait v Gloucestershire Hospitals NHS Foundation Trust*.[40] Despite a claim for £107 an hour actually being paid for case management in *Manna* above, Cox J allowed [217] only £95 an hour, accepting the defendant's evidence that £107 an hour was beyond the normal range. Irwin J [142] awarded £98 an hour in *AB v Royal Devon & Exeter*.
32. The required number of hours varies greatly and will be lower where there is agency care as against direct employment.

Provision for holidays, sick pay etc.

33. Where future care is to be provided through direct employment rather than agency provision, it is now customary to take into account i) paid holidays ii) higher hourly rates paid on Bank holidays iii) sick leave and iv) down time in the package for training days by adopting calculations based on a notional 60 weeks in the year.[41] While a few experts continue to use it, the alternative method

---

[39] [2008] EWHC 2234 (QC)—the transcript lacks numbered paragraphs.
[40] [2015] EWHC 848 (QB) at [92].
[41] See: *XXX v A Strategic Health Authority* above at [24] and *Whiten v St George's Healthcare NHS Trust* [2011] EWHC 2066 (QB) at [167]–[168]. For the evolution of the 60-week calculation, see the paper at footnote 1. *Streeter* above is an exception, where the experts both adopted 59.6 weeks but made an additional allowance on Bank holidays—ruled on by Baker J in line with Mrs Gough at £1 an hour uplift.

It is clear that down time for training days, additional pay for bank holidays etc. are included in the 60-week calculation. Those care experts who take 60 weeks and routinely bill for training time and so on in addition might be said to be trying too hard. The taking of 60 weeks, however, might be distinguished up or down for the specific training etc. requirements of any case since it has evolved out of the bigger cases—it might be easier to distinguish down rather than up (or the attempt not worth the effort). See also the discussion below in the main text with regard to liaison and MDT meetings as within the 60-week calculation.

In *HS v Lancashire Teaching Hospitals NHS Trust* [2015] EWHC 1376 (QB), the claimant's care expert asked for a 5%

of taking 52 weeks in the year and a percentage uplift to cover the required extras (which started at around 27 per cent and rose steadily) has fallen out of favour in reported cases. Jay J in *Farrugia* above described [100] taking a 60-week year as "standard practice".

ERNIC

34. Calculation of ERNIC on carers' wages was often misunderstood. It is currently (tax year 2018/19) payable at 13.8 per cent on wages above the secondary threshold[42] (£162 a week × 52 weeks = £8,424 p.a.) So, to reach the annual sum of ERNIC, calculate the annual wages bill and deduct from it (£8,424 × the likely number of carers in the package) to give the sum on which 13.8 per cent is likely to be paid. There is controversy over whether the £3,000 Employment Allowance should or should not be offset–it appears to depend on how/by whom the carers are employed, which may change over time. Perhaps "a loss of chance" approach might set off half unless a care expert can explain things convincingly?

NEST pension contributions

35. The following information comes from the NEST website on 1 March 2018.[43]
36. If enrolled within the scheme, employers pay a percentage of *qualifying earnings*: for tax year 2018/19 this is between £6,032 and £46,350 p.a. if implemented as proposed.
37. Enrolment is compulsory for all workers aged at least 22 but under State retirement age who earn at least £10,000 p.a. from that employer, who work (or normally work) in the UK and who are not already an active member of a qualifying scheme with that employer.
38. Enrolment is at a worker's own option if aged at least 16, with the employer having to contribute if they have *qualifying earnings,* i.e. earn over £6,032 p.a.
39. The staged introduction of the duties is now completed.
40. The full impact of the contributions is still being phased in:

	Minimum percentage of qualifying earnings that must be paid in total	Minimum percentage of qualifying earnings that *employers* must pay
Lately	2 per cent	**1 per cent**
April 2018 to end March 2019	5 per cent	**2 per cent**
April 2019 onwards	8 per cent	**3 per cent**

Child care

41. The possible costs of caring for children have been claimed recently in *Totham* and *Robshaw*, both above. They were cases of cerebral palsy and the claims were resisted on the basis that neither claimant would realistically have children. The defences succeeded with slightly different formulations in the rationale. In *Totham*, Laing J found [71] that she was "not satisfied that there is a more than fanciful chance that Eva will have children". In *Robshaw*, Foskett J [191] would not go so far as to say the chance was "merely speculative or fanciful" but nevertheless said that the

---

contingency uplift (5% × 60 weeks = 3 more weeks) "in order to cover holidays, sickness and other unexpected and sudden absences on the part of employed carers". William Davis J rejected the argument at [31] on the basis that the 60-week calculation included holidays and sickness. He continued: "Any maternity leave will be funded from the public purse given the number of employees. Any other absences will almost certainly be accommodated with the carers' shift patterns."

[42] There is an upper ceiling; but no carer is ever paid enough to bring it into play.
[43] See *http://www.nestpensions.org.uk/schemeweb/nest.html*.

discount for contingencies would have to be so significant that "it would reduce the figure to something that would bear no real relationship to that actual cost if the event itself materialised. An award of such a sum would, in my view, be wholly artificial." And he made no award at all [192].

42. Child care claims in less serious cases are often raised but rarely pursued fully as strictly *child care*—more often they are a facet of care of claimants themselves to enable them to provide their own child care, adding only modestly or not at all to their underlying requirements. What is left may well amount to household services rather than *care*: see Jay J in *Hayden*—"The claim is for a nanny but I see him or her as being more by way of factotum, assisting the Claimant with the heavier aspects of cleaning and childcare . . . "[44]

Parental contribution to the future care package

43. The court's attitude to any fair offset from future commercial care of very severely damaged children on account of parental involvement has evolved since 2006. The seeds sown by Sir Rodger Bell in *Iqbal*[45]—to the effect that parents are not to be presumed to take part in the care of grievously injured children requiring onerous care—have grown on strongly via Teare J in *Massey* [64], Lloyd Jones J in *A v Powys* [57] and HHJ Collender QC (sitting as a High Court Judge) in *Crofts* [120]. By the time of *Whiten* (2011) the NHSLA was no longer apparently arguing for any real offset: the only point at which the parents' potential contribution was considered relevant was in allowing for a single night sleeper in the commercial package on the basis that they would be available in an emergency [205]. In *Farrugia* above [96], care was awarded for 14 hours a day x 2 commercial carers except when a family member would take the place of one commercial carer in outings spread over 10 hours each week. This modest adjustment to the rates for family provision covered only 48 weeks in the year up to the claimant's age of 49. While not arguing for any offset in *Robshaw* above (claimant 12 years old), the NHSLA renewed its fight in *HS v Lancs*.[46] (claimant only eight) but were again unsuccessful.

Pre-existing conditions—a matter of causation or deduction?

44. In *Huntley*[47] the claimant's pre-accident problems had not led to any prior requirement for care and attendance. In other cases, later negligence increases a pre-existing need for care, accommodation and therapies above those that would have been required anyway. How should the court approach the task? Is it a matter of *causation* so that, when damages are assessed, it is only in respect of the strictly increased elements satisfying the prior test of causation? Or, is it a matter of *quantification of damage* so that the whole of the reasonable needs are taken as the starting point and the pre-existing needs considered only as a matter of potential deduction? If the latter, a claimant can recover damages for the whole of his condition on a commercial basis and, if the pre-existing needs would have been satisfied at essentially no cost to him (family or local authority care), giving little or no credit.

45. In *Sklair v Haycock*,[48] the claimant (49 and looked after informally by his "Bohemian" father) had suffered with Asperger's Syndrome and Obsessive Compulsive Disorder. Edwards-Stuart J found that the claimant's elderly father would have continued to look after him for 5–10 years longer, when his wider family would have looked after him at a financial cost to them of £150–£200 per week for 5–10 years, after which a residential placement in local authority care would have been

---

[44] [2016] EWHC 3276 (QB) at [214]: " . . . I allow £9,082 per annum until the Claimant's youngest child reaches the age of 5. Thereafter, I allow 4 hours a week at £12 per hour. The Parties have agreed a multiplier of 7.05."
[45] [2006] EWHC 3111 (QB) [20].
[46] [2015] EWHC 1376 (QB).
[47] [2009] EWHC 405 (QB).
[48] [2009] EWHC 3328 (QB).

likely. The accident had turned the claimant's need for this lower level of care (as a matter of fact) into a reasonable need for 24-hour commercial care [80.] The findings of Edwards-Stuart J amounted to deciding the causation issue on the basis that the negligence had caused the whole of the need for care (awarding the full commercial cost) and he then made, as a matter of quantification of the damages, a small deduction only for the short period when modest financial cost would have been incurred.

46. In *Reaney v Various Staffs NHS Trusts*,[49] the claimant's spinal cord condition had been made worse by clinical negligence: she would have needed some more modest care etc. anyway but now needed, on Foskett J's findings, an intensive commercial package. He too decided that the negligence had caused the whole of the need for commercial care etc. and made no real deduction in respect of the prior needs. He went so far as to say that the principle of *material contribution* would have led him to a similar result [71].

47. The defendant appealed in *Reaney* where the Master of the Rolls overturned the reasoning and remitted the case for further consideration. The essential question is one of *causation* not *deduction*. Where negligence increases a claimant's needs *quantitatively* (even if *significantly* or *substantially* so—"more of the same") [21], a defendant's negligence only *causes* the additional need, not the underlying one: *Performance Cars Ltd v Abraham*[50] followed, as applied in *Steel v Joy*.[51] How the need would have been/will now be supplied (whether at commercial cost or free) is irrelevant to the causation question [33].

48. If, however, the negligence makes a *qualitative* difference—the needs are no longer of the same type—it has *caused* the whole of it in its different form. The Master of Rolls agreed with counsel for the appellant that the causation result in *Sklair* might be explained on the basis that the care need before and after the negligence was indeed qualitatively different—the difference between "personal support in a 24-hour care regime and general supervisory care of an essentially independent life" [32]. Nothing was said, in that event, as to the correctness of making even a small deduction at the quantification stage. In *Reaney*, however, despite the findings of Foskett J for very substantially increased needs, they did not go far enough to move the case across the line between the negligence having made merely a *quantitative* as against a *qualitative* difference.

49. Further he had been wrong to have recourse to ideas of *material contribution* and invocation of the principle (described by the MR as an "accurate distillation of the law") in *Bailey v MoD*.[52] Since there was no doubt as to the claimant's needs before and after the negligence, the principle could have no application. See the discussion at [36].

50. Whipple J distinguished *Reaney* and instead applied *Rahman v Arearose Ltd*[53] in the case of *XP v Compensa Towarzstwo SA & Przeyslaw Bejger*.[54] In *Reaney* the claimant was already paralysed before the clinical negligence and there was a clear baseline against which the Court could assess how much, if any, additional or different care was needed. Whipple J contrasted the *Reaney* position [93] with the one before her: two accidents on top of each other and no clear baseline to determine condition and prognosis after the first accident compared with the position after the second. She found the facts of the case not to be capable of such neat separation as envisaged in *Reaney* [95] on some heads of damage; she there applied the broader brush of the Court of Appeal in *Rahman*, coming to a "just conclusion" with a 75:25 split.

Resident carers

51. The old arguments for residential agency care have almost completely fallen away in the most serious cases. There may still be a place for such a provision, however, in cases requiring a lighter

---

[49] [2014] EWHC 3016 (QB).
[50] [1962] 1 QB 33.
[51] [2004] 1 WLR 3002.
[52] [2007] EWHC 2913 (QB).
[53] [2001] QB 351.
[54] [2016] EWHC 1728 (QB).

K1: Care and attendance

touch, as with care of the partial tetraplegic claimant in *Davies*[55] (between the ages of 70 and 75, after which extensive top up for double up hours was added.) The last gasp of the argument for residential care in the most serious cases came when the NHSLA in *Whiten* above tried to run a *Davies*-post-75-style argument in the case of a grievously injured child with mixed spastic-dystonic, severe, quadriplegic cerebral palsy. It suggested the bedrock of a care package through a residential agency carer with extensive hourly top up. Swift J rejected that potential solution without hesitation [204].

52. Nevertheless, in the unusual case of *AB v Devon & Exeter NHS Foundation Trust*[56]—a high paraplegic with severe spasm—a single resident carer was the answer to age 55 and two resident carers, overlapping and doubling up sensibly, from that age onwards. The annual multiplicands for the packages, including case management, were £79,420 [142] and £150,140 [145].

Risk/benefit applied to care regimes

53. *Davies* and *C v Dixon*, both above, have also been interesting in the detailed way in which Wilkie J and King J balanced risk and benefit to the claimant in reaching the appropriate care package. In each case the defendant argued that the package suggested by the claimant's experts amounted to substantial over-provision and would be stifling of the claimant. In *Davies* some risk of falling was found to be acceptable without a resident carer always on hand before the age of 70: a resident carer package before that age did not take into account the contribution which a degree of self-reliance has to a person's sense of worth and well-being [110]. In *C v Dixon* the claimant was not to be wrapped in cotton wool [35] with unnecessary commercial and double-up provision—he could have the required 24-hour care in a looser sense, including some down time in the package as long he had someone to contact in an emergency. Since his partner was assumed to be with him for the next 10 years, there was no need for commercial overnight care during that period.

54. In the moderate (general damages £147,500—July 2013) brain injury case of *Ali v Caton & MIB* above Stuart-Smith J described the scope of the care package there allowing 15 hours a week of support as follows [331ii]:

> "The purpose of the future care regime should be to provide sufficient support to enable [the claimant] to pursue a structured and constructive existence so far as possible, reinforcing constructive routines and being available to assist when he is confronted by the new, the unfamiliar or the complex."

Two carers throughout the day

55. Until *Manna* in 2015, whether two carers are required throughout the day had not been litigated for a while to a formal decision—it was common ground in the 2014 case of *Farrugia* above (severe brain injury) that it was necessary and in *Streeter* above in 2013 (C5/6 motor tetraplegia) that it was not. In *A v B*[57] two carers were required throughout waking hours (essentially in respect of transfers for toileting which could not be forecast as to timing) in a case of severe compromise in dystonic athetoid tetraplegic cerebral palsy. A similar result ensued in *XXX*. In both cases the claimants had little or no appreciation of their predicament but swift availability of changing was necessary for their health and comfort. The result was the same in *Massey* for a different reason: here the claimant had substantially retained intellect in a grossly malfunctioning body: for him the availability of two carers was essential for transfers and transport so that he could exercise

---

[55] [2008] EWHC 740 (QB) Wilkie J.
[56] [2016] EWHC 1024 (QB) Irwin J.
[57] [2006] EWHC 1178 (QB).

autonomy and make decisions to act on impulse rather than live in the straightjacket of double-up provision which was less than continuous and at fixed hours of the day.

56. In *Farrugia* above, while awarding care based on two carers in attendance during waking hours, Jay J said this when considering whether two *commercial* carers had to be present throughout:

> "I do not accept . . . that Jack should, in effect, be free to do whatever he wishes at the spur of the moment. I do not consider that Jack's personal autonomy is overridden, or the dictates of spontaneity are unreasonably quelled, by providing for a regime which presupposes a modest degree of pre-planning and organisation. This, after all, reflects the realities of ordinary life."

57. The case for two carers in respect of a sentient adult who can give basic cooperation with hoisted transfers (in the sense of not lashing out or being subject to spasm) has not yet been clearly made out for transfers within the home. While the NHS commonly uses two nurses for such transfers even with a hoist on hospital wards, that appears to be at least partly because two nurses are available in such a setting and the use of two speeds things up.

58. *Manna* above saw the principal dispute at trial focus on the amount of double up care for an ambulant young man with profound cognitive problems and prone to outbursts: 14+14 hours per day—total daytime double-up—was found to be reasonable because of the unpredictability of outbursts [209]; it would simply be too much for one person alone to provide the required structured care all day [211]; 28 hours of double-up *per week* was rejected.

Day centre provision

59. The argument for offset from a commercial care package for down time while an adult claimant attends a local authority day centre was never strong. With its lack of forensic success, coupled with further funding cuts and closure of day centres, the argument is not currently being aired.

Team leaders

60. Although the payment of a higher rate to a member of the support worker team did not find favour over 10 years ago now in *Crofton* or *Iqbal*, the allowance of a team leader (reducing the amount and cost of case management intervention) has become pretty standard more recently in really serious cases. An extra £2 an hour was conceded in *XXX*. In *Whiten* the principle was disputed; and as a fall back it was suggested by the defendant that any provision could be by reference to a small proportion of the hours worked by the team leader, i.e. only those hours when in fact engaged on team leader duties. Swift J [164] rejected that line and allowed 30 hours a week at a weekday rate enhanced by £3 an hour (London). The whole point was to attract someone to the post with experience and ability: the defendant's suggestion would not achieve the aim. Contrast *Farrugia*, in which Jay J awarded an increase of £5 an hour (Hants.) [104] but over only 22 hours a week [103], commenting that he simply could not accept that a full week's work was required for the combination of tasks required of the team leader. In *Streeter*, Baker J allowed an increment of £2 an hour over 15 hours a week.[58] In *Robshaw*, Foskett J [183]–[184] allowed an enhanced rate of £4 an hour for 30 hours a week to age 19; £5 an hour (the gap being said to grow over time) over 25 hours a week from that age onwards. In *HS v Lancs.* William Davis J awarded 33.5 hours a week at unspecified team leader rates. In *Manna* Cox J awarded £5 an hour uplift but the number of hours is unclear. In *JR v Sheffield*[59], the parties compromised at £4 an hour uplift [55].

---

[58] See footnote 34.
[59] [2017] EWHC 1245 (QB).

61. Much appears to depend on the precise nature of the case, the experts and the judge as to how things are expressed.

Hand over meetings

62. Claiming hand over periods of up to half an hour at the conclusion of each shift has never appeared an attractive argument and is not generally being run at the moment unless in unusual circumstances.

Liaison/team meetings

63. These were not contended for in *Whiten* or *Farrugia*; allowed as to merely one hour a month in *C v Dixon*, and substantially conceded in *XXX*. There may have been oversight when these allowances have been made or conceded: as the "60 weeks in the year" evolved, it was probably supposed to take into account a routine allowance for training and team meetings—see the discussion of the evidence in the Judgment of Penry-Davey J in *Smith* above.
64. The result was more complicated in *Robshaw* above, where Foskett J allowed for the costs of therapists attending multi-disciplinary meetings but decided—in line with the above discussion—that the attendance of the case manager, team leader and support workers should be funded out of the normal working time already awarded within the 60-week year. He allowed five meeting in the first year; four per annum then until age 18; three per annum then to age 25; the claim was limited to one per annum then for life but he would have awarded two per annum. All meetings were said to require two hours allocated to them and should not be rushed. See [474]–[479].

The status of family choice on behalf of a claimant

65. The issue of the status of a future family choice on behalf of a claimant raised its head in the case of *Harman v East Kent Hospitals NHS Foundation Trust*.[60] The claimant, aged 13 and suffering severe autism with significant cognitive impairment, was being cared for in a specialist placement funded by the LEA but spending eight weeks a year at home. The issue was where the claimant would live when his education came to an end in 12 years at age 25: the parents wanted him then to come home. Turner J found in favour of that course, following expert evidence that a care package which met with the aspirations of the parents would be more likely to succeed than one which did not [38]. As to the underlying point of law, however, the parents' choice did not trump the view of the court of the primary measure of damage in the future:

> "[36] Care must be taken in cases such as this not to equiparate the preferences of relatives with the regime of care and support the cost of which should be the basis of reasonable compensation. Each case must be looked at on its own facts. There may well be circumstances in which, however strong and genuine the desire of the parents or a spouse or partner may be to have the claimant home, there are good reasons for taking a contrary course. The purpose of damages in a personal injury claim is to compensate the victim and not to accommodate the wishes of his family whatever the extent of the inevitable personal sympathy one might have for those who are left to pick up the pieces and suffer the inevitable and sustained emotional impact of serious injury to someone dear to them."

---

[60] [2015] EWHC 1662 (QB).

Chance contingencies and PPOs for care

66. *Huntley* above illustrates that the essential chance assessment of damages for future loss has survived the new PPO regime, which purports to trace everything back to a claimant's needs. There the claimant, who had suffered a frontal lobe injury and whose rehabilitation had not gone well up to trial, contended for 24 hours of care per day as the long term solution: the defendant submitted for 21 hours per week. Underhill J (as he then was) approached matters by evaluating first of all the hard-core minimum level that he thought was reasonable, which he assessed at six hours a day [109]. This hard-core cost he would have put within a PPO [114] but not the full chance reasonable amount that he went on to evaluate as follows. He uplifted the package by 50 per cent from six hours to nine hours a day with a broad brush for all the possibilities of needing greater care. He then discounted that back by one hour to eight hours a day for the chance that the claimant would not in fact engage all the care that he might reasonably require. There was a real chance that he would reject care (as he would if he entered a stable relationship) and small chances of imprisonment and detention under the Mental Health Act. The resulting additional two hours a day beyond the core six hours Underhill J would have provided within an additional lump sum award; but the whole PPO submission was withdrawn when the claimant did not recover for 24-hour care.

67. For a further example taking contingencies into account, see the decision of Kenneth Parker J in *Tate v Ryder Holdings* above [38]–[42] where he averaged the cost of caring for the claimant in his own and residential accommodation, catering for different times in his life, and adjusted further for the chances of non-compliance by 20 per cent for reasons similar to those set out by Underhill J in *Huntley*. As in *Huntley*, the adjustments led to a lump sum award rather than PPO.

K1: Care and attendance

National Joint Council Payscales – Spinal Column Point 8

Year	Time of day	Hourly rate £	Hours pw	Cost pw £	Divided by hours pw	Aggregate rate	Day (9am to 8pm) aggregate rate (i.e. inc. w/ends)
Apr 1998 to Mar 1999	Basic Evening Saturday Sunday	£4.98 £6.22 £7.47 £9.96	55 65 24 24	£273.90 + £404.30 + £179.28 + £239.04 = £1,096.52	168	£6.53	£6.05
Apr 1999 to Mar 2000	Basic Evening Saturday Sunday	£5.13 £6.41 £7.69 £10.26	55 65 24 24	£282.15 + £416.65 + £184.56 + £246.24 = £1,129.60	168	£6.72	£6.23
Apr 2000 to Mar 2001	Basic Evening Saturday Sunday	£5.29 £6.61 £7.93 £10.58	55 65 24 24	£290.95 + £429.65 + £190.32 + £253.92 = £1,164.84	168	£6.93	£6.42
Apr 2001 to Mar 2002	Basic Evening Saturday Sunday	£5.49 £6.86 £8.23 £10.97	55 65 24 24	£301.95 + £455.90 + £197.52 + £263.28 = £1,208.61	168	£7.19	£6.66
Apr 2002 to Sep 2002	Basic Evening Saturday Sunday	£5.65 £7.06 £8.47 £11.30	55 65 24 24	£310.75 + £458.90 + £203.28 + £271.20 = £1,244.13	168	£7.41	£6.86
Oct 2002 to Mar 2003	Basic Evening Saturday Sunday	£5.71 £7.14 £8.56 £11.42	55 65 24 24	£314.05 + £464.10 + £205.44 + £274.08 = £1,257.67	168	£7.49	£6.93
Apr 2003 to Mar 2004	Basic Evening Saturday Sunday	£5.90 £7.37 £8.85 £11.80	55 65 24 24	£324.50 + £479.05 + £212.40 + £283.20 = £1,299.15	168	£7.73	£7.16
Apr 2004 to Mar 2005	Basic Evening Saturday Sunday	£6.06 £7.57 £9.09 £12.12	55 65 24 24	£333.30 + £492.05 + £218.16 + £290.88 = £1,334.39	168	£7.94	£7.36
Apr 2005 to Mar 2006	Basic Evening Saturday Sunday	£6.24 £7.80 £9.36 £12.48	55 65 24 24	£343.20 + £507.00 + £224.64 + £299.52 = £1,374.36	168	£8.18	£7.58
Apr 2006 to Mar 2007	Basic Evening Saturday Sunday	£6.43 £8.04 £9.65 £12.86	55 65 24 24	£353.65 + £522.60 + £231.60 + £308.64 = £1,416.49	168	£8.43	£7.81
Apr 2007 to Mar 2008	Basic Evening Saturday Sunday	£6.59 £8.24 £9.88 £13.18	55 65 24 24	£362.45 + £535.60 + £237.12 + £316.32 = £1,451.49	168	£8.64	£8.00

K1: Care and attendance

Year	Time of day	Hourly rate £	Hours pw	Cost pw £	Divided by hours pw	Aggregate rate	Day (9am to 8pm) aggregate rate (i.e. inc. w/ends)
Apr 2008 to Mar 2009	Basic Evening Saturday Sunday	£6.75 £8.44 £10.13 £13.50	55 65 24 24	£371.25 + £548.60 + £243.12 + £324.00 = £1,486.97	168	£8.85	£8.20
Apr 2009 to Mar 2013	Basic Evening Saturday Sunday	£6.85 £8.56 £10.28 £13.70	55 65 24 24	£376.75 £556.40 £246.72 £328.80 = £1,508.67	168	£8.98	£8.32
April 2013 to Dec 2014	Basic Evening Saturday Sunday	£6.90 £9.21 £10.36 £13.81	70 50 24 24	£483.32 £460.31 £248.57 £331.42 = £1,523.62	168	£9.07	£8.38
Jan 2015 to 31 Mar 2016	Basic Evening Saturday Sunday	£7.19 £9.59 £10.78 £14.38	70 50 24 24	£503.28 £479.31 £258.83 £345.11 = £1,586.53	168	£9.44	£8.73
April 2016 to 31 Mar 2017	Basic Evening Saturday Sunday	£7.66 £10.21 £11.48 £15.31	70 50 24 24	£535.93 £510.41 £275.62 £367.50 = £1,689.46	168	£10.06	£9.30
April 2017 to 31 Mar 2018	Basic Evening Saturday Sunday	£7.90 £10.54 £11.85 £15.80	70 50 24 24	£553.17 £526.83 £284.49 £379.32 = £1,743.81	168	£10.38	£9.60
April 2018 to 31 Mar 2019	Basic Evening Saturday Sunday	£8.62 £11.49 £12.93 £17.24	70 50 24 24	£603.24 £574.51 £310.24 £413.65 = £1,901.64	168	£11.32	£10.46
April 2019 to 31 Mar 2020 **NB NOW SPINAL POINT 2**	Basic Evening Saturday Sunday	£9.18 £12.24 £13.77 £18.36	70 50 24 24	£642.61 £612.01 £330.48 £440.64 = £2,025.74	168	£12.06	£11.15

Notes for 2018/19 and 2019/20

Agreement between the LGA and NJC trade union side was reached in April 2018, with uplifted rates being applicable from 1 April 2018 and 1 April 2019 respectively.

The rates for 2018/19 represent a 9.052 per cent uplift on the 2017/18 rates.

NB **From 1 April 2019** it has been agreed to re-structure the NJC pay spine. Therefore from this date the relevant pay point for gratuitous family care will be **SPINAL POINT 2**.

Bank holiday pay is not incorporated into the above as the LGA provision is for staff to be paid at the normal rate for the period in question and to take either a half or full day time off in lieu, according to time worked. Specific calculation is therefore difficult and is likely to make minimal difference at 0.03 per cent overall.

Source for the above rates: National Joint Council for Local Government Services

K2: Nannies, cleaners and school fees

The death or incapacity of a spouse frequently involves incurring the costs of a nanny or a housekeeper or of sending a child to boarding school so that the surviving parent can continue working. Also, with some employments, typically when they involve overseas postings or frequent moves, school fees are part of the remuneration and will be lost if the employee dies or is disabled from that particular employment.

Nannies

	Live-out		Live-in	
	Weekly gross	Annual gross	Weekly gross	Annual gross
Central London	£617	£32,110	£438	£22,765
Outer London/Home Counties	£564	£29,328	£412	£21,431
Other areas	£506	£26,286	£386	£20,072

The figures are derived from the 2017 survey by *Nannytax*. The total cost to the client will be more than the gross wage as it is necessary to pay for holidays, sickness, employer's national insurance contribution, agency fees and so on. (See the discussion in the notes to Table K1: Care and attendance.)

Cleaners

The services of cleaners in London are currently (March 2018) advertised at the following rates. These are commonly for three or more hours a week: one-off visits usually cost more.

Homeclean	£8.73 per hour	(three hours a week)
	£9.09 per hour	(two hours a week: the cleaner is paid separately avoiding VAT; and there is an annual agency fee which is greater in the first year)
Housekeep	£13.50 per hour	(Minimum visit: two hours)
Amy Cleaning	£12.00 per hour	(Varies. The cleaner is paid separately, avoiding VAT; there is also an agency fee).

School fees

Annual school fees for a three-term year are as follows.

Public school		**Independent Schools Council (average)**	
Boarders (Upper school)	£37,740	Boarder	£33,684
Day pupils (Upper school)	£26,130	Day pupil (boarding school)	£18,750
Day pupils (Under school or preparatory school)	£18,336	Day pupil (day school)	£13,854

Notes:

1. Fees for pupils entering in the sixth form may be higher.

2. Fees for weekly as opposed to full-time boarders may be lower.

The information has been obtained from the websites of Nannytax, Homeclean, Housekeep, Amy Cleaning, Westminster School, and the Independent Schools Council.

K3: DIY, gardening and housekeeping

1. The sort of injury which limits one's capacity to earn will often also limit one's capacity to do jobs around the house. Depending on the kind of injury and the claimant's pre-accident talents, these may range from the skilled, such as plumbing or electrical work, to the mundane, such as washing up and putting out the bins.

2. It is well established that these skills have a monetary value[1] and that "the loss of ability to do work in the home is a recoverable head of damages and includes 'services' such as general housekeeping, gardening and maintenance".[2]

3. The Court of Appeal decided in *Daly v General Steam Navigation Co*[3] that *special* damages for past loss must comprise actual expenditure (or presumably the value of gratuitous care actually provided by others). Absent actual expenditure or gratuitous care, loss of capacity before trial is reflected in enhanced *general* damages. With regard to future loss, however, the court held that the claimant need not prove an actual intention to employ replacement services (paid or unpaid). Bridge LJ said:

   " . . . it seems to me that it was entirely reasonable and entirely in accordance with principle in assessing damages, to say that the estimated cost of employing labour for that time, . . . , was the proper measure of her damages under this heading. It is really quite immaterial, in my judgment, whether . . . the plaintiff chooses to alleviate her own housekeeping burden . . . by employing the labour which has been taken as the estimate on which damages have been awarded, or whether she continues to struggle with the housekeeping on her own and to spend the damages which have been awarded to her on other luxuries which she would otherwise be unable to afford."

4. One difficulty is finding an appropriate rate and working out a number of hours per week which these tasks take. People in rented accommodation may do little maintenance, and older people often, though not invariably, find their appetite for such tasks diminishes. The claimant will need evidence that he or she would be carrying out the work personally if it had not been for the injury. The evidence may include (in addition to witness statements) photographs, estimates from those providing such services locally (for labour only), and reports from a local surveyor and/or an independent agency. There are however differences of judicial opinion as to the utility of expert evidence: some judges accept it[4], whilst Mackay J in *Fleet v Fleet*[5] derived his own figure from experience, saying, "It would be dismal if experts had to be called to say how much it costs to mow a lawn or paint a room."

5. The courts have made a range of awards, sometimes using a multiplier/multiplicand approach and sometimes making a global award.[6] Cases in *Kemp & Kemp* show (adjusted for inflation to 2018) multiplicands for DIY and gardening of the order of £1,340–£2,200, and global awards of some £16,400–£22,200.

---

[1] *Phipps v Brooks Dry Cleaning Services* [1996] P.I.Q.R. Q 100.
[2] "Damages for Personal Injury: Medical, Nursing and Other Expenses", Law Commission, Law Com. No.262 (1999), para.2.34.
[3] [1981] W.L.R. 120,127.
[4] e.g. *Smith v East and North Hertfordshire Hospitals NHS Trust* [2008] EWHC 2234 (QB).
[5] [2009] EWHC 3166 (QB).
[6] See the analysis in *Kemp & Kemp* Vol. 1, Ch. 17.

K3: DIY, gardening and housekeeping

Handyman, gardening and housekeeping services are being advertised in March 2018 at the following rates:

	London	**Home Counties**	**Rest of country**
Handymen per hour	£58 per hour	£25 per hour	£30 per hour
Handymen half-day	£192 per half-day	£100 per half-day	£110 per half-day
Handymen day rates	£319 per day	£200 per day	£200 per day
Gardening—(for team of two)	£48.50 per hour	£42 per hour	£38 per hour
Cleaning and housekeeping	£12 per hour	£13 per hour	£11 per hour

Notes to the table:

- The figure in the table is generally the median.
- Charges for handymen and gardeners vary with the type of work. Plumbing and electrical work is usually dearer than decorating and putting up shelves. Garden design and planting may cost more than garden maintenance such as mowing the lawn and trimming the hedge.
- There is often a minimum period or a supplemental charge for the first hour.
- Charges are generally higher in the evenings and at weekends.
- Some firms prefer to quote for a specified job and do not advertise an hourly rate.
- Some firms provide services at a reduced rate for pensioners and those on a low income. These are not reflected in the table.

K4: Hospital self-pay (uninsured) charges

The following figures are inclusive of hospital charges and surgeons' and anaesthetists' fees. The charges are approximate, as certain factors affecting cost, such as length of stay or prosthesis used, vary from patient to patient. It should be borne in mind that the figures in the "National Average" column are derived from a database that includes the London figures.

	London average (median)	National average (median)
Arthroscopy (hip)	6,503	5,990
Arthroscopy (knee)	3,836	3,523
Arthroscopy (shoulder)	4,438	4,695
Breast lump removal	585	1,830
Carpal tunnel release	2,462	1,719
Cataract removal	2,950	2,425
Circumcision	1,800	1,902
Colonoscopy	1,950	1,832
Coronary artery bypass graft	17,500	17,500
Cruciate knee ligament repair	8,403	6,000
CT scan	914	500
Cystoscopy	1,850	1,625
Epidural injection	1,250	1,459
Gall bladder removal – laparoscopic	6,350	6,212
Facet joint injection	1,750	1,990
Gastric banding	7,640	6,450
Gastric balloon insertion	4,475	4,085
Gastric bypass	10,900	10,495
Gastroscopy	1,450	1,447
Grommets insertion	2,600	2,243
Haemorrhoids removal	2,695	2,829
Hernia repair (inguinal)	3,250	2,695
Herniated disc removal	6,423	7,345
Hip replacement – total	13,660	10,761
Hip replacement – revision	12,306	12,306
Hysterectomy	7,550	6,545
Hysteroscopy	2,350	2,054
Knee arthroscopy	3,950	3,923
Knee replacement – total	13,250	11,434
Knee replacement – revision	18,204	18,204
Laparoscopy	3,450	3,450
Prostate removal	14,595	14,595
Sigmoidoscopy	1,550	1,743
Vaginal prolapse repair	5,950	5,199
Varicose vein ablation (one leg)	2,526	2,851
Vasectomy	1,650	1,045
Vasectomy reversal	3,850	2,830

These figures are drawn from around the country. Charges vary from hospital to hospital and between different areas of the country. They are generally higher in London than elsewhere. All figures have been sourced from www.privatehealth.co.uk and are correct as at 21 March 2018.

K5: NHS charges

NHS prescriptions (from 1 April 2018)

Charge per prescribed item		£8.60
Prescription prepayment certificate:	three months	£29.10
	12 months	£104.00

For items dispensed in combination (duo) packs, there is a charge for each different drug in the pack.

NHS dental treatment (from 1 January 2018)

If a patient is not exempt from charges, he should pay one of the following rates for each course of treatment he receives:

Course of treatment	Cost	Scope
Band 1	£21.60	This covers an examination, diagnosis (e.g. x-rays), advice on how to prevent future problems, and a scale and polish if clinically needed, and preventative care such as the application of fluoride varnish or fissure sealant if appropriate.
Band 2	£59.10	This covers everything listed in Band 1 above, plus any further treatment such as fillings, root canal work or removal of teeth but not more complex items covered by Band 3.
Band 3	£256.50	This covers everything listed in Bands 1 and 2 above, plus crowns, dentures or bridges and other laboratory work.

Notes

1. These are the only charges for NHS dental treatment.
2. A patient only has to pay one charge for each course of treatment, even if it takes more than one visit to the dentist to finish it.
3. If the patient needs more treatment within the same or lower charge band (e.g. an additional filling), within two months of completing a course of treatment, there is no extra charge.
4. There is no charge for repairing dentures or for having stitches removed.
5. Children under 18, and many adults, do not have to pay NHS charges. (See form HC11, "Help with Health Costs", which can be found on the Department of Health website: *http://www.dh.gov.uk*.)

K6: The 2015 Rehabilitation Code

(Code of Best Practice on Rehabilitation, Early Intervention and Medical Treatment in Personal Injury Claims)

INTRODUCTION

The Code promotes the collaborative use of rehabilitation and early intervention in the compensation process. It is reviewed from time to time in response to feedback from those who use it, taking into account the changing legal and medical landscape.

The Code's purpose is to help the injured claimant make the best and quickest possible medical, social vocational and psychological recovery. This means ensuring that his or her need for rehabilitation is assessed and addressed as a priority and that the process is pursued on a collaborative basis. With this in mind, the claimant solicitor should always ensure that the compensator receives the earliest possible notification of the claim and its circumstances whenever rehabilitation may be beneficial.

Although the objectives of the Code apply whatever the clinical and social needs of the claimant, the best way to achieve them will vary depending on the nature of the injury and the claimant's circumstances. The Code recognises that the dynamics of lesser-injury cases are different to those further up the scale. A separate process is set out for claims below £25,000 (in line with the Civil Procedure Rules definition of low value). Separate provision is also made for soft tissue injury cases as defined in paragraph **1.1(16A)** of the Pre-Action Protocol for Low Value Personal Injury Claims in Road Traffic Accidents.

It is important to stress, however that even low value injuries can be life-changing for some people. The projected monetary value of a claim is only a guide to the rehabilitation needs of the injured person. Each case should be taken on its individual merits and the guidelines for higher- value injuries will sometimes be more appropriate for those in the lowest category.

Sections 1 to 3 set out the guiding principles and the obligations of the various parties, and apply to all types of injury. After that, the sections diverge significantly depending on the size of claim.

Although the Code deals mainly with the Immediate Needs Assessment it encourages all parties to adopt the same principles and collaborative approach right up until the case is concluded. In doing so it does not stipulate a detailed process. Rather, it assumes that the parties will have established the collaborative working relationships that render a prescriptive document unnecessary.

Ten 'markers' that can affect the rehabilitation assessment, and therefore the treatment are to be found in the Glossary at the end of the Code. They should be considered in all cases.

With the more serious injuries, it is envisaged that Case Managers will have an essential role to play in assessing the claimant's needs and then overseeing treatment. This Code should be read in conjunction with the Guide for Case Managers and those who Commission them published separately.

1. ROLE OF THE CODE

1.1 The purpose of the personal injury claims process is to restore the individual as much as possible to the position they were in before the accident. The Code provides a framework for the claimant solicitor and compensator to work together to ensure that the claimant's health, quality of life, independence and ability to work are restored before, or simultaneously with, the process of assessing compensation.

1.2 Although the Code is recognised by the relevant CPR Pre-Action Protocols, achieving the aims are more important than strict adherence to its terms. Therefore it is open to the parties to agree an alternative framework to achieve the early rehabilitation of the claimant.

1.3 Where there is no agreement on liability the parties may still agree to use the Code. The health and economic benefits of proceeding with rehabilitation at an early stage, regardless of agreement on liability may be especially strong in catastrophic and other severe cases. Compensators should consider from the outset whether there is a possibility or likelihood of at least partial admission later on in the process so as not to compromise the prospects for rehabilitation.

1.4 In this Code, the expression 'the compensator' includes any person acting on behalf of the compensator. 'Claimant solicitor' includes any legal representative acting on behalf of the claimant. 'Case Manager' means a suitably qualified rehabilitation case manager.

2. **THE CLAIMANT SOLICITOR**

2.1 The claimant solicitor's obligation to act in the best interests of their client extends beyond securing reasonable financial compensation vital as that may be. Their duty also includes considering as soon as practicable, whether additional medical or rehabilitative intervention would improve the claimant's present and/or longer-term physical and mental well-being. In doing so, there should be full consultation with the claimant and/or their family and any treating practitioner where doing so is proportionate and reasonable. This duty continues throughout the life of the case but is most important in the early stages.

2.2 It is the duty of a claimant solicitor to have an initial discussion with the claimant and/or their family to identify:

1) Whether there is an immediate need for aids, adaptations, adjustments to employment to enable the claimant to perform their existing job obtain a suitable alternative role with the same employer or retrain for new employment. They should, where practical and proportionate, work with the claimant's employers to ensure that the position is kept open for them as long as possible.
2) The need to alleviate any problems related to their injuries.

2.3 The claimant solicitor should then communicate these needs to the compensator by telephone or email, together with all other relevant information, as soon as practicable. It is the intention of this Code that both parties will work to address all rehabilitation needs on a collaborative basis.

2.4 The compensator will need to receive from the claimant solicitor sufficient information to make a well-informed decision about the need for rehabilitation assistance including detailed and adequate information on the functional impact of the claimant's injuries. There is no requirement for an expert report at this early stage. The information should, however include the nature and extent of any likely continuing disability and any suggestions that may have already been made concerning rehabilitation and/or early intervention. It should be communicated within 21 days of becoming aware of those injuries or needs once the compensator is known.

2.5 Upon receiving a rehabilitation suggestion from the compensator, the claimant solicitor should discuss it with the claimant and/or their family as soon as practical and reply within 21 days.

2.6 Many cases will be considered under this Code before medical evidence has actually been commissioned or obtained. It is important in these situations that rehabilitation steps are not undertaken that might conflict with the recommendations of treating clinical teams. It is equally important that unnecessary delay is avoided in implementing steps that could make a material difference to the injured person or their family. Early engagement with the compensator is crucial to discuss such issues.

2.7 Whilst generally in catastrophic and other particularly severe cases, it is recommended that an appropriately qualified Case Manager should be appointed before any rehabilitation commences, this may not always be possible even though it should be a priority. Methods of selecting Case Managers are described in paragraphs 7.3 and 7.4. The aim when appointing a Case Manager should be to ensure that any proposed rehabilitation plan they recommend is appropriate and that the goals set are specific and attainable. The Case Manager should before undertaking an Immediate Needs Assessment (INA) as part of the claims process, make every attempt to liaise with NHS clinicians and others involved in the claimant's treatment, and to work collaboratively with them, provided this does not unduly delay the process. If possible, they should obtain the claimant's rehabilitation prescription discharge summary or similar, including any A&E records and/or treating consultant's report and medical records.

3. THE COMPENSATOR

3.1 It is the duty of the compensator from the earliest practicable stage, to consider whether the claimant would benefit from additional medical or rehabilitative treatment. This duty continues throughout the life of the case but is most important in the early stages.

3.2 If the claimant may have rehabilitation needs, the compensator should contact the claimant solicitor as soon as practicable to seek to work collaboratively on addressing those needs. As set out in paragraph 2.5, the claimant solicitor should respond within 21 days.

3.3 Where a request to consider rehabilitation has been communicated by the claimant solicitor, the compensator should respond within 21 days, or earlier if possible, either confirming their agreement or giving reasons for rejecting the request.

3.4 Nothing in this Code modifies the obligations of the compensator under the Protocols to investigate claims rapidly and, in any event within the relevant liability response period.

LOWER-VALUE INJURIES

4. THE ASSESSMENT PROCESS—LOWER-VALUE INJURIES

4.1 Different considerations apply for soft-tissue injury cases compared to other lower-value cases of £25,000 or below. In all cases, the claimant's solicitor should consider, with the claimant and/or the claimant's family, whether there is a need for early rehabilitation. The results of that discussion should be recorded in section C of the electronic Claims Notification Form, which will be transmitted through the Ministry of Justice Claims Portal to commence the claim. That form requires details of any professional treatment recommendations, treatment already received (including name of provider) and ongoing rehabilitation needs.

4.2 For lower-value injuries generally this might involve physiotherapy diagnostics and consultant follow-up, psychological intervention or other services to alleviate problems caused by the injury. In soft-tissue injury cases, in particular, it is understood that there is not always necessarily a requirement for a rehabilitation intervention. It is considered likely that, where there is an initial intervention it will focus on treating any physical need, for example through physiotherapy.

In all cases, the claimant solicitor should communicate with the compensator as soon as practical about any rehabilitation needs, preferably by electronic means. The mechanism of completion and transmission of the Claims Notification Form should facilitate this process and should take place before any significant treatment has been commenced, subject always to any overriding medical need for urgent treatment.

4.3 Nothing in this Code alters the legal principles that:

1. Until there has been a liability admission by a compensator (through the Compensator's Response in the Claims Portal), the claimant can have no certainty about the prospect of recovery of any treatment sums incurred.
2. Until the compensator has accepted a treatment regime in which the number and price of sessions have been agreed, the level of recovery of any such sums will always be a matter for negotiation (most likely through exchange of offers in the portal system) unless the subject of a Court order.
3. Where a claimant has decided not to take up a form of treatment that is readily available in favour of a more expensive option the reasonableness of that decision may be a factor that is taken into account on the assessment of damages.

4.4 Unless there is a medico-legal report containing full recommendations for rehabilitation, which both parties are happy to adopt, an initial Triage Report (TR) should be obtained to establish the type of treatment needed. In most cases, the Triage Report will be the only report required Where both the claimant's solicitor and the compensator agree that further reports are required, the assessment process is likely to have two further stages:

(i) A subsequent Assessment Report (AR) provided by the healthcare professional who is actually treating the claimant;
(ii) A Discharge Report (DR) from the treating healthcare professional to summarise the treatment provided.

It is, however, understood within the Code that a treatment discharge summary should routinely be included within the claimant's treatment records.

It is always possible for the Assessment Report (AR) and Discharge Report (DR) to be combined into one document.

4.5 The Triage Report (TR) assessment should be undertaken by an appropriately qualified and experienced person who is subject to appropriate clinical governance structures Guidance on this may be obtained by reading the British Standards Institute standard PAS 150 or the UKRC Standards. It is permissible under the Code that the assessor providing the Triage Report could also be appointed to implement the recommendations.

4.6 The person or organisation that prepares the Triage and, if appropriate, Assessment and Discharge Reports and/or undertakes treatment should, save in exceptional circumstances, be entirely independent of the person or organisation that provided any medico-legal report to the claimant. In soft-tissue injury cases, the parties are referred to Part 45291 of the Civil Procedure Rules.

4.7 The Triage and the preparation of any subsequent Assessment and Discharge Report and/or the provision of any treatment may be carried out or provided by a person or organisation having a direct or indirect business connection with the solicitor or compensator only if the other party agrees. The solicitor or compensator will be expected to reveal to the other party the existence and nature of such a business connection before instructing the connected organisation.

4.8 The assessment agency will be asked to carry out the Triage Report in a way that is appropriate to the needs of the case, which will in most cases be a telephone interview within seven days of the referral being received by the agency. It is expected that the TR will be very simple, usually just an email.

4.9 In all cases, the TR should be published simultaneously or made available immediately by the instructing party to the other side This applies also to treatment reports (AR and DR) where the parties have agreed that they are required Both parties will have the right to raise questions on the report(s), disclosing such correspondence to the other party.

4.10 It is recognised that, for the Triage Report to be of benefit to the parties, it should be prepared and used wholly outside the litigation process Neither side can rely on the report in any subsequent litigation unless both parties agree in writing. Likewise, any notes, correspondence or documents created in connection with the triage assessment process will not be disclosed in any litigation. Anyone involved in preparing the Triage Report or in the assessment process shall not be a compellable witness at court This principle is also set out in the Protocols.

4.11 The compensator will usually only consider rehabilitation that deals with the effects of the injuries that have been caused in the relevant accident. They will not normally fund treatment for other conditions that do not directly relate to the accident unless these conditions have been exacerbated by it or will impede recovery.

5. THE REPORTS—LOWER-VALUE INJURIES

5.1 It is expected under the Code that all treatment reporting described in this section will be concise and proportionate to the severity of the injuries and likely value of the claim.

5.2 The Triage Report should consider, where relevant, the ten 'markers' identified at the end of this Code and will normally cover the following headings:

1. The injuries sustained by the claimant;
2. The current impact on their activities of daily living, their domestic circumstances and, where relevant, their employment;
3. Any other relevant medical conditions not arising from the accident;
4. The past provision and current availability of treatment to the claimant via the NHS, their employer or health insurance schemes;
5. The type of intervention or treatment recommended;
6. The likely cost and duration of treatment;
7. The expected outcome of such intervention or treatment.

5.3 The Triage Report will not provide a prognosis or a diagnosis.

5.4 The assessment reports (TR, or any AR or DR) should not deal with issues relating to legal liability and should therefore not contain a detailed account of the accident circumstances, though they should enable the parties to understand the mechanism by which the injury occurred.

5.5 Where agreed as needed, any Assessment Report (AR) will normally have the following minimum headings:

1. Nature, symptoms and severity of injury(ies);
2. Relevance of any pre-existing conditions or injuries;
3. Primary rehabilitation goal and anticipated outcome;
4. Expected duration, number, type and length of treatment sessions;
5. Impact of injuries upon work and or activities of daily living and barriers to recovery and return to work.

5.6 Where agreed as needed, such as where a treatment discharge summary is considered inadequate, any Discharge Report (DR) will normally have the following minimum headings:

1. Current nature, symptoms and severity of injury(ies);
2. Whether the primary rehabilitation goal has been attained;
3. Number, type and length of treatment sessions/appointments attended or missed/DNAs (Did Not Attend);
4. Current impact of injuries on work or activities of daily living;
5. Whether the claimant has achieved, as far as possible, a full functional recovery;
6. Whether additional treatment is required to address the claimant's symptoms.

In cases where no AR or DR has been agreed, it is expected that the notes and discharge summary of the treatment provider will contain the necessary information.

5.7 The provision as to the report being outside the litigation process is limited to the Triage Report and any notes or correspondence relating to it Any notes and reports created during the subsequent treatment process will be covered by the usual principle in relation to disclosure of documents and medical records relating to the claimant.

5.8 The compensator will normally pay for the TR within 28 days of receipt Where the claimant's solicitor and the compensator have agreed that such reports are required, the compensator will also pay for any AR and DR within 28 days of receipt. In either case, the compensator may challenge bills that they believe to be excessive or disproportionate.

5.9 The reporting agency should ensure that all invoices are within reasonable market rates, are clear and provide the following detail:

1. Type of treatment provided, eg. telephonic CBT, face-to-face physiotherapy;
2. Dates of treatments/sessions attended and DNAs of treatment sessions;
3. Total number of treatments delivered and whether those treatments were provided remotely or in person;
4. Total cost and whether this is for treatment provided or an estimate of future cost.

5.10 Where any treatment has been organised prior to notification to or approval by the compensator, any invoice submitted to the compensator will also need to be accompanied by a discharge summary recording treatment outcome in addition to the information contained in paragraph 5.9 The need for the discharge summary to be included in the treatment records is covered in paragraph 44.

5.11 The parties should continue to work together to ensure that the recommended rehabilitation proceeds smoothly and that any further rehabilitation needs continue to be assessed.

6. RECOMMENDATIONS—LOWER-VALUE INJURIES

6.1 The compensator will be under a duty to consider the recommendations made and the extent to which funds will be made available to implement the recommendations. The claimant will be under no obligation to undergo intervention, medical or investigation treatment Where intervention treatment has taken place, the compensator will not be required to pay for treatment that is unreasonable in nature, content or cost.

6.2 The compensator should provide a response to the claimant's solicitor within 15 business days from the date when the TR is disclosed. If the Insurer's Response Form is transmitted via the portal earlier than 15 business days from receipt of the CNF and the TR, the response should be included in the Response Form The response should include: (i) the extent to which the recommendations have been accepted and rehabilitation treatment will be funded; (ii) justifications for any refusal to meet the cost of recommended rehabilitation and (if appropriate) alternative recommendations. As stated in paragraph 4.3, the claimant may start treatment without waiting for the compensator's response, but at their own risk as to recovering the cost.

6.3 The compensator agrees that, in any legal proceedings connected with the claim, they will not dispute the reasonableness or costs of the treatment they have funded, provided the claimant has undertaken the treatment and it has been expressly agreed and/or the treatment provider has been jointly instructed. If the claim later fails, is discontinued or contributory negligence is an issue, it is not within the Code to seek to recover such funding from the claimant unless it can be proven that there has been fraud/fundamental dishonesty.

6.4 Following on from implementation of the assessment process, the parties should consider and agree at the earliest opportunity a process for ensuring that the ongoing rehabilitation needs of the claimant are met in a collaborative manner.

MEDIUM, SEVERE AND CATASTROPHIC INJURIES

7. THE ASSESSMENT PROCESS—MEDIUM, SEVERE AND CATASTROPHIC INJURIES

7.1 The need for and type of rehabilitation assistance will be considered by means of an Immediate Needs Assessment (INA) carried out by a Case Manager or appropriate rehabilitation professional, eg. an NHS Rehabilitation Consultant. (For further information about Case Managers, refer to the Glossary and The Guide for Case Managers and those who Commission them, published separately).

7.2 The Case Manager must be professionally and suitably qualified, experienced and skilled to carry out the task, and they must comply with appropriate clinical governance. With the most severe life-changing injuries, a Case Manager should normally be registered with a professional body appropriate to the severity of the claimant's injuries. The individual or organisation should not, save in exceptional circumstances, have provided a medico-legal report to the claimant nor be associated with any person or organisation that has done so.

7.3 The claimant solicitor and the compensator should have discussions at the outset to agree the person or organisation to conduct the INA, as well as topics to include in the letter of instruction. The INA should go ahead whether or not the claimant is still being treated by NHS physicians, who should nonetheless be consulted about their recommendations for short-term and longer-term rehabilitation. A fundamental part of the Case Manager's role is to make immediate contact with the treating clinical lead to assess whether any proposed rehabilitation plan is appropriate.

7.4. The parties are encouraged to try to agree the selection of an appropriately qualified independent Case Manager best suited to the claimant's needs to undertake the INA The parties should then endeavour to agree the method of instruction and how the referral will be made. When considering options with the claimant, a joint referral to the chosen Case Manager may maximise the benefits of collaborative working Any option chosen by the parties is subject to the claimant's agreement In all situations, the parties should seek to agree early implementation of reasonable recommendations and secure funding. In circumstances where trust has been built, it is recommended that the parties agree to retain the Case Manager to co-ordinate the implementation of the agreed rehabilitation plan.

7.5 With catastrophic injuries, it is especially important to achieve good early communication between the parties and an agreement to share information that could aid recovery This will normally involve telephone or face-to-face meetings to discuss what is already known, and to plan how to gain further information on the claimant's health, vocational and social requirements The fact that the claimant may be an NHS in-patient should not be a barrier to carrying out an INA.

7.6 No solicitor or compensator may insist on the INA being carried out by a particular person or organisation if the other party raises a reasonable objection within 21 days of the nomination. Where alternative providers are offered, the claimant and/or their family should be personally informed of the options and the associated benefits and costs of each option.

7.7 Objections to a particular person or organisation should include possible remedies such as additional information requirements or alternative solutions. If the discussion is not resolved within 21 days, responsibility for commissioning the provider lies ultimately with the claimant as long as they can demonstrate that full and timely co-operation has been provided.

7.8 A rehabilitation provider's overriding duty is to the claimant Their relationship with the claimant is therapeutic, and they should act totally independently of the instructing party.

7.9 The assessment may be carried out by a person or organisation having a direct or indirect business connection with the solicitor or compensator only if the other party agrees The solicitor and compensator must always reveal any business connection at the earliest opportunity.

7.10 The assessment process should provide information and analysis as to the rehabilitation assistance that would maximise recovery and mitigate the loss. Further assessments of rehabilitation needs may be required as the claimant recovers.

7.11 The compensator will usually only consider rehabilitation that deals with the effects of injuries for which they are liable. Treatment for other conditions will not normally be included unless it is agreed that they have been exacerbated by the accident or are impeding the claimant's recovery.

8. THE IMMEDIATE NEEDS ASSESSMENT (INA) REPORT—MEDIUM, SEVERE AND CATASTROPHIC INJURIES

8.1 The Case Manager will be asked to carry out the INA in a way appropriate to the case, taking into account the importance of acting promptly. This may include, by prior appointment, a telephone interview. In more complex and catastrophic cases, a face-to-face discussion with the claimant is likely.

8.2 As well as the ten 'markers' identified in the Glossary at the end of this Code, the INA should consider the following points, provided doing so does not unduly delay the process:

   a. The physical and psychological injuries sustained by the claimant and the subsequent care received or planned;
   b. The symptoms, disability/incapacity arising from those injuries. Where relevant to the overall picture of the claimant's rehabilitation needs, any other medical conditions not arising from the accident should also be separately noted;
   c. The availability or planned delivery of interventions or treatment via the NHS, their employer or health insurance schemes;
   d. Any impact upon the claimant's domestic and social circumstances, including mobility, accommodation and employment, and whether therapies such as gym training or swimming would be beneficial;
   e. The injuries/disability for which early intervention or early rehabilitation is suggested;

K6: The 2015 Rehabilitation Code

    f. The type of clinical intervention or treatment required in both the short and medium term, and its rationale;
    g. The likely cost and duration of recommended interventions or treatment, their goals and duration, with anticipated outcomes;
    h. The anticipated clinical and return-to-work outcome of such intervention or treatment.

8.3 The INA report will not provide a medical prognosis or diagnosis, but should include any clinically justifiable recommendations for further medical investigation, compliant with NICE guidelines and, where possible, aligned to the NHS Rehabilitation prescription, discharge report or similar. Where recommendations are in addition to or deviate from the NHS recommendations, these should be explained with appropriate justification provided.

8.4 The INA report should not deal with issues relating to legal liability, such as a detailed account of the accident circumstances, though it should enable the parties to understand the mechanism by which the injury occurred.

8.5 The Case Manager will, on completion of the report, send copies to the claimant solicitor and compensator simultaneously. Both parties will have the right to raise questions on the report, disclosing such correspondence to the other party. It is, however, anticipated that the parties will discuss the recommendations and agree the appropriate action to be taken. Subject to the claimant's consent, their GP and/or treating clinical team will also be informed of the INA and its recommendations once funding to proceed has been obtained. In most cases, the INA will be conducted, and the report provided, within 21 days from the date of the letter of referral to the Case Manager.

8.6 For this assessment report to be of benefit to the parties, it should be prepared and used wholly outside the litigation process, unless both parties agree otherwise in writing.

8.7 The report, any correspondence related to it and any notes created by the assessing agency will be deemed to be covered by legal privilege and not disclosed in any proceedings unless the parties agree. The same applies to notes or documents related to the INA, either during or after the report submission. Anyone involved in preparing the report or in the assessment process will not be a compellable witness at court. (This principle is also set out in the Protocols.)

8.8 Any notes and reports created during the subsequent case management process post-INA will be covered by the usual principle in relation to disclosure of documents and medical records relating to the claimant. However, it is open to the parties to agree to extend the provisions of the Code beyond the INA to subsequent reports.

8.9 The compensator will pay for the INA report within 28 days of receipt.

9. **RECOMMENDATIONS—MEDIUM, SEVERE AND CATASTROPHIC INJURIES**

9.1 When the Immediate Needs Assessment (INA) report is received, the compensator has a duty to consider the recommendations and the extent to which funds are made available to implement them. The compensator is not required to pay for treatment that is unreasonable in nature, content or cost. The claimant will be under no obligation to undergo treatment.

9.2 The compensator should respond to the claimant solicitor within 21 days of receiving the INA report. The response should include: (i) the extent to which it accepts the recommendations and is willing to fund treatment; and (ii) justifications for any refusal, with alternative recommendations.

9.3 The compensator will not dispute the reasonableness or costs of the treatment, as long as the claimant has undertaken the treatment and it was expressly agreed in advance (or the treatment provider had been jointly instructed). Where there is disagreement, general interim payments are recommended to provide continuity of services with an understanding that recovery of such sums is not guaranteed and will always be a matter for negotiation or determination by a court. Where a claimant has decided not to take up a form of treatment that is readily available in favour of a more expensive option, the reasonableness of that decision may be a factor that is taken into account on the assessment of damages. If the claim later fails or is discontinued or contributory negligence is an issue, the compensator will not seek to recover any agreed rehabilitation funding it has already provided unless it can be proven that there has been fraud/fundamental dishonesty.

9.4 Following implementation of the INA, the parties should consider and attempt to agree, as soon as possible, a collaborative process for meeting the claimant's ongoing rehabilitation needs.

9.5 The overriding purpose of the INA should be to assess the claimant's medical and social needs with a view to recommending treatment rather than to obtain information to settle the claim.

GLOSSARY—THE TEN 'MARKERS'

The ten 'markers' referred to in this Code that should be taken into account when assessing an injured person's rehabilitation needs are summarised below:

1. Age (particularly children/elderly);
2. Pre-existing physical and psycho-social comorbidities;
3. Return-to-work/education issues;
4. Dependants living at home;
5. Geographic location;
6. Mental capacity;
7. Activities of daily living in the short-term and long-term;
8. Realistic goals, aspirations, attainments;
9. Fatalities/those who witness major incidence of trauma within the same accident;
10. Length of time post-accident.

September 2015
The working parties that drew up the 2015 Rehabilitation Code included representatives of ABI, APIL, CMSUK, FOIL, IUA, MASS and PIBA. Although it is for the parties involved in personal injury claims to decide when and how to use the Code, it is envisaged that it should become operational from December 1, 2015.

A Summary Version of the Rehabilitation Code*

The 2015 Rehabilitation Code 96 Making a real difference to injured people

The Rehabilitation Code provides an approved framework for injury claims within which claimant representatives and compensators can work together. Whilst the Code is voluntary, the Personal Injury Pre- action Protocol provides that its use should be considered for all types of personal injury claims. The objective is to ensure that injured people receive the rehabilitation they need to restore quality of life and earning capacity as soon as possible and as much as possible. Although the principles are the same throughout, the Code recognises significant differences between the handling of lower value injuries (<£25k) and medium or catastrophic injuries.

* Although this document provides a summary, it should always be read in conjunction with the entire Code.

The important features of the Code are:

1. The claimant is put at the centre of the process.

2. The claimant's lawyer and the compensator work on a collaborative basis to address the claimant's needs, from first early notification of the claim and through early exchange of information.

3. The need for rehabilitation is addressed as a priority. Time-frames are set out in the Code.

4. Rehabilitation needs are assessed by independent professionals with appropriate qualifications, skills and experience.

5. Initial rehabilitation assessments can be conducted by telephone or personal interview, according to the type of case. The resulting report should deal with matters specified in the Code.

6. The parties may consider whether joint instruction of rehabilitation assessor and provider would aid collaborative working and be in the claimant's best interests.

7. The claimant has the ultimate say in choice of case manager, and is not obliged to undergo treatment or intervention that is considered unreasonable. A guide to appointing and working with case managers accompanies this Code, but is not part of it.

8. The case manager should seek proactively to co-operate with treating NHS clinicians.

9. The compensator will pay for any agreed assessment of rehabilitation needs, and must justify a refusal to follow any of the rehabilitation recommendations.

10. Initial assessment (including the Triage Report for lower value injuries) is outside the litigation process.

11. Where rehabilitation has been provided under the Code, the compensator will not seek to recoup its cost if the claim later fails unless fraud or fundamental dishonesty can be proven.

12. The Code recognises that lower value claims (typically < £25k) have different dynamics, and that there will sometimes be a medical need for claimant solicitors to arrange treatment before getting agreement from the compensator. In these circumstances, the compensator is not obliged to pay for treatment that is unnecessary, disproportionate or unduly expensive.

13. In the interests of streamlining the process, most lower value claims will require a Triage Report only.

14. It is the intention that the parties adopt the principles of the Code beyond the Immediate Needs Assessment and throughout the rehabilitation process.

The working parties that drew up the 2015 Rehabilitation Code included representatives of ABI, IUA, APIL, FOIL, MASS, PIBA and CMS UK.

For enquiries, please email deborah.finch@iua.co.uk

Time Scales (calendar days unless indicated otherwise)

Claimant solicitor	• Duty of every claimant solicitor to consider the need for rehabilitation from the earliest practicable stage in consultation with the claimant/their family and, where appropriate, treating physicians. • Give the earliest possible notification to compensator of the claim and need for rehabilitation. • Where the need for rehabilitation is identified by the compensator, consider this immediately with the claimant and/or their family.
Compensator	• Shall equally consider and communicate at earliest practicable stage whether the claimant will benefit from rehabilitation. • Where the need for rehabilitation is notified by the claimant solicitor, the compensator will respond within 21 days.
Both parties	• Consider choice of assessor and object to any suggested assessor within 21 days of nomination.
Immediate Needs Assessor	• Assessment to occur within 21 days of referral letter (but see below for smaller injuries). • Provide report simultaneously to parties.
Compensator	• Pay for report within 28 days of receipt. • Respond substantively to recommendations to the claimant solicitor within 21 days of receipt of report.
Lower value injuries (<£25k)	• As above, save that in the interests of speeding up the process, there will sometimes be a medical need for the claimant and/or their solicitor arrange treatment before the compensator has had time to approve it. In these circumstances, the compensator is not obliged to pay for treatment that is unnecessary, disproportionate or unduly expensive. • The claimant solicitor should communicate any rehabilitation needs to the compensator as soon as practical using the Claims Notification Form in the MoJ Portal. • The Triage Report, which will normally form the basis of treatment, should be made available simultaneously to both parties. • The compensator will respond to the report within 15 working days and pay for it within 28 days of receipt.

K7: APIL/FOIL Serious Injury Guide

The Serious Injury Guide is published by APIL and FOIL
Last updated 6 July 2017

INTRODUCTION

This best practice Guide is designed to assist with the conduct of personal injury cases involving complex injuries, specifically cases with a potential value on a full liability basis of £250,000 and above and that are likely to involve a claim for an element of future continuing loss. The parties may well agree to operate the Guide in relation to lower value multi track cases. The Guide excludes clinical negligence and asbestos related disease cases.

The Guide is intended to help parties involved in these multi track claims resolve any/all issues whilst putting the claimant at the centre of the process. It puts in place a system that meets the reasonable needs of the injured claimant whilst ensuring the parties work together towards resolving the case by cooperating and narrowing the issues.

This Guide creates an environment that encourages positive collaborative behaviour from both sides, and will work in parallel with the Civil Procedure Rules.

Nothing within this document affects a solicitor's duty to act in the best interests of the client and upon their instructions.

It is recognised that there will be occasions when the defendant[1] insurer and or agent cannot commit a commercial client for whom they are handling agents to comply with the Guide. The claimant representative will be notified of this issue immediately.

It is recognised that there will be occasions where either the claimant or the defendant insurer /and or the claims handling agent are unable to comply with the Guide. Where this occurs it is expected that notification of this fact to the opposing party should be made immediately.

This Guide comprises the following:

- Objectives
- Guidance
- Collaboration
- Early notification
- First contact
- Rehabilitation
- Ongoing review and case planning
- Dispute resolution and escalation
- Costs

OBJECTIVES

The principal aims are as follows:

- to resolve liability as quickly as possible;

---

[1] Any reference to defendant or defendant insurer can be taken to be singular or pleural when more than one defendant or insurer is involved or potentially involved.

K7: APIL/FOIL Serious Injury Guide

- where beneficial to the claimant to provide early access to rehabilitation to maximise their recovery;
- to resolve claims in a cost appropriate and proportionate manner;
- to resolve claims within an appropriate agreed time frame;
- resolution through an environment of mutual trust, transparency and collaboration;

To achieve the above the parties agree to work collaboratively bringing tangible benefits to all parties.

The key objectives are:

i. Notification

Early notification of claims to defendants and their insurers when known, with a view to achieving resolution of the case as quickly as possible and where liability is admitted or established, providing compensation.

ii. Case planning

Collaboration and dialogue are a central objective to achieve efficient case progression through an agreed action plan, dealing with but not limited to liability resolution, rehabilitation, quantum evidence and overall settlement.

iii. Liability

In all cases handled under the Guide a commitment to resolve liability by agreement, with a view to this being finalised within a maximum period of six months from the date of first notification. Where this is not possible, to identify the barriers that are stopping liability being resolved and to agree an action plan to conclude the issue at the earliest opportunity. The plan can include trial or alternative dispute resolution as appropriate.

For cases handled in accordance with this Guide the withdrawal of an admission would only be in exceptional circumstances and an admission made by any party may well be binding on that party in the litigation. The rules concerning admissions at CPR 14.1A continue to apply.

iv. Considerations on resolution of liability

A commitment to an early interim payment of disbursements (the subject matter of which has been disclosed) in addition to base costs related to liability once resolved. If the parties are unable to agree the amount of contribution an action plan will be developed to conclude the issue at the earliest opportunity.

The objectives and processes set within the Guide do not prevent the parties agreeing to additional items such as payment of interest on general damages, stay of proceedings or on any other issue in the course of the claim, all such discussions being in the spirit of the Guide.

v. Rehabilitation

Discussion at the earliest opportunity by all parties to consider effective rehabilitation where reasonably required.

Appointment, where necessary, of an independent clinical case manager instructed by the claimant, or subject to the claimant's agreement, on a joint basis.

K7: APIL/FOIL Serious Injury Guide

vi. Interim damages

A willingness to make early and continuing interim payments where appropriate.

vii. Part 36/Calderbank offers

No Part 36/Calderbank offers unless or until the parties have tried to agree an issue through dialogue and negotiation but cannot do so.

viii. Documents

Commitment by all parties to obtain and disclose promptly all relevant documents, such as

   a. liability documents
   b. police reports in road accident cases (police guidance on disclosure of information to third parties in relation to civil claims can be found at *www.seriousinjuryguide.co.uk* and at National Police Library Online).
   c. accident report documentation
   d. medical notes and records
   e. documents relating to past loss
   f. case manager records
   g. other relevant non-privileged material

Where possible, all parties are to obtain evidence in such a way as to avoid duplication of effort and cost.

GUIDANCE: ACHIEVING THE OBJECTIVES

1. COLLABORATION AND CASE PLANNING

1.1. The aims and objectives of this Guide will be achieved through the parties working together, allocating tasks where appropriate, narrowing the issues throughout the claim, leading to resolution at the earliest time.

1.2. Collaboration begins with a commitment to early notification of a claim to the potential defendant.

Collaborative working between the parties should continue throughout the life of the claim with the objective of achieving:

- early liability resolution
- maximising rehabilitation opportunities
- making provision for early interim payments
- emphasising restitution and redress, (rather than just compensation)
- early identification of issues not in dispute
- flexible approaches to resolution of issues in dispute

1.3. The parties should aim to agree a framework/timetable for engaging on a regular basis in order to bring the case to conclusion.

2. EARLY NOTIFICATION

2.1. The claimant's solicitor should ensure that the defendant and their insurers / handling agents are given early notification of the claim. The recommended contents of the early notification letter are set out below. The early notification point for each insurer can be found at *www.seriousinjuryguide.co.uk*.

2.2. A full formal detailed letter of claim is not expected (in the first instance). The aim is to alert the proposed defendant and insurer / handling agent to the potential claim, applicability of this Guide and to enable:

- an initial view for the purpose of understanding the nature of the claim and severity of injuries
- allocation of the case to an appropriate level of file handler within their organisation
- liability to be resolved promptly without further investigation by the proposed claimant.

2.3. The claimant's solicitors should aim to send a written notification within 7 calendar days of instruction. This should include where available but not be limited to:

- Name, address, date of birth and NI number of claimant (Such personal data should not be sent in one letter because of the risk of fraud.)
- Date, time and place of accident or date of onset of condition giving rise to the claim
- Factual outline of accident and injury if available
- Who is said to be responsible and relationship to claimant
- Any other party approached
- Occupation and approximate income
- Name and address of employer if there is one
- Current medical status in summary form (e.g. inpatient or discharged)
- Any immediate medical or rehabilitation needs if known
- The identity of the firms' escalation point of contact (see escalation section) and email address
- Protected party status on a without prejudice basis
- A reference to the claim being conducted within the Guide.

2.4. In the notification letter, the name of file hander with conduct at the claimant's solicitor's firm and immediate line manager/supervisor should be identified. Relevant e-mail addresses and telephone numbers should also be included.

2.5. The solicitors representing the claimant should take all reasonable steps to locate and notify the appropriate insurer / handling agent. Where known the letter should be sent to an established address to enable the file to be allocated at the correct handling level within the insurance company / handling agents.

2.6. If an insurer or handling agent is unknown, a short notification letter should be sent to the proposed defendant with a request to pass it on to any relevant insurer. In RTA cases, the MIB should be approached in the absence of an alternative insurer.

2.7. In the event that more than one potential defendant is identified details should be communicated to all other defendants (see section 4 below).

2.8. The reasonable costs of the solicitor in complying with this section will not be challenged for the lack of a retainer at this point in time.

3. FIRST CONTACT

3.1. At the earliest opportunity but no later than:

3.1.1. 14 calendar days of receipt of the notification letter, the defendant insurer / handling agent must acknowledge the correspondence in writing and confirm it is with the correct handler, confirming the name of the file handler, escalation contact point, as well as e-mail addresses and telephone numbers of the same.

3.1.2. 28 calendar days of receipt of the notification letter, the defendant insurer shall make contact with the claimant solicitor. The purpose of this first contact is to establish lines of communication between the parties, to include but not limited to:

- the parties' views on liability
- update on injuries
- any rehabilitation needs identified
- other potential defendants
- agreement as to when to hold further discussions.

4. CLAIMS INVOLVING MULTIPLE DEFENDANTS

4.1. The claimant solicitor must be kept informed in the event that additional defendants are identified.

4.2. In the event that there is more than one potential defendant it is expected that one defendant will coordinate correspondence with the claimant representatives. The identity of the coordinating party in such cases ought to be communicated within 28 calendar days of the last letter of claim where more than one is sent.

4.3. Where a coordinating contact point is offered the claimant representative shall restrict communication to that party, save that in the event that they consider there is a failure to make satisfactory progress in accordance with this Guide, all other known defendants should be alerted to the concern(s) raised. It is expected that this step will not be taken unless the escalation procedure has been tried first.

4.4. The defendants should confer within a maximum of 28 days in order to agree a response or to appoint a replacement coordinating defendant.

4.5. It may be that a coordinating defendant cannot be agreed between the defendants. In such cases the claimant must be notified of the fact immediately. However there is a continuing expectation that the defendants will, as soon as possible, agree a coordinating defendant.

5. ONGOING REVIEW AND FORWARD PLANNING

5.1 Regular on-going dialogue should take place between the parties with a view to agreeing the next steps required to progress the case. Material changes in circumstances should be communicated immediately (e.g. death of the claimant, loss of capacity, significant medical deterioration, material change in care regime costs, risk of loss of employment etc).

5.2 The claimant solicitor should give reasonable access for medical facilities when requested by the defence insurer. The parties should liaise on the issue of selection of any expert and the status thereof as part of the planning process.

K7: APIL/FOIL Serious Injury Guide

6. REHABILITATION

6.1. One of the overriding aims of the Guide is to help claimants to access rehabilitation when appropriate. At the earliest practical stage the parties should, in consultations with the claimant and/or the claimant's family, consider whether early intervention, rehabilitation or medical treatment would improve the present or long term situation. Defendants should reply promptly to any request to rehabilitation, and in any event within 21 days.

6.2. Further guidance can be found in the following material:

6.2.1. APIL's **Think Rehab! Best Practice Guide** on rehabilitation and the parties *http://www.apil.org.uk/files/pdf/rehabiliation-guide-to-best-practice.pdf*

6.2.2. The **Guide to Best Practice at the Interface Between Rehabilitation and the Medico-legal Process** endorsed by BSRM, APIL and the Royal College of Physicians published November 2006, *http://www.bsrm.co.uk/publications/Guide2BestPracticeIntRehabMedLegal.pdf*

6.2.3. The Rehabilitation Code 2015 (official implementation 1 December 2015) *http://iual.informz.ca/IUAL/data/images/2015%20Circular%20Attachments/067%20REHAB%20CODE.pdf*

6.2.4. The Guide to Case Managers 2015 (official implementation 1 December 2015) *http://iual.informz.ca/IUAL/data/images/2015%20Circular%20Attachments/067%20CM%20GUIDE%20MASTE R2.pdf*

6.3. The parties are encouraged to try to agree the selection of an appropriately qualified case manager best suited to the claimant's needs.

6.4. The insurer and/or appointed solicitor will be kept up to date with rehabilitation progress as part of the case planning process, by whatever means is agreed between the parties or generally.

6.5. Rehabilitation reports and case management material should be provided to the insurer on a regular basis.

6.6. The parties should seek to agree the frequency with which records and documents should be disclosed.

6.7. The parties should seek to agree the frequency of meetings or conference calls with the case manager (if such meetings or calls are appropriate).

7. ESCALATION PROCEDURE

7.1. In the event that either party feels that the opposing handler is not acting in accordance with the spirit of the Guide the first step must always be to exhaust attempts to resolve the point of concern by dialogue or a meeting.

7.2. If such dialogue still fails to allay the concerns, contact should be made with the nominated contact point at the firm/insurer/handling agent (see notification stage above) in order to try to deal with the issue.

7.3. In circumstances where a defendant solicitor has been instructed, the signatory insurer escalation point will remain the nominated contact point for the purposes of the Serious Injury Guide. The claimant solicitor should contact the signatory insurer escalation point directly with any escalation procedure issues, and in doing so, there will be no issue raised in relation to the Code of Conduct. The defendant solicitor should be notified of the intention to escalate, and should be copied into the correspondence sent to the insurer escalation contact point.

7.4. All parties are expected to adhere to the objectives set out above.

8. DISPUTE RESOLUTION

8.1. Ongoing dialogue is fundamental to the process. The parties will continue to discuss the case on a regular basis and at the times agreed. There may be occasions when issues arise that cannot be resolved through discussion.

8.2. On those occasions the parties should consider and agree if possible how they will approach such disputes. Such an approach should be adopted when any dispute emerges in the case, whether it relates to a discrete issue or resolution of the dispute generally.

8.3. All methods of dispute resolution should be considered. Including:

- Stocktake/cooling off period before the parties re-engage
- Early Neutral Evaluation
- Joint Settlement Meeting
- Mediation
- Arbitration

8.4. Considering other methods of dispute resolution does not prevent the parties from starting legal proceedings including Detailed Assessment if needed.

9. COSTS

9.1. Where the stage has been reached in the case where it looks like there stands a good prospect of resolution, the parties should also consider how to resolve costs promptly. For example, if there is a Joint Settlement Meeting, then the Defendants are entitled to expect the Claimant to provide cost details to be served 7 days prior to the JSM; the parties should agree the manner in which the cost details will be given (by way of a schedule, some other form or draft Bill of costs). The parties should agree whether cost lawyers need to be available at the meeting in order to facilitate resolution of costs. If it is not possible to resolve costs at the meeting, the parties should agree a 28 day period following the meeting to enable without prejudice discussions with a view to finalising the costs issues.

9.2. Where the case is resolved by acceptance of written offer, the parties should be prepared to engage immediately in discussion concerning costs. Agreement should focus on the information that is to be provided by the receiving party to the paying party, and a without prejudice timescale established, normally 28 days after acceptance of offer, to try and resolve costs once and for all prior to commencing the costs procedure.

9.3. Following resolution of liability, the Guide recognises an early commitment to pay an interim payment towards disbursements and a contribution towards base costs. See objective (iv) above.

Signatories:

The following general insurers and claimant firms and professional organisations have agreed to follow this Guide. See www.seriousinjuryguide.co.uk for a full and up-to-date list. All named firms

K7: APIL/FOIL Serious Injury Guide

commit that all handlers within their organisations will follow the Guide in all respects including the escalation process.

Acromas
Admiral
Allianz
Aviva
AXA
   Swiftcover
Direct Line Group
   Churchill
Esure
Hastings (on behalf of Advantage Insurance Company Ltd)
LV/Highway
Motor Insurers' Bureau
NFU Mutual
QBE
RSA
Access Legal Solicitors (Shoosmiths)
Admiral Law
ASB Aspire
Ashton Legal
Aspire Law
Atherton Godfrey
Barlow Robbins Solicitors
Barr Ellison Solicitors
Barratts Solicitors
Beardsells Personal Injury
Beecham Peacock Solicitors
Birchall Blackburn Law
Blakeley Solicitors
Blaser Mills
Bolt Burdon Kemp
Boyes Turner
Boys and Maughan Solicitors
Brethertons LLP Solicitors
Carpenters
Cartridges Law
CFG Law
Clarke Willmott
Clear Law
Coles Miller LLP Solicitors
Coole and Haddock
QualitySolicitors Dunn and Baker
Field Fisher
Fletchers Solicitors
Foot Anstey

Ford Simey LLP
Freeths
George Ide LLP Solicitors
Goughs Solicitors
Gotelee Solicitors
Healys
Higgs and Sons Solicitors
Hodge Jones and Allen
Hudgell Solicitors
Hugh James
Holmes & Hills
Irwin Mitchell Solicitors
JNP Legal
Leigh Day
Liddy's Solicitors
Mason Baggott and Garton
Minster Law Solicitors
Moore Blatch
Morrish LLP Solicitors
Nash and Co Solicitors
Novum Law
Osbornes Law
Pattinson Brewer Solicitors
Patrick Blackmore
Peace Legal
Penningtons Manches
Pierre Thomas and Partners
Potter Rees Dolan
Pudsey Legal
Serious Law
Sills and Betteridge Solicitors
Simpkins and Co Solicitors
Simpson Millar LLP Solicitors
Slater & Gordon Lawyers
Slater Heelis LLP Solicitors
Smith Jones
Stewarts Law
Thomas Dunton Solicitors
Thompsons Solicitors
Trethowans Solicitors
Trowers & Hamlins
Whitestone Solicitors
Watsons Solicitors
Wolferstans Solicitors

Group L
Motoring and Allied Material

L1: **Motoring costs**

L2: **Taxation of car and fuel benefits**

L3: **The Motability Scheme**

L4: **The costs of buying and replacing cars**

L5: **Time, speed and distance**

L1: Motoring costs

Illustrative vehicle running costs

RAC Motoring Services, in conjunction with Emmerson Hill Associates (Vehicle Management Consultants), have compiled the following illustrative vehicle running costs. The figures represent a guide to the cost of running, from new, a privately-owned petrol or diesel car for a period of three years with an annual mileage of **10,000 miles**.

Petrol cars

Engine size (cc)	1000	1200	1400	up to 1800	2000	2500	3000	over 3000
Assumed fuel consumption	58	50	46	40	36	31	27	25
CO_2 emissions level g/km	Under 120	121-150	151-165	166-185	186-225	226-255	226-255	255 plus
New cost incl. first year VED	8450	9650	10950	14750	16950	21750	24950	29750
Average value at 3 years	3450	3950	4250	4950	5750	6500	7250	9500
Projected depreciation	5000	5700	6700	9800	11200	15250	17700	20250
Finance charge @4.8% APR	625	714	810	1092	1254	1610	1846	2202
Servicing and maintenance	550	575	600	700	880	1070	1200	1375
Tyres and replacement parts	340	370	415	500	600	760	790	835
Insurance premiums 3 years	1005	1185	1230	1500	1860	2775	3150	3600
Excise licences next 2 years	280	280	280	280	280	280	280	280
RAC membership 3 years	495	495	495	495	495	495	495	495
Total cost over 3 year period excl. petrol	8295	9319	10530	14367	16569	22240	25461	29037
Annual cost	2765	3106	3510	4789	5523	7413	8487	9679
Cost per mile in pence excl petrol	27.65	31.06	35.10	47.89	55.23	74.13	84.87	96.79
Fuel cost pence per mile @ 1.10/litre	8.59	9.97	10.83	12.46	13.84	16.07	18.46	19.93
Standing cost per mile	24.68	27.91	31.72	43.89	50.30	68.03	78.24	89.42
Running cost per mile	11.56	13.12	14.22	16.46	18.78	22.17	25.09	27.30
Adjustment for change in fuel price of 1p +/−	0.08	0.09	0.10	0.11	0.13	0.15	0.17	0.18

Diesel cars

Engine size (cc)	Up to 1400	Up to 1400	1401-2000	2001-2200	2001-2200	2201-2500	2501-3000	over 3000
Assumed fuel consumption	60	58	53	42	40	39	36	34
CO_2 emissions level g/km	Under 120	121-150	151-165	166-185	186-225	226-255	255 plus	255 plus
New cost incl. first year VED	9750	9950	13750	20450	22500	25950	31650	33000
Average value at 3 years	3950	4250	5750	7950	8250	9450	11250	12250
Projected depreciation	5800	5700	8000	12500	14250	16500	20400	20750
Finance charge @4.8% APR	722	736	1018	1513	1665	1920	2342	2442
Servicing and maintenance	520	520	760	1075	1075	1440	1520	1650
Tyres and replacement parts	350	350	475	595	595	625	650	750
Insurance premiums 3 years	1185	1185	1500	1860	1860	2850	3600	4200
Excise licences next 2 years	280	280	280	280	280	280	280	280
RAC membership 3 years	495	495	495	495	495	495	495	495
Total cost over 3 year period excl. diesel	9352	9266	12528	18318	20220	24110	29287	30567
Annual cost	3117	3089	4176	6106	6740	8037	9762	10189
Cost per mile in pence excl diesel	31.17	30.89	41.76	61.06	67.40	80.37	97.62	101.89
Fuel cost pence per mile @ 1.10/litre	8.31	8.59	9.40	11.86	12.46	12.78	13.84	14.66
Standing cost per mile	28.27	27.99	37.64	55.49	61.83	73.48	90.39	93.89
Running cost per mile	11.21	11.49	13.52	17.43	18.02	19.66	21.08	22.66
Adjustment for change in fuel price of 1p +/−	0.08	0.08	0.09	0.11	0.11	0.12	0.13	0.13

Sweet & Maxwell

L1: Motoring costs

Note to the RAC vehicle running figures above:

The standing and running costs per mile and the adjustment for changes in fuel price have been calculated by the editors from the RAC figures.

Standing costs include Vehicle Tax, insurance, finance charges, depreciation and RAC membership.

Running costs include fuel, tyres and replacement parts, service and maintenance.

Illustrative motorcycle running costs

RAC Motoring Services, in conjunction with Emmerson Hill Associates (Vehicle Management Consultants), have compiled the following illustrative motorcycle running costs. The figures represent a guide to the cost of running a privately-owned motorcycle for a period of three years with an annual mileage of **6,000 miles**.

Motorcycles

Engine size (cc)	100	125	250	up to 400	up to 600	up to 750	up to 1000	over 1000
Assumed fuel consumption	80	68	56	48	45	43	37	33
Average cost new	1,950	2,150	2,950	4,250	4,500	5,250	6,150	7,750
Average value at 3 years	950	1,250	1,850	2,150	2,650	3,100	3,500	4,450
Projected depreciation	1,000	900	1,100	2,100	1,850	2,150	2,650	3,300
Finance charge @4.8% APR	144	159	218	315	333	389	455	574
Fuel cost @ 1.10/litre	1,125	1,323	1,607	1,875	2,000	2,094	2,432	2,727
Insurance and repairs 3 years	715	910	1,075	1,155	1,460	1,475	1,710	1,790
Servicing and maintenance	250	295	525	550	600	725	795	825
Tyres and replacement parts	350	450	650	690	740	820	820	900
Excise licences 3 years	54	54	123	123	186	255	255	255
RAC membership	150	150	150	150	150	150	150	150
Protective clothing and helmet	425	425	525	525	525	525	525	525
Total cost over 3 year period	4,213	4,666	5,973	7,483	7,844	8,583	9,792	11,046
Annual cost	1,404	1,555	1,991	2,494	2,615	2,861	3,264	3,682
Cost per mile in pence	23.41	25.92	33.18	41.57	43.58	47.68	54.40	61.37
Standing cost per mile	13.82	14.43	17.73	24.27	25.02	27.47	31.92	36.63
Running cost per mile	9.58	11.49	15.46	17.31	18.56	20.22	22.48	24.73
Adjustment for change in fuel price of 1p +/−	0.06	0.07	0.08	0.09	0.10	0.11	0.12	0.14

Note to the RAC motorcycle figures above:

The standing and running costs per mile and the adjustment for changes in fuel price have been calculated by the editors from the RAC figures.

Standing costs include Vehicle Tax, insurance and repairs, finance charges, depreciation, protective clothing and RAC membership.

Running costs include fuel, tyres and replacement parts, service and maintenance.

Vehicle Tax

Vehicles registered before March 2001

If the engine capacity is 1,549 cc or less the duty is £155; if it is over 1,549 cc the duty is £255. (Vehicles registered more than 40 years before 1 January in the current year are entitled to exemption from Vehicle Tax.)

Vehicles registered between 1 March 2001 and 31 March 2017

The tax depends on the fuel type and the emissions of carbon dioxide in the legislated Type Approval tests. In the tables, averages for the price groups are used for the tax rate. There is a first year rate (for new car purchases only) and a standard rate for all subsequent years.

Bands	CO_2 Emission (g/km)	Petrol or Diesel Car Standard rate £
Band A	Up to 100	0
Band B	101–110	20
Band C	111–120	30
Band D	121–130	120
Band E	131–140	140
Band F	141–150	155
Band G	151–165	195
Band H	166–175	230
Band I	176–185	250
Band J	186–200	290
Band K*	201–225	315
Band L	226–255	540
Band M	Over 255	555

* Band K includes cars with a CO_2 figure over 225 g/km which were registered before 23 March 2006.

An alternative fuel car has a discount of £10 for all bands. A fully electric vehicle is exempt from tax.

The CO_2 emission of a particular vehicle can be found at a website provided by the Vehicle Certification Agency (VCA): *www.carfueldata.direct.gov.uk*. It is also on the V5 registration document.

Vehicles registered on or after 1 April 2017

Only vehicles with zero emissions will benefit from zero tax. An alternative fuel car has a discount of £10.

There is a premium of £310 in years 2–6 on all cars costing over £40,000, even if they have zero emissions; the premium depends on *list price*, not the actual purchase price.

L1: Motoring costs

CO₂ Emission Years 2–6—cars >£40k (g/km)	First year rate Petrol (new cars only) from 1.4.18 £	First year rate Diesel (new cars only) from 1.4.18 £	Standard rate Petrol/Diesel Year 2 onwards— cars not >£40k Year 7 onwards— cars >£40k £	Premium Petrol/Diesel rate Year 2–6— cars >£40k £
Zero	0	0	0	310
1–50	10	25	140	450
51–75	25	105	140	450
76–90	105	125	140	140
91–100	125	145	140	450
101–110	145	165	140	450
111–130	165	205	140	450
131–150	205	515	140	450
151–170	515	830	140	450
171–190	830	1,240	140	450
191–225	1,240	1,760	140	450
226–255	1,760	2,070	140	450
Over 255	2,070	2,070	140	450

L2: Taxation of car and fuel benefits

Car benefit 2009/10 to 2018/19

				CO₂ emissions (g/km)						Percentage of car's price taxed if car does not run solely on diesel	Percentage of car's price taxed if car does run solely on diesel	
											Up to and including 2017/18	From 2018/19
2009/10	2010/11	2011/12	2012/13	2013/14	2014/15	2015/16	2016/17	2017/18	2018/19	(%)	(%)	(%)
	1-75	1-75	1-75	1-75	1-75	0-50				5	8	9
							0-50			7	10	11
						51-75		0-50		9	12	13
0-120	76-120	76-120	76-99	76-94			51-75			10	13	14
			100-104	95-99	76-94		51-75			11	14	15
			105-109	100-104	95-99					12	15	16
			110-114	105-109	100-104	76-94		51-75	0-50	13	16	17
			115-119	110-114	105-109	95-99				14	17	18
121-139	121-134	121-129	120-124	115-119	110-114	100-104	76-94			15	18	19
140-144	135-139	130-134	125-129	120-124	115-119	105-109	95-99		51-75	16	19	20
145-149	140-144	135-139	130-134	125-129	120-124	110-114	100-104	76-94		17	20	21
150-154	145-149	140-144	135-139	130-134	125-129	115-119	105-109	95-99		18	21	22
155-159	150-154	145-149	140-144	135-139	130-134	120-124	110-114	100-104	76-94	19	22	23
160-164	155-159	150-154	145-149	140-144	135-139	125-129	115-119	105-109	95-99	20	23	24
165-169	160-164	155-159	150-154	145-149	140-144	130-134	120-124	110-114	100-104	21	24	25
170-174	165-169	160-164	155-159	150-154	145-149	135-139	125-129	115-119	105-109	22	25	26
175-179	170-174	165-169	160-164	155-159	150-154	140-144	130-134	120-124	110-114	23	26	27
180-184	175-179	170-174	165-169	160-164	155-159	145-149	135-139	125-129	115-119	24	27	28
185-189	180-184	175-179	170-174	165-169	160-164	150-154	140-144	130-134	120-124	25	28	29
190-194	185-189	180-184	175-179	170-174	165-169	155-159	145-149	135-139	125-129	26	29	30
195-199	190-194	185-189	180-184	175-179	170-174	160-164	150-154	140-144	130-134	27	30	31
200-204	195-199	190-194	185-189	180-184	175-179	165-169	155-159	145-149	135-139	28	31	32
205-209	200-204	195-199	190-194	185-189	180-184	170-174	160-164	150-154	140-144	29	32	33
210-214	205-209	200-204	195-199	190-194	185-189	175-179	165-169	155-159	145-149	30	33	34
215-119	210-214	205-209	200-204	195-199	190-194	180-184	170-174	160-164	150-154	31	34	35
220-224	215-119	210-214	205-209	200-204	195-199	185-189	175-179	165-169	155-159	32	35	36
225-229	220-224	215-119	210-214	205-209	200-204	190-194	180-184	170-174	160-164	33	36	37
230-234	225-229	220-224	215-119	210-214	205-209	195-199	185-189	175-179	165-169	34	37	37
235+	230+	225+	220+	215+	210+	200-204	190-194	180-184	170-174	35	37	37
						205-209	195-199	185-189	175-179	36	37	37
						210+	200+	190+	180+	37	37	37

Notes

1. From 6 April 2002, although the benefit of a company car is still to be calculated as a percentage of the price of the car (normally list price), the percentage is graduated according to carbon dioxide (CO_2) emissions and adjustments for business mileage and older cars no longer apply.
2. There are discounts for certain cleaner alternatively-propelled cars, which may reduce the minimum charge to that shown in the table.
3. The diesel supplement and the discounts for cleaner alternatives apply only to cars first registered on 1 January 1998 or later.
4. Cars without an approved CO_2 emissions figure are taxed according to engine size. This includes all cars registered before 1998 but only a tiny proportion of those registered 1998 and later.
5. Except where otherwise indicated, the exact CO_2 figure is rounded down to the nearest five grams per kilometre when using the above table.
6. From 6 April 2008 there was a new lower rate of 10 per cent (13 per cent for diesel) for cars with CO_2 emissions of 120 grams per kilometre or less.
7. From 6 April 2010 cars and vans with zero CO_2 emissions were exempt from company car tax for five tax years.
8. From 6 April 2010 an ultra low carbon cars band was introduced for five years.

L2: Taxation of car and fuel benefits

9. From 6 April 2018 the differential between petrol and diesel cars was increased to 4 per cent (previously a 3 per cent differential). However, a maximum taxable value of 37 per cent applies to both petrol and diesel cars.

Car fuel benefit — petrol and diesel — cash equivalent 2003/04 to 2018/19

Notes

1. From 6 April 2003, the car fuel benefit is, like the car benefit, linked directly to the CO_2 emissions of the company car.
2. There are the same diesel supplement and discounts for cleaner alternatively-propelled cars as there are in calculating the car benefit.
3. To calculate the car fuel benefit the percentage in the table used for calculating car benefit is multiplied against a set figure for the year:

2003/04 to 2007/08	£14,400
2008/09 to 2009/10	£16,900
2010/11	£18,000
2011/12	£18,800
2012/13	£20,200
2013/14	£21,100
2014/15	£21,700
2015/16	£22,100
2016/17	£22,200
2017/18	£22,600
2018/19	£23,400

    Thus, if the car benefit percentage for 2018/19 is 23 per cent, the fuel benefit would be £23,400 × 23% = £5,382.
4. For cars registered before 1 January 1998 and cars with no approved CO_2 emissions figure, the percentage to be applied is the same as that used to calculate the car benefit.

Authorised Mileage Allowance Payments — tax-free rates in pence per mile 2002/03 to 2018/19

	Annual mileage	Pence per mile
Cars and vans	Up to 10,000	45p*
	10,001 +	25p
Motorcycles		24p
Bicycles		20p
Business Passengers		5p

* For 2002/03 to 2010/11 (inclusive) this rate was 40 pence per mile

L3: The Motability Scheme

Disabled people who need a motor vehicle may obtain one by utilising most if not all of the Higher Rate component of the Disability Living Allowance, the Enhanced Rate Mobility Component of Personal Independence Payment, the War Pensioner's Mobility Supplement or the Armed Forces Independence Payment. However, to lease a car using DLA you must have at least 12 months of any award left. Motability is only available to those in receipt of any of these benefits who assign all or some of them to the scheme for the duration of the contract. Because of the very wide range of physical and mental disabilities of those in receipt of them the scheme does not require the person seeking to use it to be a driver: anyone in receipt of one of these allowances who is over three is entitled to use it. Under the Scheme there are three available options:

1. A new car can be obtained on a three-year lease hire contract.
2. A wheelchair accessible vehicle (WAV) can be obtained on a five-year lease hire contract or three-year for a secondhand one.
3. A powered wheelchair or scooter may be taken on a three-year contract hire.

A national network of some 4,500 dealers provides a wide range of suitably adapted new and used cars. In the case of any option, the scheme requires a capital sum and a monthly payment which is provided for by the assignment of the relevant state benefit to the scheme. As well as the adapted vehicle, all maintenance is provided to include the cost of tyres, as is insurance for two named drivers who are over 25, annual road fund disc and roadside recovery. Fuel, oil and other incidentals are the responsibility of the driver. There is a 60,000 mile limit on use over a three-year contract or 100,000 miles over a five-year contract. Any mileage over that limit attracts a penalty of 5p per mile. At the end of the contract period the car reverts to the scheme. Hire purchase is no longer available.

When costing, care must be taken to distinguish between the three elements of any claim:

(i) the capital cost of both purchase and adaptation which recur every three years;
(ii) the monthly running costs covered by the Motability Scheme; and
(iii) the running costs not covered by the scheme such as oil, petrol and car washes.

Not all cars are available and advice must be obtained as to whether what is available adequately meets the needs of the disabled person. When experts have recommended that a car be obtained under the scheme practitioners should ensure that they are clear which option is being recommended and ensure that they compare like for like.

The condition precedent for using the Motability Scheme is that the beneficiary is in receipt of a state benefit which falls within the Second Schedule of the Social Security (Recovery of Benefits) Act 1997. It is now clear, following *Eagle v Chambers (No.2)* [2004] EWCA Civ 1033, that s.17 of the Act precludes a court from insisting that the mobility component of the Disabled Living Allowance should be used by any recipient to mitigate her loss. Henceforth no defendant can insist that a claimant use the mobility allowance to participate in the Motability Scheme.

DLA, hitherto the gateway into Motability, is being replaced by the Personal Independence Payment (PIP). When this is fully implemented only those receiving the enhanced rate of the mobility component of PIP will be eligible to use the Motability Scheme. During the transitional period those with the higher rate of the mobility component of DLA continue to be eligible although the requirement of having a year remaining will prevent many from taking on a new lease. PIP is assessed in a less generous way than DLA and it is likely that as the shift occurs to PIP some will cease to be eligible for Motability.

Further reading and assistance in specific cases can be obtained at:
http://www.motabilitycarscheme.co.uk and Customer Services (0300) 456 4566.

L4: The costs of buying and replacing cars

There are a number of commonly encountered calculations involving the cost of cars. This section contains tables and examples of calculations dealing with the following and should be read along with the table of Motoring costs in section L1:

1. Cost of future replacements.

2. Cost of more frequent replacement.

3. Cost of automatic cars.

4. Cost of additional mileage.

5. Cost of professional servicing.

6. Cost of Assessment.

We have classified cars as follows:

Mini:	Most cars of 1.1 litre or under, such as Toyota Aygo 1.0, Vauxhall Corsa 1.0
Super mini:	Similar cars between 1.1 and 1.4, Ford Fiesta 1.25, Suzuki Swift 1.2
Small:	Cars of the smaller Ford Focus, VW Golf type, mostly 1.3–1.6 litre
Medium:	The Ford Mondeo, VW Passat type, mostly cars from 1.6–1.9 litre
Executive:	The larger Passat, Volvo S60 type, mostly 2.0–2.8 litre
Prestige:	The BMW 330d, Jaguar 3.0, mostly up to 3.5 litre
Luxury:	The Jaguar XJ, Audi A8 4.2, mostly over 3.5 litre and expensive
Estate etc:	Self-explanatory

Notes:

1. Depreciation: Different cars, even produced by the same manufacturer, depreciate at different rates. As a model of car may change after a few years even if the same name is retained, losses over a long period cannot be calculated for individual models but only by reference to the general position.

2. Automatics: The comparison of manual and automatic cars is similarly a generalisation. The calculation for depreciation assumes that the new price of the automatic is *higher* than for the manual model. There is considerable variation, even among cars of similar type with similar new prices, in the rate at which the premium for the automatic version is eroded. With some cars the gap disappears very quickly: with some the premium for the automatic version is actually greater for used cars than for new ones.

3. Where the current new price of the manual and automatic versions is the same, which is often the case with expensive cars, the used automatic tends to retain its value *better* than the manual model. It may nevertheless have higher fuel consumption but whether it will be more expensive overall may depend on the mileage.

L4: The costs of buying and replacing cars

1. Cost of future replacements

Table 1 below has representative trade-in values of used *manual* cars expressed as a proportion of the *current* new price (calculated from material in *Parker's Car Price Guide*). Automatic cars may depreciate faster. Where the new price of an automatic car is *higher* than that of the corresponding manual car, there is a tendency for the automatic to depreciate by about one per cent more (altogether, not per year).

Table 1 Trade-in values of used manual cars

Age of car	Residual value	Loss of value	Equivalent annual depreciation
1	0.64	0.36	0.360
2	0.50	0.50	0.256
3	0.41	0.59	0.204
4	0.36	0.64	0.168
5	0.33	0.67	0.143
Adjustment for automatics	−0.01	+0.01	

The table can be used to calculate the future net costs of replacements where the replacements will be second hand as well as where they will be new.

Example 1: The claimant is 54 and needs a people carrier such as a Chrysler Grand Voyager 3.3 LE Auto 5d, automatic version. He will need to replace it every four years, the final replacement being when he is 70. He would not otherwise have had a car (or the car is additional to whatever vehicle would have been bought in any event).

Initial price of people carrier, say		£32,995.00
Proportion of price lost at each replacement		
(Table 1 above, + 0.01)	0.65	
Cost of each replacement	0.65 × 32,995 = 21,446.75	
Multiplier for 16 years (table A5, -0.75%, four-yearly)	4.32	
Cost of future replacements	4.32 × 21,446.75 =	£92,649.96
Total		£125,644.96

Example 2: The same claimant currently runs a manual Volvo S80 2.4 SE and will replace it with the Chrysler people carrier. The additional cost is the future cost of the Chryslers *minus* the corresponding figure saved on Volvos. (If either both cars are manual or both automatic the calculation is simpler.)

Initial price of Volvo saved, say		£28,245.00
Proportion of price saved at each replacement		
(Table 1 above, manual)	0.64	
Cost of each replacement	0.64 × 28,245.00 = 18,076.80	
Multiplier for 16 years (table A5, -0.75%, four-yearly)	4.32	
Cost of future replacements saved	4.32 × 18,076.80 =	£78,091.78
Total		£106,336.78
Net future cost of Chryslers instead of Volvos	=	£19,308.18
(125,644.96 − 106,336.78)		

L4: The costs of buying and replacing cars

2. Cost of more frequent replacement

Claimants are sometimes advised that because of their condition they need a more reliable car and should therefore replace it more often than they needed to do before the injury. Table 2, which is derived from Table 1, shows the additional annual cost, expressed as a proportion of the new price. Find the row corresponding to the new interval in years and the column corresponding to the old interval.

Note that the table expresses the multiplier as an *annual* cost, not the cost *on each exchange*. Thus in row 2, column 4, the figure 0.088 means that the additional expense of replacing a car every two years, instead of every four years, is 8.8 per cent of the price of the car per year for however long the claimant continues to drive.

Table 2 Multipliers for additional annual cost of replacing car more frequently

		Old interval in years			
New interval in years	1	2	3	4	5
1	0	0.104	0.156	0.192	0.217
2		0	0.052	0.088	0.113
3			0	0.036	0.061
4				0	0.025
5					0

Example: The claimant is 40 and drives a car currently costing £11,995 new. She has just bought one. She can continue to drive a similar car, with modifications. She has been advised that because of her disability she should now change it every three years rather than every five as she has until now. She should stop driving at about 73, so the last change will be at about age 70.

Multiplier for additional annual cost from table above		
– new frequency three years, old frequency five years	0.061	
Multiplier for woman of 40 until age 70 (Table A1)	32.56	
Multiplier for additional cost of more frequent replacement	0.061 × 32.56	= 1.99
Current cost of car		£11,995.00
Additional cost of replacing car more frequently until age 70		£23,870.05

3. Cost of automatic cars

Claimants' injuries sometimes make it necessary for them to have an automatic car which they would not otherwise have needed. Generally this involves additional costs in three respects: the automatic car is more expensive to buy, is more expensive to run and tends to depreciate faster than the corresponding manual model (but see the notes in the introduction).

L4: The costs of buying and replacing cars

Table 3 Added cost of automatic cars

		Mini and Super Mini	Small	Medium and Executive	Prestige and Luxury	Estate, 4×4 and MPV
Added cost of new car in £		850	1,075	1,145	1,275	1,245
Added cost of **Petrol** in pence per mile	At 129.0p per litre	3.42	1.73	1.42	0.41	–
	For every penny more/less, add/subtract	0.030	0.015	0.012	0.004	–

Greater depreciation

Where the new price of an automatic model of a car is *higher* than that of the corresponding manual car, there is a tendency for the automatic to depreciate by about one per cent more (altogether, not per year)—see Table 1 above. Thus:

New manual model	£11,000	three-year-old manual	11,000 × 0.41 = £4,510
New automatic	£12,000	three-year-old automatic	12,000 × 0.40 = £4,800

Example: The claimant is 48. He drives a manual car of medium type whose price new is about £16,000. He drives about 10,000 miles a year and changes his car every three years. Because of his injury he now needs an automatic at a cost of £17,145. He is likely to stop driving in about 30 years.

Extra cost of automatic car:
On first purchase (from Table 3, column 3 above): £1,145.00

Cost at each replacement of automatic (Table 1, row 3): 17,145 × 0.60 = 10,287.00
less cost at each replacement of manual   16,000 × 0.59 = 9,440.00
Additional cost at each replacement   £ 847.00
Crude multiplier for replacements (Table A5, 27 years, three-yearly) 10.09
Multiplier for 27 years certain (Table A5, cont's loss)   29.94
Multiplier for man of 48 until age 75 (Table A1)   27.56
Multiplier discounted for mortality   (10.09 × 27.56/29.94) =   9.29   = £7,868.63

Extra cost per mile, petrol at 135.7 p/litre (Table 3, column 3) =
    1.42 + (6.7 × 0.012) = 1.50 pence
Extra running cost 10,000 miles pa   £150.00
Crude multiplier (Table A5, 30 years, cont's loss)   33.66
Multiplier discounted for mortality (33.66 × 27.56/29.94) =   30.98   £4,647.00

Total extra cost: £13,660.63

Sweet & Maxwell

L4: The costs of buying and replacing cars

4. Cost of additional mileage

The RAC figures for *running* costs at Table L1 do not include depreciation. Mileage reduces the value of a car by a factor which varies with the type of car and its age on resale. Age on resale is not necessarily the length of time the claimant had the car. The categories A, B, C, etc. are derived from *Parker's Price Guide*.

The table may not be appropriate for mileages below 1,000 miles a year or above 30,000 miles a year.

Table 4 Adjustment for depreciation for extra mileage

Age on resale	A	B	C	D	E	F	G	H
1	3.00	4.00	5.00	6.00	7.00	8.50	10.50	13.50
2	2.50	3.50	4.50	5.50	6.50	7.50	9.00	11.00
3	2.00	3.00	3.50	4.50	5.00	6.00	7.50	10.00
4	1.20	2.00	2.50	3.50	4.00	5.00	6.00	8.00
5	1.00	1.50	2.00	2.50	3.00	4.00	5.00	7.00
6	0.70	1.20	1.50	2.00	2.50	3.00	4.00	6.00
7	0.50	0.90	1.00	1.50	2.00	2.50	3.50	5.00
8	0.40	0.60	0.90	1.00	1.50	2.00	2.50	4.00

Depreciation in pence per mile

Example: The claimant would have had a car anyway. His mileage is increased by 4,000 miles a year because of his injury. He buys a one-year-old car and changes it after four years, with a 1.3 litre engine, in category C in the mileage adjustment table. Petrol costs 116.7 pence per litre.

Running cost per mile from RAC figures (Table L1)	14.22 pence
Adjustment for petrol price (from Table L1) (6.7p × 0.10)	0.67
Adjustment for mileage (category C, Four years old)	2.50
Total per mile	17.39 pence
Total annual cost (4,000 × 17.39)	£ 695.60

5. Cost of professional servicing

Some claimants will have carried out the routine servicing of their cars themselves, but their injury may make that impracticable and they will in future need to have the car serviced professionally.

The resulting increased cost consists essentially in the labour element in the cost of servicing. Costs such as the cost of the Ministry of Transport test itself will remain the same and will not form an element of the loss. There will be *some* increase in the cost of materials such as replacement parts and oil, as these may be less expensive online or at a supermarket rather than at a garage. On the other hand, particularly with newer models, the more complex servicing tasks may not be feasible without specialised equipment, and so even mechanically minded car owners may be unable to do these jobs themselves. This section therefore takes the loss as equivalent to the cost of labour and treats these other factors as neutral overall.

Labour costs vary between main dealers and independent garages, and between different parts of the country. They are generally cheaper in the north and away from London, but do not conform to any clear pattern. In a 2011 survey Gwynedd was one of the most expensive areas, but Clwyd, not far away, was one of the cheapest. Also, as will be seen from the figures in Table L1: Motoring Costs, the most powerful cars involve higher labour costs but the least powerful are not particular cheaper to service than those with slightly larger engines. For those reasons it is not straightforward to try to produce figures independently on the basis of time estimates and hourly labour charges, and the editors recommend using the following figures derived from Table L1.

Table 5 Additional cost of professional servicing

Additional cost in pence per mile

Engine size (cc)	1000	1200	1400	1800	2000	2500	3000	over 3000
Petrol cars	1.83	1.92	2.00	2.33	2.93	3.57	4.00	4.58
Engine size (cc)	up to 1400	up to 1400	1401-2000	2001-2200	2001-2200	2201-2500	2501-3000	over 3000
Diesel cars	1.73	1.73	2.53	3.58	3.58	4.80	5.07	5.50
Engine size (cc)	100	125	250	400	600	750	1000	over 1000
Motorcycles	1.39	1.64	2.92	3.06	3.33	4.03	4.42	4.58

Example: The same claimant as in section 5 used to do his own servicing and because of his injury is now unable to do so. His car has a 1.3 litre engine. Before the accident he drove 12,000 miles a year, but because of the accident he must now drive a further 4,000 miles, making 16,000 miles in all. He incurs the additional cost of professional servicing, as well as the additional cost of extra mileage.

Extra cost of professional servicing per mile	2.00 pence
Annual cost (for 12,000 miles) 12,000 × 2.00 pence	£240.00
Cost of additional 4,000 mileage (from section 4 example)	£695.60
Total annual cost	£935.60

Note that the figure for running costs used to calculate the cost of additional mileage already includes service labour costs. The extra cost of servicing must therefore be based on the pre-accident 12,000 miles: there will be double counting if it is calculated on the basis of the post-accident 16,000 miles.

6. Cost of assessment

At the QEF Mobility Centre in Carshalton, Surrey, the Queen Elizabeth Foundation for Disabled People conducts a variety of driving assessments, such as car adaptation assessments, for people with disabilities, and will provide a report. The centre also provides advice and training but does not provide costings or carry out adaptations itself.

The cost of an assessment for litigation purposes is £1,080 (including VAT).

There is a lower, subsidised, rate for individuals not requiring the report for litigation, but the Centre will then deal only with the client personally, and not with others such as solicitors or case managers.

Sections 1–4 are based on figures in *Parker's Car Price Guide* and from the websites of the Vehicle Certification Agency and the United States Department of Transportation.

L5: Time, speed and distance

Table of speeds and distances

Speeds				Distances in yards																
mph	km/h	yd/sec	m/sec	5	10	15	20	25	30	40	50	60	75	100	125	150	175	200	225	250	300	400	500
5	8.0	2.44	2.24	2.0	4.1	6.1	8.2	10.2	12.3	16.4	20.5	24.5	30.7	40.9	51.1	61.4	71.6	81.8	92.0	102.3	122.7	163.6	204.5
10	16.1	4.89	4.47	1.0	2.0	3.1	4.1	5.1	6.1	8.2	10.2	12.3	15.3	20.5	25.6	30.7	35.8	40.9	46.0	51.1	61.4	81.8	102.3
15	24.1	7.33	6.71	0.7	1.4	2.0	2.7	3.4	4.1	5.5	6.8	8.2	10.2	13.6	17.0	20.5	23.9	27.3	30.7	34.1	40.9	54.5	68.2
20	32.2	9.78	8.94	0.5	1.0	1.5	2.0	2.6	3.1	4.1	5.1	6.1	7.7	10.2	12.8	15.3	17.9	20.5	23.0	25.6	30.7	40.9	51.1
25	40.2	12.22	11.18	0.4	0.8	1.2	1.6	2.0	2.5	3.3	4.1	4.9	6.1	8.2	10.2	12.3	14.3	16.4	18.4	20.5	24.5	32.7	40.9
30	48.3	14.67	13.41	0.3	0.7	1.0	1.4	1.7	2.0	2.7	3.4	4.1	5.1	6.8	8.5	10.2	11.9	13.6	15.3	17.0	20.5	27.3	34.1
35	56.3	17.11	15.65	0.3	0.6	0.9	1.2	1.5	1.8	2.3	2.9	3.5	4.4	5.8	7.3	8.8	10.2	11.7	13.1	14.6	17.5	23.4	29.2
40	64.4	19.56	17.88	0.3	0.5	0.8	1.0	1.3	1.5	2.0	2.6	3.1	3.8	5.1	6.4	7.7	8.9	10.2	11.5	12.8	15.3	20.5	25.6
45	72.4	22.00	20.12	0.2	0.5	0.7	0.9	1.1	1.4	1.8	2.3	2.7	3.4	4.5	5.7	6.8	8.0	9.1	10.2	11.4	13.6	18.2	22.7
50	80.5	24.44	22.35	0.2	0.4	0.6	0.8	1.0	1.2	1.6	2.0	2.5	3.1	4.1	5.1	6.1	7.2	8.2	9.2	10.2	12.3	16.4	20.5
60	96.6	29.33	26.82	0.2	0.3	0.5	0.7	0.9	1.0	1.4	1.7	2.0	2.6	3.4	4.3	5.1	6.0	6.8	7.7	8.5	10.2	13.6	17.0
70	112.7	34.22	31.29	0.1	0.3	0.4	0.6	0.7	0.9	1.2	1.5	1.8	2.2	2.9	3.7	4.4	5.1	5.8	6.6	7.3	8.8	11.7	14.6
80	128.7	39.11	35.76	0.1	0.3	0.4	0.5	0.6	0.8	1.0	1.3	1.5	1.9	2.6	3.2	3.8	4.5	5.1	5.8	6.4	7.7	10.2	12.8
90	144.8	44.00	40.23	0.1	0.2	0.3	0.5	0.6	0.7	0.9	1.1	1.4	1.7	2.3	2.8	3.4	4.0	4.5	5.1	5.7	6.8	9.1	11.4
100	160.9	48.89	44.70	0.1	0.2	0.3	0.4	0.5	0.6	0.8	1.0	1.2	1.5	2.0	2.6	3.1	3.6	4.1	4.6	5.1	6.1	8.2	10.2

Seconds

Notes:

1. The table shows the time taken to cover a given distance at a given speed, to the nearest $\frac{1}{10}$ second.

2. The table can also be used to ascertain the approximate speed of a vehicle, if the time and distance are known.

3. As an example, to find how long it would take to cover 125 yards at 35 mph, follow the vertical column down from the figure 125 and follow the horizontal row across from the figure 35: they meet at the figure 7.3, which is the number of seconds taken to cover the distance.

4. A speed of z miles per hour approximately equals [0.5z] yards per second.

5. The general formula for the number of seconds to cover a given distance at a given speed is approximately:

$$\frac{\text{distance in yards} \times 2.04545}{\text{speed in miles per hour}}$$

Typical Stopping Distances (average car length = 4 metres)

Speed (mph)	Thinking Distance (metres)	Braking Distance (metres)	Total Stopping Distance (metres)	(car lengths)
20	6	6	12	3
30	9	14	23	6
40	12	24	36	9
50	15	38	53	13
60	18	55	73	18
70	21	75	96	24

Extracted from *The Highway Code*, published by The Stationery Office.

Group M
Other Information

M1: **Senior Court Costs Office Guideline Rates for Summary Assessment**

M2: **Conversion formulae**

M3: **Perpetual calendar**

M4: **Religious festivals**

M5: **Medical reference intervals and scales**

M1: Senior Court Costs Office Guideline Rates for Summary Assessment

Band One	A	B	C	D
2011–present	217	192	161	118
2010	217	192	161	118
2009	213	189	158	116
2008	203	180	151	110
2007	195	173	145	106

Aldershot, Farnham, Bournemouth (including Poole), Birmingham Inner, Bristol, Cambridge City, Harlow, Canterbury, Maidstone, Medway and Tunbridge Wells, Cardiff (Inner), Chelmsford South, Essex and East Suffolk, Chester, Fareham, Winchester, Hampshire, Dorset, Wiltshire, Isle of Wight, Kingston, Guildford, Reigate, Epsom, Leeds Inner (within two-kilometres radius of the City Art Gallery), Lewes, Liverpool, Birkenhead, Manchester Central, Newcastle—City Centre (within a two-mile radius of St Nicholas Cathedral), Norwich City, Nottingham City, Oxford, Thames Valley, Southampton, Portsmouth, Swindon, Basingstoke, Watford.

Band Two	A	B	C	D
2011–present	201	177	146	111
2010	201	177	146	111
2009	198	174	144	109
2008	191	168	139	105
2007	183	161	133	101

Bath, Cheltenham and Gloucester, Taunton, Yeovil, Bury, Chelmsford North, Cambridge County, Peterborough, Bury St E, Norfolk, Lowestoft, Cheshire and North Wales, Coventry, Rugby, Nuneaton, Stratford and Warwick, Exeter, Plymouth, Hull (City), Leeds Outer, Wakefield and Pontefract, Leigh, Lincoln, Luton, Bedford, St Albans, Hitchin, Hertford, Manchester Outer, Oldham, Bolton, Tameside, Newcastle (other than City Centre), Nottingham and Derbyshire, Sheffield, Doncaster and South Yorkshire, Southport, St Helens, Stockport, Altrincham, Salford, Swansea, Newport, Cardiff (Outer), Wigan, Wolverhampton, Walsall, Dudley and Stourbridge, York, Harrogate.

Band Three	A	B	C	D
2011–present	201	177	146	111
2010	201	177	146	111
2009	198	174	144	109
2008	174	156	133	99
2007	167	150	128	95

Birmingham Outer, Bradford (Dewsbury, Halifax, Huddersfield, Keighley and Skipton), Cumbria, Devon, Cornwall, Grimsby, Skegness, Hull Outer, Kidderminster, Northampton and Leicester, Preston, Lancaster, Blackpool, Chorley, Accrington, Burnley, Blackburn, Rawenstall and Nelson, Scarborough and Ripon, Stafford, Stoke, Tamworth, Teesside, Worcester, Hereford, Evesham and Redditch, Shrewsbury, Telford, Ludlow, Oswestry, South and West Wales.

London City [EC1–4]	A	B	C	D
2011–present	409	296	226	138
2010	409	296	226	138
2009	402	291	222	136
2008	396	285	219	134
2007	380	274	210	129

M1: Senior Court Costs Office Guideline Rates for Summary Assessment

London Central [W1, WC1, WC2, SW1]	A	B	C	D
2011–present	317	242	196	126
2010	317	242	196	126
2009	312	238	193	124
2008	304	231	189	121
2007	292	222	181	116
London Outer [N, E, SE, W, SW, NW, Bromley, Croydon, Dartford, Gravesend and Uxbridge]	A	B	C	D
2011–present	229–267	172–229	165	121
2010	229–267	172–229	165	121
2009	263–225	225–169	162	119
2008	256–219	219–165	158	116
2007	246–210	210–158	152	111

A – Solicitors and Fellows of CILEx with over eight years' post-qualification experience including at least eight years' litigation experience.
B – Solicitors, legal executives and costs lawyers with over four years' post-qualification experience including at least four years' litigation experience.
C – Other solicitors and legal executives, costs lawyers and fee earners of equivalent experience.
D – Trainee solicitors, paralegals and fee earners of equivalent experience.
Note: "Legal Executive" means a Fellow of the Institute of Legal Executives.

Entitlement to VAT on Costs

DATE	VAT RATE
1 April 1991–30 November 2008	17.5%
1 December 2008–31 December 2009	15%
1 January 2010–3 January 2011	17.5%
4 January 2011 to date	20%

Costs PD 44 para.2.3 deals with entitlement to VAT on Costs. It provides:

"VAT should not be included in a claim for costs if the receiving party is able to recover the VAT as input tax. Where the receiving party is able to obtain credit from HM Revenue and Customs for a proportion of the VAT as input tax, only that proportion which is not eligible for credit should be included in the claim for costs."

Costs PD 44 para.2.7 deals with the form of a Bill of Costs where the VAT Rate changes. It provides:

"Where there is a change in the rate of VAT, suppliers of goods and services are entitled by ss.88(1) and 88(2) of the VAT Act 1994 in most circumstances to elect whether the new or the old rate of VAT should apply to a supply where the basic and actual tax points span a period during which there has been a change in VAT rates."

Costs PD 44 para.2.8 provides:

"It will be assumed, unless a contrary indication is given in writing, that an election to take advantage of the provisions mentioned in paragraph 2.7 and to charge VAT at the lower rate has been made. In any case in which an election to charge at the lower rate is not made, such a decision must be justified to the court assessing the costs."

Costs PD 44 para.2.9 deals with apportionment. It provides:

"Subject to 2.7 & 2.8 all bills of costs, fees and disbursements on which VAT is included must be divided into separate parts so as to show work done before, on and after the date or dates from which any change in the rate of VAT takes effect. Where, however, a lump sum charge is made for work which spans a period during which there has been a change in VAT rates, and paragraphs 2.7 and 2.8 above do not apply, reference should be made to paragraphs 30.7 or 30.8 of the VAT Guide (Notice 700) (or any revised edition of that notice) published by HMRC. If necessary, the lump sum should be apportioned. The totals of profit costs and disbursements in each part must be carried separately to the summary."

M2: Conversion formulae

	To convert	Multiply by	To convert	Multiply by
Area	square inches to square centimetres	6.452	square centimetres to square inches	0.1555
	square feet to square metres	0.0929	square metres to square feet	10.7638
	square yards to square metres	0.8361	square metres to square yards	1.196
	square miles to square kilometres	2.590	square kilometres to square miles	0.3861
	acres to hectares	0.4047	hectares to acres	2.471
Length	inches to centimetres	2.540	centimetres to inches	0.3937
	feet to metres	0.3048	metres to feet	3.281
	yards to metres	0.9144	metres to yards	1.094
	miles to kilometres	1.6093	kilometres to miles	0.6214
Temperature	Fahrenheit to Celsius	$-32 \times 5 \div 9$	Celsius to Fahrenheit	$\times 9 \div 5 + 32$
Volume	cubic inches to cubic centimetres	16.39	cubic centimetres to cubic inches	0.06102
	cubic feet to cubic metres	0.02832	cubic metres to cubic feet	35.31
	cubic yards to cubic metres	0.7646	cubic metres to cubic yards	1.308
	cubic inches to litres	0.01639	litres to cubic inches	61.024
	gallons to litres	4.545	litres to gallons	0.22
Weight	grains to grams	0.0647	grams to grains	15.43
	ounces to grams	28.35	grams to ounces	0.03527
	pounds to grams	453.592	grams to pounds	0.0022
	pounds to kilograms	0.4536	kilograms to pounds	2.2046
	tons to kilograms	1016.05	kilograms to tons	0.0009842
Speed	miles per hour to kilometres per hour	1.6093	kilometres per hour to miles per hour	0.6214
Fuel cost	pence per litre to pounds per gallon	0.045	pounds per gallon to pence per litre	22.00
USA measures (dry)	USA pint to UK pint	0.9689	UK pint to USA pint	1.032
	USA pints to litres	0.5506	litres to USA pints	1.816
	USA bushel to UK bushel	0.9689	UK bushel to USA bushel	1.032
	USA bushels to litres	35.238	litres to USA bushels	0.0283

M2: Conversion formulae

	To convert	Multiply by	To convert	Multiply by
USA measures (liquid)	USA pint to UK pint	0.8327	UK pint to USA pint	1.2
	USA pints to litres	0.4732	litres to USA pint	2.113
	USA gallon to UK gallon	0.8327	UK gallon to USA gallon	1.2
	USA gallons to litres	3.7853	litres to USA gallons	0.2641

Clothing

Shirts

UK/USA	14	$14\frac{1}{2}$	15	$15\frac{1}{2}$	16	$16\frac{1}{2}$	17	$17\frac{1}{2}$
Europe	36	37	38	39	40	41	42	43

Ladies clothes

UK							
Size code	10	12	14	16	18	20	22
Bust/hip inches	32/34	34/36	36/38	38/40	40/42	42/44	44/46
Bust/hip cm	84/89	88/93	92/97	97/102	102/107	107/112	112/117

USA							
Size code	6	8	10	12	14	16	18
Bust/hip inches	$34\frac{1}{2}/36\frac{1}{2}$	$35\frac{1}{2}/37\frac{1}{2}$	$36\frac{1}{2}/38\frac{1}{2}$	$37\frac{1}{2}/39\frac{1}{2}$	38/40	$39\frac{1}{2}/41\frac{1}{2}$	41/43

European sizes vary from country to country

Footwear—Men

British	6	7	8	9	10	11	12
American	$6\frac{1}{2}$	$7\frac{1}{2}$	$8\frac{1}{2}$	$9\frac{1}{2}$	$10\frac{1}{2}$	$11\frac{1}{2}$	$12\frac{1}{2}$
Continental	40	41	42	43	44	45	46

Footwear—Women

British	3	4	5	6	7	8	9
American	$4\frac{1}{2}$	$5\frac{1}{2}$	$6\frac{1}{2}$	$7\frac{1}{2}$	$8\frac{1}{2}$	$9\frac{1}{2}$	$10\frac{1}{2}$
Continental	36	37	38	39	40	42	43

Children's clothes

UK												
Age	1	2	3	4	5	6	7	8	9	10	11	12
Height/inches	32	36	38	40	43	45	48	50	53	55	58	60
Height/cm	80	92	98	104	110	116	122	128	134	140	146	152

USA												
Boys' size code	1	2	3	4	5	6	8		10		12	
Girls' size code	2	3	4	5	6	6x	7	8	10		12	

Europe												
Height/cm	80	92	98	104	110	116	122	128	134	140	146	152

M3: Perpetual calendar

The number opposite each of the years in the list below indicates which of the calendars on the following pages is the one for that year. Thus the number opposite 2000 is 14, so calendar 14 can be used as a 2000 calendar.

Leap years

Years divisible by four without remainder are leap years with 366 days instead of 365 (29 days in February instead of 28). However, the first year of the century is not a leap year except when divisible by 400.

Year	Calendar	Year	Calendar	Year	Calendar	Year	Calendar	Year	Calendar	Year	Calendar
1980	10	1992	11	2004	12	2016	13	2028	14	2040	8
1981	5	1993	6	2005	7	2017	1	2029	2	2041	3
1982	6	1994	7	2006	1	2018	2	2030	3	2042	4
1983	7	1995	1	2007	2	2019	3	2031	4	2043	5
1984	8	1996	9	2008	10	2020	11	2032	12	2044	13
1985	3	1997	4	2009	5	2021	6	2033	7	2045	1
1986	4	1998	5	2010	6	2022	7	2034	1	2046	2
1987	5	1999	6	2011	7	2023	1	2035	2	2047	3
1988	13	2000	14	2012	8	2024	9	2036	10	2048	11
1989	1	2001	2	2013	3	2025	4	2037	5	2049	6
1990	2	2002	3	2014	4	2026	5	2038	6	2050	7
1991	3	2003	4	2015	5	2027	6	2039	7	2051	1

1

	January	February	March	April
M	2 9 16 23 30	6 13 20 27	6 13 20 27	3 10 17 24
T	3 10 17 24 31	7 14 21 28	7 14 21 28	4 11 18 25
W	4 11 18 25	1 8 15 22	1 8 15 22 29	5 12 19 26
T	5 12 19 26	2 9 16 23	2 9 16 23 30	6 13 20 27
F	6 13 20 27	3 10 17 24	3 10 17 24 31	7 14 21 28
S	7 14 21 28	4 11 18 25	4 11 18 25	1 8 15 22 29
S	1 8 15 22 29	5 12 19 26	5 12 19 26	2 9 16 23 30

	May	June	July	August
M	1 8 15 22 29	5 12 19 26	3 10 17 24 31	7 14 21 28
T	2 9 16 23 30	6 13 20 27	4 11 18 25	1 8 15 22 29
W	3 10 17 24 31	7 14 21 28	5 12 19 26	2 9 16 23 30
T	4 11 18 25	1 8 15 22 29	6 13 20 27	3 10 17 24 31
F	5 12 19 26	2 9 16 23 30	7 14 21 28	4 11 18 25
S	6 13 20 27	3 10 17 24	1 8 15 22 29	5 12 19 26
S	7 14 21 28	4 11 18 25	2 9 16 23 30	6 13 20 27

	September	October	November	December
M	4 11 18 25	2 9 16 23 30	6 13 20 27	4 11 18 25
T	5 12 19 26	3 10 17 24 31	7 14 21 28	5 12 19 26
W	6 13 20 27	4 11 18 25	1 8 15 22 29	6 13 20 27
T	7 14 21 28	5 12 19 26	2 9 16 23 30	7 14 21 28
F	1 8 15 22 29	6 13 20 27	3 10 17 24	1 8 15 22 29
S	2 9 16 23 30	7 14 21 28	4 11 18 25	2 9 16 23 30
S	3 10 17 24	1 8 15 22 29	5 12 19 26	3 10 17 24 31

2

	January	February	March	April
M	1 8 15 22 29	5 12 19 26	5 12 19 26	2 9 16 23 30
T	2 9 16 23 30	6 13 20 27	6 13 20 27	3 10 17 24
W	3 10 17 24 31	7 14 21 28	7 14 21 28	4 11 18 25
T	4 11 18 25	1 8 15 22	1 8 15 22 29	5 12 19 26
F	5 12 19 26	2 9 16 23	2 9 16 23 30	6 13 20 27
S	6 13 20 27	3 10 17 24	3 10 17 24 31	7 14 21 28
S	7 14 21 28	4 11 18 25	4 11 18 25	1 8 15 22 29

	May	June	July	August
M	7 14 21 28	4 11 18 25	2 9 16 23 30	6 13 20 27
T	1 8 15 22 29	5 12 19 26	3 10 17 24 31	7 14 21 28
W	2 9 16 23 30	6 13 20 27	4 11 18 25	1 8 15 22 29
T	3 10 17 24 31	7 14 21 28	5 12 19 26	2 9 16 23 30
F	4 11 18 25	1 8 15 22 29	6 13 20 27	3 10 17 24 31
S	5 12 19 26	2 9 16 23 30	7 14 21 28	4 11 18 25
S	6 13 20 27	3 10 17 24	1 8 15 22 29	5 12 19 26

	September	October	November	December
M	3 10 17 24	1 8 15 22 29	5 12 19 26	3 10 17 24 31
T	4 11 18 25	2 9 16 23 30	6 13 20 27	4 11 18 25
W	5 12 19 26	3 10 17 24 31	7 14 21 28	5 12 19 26
T	6 13 20 27	4 11 18 25	1 8 15 22 29	6 13 20 27
F	7 14 21 28	5 12 19 26	2 9 16 23 30	7 14 21 28
S	1 8 15 22 29	6 13 20 27	3 10 17 24	1 8 15 22 29
S	2 9 16 23 30	7 14 21 28	4 11 18 25	2 9 16 23 30

M3: Perpetual calendar

3

	January	February	March	April
M	7 14 21 28	4 11 18 25	4 11 18 25	1 8 15 22 29
T	1 8 15 22 29	5 12 19 26	5 12 19 26	2 9 16 23 30
W	2 9 16 23 30	6 13 20 27	6 13 20 27	3 10 17 24
T	3 10 17 24 31	7 14 21 28	7 14 21 28	4 11 18 25
F	4 11 18 25	1 8 15 22	1 8 15 22 29	5 12 19 26
S	5 12 19 26	2 9 16 23	2 9 16 23 30	6 13 20 27
S	6 13 20 27	3 10 17 24	3 10 17 24 31	7 14 21 28

	May	June	July	August
M	6 13 20 27	3 10 17 24	1 8 15 22 29	5 12 19 26
T	7 14 21 28	4 11 18 25	2 9 16 23 30	7 14 21 28
W	1 8 15 22 29	5 12 19 26	3 10 17 24 31	6 13 20 27
T	2 9 16 23 30	6 13 20 27	4 11 18 25	1 8 15 22 29
F	3 10 17 24 31	7 14 21 28	5 12 19 26	2 9 16 23 30
S	4 11 18 25	1 8 15 22 29	6 13 20 27	3 10 17 24 31
S	5 12 19 26	2 9 16 23 30	7 14 21 28	4 11 18 25

	September	October	November	December
M	2 9 16 23 30	7 14 21 28	4 11 18 25	2 9 16 23 30
T	3 10 17 24	1 8 15 22 29	5 12 19 26	3 10 17 24 31
W	4 11 18 25	2 9 16 23 30	6 13 20 27	4 11 18 25
T	5 12 19 26	3 10 17 24 31	7 14 21 28	5 12 19 26
F	6 13 20 27	4 11 18 25	1 8 15 22 29	6 13 20 27
S	7 14 21 28	5 12 19 26	2 9 16 23 30	7 14 21 28
S	1 8 15 22 29	6 13 20 27	3 10 17 24	1 8 15 22 29

4

	January	February	March	April
M	6 13 20 27	3 10 17 24	3 10 17 24 31	7 14 21 28
T	7 14 21 28	4 11 18 25	4 11 18 25	1 8 15 22 29
W	1 8 15 22 29	5 12 19 26	5 12 19 26	2 9 16 23 30
T	2 9 16 23 30	6 13 20 27	6 13 20 27	3 10 17 24
F	3 10 17 24 31	7 14 21 28	7 14 21 28	4 11 18 25
S	4 11 18 25	1 8 15 22	1 8 15 22 29	5 12 19 26
S	5 12 19 26	2 9 16 23	2 9 16 23 30	6 13 20 27

	May	June	July	August
M	5 12 19 26	2 9 16 23 30	7 14 21 28	4 11 18 25
T	6 13 20 27	3 10 17 24	1 8 15 22 29	5 12 19 26
W	7 14 21 28	4 11 18 25	2 9 16 23 30	6 13 20 27
T	1 8 15 22 29	5 12 19 26	3 10 17 24 31	7 14 21 28
F	2 9 16 23 30	6 13 20 27	4 11 18 25	1 8 15 22 29
S	3 10 17 24 31	7 14 21 28	5 12 19 26	2 9 16 23 30
S	4 11 18 25	1 8 15 22 29	6 13 20 27	3 10 17 24 31

	September	October	November	December
M	1 8 15 22 29	6 13 20 27	3 10 17 24	1 8 15 22 29
T	2 9 16 23 30	7 14 21 28	4 11 18 25	2 9 16 23 30
W	3 10 17 24	1 8 15 22 29	5 12 19 26	3 10 17 24 31
T	4 11 18 25	2 9 16 23 30	6 13 20 27	4 11 18 25
F	5 12 19 26	3 10 17 24 31	7 14 21 28	5 12 19 26
S	6 13 20 27	4 11 18 25	1 8 15 22 29	6 13 20 27
S	7 14 21 28	5 12 19 26	2 9 16 23 30	7 14 21 28

5

	January	February	March	April
M	5 12 19 26	2 9 16 23	2 9 16 23 30	6 13 20 27
T	6 13 20 27	3 10 17 24	3 10 17 24 31	7 14 21 28
W	7 14 21 28	4 11 18 25	4 11 18 25	1 8 15 22 29
T	1 8 15 22 29	5 12 19 26	5 12 19 26	2 9 16 23 30
F	2 9 16 23 30	6 13 20 27	6 13 20 27	3 10 17 24
S	3 10 17 24 31	7 14 21 28	7 14 21 28	4 11 18 25
S	4 11 18 25	1 8 15 22	1 8 15 22 29	5 12 19 26

	May	June	July	August
M	4 11 18 25	1 8 15 22 29	6 13 20 27	3 10 17 24 31
T	5 12 19 26	2 9 16 23 30	7 14 21 28	4 11 18 25
W	6 13 20 27	3 10 17 24	1 8 15 22 29	5 12 19 26
T	7 14 21 28	4 11 18 25	2 9 16 23 30	6 13 20 27
F	1 8 15 22 29	5 12 19 26	3 10 17 24 31	7 14 21 28
S	2 9 16 23 30	6 13 20 27	4 11 18 25	1 8 15 22 29
S	3 10 17 24 31	7 14 21 28	5 12 19 26	2 9 16 23 30

	September	October	November	December
M	7 14 21 28	5 12 19 26	2 9 16 23 30	7 14 21 28
T	1 8 15 22 29	6 13 20 27	3 10 17 24	1 8 15 22 29
W	2 9 16 23 30	7 14 21 28	4 11 18 25	2 9 16 23 30
T	3 10 17 24	1 8 15 22 29	5 12 19 26	3 10 17 24 31
F	4 11 18 25	2 9 16 23 30	6 13 20 27	4 11 18 25
S	5 12 19 26	3 10 17 24 31	7 14 21 28	5 12 19 26
S	6 13 20 27	4 11 18 25	1 8 15 22 29	6 13 20 27

6

	January	February	March	April
M	4 11 18 25	1 8 15 22	1 8 15 22 29	5 12 19 26
T	5 12 19 26	2 9 16 23	2 9 16 23 30	6 13 20 27
W	6 13 20 27	3 10 17 24	3 10 17 24 31	7 14 21 28
T	7 14 21 28	4 11 18 25	4 11 18 25	1 8 15 22 29
F	1 8 15 22 29	5 12 19 26	5 12 19 26	2 9 16 23 30
S	2 9 16 23 30	6 13 20 27	6 13 20 27	3 10 17 24
S	3 10 17 24 31	7 14 21 28	7 14 21 28	4 11 18 25

	May	June	July	August
M	3 10 17 24 31	7 14 21 28	5 12 19 26	2 9 16 23 30
T	4 11 18 25	1 8 15 22 29	6 13 20 27	3 10 17 24 31
W	5 12 19 26	2 9 16 23 30	7 14 21 28	4 11 18 25
T	6 13 20 27	3 10 17 24	1 8 15 22 29	5 12 19 26
F	7 14 21 28	4 11 18 25	2 9 16 23 30	6 13 20 27
S	1 8 15 22 29	5 12 19 26	3 10 17 24 31	7 14 21 28
S	2 9 16 23 30	6 13 20 27	4 11 18 25	1 8 15 22 29

	September	October	November	December
M	6 13 20 27	4 11 18 25	1 8 15 22 29	6 13 20 27
T	7 14 21 28	5 12 19 26	2 9 16 23 30	7 14 21 28
W	1 8 15 22 29	6 13 20 27	3 10 17 24	1 8 15 22 29
T	2 9 16 23 30	7 14 21 28	4 11 18 25	2 9 16 23 30
F	3 10 17 24	1 8 15 22 29	5 12 19 26	3 10 17 24 31
S	4 11 18 25	2 9 16 23 30	6 13 20 27	4 11 18 25
S	5 12 19 26	3 10 17 24 31	7 14 21 28	5 12 19 26

7

	January	February	March	April
M	3 10 17 24 31	7 14 21 28	7 14 21 28	4 11 18 25
T	4 11 18 25	1 8 15 22	1 8 15 22 29	5 12 19 26
W	5 12 19 26	2 9 16 23	2 9 16 23 30	6 13 20 27
T	6 13 20 27	3 10 17 24	3 10 17 24 31	7 14 21 28
F	7 14 21 28	4 11 18 25	4 11 18 25	1 8 15 22 29
S	1 8 15 22 29	5 12 19 26	5 12 19 26	2 9 16 23 30
S	2 9 16 23 30	6 13 20 27	6 13 20 27	3 10 17 24

	May	June	July	August
M	2 9 16 23 30	6 13 20 27	4 11 18 25	1 8 15 22 29
T	3 10 17 24 31	7 14 21 28	5 12 19 26	2 9 16 23 30
W	4 11 18 25	1 8 15 22 29	6 13 20 27	3 10 17 24 31
T	5 12 19 26	2 9 16 23 30	7 14 21 28	4 11 18 25
F	6 13 20 27	3 10 17 24	1 8 15 22 29	5 12 19 26
S	7 14 21 28	4 11 18 25	2 9 16 23 30	6 13 20 27
S	1 8 15 22 29	5 12 19 26	3 10 17 24 31	7 14 21 28

	September	October	November	December
M	5 12 19 26	3 10 17 24 31	7 14 21 28	5 12 19 26
T	6 13 20 27	4 11 18 25	1 8 15 22 29	6 13 20 27
W	7 14 21 28	5 12 19 26	2 9 16 23 30	7 14 21 28
T	1 8 15 22 29	6 13 20 27	3 10 17 24	1 8 15 22 29
F	2 9 16 23 30	7 14 21 28	4 11 18 25	2 9 16 23 30
S	3 10 17 24	1 8 15 22 29	5 12 19 26	3 10 17 24 31
S	4 11 18 25	2 9 16 23 30	6 13 20 27	4 11 18 25

8

	January	February	March	April
M	2 9 16 23 30	6 13 20 27	5 12 19 26	2 9 16 23 30
T	3 10 17 24 31	7 14 21 28	6 13 20 27	3 10 17 24
W	4 11 18 25	1 8 15 22 29	7 14 21 28	4 11 18 25
T	5 12 19 26	2 9 16 23	1 8 15 22 29	5 12 19 26
F	6 13 20 27	3 10 17 24	2 9 16 23 30	6 13 20 27
S	7 14 21 28	4 11 18 25	3 10 17 24 31	7 14 21 28
S	1 8 15 22 29	5 12 19 26	4 11 18 25	1 8 15 22 29

	May	June	July	August
M	7 14 21 28	4 11 18 25	2 9 16 23 30	6 13 20 27
T	1 8 15 22 29	5 12 19 26	3 10 17 24 31	7 14 21 28
W	2 9 16 23 30	6 13 20 27	4 11 18 25	1 8 15 22 29
T	3 10 17 24 31	7 14 21 28	5 12 19 26	2 9 16 23 30
F	4 11 18 25	1 8 15 22 29	6 13 20 27	3 10 17 24 31
S	5 12 19 26	2 9 16 23 30	7 14 21 28	4 11 18 25
S	6 13 20 27	3 10 17 24	1 8 15 22 29	5 12 19 26

	September	October	November	December
M	3 10 17 24	1 8 15 22 29	5 12 19 26	3 10 17 24 31
T	4 11 18 25	2 9 16 23 30	6 13 20 27	4 11 18 25
W	5 12 19 26	3 10 17 24 31	7 14 21 28	5 12 19 26
T	6 13 20 27	4 11 18 25	1 8 15 22 29	6 13 20 27
F	7 14 21 28	5 12 19 26	2 9 16 23 30	7 14 21 28
S	1 8 15 22 29	6 13 20 27	3 10 17 24	1 8 15 22 29
S	2 9 16 23 30	7 14 21 28	4 11 18 25	2 9 16 23 30

Sweet & Maxwell

M3: Perpetual calendar

9

	January	February	March	April
M	1 8 15 22 29	5 12 19 26	4 11 18 25	1 8 15 22 29
T	2 9 16 23 30	6 13 20 27	5 12 19 26	2 9 16 23 30
W	3 10 17 24	7 14 21 28	6 13 20 27	3 10 17 24
T	4 11 18 25	1 8 15 22 29	7 14 21 28	4 11 18 25
F	5 12 19 26	2 9 16 23	1 8 15 22 29	5 12 19 26
S	6 13 20 27	3 10 17 24	2 9 16 23 30	6 13 20 27
S	7 14 21 28	4 11 18 25	3 10 17 24 31	7 14 21 28

	May	June	July	August
M	6 13 20 27	3 10 17 24	1 8 15 22 29	5 12 19 26
T	7 14 21 28	4 11 18 25	2 9 16 23 30	6 13 20 27
W	1 8 15 22 29	5 12 19 26	3 10 17 24 31	7 14 21 28
T	2 9 16 23 30	6 13 20 27	4 11 18 25	1 8 15 22 29
F	3 10 17 24 31	7 14 21 28	5 12 19 26	2 9 16 23 30
S	4 11 18 25	1 8 15 22 29	6 13 20 27	3 10 17 24 31
S	5 12 19 26	2 9 16 23 30	7 14 21 28	4 11 18 25

	September	October	November	December
M	2 9 16 23 30	7 14 21 28	4 11 18 25	2 9 16 23 30
T	3 10 17 24	1 8 15 22 29	5 12 19 26	3 10 17 24 31
W	4 11 18 25	2 9 16 23 30	6 13 20 27	4 11 18 25
T	5 12 19 26	3 10 17 24 31	7 14 21 28	5 12 19 26
F	6 13 20 27	4 11 18 25	1 8 15 22 29	6 13 20 27
S	7 14 21 28	5 12 19 26	2 9 16 23 30	7 14 21 28
S	1 8 15 22 29	6 13 20 27	3 10 17 24	1 8 15 22 29

10

	January	February	March	April
M	7 14 21 28	4 11 18 25	3 10 17 24 31	7 14 21 28
T	1 8 15 22 29	5 12 19 26	4 11 18 25	1 8 15 22 29
W	2 9 16 23 30	6 13 20 27	5 12 19 26	2 9 16 23 30
T	3 10 17 24 31	7 14 21 28	6 13 20 27	3 10 17 24
F	4 11 18 25	1 8 15 22 29	7 14 21 28	4 11 18 25
S	5 12 19 26	2 9 16 23	1 8 15 22 29	5 12 19 26
S	6 13 20 27	3 10 17 24	2 9 16 23 30	6 13 20 27

	May	June	July	August
M	5 12 19 26	2 9 16 23 30	7 14 21 28	4 11 18 25
T	6 13 20 27	3 10 17 24	1 8 15 22 29	5 12 19 26
W	7 14 21 28	4 11 18 25	2 9 16 23 30	6 13 20 27
T	1 8 15 22 29	5 12 19 26	3 10 17 24 31	7 14 21 28
F	2 9 16 23 30	6 13 20 27	4 11 18 25	1 8 15 22 29
S	3 10 17 24 31	7 14 21 28	5 12 19 26	2 9 16 23 30
S	4 11 18 25	1 8 15 22 29	6 13 20 27	3 10 17 24 31

	September	October	November	December
M	1 8 15 22 29	6 13 20 27	3 10 17 24	1 8 15 22 29
T	2 9 16 23 30	7 14 21 28	4 11 18 25	2 9 16 23 30
W	3 10 17 24	1 8 15 22 29	5 12 19 26	3 10 17 24 31
T	4 11 18 25	2 9 16 23 30	6 13 20 27	4 11 18 25
F	5 12 19 26	3 10 17 24 31	7 14 21 28	5 12 19 26
S	6 13 20 27	4 11 18 25	1 8 15 22 29	6 13 20 27
S	7 14 21 28	5 12 19 26	2 9 16 23 30	7 14 21 28

11

	January	February	March	April
M	6 13 20 27	3 10 17 24	2 9 16 23 30	6 13 20 27
T	7 14 21 28	4 11 18 25	3 10 17 24 31	7 14 21 28
W	1 8 15 22 29	5 12 19 26	4 11 18 25	1 8 15 22 29
T	2 9 16 23 30	6 13 20 27	5 12 19 26	2 9 16 23 30
F	3 10 17 24 31	7 14 21 28	6 13 20 27	3 10 17 24
S	4 11 18 25	1 8 15 22 29	7 14 21 28	4 11 18 25
S	5 12 19 26	2 9 16 23	1 8 15 22 29	5 12 19 26

	May	June	July	August
M	4 11 18 25	1 8 15 22 29	6 13 20 27	3 10 17 24 31
T	5 12 19 26	2 9 16 23 30	7 14 21 28	4 11 18 25
W	6 13 20 27	3 10 17 24	1 8 15 22 29	5 12 19 26
T	7 14 21 28	4 11 18 25	2 9 16 23 30	6 13 20 27
F	1 8 15 22 29	5 12 19 26	3 10 17 24 31	7 14 21 28
S	2 9 16 23 30	6 13 20 27	4 11 18 25	1 8 15 22 29
S	3 10 17 24 31	7 14 21 28	5 12 19 26	2 9 16 23 30

	September	October	November	December
M	7 14 21 28	5 12 19 26	2 9 16 23 30	7 14 21 28
T	1 8 15 22 29	6 13 20 27	3 10 17 24	1 8 15 22 29
W	2 9 16 23 30	7 14 21 28	4 11 18 25	2 9 16 23 30
T	3 10 17 24	1 8 15 22 29	5 12 19 26	3 10 17 24 31
F	4 11 18 25	2 9 16 23 30	6 13 20 27	4 11 18 25
S	5 12 19 26	3 10 17 24 31	7 14 21 28	5 12 19 26
S	6 13 20 27	4 11 18 25	1 8 15 22 29	6 13 20 27

12

	January	February	March	April
M	5 12 19 26	2 9 16 23	1 8 15 22 29	5 12 19 26
T	6 13 20 27	3 10 17 24	2 9 16 23 30	6 13 20 27
W	7 14 21 28	4 11 18 25	3 10 17 24 31	7 14 21 28
T	1 8 15 22 29	5 12 19 26	4 11 18 25	1 8 15 22 29
F	2 9 16 23 30	6 13 20 27	5 12 19 26	2 9 16 23 30
S	3 10 17 24 31	7 14 21 28	6 13 20 27	3 10 17 24
S	4 11 18 25	1 8 15 22 29	7 14 21 28	4 11 18 25

	May	June	July	August
M	3 10 17 24 31	7 14 21 28	5 12 19 26	2 9 16 23 30
T	4 11 18 25	1 8 15 22 29	6 13 20 27	3 10 17 24 31
W	5 12 19 26	2 9 16 23 30	7 14 21 28	4 11 18 25
T	6 13 20 27	3 10 17 24	1 8 15 22 29	5 12 19 26
F	7 14 21 28	4 11 18 25	2 9 16 23 30	6 13 20 27
S	1 8 15 22 29	5 12 19 26	3 10 17 24 31	7 14 21 28
S	2 9 16 23 30	6 13 20 27	4 11 18 25	1 8 15 22 29

	September	October	November	December
M	6 13 20 27	4 11 18 25	1 8 15 22 29	6 13 20 27
T	7 14 21 28	5 12 19 26	2 9 16 23 30	7 14 21 28
W	1 8 15 22 29	6 13 20 27	3 10 17 24	1 8 15 22 29
T	2 9 16 23 30	7 14 21 28	4 11 18 25	2 9 16 23 30
F	3 10 17 24	1 8 15 22 29	5 12 19 26	3 10 17 24 31
S	4 11 18 25	2 9 16 23 30	6 13 20 27	4 11 18 25
S	5 12 19 26	3 10 17 24 31	7 14 21 28	5 12 19 26

13

	January	February	March	April
M	4 11 18 25	1 8 15 22 29	7 14 21 28	4 11 18 25
T	5 12 19 26	2 9 16 23	1 8 15 22 29	5 12 19 26
W	6 13 20 27	3 10 17 24	2 9 16 23 30	6 13 20 27
T	7 14 21 28	4 11 18 25	3 10 17 24 31	7 14 21 28
F	1 8 15 22 29	5 12 19 26	4 11 18 25	1 8 15 22 29
S	2 9 16 23 30	6 13 20 27	5 12 19 26	2 9 16 23 30
S	3 10 17 24 31	7 14 21 28	6 13 20 27	3 10 17 24

	May	June	July	August
M	2 9 16 23 30	6 13 20 27	4 11 18 25	1 8 15 22 29
T	3 10 17 24 31	7 14 21 28	5 12 19 26	2 9 16 23 30
W	4 11 18 25	1 8 15 22 29	6 13 20 27	3 10 17 24 31
T	5 12 19 26	2 9 16 23 30	7 14 21 28	4 11 18 25
F	6 13 20 27	3 10 17 24	1 8 15 22 29	5 12 19 26
S	7 14 21 28	4 11 18 25	2 9 16 23 30	6 13 20 27
S	1 8 15 22 29	5 12 19 26	3 10 17 24 31	7 14 21 28

	September	October	November	December
M	5 12 19 26	3 10 17 24 31	7 14 21 28	5 12 19 26
T	6 13 20 27	4 11 18 25	1 8 15 22 29	6 13 20 27
W	7 14 21 28	5 12 19 26	2 9 16 23 30	7 14 21 28
T	1 8 15 22 29	6 13 20 27	3 10 17 24	1 8 15 22 29
F	2 9 16 23 30	7 14 21 28	4 11 18 25	2 9 16 23 30
S	3 10 17 24	1 8 15 22 29	5 12 19 26	3 10 17 24 31
S	4 11 18 25	2 9 16 23 30	6 13 20 27	4 11 18 25

14

	January	February	March	April
M	3 10 17 24 31	7 14 21 28	6 13 20 27	3 10 17 24
T	4 11 18 25	1 8 15 22 29	7 14 21 28	4 11 18 25
W	5 12 19 26	2 9 16 23	1 8 15 22 29	5 12 19 26
T	6 13 20 27	3 10 17 24	2 9 16 23 30	6 13 20 27
F	7 14 21 28	4 11 18 25	3 10 17 24 31	7 14 21 28
S	1 8 15 22 29	5 12 19 26	4 11 18 25	1 8 15 22 29
S	2 9 16 23 30	6 13 20 27	5 12 19 26	2 9 16 23 30

	May	June	July	August
M	1 8 15 22 29	5 12 19 26	3 10 17 24 31	7 14 21 28
T	2 9 16 23 30	6 13 20 27	4 11 18 25	1 8 15 22 29
W	3 10 17 24 31	7 14 21 28	5 12 19 26	2 9 16 23 30
T	4 11 18 25	1 8 15 22 29	6 13 20 27	3 10 17 24 31
F	5 12 19 26	2 9 16 23 30	7 14 21 28	4 11 18 25
S	6 13 20 27	3 10 17 24	1 8 15 22 29	5 12 19 26
S	7 14 21 28	4 11 18 25	2 9 16 23 30	6 13 20 27

	September	October	November	December
M	4 11 18 25	2 9 16 23 30	6 13 20 27	4 11 18 25
T	5 12 19 26	3 10 1 24 31	7 14 21 28	5 12 19 26
W	6 13 20 27	4 11 18 25	1 8 15 22 29	6 13 20 27
T	7 14 21 28	5 12 19 26	2 9 16 23 30	7 14 21 28
F	1 8 15 22 29	6 13 20 27	3 10 17 24	1 8 15 22 29
S	2 9 16 23 30	7 14 21 28	4 11 18 25	2 9 16 23 30
S	3 10 17 24	1 8 15 22 29	5 12 19 26	3 10 17 24 31

M4: Religious festivals

	2017	
☬	Birthday of Guru Gobind Singh	5 January
✝	Ash Wednesday	1 March
✡	Purim	12 March
ॐ	Holi	12 March
☬	Hola Mohalla	13 March
✡	Passover	11 April
☬	Baisakhi Day	14 April
✝	Good Friday	14 April
✝	Easter Sunday	16 April
✝	Easter Monday	17 April
✝	Ascension Day	25 May
☪	Ramadan begins	27 May
✡	Shavuot	31 May
✝	Pentecost	4 June
☪	Eid al-Fitr	26 June
☪	Eid al-Adha	1 September
✡	Rosh Hashanah	21 September
☪	Hijra – New Year	21 September
✡	Yom Kippur	30 September
ॐ	Dasarah	30 September
☪	Ashurah	1 October
✡	Succot	5 October
ॐ	Diwali	19 October
☬	Birthday of Guru Nanak	4 November
☪	Mawlid-al-Nabi	1 December
✡	Chanukah	13 December
✝	Christmas Day	25 December

	2018	
☬	Birthday of Guru Gobind Singh	5 January
✝	Ash Wednesday	14 February
✡	Purim	28 February
ॐ	Holi	2 March
☬	Hola Mohalla	2 March
✝	Good Friday	30 March
✡	Passover	31 March
✝	Easter Sunday	1 April
✝	Easter Monday	2 April
☬	Baisakhi Day	14 April
✝	Ascension Day	10 May
☪	Ramadan begins	16 May
✡	Shavuot	20 May
✝	Pentecost	20 May
☪	Eid al-Fitr	15 June
☪	Eid al-Adha	22 August
✡	Rosh Hashanah	10 September
☪	Hijra – New year	11 September
✡	Yom Kippur	19 September
☪	Ashurah	21 September
✡	Succot	24 September
ॐ	Dasarah	18 October
ॐ	Diwali	7 November
☪	Mawlid-al-Nabi	21 November
☬	Birthday of Guru Nanak	23 November
✡	Chanukah	3 December
✝	Christmas Day	25 December

	2019	
☬	Birthday of Guru Gobind Singh	13 January
✝	Ash Wednesday	6 March
ॐ	Holi	20 March
✡	Purim	21 March
☬	Hola Mohalla	21 March
☬	Baisakhi Day	14 April
✝	Good Friday	19 April
✡	Passover	20 April
✝	Easter Sunday	21 April
✝	Easter Monday	22 April
☪	Ramadan begins	5 May
✝	Ascension Day	30 May
☪	Eid al-Fitr	4 June
✡	Shavuot	9 June
✝	Pentecost	9 June
☪	Eid al-Adha	11 August
☪	Hijra – New Year	1 September
☪	Ashurah	10 September
✡	Rosh Hashanah	30 September
ॐ	Dasarah	7 October
✡	Yom Kippur	9 October
✡	Succot	14 October
ॐ	Diwali	27 October
☪	Mawlid-al-Nabi	10 November
☬	Birthday of Guru Nanak	12 November
✡	Chanukah	23 December
✝	Christmas Day	25 December

✝	Christian
ॐ	Hindu
✡	Jewish
☪	Muslim
☬	Sikh

Note: all Islamic and Jewish holidays begin at sundown on the preceding day.

M5: Medical reference intervals and scales

Haematology—reference intervals

Measurement	Reference interval
White cell count	$4.0–11.0 \times 10^9/l$
Red cell count – Male: Female:	$4.5–6.5 \times 10^{12}/l$ $3.9–5.6 \times 10^{12}/l$
Haemoglobin – Male: Female:	13.5–18.0 g/dl 11.5–16.0 g/dl
Platelet count	$150.0–400.0 \times 10^9/l$
Erythrocyte sedimentation rate (ESR) – Male: Female:	Up to age in years divided by two. Up to (age in years plus 10) divided by two.
Prothrombin time (factors II, VII, X)	10–14 seconds
Activated partial thromboplastin time (VIII, IX, XI, XII)	35–45 seconds

Target INR (international normalized ratio) for acute venous thromboembolism (British Society for Haematology Guidelines on oral anticoagulation with Warfarin, 4th edition, 2011)

First episode of venous thromboembolism (VTE)	INR target 2.5
Recurrent VTE whilst anticoagulated within the therapeutic range	INR target 3.5

Cerebrospinal fluid—reference intervals

Opening pressure (mmCSF)	Infants: < 80; children: < 90; adults: < 210

Substance	Reference interval
Glucose	3.3–4.4 mmol/l or $\geq 2/3$ of plasma glucose
Chloride	122–128 mmol/l
Lactate	< 2.8 mmol/l

M5: Medical reference intervals and scales

Biochemistry—reference intervals

Substance	Specimen	Reference Interval
Albumin	P	*35–50 g/l
a-amylase	P	0–180 Somogyi U/dl
Bicarbonate	P	*24–30 mmol/l
C reactive protein (CRP)	P	< 6 mg/l
Calcium (ionised)	P	1.0–1.25 mmol/l
Calcium (total)	P	*2.12–2.65 mmol/l
Chloride	P	98–107 mmol/l
Cholesterol	P	3.3–6.2 mmol/l
Creatinine	P	*58–110 mmol/l
Glucose (fasting)	P	3.5–5.5 mmol/l
Glycosylated haemoglobin	B	5–8%
Phosphate	P	0.8–1.45 mmol/l
Potassium	P	3.6–5.0 mmol/l
Protein (total)	P	60–80 g/l
Sodium	P	*137–145 mmol/l
Urea	P	*2.5–7.5 mmol/l

Key: P = plasma; B = whole blood

* Reference intervals for these substances differ in pregnancy. Reference intervals in pregnancy are not reproduced here.

Arterial blood gases—reference intervals

pH:	7.35–7.45
PaO$_2$:	>10.6 kPa
PaCO$_2$:	4.7–6.0 kPa
Base excess	±2 mmol/l
NB: 7.6 mmHg = 1 kPa (atmospheric pressure = 100 kPa)	

M5: Medical reference intervals and scales

Apgar scoring chart

A baby's condition is assessed at one and five minutes after birth by means of the Apgar score. This system observes five signs. A score of nought, one or two is awarded for each sign.

Sign	0	1	2
Heart rate	absent	slow (below 100)	over 100
Respiratory effect	absent	weak cry, hypoventilation	good cry
Muscle tone	limp	some flexion of extremities	well flexed
Reflex irritability	no response	some motion	cry
Colour	blue, pale	body pink, extremities blue	completely pink

NB: An Apgar score of 10 represents optimal condition. A score of three or less indicates a markedly asphyxiated infant.

Glasgow coma scale

Three types of response are assessed:

	Score	
Best motor response	6	Obeys commands
	5	Localises to pain
	4	Flexion/withdrawal to pain
	3	Abnormal flexion
	2	Abnormal extension
	1	None
Best verbal response	5	Oriented
	4	Confused
	3	Inappropriate words
	2	Incomprehensible sounds
	1	None
Eye opening	4	Spontaneously
	3	To speech
	2	To pain
	1	None

The overall score is the sum of the scores in each area, e.g. no response to pain + no verbal response + no eye opening = three.

In severe injury the score is eight or under.
In moderate injury the score is nine–12.
In minor injury the score is 13–15.

PULHHEEMS rating

This is a "qualitative" system of physical and mental assessment and grading for Armed Forces Personnel. It is taken from the joint Services publication JSP950 and is issued to all Service and Civilian medical practitioners who are required to examine applicants for entry to the Armed Forces. It is carried out on new recruits, and repeated at five-yearly intervals after the age of 30. After the age of 50, it is performed at two-yearly intervals. Service Medical Boards are also conducted throughout service to "assess and re-grade personnel following changes in their functional capacity and medical employability resulting from illness and/or injury, either on a temporary or permanent basis".

PULHHEEMS is an abbreviation for the qualities to be tested. These include:

P	Physique/Age/Strength/Stamina
U	Upper limbs; Strength/Range of Movement
L	Lower limbs, pelvis and back; Strength/ROM [range of movement]
H	Hearing in the left ear
H	Hearing in the right ear
E	Visual acuity—left eye
E	Visual acuity—right eye
M	Mental Capacity
S	Stability (emotional)

Interpretation of a value in each field describes function and determines the grading used. In general, a "lower" number indicates a "higher" level of physical prowess in all areas. For example "P2" equates to satisfactory level of ability in all areas, whereas a score of P7 would indicate "medical fitness but with major employment limitations". A score of S8 renders the individual unfit for service—i.e. "defect of emotional stability such that the individual is below P7 criteria". In the form this appears in a table as follows (Lord Nelson taken as an example):

P	U	L	H	H	E	E	M	S
2	7	3	2	2	2	8	2	2

M5: Medical reference intervals and scales

FDI World Dental Federation notation

FDI Two-Digit Notation

Permanent Teeth

upper right								upper left							
18	17	16	15	14	13	12	11	21	22	23	24	25	26	27	28
48	47	46	45	44	43	43	41	31	32	33	34	35	36	37	38
lower right								lower left							

Deciduous teeth (baby teeth)

upper right						upper left					
		55	54	53	52	51	61	62	63	64	65
		85	84	83	82	81	71	72	73	74	75
lower right						lower left					

Codes, names and usual number of roots

Codes		Names	Usual number of roots
11	21	maxillary central incisor	1
41	31	mandibular central incisor	1
12	22	maxillary lateral incisor	1
42	32	mandibular lateral incisor	1
13	23	maxillary canine	1
43	33	mandibular canine	1
14	24	maxillary first premolar	2
44	34	mandibular first premolar	1
15	25	maxillary second premolar	1
45	35	mandibular second premolar	1
16	26	maxillary first molar	3
46	36	mandibular first molar	2
17	27	maxillary second molar	3
47	37	mandibular second molar	2
18	28	maxillary third premolar	3
48	38	mandibular third premolar	2

How the codes are constructed

Syntax: <quadrant code><tooth code>

Quadrant codes

1	upper right
2	upper left
3	lower left
4	lower right

Tooth codes

1	central incisors
2	lateral incisors
3	canines
4	1st premolars
5	2nd premolars
6	1st molars
7	2nd molars
8	3rd molars